A-Z OF FORMULA
RACING CARS

A-Z OF FORMULA
RACING CARS

DAVID HODGES

Edited and with contributions by Mike Lawrence

Published 1990 by
Bay View Books Ltd
13a Bridgeland Street
Bideford, Devon EX39 2QE

Designed by Gerrard Lindley
Typeset by Lens Typesetting, Bideford

ISBN 1 870979 16 8

Printed in Hong Kong by Leefung Asco Printers Ltd

ACKNOWLEDGMENTS

Most of the photographs in this book are from the author's
collection – he took many of them – and the publisher is also
grateful to constructors, teams, sponsors, libraries and
photographers, including: Abarth, Stan J. Alexander,
Autosport, Patrick Benjafield, Jeff Bloxham, BMW, BP,
Bridgestone, Peter Browning, Neill Bruce (Peter Roberts
Collection), Malcolm Bryan, Peter Burn, Camel, Gianni
Cancellieri, Canon, Paul Cohen, Johannes Czernin, Data
General, Denim, Elf, Embassy, Fiat, Brian Foley, Ford, Gitanes,
Guinness, Gulf, F. Hall, Peter Hampsheir, Hawke, Jeff
Hutchinson, Jewson, Larrousse-Calmels, Leyland, Lotus, Lucas,
Peter McFadyen, March, Martini, Matchbox, Philip Morris
(Marlboro), MRE, National Motor Museum, Olympus, Francis
Penn, Martin Pfunder, David Phipps, Pininfarina, Pirelli,
Planners International, John Player, Cyril Posthumus, Pygmée,
Q8, Duncan Rabagliati, Renault, Maurice Rowe, Saab, Bertram
Schafer Racing, STP, Gerry Stream, Marian Suman-Hreblay,
Sutton Photographic, Texaco, Tim Tyler, Unipart, Volkswagen,
West, Chris Willows, Yardley, Zoom.

CONTENTS

INTRODUCTION

It is customary to outline the terms of reference of an A-Z. Here the intention was simple: provide brief information on racing cars built to the principal international categories through four decades. 'Formula' has become widely used, but in this A-Z it refers to the mainstream categories, F1, F2, F3, F Junior and F3000. These cannot be totally isolated, so there are references to other categories, for example to USAC or CART, to F5000, or to the lesser Formula Ford, *Formule Renault*, and so on, while some of the cars built between the end of the Second World War and the introduction of formulae as we soon came to know them are included.

Even so, the 'five formulae' approach has meant that as marque histories some entries are fragmentary, and there are some cases where cars outside the terms of reference are fundamental to a marque and have been included. Surtees' F5000 cars are an example, and it seemed appropriate to record the last of the Cooper line, while equivalent McLaren contemporaries are ignored – but then it would have been most odd to include McLaren or Lola F5000 cars and ignore the much more important USAC or CART cars built by those constructors. Similarly, engines have been taken for granted; lines had to be drawn.

A rigid framework would have made the work impossible, but the general approach has been to recall the overall history of a marque that has a history, to describe its cars in chronological order and apply the filter of perspective (be it an opinion or an assessment), to list the drivers of F1 cars, at least those who started in Grands Prix, and to illustrate many of the entries. In this context the drivers and their championships are not a major factor, but as well as a summary of the regulations and the Constructors' Championship in appendices the opportunity has been taken in the index to bring together the other personalities involved in formula cars – if nothing else, this suggests how many marques and cars some designers have been associated with.

The existence of many one-off cars is recorded, but in the knowledge that the book is not comprehensive in an area that can be grey. Supposition plays no part, and questionable references have been set aside. A handful of F3 cars that have fleetingly appeared in national championship races in the last dozen years are not here: Focus, Pellini or Seymaz, for example, or CRS, MGM and MP. There were more back in the half-litre days, but those that have some merit are here, as well as many that the racing world did not miss when they disappeared. The publisher has already been very tolerant, and anticipates that a price to be paid for finally imposing a deadline could be a post bag of letters from readers who know all about – say – the Alfa-engined Formula 2 car that Signor Monguzzi reputedly laid down in Milan in 1968 . . .

Many people have helped in the preparation of this book. First and foremost I am grateful to Mike Lawrence, who read the manuscript, supplemented some entries, corrected others, and contributed entries, particularly for many of the half-litre cars of the 1950s. He also produced most of the material for the Lola and March entries – he is of course author of a widely-acclaimed history of March. I am also grateful to Rod Barrett, Donatella Biffignandi of the Museo dell'Automobile Carlo Biscaretti di Ruffia, Gianni Cancellieri, Esteban Delgado, Ian Flux, Mark Gallagher, Peter Hampsheir, Fernando Hoyos, Peter Kirchberg, Franco Lini, Wolfgang Monsehr, Jimmy Piget, Cyril Posthumus, Marcus Pye, Duncan Rabagliati, Jo Saward, Meyk Schmidt, Paul Sheldon, Tommy Sjoberg, Marian Suman-Hreblay, John Surtees, Ron Tauranac and Chris Willows. Peter Foubister gave me unstinted access to the archive of *Autosport*, and other journals consulted have included *Auto*, *Autocar*, *Autosprint*, *Motor*, *Motoring News*, *Motor Sport*, *Road and Track* and *Sport Auto*, as well as the invaluable annuals *Autocourse*, *Automobile Year*, *Autosprint Anno*, *Formula One* and *Grand Prix*, and marque histories.

David Hodges
June 1990

A
ABARTH

Carlo Abarth had a wide repertoire of competition cars in the twenty years that his company existed, from the time he set it up when the Cisitalia Grand Prix project collapsed until its absorption by Fiat, with machines ranging from ferociously hot little saloons to record cars and the sports-racing cars that were to undermine the business. Armando Scagliarini, a minor-category driver, backed Scuderia Abarth and helped set up the company. A 204-A (neé Cisitalia) sports car stripped of its cycle wings and lights was essayed as an F2 car in 1950, with no more success than drivers with regular 204 Spyders achieved.

A single-seater racing Abarth was, however, a rarity. Nothing came of the rumoured twin-ohc V-8 F2 project for 1950 or the widely reported F1 project in the second half of the 1960s – that car was apparently to use a 3-litre version of the 2-litre V-8, which did in fact appear in a sports-racing car and in hill climbs – but the 1-litre F2 that had come in 1964 was obviously very attractive, not least because Abarth could pick around his assortment of Fiat-based 1-litre engines. (He had a working agreement for engine development with Fiat from 1960 until Fiat took over his company in 1971.)

The Type 232 F2 car was announced in the Spring of 1964, and seemed promising. It had a sturdy space frame chassis and suspension on 'British lines' and clean bodywork. The 995cc (76 x 55mm) engine was said to produce 120bhp and drove through a six-speed gearbox. Power of that order should have compensated for any chassis shortcomings as Abarth felt its way into formula racing, and indeed the car did show a little better on fast Avus than it did at the Nürburgring. But in the hands of 'Geki' it was never competitive; he didn't match up to the likes of Clark, and Italian horsepower did not match Cosworth's.

Allegiances to Fiat are proclaimed on the nose of the first 232 as is the Scorpio birth sign Abarth adopted as his marque's badge.

ABBOTT

A neat and compact F3 car built by Norman Abbott. It was a one-off run in the 1-litre F3 as late as 1970 (it originated in 1966) without a record of achievement beyond a second place in a secondary Silverstone race in 1970, but presumably with satisfaction for its constructor.

AFM

The first F2 gave German constructors an opportunity to get back into front-line racing, modestly perhaps but at least on paper as equals of the Italian front runners. Alex von Falkenhausen was prominent in this revival, his AFM firm initially developing BMW 328s, then converting some to single-seaters. This led to a car designed as a single-seater, conventional in its tubular chassis, twin-wishbone ifs and de Dion rear suspension and initially powered by a developed version of the BMW straight six.

Several appeared in F2 in 1949-50, usually beaten in German events by Veritas, although Hans Stuck had a moment of glory in 1950 when he drove an AFM to win a heat of the Monza Autodrome GP. Later that year a light-alloy twin-cam V8 designed by Richard Küchen was fitted into the works AFM, and was used through 1951-3. The car was driven by Stuck, but was seldom more than a mid-grid qualifier in major races, and it was unreliable.

The Küchen-engined AFM, driven by Hans Stuck.

AGS

Automobiles Gonfaronnaise Sportives started small and although it moved into Grand Prix racing in 1986 it has remained small. This may be why it has not been glamorous or particularly successful in the big league, has made friends and few enemies and, at least until several key personnel left in 1988, seemed harmonious. The president since 1989 has been Cyril de Rouvre, but at least until that season AGS was essentially Henri Julien's outfit. He was a part-time racing car builder and driver in the 1960s, and towards the end of that decade ran F3 Matras for up-and-coming French drivers. That led to AGS building its first cars in 1970 – the *Formule France* JH1 designed by Christian Vanderpleyn. Cars for the 'French categories' followed in the 1970s, and there was a short-lived F3 car. None were outstanding, or notably successful, so it was perhaps surprising that AGS should move on to F2 in 1978, with the JH15.

Two seasons passed before an AGS driver scored European F2 Championship points, but at least Dallest then did so in style, with a maximum score at Pau. Although 1981 was a disappointing year for points, AGS drivers generally showed acceptably well on end-of-season tables until F2 ran its term in 1984. By then AGS people had looked at the possibility of a Cosworth-powered F1 car, but that dream was set aside.

Rather in the face of expectations, Julien took AGS into F3000, but then at the 1986 Italian GP the team's first F1 car made its debut. It had a somewhat rustic air, and indeed expedient use had been made of Renault left-overs to create a Grand Prix car (but less convincing contraptions have been seen in F1). AGS stuck to it and in the 1987 Australian GP actually scored a Constructors' Championship point. There was another one in 1989, to help sustain a team that was competing hopefully. For the following season the team looked for more than hope, as it was restructured and relocated in a new factory alongside the Var circuit at Le Luc en Provence. Hughes de Chaunac became technical and sporting director and Michel Costa took on the design role, while founder Henri Julien became a consultant.

JH5 This Vanderpleyn-designed F3 car was completed early in 1972 but turned out not to be the first of a line, as might have been anticipated. It was a monocoque car, with a tubular sub frame for its Nova engine, front radiator and orthodox suspension. It was seldom raced by Francois Guerre-Berthelot, for whom it was built. In 1989 he became AGS's F1 team manager.

JH15 A small and neat monocoque F2 car, unpretentious and conventional in a manner being out-moded by ground effects. It was powered by the familiar BMW M12, driving through a Hewland gearbox. The debut came at Thruxton in 1978, when Dallest qualified the JH15 reasonably well and was running at the end of its first race, albeit last and not classified. He started in half the Championship races, with two place finishes but also two DNQs in his six races while Dolhem failed to qualify once and failed to finish the two races he started.

JH16 This amounted to a facelift for the JH15, but more was called for in 1979 and this car was never convincing on the circuits. Nevertheless, Couderc placed it seventh at Vallelunga, the best AGS F2 performance in two years. This car was intended to serve while a new car was developed, but the JH17 did not appear until March 1980.

The first F2 cars from AGS, JH15 and JH16, were tidy and competent, but lacked the 'extra ingredient' that might have made them front runners. This is Jose Dolhem in a commendably clean JH16 at Donington in 1979.

JH17 A ground effects car, this was large compared with its predecessor, with a wide track and long wheelbase. When it was announced, a horses-for-courses policy was outlined, suggesting for example a narrow-track variant for fast circuits, but the JH17 was mediocre on such circuits, lacking straight line speed. It was an aluminium monocoque car, with full-length side pods, inboard front suspension, inboard rear

The JH17 was big, a fact hidden by its well-balanced lines. Despite the outward signs, sponsorship in 1980 was no more than adequate for a small team.

brakes, Kevlar bodywork, BMW engine and a Hewland gearbox. It looked the part, and concentrating the effort on one driver was sensible (originally he was to be Gaillard, but Richard Dallest occupied the cockpit). The JH17 worked best on twisty circuits and in wet conditions – Dallest won at Pau and Zandvoort.

JH18 Outwardly similar to JH17, this car was sleeker and smaller in its wheelbase, length and height. The basic monocoque was retained, but the Mader-BMW engine was used as a semi-stressed member. Improvement in straight-line speed was not found, reliability was suspect and the season started badly when Dallest had a big accident (JH17 had to be used on occasion). There were only two scoring finishes in 1981, at the end of the year, and the retirement rate was over 50 per cent. JH18 was used as a reserve car in Europe in 1982, and towards the end of that year was raced in the final round of the Japanese Championship (the JAF Grand Prix, when Eje Elgh placed it sixth).

JH19 This basic design carried AGS through the last F2 seasons, and the first car was in any case a derivative. Julien went for a longer wheelbase again, otherwise it was similar to JH18 and still lacked out-and-out speed. There were problems with a questionable skirt system, but few with its Michelin tyres. Two were run for drivers from F3 – Streiff acclimatized well and was sixth in the Championship, while Fabre was 15th.

The car appeared in 'B' form in 1983. It was lighter, the monocoque was retained but with some bodywork revision and there was a rear suspension arrangement in which the coil spring/damper units were mounted horizontally atop the gearbox. Carbon fibre brakes were tried, and used on into 1984. Within the constraints of a tight budget the JH19B was developed through the season and the last races saw Streiff placed 2,3,3, and fourth in the Championship. Ballabio bought a drive in a JH19 for half of the season.

The single JH19C built for 1984 was very similar, save in its pullrod front suspension and bodywork details. Streiff scored two second places in the summer and then won the very last European F2 Championship race, at Brands Hatch.

JH19B looked a bulky car, but it was close to the 515kg minimum weight. Streiff is the driver.

JH19C appeared sleeker – in bodywork details such as the engine cover and curves inside the rear wheel. Streiff is driving the JH19C during practice at Brands Hatch, where he went on to win the race and secure a tiny niche in history.

Last of the old-order front-engined Grand Prix cars in 1960. The Ferrari Dino 246 (**top**) was the most thoroughly race-developed of the type but even on an ultra-fast circuit such as Reims, where engine power paid dividends, Phil Hill could only just stay on terms with the works Coopers. In any case, his car did not last through this French GP.

That race saw the last Grand Prix appearance of the Vanwall team, and perhaps heart ruled head, for it was a one-off race for VW11 (**above**), the low and light car. It was unimpressive in practice at Reims (Brooks started it from row 6 of the grid after a troublesome practice) and it completed only eight laps in the race.

The outstanding car/engine and driver combination of the last two seasons of 2.5-litre F1 racing, Cooper-Climax and Jack Brabham (**top**). The car here is the 'low line' T53 driven by Brabham to win five World Championship races in 1960. While suspension improvements cannot be seen, it obviously has a low frontal area and a lean nose for good penetration.

The Lotus 18 (**above**) looked unsophisticated beside a works Cooper in 1960 – but looks misled – while the Cooper T51 introduced only a year earlier looked a very bulky old thing in the company of the Lotus. Innes Ireland is driving the works 18 at Reims, while Olivier Gendebien is in the Yeoman Credit team Cooper.

The Lotus 25, and the derivative 33, was the outstanding F1 car of the 1.5-litre Formula, with a monocoque hull that by modern standards was very simple, beautifully clean lines and apparently skimpy suspension, very successful and for ever associated with Jim Clark (driving here).

BRM responded positively to the Lotus lead, with the P61 and P261 (or P61/2). This was more successful in its second form in 1964, when it had stressed-skin extensions to its central monocoque in place of the tubular sub frames front and rear. Dark green was favoured by the team until its cars were sponsored in 1970, but BRMs run by independent teams appeared in light green, red and blue. This P261 is being driven by Graham Hill, on his way to second place in the 1964 British GP at Brands Hatch.

Ferrari 158 matched its British V-8-engined rivals in sleek good looks in 1964. This 158 is driven by Bandini.

There was little conformity to Grand Prix grids in 1965: 3-2-3 was usual and 2-2-2 grids formed up at Monaco, Watkins Glen and Mexico City, but Silverstone and the Nürburgring quite comfortably accommodated 4-3-4 grids. The British GP front row quartet was Clark (Lotus 33), Hill (BRM P261), Ginther (Honda R272) and Stewart (BRM).

A Honda led a Grand Prix for the first time at Silverstone in 1965, and Richie Ginther was to win in one of the Japanese cars at the end of that season. Here he concentrates as the British GP field is assembled. His car has clean bodywork, but the suspension has a well-used look to it. The inboard layout compares interestingly with the cluttered appearance of the front suspension of Bob Anderson's private Brabham BT11 behind it.

JH20 This F3000 car marked a step towards F1, and by AGS standards it was nearly all new. Its carbon composite monocoque was developed from the Duqueiene VG4 (see Duqueiene), and in the double wishbone pushrod front suspension the coil springs/dampers were mounted horizontally within the nose, while the rear suspension followed JH19B lines. The association with Mader was retained as the Swiss specialist was responsible for the team's DFVs; drive was through a Hewland DG400. In racing reliability was suspect and Streiff's best run of finishes (5,3,5) came at the end of the year; he was eighth in the Championship.

The monocoque was used in the JH20B, which had revised suspension and fuller bodywork. It was run by the Danielsson team in 1986, but raced only four times as worthwhile sponsorship did not materialize (the only scoring finish was Dallest's fourth at Pau).

JH20 had a spindly and unfinished look – the lines were attractive from the nose to the back of the cockpit, but around the exposed DFV the car seemed incomplete.

JH21C The 30th AGS, if rebuilds and conversions are excluded, this was another one-off. A substantial and overweight F1 machine incorporating major Renault components, including a remodelled monocoque, double wishbone suspension and brakes, it was powered by the Motori-Moderni turbocharged V-6. It made its debut in the 1986 Italian GP, and failed to finish in its two races that year.

Driver: Ivan Capelli.

JH22 The designation changed, as did the power unit, but a lot of JH21C and four-year-old Renault technology remained. There was a normally-aspirated Cosworth DFZ engine in the back, two cars were built and there was detail change if not development through the year. The worthwhile change came at the end of the season, when Roberto Moreno took Fabre's place in the cockpit and scored in the Australian GP – his first point, and AGS's first Constructors' Championship point. Otherwise, Fabre had usually qualified (eleven times in 14 attempts) and had a best race placing of ninth.

One of the cars was to be used as a test bed for the Negre W-12 engine in 1988, but this combination did not run on a circuit until Autumn 1989.

Drivers: Pascal Fabre, Roberto Moreno.

The white and red colour scheme did not flatter JH22, which in any case was cumbersome in appearance as well as in track behaviour. The engine air intake above the cover was one of the bodywork variables, and the wings were modified on and off through the year. The venue is Silverstone, during practice for the British GP. In the race Fabre scored one of his two top-ten placings.

JH23 This car came in a season overshadowed by off-track problems, with sponsors and with rumours of a take over (that came to pass early in 1989 and with the loss of most of the technical staff). So the JH23 was Vanderplyen's last AGS. It was simple and slender, with only minor components carried over from the JH22. There was nothing in the specification to mark it out, in its monocoque, double wishbones pushrod suspension or DFZ V-8, but this time AGS was rated unlucky not to score points. Streiff's return helped – he was a consistent mid-grid qualifier, and although he finished only four races he had sometimes run with the big boys.

The car was uprated as the JH23B for 1989 with DFR engines. One was destroyed in Streiff's very serious Brazilian test accident. Joachim Winkelhock was never able to pre-qualify and was replaced in mid season; Tarquini invariably qualified and scored a point in Mexico.

Drivers: Philippe Streiff, Gabriele Tarquini.

Visually there was little to distinguish this AGS, here in its 1989 JH23B form and driven by Winkelhock in one of his fruitless attempts to pre-qualify the car.

JH24 This car came late, understandably as new technical manager/designer Claude Galopin joined the team after the 1988 'defections'. It had a stiffer monocoque in carbon fibre/kevlar, largely JH23 suspension, a lower mounting for the DFR (2.5cm makes a difference in weight distribution), and the six-speed gearbox used on JH23B. Outwardly it had shorter and lower side pods and engine cover. It first appeared in practice for the French GP, and was expected to run in the British GP. However, for the rest of the season the team failed to qualify a single car. Three JH24s were built, and second driver Dalmas had one for the last two races, but he repeated Winkelhock's early-season DNPQ record.

JH24 looked the part, but Gabriele Tarquini could not get it onto the grid for a race in 1989. This is a practice shot from French GP practice, where the car first appeared.

AHE

Alan Eyre, an Australian, built this stubby but otherwise conventional tubular frame 500cc car which appeared in 1955.

ML

AIKENS

Frank Aikens' 500cc special of 1946-7 had a Fiat 500 chassis, with the rear axle modified to take a chain drive, and a vertical twin Triumph engine and Norton gearbox mounted at the back. Aikens was a pilot in the R.A.F. and on his home base was a German P.o.W. who had once been a racing mechanic and was only too delighted to become involved in the project. With then rare tuning components they made the Triumph engine a very potent motor indeed. The driver was not helped by an uncomfortable 'knees under the chin' driving position but Aikens drove well, although the car was often unreliable.

ML

AJB

In the late 1940s Archie Butterworth designed a Grand Prix car in his spare time. This was to have a 4425cc (89 x 89mm) air-cooled V-8 mounted in an independently sprung frame with torsion bar suspension and four-wheel drive. Braking was to be by hydraulic discs all round and among several patented features was a five-speed gearbox with twin-pedal change. This progressed as far as the chassis frame but in the meantime he found a couple of air-cooled 3.7-litre V-8 Steyr engines complete with three-speed gearboxes.

One was put into a crude chassis with quarter elliptic springs all round, and boxed-in Jeep side members, but its transmisssion was ingenious. From the gearbox the power was transmitted to a transfer box which offset the drive to a central differential. From there prop shafts took the power front and rear to standard Jeep axles which, of course, were 'live'. The Steyr's capacity was increased to 4425cc (87.5 x 92mm) and power output from 85bhp to 260bhp.

This special scored some successes in sprints and hill climbs and in 1950 it took part in the International Trophy at Silverstone. Unfortunately the aluminium crankcase flexed and it ran its bearings after just one lap.

Later Butterworth built and ran an ingenious transmission in which gears were changed by pressing one of two clutch pedals; this was taken up by Lotus but Chapman's ideas clashed with Butterworth's and it was dropped.

The 1949 AJB was primarily intended for sprints and (as here) hill climbs, but this imposing, noisy and ingenious device did appear on a circuit.

At the beginning of 1952 Butterworth completed the first stage of an air-cooled flat four engine project. By changing the cylinder barrels the engine could be made in sizes between 1.5-litres and 2.5-litres. For the 1952 season he had made up parts for six of these units in 2-litre form (87.5 x 82.5mm). One of these engines went to Kieft and was fitted with Norton barrels but Kieft could not cool it properly and it was sold on to later appear in Graham Eden's F2 Cooper (entered as the 'Cooper-Arden'). This ran in only one club race. Two other engines were used in the Aston-Butterworths.

In 1957 the final version AJB engine appeared, when it was run in an Elva sports car driven by Archie Scott-Brown. It won only one race, a five-lapper at Brands Hatch, although with a claimed 158bhp it was one of the most powerful 1.5-litre engines in the world. Once the problem with exhaust valves was identified Butterworth began to modify a Cooper chassis to take the engine. It was to have been driven in F2 by Archie Scott-Brown and then enlarged to 2.5-litres to run in F1. An entry was filed for the Monaco GP, which had an F2 class, but the car was not ready so Scott-Brown drove the works Lister-Jaguar at Spa where he crashed and died of his injuries. Butterworth then turned his back on motor racing.

ML

AJS

Despite the name, this car had no official connection with AJS the motorcycle manufacturer although it did use its engines. The cars were slim Cooper copies made in Casablanca which was then in French Morocco. It is said that two of them scored a resounding 1-2 on their debut in a race in Morocco of which no record exists, but after that triumph nothing further was heard of it in Europe.

ML

ALBA

Giorgio Stirano was an engineer with Osella until 1981, when he left and built his first Alba ('dawn'). Although the marque was to become associated with sports-racing cars, this one-off was the F3 AR1. It was entirely conventional, with an Alfa Romeo engine, and made no impression before being set aside as Stirano concentrated on his first Group C Junior car. It was raced by Pavia in 1982.

The F3 Alba had a well-used look when it first appeared in the Autumn of 1981.

ALEXIS

Alex Francis' first competition cars were trials specials, the first for his own use in 1953 and the last of a small production batch coming in 1964. By that time the Alexis company was five years old, having been set up by Francis and Bill Harris, designer of the Flather Special F3 car, to build a Formula Junior car. When Harris returned to Australia in 1965 Allan Taylor effectively took his place and in the second half of the 1960s built Alexis up as a racing car constructor.

The first Juniors gave way to professional Juniors as Alexis moved on from the Mk1, for Francis and Harris to race as amateurs, to cars for the professional Team Alexis, and then for sale. Alexis naturally entered F2 and F3 as these took the place of FJ and the marque's racing high point came when Paul Hawkins won the F2 Eifelrennen in 1965. There were also failures, with later F2 and F3 efforts, but in business terms there was a successful liaison with the Jim Russell Racing Drivers' School which led to the production of 57 Russell-Alexis Formula Ford cars in 1967-8.

Lesser categories were to keep bread and butter work flowing for the Alexis plant at Coleshill from 1970 onwards. F3 cars were listed through much of the decade, but in that category Alexis rather lost its way and its cars did not actually feature on F3 grids. Incidentally, Terry Ogilvie-Hardy's 'Project X' offerings tended to be based on Alexis.

Mks 1 and 2 These 1959 and 1960 FJ cars were front-engined one-offs, the second being a logical refinement. Both had space frame chassis with offset cockpits and shapely aluminium bodies. Wishbone ifs was used, but the rigid rear axles of the first car gave way to an independent arrangement of lower wishbones, top links (the driveshafts) and radius arms on the Mk2. Both had BMC engines driving through BMC gearboxes, although in Mk2 a Ford 105E was to take the place of the A-series engine. These cars were successful at club level, but that was not what FJ was about, or where Alexis wanted to be.

Among front-engined cars, Mk2 was outstandingly compact, although this was at the expense of a cramped cockpit which enforced the close-to-the-wheel driving position that returned to racing favour among saloon drivers of the late 1980s (and meant that an Alexis driver of average stature towered above the roll-over bar). Cooper wheels were used, but in components like that Alexis was soon to be self-sufficient. This car, which is being driven at Goodwood by Gerry Ashmore, later became the basis of a Project X car.

Mk3 A Junior introduced for 1961 with a Ford engine behind the cockpit and driving through a VW gearbox. Otherwise this car was very similar in make-up to the Mk2. A pair was built for Team Alexis, for whom Jack Pitcher scored a first victory, in a minor race at Cadwell Park in the Spring. Generally Peter Procter was the lead driver.

Mk4 Another pair for the team, straightforward successors to the Mk3s. The suspension was modified for smaller and wider wheels, disc brakes took the place of drums, and there was a Hewland gearbox. It did not appear until May, and the summer of 1962 was passing before John Rhodes took a top sixth place in a Mk4. In the following year Australian John Ampt was second in a Mk4 in races at Silverstone and Chimay.

Mk5 A one-off Junior for 1963, again similar in mechanical respects, a little smaller than the Mk4 and with fibreglass bodywork. It was run alongside the older cars, usually driven by Ampt, then it had a second life in F3 as DAF bought it to race-test the Variomatic transmission.

Mk6 Harris laid this out as a dual-purpose (F2//F3) chassis, but the pair built were used in F3 form and when an F2 car was completed it was designated Mk7 (although confusingly Chris Meek ran a Mk6 in three F2 races in 1967). The design followed lines established with the Juniors but there was little return from major races (Ampt was sixth in a Monza F3 race).

Mk7 The F2 variant of the Mk6, with Cosworth SCA and Hewland gearbox. In 1964 it was never quite the equal of the Lotus 32, or the Brabhams and Lolas, but Peter Revson was fourth at Pergusa and fourth in a heat at Vallelunga, where Ogilvie-Hardy was fifth in the final. Although Paul Hawkins won the Eifelrennen in 1965 there were no other worthy results and that was Alexis' only win in the three 1-litre F2 seasons.

Mk8 Harris' last Alexis was another dual-purpose design, and another evolutionary design, using a shorter space frame chassis with modified suspension and bodywork. Three were built and little was achieved in F3 racing (Alexis did not appear in F2 in 1966), but one car was run with a BRM F2 engine in 1967.

Mk9 Allan Taylor's one-off 1966 F3 car, which marked a new departure but not a comeback. The intention to build a sturdier car was carried through, and the lack of competitiveness tended to be attributed to the team's Cosworth MAEs. That perhaps was a lead to its programme to develop its own MAEs and enter into a joint F2 engine programme with Vegantune, which led nowhere.

Mk10 This unsuccessful car marked a serious F2 endeavour. It had a contracted-out space frame design, Cosworth FVA and Hewland gearbox. Alexis did not have the resources to develop it – contracted driver David Hobbs drove just one race in a Mk10, and Taylor had a few outings later in 1967 but nothing came of them.

Mk12 This F3 car was introduced when the 1968 season was under way, and that, perhaps, accounts for the fact that only three were built when, on paper, it was a sound design. It was conventional, with a new space frame, suspension that followed the general lines used for years, and Alexis' downdraught MAE (in the summer Ogilvie-Hardy ran a car with a Cosworth engine, and drove it to seventh place at Chimay).

Mk16 Taylor's 1969 F3 car had a refined space frame and outwardly followed the wedge fashion of the time. But the in-house engines never delivered competitive power and that perhaps overshadowed other shortcomings.

Mk17 The space frame was carried over to 1970, with neat new bodywork, a Holbay engine and a Hewland gearbox. A works car was run but development could hardly be progressive as several drivers occupied its cockpit through the season, none of them a top driver or one with a reputation for development work. A sixth place in one of the British series races was the only top-six achievement.

Mk20 The 1971 F3 car, with revised front suspension, side radiators and a pronounced wedge nose that made for a sleek overall appearance. A Vegantune engine was used in the development car, but once again there appeared to be little development and this car did not impress. Effectively Alexis was a spent force in F3, although the Mk25 and Mk27 were listed as F3/F Atlantic models in 1975-6.

ALFA DANA

This Danish name turned up in F3 in the second half of the 1950s, as a one-off driven by Rasmussen. Then it reappeared with a Formula Junior venture, on Stanguellini lines after these were outmoded. Remarkably, two cars survived in local racing into the 1-litre F3 years, fitted with BMC A Series-based engines, but as front-engined cars they were archaic.

ALFA ROMEO

Alfa Romeo is one of the great names of the middle period of racing, and its cars dominated the first two World Championship seasons. Sadly, it did not live up to its past in the early 1980s, when its Autodelta competitions subsidiary brought the name back into Grand Prix. To a degree that reflected an approach that was of the past – the principal personality at Autodelta was Carlo Chiti, whose most successful F1 work was on Ferrari engines of the early 1960s and who often seemed very much a man of racing in the 1950s. He took Alfa Romeo into sports car racing in the 1960s, and engines from that programme were used in McLaren and March F1 cars, while the twelve-cylinder engines from it were developed for Brabham under an arrangement that was exclusive until the decision to run Alfa Romeo F1 cars was taken.

The return in 1979 was widely welcomed. The team tried hard for three seasons while the parent company struggled. Then racing responsibilities were divided – Autodelta continued to build the machines, but Paolo Pavanello's Euroracing outfit ran them. That arrangement lasted for three seasons. Throughout there were personality clashes and hirings and firings, most notably concerning Chiti and Ducarouge.

Those six full seasons produced little in terms of results and championship points. The Alfa Romeo Grand Prix line faded away at the end of 1985 and it seemed unlikely that it would have continued when Fiat took control, as their GP arm was Ferrari. Alfa engines continued to be used by other minor constructors until 1988 and an Indycar engine programme came in the following year.

158 This very straightforward car was designed for *vetturetta* racing by Gioacchino Colombo, working at Ferrari's Modena plant (Enzo Ferrari initiated the design, and for a while he managed Alfa Corse, which ran the 'Alfetta' in what amounted to second-division racing). The cars were raced in 1938 – Villoresi won in a 158 first time out – and through to 1940. They were brought out again in 1946, and then became Grand Prix cars as they complied with the regulations that came in 1947.

Heart of the 158 was a twin-ohc supercharged straight eight (58 x 70mm, 1479cc), which produced 275bhp in 1947. The chassis of oval-section tubes was orthodox, as was the independent front suspension and swing axle at the rear. But in performance there was nothing ordinary about these cars – in 1947-8 the 158s won every time they started and after a sabbatical in 1949 they won every time out in 1950, when their drivers (Farina, Fangio, Fagioli) were 1-2-3 in the first World Championship. That year the engine was rated at 350bhp, and was becoming hugely thirsty for the methanol fuel used. Further development led to redesignation, as the 159.

Drivers (post war races): Luigi Fagioli, Juan Manuel Fangio, Giuseppe Farina, Alessandro Gaboardi, Emanuel de Graffenried, Battista Guidotti, Reg Parnell, Consalvo Sanesi, Piero Taruffi, Carlo Felice Trossi, Achille Varzi, Jean-Pierre Wimille.

Two winners in Switzerland – **above**, the first world champion, Giuseppe Farina, in a 158/50 in the 1950 GP and, **below**, Fangio on the Bremgarten cobbles in a 159 in 1951.

159 First raced late in 1950, this was a development of the 158, with engines that eventually gave up to 425bhp (but absorbed 135bhp in supercharger drive, and had a fuel consumption of 1.6mpg), minor chassis revisions and on some 159M cars a de Dion rear suspension. In 1951 Ferrari's cars matched the Alfas – the 27th consecutive victory for the 158/159 came in the French GP, then a Ferrari won the British race, and Fangio drove a 159 to win its last race, the Spanish GP. Some work was done on a successor, but the Alfa management realistically decided to abandon Grand Prix racing.

Drivers: Felice Bonetto, Juan-Manuel Fangio, Giuseppe Farina, Emanuel de Graffenried, Paul Pietsch, Consalvo Sanesi.

177 The Alfa Romeo return to Grand Prix racing was gradual and less than glorious, with a car that had been driven through a year of development before it was raced in 1979. It was a corpulent car in Alfa's traditional dark red, with the flat twelve engine (77 x 53.6mm, 2995cc) that had sports car origins and F1 development through the Brabham liaison. It was raced three times (Belgium, France, Italy), recording no finishes.

Driver: Bruno Giacomelli

177 was a bulky car which proved almost surprisingly competitive in its first race outing, suggesting it might to advantage have been raced a year earlier. Its 1979 driver was Giacomelli, here in the Belgian GP.

179 In many ways a derivative of the 177, but with the 1260 series V-12 (78.5 x 51.5mm, 2995cc) and ground effects aerodynamics by Frenchman Robert Choulet, this car first appeared at the 1979 Italian GP and was extensively revised for its full season in 1980. Revision continued through the season as Autodelta groped towards competitive performance. In this the team was cruelly set back when Depailler was killed in a test accident at Hockenheim. Autodelta seemed to come to terms with ground effects but was then wrong-footed by the ban on sliding skirts in 1981. For that year the 179s had been updated as 179Cs. An attempt to devise a hydropneumatic suspension lowering system failed. A lower D version appeared in mid-season, and fared no better. Ducarouge joined and reworked the ground effects again. At the very end of the 179's life a 179F with a carbon-fibre monocoque appeared, and in 1982 a 179 was converted for development purposes with a turbocharged 1.5-litre V-8.

Drivers: Mario Andretti, Vittorio Brambilla, Patrick Depailler, Andrea de Cesaris, Bruno Giacomelli.

A 179 in C form, driven by Andretti at Long Beach, where he finished fourth.

182 This appeared almost as bulky as the 179s, but with a British carbon fibre monocoque in place of the aluminium honeycomb chassis it was substantially lighter. The suspension arrangement of top rocker arms and lower wishbones was retained. The design was largely the work of Ducarouge. The V-12 produced some 530bhp, but in a world where turbos ruled and 600bhp was called for.

Alfa's turbocar made its public debut during Italian GP practice. This 182T had a narrower monocoque (already seen on the 182D) and several other modifications, while the 890T 90-degree V-8 (74 x 43.5mm, 1496cc) was rated at 600bhp. It was not raced in 1982.

At the end of that year Alfa president Ettore Massacesi announced that the racing equipment and many of the personnel were to be handed over to Euroracing. That was at least better than the closure that had been anticipated.

Drivers: Andrea de Cesaris, Bruno Giacomelli.

One of the better finishes for the Autodelta team was the third place gained by de Cesaris in this 182T at Monaco in 1982. Everything about the car, even the suspension fairings, looks big (overall length was actually 439cm and width 215cm).

183T The 182T was the basis for the 1983 car, to the 'flat-bottom' regulations (the sole 182T was converted as the first of five 183Ts). The later cars were revised as the season went on, but not under the direction of Ducarouge, who was fired in mid-summer; Luigi Marmiroli took his place. It was an encouraging season, with two second places falling to the team.

Drivers: Mauro Baldi, Andrea de Cesaris.

184T Marmiroli's 184T in Benetton colours had more angular lines, pushrod front suspension, pullrod rear suspension, and the turbo V-8 rated at 670bhp. That was not enough, and in terms of results the team slipped. In mid-summer Chiti was eased out and his place was taken by Giovanni Tonti. Two of the cars had to be brought out again in mid-1985, when a 185T was also converted to 184T specification.

Drivers: Eddie Cheever, Riccardo Patrese.

New colours and a new shape brought no improvement in Alfa Romeo GP fortunes. This is Patrese in 184T/2 in the British GP.

185T A redesign by John Gentry, who left before development started. The team despaired of it, brought out 184Ts and managed just seven finishes all year, one scoring points. Almost inevitably, 1985 was the last season for an Alfa Romeo GP team, although engines were supplied to another second-rank outfit through to the end of the turbo era (in 1988 with 'Osella' on the cam covers).

Drivers: Eddie Cheever, Riccardo Patrese.

ALFA SPECIAL

Probably the best of the specials which ran in the South African Gold Star series and which was also turned out for local F1 races, this car was built by Piet de Klerk, who had worked at Lotus and then returned home to construct his car. It was a typical South African special of its time with space frame, all independent suspension by coil springs and wishbones, and an enlarged and tuned Alfa Romeo Giulietta engine because the Gold Star series was limited to four cylinder engines.

Apart from Gold Star success de Klerk qualified the car eleventh in the 1963 South African GP, within 0.8s of McLaren and Maggs in the works Coopers, but his fine effort came to an end at two-thirds distance with a broken gearbox. In the 1965 Grand Prix de Klerk qualified 17th in a field of 20, and finished tenth, the quickest of all the locals. That may not appear to be a remarkable feat, but it was achieved in a three-year-old special with a modified production car engine in a World Championship event.   ML

ALPINE

Jean Redelé formed Alpine at Dieppe in 1951. This started an association with Renault that was to lead to the company becoming the Régie's competitions arm, to the point where it was responsible for the A500 'Laboratoire' that was the direct forerunner of the turbocharged GP Renaults. Alpine's reputation perhaps rested on its rally coupés, sports-racing cars and road-going sports cars, but from the mid-1960s it had an important role in the revival of French single-seater racing fortunes.

The first Alpine *monoplace*, which came in 1964, was an F2/F3 car with strong Brabham resemblances – Ron Tauranac had a design consultant role. The weak point tended to be the Renault-based engines, and for that reason F2 was set aside. By 1968 sports cars and *Formule France* – less competitive and immediately more rewarding – were taking priority over F3, but there was a stillborn F1 project. Although *Formule Renault* had become important by the early 1970s, Alpine had become a force again in F3 from 1969, with a string of *comingmen* – Depailler, Jabouille, Leclère and Tambay among them – winning their spurs with the oddly-shaped but effective cars.

At the same time the Alpine A110s enjoyed a successful run in major rallies and the Renault-Alpine sports-racing cars were being developed. In business terms, however, Alpine was running into trouble and was to be saved by a complete Renault takeover in 1974. Apart from the A500, the emphasis at Dieppe shifted to the A440-441-442 sports-racing cars and the single-seater line ended.

1964-5 The first F2 and F3 Alpines had many common components, with tubular space frames and suspension that were closely similar to the 1963 Formula Junior Brabham, while the body attributed to Marcel Hubert had Brabham lines.

The F2 car used the twin-ohc Gordini-developed Renault engine, which was rated at 105bhp. This was some 10bhp less than the Cosworth SCA used by most other constructors, which was out of the question for Alpine because of its Ford associations. Nominally the works pair were run 'for experience', and while Mauro Bianchi and Jose Rosinski achieved some reasonable results early in 1964 the F2 Alpine was soon eclipsed.

The F3 car fared better, with the robust Mignotet-prepared R8 engine giving 80bhp. While the F2 car had a five-speed Hewland gearbox, the F3 version had a Renault four-speed unit. Development away from the Brabham-like origins started, but the car was soon to be overwhelmed by Matras. Before that happened, Henry Grandsire and Mauro Bianchi scored some good Alpine wins in 1964 French races and Grandsire won the French F3 championship. A few cars were sold to independents.

The first single-seater to come from the Dieppe specialist constructor at its early-1964 debut. This is the F3 car, with one of the works drivers, Mauro Bianchi, in the cockpit and F2 driver Rosinski beside it.

1966-7 These were low-key seasons, largely because Matra had no inhibitions about using British engines and so became the dominant French single-seater marque, and Alpine backed away from F2 and did not mount a major effort in F3. The cars followed the established Alpine pattern, with revised suspension, still outboard all round, and a modified space frame for the 1967 F3 car. Rory Weber salvaged some good results in 1966 (he was second in the French Championship), while Cévert and Depailler moved up into F3 driving Alpines. Early in that year, Bianchi and Grandsire did well with Alpines in Argentine F3 Temporada races.

There was less Brabham influence by 1966, whatever appearances may suggest, and the Alpines had clean lines. This is Bianchi, letting the tail slide in Argentina in 1966.

A330 The 1968 F3 car, which had a reputation for handling well, had a shorter chassis (still a space frame but with little left of the original Tauranac work). Outside East European F3 this was the only car not powered by a Ford-based engine – an output of the order of 115bhp was claimed, but that had to be matched against the 120-125bhp of the opposition. *Formule France* took priority and a minimal budget hamstrung F3 development – one car was run for Depailler, attended by two mechanics. He showed what might have been, with three good second places and other top-five finishes in French races. In 1969 this car was still used, alongside that year's A360. Depailler drove it, and was fourth in the French championship behind team mate Jabouille.

A360 To all intents and purposes this F3 car started as a long wheelbase version of A330, and Jabouille won with it at Montlhéry. After a dormant season, when the only Alpine around was the A330 with a Novamotor engine, the A360 was revived, with striking bodywork.

The 1971 A360 had a similar space frame, wider (as was the track) and longer to accommodate a single fuel tank behind the driver. Unequal-length wide-based wishbones were used in the front suspension, with lower wishbones, top links and radius arms at the rear. The Renault R16-based engine produced just over 120bhp for 1971, and drove through a Hewland Mk8 five-speed 'box. The usual nose looked substantial but a narrow one was sometimes seen, the centre section was slim and the tail was high, multi-louvred and apparently efficient, while midriff bulges were to improve aerodynamic qualities.

Just two works cars were run in 1971 when they won consistently in France (Depailler was Champion) and one even crossed the line first at Brands Hatch, only for that very rare victory to be disallowed. Lucien Guitteny ran one of these cars independently in 1972, with some success.

First time around – the original A360 at Montlhéry in 1969.

In familiar form – the bluff-wide-nosed A360 in 1971. The car was sometimes run in a 'narrow-nose' form, that is without the suspension-shrouding parts bearing the word 'Elf'. This car is on hostile ground, at Mallory Park.

At the Paul Ricard circuit, this car driven by Jabouille is running in 'fast circuit' form with no aerofoils at all – a most unusual condition for a formula single-seater by that time.

A364 This car served through the last two seasons of 1.6-litre F3 racing, in 1973 in 'B' form, and unlike its predecessors was built for sale to independents. It had a new space frame designed by André de Cortanze, which in large part was to be carried over to the Elf 2 F2 car in 1974, and revised suspension. While the bodywork theme was similar, the A364 was a sleeker car. The works cars were run in distinctive Renault house colours which complemented the work of aerodynamicist Hubert. Dudot-Renault engines were standard, and in 1973 these matched the Ford-based units in terms of power output.

The works pair, Leclère and Serpaggi, were top contenders in 1972-3, Depailler stepped back down to F3 to win the Monaco race in 1972 and Guitteny scored well. In 1973 the 'domestic' challenge from Martini led to suspension revisions. Then with the end of the formula, the Alpine *monoplace* line abruptly ended – any other considerations apart, there were no suitable Renault engines for the 2-litre F3.

A500 Alpine built two F1 cars that were never raced. The first, tested in 1968 by Mauro Bianchi, was a conventional machine with a 3-litre V-8 and Hewland gearbox, apparently built without full authority or even the agreement of Redelé and therefore set aside. The second, designed by André de Cortanze, was the Laboratoire, forerunner of the Renault turbocharged F1 cars. It was a monocoque car, using the suspension layout from the A442 sports-racing car, as well as the turbo engine. Extensive tests were run at French circuits, and at Jarama, in 1976.

The 'business end' of A500, with part of the turbo V-6 showing and a piece of metal sheet on the otherwise sinister black bodywork suggesting that variations were being tested. In most respects, the car looks as if it could have been raced.

ALTA

The origins of Geoffrey Taylor's Alta marque were in a sporting car of the late 1920s; the first single-seater came in the next decade and from 1937 Alta was a challenger in the *voiturette* category. Plans for a Grand Prix car were announced late in 1945, but this took shape in the metal very slowly and the first did not appear at a race meeting until 1948 – Alta resources were always stretched thin. A second car came in 1949, the third in 1950.

The Alta was a good-looking car, with a sturdy tubular chassis and independent suspension all round, and with double wishbones and circular rubber blocks in compression as the springing medium. The 'square' (78 x 78mm, 1485cc) engine initially had single-stage supercharging, but in the third car had two-stage supercharging and gave 230bhp. It drove through Alta's own four-speed all-synchromesh gearbox.

The Grand Prix car first ran, briefly, in the 1948 British Empire Trophy race, and its Grand Prix debut came in Switzerland. The first worthwhile race placings did not come until 1949, when Abecassis was seventh in the British GP. Remarkably Geoffrey Crossley, a complete novice in Grand Prix and Continental racing terms, then placed his car seventh in the Belgian GP. Those were the highlights, however, for the chassis (reputedly following a 1939 Mercedes) was heavy, the rubber in the suspension behaved inconsistently and the engine (reputedly following Maserati lines – the internal dimensions were no coincidence) seldom delivered its full power.

The third car went to Joe Kelly, and in 1952 it was the basis of his Bristol-engined IRA (Irish Racing Automobiles).

In 1951 Alta built three 2-litre F2 cars, which were as disappointing – the HWMs and Coopers using Alta engines were much more successful. The 1970cc (83.5 x 90mm) version of the engine was rated at 140bhp, improved to 150bhp in the last two Alta cars built, in 1952. As Geoff Taylor followed the lines of his 1.5-litre supercharged car in the F2 chassis and running gear this car was even more overweight in power/weight ratio terms.

Some work was done on a car for the 2.5-litre formula but this was never built. The engine intended for it was successful in Connaughts (who reached an exclusive deal with Alta when it was clear that Coventry Climax would not release its FPE 'Godiva' engine).

Drivers (GPs): George Abecassis, Geoffrey Crossley, John Heath, Joe Kelly, Graham Whitehead.

The 1.5-litre supercharged Alta was a big car, with lines very much in keeping with its late-1940s contemporaries. This first car has been rebuilt with a higher and shorter tail and exhaust running past the cockpit just below the rear-view mirror. The driver in the very old-fashioned position in this shot is John Heath, in the 1948 French GP.

AMON

New Zealander Chris Amon was an immensely talented racing driver, universally adjudged unlucky never to win a Grand Prix. That streak of misfortune continued as he became a driver-constructor in 1974, with the Amon AF101. This car, which turned out to be a one-off, was designed by Gordon Fowell ('F' in the designation) and financed in large part by John Dalton. It was not the simplest of designs – following Lotus lines rather than March lines among its contemporaries – and development was beyond the team's resources. The AF101 was built around a slim aluminium monocoque, with the fuel carried between its cockpit and DFV engine, torsion bar suspension and apparently sophisticated aerodynamics. It suffered component failures and accidents, and was qualified to start in only one GP (the 1974 Spanish race, when it failed to finish).

Drivers: Chris Amon, Larry Perkins

The AF101 during practice at Monaco, when hub problems led to its withdrawal. Usually the light blue car was run with a simpler conventional single front wing.

AMS

This Italian F2 car had more than a passing resemblance to the March 782, but it was powered by AMS's own V-6 engine, which made it unusual among F2 cars. The AMS 279 appeared at only one race meeting, the 1979 European Championship round at Misano, where it did not come to the grid as its driver, Piero Necchi, was involved in a fracas with a marshal after practice. A two-car team was announced for 1980, but failed to materialize.

AMWEG

Alfred Amweg was optimistic when he presented his BMW-engined AA1 F2 car for practice at Hockenheim in June 1976. It was distant from the pace, failed to qualify, and was not seen again.

ANSON

Gary Anderson and Bob Simpson battled for years to break the F3 mould with their Ansons, and sometimes seemed to, as when Franz Konrad won the 1983 German Championship with an SA4. Major success, however, eluded Anson, although the cars showed real promise in F3 and did well in Super Vee in the USA.

The first SA1 (1975) was basically a Brabham BT38 reworked in a small garage and driven by Anderson in *formule libre*; the second SA1 was an original design which appeared in F3 in 1976. The partners gave up work as senior F1 technicians to build the SA2, but then returned to major teams as backing for their F3 project fell through. With Jeff Hills they formed Anson Ltd. in 1980 to make specialized racing parts, before picking up the F3 thread again and continuing with it through to the SA6 of the mid-1980s. The SA6 was built by Pacemaker, and there was talk of Formula Atlantic and F3000 cars, but Pacemaker got into financial difficulties early in 1987 and the single-seater rights were sold to a US company, which intended to continue FSV production. Gary Anderson worked for a while with Galles' Indycar team, then returned to European racing as race engineer with F3000 teams.

SA2 This was laid down as an F3 car for a proposed 1977 Unipart team (which eventually came into being with March chassis). Only one car was completed. Anticipating later Ansons, it was flat sided, and had a full-width nose. Lack of resources meant it was not developed, and it made no impression.

SA3 With this car Anson gained a foothold in F3, and the SA3V variant was well received in US Super Vee circles. It was introduced early in 1981, with the slogan 'Simple, Safe and Swift', which sounded more appropriate to a cyclecar of the 1920s.

The SA3 had a honeycomb panel monocoque, top rocker arm/bottom wishbone suspension front and rear, an original approach to aerodynamics with a 'rear pod' incorporating the engine cover and a low aerofoil and short side pods. By the time it was raced it had a normal rear wing and pods extending full length between the wheels. The SA3C (1982) had minor bodywork improvements, and suspension changes came in mid-season. It was basically a precise car and F3 drivers preferred the 'lazier' Ralt chassis.

The driver sat well forward in the SA3 – the front coil spring/damper units were mounted to the instruments bulkhead, while the adjustable anti-roll bar was under his knees. This is an SA3C during tests early in 1982.

SA4 This car was similar to its predecessor in constructional detail, outwardly with a long flat deck behind the cockpit and full-length pods between the wheels. Development time was wasted with unsuitable tyres, but in 1983 there were really quite enough orders for Anson's modest Tamworth base, particularly from Germany for F3 cars and from the USA for Super Vees. In 1984 when the developed SA4B was offered the accent tended to be on Super Vees. Claudio Langes showed this Anson's potential in 1983 European F3 races, with an Alfa-engined car; Tommy Byrne was sixth in the 1984 European championship, starting the year with Alfa engines before switching to VW units. SA4s were not campaigned in the important British F3 series in those seasons.

SA4 was perhaps the most attractive Anson, in part because it was less angular than the others. This is a 1984 'B' car, with Novamotor-Alfa engine. Tommy Byrne is in the cockpit with Gary Anderson beside it.

SA6 Pacemaker Performance Cars of Bridgnorth undertook production of this rather bulky Anderson design, which had lines determined by its deep monocoque and was another dual-role car, intended for FSV as well as F3. Keith Fine placed the Mike Rowe SA6 in the top ten of a British F3 race early in 1985, then Anson faded away.

Perhaps the kindest one-word description of the SA6 was 'distinctive', for the lines of its prominent side pods were at odds with the slope of the nose and the curving engine cover. Driver is Keith Fine, kerb-hopping at Thruxton's chicane.

APACHE

Appropriately originating from West Creek in California, the Apache was a front-engined Junior line which ran to two models in 1959-60. It was offered with a variety of power units, including MG TD-based engines complying with the American Formula Junior regulations which briefly admitted engines up to 1.5 litres with a weight penalty. The Apache had a tubular chassis, broad wishbone independent suspension front and rear and transmission offset to the right to give a lower driver position. The cars do not feature in contemporary race results.

APOLLON

The Jolly Club of Switzerland attempted to run Williams FW03 under this name in 1977, two years after its heyday and with a predictable lack of success.

ARC

This French sports car constructor built a one-off Toyota-engined F3 car in 1982, and apparently abandoned it after it had appeared at one early-Autumn race meeting.

ARENGO

The Arengo was a 500cc special from Bristol which caused something of a stir when it was announced during the winter of 1949-50 because the maker claimed 52bhp from a special three-valve head bolted to the top of a JAP engine (at the time a Norton gave about 46bhp) and that in a car with an all-up weight of 350lb against the 600lb for a Cooper. The car had a ladder frame with stressed substructures to carry the four corners which were independently sprung by transverse quarter-elliptical springs (double wishbones at the front, swing axles at the rear).

Joe Fry drove the prototype to score a debut win but that was against poor opposition in a minor race at a long-forgotten airfield circuit (Lulsgate). When the Arengo (at least three were made) came across serious opposition it proved unequal to the job.   ML

ARGO

Out of the collapse of one British specialist constructor, Modus, another came into being. Anglia Cars once seemed on the verge of becoming firmly established in F3 but that never quite came to pass, although its Argo cars were sometimes front runners. Key to its formation was Jo Marquart, a Swiss designer from a background with McLaren, Huron, GRD and Modus, and it was the failure of the Modus group that led him to start on the first Argo in a domestic garage at Wymondham in Norfolk. He was joined by John Peterson, American one-time driver and co-founder of the British Novamotor agency, and one-time mechanic Nick Jordan.

The first Argo echoed Marquart's Modus and was completed in February 1977. It had a successful debut and there were good race results in the second half of that year, but this was followed by a down season, and that seemed to set a pattern for Argo. For example, JM6 worked well in F3, Super Vee and Formula Atlantic in 1980, but the JM8 was a failure in 1981. Eventually Argo backed away from F3 and hopes of a resurgence in the category in 1989 came to nothing.

JM1 Essentially this was an F3 Modus carrying less bodywork. It was conventional, with double wishbone front suspension and a lower wishbone/top link arrangement at the rear; coil springs/dampers were outboard at the front, but if the bodywork line of the bulged flanks had been carried through to the back of the engine it would have enclosed them at the rear. Outwardly there was a prominent full-width nose and deep cockpit surround. Nova Toyota engines were normally used, with Hewland 'boxes. Stefan Johansson scored the first Argo F3 victory at Anderstorp in August 1977 and later that year David Kennedy was second in two European Championship races. Johansson had a relatively good season with an under-financed JM1 in the 1978 British series.

The first Argo, brand new and shining early in 1977. The nose and radiators strongly echo Marquart's Modus F3 car.

JM3 This was a tidied up derivative wing car, which was disappointing for much of the 1979 season. It had one-piece bodywork, clothing a slim monocoque and wide side pods and a revised engine bay. This would accept Toyota or VW engines (the former were normal), and the Hewland Mk9 gearbox was specified. Racing Team Holland ran a pair, but as a works-associated effort this failed to produce results or development so attention shifted to Roberto Guerrero. A revised car with stiffer monocoque and suspension was developed late in the season.

JM6 The 1980 F3 car, developed from the JM3, was very successful in the British Championship but not seen in Continental races. Guerrero had an excellent working relationship with the Argo personnel and by the summer the JM6 was rated the car to beat (it was beaten, in that Johansson switched from March to Ralt and won the title at the final round). Guerrero won five races and was equal second in the Championship; Tassin won two and was fourth at the end of the year, while Sears was eighth in a JM6. That was Argo's best F3 season. Dave Scott started his 1981 season with a JM6.

JM6 looked more bitty than its predecessors but was effective, although as a wing car it was surpassed by Ralt towards the end of the season. The driver is Thierry Tassin.

JM8 This was Argo's first full ground effects car, built around a slim aluminium panel monocoque with fuel tank on the centre line between cockpit and engine, and oil tank between engine and gearbox. The underside was smooth, suspension members were inboard (save for wishbones and top rocker arms, of course), while brakes were outboard all round. It all looked promising, and that seemed to be confirmed during tests, but in racing the car was a failure. Drivers turned away from it, Brett Riley was called in to develop it, and a JM6 had to be loaned to one customer as his JM8 was so far off the pace.

Aesthetically the lines of JM8's nose complemented the line of the side pods with their flush radiator intakes, but the whole car appeared bulky. Tassin, the driver here, soon abandoned the JM8 as beyond hope.

JM10 If Argo was to stay in F3 a new design was essential, and it came in the form of JM10. This had an aluminium monocoque extended rearwards to provide support for semi-stressed engines (there was no sub frame for this purpose), and wide side pods were featured again, with inboard suspension. The programme ran late, testing was further set back by an accident, and when the car did race in May 1982 it was immediately withdrawn 'for development'. That year nobody scored in an Argo, and Argo cars made only occasional F3 appearances after that, a JM10 running in a couple of 1984 British races. Then there were no Argos in F3 for some time, until the JM18 which had been announced for this category in 1989 made its debut at a French meeting in April 1990.

JM10 looked straightforward, and ordinary, after JM8, but it was never developed into a raceworthy car.

ARIEL SPECIAL

An early Australian 500 car built by R. Barnard on Cooper lines.   ML

ARNO

An F3 Arno one-off appeared in a late-1983 Italian race, when it was reported to have wayward handling, to the extent that its experienced driver, Fabio Mancini, found it very difficult to set up. This car, however, was a forerunner, and Arno Racing made a determined effort in the Italian Championship in the next two seasons. Three cars were built for 1984, and four to a similar design for 1985; Mancini continued as the leading driver.

The A02/384 was built around a honeycomb monocoque, with pushrod double wishbone suspension, and an Alfa engine. In 1984 the best race result was a third place, scored by Mancini, who was tenth in the Championship. Arno claimed to have built on experience in the A03/385, but this did not show in the race results of 1985, or in the flickering efforts in 1986.

ARNOTT

In 1953 Arnott seemed to be emerging as a possible challenger to Cooper in British F3 racing. Around a dozen were built but they failed to attract leading drivers. The car was designed for Daphne Arnott by George Thornton along fairly conventional chassis lines, but with double wishbone and longitudinal torsion bar suspension and distinctive looks stemming from its short wheelbase, flank fuel tanks and wide open cockpit. Ivor Bueb modified his Arnott, using coil springs, extending the wheelbase and replacing the pannier tanks with one behind the cockpit, but he soon turned to a Cooper, which is an indication of poor Arnott potential.

Among the mass of rear-engined F3 cars of 1953 the Arnott did at least look different, although to modern eyes fuel and driver look terribly vulnerable. As this Arnott driver sorts out his problems at Brands Hatch another unusual car, a front wheel drive Emeryson, is driven round him.

The first car was completed in 1952, which was regarded as a development year although there were encouraging wins in 'junior' events. In 1953 the best showing in a major half-litre event was John Brise' fourth in a Silverstone 100-mile race. That year a fully-enclosed car was built for 350/500cc record attempts and some effort was put into developing a desmodromic-valve JAP engine before Arnott turned to sports cars.

ARROWS

The Arrows Racing Team survived a welter of controversy and problems through its first seasons, then settled to a chequered career when it sometimes seemed to be on the verge of a breakthrough to real success.

It was launched by a group of ex-Shadow personnel, with backing from Franco Ambrosio (soon to fall foul of the Italian authorities, and courts, because of financial irregularities), and took its name from the principals' initials: Ambrosio (AR), Alan Rees (R), Jackie Oliver (O), Dave Wass (W) and Tony Southgate (S). A base was set up at Milton Keynes and the first Arrows F1 car designed and built in 60 days, in time for the second Grand Prix of 1978 – an important deadline for the team, as it qualified Arrows for FOCA membership. However, the FA1 was shown to be just too similar to the Shadow DN9, and after a London High Court case brought by Shadow's Don Nichols it had to be withdrawn. Designer Southgate and draughtsman Wass produced the A1 in 52 days, and the team did not miss a race.

A first period of promise was followed by one when lack of success came hand-in-hand with financial problems. That phase passed, too, although Arrows was never one of the lavishly-endowed F1 teams. In 1987 it became USF&G Arrows, for its primary sponsor (US Finance & Guaranty), which saw it through until the Japanese Footwork Group acquired a major shareholding late in 1989, (Footwork had failed to make any impression with its own F3000 car and its credentials for an entry into F1 were questionable). That year a well-equipped new Arrows factory had been topped out, while the adjacent first plant was retained. At the end of the season there was something of a clean sweep, designer Brawn and the two drivers leaving, while principals Oliver and Rees remained. From a new position of strength a deal to use a Porsche engine from 1991 was concluded. Through the ups and downs the approach had always been professional, the personnel were prepared to graft, and some very talented drivers occupied Arrows cockpits, but that first Grand Prix victory was very elusive.

FA1 The first Arrows was an effective car, in that Patrese in FA1/1 led the second race in which it was run (the 1978 South

The long nose, prominent stepped side pods and hump-backed profile characterized the FA1. This first car was rushed through for the 1978 Brazilian GP, which the team had to contest in order to qualify for FOCA membership benefits. It was photographed in January; soon it was to wear gold Warsteiner colours.

African GP) and then scored points with it until it was ruled out as 40 per cent of its components were shown to be copied from Shadow DN9 drawings. The four cars that had been built were to be broken up.

This short-lived car was a ground effects design, with double wing sections flanking a slim monocoque and Cosworth engine, although the ground effects were to a degree undermined as the suspension members at the rear were mounted outboard, in the airflow.

Drivers: Riccardo Patrese, Rolf Stommelen.

A1 Anticipating a judgement against Arrows and the FA1, the team had the first two A1s ready for a press launch three days after the court case ended and the type made its race debut in the Austrian GP, where Patrese qualified it well, only to be eliminated in a race accident (the same fate befell him in the next race, in Holland, when the first of 1978's three A1s was effectively written off).

There was a 'family resemblance' in the lines and specification of the A1, although it had a wider track and longer wheelbase than the FA1, and there was inboard rear suspension and other changes. None seemed to be for the better, until the last race of the year when Patrese was fourth in Canada – a result which might be seen as his response to a vendetta against him after the Peterson accident in which he was wrongly identified as the culprit. The cars were revised as A1Bs for 1979, when three were built to this specification, with changes to the suspension and aerodynamic refinements. Performances in the early races showed that a new car was badly needed (to the time when the A2 appeared, Arrows scored just three points). In 1980 a car dubbed 'A1G' was run in the British national series; Guy Edwards won one race with it, but even in that category it was hardly a match for the Williams FW07s.

Drivers: Jochen Mass, Riccardo Patrese, Rolf Stommelen.

Patrese in an A1 in the 1978 Canadian GP, apparently with a sticking skirt. Around the cockpit it is particularly reminiscent of the FA1.

A2 This was to be a total wing car, giving exceptional downforce with low drag penalties, and as soon as it was run at a race meeting (the 1979 French GP) the team knew that it had created a lemon, despite brave assertions that 'Tony Southgate's revolutionary design is a massive leap forward'. It had a short 'bullet' nose, faired-in front suspension members which governed the airflow to the side pods, a cockpit well forward, engine and gearbox tilted upwards to the rear to allow for a full-width underside aerofoil section, and inboard suspension all round. The car was far from nimble on slow corners, and it suffered badly from 'porpoising' elsewhere – the unlovely thing was so far from competitive that within weeks of its first race work had started on its successor, and A1Bs were sometimes brought back into service in 1979.

(Southgate had generated massive downforce but had not learned how to harness it in a balanced car – nobody fully understood ground effects at that time.)

Drivers: Riccardo Patrese, Jochen Mass.

The unusual lines of the A2, and the inclined mounting of the DFV, are shown in this shot of Mass in practice at Silverstone. Although it was designed to run without wings, one soon appeared between the large side plates at the rear.

A3 Southgate and Wass played safe with the 1980 Arrows, which almost inevitably reflected the Williams lines that had been so successful. The A3 was compact, with short wheelbase and narrow track, had normal nose and tail 'foils, and no aerodynamic novelties save a gearbox enclosure to reduce drag. Its track behaviour was better than the A2's and effforts were made to improve it through 1980. Patrese placed one second at Long Beach, and overall Arrows was seventh in the Constructors' Championship.

The A3 had to serve in 1981, when the team was caught out by Brabham's suspension-lowering ploy and if for no other reason than slender resources was unable to match it. The car had to use Pirelli tyres which were no match for Michelins in terms of grip. All this offset the work Wass had done on the car's suspension since Southgate left in 1980. Nevertheless, good early-season results saw Arrows eighth at the end of the year.

Drivers: Jochen Mass, Riccardo Patrese, Siegfried Stohr.

The A3 was an entirely conventional car by 1980 standards, built around a narrow and rigid honeycomb monocoque and inboard suspension. Outwardly, Warsteiner colours made its lines appear sleeker.

A4 This was another state of the art car, for the team could not afford to be adventurous. Wass laid it out as a compact and light wing car, with a honeycomb monocoque and pullrod suspension. It was good enough to pick up odd points, Baldi, Surer and Tambay all scoring modestly with it (five cars were built and between them these three drivers scored five points).

Drivers: Mauro Baldi, Brian Henton, Marc Surer, Patrick Tambay.

Baldi in the fifth A4 in the Austrian GP. It was a competent car, at a time when a little more was called for.

A5 This appeared as a one-off in the late summer of 1982, and was used in three autumn races. It was a Williams FW08 lookalike, lighter than the A4 with similar aerodynamic qualities to that car, with an all-honeycomb monocoque and a new pullrod front suspension layout. It was intended to be a development car, and in fact was to be converted to A6 specification.

Drivers: Mauro Baldi, Marc Surer.

A6 Hopes that the A4 or A5 would be the last DFV-powered Arrows were dashed and the team moved into the flat-bottom era with the Cosworth V-8 behind the drivers of the A6s. This was a good car among the normally-aspirated runners in 1983 and the four points scored by Surer kept the team respectable. It was another straightforward Wass design, still using a honeycomb monocoque (a carbon fibre chassis was an expensive item for a team which started the season without a sponsor) and orthodox inboard suspension. Slightly modified, the cars continued in use through to the Spring of 1984.

Drivers: Thierry Boutsen, Alan Jones, Chico Serra, Marc Surer.

Alan Jones was tempted out of single-seater retirement to drive the first A6 at Long Beach, where it was only too obviously unsponsored – at least the unbroken white shows off the clean lines of the bodywork. That was Jones' only race for the team, and he retired at two-thirds distance.

A7 Late in the day, Arrows finalized a contract to use BMW turbo engines in 1984, although these were not to be the 'front-line' engines as supplied to Brabham but Mader-prepared units. Perforce, the A7 followed the lines of the A6 and it was therefore an interim car which at least enabled the team to find its feet in the turbo era (half of Arrows' six points in 1984 were scored with A6s).

Drivers: Thierry Boutsen, Marc Surer.

Like many first-generation turbo cars, the Arrows A7 was not attractive. It retained the compact proportions of the preceding DFV-powered cars, but the short wheelbase was not ideal for turbo power. Normally an engine cover was fitted.

A8 Unlike the A7, this was a purpose-designed turbo car, with a longer chassis – Wass' first carbon fibre monocoque, made by Advanced Composites for lightness and stiffness. In the A7, BMW engine installation specifications were followed, but in the A8 Wass devised Arrows' much more rigid installation, as he did for the turbo ancillaries. Pushrod suspension was used at the front, pullrod at the rear.

The driver pairing was strong, the car was more competitive, and it was reliable – factors that resulted in Arrows scoring 14 points in 1985, more than in any previous year. However, the cars were not competitive in 1986, when as only one A9 was completed they had to serve through to the end of the year.

Drivers: Gerhard Berger, Thierry Boutsen, Christian Danner, Marc Surer.

The A8 gave Arrows it best year in 1985, the car living up to its looks. Driver is Berger in the GP d'Europe at Brands Hatch.

A9 A one-off, this appeared in the summer of 1986 but was raced only three times after its German GP debut in Boutsen's hands. It was Wass' last design for the team and had a sub-contracted all-carbon monocoque. One change was the

The single A9 was wheeled out when Arrows' new headquarters was formally opened in 1989. Otherwise it is a best-forgotten piece of fairly bulky machinery.

position of the gear cluster, ahead of the differential. Pushrod suspension was used, but an A8 rear end was soon grafted onto the car. A9 was used in only three races and was neglected as Gordon Coppuck temporarily took on the Arrows design role on a freelance basis.

Drivers: Thierry Boutsen, Christian Danner.

A10 Much changed for 1987. The budget seemed adequate, with USF&G becoming more prominently the major sponsor. Ross Brawn joined, to design a clean low-lined car, although he did not go to the excessive lengths represented in the previous year's Brabham. The engine was installed upright in the largely carbon fibre chassis and pushrod suspension was used. A USF&G subsidiary, Megatron, acquired the stock of 'upright' BMW engines, which were to be renamed Megatron and were the team's weakness – the erstwhile Bee Emm was a relatively old and unsophisticated design, it was not very reliable and was not notably fuel-efficient.

There was a new driving pair, Warwick and Cheever (and they were to stay with Arrows to the end of 1989). Achievement in 1987 was not outstanding, Arrows ending the season equal sixth in the Constructors' Championship.

The design was refined in the A10B of 1988, and as far as chassis and running gear were concerned this meant paring weight. Through the season there were to be minor changes in areas such as suspension and aerodynamics. Mader developed the engine, which at the lower boost restriction in force was more reliable and less thirsty. The outcome was Arrows' best year in Championship terms, fourth on the table with 23 points.

Drivers: Eddie Cheever, Derek Warwick.

In the A10 Ross Brawn achieved low clean lines, despite having to fit in an upright four-in-line engine. This is Eddie Cheever in an A10B at Silverstone, when the sun shone on practice for the 1988 British GP.

A11 Outwardly, Brawn's slimline design followed the general trend in 1989, while for a power unit Arrows turned to the DFR. It followed the A10 in its suspension, pushrod at the front

A11 was workmanlike, but in no way distinctive on a 1989 grid. Derek Warwick, before his last season with the team, poses with the car during tests at the Paul Ricard circuit.

and pullrod at the rear, and a new Arrows-designed (Hewland internals) six-speed transverse gearbox was used. The carbon fibre/honeycomb composite chassis was at least as stiff as the A10's and the car followed the narrow-nose trend.

In racing terms, Arrows slipped back again, to seventh in the Constructors' Championship.

Drivers: Eddie Cheever, Derek Warwick.

ARZANI-VOLPINI

This brave but misguided one-off was an attempt to make a 1955 2.5-litre F1 car out of the 1.5-litre supercharged Maserati-Milano of 1950, with its four-cylinder engine enlarged to 2492cc and no longer supercharged. Its ladder chassis was clothed in very attractive bodywork, but the car was heavy and probably sadly underpowered.

Its inexperienced amateur driver Alborghetti was killed when he crashed at Pau in the car's first race, in 1955. That turned out to be its only race for although it was entered for that year's Italian GP it failed to appear. Egidio Arzani and Gianpaolo Volpini abandoned it. The name Volpini later appeared on a short-lived Formula Junior car.

ASA

Forbes Clark unashamedly copied the contemporary Cooper when be built this 500cc car in 1948. It did not, however, achieve Cooper-like results, partly due to the fact that it had a Rudge engine which was not quite up to the job. Later it appeared, modified, as the Rippon.

ASSEGAI

Tony Kotze built the Assegai for the South African Gold Cup series and like most South African specials it had a four-cylinder 1493cc Alfa Romeo engine, a five-speed Colotti gearbox and followed the broad layout of a Cooper. It was, however, very slim and claimed to be substantially lower than any previous F1 car while its 3½in ground clearance was then unprecedented. That was its only distinction for Kotze failed to qualify for the 1962 Rand Grand Prix, the only F1 race in which the Assegai was entered. ML

ASTON-BUTTERWORTH

In 1952 Bill Aston, a former motorcycle racer of mature years, built a near copy of the 'box section' Cooper F2 chassis, with swing axles at the rear. In order to be able to offer race organisers something different he looked for an unusual engine and found it in Archie Butterworth's air-cooled flat four. This was the interim AJB unit of 1983cc (87.5 x 82.5mm) which was fitted with Steyr barrels and heads and produced about 140bhp. This was a much lower engine than the usual Bristol unit. Transmission was via a four-speed MG gearbox and to keep the drive line low the prop shaft passed under the chassis-mounted EMV differential from where the power was transferred upwards by a couple of straight-cut spur gears. As work progressed Robin Montgomerie-Charrington ordered a car, though he specified Dunlop alloy wheels.

Named Aston-Butterworths these were perhaps the lightest cars in F2 and, initially, could match the pace of some of the Cooper-Bristols, but it was beyond the resources of two enthusiastic amateurs to develop the concept. Both cars suffered reliability problems and an early modification was to put double CV joints into the drive shafts.

Montgomerie-Charrington had the best Championship outing result in 1952, when he qualified 15th in Belgium and was seventh when he came in to refuel – but the wrong mixture was poured into the tank. In non-Championship events the best showing was at Chimay in a large field of privateers where Montgomerie-Charrington finished third despite running out of fuel on his last lap.

Aston made a few unsuccessful appearances in 1953, and then put the car away. It seems he could not crack the problem of fuel supply – it often suffered from fuel starvation and sometimes caught fire. Later Aston's car was converted into a sports car while Montgomerie-Charrrington's survives as raced.   ML

By the time the F1 Aston Martins started in a race, the whole line of development they represented was on the verge of extinction and the cars proved ineffectual. This is Carroll Shelby in the second team car in the 1959 International Trophy at Silverstone.

DBR5 A pair of lighter cars, one with independent rear suspension, was built for 1960. They were little raced, and promised to be no more than mid-field runners. An eleventh place (at Silverstone) was the best Grand Prix showing.

Drivers: Roy Salvadori, Maurice Trintignant.

ATLAS

A successful early German 500cc car, this was in fact an unmodified Cooper given a new name.   ML

ATS (D)

This team was created by Hans Gunther Schmid to promote his ATS wheels company and entered F1 racing when he bought Penske PC4s in 1977. These were modified to become ATS HS-1, while in parallel Schmid acquired the March F1 interests for 1978 and the first ATS as such was built.

Schmid gained a reputation for idiosyncratic behaviour and his team had several managers, including Opert, Elford, Heavans, Ramirez and Caldwell, several designers and some good drivers as well as some who made up the numbers in ATS' eight seasons. Altogether this ATS team's cars made 311 appearances in Championship races, and scored a grand total of eight points. Its last season was 1984, but Schmid set up the Rial team three years later.

PC4/HS-1 An erstwhile Penske first appeared in the ATS black and yellow colours at Long Beach in 1977, when Jarier placed it sixth. There were no more scoring finishes that year, and for 1978 the cars were developed by Robin Herd and

A flat four engine made for low lines, but a high seating position meant that quite a lot of driver (here Montgomerie-Charrington) was added to the frontal area.

ASTON MARTIN

It seemed logical for Aston Martin to extend their 1950s racing programme to single-seaters, based on successful sports cars. A tentative start was made with a car based on the DB3S, which was raced in New Zealand without conspicuous success in 1956. The F1 cars which followed later in the decade took shape slowly – the sports car programme had priority – and when they appeared they were outmoded. In Europe in 1959-60 little was achieved; two of the cars were revised for Tasman racing in 1960, and Lex Davison drove one of these to second place in the Australian GP, while Bob Stilwell won a race at Warwick Farm in the other.

DBR4/250 Four of these space-framed front engined cars were built, with twin-cam straight six engines (up to 280bhp was eventually and perhaps optimistically claimed) and de Dion rear suspension – the last new GP car to use the system. They were handsome cars, but obviously bulky compared to contemporary Coopers when they first came to a grid, for the 1959 International Trophy at Silverstone. In that race Salvadori achieved the team's best result, second, but the best in Grands Prix were sixth placings in Britain and Portugal.

While the concept was obsolete, the cars were overweight and development was sluggish, most of the early problems were rather surprisingly with the engine – as the basic unit had been proved in sports cars, reliability might have been expected in this area. Eventually, oil circulation modifications improved matters.

One of the cars was brought out again early in 1960.

Drivers: Roy Salvadori, Carroll Shelby.

From this angle the most obvious differences between the Penske PC4 and the ATS HS-1 are in the flatter nose and smoother engine cover, with shoulder intakes deleted. Rosberg is the driver, in the British GP.

redesignated HS-1. Despite the efforts of drivers of the calibre of Mass and Rosberg, the team failed to score in 1978.

Drivers: Hans Binder, Michael Bleekemolen, Alberto Colombo, Harald Ertl, Jean-Pierre Jarier, Jochen Mass, Keke Rosberg.

D1 John Gentry undertook a more susbstantial revision of the design, making it a skirt car with wider track and side pods. It started in the last two races of 1978.

Driver: Keke Rosberg.

D2-D4 The D2 was designed by Giacomo Caliri on Lotus 79 lines, and three were built for the team's single driver. It proved an ill-handling machine and Stuck finished only two races in it before the D3 appeared in mid-season. Designed by Nigel Stroud, this was outwardly similar to the D2, with a new monocoque and suspension. It was more promising, and Stuck actually scored two points with it, in the last race of 1979.

The single 1979 D3 was brought out at the start of the next season, alongside one of two new D3s. These were to be remodelled as D4s by the spring, and more built, design being credited to Gustav Brunner and Tim Wardrop. A resemblance to the Williams FW07 was now remarked. These cars were generally reliable qualifiers through 1980 and served on into 1981, when the first race saw several personnel quit as Herr Schmid gave expression to another executive whim. Driver Jan Lammers failed to qualify twice in four attempts before he left.

Drivers: Slim Borgudd, Jan Lammers, Hans Stuck, Marc Surer.

The 'Lotus lines' of the D3 are apparent in this shot of Stuck in the 1979 Dutch GP. It appears a neat clean-lined ground effects car, but imitation seldom works and D2-D4 performances were disappointing.

HGS1/D5 Designed by Hervé Guilpin, this more compact car appeared in the Spring of 1981, when Borgudd was the team's driver and had the task of sorting it out. After failing to qualify in his first four attempts, he then scored a point in the British GP.

The straightforward design was revised as the D5 for 1982, ATS' final season with DFV engines. In terms of championship scores, this was the team's best season as two fifth places gained four points.

Drivers: Slim Borgudd, Eliseo Salazar, Manfred Winkelhock.

D5 was another Cosworth kit car, with good looks but no other notable qualities. Chilean driver Eliseo Salazar placed one fifth in the San Marino GP, although this race was not contested by a full F1 contingent.

D6-D7 Schmid obtained BMW turbo engines in 1983, and there was a new car designed by Brunner, who had a 'clean sheet of paper' brief. It was up to the minute in its specification – carbon fibre monocoque, pullrod suspension, and so on – and with that power unit should have been a contender for top honours. The car, however, was let down by the continuing turmoil within the team, and Winkelhock finished only four times in 15 starts.

Three were built, followed by two more, slightly modified and designated D7, for 1984. Winkelhock recorded two finishes in 14 attempts, but in the summer Berger came into the team and achieved three finishes from four starts, his best being sixth at Monza (that did not earn a point, as ATS had been entered as a one-car team at the beginning of the season). At the end of the year BMW cut off the supply of engines and the team was closed down.

Drivers: Gerhard Berger, Manfred Winkelhock.

The D6 had typical turbo car lines, with very large aerofoils and substantial side pods for radiators and turbo ancillaries. Driver is Winkelhock, during Rio tests.

ATS (I)

Automobili Turismo e Sport was set up in 1961 by a group of Ferrari defectors, including designer Carlo Chiti and team manager Romolo Tavoni, with backing from a group headed by Count Giovanni Volpi. An early intention had been that the marque should carry the name of his Scuderia Serenissima, but this Italian F1 challenge to Ferrari emerged late in 1962 as the ATS.

The Tipo 100 looked sleek, although not robust in the manner of its contemporaries. It was built around a space frame, with straightforward independent suspension (the coil spring/damper units were inboard at the front). The engine

ATS on a grid for the first time, at Spa in 1963. A low nose and high engine cover gave it distinctive proportions among the dominant Coventry Climax engined cars but even its appearance was not convincing. This is Phil Hill's car; behind it, wearing the flat 'at, is Carlo Chiti.

was a 90-degree V-8 (66 x 54.6mm, 1494cc), initially with four Webers but later with Lucas fuel injection, for which 190bhp at 10,000rpm was claimed. It drove through a Colotti six-speed gearbox.

Jack Fairman carried out a test programme and Phil Hill and Giancarlo Baghetti gave the ATS its race debut in the 1963 Belgian GP, when it was far from competitive. That state of affairs did not improve, and at the end of the season the team collapsed. One of the cars was susbstantially reworked by Alf Francis in 1964 and appeared in the Italian GP as the 'Derrington-Francis' (qv).

Drivers: Giancarlo Baghetti, Phil Hill.

AUSPER

Goldhawk Road, London W12 sounds an improbable address for Competition Cars of Australia, but that is where a would-be constructor built a handful of Formula Junior cars in 1961-2. The Auspers showed some promise in the hands of Ouvaroff in 1961 and Rhodes in 1962.

They were space frame cars, with aluminium bodywork, double unequal length wishbone front suspension and lower wishbone, top strut acting as a wishbone and twin radius arms at the rear in 1961 (the 1962 car had double wishbones at the rear) and 2LS drum brakes outboard all round. Cosworth engines were specified, with a Renault-based gearbox.

The 1961 car had a curiously flattened appearance, as it was low with wide bodywork and the bottom line of the tail upswept. The 1962 car was more angular, very sleek with mirrors faired into the body, and at a height of 24in to the top of the body very low. Ausper's specification sheet does not give it a designation, but it came to be known as T4. John Rhodes seemed to get it away to a good start at Silverstone, when he ran with the leaders and finished fourth in a top-class field, but then he moved on to another team. Ausper had plans to enter F1 using the Australian Clisby V-6 engine but problems with that unit meant it never appeared and Ausper's F1 plans faded with it.

The first FJ Ausper had bulbous but sleek bodywork. There was presumably a roll over bar in that low fairing behind the driver's head.

AUSTIN SPECIAL

An Austin 7 Special fitted with a JAP engine appeared briefly in 1951 British F3 races, without success. The only thing which makes it interesting is that the constructor/driver was Arthur Mallock, who went on to establish the company which bears his name.   ML

AVIA

Václav Lím made his name as a constructor with a series of attractive and successful Formula Easter cars (1.3-litre production-based engines, with all components to be derived from Eastern bloc cars), and he also drove his Avias to win races and local championships. However, his first efforts as a constructor had been with two F3 cars, in 1970 and 1972 (the year the Czech organizers were bidden to turn their backs on F3), both cars using Ford-based engines. It can only be assumed that Lím faced the same problems in obtaining specialist components that deterred some of his compatriots, for nothing came of his Avia F3 cars.

AVIDESA

Selex, the Barcelona-based constructor, built the cars for an Avidesa team run in the 1983 European F3 Championship and named after their sponsor. The Avidesa 383 was a sleek Alfa-engined car based on the 1982 Selex, at first distinguished by a swept-back rear wing reminiscent of similar devices of doubtful value. The best placing for an Avidesa was seventh, scored by Adrian Campos in a Jarama race when he had the benefit of the very best of Michelins. But Campos, and team mate Jose-Luis Llobelli, both scored top-ten places in races outside Spain, suggesting that if they had been more experienced or less tempestuous the Avidesa (or Selex) might have got somewhere. As it was Avidesa backed a Ralt RT3 for Campos in 1984.

The Avidesa was a tidy car in all respects save the rear aerofoil, where variations tended to extremes (in this case obviously a late addition as it has not been painted to match the car). Driver is Jose-Luis Llobelli.

B

BAIRD-GRIFFIN

Bobby Baird was the heir to a large publishing business in Belfast and he set up a team with a well-equipped workshop. He bought the Lagonda-engined Emeryson Special and fitted it with the ex-Whitney Straight 4.5-litre Duesenberg unit, which proved too powerful for any available gearbox, and during 1951 he laid plans to build a new F1 car using Maserati parts. This had a ladder frame chassis with Simca front suspension and a de Dion rear axle with long fabricated radius arms and Morris torsion bars. The engine, built by Dennis Griffin, was based on a Maserati 4CLT unit with many of its major components being made new, and it drove through a rear-mounted four-speed gearbox.

As soon as it was no longer the World Championship category, F1 became a lost cause and the Baird-Griffin appeared in only two minor races where it was outclassed. 'Bobby Baird' was fatally injured in a practice accident at Snetterton in 1953. ML

BALDOCK

A British 500 special which mated a modified and lowered Austin Seven chassis and a near-standard Velocette engine. It was all done on a shoestring in the spirit of the earliest 500 cars but by the time it was ready, in 1949, the builder was already bemoaning the lack of opportunities for novice special builders. There is no known racing history. ML

BALSA

This was an abortive French project for the second Formula 2, powered by a modified Peugeot engine. It never got to a race grid, but later came into the possession of Henri Julien (of AGS) and in the late 1980s appeared as a static exhibit at French historic car shows.

BANDINI

This Italian Formula Junior car might have got by in the first year of the category, but in 1961 – only the second year of international FJ racing – it was obsolete before it was built: a front-mounted Fiat engine in tubular chassis and with a de Dion rear end was not a recipe for a competitive car.

BARDON-TURNER

Don Truman found shortcomings in the Marwyn he bought in conjunction with Barbara Longmore and her brother and by the end of 1948 it had been extensively lightened, lowered and given a new body. Thus was born the 'Bardon' (BARbara and DON) which was a huge improvement over the original and although it was not a winner with a JAP engine, Don was awarded a special 'Good Loser' trophy in 1949. Jack Turner then took on the car and gave it better brakes, all-independent suspension and alloy wheels but failed to make it truly competitive. ML

BARNETT

This was a one-off F3 venture in 1966, apparently conventional and well-made – it appeared at only one race meeting, for a minor F3 event at Castle Combe.

BARRON

Through the 1980s several successful F3 teams aspired to constructor status, and most found the giant stride from aspiration to realization was beyond them. The Barron Racing Team was even more ambitious, attempting the move with 'the first professional Dutch F3 car' – which leaves one to speculate on the blurred divide between a Daf built overseas and a Barron F31 with most of its major components originating outside Holland.

The car completed late in 1984 to a design by Kees van der Grint was exploratory for the team but largely orthodox in its make-up. A narrow track made it look long and slim while its flat engine deck and faired-in roll cage was also distinctive. It had a bonded and riveted sandwich monocoque, Toyota engine and Hewland gearbox, but did not feature in 1985 F3 racing. In that year Barron Tyrrell 012s made a few appearances in F3000 before the team gave up in mid-season (it did achieve the best result with an ex-F1 car in F5000 racing, third).

BC

This was a Milanese one-off Junior, its wire wheels visually at odds with designer Crespaldi's layout which put the engine behind the cockpit. That engine was a Fiat 1100, driving through a Fiat 600 gearbox – as in most 1959 Italian Juniors. There was a multi-tubular frame, wishbone and coil spring ifs, and swing axle at the rear.

BEAGLE

Jim Yardley was a very successful hobby constructor, who raced his own cars in Britain in 750 MC and Monoposto categories in the 1960s and 1970s, and part-way through the first decade introduced the name Beagle. Mk I in 1966 was a rear-engined monocoque construction car, which was raced in national category events before it was adapted for F3 in 1970. Yardley was racing as an enthusiast, not seeking top honours, and although he looked again at F3, in particular a front-engined car with beam front axle which appeared in a couple of races, he put it away again and concentrated on building Beagles for lesser classes.

BEATRICE

Beatrice Companies Inc was a sponsor and the corporate name was included in the team's car designations, hence Beatrice-Lola-Hart THL1. There were further complications in that while the car brought the name Lola back into Grand Prix racing it was built by FORCE (Formula One Race Car Engineering Ltd.) in a plant near London Airport, many miles from the Lola factory, to designs by Neil Oatley and John Baldwin, and run by Team Haas (USA) Ltd. The list of personnel was impressive, reflecting the initial funding of the parallel F1 and Indycar operations, but quite early in the team's first full season (1986) Beatrice management changes led to the conglomerate starting to withdraw from its racing commitment. The team saw out the 1986 F1 season, when it gained six Championship points, then disappeared.

THL1 This was a straightforward car powered by the Hart 415T while Duckworth's turbo engine for Ford was developed. To get the team up and running it was entered in the last three races of 1985, driven by Alan Jones, and THL1s started in five races in 1986. Those eight starts brought one finish, when Tambay was eighth in the 1986 Spanish GP.

Drivers: Alan Jones, Patrick Tambay.

The first Beatrice-Lola, immaculate in a predominantly red and white colour scheme. The THL2 was virtually identical, with some changes to ducting on the tops of the side pods and blue Ford decals on the nose, engine cover and rear wing end plates.

Beatrice THL2 The Ford-powered version of the car made its debut at Imola, and was to show some promise – its reputation was as a well-mannered but under-powered car, which suffered too many minor failures in races. Its best placing was fourth by Jones in the Austrian GP.

Drivers: Eddie Cheever, Alan Jones, Patrick Tambay.

BEELS

Lex Beels was a Dutchman who somehow managed to drive both in Holland and in British non-international events in a 500cc Cooper-JAP. When the 500 movement got under way in Holland in 1949 many people wanted to buy Coopers but because of prevailing conditions they were impossibly expensive so Beels made Cooper copies under his own name. As is usual with copies, they were not quite as good as the originals.   ML

A JAP-engined Beels at Brands Hatch in August 1950, looking very much the Cooper copy that it was. The driver is J. Richardson.

BELGICA

A modified F3 Brabham BT15, obviously from Belgium, which made no impression in its few 1966-7 appearances.

BELLASI

Vittorio Bellasi was a fringe constructor in the late 1960s, trying to establish a foothold in the Tecno-dominated Italian market, when his name rather surprisingly appeared on a short-lived F1 car. A one-off Bellasi on Brabham lines was raced in Italian F3 events by Giugliemo Bellasi in 1966, and in the following year a monocoque F3 car was introduced. The F3 Bellasi which ran in 1969 Italian races was a noticeably petite tubular-chassis car with a pronounced wedge body on Lotus 61 lines (it was dubbed 'Cuneo'). It had an untidy outboard suspension all round and the peculiarity of a rear-mounted water radiator, where the coolant was apparently warmed by the exhaust. The cars made no impression, although one was driven by Giorgio Pianta.

Nevertheless, Silvio Moser, who had been racing a Brabham BT24 with a DFV in place of the Repco V-8, commissioned Bellasi to produce an F1 car for 1970. This appeared for the 1970 Dutch GP, as a fairly simple monocoque car with the engine used as a stressed member and sensible outward lines. The DFV and gearbox from Moser's Brabham were used, and the suspension was inspired by that car.

Moser failed to qualify it for the grid at its Zandvoort debut, but later started in the Austrian race, retiring after 13 laps when running last. Moser failed to make the grid at Monza in 1970, but did so in the car's fourth and last Championship race meeting appearance, retiring from the Italian GP after six laps.

The F1 Bellasi was a bulky machine, with outward lines accurately reflecting its unsophisticated construction (Moser needed a monocoque replacement for the Brabham he had been racing because of regulations calling for bag fuel tanks). He is driving it in his first attempt to qualify it, at Zandvoort in 1970.

BENDY

Vic Cavanagh built South Africa's first 500cc car in 1947, using Fiat Topolino front suspension, while the rear was almost solid and the back wheels set close together, rather like an Isetta bubble car. It got its name because the rear-mounted Sunbeam sprint engine had a habit of bending the back axle. A MkII version maintained the tradition by bending its engine mountings and also featured 'crab' (very narrow) rear track and so had a tendency to roll.   ML

BENETTON

The Benetton name came into F1 in 1983, as a Tyrrell sponsor, then there were sponsorship associations with Alfa Romeo and Toleman, before Benetton Formula Limited took over the Toleman team early in 1986, the Witney base being retained. Designer Rory Byrne and manager Peter Collins stayed with the team, but Collins left in the summer of 1989 and Gordon Message took his place.

In the team's first season Berger won the Mexican GP in one of their multi-coloured cars; Benetton always seemed on the threshold of great things, but somehow never quite made the final breakthrough. Nevertheless, sixth, fifth and third in the 1986, 1987 and 1988 Constructors' Championships showed real progress, especially as engine changes meant that a new car had to be designed and developed for each season. Quite apart from those United Colours of Benetton, Byrne's cars were always distinctive.

From 1987 Benetton was firmly associated with Ford, to the point of exclusivity as far as new engines were concerned. Indeed, Ford announced John Barnard's appointment as Technical Director of the Benetton Group towards the end of the 1989 season. This was an unexpected coup, and Barnard was to set up a new high technology research and development centre, to direct a group covering virtually every aspect of F1 cars.

B186 Virtually nothing was carried over from the Hart-powered Toleman T185 to this BMW M12/13-engined car, although there were obvious similarities in major components such as the carbon composite monocoque. The engine was used as a semi-stressed member, while a tubular frame made for rigidity. The Bee Emm units came as a package that included engine management and heat exchanger, so in part Byrne was able to concentrate on aerodynamics and his self-imposed task of reducing cross-section as much as possible. Suspension was inboard, pullrod at the front, pushrod at the rear. A modified six-speed Hewland DG gearbox was used.

The late start meant that chassis construction continued well into the year – seven were eventually built – and development had to run in parallel with race preparation. Towards the end of the year Berger scored that Mexico win – Pirelli's only win before they 'retired' until 1989.

Drivers: Gerhard Berger, Teo Fabi.

B187 Benetton took over the Ford-Cosworth turbo V-6 programme as the Haas (née Beatrice) team folded, so once again a new car had to be designed and developed in a hurry. Its slim monocoque turned out to be marginally suspect and had to be strengthened after a Monaco accident. This engine was stressed to play a full load bearing role, and its wide-angle vee made for a very low rear deck. Pushrod suspension was used front and rear, with the front shock absorbers mounted on top of the chassis. Various aerofoil arrangements, including vertical deflectors, were used through the year.

The car was quick in its first race but did not fulfil early hopes. The best race placing was Boutsen's third in the Australian GP.

Drivers: Thierry Boutsen, Teo Fabi.

Deep but slender nose, low lines behind the cockpit and prominent curvaceous rear wing supports were external characteristics of the B187. This is Fabi, in practice at Silverstone.

B188 The change to a normally-aspirated engine, and a regulation requiring that a driver's feet be placed behind the axle line of the front wheels, meant another new car for 1988. The actual mounting for the 3.5-litre Ford Cosworth DFR was similar, but the six-speed gear cluster was positioned between the engine and the rear axle line. In the pullrod front suspension the spring/damper units were under the driver's heels, operated by bell cranks. The wide-based upper and lower wishbone arrangement was retained at the rear.

The car was overweight, and the engine did not deliver the anticipated power. The 600bhp looked for before the season was there, but hardly the 650bhp sought as the series got under way (the Yamaha-designed five-valve heads gave no advantages and were set aside).

During the year a B188 was used in developments tests with an 'active' – or maybe 're-active' – suspension system and these trials continued into 1989. In 1988 the team scored no less than eight third places (Boutsen six, Nannini two), and while Benetton's third place in the Championship was remote from the winning score in points terms, it was well clear of the rest. The B188s were used into 1989.

Drivers: Thierry Boutsen, Johnny Herbert, Alessandro Nannini.

Brand new B188, with Byrne trade marks such as the broad-chord curly front wing.

B189 Another new engine brought another new car, although the B189 followed the B188 lines. The first half of the season passed before the B189s came into general use, while problems of aerodynamics, balance and traction were sorted out. The B189 race debut came in the French GP. Byrne, with Dave Wass and Paul Crooks, sought to package the whole car as neatly as possible. The 75-degree Ford HB V-8 was commendably compact and, with light alloys used extensively, it was lighter than the DFR. It was a V-8, and in theory V-8s were not the engines to win races in 1989, but late in the year it was the equal of all but the Honda engine – and in Japan a Benetton did win with a V-8.

B189 had a finer nose, in common with all 1989 F1 cars, and slab sides, but visually followed the Benetton line very clearly.

Through the year the team had been in some disarray. Collins boldy stuck to his decision to pair Herbert with Nannini, although the young British driver was by no means fully recovered from an F3000 accident in 1988 and was 'rested' in mid-season – not long before Collins' departure. The first good result for a B189 was Nannini's third in the British GP, and then he was placed first in Japan. Benetton was fourth in the 1989 Constructors' Championship, just out of touch with the top three.

Drivers: Johnny Herbert, Alessandro Nannini, Emanuele Pirro.

BENNETT

A.D. Bennett's fourth one-off car was a front-engined Formula Junior, following a speedway car, and 750 and 1172 clubman's cars. It was a slender space frame machine, on the lines of the preceding pair, and in 1965 Derek Bennett was to pick up the clubman's theme again in the first of his Chevrons.

Derek Bennett in his F Junior car at Oulton Park in 1960.

BERNADET/JB

A high, chubby, and stubby little French 500 car, Jean Bernadet's design had an sohc Norton, cast alloy wheels similar to the DB and all independent suspension by parallel links. As though embarrassed by the fact that it was rear-engined it also had a wide and completely unnecessary open 'radiator grill' which did nothing for the aerodynamics. It did not make a mark in circuit racing but was quite successful in hill climbs.

After that Bernardet made a more conventional 500 car with double wishbone and rubber band suspension all round. This went into small scale production and, fitted with a variety of engines, was one of the most successful of all French F3 cars.

ML

BERTA

Oreste Berta has survived as a constructor in a difficult environment since the early 1970s and in local terms has flourished, although his odd ventures with cars for international formulae have not been successful. He began by undertaking an F5000 project for local driver Vega and that led him to turn away from his straightforward garage business and set up as a constructor, based near Cordoba in Argentina.

Although nothing came of the Vega-inspired F5000 project a car was built in 1974 and taken to the USA, where it made no impression and disappeared. At the end of that year a Berta F1 car was widely reported and described in some detail (it had a Berta V-8 on DFV lines, a body on contemporary Chevron lines, with a nose on Brabham BT34 lines). It was even said to have been track tested by Vega, but it was never seen at a race meeting. However, Berta did get to international grids in the 1970s with a Lola-inspired DFV-powered sports-racing car, the LR.

Success in Sudam F2 and F3 races, run to regulations that did not correspond with the international formulae, led to a venture into German F3 racing in 1988 with Marc Hessel. The car had an aluminium honeycomb and carbon fibre chassis, conventional suspension, and a Berta-tuned Renault 18 engine driving through a Meriggi Renault-based gearbox. If the decision to campaign it was based on relative performances by European cars such as Dallaras in Sudam, it misled, for the Berta proved far from competitive in Europe.

The F3 Berta had lines similar to the contemporary Dallara, although its construction followed the company's Sudam F3 lines; obviously it had to be a flat-bottom car, with appendages such as tyres and aerofoils also complying with international regulations. Driver is Victor Rosso, who set up the short-lived European campaign.

BERTE

René Berte, a Belgian, built this early 500 car along conventional lines except that the swing axle rear suspension was sprung by a low mounted transverse leaf spring with the dampers at the rear running down from the rear uprights to the bottom of the frame. He opted for a twin-cylinder AJS engine.

BERTOCCO

This car was actually a Cooper, adapted to take an Alfa Romeo engine by F. Vento. Luigi Bertocco started it in one race, at Vallelunga at the end of the 1967 season. He retired and did not run the car in F2 again.

BF

Two gentlemen of Rome, Brachetti and Ferrari, built a Stanguellini-type Junior in 1959, using the customary Fiat elements. The 1100 engine was offset at the front, in a semi-space frame, and suspension comprised wishbones and transverse leaf spring at the front, while there was a de Dion rear end. The Faccioli Junior was sometimes referred to as a BF.

BIREL

There was only one Italian F3 car constructor of substance in the late 1960s, Tecno, but there were inducements to run Italian cars in the category, so the Brambillas got behind an effort to build a local machine. This turned out to be a copy of the Brabham BT21B, which Vittorio Brambilla drove with some success in 1969 (a win at Vallelunga and some good placings). It was set aside for a while as the brothers concentrated on karts, then overhauled as the Birel 71, taking on some Alpine characteristics. Vittorio started the season with an Alfa Romeo-based engine, winning the first of the eight races in the Italian Championship, then used a Nova (Ford) engine and won two more races. He tried four races with a Wainer-tuned Alfa engine in 1972, and two with a Nova, while Ernesto had five outings with the Alfa-powered version. Each brother scored one point with a Birel, then turned to Brabhams, while one Roberto Manzoni tried a Birel, unsuccessfully, and this very minor marque petered out.

BIRRANA

This short-lived but very successful Adelaide constructor was formed in 1971 by Malcolm Ramsay and designer Tony Alcock, who had considerable experience with leading British teams. The first Birrana was a Formula Ford car, but most were built for Australian F2 (ANF2), which in the mid-1970s was open to cars with engines of 1.1-1.6 litres with no more than two valves per cylinder. The Australian championship fell to Birrana drivers 1973-6. Two of the ANF2 274s were taken to Britain in 1975 and run in Formula Atlantic events, and one of these became the 1976 F2 Minos (see Minos). The company was wound up soon after Alcock's death in Graham Hill's aircraft accident.

BLW

Another of those not-so-rare US Juniors, built in Spokane. It had a rear-mounted DKW engine – as with some other constructors, this was referred to as an Auto Union engine – in a tubular chassis, with swing axle at the rear. Its racing record is not known.

BMC

This BMC was British Motor Car Distributors, of San Francisco, which is particularly remembered for abortive Indianapolis machines such as the MG Liquid Suspension Special. In a response to the American enthusiasm for Formula Junior in its

The first Formula Junior BMC was one of the neatest of all front-engined racing cars.

first two years, BMCD built small runs of cars designed by Joe Huffaker, a West Coast sports-racing car exponent.

The first was a little front-engined car, even more tightly packaged than Colin Chapman's first single-seaters. The space frame largely comprised square-section tubes, suspension was independent all round, a BMCD-tuned BMC A-series engine was used, inclined to the left at almost 45 degrees, with the transmission running to the right of the cockpit, which was offset to the left.

This car was effective in 1960, but soon outclassed by imports, so BMCD took a leaf out of the British book and produced an orthodox rear-engined FJ car early in 1961. This made little impression, in part because of the power unit, for BMCD tuning produced a shade under 90bhp. In one of the oddities of racing history, one of these cars appeared as a paper entry for a British F2 race in 1964.

BMW

In racing, BMW is usually recalled for a long and illustrious run of outstanding touring cars or as engine suppliers, above all for F2 and F1. The forerunner of most F2 engines, and more distantly the F1 turbo, was introduced as a 1.5-litre road car unit in 1962; among its racing derivatives, the M12 2-litre F2 engine was the category's mainstay for a decade, with more than 500 being made between 1973 and 1981.

The company's own first F2 ventures had come earlier, in 1967, stemming from an entry into hill climbing with an adapted F1 Brabham in 1966. That car was powered by a 2-litre engine with the notoriously unreliable Apfelbeck radial-valve head. For the F2 that came into force in 1967 a 1.6-litre version was devised and used in Lola T100 chassis run by John Surtees' Lola team. These cars had a white and blue colour scheme, carried BMW badges and scant evidence of Lola origins. Hahne (BMW) appeared in twelfth place on the 1967 F2 Championship table.

For 1968 a pair of Lola T102s was built expressly as the BMW team cars; there were no other T102s, and these were commonly entered as 'BMW T102', so they can be regarded as BMWs. They served the team well, as did the Len Terry design that followed. These cars were built by Dornier. At the end of the 1970 season the team was wound up as the company directed its attention to other types of racing, and to supplying the engines that were to dominate F2 for a long period.

T102 This car followed the then-usual Lola bathtub monocoque pattern, with suspension on Lola lines and differing from the T100 in details such as the tubular engine sub frame. Outwardly the cars were slim, as far as the back of

The lines of the Lola T102 can be made out in this later 1968 shot of the revised car, which was notably tidier behind the cockpit. Far from tidy, however, are two gross sponsons between the wheels. These were full of nothing but air as they performed an aerodynamic function, and were sometimes seen on fast circuits. Germans sometimes preferred to designate this car 'F268'. Driver in this shot is Jo Siffert.

the cockpit; behind it, Ludwig Apfelbeck's masterpiece projected untidily above the body lines. In that form the car was not successful.

Before the end of the 1968 season BMW discarded the Apfelbeck device, and modified the T102s with more compact power units and tidier rear ends. In this form they were used in 1969, when they came good (in April, Hahne was second overall in the AvD Trophy but first non-graded driver, thus earning a first European Championship maximum points score for a BMW F2 driver).

F269-270 Len Terry was commissioned to design a successor to the Lolas and he instinctively followed the path of orthodoxy. Unlike the Lolas a full monocoque was used, wearing normal and streamlined bodies, the former sometimes with an enormous rear aerofoil and the latter with detail changes as the team sought handling improvements. The engine was a conventional four-valve straight four, initially rated at 225bhp, with 240-250bhp being claimed in 1970. Two cars were built in 1969 and two more for 1970, when BMW also bought a March 702 'for test purposes'.

These BMWs were effective on fast circuits because of engine power rather than slippery shapes. Ickx, Quester, Hahne and Siffert all won races with them in 1970, when in non-graded terms Quester scored best in the European Championship, where he was fifth. Final races were at Neubiberg (Munich) in October 1970, and at Macau later that year.

Full house – all four BMWs in the Thruxton paddock in 1970 (**above**), with normal bodies and rear aerofoils. Front to rear the cars are 270/2 (Siffert), 270/1 (Ickx), 269/4 (Quester) and 269/2 (Hahne). (**Below**) One version of the streamlined bodywork. Others had strakes on the nose, streamlined headrests, or rear aerofoils. Driver is Hubert Hahne at Hockenheim late in 1970.

BODE

An early German Formula Junior car which, like most of its contemporaries, used DKW components, in this case the front wheel drive transmission as well as the temperamental two-stroke engine. (A story current in the late 1950s was that above-average engines were selected from the Auto Union production line for sporting use in Juniors or 1000SP rally cars.) The Cologne-built Bode had a simple box section chassis, wishbone and top leaf spring front suspension and a leaf-sprung rigid rear axle. With that sort of specification it was not going anywhere.

BOND

Laurie Bond combined simplicity, light weight and front wheel drive in several competitions cars, the first a tiny hill climb car in 1947. The Bond Type C was a well proportioned 500cc F3 car, with a JAP engine driving the front wheels by chain and echoes of old cyclecar practices in wire-and-bobbin steering and cable-operated brakes, contrasting oddly with its monocoque construction. It made no impression on the circuits. Bond tried again with a Formula Junior car in 1961. This had its Cosworth-Ford engine mounted back to front, driving through a Ford gearbox to a differential/transfer box and the front wheels, plus a fibreglass monocoque. It was no more successful than the other front wheel drive cars built to post-1945 regulations, and they have been few in number.

The 1961 Bond was a well-proportioned little car, but quite ineffectual in the forcing house of Formula Junior.

BONNET

After Charles Deutsch and René Bonnet – DB – had gone their separate ways in 1962 Bonnet turned to rear-engined cars, notably the Djet sports car. He also essayed a Junior, using Renault components, and in 1964 an F2 car appeared briefly. This followed the Junior in having a semi-monocoque – perhaps quasi-monocoque would be more accurate – chassis contrived by rivetting sheet aluminium to the outside of a tubular frame with fibreglass panels bonded to the inside. Double wishbone suspension was used front and rear, with inboard coil spring/damper units (coupled with a low frontal area, this gave an impression of sleekness). Renault engine, gearbox, suspension uprights and so on were used. This Bonnet made no impression in F2, and the marque's short life ended as it was 'taken over' (rescued) by Matra to become the basis of Matra Sports. René Bonnet died in 1983.

BOVY

Belgian F3 driver Quirin Bovy built this car on Dallara lines for his own use in 1980, and proposed to offer replicas for sale. The Bovy was exhibited with a Nova-Toyota engine early in 1980, but did not feature in races that year.

BOXER

Brian Lewis worked with sports car and F2 teams in the 1960s and formed his own company in 1972 to run independent cars, most notably the Bang and Olufsen March pairs in F2 and F3 in 1975. Late that year he built his own first car, provisionally named Boxer as the intention was that it would carry the name of a sponsor. It actually went through life as the Boxer.

John Clarke designed a straightforward orthdox F2/Formula Atlantic car around a square-sided monocoque in sheet aluminium, with a full-width nose and rear sub frame. This PR276 was first shown with a BMW engine, but first raced with a Swindon BDX. Tony Rouff drove it in two 1976 F2 Championship events, being placed eighth at Thruxton and second at the Nürburgring, but failing to qualify twice. It was also run in F Atlantic guise.

The car came out again in 1977 for F2, with a Hart engine. Brian Henton started four times before money ran out, scoring a win at Thruxton and a fifth at Hockenheim. Then Danny Sullivan had six F2 races in it, the future Indycar champion scoring two Championship points. It was also run in odd ShellSport races and was brought out again for two early 1978 F2 races. Meanwhile Lewis' plans to build an F1 car, primarily for the British series, had been abandoned.

Narrow track accentuated the bluff appearance of the full-width nose, which housed the water radiator. A proposed F3 version would have been slimmer.

BRABHAM

Jack Brabham and Ron Tauranac set up Motor Racing Developments as an offshoot of Jack Brabham (Motors) Ltd in 1961, built their one and only MRD car in secret that year, then while retaining the Motor Racing Developments company name turned to the marque name 'Brabham' for the cars produced by Brabham Racing Developments. That company was established in 1962, with the aim of building single-seaters and sports-racing cars, and running a team up to the level of F1, with the works efforts being run by the Brabham Racing Organisation.

Both men were shrewd and practical, and between them had a wide range of talents which were the resources behind the business, rather than large financial backing. Their partnership lasted for less than a dozen years, after which Tauranac ran it briefly, then C.B. (Bernard) Ecclestone bought in, buying up when Tauranac went off on his own. Ecclestone soon discontinued the line of customer cars and Brabham became an F1 constructor, that phase lasting half as long again as the first one. Bernie Ecclestone then moved out, as his two roles as team supremo and prominent official of the governing body were incompatible bedfellows.

After a year's enforced sabbatical, a Brabham team was back in racing in 1989, under new and troubled ownership, run with ability rather than the flair that had so often been a hallmark of its earlier years. Through those earlier years, it had two main designers: Ron Tauranac and Gordon Murray. The Grand Prix cars they laid down had won 35 championship races, from a total of 343 contested – a better than ten per cent success rate. Brabham had also built some very successful private cars, and by no means least Jack Brabham had won the World Championship driving cars bearing his own name.

Through to the end of the 1960s the cars were known as Repco Brabhams, and they all carried the BT (Brabham Tauranac) designation that was retained after both men had left the company. From 1967 the letters also became part of the chassis number, in place of the earlier system that had used prefix letters denoting the type – for example, FJ. Economy was a watchword, perhaps exemplified in the single-fold brochure for the 1965 models ('Brabham Racing Developments announce the following range of three "Repco" Brabham single seat racing cars, all of which are developed from the French Championship series winning Formula two car'); and it was this attitude, perhaps, which cost the Brabham Racing Organisation some races. In another example of that economy of effort those same 1965 cars had a common specification, save in components such as engine and gearbox. A BT15 F3 car with Cosworth MAE was priced at all of £2000, or £2025 with a Holbay R65.

Through to the BT33 all the circuit cars had space frames, although on the BT26 there was stressed-skin stiffening and the BT25 Indianapolis car had a monocoque construction.

From the days when Jo Schlesser scored the marque's first international win, in a Formula Junior race at Montlhéry, and in the French FJ series that year won its first Championship, the customer cars were usually competitive, too – small wonder that as the 1970s opened some 500 Brabhams had left the small factory near Weybridge. More than most, the early Brabhams seemed to be subjected to modification and adaptation by their owners, and to lead long and useful competition lives (and, in turn, to confuse later chassis number collectors).

In the early Ecclestone years the team was not necessarily well endowed, in fact, the second car tended to be occupied on a rent-a-drive basis. Commercial factors doubtless came into play when Ecclestone turned the team away from Murray's first very elegant and effective F1 Brabhams to the Alfa-engined cars that were erratic performers. A return to elegance and competitiveness came with the Cosworth-engined cars at the very end of the 1970s, and this was carried through into the period when the team used BMW turbo engines – after a difficult start, these became reliable and powered some beautiful cars. Both Cosworth and BMW cars had simple and attractive white and dark blue colour schemes which enhanced their lines.

In the mid-1980s Brabham slipped into decline, beginning with Murray's unsuccessful ultra-low car and engines that were no longer competitive. After a year out of racing the team returned in 1989 under rather uncertain circumstances. There was a background of dispute and litigation as various parties claimed control. Swiss financier Joachim Luhti apparently won these battles, but by the middle of the year he had fallen foul of the Swiss banking authorities about unrelated matters. However, with Japanese sponsorship, there were resources to carry the team through a full season, although its cars did not live up to early promise, or Brabham's past. Then 1990 opened with injunctions and contractual problems seemingly the most important factor in determining a once-great marque's future. Days before the first Grand Prix of the year this was assured as a Middlebridge Group buy out went ahead.

BT2 The 1962 FJ Brabham was developed from BT1, the solitary MRD that had been raced by Gavin Youl in 1961. There was no call for Jack Brabham to be tactful in his choice of make name in 1962, for he had broken with Cooper and his own early-season F1 races were in a private Lotus 24. The BT2 was a conventional space frame car, well made and strong, which was not an instant success but performed well enough. Schlesser's blue car was the only one to actually win in 1962, Frank Gardner scored top five placings in a works car while team mate Youl faded, Bob Olthoff took a third place with a BMC-engined BT2 (most had Ford-based engines), and in the USA Augie Pabst was prominent in a Brabham run by Briggs Cunningham. The 11 cars built got the new marque away to a solid start.

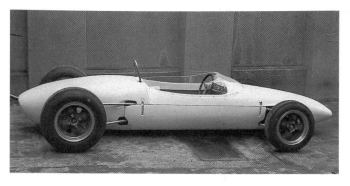

The first Brabham . . .

BT3 Brabham's first F1 car was designed and built during the first half of 1962, making its race debut on August 5 in the German GP. In it Tauranac followed the broad lines that featured in most Brabhams through to the end of the decade. The chassis was stiff by space frame standards, outboard coil spring/damper suspension was used all round, with leading top wishbone and trailing lower wishbone at the front, twin wishbones and radius arms at the rear, and outboard brakes. There were fuel tanks alongside the driver and behind his seat. The water radiator was in the nose, with pipe runs partly exposed. The Coventry Climax V-8 drove through a Colotti-Francis six-speed gearbox.

This one-off car was raced by Brabham in 1962, when it retired after nine laps of the German GP, was third in the Oulton Park Gold Cup, was fourth in the US Grand Prix (when Jack became the first driver to score Championship points in a car bearing his own name) and second in the Mexican GP. In 1963 it was modified with a fuel-injection V-8 and Hewland five-speed 'box, and was used by Brabham early in the year, before Denny Hulme drove his first F1 races in it.

It then passed to Ian Raby, who ran it in a few F1 races with a BRM V-8, and was sold on to be modified as a *formule libre* car before being restored to its original condition for the Donington Museum.

The BT4 was a closely similar Intercontinental/Tasman car with a Coventry Climax FPF engine.

Drivers: Jack Brabham, Denny Hulme, Ian Raby.

In 1962 the BT3 was run in overall turquoise blue, but for 1963 was repainted in the green and gold colours that were to become familiar. Driver here is Jack Brabham, in the car's debut race at the Nürburgring.

BT6 The 1963 FJ car was essentially a development of the BT2. By coincidence, one of the very last important Junior races was won by Schlesser, in a Brabham, at Montlhéry. In that last season of Junior racing, more than a dozen top events fell to Brabham drivers and the marque was second only to Lotus. Twenty BT6s were built (the sole works car being driven by Hulme), and some were adapted for F2/F3 in 1964.

Formula Junior lingered on briefly into 1964 in Argentina, where Silvio Moser was successful in a Brabham (here at Buenos Aires).

BT7 This was a development of the BT3 design for the two-car F1 team run from 1963. The suspension was revised, with an upper wishbone and lower transverse link at the rear, the wheelbase was longer and the bodywork more effective after Tauranac had taken aerodynamic advice from Jaguar's Malcolm Sayer. Short-stroke Coventry Climax V-8s were used, with five-speed Hewland gearboxes.

Dan Gurney had a BT7 for the whole Championship season, while Brabham had to wait until the summer for the second. They served the team well in 1963, when Gurney was second in the Dutch and South African GPs and fifth in the Drivers' Championship, while the Brabham team was third in the Constructors' Championship, ahead of Ferrari.

The two cars were modified for 1964, in particular for the new wide Dunlops. While the championship tables suggested that Brabham was less competitive (fourth in the Constructors' Championship), it was a breakthrough season in that Brabham won the International Trophy and Gurney won the French GP. Later in the year one BT7 was sold to Rob Walker, for Jo Bonnier to drive, and he continued to race it in 1965, several times finishing seventh, while the works team retained and occasionally raced the other.

Drivers: Giancarlo Baghetti, Jo Bonnier, Jack Brabham, Dan Gurney, Denny Hulme.

BT7 does not look very tidy from this angle, which accentuates the suspension 'clutter'. But on this particular late June day in 1964 it was a very effective car – the driver is Dan Gurney, on his way to Brabham's first World Championship race victory.

BT9 The 1964 F3 car was derived from the preceding Junior. It maintained its reputation for road-holding, but the success record for the 13 built was not outstanding – only four major F3 races fell to a Brabham driver, Silvio Moser, in large part because this was the year when F3 was dominated by Stewart-Tyrrell-Cooper, and in part because the engine situation was unsettled.

BT10 This was Brabham's first car for the 1-litre F2, usually powered by Cosworth SCA engines (a Giannini team occasionally turned out 'Giannini-Brabhams' with a stroked version of the power unit that had its origins in Italian 750 racing of the 1950s). The chassis followed the BT6, but with some sheet steel welded to the bottom tubes (this added stiffness, and as the cars were underweight it was no problem in that respect). Outboard suspension was retained, in common only with Alpine among 1964 F2 cars, and the French car in any case 'borrowed' from the Brabham design. The suspension differed from the Junior only in details of geometry, although there was reinforcing sheet metal around the mounting points.

These cars were much more successful than the parallel F3 cars, winning nine of the 18 races in 1964. Successful drivers were Brabham and Hulme in works cars, Rees in a Winkelmann car, Schlesser in a Ford France car and private entry sensation of the year, Jochen Rindt. Some BT10s were converted to F3 specification in 1965.

The BT10 appeared a little bulkier than rival F2 cars, but the greater frontal area was no handicap. This works car is driven by Jack Brabham, on his way to victory in a hard-fought Oulton Park Gold Cup.

BT11 This appeared as the 'customer' version of the BT7, then in an unusual reversal the works team had the last two of the five built in F1 form (five BT11A Tasman cars were also made). Two of the BT11s delivered in the Spring of 1964 had BRM engines, ('delivery' is perhaps mis-applied, for Rob Walker's

car was completed by his mechanics) but Bob Anderson's Climax V-8-engined example was the first to race, in the Silverstone International Trophy.

Anderson and Siffert each scored a third place finish in a Championship race (in Austria and the USA respectively), while Siffert won a non-Championship race at Enna in the Walker Brabham-BRM. This car was bought by Willment, and Graham Hill drove it to win the 1964 Rand GP, before Gardner raced it in 1965 GPs. Brabham drove the first works BT11 towards the end of 1964 and there was a pair in 1965. Gurney's second places in the USA and Mexico were the team's best performances, for there were engine problems with both 16- and 32-valve V-8s.

The private cars served on through the first 3-litre F1 seasons, one appearing on the 1968 South African GP grid. Coventry Climax 2.7-litre FPF engines were used by Anderson, others had 2-litre BRM V-8s. Anderson scored Championship points, before he was killed in a sad test accident at Silverstone in the summer of 1967; John Taylor had been fatally injured at the Nürburgring in Bridges' ex-Willment ex-Walker BT11 in 1966.

Drivers: Chris Amon, Bob Anderson, Jo Bonnier, L. Botha, Jack Brabham, Dave Charlton, Frank Gardner, Dan Gurney, Graham Hill, Denny Hulme, Hap Sharp, Jo Siffert, John Taylor.

BT11 in its original form, in this case Anderson's car with a carburettor Coventry Climax V-8. BRM-powered cars had less prominent engine air intakes. The car is at Monaco in 1964, and the bodywork is picking up reflections from a Tabac advertising banner.

BT15 The 1965-6 F3 car, which had the same space frame/bodywork/suspension specification and dimensions as the BT16 F2 car and the BT14 *formule libre* car. Fifty-eight were made and all the successful cars were Cosworth-powered. Success came in full measure in 1965, when winning Brabham drivers included Pike, Courage, Ahrens, Troberg, Williams, Moser, Crichton-Stuart, Irwin, Mohr and Troberg, between them picking up victories in 42 major races.

BT16 The F2 version of the 1965 works/customer cars for secondary formulae, with most differences at the back. The favoured engine of the year was again supplied by Cosworth and Brabhams powered by the Northampton engines won four F2 races (two victories to the works team, two to Winkelmann) while Hill won one dramatic race at Snetterton in a car with the BRM F2 engine. These two units gave just under or fractionally over 130bhp, or so it was claimed; there seemed no question about the 130bhp produced by a new power unit, the twin-ohc Honda engine which Brabham used in three races, in preparation for 1966. Jack Brabham himself came close to winning with one of these engines in the last F2 race of the year, at Albi. Some BT16s served on quite adequately in 1966.

With these cars Brabham noses seemed to be slimmer. Certainly there were no complaints about penetration, and the BT16s were a match for similarly-powered cars in a straight line. This is Hulme, at Karlskoga.

BT18 Tauranac modified his successful design for a fourth season, and for 1966 one main designation sufficed, covering BT18, the works Brabham-Honda; BT18A, the F3 car; and BT18B, the customer F2 cars, normally with Cosworth engines. The F2 cars had apparently slight advantages in specification and these were sufficient to persuade some entrants to use F2 chassis for F3 cars.

In F2 the chassis was a known quantity, and the Honda engine turned out to be powerful and reliable. The works drivers, Brabham and Hulme, won 12 of the year's 15 races and were first and second six times, while stand-in Chris Irwin took a third place. The second most successful team was Winkelmann's, with Cosworth-engined Brabhams (Rindt won two races, Rees scored two second placings). Ahrens also finished in the top three in one race with a BT18B, and had a good season with Brabhams in F3 as well. In that category the works was represented by the Chequered Flag team and Chris Irwin won nine races in its cars.

Another neat car, and the dominant one in the 1966 F2 series. At last Tauranac seems to be accepting that the idea is not to protect a roll-over bar with a driver's head, but vice-versa. This car at Pau is driven by Hulme.

BT19 This was one of the most remarkable one-off lash-ups in the history of racing. It was laid down in 1965 for the Coventry Climax flat-16 engine, and when that was stillborn it was set aside until quite late in the year when it was modified to accept the 3-litre version of the Repco V-8. This had been developed on the basis of an Oldsmobile aluminium unit by Frank Hallam and Phil Irving for Tasman racing; its 2.5-litre capacity was increased to 2994cc (88.9 x 60.3mm) and as the Type 620 it produced almost 300bhp. The team's engine man was John Judd.

Tauranac had introduced some oval-section tubes around the cockpit to strengthen a weak area in a space frame car. Suspension was still outboard front and rear and 15in wheels soon replaced the first 13in wheels. Initially a Hewland HD transmitted the power, but it soon gave way to a sturdier DG.

The BT19 was only raced by Jack Brabham in 1966, and at Reims on July 3 he drove it to win the French GP. That was the first Championship race victory for a driver in a car bearing his name. Moreover, it was the first of four successive Grand Prix victories, and that run gained the World Championship. The unique BT19 was brought out for three 1967 Grands Prix, with the 740 engine, Brabham placing it second in Holland. Then it was driven by Gardner in the Oulton Park Gold Cup and Brabham in a non-Championship race at Jarama to come third.

Drivers: Jack Brabham, Frank Gardner.

Hastily-adapted BT19 looked solidly purpose-built, and typically 'Brabham'. The four-into-one exhausts seem in danger of becoming entangled in the suspension, and in this British GP shot the car has 13in front wheels, 15in rears.

BT20 This can be regarded as an improved BT19, with a longer wheelbase and wider track, double tubes around the cockpit in place of the oval tubes and other minor changes. The first was completed for Hulme to race in the 1966 French GP, when he was third on a triumphant Brabham day, and the second was ready for the late-season races. The BT20s did not have a long front-line career, being used in only eleven GPs (14 starts) before they were superseded by the BT24. Only one Championship race fell to a BT20, when Hulme won at Monaco in 1967. Both had further lives, the original car going to John Love, the second to a French rugby player, Guy Ligier, who scored his only World Championship point with it in Germany in 1967. Silvio Moser started in two 1968 Grands Prix in it, achieving his best-ever placing (fifth) in Holland.

Drivers: Jack Brabham, Denny Hulme, Guy Ligier, John Love, Silvio Moser.

BT20 seemed a slightly tidier BT19. The fuel tank alongside the cockpit is more apparent in this shot than on the BT19. Denny Hulme is the driver, at Monaco in 1967.

BT21 These cars were built in greater numbers than any other customer Brabham, 110 being recorded. Most were F3 cars but with a substantial number in BT21B (Formula B in America) and BT21C *formule libre* form. The last, usually referred to as 'BT21X', was actually the prototype of the 1968 BT28 F3 car. The first BT21s came at the end of 1966 and showed few changes – the chassis was a little shallower than the BT18, the suspension was modified in detail and the bodywork was new. Normal engines were Cosworth MAE or Lucas units giving 105-115bhp in 1967, and Holbay or Lucas engines giving up to 120bhp in 1968, naturally driving through Hewland 'boxes.

Private owners, or teams such as Felday, had a good season with Brabhams in 1967 (the formidable Matra team just failed to match Brabham's score in international or major national races, by 23 to 26), but then in 1968 Tecno proved more than a match. There were only minor modifications in the BT21B, primarily to accommodate wider wheels, and only seven races of comparable status fell to Brabham drivers. Late that year the BT21X appeared, with a much more rigid space frame (deriving from BT23 rather than BT21), which overcame most of the shortcomings.

Brabhams still seemed to be getting slimmer in 1967. This BT21 is being driven by Peter Gethin.

BT22 A one-off with a Coventry Climax 2.75-litre FPF engine, used by Hulme in five early-1966 races while the first BT20 was being completed. Its only finish was fourth in the International Trophy.

BT23 This designation covered Formula B and Tasman cars as well as two F2 models, BT23 (1967) and BT23C (1967-8) – the differences were minimal. The space frame was stiffened with stress-bearing panels, the upper right and lower left main tubes were larger than the others as they carried coolant and the engine bay was stiffened with small tubes. The suspension followed well-tried lines. The 200-plus bhp Cosworth FVA drove through a Hewland FT200 gearbox.

Jochen Rindt dominated the 1967-8 seasons in Winkelmann Brabhams, winning nine (of 15) races in a BT23 and six (from twelve starts) in a BT23C, but as a graded driver he could not claim the Championship. The works team run in 1967 was dogged by minor problems, but these were good independent team cars, driven by the likes of Kurt Ahrens, Derek Bell, Piers Courage, Peter Gethin, Rob Widdows and Jonathan Williams. Chris Lambert died in a Zandvoort accident in a BT23C.

Without the infant aerofoil and outboard suspension, BT23C would have been another clean-lined car. This one is driven by Rindt on home ground at Langenlebarn, hence presumably the additional decals.

BT24 These cars followed the Repco V-8-engined Tasman BT23A and, save in the larger engine bay, were as compact as the F2 car – therefore slightly shorter and narrower than the BT20s (from which the suspension was derived). In summary, this was an F2 chassis with suspension, wheels, brakes and DG300 to cope with the 330bhp of the Repco 740 engine.

That power output was by no means sufficient to match the Cosworth-engined Lotus 49 in 1967, but the BT24s were nimble cars and the pair used in that season were placed first and second in three Championship races. A BT24 was first raced in the Belgian GP, and after that Brabham won in France and Canada and Hulme in Germany, but Denny beat an unamused Jack into second place in the Drivers' Championship while the team won the Constructors' title. A third car was built, but the BT24s were little used by the team in 1968 although they lingered on in 1969 with independents.

Drivers: Kurt Ahrens, Jack Brabham, Dan Gurney, Denny Hulme, Silvio Moser, Jochen Rindt, Sam Tingle.

BT24 was another workmanlike little car. Here in its debut race at Spa in 1967 it has a pair of tiny aerodynamic trim tabs on the nose. The driver is Jack Brabham.

BT26 This car came for the 1968 Grand Prix season, which was disastrous from Brabham's point of view. The four-valve centre-exhaust 860 engine Repco had devised, with John Judd and Norman Wilson undertaking design work, turned out to be hopelessly unreliable. The car was longer than the BT24 and its track was wider as tyres got fatter. It was the last F1 Brabham to have a tubular chassis (not quite a space frame as sheet panels were used instead of triangulated tubes). At the Belgian GP in 1968 the cars appeared with a modest strut-mounted rear aerofoil, and small nose tabs. The aerofoil business was to grow apace and outgrow itself.

In the 1968 Grand Prix the team recorded just two scoring finishes with BT26s, both at a wet Nürburgring, and slumped to eighth in the Constructors' Championship. For 1969 the BT26 was reworked to accommodate the Cosworth DFV. The

The BT26 looked fine, but engine component failures let it down in 1968. At Zandvoort that year it is wearing big fat Goodyears and tiny wings. The driver is Rindt.

original car was acquired by Frank Williams while the works had the use of three. In this form it was successful. Jack Brabham scored the first win in a BT26, in the International Trophy, Ickx its Grands Prix wins, in Germany and Canada, and Courage was second in the Williams' car in the USA. Brabham came second in the Constructors' Championship.

Drivers: Derek Bell, Jack Brabham, Piers Courage, Pieter de Hierte, Jacky Ickx, Jochen Rindt.

At Mosport towards the end of 1969 the BT26 driven by Ickx had a DFV in place of the Repco V-8, big fat tyres, and a lot of aerofoiling.

BT28 This was intended to be Brabham's front-line F3 car for 1969, but despite the development period with the BT21X, cars were completed and delivered only slowly. As far as independents were concerned it became the car for 1970 and beyond, as it was easily updated to BT35 specification. The make-up was familiar – space frame and outboard suspension, with a slippery body (and cramped cockpit). Tim Schenken drove the quasi-works Sports Motors car, tried assorted wings and ironed out problems, so that the BT28 developed as the controllable and viceless machine Brabham customers tended to expect. Schenken also won races in Britain, and late in the year Scandinavian drivers started winning too. There were more BT28s around in 1970, and 23 of the 60 major races fell to their drivers – British, French, Italian, Swedish – in races throughout Europe.

The effective aerodynamic lines of the BT28 show well in this shot of the Sports Motors Lucas-engined car, driven by Schenken at Brands Hatch in the Autumn of 1969.

BT29 This was a Formula B car introduced in 1969, but odd examples were later uprated for use in F2, without success.

BT30 The F2 'companion' to the BT28, sharing the more complex space frame and early production delays in 1969. Wings were worn early in that year, then became less outrageous. Cosworth FVAs were the usual engines in 1969-70, giving up to 230bhp. The aluminium fuel tanks had to go

for 1970 when the car was little changed, but midfriff bulges showed where the mandatory bag tanks were housed.

In 1969 Piers Courage with the Williams' BT23C and BT30 was the leading Brabham driver, fifth in the Championship with Peter Westbury sixth with the Felday BT30. That year there were more points-scorers in BT23s than in BT30s, but of the 40 drivers who scored points in the 1970 Championship no fewer than 22 did so in BT30s and Derek Bell was runner-up in the Championship, with a Wheatcroft BT30. The car was still widely used in the last 1.6-litre F2 season of 1971.

BT30 in its 1970 form, with a bag tank bulge showing behind the front wheel. Driver is Derek Bell, at Pau.

BT33 Necessarily a monocoque car, as changes in regulations called for enclosed fuel cells, the BT33 could have been built and run in 1969. It came for the start of the 1970 season and, but for a couple of silly errors, could have brought Jack Brabham a fourth World Championship, despite the team's very tight budget that year. Tauranac used the DFV as a stressed member, with a straightforward riveted sheet aluminium bathtub monocoque. The main fuel tanks were in the side members with supplementary fuel capacity under the driver's knees. The rear suspension was mounted to a steel ring member attached to the casing of the DG300. At the front there was a fabricated rocker arm, lower wishbone, and inboard coil spring/damper units. Neat bodywork by Specialised Mouldings featured the nose lines of the BT28/30, (on the first car the nose was from that production source), with top air exits on McLaren lines. The works car was coloured 'peacock blue', not far removed from the turquoise of the original GP Brabham, with a broad yellow stripe.

Brabham was the works driver in 1970, the second car being run by the team for Rolf Stommelen. Brabham started well with a win in South Africa, and that turned out to be his last GP victory. He should have won at Monaco and Brands Hatch. Stommelen, having his only good F1 year, contributed ten points to push Brabham into a by no means disgraced fourth place in the Constructors' Championship. At the end of the season Brabham retired and returned to Australia, selling his share of MRD to Ron Tauranac.

BT33 was a good-looking and workmanlike car, which changed little through two full seasons and served its drivers well. This is Schenken in the first BT33, on his way to third place in the 1971 International Trophy.

Fortunes slumped in 1971, when Tim Schenken in a BT33 was run alongside Graham Hill in the BT34, while Chris Craft had a few outings in Alan de Cadenet's BT33 and Carlos Reutemann an F1 run in a late-season non-Championship race at Brands Hatch. Five points saw Brabham ninth in the Constructors' Championship .

Tauranac tired of running the factory and the team, and early in 1972 he followed Brabham to temporary retirement in Australia. In the period of transition, as Tauranac bowed out, a BT33 was uprated for early-1972 races and Hill scored one point with it in South Africa.

Drivers: Jack Brabham, Dave Charlton, Chris Craft, Wilson Fittipaldi, Graham Hill, Carlos Reutemann, Tim Schenken, Rolf Stommelen.

BT34 A one-off, built for Graham Hill's exclusive use in 1971, when he drove it to his last F1 victory, in the International Trophy at Silverstone. It was distinctive, its twin water radiator nacelles ahead of the front wheels with an adjustable aerofoil linking them and air exhausted into an area where the airflow was in any case disturbed (Tauranac reverted to outboard suspension on this car). The steering rack was behind the hub line and the cockpit was forward in the wheelbase, so that a 63-litre under-seat fuel tank could be added to the two 73-litre side tanks. It was flat-sided, sometimes run with the DFV covered, and an oil radiator projected on the right, level with the substantial roll-over bar. A Hewland FG400 gearbox was used. The BT34 was slightly revised to be used by Reutemann and Wilson Fittipaldi in 1972, when the Argentine drove it to win the non-Championship Brazilian GP (its best Championship race placing had been Hill's fifth in Austria in 1971).

Drivers: Wilson Fittipaldi, Graham Hill, Carlos Reutemann.

The 'lobster claw' BT34 in its first race, the 1971 Race of Champions at Brands Hatch. Towards the summer the engine cover tended to be discarded and the mirrors were mounted on spindly outriggers.

BT35 This designation was applied to Formulae 3, B and Atlantic cars. They were very much 'Tauranac Brabhams', with space frames and outboard suspension (but inboard rear brakes) and they were popular with independents, particularly outside Britain. However, there were few victories in 1971, and just a few top-six placings in 1972.

This F3 car looks strangely naked without aerofoils, although that was customary in 1971. Driver is Brazilian Ronald Rossi, at Brands Hatch.

BT36 This F2 car had much in common with the BT35, but with a Hewland FT200 to cope with the power of an FVA and wider wheels to put it on the road. Larger fuel cells and other detail changes were made to suit the purpose. As the 2-litre F2 was introduced in 1972 some cars were fitted with BDAs. In 1971 Reutemann was second in the European Championship, driving BT30 and BT36, while Schenken was fourth with a Rondel BT36.

Every inch a Brabham, but in a Tauranac line that was ending. Tim Schenken is in the cockpit of this BT36, the rather morose character on the right rear wheel is Ron Dennis, his Rondel partner Neil Trundle is on the other side. They took great pride in the turn-out of their cars. Dennis still does.

BT37 The change of management led to a holding season at MRD, when the team had to run three types of F1 car, among them the interim BT37 devised by Ralph Bellamy, which was basically the BT34 with a conventional nose radiator arrangement. The white cars looked smart, but in 1972 the best placing was Reutemann's fourth in Canada, and that was matched by de Adamich in Belgium in 1973 with a Ceramica Pagnossin backed car. After he crashed in the British GP, and Watson had an outing in that race, the BT37s were retired. They had contributed to Brabham's ninth place in the 1972 Championship.

Drivers: Andrea de Adamich, Wilson Fittipaldi, Graham Hill, Carlos Reutemann, John Watson.

BT38 This was a completely new customer model, the basic designation applying to F2, F3 and FB/Atlantic versions. Designed by Geoff Ferris, it was the first monocoque production Brabham, with a square-section hull in aluminium to the back of the cockpit, a steel bolt-on structure for everything behind it and a three-section glassfibre body to clothe it. Weybridge tradition was followed in some other respects, such as suspension: unequal length wishbones at the front, single top link, lower wishbones and twin radius arms at the rear, with outboard coil springs/dampers at both ends, but inboard rear brakes. Components such as wheels and foam-filled fuel tanks varied according to the intended category.

Before the formal announcement some 40 cars had been ordered, including four for the ambitious Motul-backed Rondel F2 team, but many deliveries were late and by and large development was left to customers. Professional F2 teams could handle that – Jaussaud was second in the championship with an ASCA car, Reutemann and Wollek fourth and seventh in Rondel cars – but the only driver to win with a BT38 in F3 was Tony Brise, and he had a degree of works assistance.

Outwardly the flat nose and side radiators characterized the BT38. This is an F2 car, and photographed from this angle makes an interesting comparison with BT36 and BT40.

BT39 An F1 experiment built up around a BT38 monocoque and suspension, with large fuel tanks on each flank and a broad twin-radiator nose on BT34 lines, powered by the Weslake V-12. This had its origins in the Gurney-Weslake engine and had been developed with Ford backing as a sports car unit. The car was tested in the late summer of 1972, and very quickly set aside as the power output of the V-12 did not seem to be of the order of the claimed 445bhp.

BT40 With its BT41 F3 counterpart, this F2 car designed by Geoff Ferris marked the end of the Brabham production line, apart from a few redundant F1 cars to be sold to independents, and the BT43 F5000 car.

The BT40 was an angular car with an aluminium monocoque, partly closed above the driver's legs. The general layout followed BT38, but in detail there were no external pipes, NACA ducts on the full-width nose gave a clean appearance, and the whole car sat lower. A works car was run for a few races with a BMW engine, but the BDA was again usual, and MRD suggested the use of an FG400 'box for F2 power in 1973.

In Watson's hands the works car showed promise, and de Adamich did well with a BDA-engined car, but there were few customers as Brabham faded in this category.

Clean lines, and perfectly presented for inspection at Bexleyheath, this BT40 has its designation shown for all to read.

BT41 Outward differences on the F3 version were in the conventional nose, smaller rear wing, and engine bay (cars were usually run with this open to the elements). Suspension was common to BT40 and BT41, but the monocoque of the F3 car had a mild steel inner skin, partly to bring it up to the minimum weight. Few reached the circuits, and a high point was perhaps Magee's third place at Monaco.

BT41 was a smart little device, which perhaps through lack of application has gone down as a failure. This is Magee, in Brown's car at Oulton Park.

BT42 Gordon Murray, an assistant designer at MRD, stepped out of the shadows with the BT42 which restored the Brabham team's fortunes. It was a short-wheelbase car with a pronounced pyramid cross section making for unusual lines that were accentuated by the engine airboxes coming into vogue in 1973. There was nothing of significance common to the BT37 and BT42, but Tauranac's twin-radiator idea reappeared in a nose that was more unified than on the earlier car. Suspension was outboard again, with double wishbones at the front and a top link, lower parallel links and twin radius rods at the rear. The DFV was a stressed member, as a matter of course, and FG gearboxes were used. Deformable structure requirements were taken care of with a plastic sandwich filling between the monocoque skins.

The first car was written-off in its debut race at Brands Hatch, but BT42s showed well in their first GPs, Reutemann scoring the first points with a new car in Sweden. Brabham finished the season in a respectable fourth place in the Championship.

The cars were little used by the team in 1974 but passed to independents – Pagnossin for de Adamich and Stommelen, Hexagon for Watson, Finotto for Larrousse. The only scoring finish was Watson's sixth at Monaco.

Drivers: Andrea de Adamich, Wilson Fittipaldi, Loris Kessel, Gérard Larrousse, Carlos Pace, Teddy Pilette, Carlos Reutemann, Richard Robarts, Rolf Stommelen, John Watson, Eppie Wietzes.

The rear wheel makes BT42/3 (in its first Grand Prix) look a very small car. Argentine sponsorship marks it out as Reutemann's – Fittipaldi's carried Brazilian decals.

BT44 In many respects this was a cleaned-up derivative – and most attractive. Among the changes there was pullrod semi-inboard front suspension and all-round dimensions were increased. Reutemann led the early-1974 Grands Prix and won the South African race, then suffered a string of failures and incidents before winning again in Austria and the USA. His early team mates that year were rent-a-drivers Richard Robarts and Rikki von Opel, but in mid-season Carlos Pace joined to give Brabham a strong pair.

For 1975 the cars were revised to 'B' standard, with a stiffer monocoque, narrow front track, some loss of weight and revised bodywork which proclaimed sponsorship from Martini and Rossi. During the year there were tentative aerodynamic experiments, but attention necessarily switched to the BT45. Pace won in his native Brazil, Reutemann won in Germany and Brabham was second in the Championship. Then the BT44Bs were sold to John Macdonald, who aspired to a GP team, but he had no success. Among his drivers Magee, Nelleman and Villota failed to qualify, then Macdonald ran into legal problems when a disgruntled driver sued, and the team folded in mid-season.

Drivers: Bob Evans, Loris Kessel, Lolla Lombardi, Carlos Pace, Carlos Reutemann.

The BT44B in 1975, with extemporized extra cool air intakes spoiling its lines. The main bodywork is nicely of-a-piece, even the little aerodynamic add-ons. The driver is Reutemann.

BT45 Bernie Ecclestone presumably had good reasons for committing the Brabham team to the Alfa Romeo flat twelve engine. Like many of Ing. Chiti's children, this one had been temperamental and weakly, yet showed some promise; beyond that it was different in the DFV age, it fitted the sponsor's image and it came at no direct cost. The cost in other respects was considerable.

Starting from scratch, Murray designed a wide monocoque, with two pontoons extended rearwards to carry the engine and containing four cells for fuel to satisfy its thirst. At the back the Hewland gearbox, 5- or 6-speed, was a known and trusted component. The car showed no promise in its early outings, from the start of the 1976 season to the point where Reutemann decided to quit. Pace persisted, and his death in an aircraft accident early in 1977 was a great blow. Meanwhile the team had been a lowly ninth in the 1976 Championship, with the best race placing being Pace's third in the French GP.

The following year started well, with Pace second in Argentina, and the introduction of the 'B' version at the South African GP. This had revised rear suspension and engine mounting, and among detail improvements had a lighter gearbox. John Watson placed one second in France, and the team ended the year fifth in the Championship.

As the first BT46 did not work, the BT45 was uprated for early-season 1978 races, with the most obvious change in this

In its original form the BT45 was unlike anything else on the mid-1970s grids, but those extraordinary engine air intakes soon went, and the overall colour changed to red.

Ferrari was expected to dominate Grand Prix racing in the first 3-litre season, 1966, for the team was seemingly well prepared with V-12s, even if these were not quite as powerful as outsiders assumed. This 312 (**top**) is driven by Bandini at the fast Reims circuit, where it had the legs of every other car but was put out of contention with a broken throttle cable.

Surprisingly, the 1966 titles fell to Jack Brabham and his 'simple' cars. He was securely champion before the last race of the year in Mexico, when he had awarded himself a 'golden' helmet. He drove a BT20 in this race (**above**), instead of the BT19 he used through the European season.

The real standard for the early 3-litre years was set by the Lotus 49, from 1967. In the old Team Lotus colours it was a car of beautiful simplicity, if not (in another Lotus tradition) total reliability. Graham Hill undertook its early development driving, and here lends a hand with final preparation before the car's debut race in Holland in 1967.

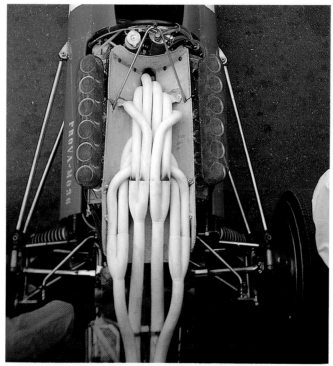

The Lotus 49 (**left**) was created for the Ford-backed Cosworth DFV engine, which had been laid down as a result of a Chapman initiative. This is another photograph from Zandvoort in 1967 – Jim Clark is in the cockpit of the car, engine designer Keith Duckworth is beside it.

In those early 3-litre years pundits insisted that at least 12 cylinders would be necessary. A V-12 was a natural format for Ferrari (**top**), here in a 1967 car with a wondrous gathering of exhausts in the vee. From above Dan Gurney's Eagle (**above**) looked less tidy than it did from the trackside, in part because of the exhausts of the Weslake V-12.

Matra was in the forefront of the French racing revival in the 1960s, although F1 success in that decade was achieved by Ken Tyrrell's very English team with its highly talented Scottish driver and a DFV engine/Hewland gearbox combination at the back of Matra chassis. This is Stewart's MS10 (**inset**) at Monza in 1968, carrying a very spindly rear aerofoil.

The 'Matra-Matra', the MS11, in its race debut at Monaco in 1968. The camera does not lie – this was not a pretty car. The driver is Jean-Pierre Beltoise.

From above the broad shape of the BT45B shows how Murray had to go to the dimensional limits permitted in order to accommodate the boxer engine and its fuel. The driver is John Watson.

BT45C being the slim full-width nose radiator. Lauda started well with Brabham, placing one of these cars second and third in the first two races. Then the revamped BT46 was brought into service.

Drivers: Niki Lauda, Carlos Pace, Larry Perkins, Carlos Reutemann, Rolf Stommelen, Hans Stuck, John Watson.

BT46 This type number stands out, for two audacious cars that came out of the new Chessington base in 1978, and for the only Brabham-Alfa victories in Championship races. The first BT46 had a slim nose, a triangular cross section and, bearing in mind that engine, a small frontal area. There were no conventional radiators but surface heat exchangers along the flanks were used to cool water and oil. Beyond that there was digital instrumentation and on-board jacking. The rising rate suspension was carried over and the engine supposedly produced 520bhp.

The cooling system did not work, in large part for aerodynamic reasons, so the cars were revised with orthodox radiators and Watson was third in the BT46 race debut in South Africa. Like other designers, Murray was soon seeking an answer to Lotus' superiority, gained through ground effects, and since the boxer engine ruled out venturi side pods

he had to seek an alternative route, coming up with a radical solution in the BT46B. He put a large fan at the rear which sucked air from the sealed engine bay through a horizontal radiator. It thus served two purposes, it cooled the engine and sucked the car to the ground, and the original slim nose could be used again. This was a first-stage system, but there were howls of protest about the 'fan car' system both before the 1978 Swedish GP and after Lauda had won it. The race result stood, but the car was banned thereafter on the grounds that the fan was a moveable aerodynamic device (Murray insisted that its primary purpose was cooling) and the BT47 project for a more advanced fan car was abandoned.

The BT46C was quickly devised, with radiators behind the front wheels and the slim nose, and even more quickly abandoned. The 'normal' BT46s saw out the season, with a win for Lauda at the sombre Italian GP meeting. Brabham's third place in the Championship was well deserved.

Drivers: Niki Lauda, John Watson.

A brilliant concept but a practical failure – the first BT46, with heat exchangers lining its flanks.

The 'fan car', with the water radiator just visible as the flat area behind the cockpit. There was also a change of primary sponsor. The driver is Lauda, on his way to victory in Sweden.

BT48 Brabham had to have a full wing car, and towards that end a vee engine. Autodelta obliged very quickly, with the 1260 Alfa V-12 (78.5 x 51.5mm, 2991cc). It used many parts from the flat twelve and was used as a stressed member. It was supposed to produce 525bhp at 12,300rpm.

The main monocoque was in sheet aluminium, with carbon fibre composite panels, the first in a racing car. It had full undercar aerodynamics and initially there was no conventional rear wing – one was hastily added when the car proved virtually undriveable. Pullrod double wishbone suspension was used front and rear, with coil spring/damper units tucked inboard out of the underwing airflow.

This car recorded one non-Championship win, ironically scored by Lauda in his last race before his much-publicized retirement and in the last race for a Brabham-Alfa. Brabham was eighth in the Championship, the new DFV-engined car looked stunning and promised well.

Drivers: Niki Lauda, Nelson Piquet.

BT49 Brabham had enough problems with Alfa engines in any season but the position worsened as Autodelta began to work up its own F1 programme in 1979, and although the season was well under way that led to the decision to return to Cosworth engines. Within weeks the first BT49s were built, using quite a lot of the BT48, but it was new from the cockpit back, with new side pods, reduced fuel tank capacity and reduced weight. In their first race appearance, in Canada, these cars showed immediate promise, although this was to be overshadowed by Lauda's abrupt departure.

The car was refined through the winter, and in the spring ran its first race with a Weismann five-/six-speed transverse shaft gearbox, which was compact and hardly interfered with ground effects airflow. This needed development, and did not finish a race until the summer. Meanwhile Piquet won at Long Beach, then at Zandvoort and Monza, and Brabham took third place in the 1980 Championship.

For 1981 the car was revised as the BT49C – lighter and with more carbon fibre parts. In the year when sliding skirts were banned, and an unenforceable 6cm ground clearance rule introduced, Murray devised a hydro-pneumatic system which meant that a car would settle lower when running and return to its legal 'clearance height' state as it stopped. The wrangles lasted through the year but most teams copied the ploy. Piquet won three Grands Prix, and Brabham was second in the Championship.

The BT50 with a BMW turbo engine had been seen in public during practice for the 1981 British GP but it had a most unhappy debut in the first 1982 race. Uprated Cosworth cars were used for the next two events and then run in parallel with BT50s for a while. The D was lighter and lower, with carbon fibre disc brakes which were 'water-cooled' in common with some other DFV-engined cars – a means of bringing underweight cars up to the formula limit by carrying disposable ballast. Piquet was first across the line in Brazil, but disqualified when the system was successfully protested. There was to be one more victory for a BT49, a rather odd one gained by Patrese at Monaco, then after one more race the BT49s were retired. The type had a long front-line life – September 1979 to June 1982, by a fluke from Canadian GP to Canadian GP – and seven Championship victories had been scored by the 18 cars built.

Drivers: Riccardo Patrese, Nelson Piquet, Hector Rebaque, Ricardo Zunino.

The BT49 had started life as a hasty design to meet a situation, yet it always had elegant lines. Obsolescence was looming as it reached this BT49C form in 1982, when it was a very good looking car indeed. This car is being driven by Piquet in Brazil, towards a victory that was disallowed.

BT50 BMW had been attracted to F1 before coming to an agreement with Brabham in the summer of 1980, and the combination was to go through a period of trials and tribulations before success eventually came. The engine carried a sub-designation in the M12 series, for chief designer Paul Rosche based it on the production straight four. As the F1 M12/13, it had a capacity of 1499cc (89.2 x 60mm) with a KKK turbocharger. Its initial output was claimed to be 570bhp, but it had a distressing tendency to fall apart and full reliability was to prove elusive. The BT50 carried on from the BT49s, with the C monocoque and pullrod double wishbone suspension, only slightly longer in the wheelbase and naturally a little heavier, with a higher spine behind the cockpit betraying the larger fuel cell.

The Brabham-BMW story began badly, and acrimoniously, with a succession of failures. Piquet's victory at Montreal in June 1982 unexpectedly relieved gloom, but there were only three more points-scoring finishes for the five BT50s that were used. In the second part of the season Brabhams ran on half-full tanks and reintroduced fuel stops, but it was some time before one made it to half distance. The BT50's short career ended as the season finished.

Drivers: Riccardo Patrese, Nelson Piquet.

The BT50 looked much more substantial than BT49. This is an early test shot, with a substantial aerial for the telemetry equipment used by BMW technicians. The driver is Hector Rebaque.

BT51 Outwardly this appeared to be a ground effects turbo car with low BT49 lines behind the cockpit, for refuelling stops were assumed. The ban on skirt ground effects cars for 1983 was not overruled, so BT51 was never raced.

BT52 This dramatic car was used through 1983, with considerable success – three Grands Prix fell to Piquet, one to Patrese, and the Brazilian gained his second drivers' title.

The concentration of weight towards the rear of the BT52 meant that the cockpit was further back than had become customary.

Outwardly, the rearward weight bias was readily apparent, and this was a car without side pods at a time when they had become universal. The lower part of the monocoque was in aluminium sheet, the upper part was moulded in carbon fibre composite, while the engine was in a steel frame bolted to the rear. Pushrod double wishbone suspension was used and coil spring/damper units were inboard, as were the carbon fibre disc brakes at the rear. The engine was rated at 640bhp, or 750bhp in qualifying trim, and drove through a Brabham five-/six-speed gearbox (which had Hewland internals). In that brief fuel-stop era pneumatic jacks were built in.

This was the most successful of Brabham-BMWs, the six cars producing 72 Championship points, for third place in the Constructors' Championship.

Drivers: Riccardo Patrese, Nelson Piquet.

BT53 The 1984 season was altogether less happy, for although Piquet won two Championship races the team achieved only twelve finishes from 32 starts. The car was a development of the BT52, with 850bhp engines and larger fuel cells as fuel stops were banned. A mid-season revision, as the BT53B with new rear wing and other aerodynamic improvements and changes to engine ancillaries, was not successful, although some of the work was applied to BT53s. The high proportion of failures was due to engine problems, particularly with turbochargers, which accounted for eight retirements.

Drivers: Teo Fabi, Nelson Piquet, Manfred Winkelhock.

Some of the simple elegance of line was lost in the BT53, although in large part that visual impression is due to aerofoils, at the front and in those rear 'winglets'. This is Piquet at Brands Hatch.

BT54 There was another substantial new element in the Brabham make-up in 1985, Pirelli tyres, which were really successful only in the very hot conditions in which the French GP was run, when Piquet won his only Grand Prix of the year. In this car Murray stayed with an aluminium sheet

The BT54 was another car with superbly balanced lines, but some of its advantages were offset as the team worked to come to terms with Pirelli rubber – or maybe Pirelli attempted to come to terms with Brabham's level of performance.

monocoque with a moulded carbon-composite top and with double wishbone suspension. There were detail advances over the BT53, and BMW improved reliability in the engine, which was rated at 850bhp in race trim. This time nine cars were built, and were not subject to mid-season revision. The team relied on Piquet, who scored 21 of its 26 points, although when Surer was brought in to replace Hesnault after four races there was some back-up strength. A pair of BT54s was brought out in mid-1986 and one raced to give a comparison with the hapless BT55.

Drivers: Francois Hesnault, Nelson Piquet, Marc Surer.

BT55 This was an unhappy season. In theory this 'lowline' design offered considerable advantages, not just in frontal area and therefore straight-line speed, but in effective airflow over the rear wing. To that end, the engine was inclined at 72 degrees, which it did not like. To compound the problem the Weismann seven-speed gearbox was unreliable.

The shallow monocoque was a carbon fibre/Kevlar moulding. Double wishbone suspension was perpetuated, pullrod operated and with the coil spring/damper units tucked further inboard. Eight chassis were built. Patrese scored the team's only points when he finished sixth at Imola and Detroit, and at the end of the San Marino race he was not running. When the immensely talented Elio de Angelis was killed in a test accident at le Castellet, in the Brabham team's first fatal accident, Derek Warwick was recruited for the remainder of the season.

Drivers: Elio de Angelis, Riccardo Patrese, Derek Warwick.

The extraordinary lines of the BT55 were best appreciated from ahead or in side elevation. Warwick is the driver in this British GP shot.

BT56 Brabham was a team struggling to escape the doldrums in 1987, and it did not help that its principal, Mr Ecclestone, was engrossed in the affairs of FISA while its gifted designer had departed after the near-fiasco of BT55. David North, Sergio Rinland and John Baldwin laid out the new car, and they had to use the 'laydown' BMW engine again as the upright units had gone to Megatron. In its make-up the car followed a pattern going back to the BT49, and outwardly it was another good looking machine. Its drivers both visited podiums with

Once again the blue and white colour scheme was very smart. The BT56 lines ran from a fine nose to a rather heavy rear wing, and for a Brabham there was the unusual feature of a radiator air exit on top of the side pods. Driver is de Cesaris, at Imola.

third-place finishes, de Cesaris in Belgium (he managed only one other finish all year) and Patrese in Mexico. So the team did stage something of a recovery in Constructors' Championship terms, coming eighth with ten points. It was then granted the dubious recovery period of a year's sabbatical, while its future was resolved.

Drivers: Andrea de Cesaris, Riccardo Patrese.

BT58 New owner Joachim Luhti sent Brabham back into the fray in 1989, then faced up to a sticky year. Against a background of company difficulties a straightforward car designed quickly by Rinland and built very quickly (for bedding-in tests just before its first public appearance in Brazil) did not let the team down. Its running gear followed the established pullrod suspension pattern and there was nothing novel in the monocoque but the engine was a Judd V-8, and the BT58s ran on Pirelli tyres. Initially the team had to pre-qualify, but good results at Monaco, where Modena scored four points and Brundle one, meant that it escaped that indignity at mid-season. Brabham was eighth in the Constructors' Championship, with eight points – there had been worse years. The off-season problems meant that it was a struggle just to get these cars to the first 1990 Grand Prix, when Modena nevertheless finished 'in the points'.

Drivers: Martin Brundle, Gregor Foitek, Stefano Modena.

The rear-engined Junior was a plump car, with suspension components that looked exceptionally sturdy and a fuel tank above the driver's leg.

The names re-emerged with the new F3 in 1964, on cars with Brabham space frame lines and Ford engines. These were prominent in Italian F3 races in 1964, with several top-six places. The following season was barren, and in 1966 only one reasonable placing was recorded for a Branca, when Baghetti was fourth in a Monza race, and the one-time Ferrari driver won a race at the same circuit in 1967. That year there was a monocoque Branca F3 car, which was later given wedge lines.

There was a short-lived spurt of activity by Branca in the early 1970s, with an angular Nova-engined car designated Branca 71 although it did not appear until the summer of that year. Giovanni Salvati drove it to win an autumn Monza race, and in 1972 six drivers raced a Branca-Nova at least twice, but the best placing was sixth, gained by Bergami at Monza. Then the marque faded, with odd F3 cars appearing through to 1978.

The BT58 was a wholly conventional 1989 car, in make-up as well as appearance. Driver is Stefano Modena, in the Silverstone pits lane.

BRANCA

This Milan constructor existed at a modest level for two decades, building only a few cars, some carrying the name Moretti and some named Branca to avoid confusion with a Torinese specialist car manufacturer, later just a Fiat conversion specialist, Fabbrica Automobili Moretti. Aquilion Branca's Moretti company built some sports-racing cars in the 1960s, and its first F3 car in 1952. This had its Gilera engine behind the cockpit in a tubular chassis, with wishbone front suspension and a de Dion arrangement at the rear. It also appeared with a dohc Fiat-based engine.

There was little Italian interest in the first F3, and the 750 formula that led to Formula Junior was preferred. There was the promise of a worthwhile market in FJ and Branca produced the first Moretti Junior using sports car components and in-house Fiat tuning expertise (some 85bhp was given by its *millecento* units). That front-engined car was very quickly followed by a rear-engined model, using the same Fiat 1100 engine and 600 gearbox. The rear-engined car had a semi-space frame wishbone and coil spring independent suspension. It made little impact in the Stanguellini-dominated races of 1959, and then came the British new wave.

Sturdy suspension was also a feature of Branca's late F3 cars, seeming to offset the frontal area advantages of the slim hull. This is Bozzetto at Monza in 1978.

BRITANNIA

John Tojeiro's first single-seater design was for Ackland Geddes' Britannia Cars. It was announced in the Spring of 1960, rather late in the season for the very competitive British market, so most of Britannia Cars' limited production went from the Hertfordshire factory to the USA. In its space frame, double wishbones, coil springs and damper suspension, inboard rear brakes and Ford 105E-based engine there was nothing out of the ordinary, save that engine development for the first car was by Basson rather than one of the usual tuners. The Britannia made little impression on circuits.

When Britannia Cars went into liquidation, Tojeiro bought parts for six Formula Junior cars which he made up and sold as 'Tojeiros'. This exercise proved that a change of name does not improve a car's performance.

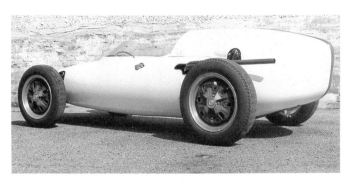

The FJ Britannia was a compact car, and its high tail was its only distinctive feature on the FJ grids of the early 1960s.

BRM

British Racing Motors was formed in 1947, as a trust with the collaborative aim of bringing into being a Grand Prix project conceived by Raymond Mays just before the end of the Second World War, and carried forward to the design phase by Mays and Palin 'Peter' Berthon. Their Type 15 took shape as a car slowly, and the prototype was not completed until late in 1949. On paper it could have been a contender in the first Championship season, but its complexity would have stretched the resources of one of the pre-war German teams, so it was remarkable that a small and under-funded team managed to put it together and get it running – an achievement that tended to be overlooked.

The car performed quite well in *formule libre* races after the World Championship had moved on, and in its MkII form was almost convincing, as well as occasionally spectacular. BRM turned to an apparently ultra-simple car for the 2.5-litre formula, only to encounter seemingly endless problems. Nevertheless, Alfred Owen, who had taken on the team's backing late in 1952, continued his support and eventually a BRM won a Grand Prix in 1959.

A threat of closure hung over the team in the opening season of the 1.5-litre formula but in its second the programme at last came good, with both Championships in 1962. A false step back to complexity was taken in the early 3-litre seasons, then things went well again, into the early 1970s. By then Sir Alfred Owen had passed control to his sister Jean, and effectively to her husband, one Louis Stanley.

Several managerial virtues were seldom in evidence, among them realism, and BRM went into a terminal decline. There was a last Grand Prix victory at Monaco in 1972, but Rubery Owen support ended as Owen died in 1974. The BRM company was put into liquidation at the end of that year, when

Stanley-BRM appeared, sponsors were lost (among them the cigarette company that by the end of the 1980s had the longest record of motor sport sponsorship), and the team struggled on with dwindling resources and ageing equipment. There was a final pathetic effort as Stanley-BRM in 1977. Nothing came of an attempt to revive the marque by John Jordan and Derick Bettridge in 1979.

Type 15 The pale green cars brought ignominy rather than the prematurely-trumpeted glory to the Bourne venture, and a change to dark green saw little change in fortune. The car had features such as pneumatic strut suspension, with trailing links at the front and a de Dion rear end, but the chassis was straightforward and in many respects of the 1930s. The centrifugally supercharged V-16 (49.53 x 48.26mm, 1488cc) was another matter, and at times potentially the most powerful GP engine around, giving 330bhp at 10,250rpm early in its life, 525bhp on test in 1952, and more was claimed but seldom, if ever, produced. It may be that 440bhp was a reliable figure. There was scant reliability and only flashes of vivid performance. In MkI form this BRM won 13 minor races, including heat victories, and ran in only one GP.

Beginnings – Raymond Mays in the first BRM at Folkingham (**above**). It later sprouted many intakes and louvres and is shown (**below**) in its most extreme form at Goodwood in 1953, driven by Fangio.

The end as Ron Flockhart pedals a MkII around Castle Combe in October 1955.

The MkII was lighter and more compact, and quite successful in local *formule libre* races in 1954-5 – there were six victories in insignificant races – and there is the memory of the exhilarating scream of 16 tiny cylinders.

Drivers: Peter Collins, Ron Flockhart, Juan-Manuel Fangio, Froilan Gonzalez, Stirling Moss, Reg Parnell, Raymond Sommer, Peter Walker, Ken Wharton. (Only Parnell and Walker drove a V-16 BRM in a Championship race.)

P25 On the face of it BRM turned to simplicity for the 2.5-litre formula car with the handsomely proportioned little P25. This had a 2491cc (102.87 x 74.93mm) four-cylinder engine designed by Stuart Tresilian. The car showed speed but had tricky handling, and there were persistent problems with valves, the single rear transmission brake and with putting the whole project together. Issigonis advised, Moulton advised, Chapman reworked the de Dion rear suspension and replaced the oleo struts with conventional coil springs and dampers, Rudd revised the front suspension and for 1959 Berthon reworked the engine to accommodate AvGas as it became obligatory. The products of all that effort were victories in secondary races, and Jo Bonnier's victory in the Dutch GP. Soon there was pressure from within the team for a rear-engined replacement, but third place in the 1959 Constructors' Championship was an achievement for the Bourne team.

Drivers: Jean Behra, Tony Brooks, Jo Bonnier, Peter Collins, Jack Fairman, Ron Flockhart, Mackay Fraser, Mike Hawthorn, Hans Herrmann, Les Leston, Stirling Moss, Roy Salvadori, Harry Schell, Maurice Trintignant.

Peter Collins in the compact P25 at the car's debut meeting, at Aintree in September 1955.

The lines of this BRM changed little through its long career. Here near its end, Harry Schell in a works car on his way to seventh place in the 1959 French GP passes the pale green car that had been loaned to BRP and was driven in this race by Moss, resting from his futile efforts to push restart it in the Reims heat.

P48 Late in 1959 the first of the P25s to be converted into rear-engined P48s appeared. Run through 1960, these somewhat extemporary cars had rear suspension and braking shortcomings, and engines that often lacked power. In 1960 a MkII version came with revised chassis and rear suspension, and conventional rear brakes in a sensible effort to overcome that lingering BRM weakness.

In all, eight were built, and run in Tasman and Inter-Continental events as well as F1. In GPs they recorded just four finishes and BRM was fourth in the Constructors' Championship.

Drivers: Jo Bonnier, Dan Gurney, Graham Hill.

Neat at the front, untidy at the rear with those inclined coil springs and struts, might sum up the appearance of the P48. This is Graham Hill in the 1960 British GP, when he led and put in the fastest lap.

BRM-Climax As a stopgap, cars were run as MkIIs (P48/57) with Coventry Climax FPF engines in the first season of the 1.5-litre formula with predictable niggardly points rewards, while BRM's V-8 was readied.

Drivers: Tony Brooks, Graham Hill.

The BRM-Climax was a smooth little car, but hopelessly underpowered in a season dominated by Ferrari engines. This is Hill at Reims.

P57 Very much the make or break BRM – the team was under an Owen ultimatum to succeed or fold, and happily this sleek car was a winner. Its space frame chassis was laid down by Rudd, with double wishbone and coil spring/damper suspension all round. It was powered by a fuel-injected V-8 (68.1mm x 50.8mm, 1482cc) designed by Berthon and developed by Aubrey Woods, and from 1963 a new BRM six-speed gearbox was used.

In 1962 BRM won the Constructors' Championship with GP victories in Holland, Germany, Italy and South Africa, and Graham Hill won the drivers' title. The team continued to race them early in 1963, Hill scoring his first Monaco win in one. The engine was to be used by other teams, while cars served independents Trintignant and Centro Sud as they were discarded by BRM.

Drivers: Giancarlo Baghetti, Lorenzo Bandini, Giorgio Bassi, Roberto Bussinello, Masten Gregory, Richie Ginther, Graham Hill, Maurice Trintignant.

Early in 1962 the Type 57 was run with eight separate exhausts pointing skywards, and here at Monaco (**above**) with the short nose once favoured by teams for that circuit, until aerofoils made such one-race modifications impractical. In its normal form (**below**) at Monza it was a pretty little car. The driver in both shots is Graham Hill.

P61 A stressed-skin semi-monocoque car designed by Rudd, with inboard suspension and complex linkages intended to give variable spring rates, and the V-8 with some internal redesign – lighter and producing around 200bhp. The chassis tended to distort, the weakness being at the rear where there was not a bulkhead, and the car had a reputation for being difficult to work on. It was nevertheless a front runner, with a first and second in the US GP, and for the first of three consecutive seasons BRM was runner-up in the 1963 Constructors' Championship.

Drivers: Richie Ginther, Graham Hill.

P261 This car was also known as the P61 MkII, and it was raceworthy for the start of the 1964 season; it served out the life of the 1.5-litre formula and on into the next with enlarged versions of the V-8. With rearward stressed-skin extensions to carry the engine, which was very firmly bolted in, the hull had torsional stiffness of a high order. It was a successful team car, with six GP victories 1964-6. Tim Parnell and Bernard White ran these V-8 BRMs into 1967 and Tony Dean ran one for Charles Lucas in the Gold Cup in 1969; the 2-litre V-8 also had a successful career in Tasman racing.

The '2-litre' versions were actually in three capacities, 1916cc and 1998cc giving up to 270bhp, and 2070cc producing some 285bhp.

Drivers: Bob Bondurant, Piers Courage, Richie Ginther, Graham Hill, David Hobbs, Innes Ireland, Chris Irwin, Charles Lucas, Jackie Stewart.

Jackie Stewart in a 2-litre P261 at Monaco at the beginning of the first 3-litre season, when this car was used as a stand in. He won the race.

P67 An experiment that was set aside, this four-wheel drive car used the space frame of a 1962 car with the V-8 turned through 180 degrees so that the clutch was just behind the driver. The drive was offset to the left, with the gearbox alongside the driver's legs. Ginther tested it and Attwood was nominated to drive it in the 1964 British GP. However, it never raced, and BRM learned about the shortcomings of four-wheel drive – the team was not tempted to join in this late-1960s fad. The P67 was used as a hill climb car.

P83 Here was a return to bad old ways, with an over-ambitious, over-complex car, which it has to be admitted reflected all the pundits' dictates for the 3-litre years. The shortcoming was at the rear of the 1965-style monocoque, where a heavy H-16 engine was bolted on. The engine was a stress-bearing member, and carried the gearbox and rear suspension. This 2988cc (69.85 x 49.89mm) unit in effect comprised two eight-cylinder engines, one atop the other, and initially there were two firing sequences. At that stage it produced a questionable 400bhp, ten per cent below target, and at its best was to be good for some 420bhp. There were endless problems with this engine (it powered one GP-winning car, a Lotus), and numerous revisions to the car. The P83 recorded only twelve race finishes, the best being second and fifth (Stewart and Spence) in the 1977 Belgian GP, and this type was last raced in the 1968 South African GP, when the V-12 P126 made its debut.

Drivers: Graham Hill, Chris Irwin, Mike Spence, Jackie Stewart.

Jackie Stewart in a P83 at Silverstone. From this angle the Type 75 engine does not look as bulky as it was.

P126 This car was designed by Len Terry along conventional lines, to be powered by the V-12 (74.6 x 57.2mm, 2999cc) that had been largely designed by Geoff Johnson and presented as a sports car unit, although its F1 potential was shown in McLaren's M5A late in 1967. Not only was the P126 the first

BRM not designed and built in house, it was the first not to use a BRM gearbox (a Hewland DG300 was specified). Double wishbone suspension was used, with inboard front springs and outboard rear springs. Two were initially built for Tasman racing, but converted for F1 use alongside a third. They showed well, with second placings, but were soon superseded by the P138. Parnell ran a P126 into 1969. Meanwhile, BRM was fifth in the 1968 Constructors' Championship.

Drivers: Richard Attwood, Piers Courage, Pedro Rodriguez, Mike Spence.

Rodriguez showed the potential of the P126 by leading the 1968 Spanish GP in this car. It looks untidy, but had the virtue of simplicity.

P133 This was in effect a BRM-built version of the P126, used in 1968-9. Two were built, but one was soon written off in an accident. Rodriguez led the 1968 Spanish GP in the other until he crashed, was second in the Belgian GP and twice finished third. This car was brought out again for early 1969 races.

Drivers: Jackie Oliver, Pedro Rodriguez, John Surtees.

Parnell ran the first BRM with a rear aerofoil, and the team introduced wings on the P133. The rear wing on this car driven by Rodriguez in Canada appears to be working, although it makes the car look even more of a mongrel.

P138 A modest development of the P133 put together in 1968, with a revised monocoque and BRM gearbox. In 1969 it was run with a 48-valve version of the V-12 but was not competitive.

Drivers: Bill Brack, George Eaton, Jackie Oliver, John Surtees, Bobby Unser.

P139 Another redesign, largely in the monocoque, and another failure that brought strife within the team and an upheaval – Rudd went, Tim Parnell took over as team manager, Tony Southgate joined as designer. The car was revised in mid-season, but it was never competitive; the only worthwhile finish was Surtees' third place in the US GP, albeit two laps behind the winner.

Drivers: George Eaton, Jackie Oliver, John Surtees.

P153 The clean sweep went some way to restore the team's fortunes, and so did a completely new car. Moreover, this was not in BRM's habitual dark green but the colours of a sponsor, Yardley. At Spa in 1970 Pedro Rodriguez scored BRM's first GP victory since 1966. Southgate designed a simple and light open bathtub monocoque, with low bulbous flanks containing the rubber fuel cells. Suspension was conventional but, rarely by 1970, brakes were outboard all round. The V-12 was worked over by Aubrey Wood, to give power which sometimes matched the DFV and complemented the P153's reputation for good handling. A P153 was run in 1971 for the third driver in the team, and in P153B form (with P160 suspension) was brought out again in 1972.

Drivers: George Eaton, Howden Ganley, Helmut Marko, Jackie Oliver, Pedro Rodriguez, Alex Soler-Roig.

A new look for BRM, with no sign of the previous 'tube' lines and a pronounced flat nose. Suspension members are unashamedly in the airflow. Yardley colours have yet to be applied to this first P153.

P160 A cleaned-up development of the P153 for 1971, with more rounded lines and a lower monocoque. The team won two of the fastest GPs (Austria and Italy, falling to Siffert and Gethin respectively) with these cars, victories more than offset as its leading drivers, Rodriguez and Siffert, both died in secondary races (the Swiss was the only driver to be killed in a BRM accident). BRM was second in the 1971 Constructors' Championship, and was never to reach such heights again.

Versions of the P160 were run with diminishing conviction in 1972-4, when luck saw BRM score its last GP victory as Beltoise drove a P160B to win in a downpour at Monaco. That car had a narrower monocoque and other detail changes. Through this period of decline there was little real innovation save for the deformable-structure chassis for P160E in 1973, the emphasis being on keeping ageing machinery 'in the field' and ignoring such details as proper rebuilds. That year Lauda did at least lead a late-season Grand Prix in a P160E. There was a slide in the Constructors' Championship, to seventh in 1972, sixth in 1973 and finally seventh in 1974.

Drivers: Jean-Pierre Beltoise, Howden Ganley, Peter Gethin, Niki Lauda, Helmut Marko, François Migault, Clay Regazzoni, Pedro Rodriguez, Vern Schuppan, Jo Siffert, Alex Soler-Roig, Reine Wisell.

The P160 as it was introduced. Other noses were to be used, and a high engine airbox, while in 1972-3 the cars were more extensively modified. Yardley colours were carried until the end of 1971, which was also the end of BRM's last season as a real force.

P160B in its 1972 colours, with the wide 'shovel' nose first seen in 1971. An airbox was usually worn.

Two years later the P160E looked a different car. This one is driven in practice at Monaco by François Migault.

P180 A pair of these Southgate-designed cars was built for 1972, with a low monocoque on P160 lines but with radiators at the rear alongside the gearbox. This over concentration of weight – the front of the car could be lifted quite easily by one man – did not lead to good handling qualities. The cars were troublesome and had just one late-season win in a minor race.

Drivers: Jean Pierre Beltoise, Bill Brack, Brian Redman.

P201 This compact car was designed by Mike Pilbeam and outwardly featured angular flanks terminating in prominent radiators and a deep cockpit surround, while under the skin lived elderly V-12s. Nevertheless, Beltoise placed a P201 second in the car's debut race, though much of this achievement was owed to retirements among the Kyalami runners. A single car was run spasmodically in 1975, as a Stanley-BRM (most of the BRM staff had left), and it appeared once in 1976.

Drivers: Chris Amon, Ian Ashley, Jean-Pierre Beltoise, Bob Evans, Henri Pescarolo, Mike Wilds.

Bob Evans during practice for the 1975 Race of Champions, with the new equipe proclaimed on the P201. In the race Evans placed it sixth, BRM's best of its final full season.

P207 Len Terry's bulky Stanley-BRM design showed no signs of becoming competitive, despite the 480bhp claimed for the V-12 in 1977. Perkins qualified it for two Grand Prix starts, Pilette (the original nominated driver) failed to qualify it three times, and it was withdrawn from a Brands Hatch race as the suspension was suspect. Pilette drove it in odd minor races, and that was to all intents and purposes the end of BRM, although cars lingered on the sidelines of minor British events as Jordan-BRMs into the early 1980s.

Drivers: Larry Perkins, Teddy Pilette.

The last real BRM had attractive overall lines, although these did little to conceal its bulk.

P230 This was an ersatz BRM – although it followed Woods/Terry design lines – which was built as an angular ground effects car by CTG in 1979, for patrons Derick Bettridge and John Jordan. They had only limited ambitions for this car, but even those were not followed through.

BRP

The British Racing Partnership was set up as a team to run cars for Stirling Moss, who was not always in a position to accept offers of worthwhile drives because of his clashing personal contracts with suppliers. In 1959 it ran F2 Cooper-Borgwards and an F1 BRM (which Moss drove in only two GPs, before it was demolished in Herrman's spectacular Avus accident). BRP then ran Coopers with Yeoman Credit backing and eventually UDT-Laystall Lotus 24s. These cars were outmoded, although hardly rendered obsolescent, when Lotus introduced the 25.

This led to BRP building its own monocoque car, 'designed' by Tony Robinson, which was a Lotus 25 copy although it had a thicker skin. The BRM V-8 was used, driving through Colotti-Francis five- and six-speed gearboxes. The first car was completed in the early summer of 1963 and driven by Innes Ireland, who won a minor race with it early in 1964. The team's best GP placings, all scored by Ireland, were fourth in the 1963 Dutch and Italian races, and two fifths in the 1964 Austrian and Italian races. BRP built a pair of unsuccessful Indianapolis cars for 1965 and closed down after an F1 project failed to take shape in 1966.

Drivers: Innes Ireland, Trevor Taylor.

Head-on, this trio of 1.5-litre GP cars differ only in detail and colour schemes. Ireland in the first BRP leads a BRM and a Cooper in the 1964 French GP.

BRW

A Formula Junior car of 1960 attributed to Eugene Bohringer of Stuttgart, the other two enthusiasts who contributed initials to its name being Rank and Wutherich. It was a typical local FJ car of the period in its use of German components – primarily Mitter-tuned DKW engine and Porsche gearbox and suspension components. The whole came together with a tubular frame, carried on torsion bar ifs and wishbones and coil spring/damper rear suspension. It was campaigned in German events, but did not feature among the top finishers on results sheets.

BRW was a bulky machine, and because of the characteristics of the tuned DKW engine was best suited to sprint events. Here one of its creators, Eberhard Rank, is on the Rossfeld hill climb in 1960.

BS

BS Fabrications was a leading sub-contractor to the racing industry, manufacturing complete cars and components for teams and running cars in Grands Prix and in the secondary British F1 series until 1980, when in an odd reaction to a recession in the racing car industry a BS Fabs F1 car was laid down, to designs by Nigel Stroud and with finance arranged by Argentine driver Ricardo Zunino. Early in 1981, however, the sponsors withdrew, and although the first car (which was to be DFV powered) lacked only suspension and wheels, with monocoque complete and bodywork to be finished, it was abandoned.

BSR

Bertram Schäfer was a prominent F3 driver in the mid-1970s, when he turned entrant before becoming an F3 constructor in 1988, his Birburg-based VW Motorsport team running the BSR 388. This was designed by ex-Zakspeed man Johann Knapp along conventional monocoque lines, with pullrod front suspension and pushrod rear suspension, the Shrick-VW engine driving through a Hewland 'box. It was run alongside the team's lead car, a Reynard, and through a consistent finishing record, rather than race-winning performances, Frank Kramer finished his season with fourth place in the German Championship.

This achievement encouraged Schäfer to run a pair of BSR 389s in 1989. These were handsome cars, with competitive power (a claimed 172 PS), but after the cars were first and second in the first round of the 1989 German Championship, persistent chassis problems led Schäfer to turn to Ralts for his 1990 team.

BSR 389 was a sleek car, with very clean front suspension and shallow side pods (on both sides). Driver is Ellen Lohr.

BUGATTI

There was still flickering life in the Bugatti company after the Second World War, and two racing cars appeared to carry the famous badge. Both were oddities and neither made an impression.

Type 73C This car complied with the capacity requirements of the first F1 of 1948, built late in the preceding year but never raced. T73 production car components featured in its make-up and the chassis and running gear followed 1930s Bugatti lines. It had a supercharged four-cylinder engine (76 x 82mm, 1488cc) for which 250bhp was claimed. Chassis with two body styles appeared later, but as far as can be ascertained neither was 'authentic'.

Type 251 The last Grand Prix Bugatti was undertaken to restore prestige to the once-famous name and financed by income from military contracts, which was dwindling as the car took shape. Gioacchino Colombo laid out a highly original design, the T251 having its straight eight engine mounted transversely behind the cockpit in a space frame and with novel detail work, yet with de Dion suspension front and rear. It appeared for only one race, when it was under-powered, had spiteful road holding and was far from competitive. It was not developed largely because Bugatti's cash flow dried up as military contracts withered when the Indo-China (Vietnam) conflict ended.

Driver: Maurice Trintignant.

BUZZIE

Built by one of the pioneers of the 500 movement, Jim Bosisto – a man who later became associated with Iota – this 1946 car achieved no success but gave its builder some interesting moments for a total cost of £35. The short wheelbase chassis was based on a Morris 8 frame, front suspension was Morgan sliding pillars while the independent rear suspension used a converted front end from a BSA three-wheeler. A rear-mounted Douglas D.T. engine drove through a Norton gearbox. It was slow and had a tendency to become airborne which, in the manner of the day, was blamed on its lightness.

In 1948 Bosisto built a second Buzzie based on one of the first batch of Iota frames which had Morgan ifs, coil spring rear suspension, and a Speedway JAP engine, but he sold it to W.C. Cuff who re-christened it Hell's Hammers V and enjoyed some success with it in hill climbs. ML

BWA

This minor Italian constructor, the offshoot of a road-car wheel and trim manufacturer, was active in the second half of the 1960s, building a small number of F3 cars. Until 1967 these were wholly conventional, and inevitably Ford-powered at that time. The F2 version, announced in 1966, did not materialize. In 1967 BWA introduced the slender monocoque T324, laying down ten. Development was left to teams, as that year BWA ran into financial problems, which was a pity as the car showed promise. It had commendably clean lines, with a Brabham-style nose but slender flanks, undercut along the sides of the cockpit, and a neat engine cover, wishbone suspension combined with outboard coil springs/dampers and a wide track.

BWA race victories were rare, the first coming in 1965 when Russo beat a second-line field at Barcelona. In the rest of that year there were isolated top-six placings and although a works team was run in 1966 Jonathan Williams in a De Sanctis dominated Italian F3 racing, and BWA's best showings were two second placings achieved by Boley Pittard. Enzo Corti, who stuck with BWA throughout its constructor years, gained odd top-six places in 1966-7 and in the following year, in a rare appearance of a BWA outside Italy, was second in a heat at Magny-Cours. Braga and Piazza picked up places in 1969, in 1970 Mario Bianchi won a minor race at Varano Melegari, and as late as the first year of the 1.6-litre F3 di Nuzzo was second in a Monza race. Apparently by that time most of the surviving BWA cars had been sold to South American entrants.

The second T251 at Reims for the 1956 French GP. Its lines seem almost prophetic, with full-width nose, fuel tanks alongside the cockpit and rear-mounted engine.

C

CARAVELLE

A neat Formula Junior car designed by Richard Utley, originally laid down for a Fiat engine but modified to follow the near-universal trend to Ford 105E-based units. The car's make-up was orthodox, with a space frame and aluminium bodywork. Its builder, Bob Hicks, drove it in 1960, scoring some top-ten placings and a notable sixth in a high-quality field at Oulton Park. Its promise led to thoughts of a three-car team with a developed version – basically to be longer and lower – but as 1961 came round the major constructors were squeezing the little men out of FJ.

'Home-built' sometimes has a patronizing ring, but there was nothing amateur about the presentation of the Caravelle, here driven by Bob Hicks at Silverstone in 1960.

CBP II

T.J. Clarke was one of the first buyers of an Iota 500 car and this 1951 special followed it in using Morgan style ifs. Apart from this the Ray Martin Kieft seems to have been the main influence – the car had a forward seating position, a bulbous nose (the rest of the body was distinctly untidy), a space frame and rear suspension by swing axles and rubber bands. It did not achieve much, but then a JAP engine was no way to success by the time it was raced. ML

CEGE

The work of Raymond Sonqvist, a Swede, the CEGE 500 of 1950 had a lightweight dual-member tubular chassis with Porsche-style torsion bar suspension, trailing arms at the front and swing axles at the rear. ML

CEGGA-MASERATI

Claude and Georges Gachnang were Swiss special builders who made a couple of moderately successful sports cars. In 1962 they built a 'conventional' F1 design – a copy of what they could see around them – which was fitted with a four-cylinder Maserati 150S engine and a Maserati five-speed gearbox.

The car was entered for Maurice Caillet in the non-Championship Pau and Naples Grands Prix but on both occasions he failed to start. He withdrew from Pau after qualifying nearly 15 seconds off the pace, and failed to qualify at Naples where he went much better but where only ten cars were allowed to start. The single-seater Cegga was later used for hill climbing. ML

CFS

When Charlie Smith, a motor cycle racer, was killed while practising for a sidecar event in 1949, 500 racing lost a talented designer, for apart from his own CFS he was also responsible for the first Parker Special. Designed to take both 500cc and 1,100cc engines it was a little beefier than most half-litre cars, with a multi-tubular frame (like a shallow space frame but not triangulated), Fiat 500 style front suspension and, most unusually, a de Dion rear axle located by a Panhard rod and sprung by a transverse leaf spring.

Smith was killed before it was fully developed and the car passed to Don Parker who rebuilt it and shortened the wheelbase by three inches (he was a tiny man). It became known as the Parker-CFS and was quite a successful car. ML

CHAIX

A misguided French attempt to build a 500 car, René Chaix's front-engined device was based on Simca (née Fiat) components and was enormous. It derived from Chaix' 500cc sports car with which he had been successful in hill climbs. With less than 30bhp on tap his huge single-seater was a lost cause before it turned a wheel. ML

CHEVRON

Derek Bennett's Chevron marque was best known for the elegant sports-racing and GT cars that came out of its former mill in Bolton, but the single-seaters that were built in parallel were often very effective on circuits. Bennett followed a path that was familiar in the 1950s, like Broadley, Chapman and others building 750 and 1172 one-offs in the mid-1950s, following a Speedway car. He then built and raced an FJ Bennett. He drove various cars in the early 1960s – an Elva, a Gemini, a Lotus and a Brabham, and his own Formula Junior car. In the mid-1960s he returned to clubman's two-seaters, with a 1965 design that was to become Chevron B1, and another was built for Brian Classic. In 1966 Chevron was established in part of the old cotton mill in Bolton.

The first formula single-seater Chevron, the F3 B7, came in 1967 and in the following years cars were also produced for F2, where they were usually competitive but not highly successful, and F5000 where they were more successful in terms of race wins. A highlight was the 1973 Race of Champions when Peter Gethin beat current F1 cars in an F5000 Chevron.

In the mid-1970s Bennett looked towards F1, and his first car started to take shape. Before it was completed he died in a hang-gliding accident in March 1978. The company continued, but without his flair it was soon struggling and it collapsed at the end of 1979, going into liquidation early in 1980. A Scottish consortium took over and revived production with the B52 sports-racing car. A change of control in 1983 saw it moved to a Winchester base. Eventually Chevron single-seaters, for the Formula Ford categories, appeared again.

B7 The first Chevron formula car was a space frame design for F3, built in the late summer of 1967. Raced by Bennett and Peter Gethin, it made little impact but was in effect a prototype for the B9. In 1968 the single B7 was converted for Formula B use.

B9 This 'improved version' of the B7 was marketed in 1968, when 15 were built. A 'works-associated' team, Red Rose, ran cars for Chris Williams and Alan Rollinson, who scored Chevron's first international single-seater victory at Schlieger-Dreieck in East Germany. The car did not become a real front runner, however, until quite late in the year when the B9B was introduced, with stressed panels added to the frame to stiffen the chassis. Late in 1968 Gethin and Schenken won international F3 races in Chevrons. A Formula B version was the B14.

B10 A B9 chassis adapted for F2, driven by Gethin in his first F2 races.

B15 Chevron became a leading F3 force with this car, as the category became intensely competitive again in 1969. A space frame basis was retained, with a stressed sheet centre section giving increased ridigity and housing bag fuel tanks. Double wishbone suspension was used front and rear, and coil spring/damper units were outboard all round. Once drivers had adapted to an apparently inbuilt understeer, the B15 was appreciated as a quick car that rewarded precise driving. Wisell, Hanson and Rollinson won international races with it. The B15B was the Formula B variant.

The B15 was a typically neat little car, and in F3 a challenger to Tecno and Brabham in 1969.

B17 The 1970 F3 Chevron was another derivative, with a revised frame and a quasi-monocoque centre section, new tank arrangements, modifications to the suspension and provision for nose aerofoils and chassis-mounted rear wings. The B17B was the Formula B variant, and as the car was announced in March 1970 it appeared that an independent adaptation for F2 by Paul Craven (installing an FVA engine) would be the only interest in the category. However, Wisell's late search for an F2 drive led to a hasty conversion, using B16 sports-car suspension to make up the B17C; by the time that had been developed race-by-race the B18 was almost ready. Meanwhile Dubler and Hanson had won F3 internationals in B17s, but had not offset an impression that Bennett was preoccupied with his sports cars, and this did not help sales.

B18 From a series of sleek cars, Chevron abruptly turned to very square lines in a car intended for F2, F3 and Formula Atlantic. It had a semi-monocoque built up around top and bottom square tubes, in an effort to keep damage repair simple, with a bolt-on engine sub frame to facilitate changes from one category to another. While the rear suspension followed the B17, inboard suspension was introduced at the front. The nose, with its large radiator intake, was blunt under a prominent aerofoil, giving the car a foreshortened appearance.

The B18 appeared in F2 form (B18C) late in the summer of 1970, but the promise shown then was not carried through to 1971, when the cars suffered from a lack of development work and just one point was scored by a Chevron driver (Mazet) in the European Championship, nothing being achieved by graded driver Siffert in his few races. F3 showings were no better.

Not a pretty car, although appearances were deceptive in that the B18 was fast in a straight line – shortcomings were felt to be due to the lack of a proper development programme. Jo Siffert is the driver here.

B20 Another 'multi-category' car, but this time with a works effort behind its development which paid off in F2 but was less evident in F3, where the B20 was third in line behind F2 and sports cars. In specification it was a development of the B18, outwardly with a less unattractive full-width nose.

Gethin won the 1972 Pau F2 race, although too many mechanical failures meant he was only ninth in the Championship. Watson and Morgan also drove the cars in F2, while Chris Skeaping was out of luck with the F3 car.

A shot from the same angle underlines the family resemblances between the B18 and B20.

B25 A full monocoque F2 car for 1973, retaining the suspension set-up, angular flanks and full-width nose of the preceding car. However, it was powered by the BDA engine in the year when BMW-engined cars dominated F2. Gerry Birrell was reckoned the moral winner at Thruxton, while Gethin and Watson later put in challenging drives in the works car (Birrell was killed during practice for the Rouen race).

Unmistakeably a Chevron. This is a Gunston Hart BDA-powered B25, which Tony Martin used to win the F2 section of the 1975 South African F1 championship.

B27 The 1974 F2 car was sleeker, but undermined by the lack of a proper development programme and by tyre size changes as Firestone policies changed. The intended semi-works team fell apart when nominated driver Kazato was killed in a sports car accident. As the F2 season opened, an adapted F Atlantic B27 driven by Bertil Roos suggested that a Ford-powered Chevron might challenge the BMW brigade, but Roos' best actual race placing was a sixth. The best results were achieved by Team Harper, with BMW-engined B27s – Purley took three second places in Championship events while Pryce also scored well. B27s came out again in early 1975 championship races, Ertl placing one third at the Nürburgring.

In the economy of its outward lines, the B27 marked a move back towards the early single-seater Chevrons. This is Roos at Barcelona as the 1974 season opened.

B29 The 1975 F2 car was overshadowed by Martini and March. The best Chevron finish in the Championship was a third by Ertl at the Nürburgring, ironically in a BMW-engined B27 just before he switched to a B29. Rebaque achieved two fourth places with a Hart BDA-engined B29, and Binder one after he turned to a works-loaned BMW-engined car. The French ROC team ran cars with Simca (Chrysler) engines developed by Hans Funda; these were prone to overheating, and were very unreliable.

The B29 was another compact well-balanced car. This is one of the French Simca-engined cars.

B34 This attractive car first ran in F Atlantic form late in 1975. The first production cars were pushed through for the South African series that winter while the test car was converted to F3 specification, with a Novamotor Toyota engine in place of the Hart BDA. It was a wide-track car, more systematically developed than most preceding single-seater Chevrons, in a programme carried through by Bennett and Paul Owens. The works-supported team run by Trivellato helped in development respects, and once Patrese had shown that the car was a winner Chevron's order book filled. Keegan, Lees in a semi-works car, and Spreafico also won major F3 races in B34s in 1976.

The svelte lines of the B34 shown off by a Trivellato car driven by Patrese at Monza. The F2 B35 appeared similar in many respects.

B35 The parallel F2 design for 1976, which became widely used as Chevron's single-seater fortunes picked up, despite the lack of a works team in this important category (Trivellato had close links, but other B35s were run independently, for example by Opert). BMW and Hart engines were used, the best race results being a second with each type, both scored by Laffite (at Pau and Nagaro respectively), while Jaussaud scored a point with a Simca-ROC-engined B35.

B38 A refinement of the F3 design for 1977, when it was second only to Ralt, with some 20 victories in major races scored by drivers of the calibre of De Angelis, Daly, Elgh, Gabbiani and Lees (Daly won one of the two British Championships, de Angelis the Italian title). In 1978 de Angelis won the Monaco F3 race in a B38.

Outward differences between the B38 and B35 were minimal, the most obvious in this shot of Geoff Lees at Cadwell Park being a small additional intake on the engine cover. The close relationship to the B40 is also clear.

B40 The B35 was refined for 1977 as the B40, which followed the same bathtub central monocoque layout with detachable sub frames, with conventional suspension (double wishbone at the front, transverse links, wishbones and radius rods at the rear) and bodywork on generally similar lines. BMW M12 or Hart 420R engines were normal, but Trivellato persevered with the troublesome Ferrari Dino 246-based power unit, which was eventually modified to overcome most drawbacks, except weight and installation problems. Leoni drove a Ferrari-engined B40 to win at Misano. Despite the number of

B40s raced, the works effort in ICI colours and the semi-works Trivellato team, there was only one other victory for a B40, scored by Rosberg in an Opert Hart-powered car at Enna. Nevertheless, eight of the twenty drivers who scored in the European championship drove Chevrons, and some B40s appeared again in 1978.

Ray Mallock was one of several drivers seen in cockpits of ICI/Newsweek B40s in 1977, here at Thruxton.

B41 The only F1 Chevron was completed after Bennett's fatal accident. It was too late, for although it was a practical and straightforward DFV-powered car, it was out-moded when it was eventually raced. That was in the 1979 British national series, under an award scheme to provide up-and-coming drivers with F1 experience. The ideal might have been praiseworthy, but it hardly made for continuity of development. Tiff Needell's second place in the first race of the season turned out to be the B41's best finish.

The B41 looked a purposeful car, and earlier in the 1970s it might have fulfilled a Grand Prix purpose. As it was, in the ground effects era it was obsolete when it first appeared.

B42 A development of the B40, with a revised monocoque, new front suspension, narrower track and lower body with a more prominent cockpit surround. Hart engines were most

The B42 looked good and perhaps deserved more than two mid-season victories in 1978. Prominent 'splitter' and cockpit surround and rear wing distinguish it from the B40.

commonly fitted, but odd cars were run with BMW or Ferrari engines. It first appeared late in 1977 and was used through 1978 by several teams. In ICI's second season Daly was the full-time driver (he won two races and was third in the championship) while guest drivers raced the other car of the team, to little good effect. Rosberg, Elgh, Lees, Gabbiani and Merzario all scored points in B42s; a notable novice to appear in a Trivellato BMW-powered B42 was Giacomo Agostini.

B43 The 1978 F3 car had no novelties and gained a reputation for being difficult to set up. Works backing was concentrated on European Championship contenders – Patrick Gaillard was a race winner for Chevron in Italy and Germany – and the car made no impression in British racing.

B47 Race Director Paul Owens picked up some of Bennett's design responsibilities, initiating the move to wing cars in the B47 (F3) and B48 (F2), while the bulk of the design work was undertaken by Tony Southgate, working in a freelance consultative capacity. Southgate had to use the existing chassis, but inboard front suspension was introduced together with side pods. The tub was too wide for this to be an effective ground effect machine. The B47 was heavy, and in areas such as handling failed to match up to the dominant March 793. Together with the B48 and B49 (the equivalent F Atlantic car) it marked a decline in Chevron fortunes.

Press presentation setting for a B47. Devaney was to persevere with this car through the year as the team tried to make it competitive, changing the wheelbase, adding longer side pods, and so on. Devaney's one victory owed more to his ability on a wet Silverstone circuit than to the qualities of the car.

B48 The F2 car developed in parallel by Southgate, with the monocoque deriving from the B42 and ground effects side pods added, together with inboard front suspension. Narrow and full-width noses were tried, together with a long wheelbase version. Bobby Rahal made the car look good early in the year, but scored only ten Championship points, while the only other driver to use it for a full season, Rothengatter, scored just three. Customers achieved little.

The B48 was an attractive car, with few outward Chevron characteristics. In this early-1979 shot at Thruxton it is in short wheelbase form, with the narrow nose. Driver is Rahal.

B53 This F3 car was to be the only formula chassis for 1980, albeit with the B54 F Atlantic equivalent. However, the only 1980 model completed was the prototype B51 CanAm car, which proved very disappointing in late 1979 tests. That led to the cancellation of options and was a factor in the closure of the company.

CHS

This conventional British 500 special was built by C.W.A. Heyward in 1951.   ML

Heyward's 500, looking like a Cooper to the detail of rear-view mirrors mounted on the transverse leaf spring, but with a less attractive blunt nose and one of those large steering wheels favoured in the middle period of 500cc F3. Representative of the multitude of British one-offs encouraged by that category, it is at Crystal Palace in 1953.

CISITALIA

There were two Cisitalia racing cars, the ultra-economical little design by Giacosa that was built in numbers, and the ultra-complex Typ 360 by the Porsche Design Studio that was never raced. The company was formed by racing drivers Piero Dusio and Piero Taruffi. Dusio went on to set up a one-model series for the little single-seaters, introduced attractive and effective sports cars and then commissioned the 360, which grossly over-stretched the company's resources. When the company failed he attempted to get the 360 project off the ground in Argentina; predictably he failed, for the car needed enormous development.

D46 This was designed around Fiat components, including the 1.1-litre engine tuned to give around 60-70bhp and suspension from the 500 Topolino, with a pioneering multi-tubular space frame. The D46 was the first new post-war racing car and seven had been built in time for Italy's first post-war race, at Turin in September 1946, when they beat several 'proper' racing cars. That was to become a familiar D46 role, while the one-model racing ideas foundered. Eventually 31 cars were built. By 1948 a 1.2-litre engine was offered and a works pair was run with 1.3-litre engines, modified bodies and increased fuel capacity. These were entered in the first post-war Monaco GP, when Nuvolari got one up to eighth place before retiring and Taruffi was sixth in the other at half distance, before he too retired. A dozen years later, hopeful entrants even looked to D46s as a basis for Formula Junior cars.

Normal D46s had dumpy little bodies with fairings around front suspension members, and were often run with stub exhausts. This works special with its extended nose and power bulge is a very attractive 'miniature GP car'. That impression is completed as the circuit is Monaco and the driver is Tazio Nuvolari.

Typ 360
The designation is a Porsche design number, and eventually a company like Porsche might have got the car working properly. It had a space frame, a supercharged flat-twelve mounted behind the cockpit, independent suspension all round and a two- or four-wheel drive option. As an Autoar it was run once in an obscure Argentine event; as a museum exhibit it is one of the great might-have-beens of racing.

Nuvolari was persuaded to dress up and pose in the only 360 completed, early in 1948. His slight figure makes the car appear larger than it was, and that impression is heightened by the large wire wheels and drum brakes and the skinny tyres.

CIVET

A 1960 Formula Junior car built in Detroit, with a front-mounted Triumph engine – Fiat or Ford alternatives were projected – in a straightforward tubular frame with wishbone and coil spring ifs and a swing axle and coil spring layout at the rear.

CLAYTON SCOTT

Sid Clayton built this early Australian 500 car using parts from a 1934 Singer with a rear-mounted Scott twin engine. Suspension all round was by quarter elliptical springs with a de Dion axle at the rear.   ML

CLUBMAN 500

A conventional early Australian 500 car with a BSA single cylinder engine which was built by Jack Godbehear and driven by Bert Flood with no recorded success.   ML

CMS

Designed by G.S. Styles, the CMS was a British 500 car of 1950 which resembled early Coopers in general layout and even used Fiat 500 parts. It was, however, too heavy to be competitive and its Triumph engine did not help in this respect.   ML

COBRA

Designed by Tom Bryant and Fred Corbin, the F3 Cobra had a shallow space frame and suspension all round by Morgan-style sliding pillars, while the engine installation resembled the Monaco 500 car. The sohc Norton engine was mounted as far to the rear as possible and offset to the right, the chain drive went forward to a countershaft and thence to both rear wheels. It was a short and stubby car originally designed to have a ground clearance of just three inches but when this limit was increased in 1951, just before it was finished, spacers had to be added to the suspension, which did nothing for its already mediocre handling.   ML

The Cobra, here at Silverstone in May 1950, was one of the oddities inspired by the half-litre F3. The top of its Norton engine can been seen between the right rear wheel and the fairing running back from the headrest position (there is actually no headrest), while part of the sliding pillar suspension can be seen inside the front left wheel.

COLONI

Success with teams in second-level championships and a restricting budget were not a sound basis for an entry into the Grand Prix arena in the late 1980s – in the post-turbo era racing in the premier category was not cheap or simple. Enzo Coloni, one-time Italian F3 champion and later entrant, took the plunge into F1 in 1987, introducing his FC187 late in the season, and saw Larini qualify it to start in the Spanish GP. After that a little more might have been expected than occasional appearances on grids, and a few race finishes, in the next two seasons.

FC187 Designed by ex-Dallara engineer Roberto Ori, this conventional car made its first appearance after its introduction at the Italian GP meeting, when Larini failed to qualify it with understandable 'new car' problems. FC187 had a carbon fibre/kevlar monocoque, double wishbone suspension with pullrods all round, a Cosworth DFZ and Coloni-adapted Hewland six-speed gearbox. Detail revisions were made to the aerodynamics and cooling system after its debut and it was qualified for the last place on the Spanish GP grid, only to become the first retirement in the race.

Driver: Nicola Larini.

FC188 The first 188 was a mildly revised version of the 187, with which Tarquini recorded four DNPQs, four retirements and three finishes (best eighth at Montreal). A 'B' version was introduced in which the radiators were repositioned, the bodywork revised, and there were new wings. This work did not advance the cause, as Tarquini qualified a Coloni for only one of the last five races of 1988.

Meanwhile, Coloni had taken on the AGS design team under Christian Vanderpleyn and there was a further mild redesign for the opening GPs of 1989. Moreno and Raphanel qualified once each in a total of eleven attempts that year.

Drivers: Roberto Moreno, Pierre-Henri Raphanel, Gabriele Tarquini.

C3 A pair of Vanderpleyn-designed cars was built under this new designation and the first was introduced at the 1989 Canadian GP. In many respects the design was carried over from the 1989 188s, for example in the suspension. The monocoque was slimmer and there was a new longitudinal six-speed gearbox. There seemed to be little development beyond aerodynamic tweaks through the rest of the season, when the budget and relationships within the team were strained. At the eleventh GP Enrico Bertaggia took Raphanel's place, and consistently failed to pre-qualify, while Moreno broke a DNPQ run just once.

Drivers: Roberto Moreno, Pierre-Henri Raphanel.

C3 was not the slimmest F1 car in 1989, but had overall lines as clean as most. This car is driven by Moreno.

COLT

Mitsubishi chose to use the Colt name for an exploratory entry into racing, with an F2 car for the 1969 JAF Grand Prix. It was a conventional front-radiator car with a four-cylinder 1958cc engine (for which 240bhp was claimed) driving through a Hewland gearbox. There were detail gimmicks at the rear, where bodywork wrapped around the gearbox and there was an oil cooler in the wing support. It did not lead to a sustained single-seater programme.

The conventional elements of the Colt, such as the outboard suspension, show in this photograph, while the slit in the front of the rear wing pylon hints at novelties at that end of the car.

CONDOR (D)

Not to be confused with those examples of the Scampolo fitted with BMW engines which were then called 'Condors', this German special was originally designed by José Jungbecker as a low-cost 750cc car. It easily adapted to 500 racing and enjoyed a little success in Germany. After three were built the project was sold and the new owner built one more car which, to signify its new ownership (and to drive historians into a lather), he called 'Kondor'.   ML

CONDOR (GB)

The Guildford-built Condor appeared early in 1960, and although it was among the lowest and smoothest front-engined Formula Juniors it was out-moded even then. It had a square-tube frame, independent suspension all-round and inboard rear brakes. Initially a Triumph engine was used, but the cars were raced with modified Ford 105E units. A handful were built and seen mainly in British club-level racing, although two were apparently sold to US entrants.

A rear-engined Condor SIII came in 1961, with a similar simple chassis and Ford engine driving through a modified Renault gearbox. It made no impact on FJ racing.

The first Condor Junior was a well-proportioned car and build quality was high.

CONNAUGHT

This British constructor came close to making the breakthrough from a modest contender in local events to a Grand Prix front-runner, let down by a simple lack of resources in the second half of the 1950s. In the age of sponsorship the story might have been different.

The little company was set up by designer Rodney Clarke and engineer Mike Oliver, with backing from Kenneth McAlpine, who also raced the cars in their early years.

The first Connaught was a club racing sports car, then an F2 single-seater came in 1950. This was modestly successful, but the marque's great moment did not come until late in 1955, when Tony Brooks drove a 2.5-litre B-type to win the Syracuse Grand Prix. Connaught could not afford a full works effort and contested only a few Continental GPs, concentrating on British races and on maintaining independents' cars. Operations ceased in 1957, when a space frame C-type was under construction and work had started on an advanced rear-engined monocoque-chassis D-type.

A-type The first of nine F2 cars to the same basic design came in 1950, and was raced through 1951 before more were completed. All had an orthodox tubular chassis, and initially wishbone and torsion bar suspension was used all round; at the rear this soon gave way to a de Dion layout. The 1960cc (79 x 100mm) pushrod ohv four-cylinder engine was based on an alloy Lea-Francis unit and at first was rated at a modest 135bhp. When F2 became more serious, as the World Championship category in 1953-73, various improvements were made, including fuel injection, but although up to 165bhp was to be claimed that was probably an exceptional output – certainly these Connaughts never had the power to complement their road-holding reputation.

Connaught drivers achieved reasonable placings in secondary events in 1952 – fourth and fifth in the British GP were good – but 1953 results were disappointing. Several of the cars were run in 2.5-litre races in 1954, and odd ones helped fill national race grids after that.

Drivers: Don Beauman, 'B. Bira', Johnny Claes, Ken Downing, Jack Fairman, Bill Holt, Leslie Marr, Kenneth McAlpine, Stirling Moss, André Pilette, Dennis Poore, John Riseley-Pritchard, Tony Rolt, Roy Salvadori, Ian Stewart, Eric Thompson, Leslie Thorne, Bill Whitehouse.

The A-type was a compact and well-mannered little car but sadly under-powered. This is Dennis Poore at Silverstone in 1953.

B-type This was a new design, using a 2470cc (93.5 x 90mm) twin-ohc 240bhp Alta engine, which as in the A-type drove through a pre-selector gearbox. Wishbone and coil spring front suspension was used, the de Dion arrangement being retained at the rear, and disc brakes were fitted. The first car appeared late in 1954 with full-width one-piece streamlined bodywork and a distinctive tail fin. This was vulnerable and difficult to handle, and was to be abandoned. In 1957 one of cars was rebodied with a semi-wedge body, and dubbed 'toothpaste tube'.

The B became known as the Syracuse after Brooks' victory. The works team contested only two Championship races in 1956, when Fairman was fourth in the British GP and Flockhart and Fairman were third and fifth at Monza. The last race for the works team was at Monaco in 1957 when Lewis-Evans placed the 'toothpaste tube' fourth. Two of the cars were bought by Bernie Ecclestone for Tasman racing but by 1957 they were obsolescent as far as would-be independent entrants were concerned.

Drivers: Tony Brooks, Ivor Bueb, Jack Fairman, Ron Flockhart, Bob Gerard, R. Gibson-Berry, Les Leston, Stuart Lewis-Evans, Kenneth McAlpine, Mike Oliver, Reg Parnell, Tony Rolt, Roy Salvadori, Archie Scott-Brown, Piero Scotti, Desmond Titterington, J. Young.

The B-type was another neat car, universally known as the Syracuse after Brooks' Sicilian victory. This was the first GP victory for a British driver in a British car for 31 years.

The distinctive 'toothpaste tube' was the third B, rebodied. Here it has a short 'Monaco' nose, and is being driven along the harbourside by Lewis-Evans. By simply plugging on as others retired he eventually finished fourth. This car was also raced in New Zealand with a 3.4-litre Jaguar engine, and normal bodywork.

C-type A lighter car with a space frame, revised de Dion rear end and inboard rear brakes, but with B-type front suspension and engine. The single C was completed by Paul Emery after Connaught had closed. It eventually came to a grid at Sebring in 1959. Slowest of all the F1 cars in practice for that first United States GP it was destined to be the first to retire from the race. The C was then modified, with a supercharged engine, for a vain attempt to qualify for the Indianapolis 500 in 1962.

Driver: Bob Said.

CONNEW

Peter Connew was responsible for some design work on the early Surtees cars, leaving in 1970 to start work on his own car, for F1 no less. Two simple open bathtub monocoques were completed in the lock-up garage in Romford, Essex, where Connew worked with help from friends Roger Doran and Barry Boor and some understanding assistance from 'the industry'. Bodywork and suspension were added to one tub, and with a dummy engine and gearbox PC1 001 was exhibited at the 1972 Racing Car Show. Finance to add the DFV and a Hewland DG300 came with French F2 and sports car driver Francois Migault, and as the Darnval-Connew PC1 002 it was entered for the British GP.

The car was a non-starter then, as in all its 1972 race meeting appearances save one. Migault qualified it 22nd for the Austrian GP and was running 17th in the race when a rear suspension failure led to retirement. In 1973 a Chevrolet V-8 was installed and the Connew was run inconspicuously in odd F5000 races, before a crash signalled the end of brave try.

Driver: Francois Migault.

David Purley hired the Connew for the 1972 John Player Challenge Trophy at Brands Hatch, when it was repainted in Lec colours. It was 18th fastest of the 18 F1 cars in practice (ten seconds off the pace) and failed to complete the warm-up lap because of a simple electrical component failure.

CONRERO

In a short-lived deviation from his well-established tuning business, Virgilio Conrero produced an attractive front-engine Formula Junior car in 1959. It had a multi-tubular chassis and body lines reputedly laid out by Michelotti, with independent suspension all round. A Fiat 1100 engine and 600 gearbox were specified, with the suggestion that a linered-down Peugeot 203 engine would also be suitable. It was a dead end for Conrero.

COOPER

Charles and John Cooper entered racing after the Second World War for fun, and that spirit lingered through the years when their relatively simple cars forced enormous changes in the sport. In 1946 John thought of starting in the curiously English sport of trials, but with Eric Brandon was attracted by the 500 Club and the national racing category it was developing. A car was laid down around Fiat Topolino components, largely because there was a damaged Fiat in the Cooper garage. (Seldom was the term 'laid down' more justified, as in those early years parts tended to be arranged on the garage floor and when they came together as a design the drawings were done.)

Charles Cooper had strong racing connections from the inter-war years, which proved useful when it came to getting a speedway engine for the first car – the Cooper T2. The T1 had been an Austin Seven-based special built in 1936. The T2 was rear-engined for practical reasons, and in general followed Strang's Fiat-based 500. A second car was completed and production as such was under way in 1948. As far as the 500s and stretched variants were concerned production continued until the end of the next decade. Meanwhile horizons had expanded and in the days of the 2-litre F2 the Coopers showed that they could build a 'proper' racing car (that is with its engine in front of the driver). The next F2 brought the Coopers that eventually led to an all-conquering Grand Prix team and stood the racing world on its head.

They were still simple cars and as a result a lot were used by independent entrants. One of these, Rob Walker, ran the Cooper which Moss drove to win the 1958 Argentine GP, the first World Championship race victory for a rear-engined car. Their simplicity also meant that the Coopers were able to run a World Championship team on a budget of £50,000. By all accounts Charles Cooper felt that 1960 expenditure was shocking, but if the Cooper approach had been a little less parsimonious the team might have had the best engines at the end of the 1960s and could perhaps have survived.

Cooper conservatism meant that the GP team was edged out of the limelight in the mid-1960s, and the team won only one GP in the five years of the 1.5-litre Formula. In the autumn of 1964 blunt old pragmatist Charles Cooper died, not long afterwards John was seriously injured in a road accident, and early in 1965 the Chipstead Motor Group took over the company. John Cooper remained in charge of technical matters, while Jonathan Sieff and Roy Salvadori had overall management responsibility. That was the last year that the production side was really strong, for after 1965 not even the F3 cars were built in double-figure numbers. There were two more good Grand Prix seasons before the team went into a decline as well. That reflected the enormous changes coming over top-flight racing – it was no longer the sport John Cooper had known so intimately, that had given him so much enjoyment. The Cooper Grand Prix effort faded. There were prototypes of production racing cars in 1968-9 but that activity also came to an end and many of the remaining components and drawings were sold to Canadian George Fejar. Cooper racing cars had been built for less than a quarter of a century, but they had an influence out of all proportion to the modest Surbiton plant, or indeed the Coopers, father and son.

500cc Cars Because the half-litre F3 cars were an evolving line they are grouped under one heading. Type numbers came to be applied to a year rather than a new design – a type number T8 was even given to a trailer built for the 500s, with interchangeable wheels. Generally the designer was Owen Maddocks, who went to work once the layout had been decided.

Charles and John built the T2, or prototype MkI, helped by Eric Brandon. He had the first T3, or definitive MkI, in 1947. The chassis derived from the original, which comprised the front parts of two Fiat chassis mated end to end. Suspension was by transverse leaf springs at the top and wishbones at the bottom, and shock absorbers were introduced on the first production cars, which also had cast Elektron wheels in place of wheels made from 'salvaged' aluminium. JAP engines producing some 45bhp were used at first, driving a primary chain to a Triumph motorcycle gearbox, thence by another chain to a sprocket on the rear axle. Brandon drove one to win the first-ever 500cc race, at Gransden Lodge in July 1947. With the T5 the Cooper movement began to gather momentum. Stirling Moss was a customer – it was his first racing car – so was 'Curly' Dryden, who was the first owner to install a Norton

engine, and 'Spike' Rhiando who was the first to instal a JAP twin to make a 1-litre Cooper single-seater.

That was to be reflected in the 1949 cars, the T7 500cc model and the extended-chassis T9 for 1-litre HRD or JAP engines (although the Coopers were never over-bothered with type numbers, two tended to be applied on these lines, hence T15 and T16 in 1951, T18 and T19 in 1952, and so on). Generally the twins were noted for poor reliability, but the 1-litre cars were very quick in sprint events and hill climbs, and in his first Continental race Moss was third behind a pair of V-12 Ferraris in an F2 race at Garda. This car had a fractionally longer wheelbase, and was run in 500cc and 1-litre forms, in the first case with only one cylinder of the twin as a 'sloper'. A very brief GP debut for Cooper came at Monaco, when Harry Schell started a 1.1-litre JAP-engined car from the last row of the grid and was involved in the multiple pile up towards the end of the first lap; at the same meeting, Moss lapped a 500cc car fast enough to have qualified for the eighth row of the GP grid, and he beat Schell in the final. Another driver who almost suddenly became prominent driving Coopers was Peter Collins.

In 1951 the 500cc category became the International F3. The little cars were already familiar in many countries, and orders stretched Cooper production capacity. Norton engines steadily supplanted JAP units, the Manx or if possible the 'double knocker' TT engine – expensive and not easily obtained, but giving a worthwhile power advantage. More power came three years later when nitro-methane was added to fuel. The T11 (MkIII) in 1950 followed its predecessor closely, but the 1951 car had revised bodywork, fuel system and rack and pinion steering. Some 60 were built. There was a major redesign in the T18 (MkVI) which had a tubular frame in place of the Fiat-based chassis; this was lighter and weight saving was carried right through the car. At the same time the opportunity was taken to lower the car and thus reduce frontal area. The T26 (MkVII) was very similar, but more fundamental changes came in the 1954 T38 (MkVIII). This had a new tubular frame, virtually a space frame, that some purists regarded as another Cooper aberration – essentially the tubes of a triangulated frame should be straight, but the main tubes of this Cooper curved as in effect they followed the body lines. Like many things Cooper, it worked. Three-piece bodywork was fitted, the suspension was modified and the engine (a JAP or to be installed by the owner – which meant a Norton) was mounted rigidly.

Charles (standing) and John Cooper with a pristine T3 in 1947.

Coopers were sometimes beaten, but overall they dominated F3 racing in the second half of the 1950s. International interest ended by 1958 and although Cooper 500 production lasted until the following year it served a rapidly declining demand. The T42 (MkIX) of 1955 and the T42 (1956-9, as MksX-X111) were developments, each a little lighter and a little slimmer. Drivers still came forward through their Cooper drives, among them Stuart Lewis-Evans and Trevor Taylor, but from 1960 the distinctive un-melodious racket of the single-cylinder 500s was heard only at club meetings.

John Cooper in a well used T18 at Rouen in 1952, on his way to a second successive victory.

Stirling Moss negotiating the Silverstone straw bales on his way to victory in the F3 race at the 1949 RAC GP meeting. His T7 has the prominent intakes called for when it was run as a 1-litre car. The elbow-out-of-cockpit cornering style was normal among Cooper drivers.

A streamlined body was built for a record car in 1951, and it was also used on fast circuits. Here it is driven by John Cooper at Avus in 1953, when he won despite an early-race collision which dented the car's nose.

Raymond Sommer at Zandvoort in a T11 in July 1950. He was an established Grand Prix driver, happy to race a nimble Cooper for fun, but at Cadours later that year he crashed in an 1100cc car and was the first driver to be killed in a single-seater Cooper.

Ace tuner Francis Beart developed a special car that was to be designated MkVIIIA. It was lower, with fuel tanks contrived so that the panniers could be discarded, with 'outrigged' dampers and many other modifications. The car was used by leading drivers, including Moss, here at Silverstone in 1954.

Pannier tanks came with the MkIV, and this shot of Les Leston working hard to keep his car on the island also shows off the megaphone exhaust and rear-view mirror mounted on the leaf spring.

T31 was a more sophisticated device, with the famous curved tubes in the chassis. This one is driven by Jim Russell at Brands Hatch.

Towards the end of their era, the little Coopers still provided a good race schooling, here for Henry Taylor and Trevor Taylor in MkIXs at Silverstone in 1957. These cars have 'proper' rear-view mirrors.

T20 Through the early Cooper years the F3 sequence was broken by occasional sports cars, and from 1952 by single seaters for F2 – and eventually of course for F1. Cooper customers who wanted to move up a class naturally looked to Cooper for a car, and Cooper was the constructor best able to respond quickly. Much was familiar – the suspension and wheels for example – but the engine was mounted ahead of the driver in a simple chassis frame which followed T15 lines. For a 2-litre engine, Cooper turned to the Bristol six-cylinder unit (66 x 96mm, 1971cc), which had its origins in the BMW 328 engine. It produced some 127bhp in 1952, so the Cooper had to be light and nimble if its drivers were to be able to challenge the F2 pace-setters in Italian cars.

The first T20 was shown early in 1952 and four were ready for the spring races. It was outclassed by Ferraris, but the rather hastily contrived chassis did its job, at least within the limits of the power available. Alan Brown became the first driver to score World Championship points in a Cooper; Mike Hawthorn made his name in T20s almost overnight, (he was assisted by the perfectly legal use of nitro-methane, a tweak not made public).

Drivers (GPs): Eric Brandon, Alan Brown, Mike Hawthorn, David Murray, Reg Parnell, Ken Wharton.

The T20 looked messy, with a very prominent bonnet-top air intake and rows of louvres on varying alignments. But Mike Hawthorn always looked relaxed in these Coopers (here in the French GP) and in Championship terms he was the leading 'non-Ferrari' driver at the end of 1952.

T23 The Cooper-Bristol MkII showed the benefits of a season's experience. It had a lighter tubular frame, larger brakes, a smoother body with engine air taken in between two radiator blocks and hot air exhausted through a large outlet on each side. There were variations car to car; the dozen built to 'works spec' were still Bristol powered, but other engines were to be installed in this chassis.

Coopers co-operated in the construction of a Moss Alta-engined one-off, using a T23 chassis frame with de Dion rear suspension and disc brakes, from a concept by Ray Martin. This Cooper-Alta was a failure, and in the summer of 1953 it was replaced by an Alta-engined MkII which was very fast.

In 1953 the front line MkIIs were driven by Ken Wharton and Bob Gerard, but Cooper drivers failed to score points that year. The cars lingered on after the formula ran out, and were also used in *formule libre* racing outside Europe, most notably perhaps by Jack Brabham in Australia.

Drivers (GPs): Alan Brown, Tony Crook, Bob Gerard, Stirling Moss, Rodney Nuckey, Ken Wharton, Peter Whitehead.

Brand new T23 prepared for its public debut at the 1952 London Motor Show.

The infamous Alta-engined special built up on the basis of a T23 chassis for Moss, here racing it for the last time in the 1953 French GP. Outwardly the only change since he first drove it was in the exhaust, which originally ran alongside the cockpit.

T24 Designation applied to a pair of Alta-engined F2 cars built during the 1953 season.

T40 This can be recorded as a modified 'bob-tail' central-seat sports-racing car, but in the Cooper story it was much more than that. It was the first rear-engined Cooper built to run as a Grand Prix car, conceived and largely built by a driver newly arrived from Australia, Jack Brabham. It used a T39 sports-racing car chassis lengthened by 5cm, with a Bristol engine – it was hoped that very light start line weight and the streamlined body would help offset the lowly power output of the engine (a bhp/litre handicap compounded by a capacity only four fifths of the formula maximum). The T40 ran unobtrusively from the back of the British GP grid until retirement, but later its potential was shown in minor races, and Brabham used it to win the 1955 Australian GP.

Driver: Jack Brabham.

A very youthful Jack Brabham posed as the near-complete T40 was wheeled out in July 1955. The bare aluminium body 'looks right', and indeed the performances of the equivalent sports cars, in 1.1-litre and 1.5-litre classes, show that it was.

T41 The first car for the 1.5-litre F2 that came into effect in 1957 and was anticipated in British races through the second half of the 1956 season. Salvadori in the first T41 won the first of these, beating a field of sports-racing cars in a race at the British GP meeting. In essence the car derived from the bob-tail sports car, with a narrower tubular chassis, transverse leaf suspension and a Coventry Climax FWB driving through a Citroën-based gearbox. Five were built in 1956 and continued to be raced in 1957, alongside the T43 or F2 MkII, while the works also tried a stripped bob-tail as a 'streamlined' F2 car.

Rob Walker was one customer for the spindly T41, here driven by Tony Brooks at Goodwood early in 1957.

T43 Following the T41, the MkII F2 car was larger, with a slightly modified chassis and bodywork that gave it a more solid appearance. Early in 1957 cars were run with FWBs, but the normal power unit was the twin-cam Coventry Climax FPF (in 1475cc form this was initially rated at 141bhp). Early in 1957 an enlarged FPF was devised, and entrant Rob Walker had a T43 with larger fuel tankage built to run in F1 events. As it turned out, the first Cooper-Climax to run in a Grand Prix was an F2 car hastily adapted after Brabham had a practice accident in the Walker car at Monaco. He ran third at one point, and finished the race by pushing it to the line in sixth place.

A works F1 car followed in which Roy Salvadori scored two World Championship points.

Meanwhile Coopers were numerically dominant in F2, and in 1957 were challenged only occasionally as Ferrari or Porsche made forays into the category.

The 1958 Grand Prix season opened in Argentina with the extraordinary victory for Stirling Moss in Walker's MkII, a last-minute entry, with strengthened gearbox and minimal engine tuning to adapt the FPF to the AvGas that became obligatory fuel in 1958, and run with a consummate mix of skill and guile to defeat Ferrari and Maserati. T43s were still raced in 1958, but achievements in Europe, or Brabham's New Zealand GP victory, were rightly overshadowed by that Argentine result.

Drivers (F1 GPs): Jack Brabham, Piero Drogo, Ron Flockhart, Stirling Moss, Roy Salvadori, Allessandro de Tomaso, Maurice Trintignant.

Brabham at Monaco in 1957, with an F2 T42 which had a 1960cc engine hastily installed after a practice crash in the purpose-built Walker car.

Moss in Argentina in 1958. Additional air intakes have been contrived to cool engine and driver (that deflector under the nose is not an aerodynamic aid, but intended to direct more air towards the radiator) The bolt-on wheels meant that tyre-change stops would have cost too much time, so Moss drove carefully through the closing laps on tyres worn through to the canvas.

T44 A one-off modification of a T43 by Bob Gerard, using a 2.25-litre Bristol engine.

T45 The 1958 F1/F2 car showed little change in the chassis, but several in other areas, notably in the adoption of coil spring and wishbone front suspension (the transverse leaf was retained at the rear, although it was to give way to wishbones). The engine was inclined to the left, and lower in the chassis as step-up gears were introduced, while a ZF differential was adopted for the F1 cars. Drum brakes were part of the original specification, but discs were to become an alternative. Twenty-four F2 cars were sold, and once again Coopers were very successful, as works or private entries (in particular, Bruce McLaren made his name driving them in Europe). In 1959 Brabham used 1958 cars in a team he organized, but more significantly BRP and Walker used Borgward fuel-injected engines (the former team in T51s) and Moss took the French F2 Championship with the Walker entry.

As far as F1 was concerned, Coventry Climax produced a 2.2-litre FPF, giving 194bhp, which was made available to the Cooper team, and Alf Francis produced a 2-litre FPF for the Walker cars. There were successes in early-season non-Championship races, then Trintignant drove Walker's 2-litre T45 to win the Monaco GP. Although the cars were out-powered at faster circuits there were other good placings, such as Salvadori's third at Silverstone and second at the Nürburgring. Salvadori was fourth in the Drivers' Championship, while Cooper was third in the Constructors' Championship. Rounding off the year, Moss won the Melbourne GP, and he started 1959 by winning the New Zealand GP.

Drivers (GPs): Jack Brabham, Ian Burgess, Jack Fairman, Stirling Moss, Arthur Owen, Roy Salvadori, Maurice Trintignant.

F2 T45s at Brands Hatch in August 1958, Brabham a little out of line as he fights off Stuart Lewis-Evans – and that was the order at the end of the two-heat event.

T46 This one-off appears out of sequence on the original Cooper types list, as it was put together in the summer of 1959, after cars with higher type numbers had appeared. It was another of those full-width streamliners that several constructors were tempted to essay for Reims or Monza down the years, and it followed a Walker F2 experiment a year earlier. Both were tried at Reims, neither was raced – the F1 car because it developed alarming lift at high speeds.

T51 This was the last car for the 1.5-litre F2, and naturally the design also served for F1, although only for 1959 in the latter category. In F2 BRP followed through the Borgward-engined theme with considerable success (the German engines were not available in 1960) and Maserati-engined cars were used by the Centro-Sud team. The main-line F1 cars had 2495cc FPF engines; the one-car Atkins team used a 2.5-litre Maserati engine, as did Centro-Sud; while for Walker's team Alf Francis devised a BRM-engined car that was built up in Italy using a Colotti transaxle (that car was raced once, then abandoned, but the known weakness of Cooper transmissions led the team to use Colotti boxes, which some later argued cost Moss the Championship). In 1960 Scuderia Castellotti produced two Ferrari-engined T51s. There were no great departures in the chassis.

In F2 racing Cooper fortunes began to slide as the imminent 1.5-litre F1 encouraged other constructors to put more effort into the last 1.5-litre F2 seasons; Porsche and Lotus in 1960 tended to beat the Coopers, sometimes rather convincingly, and that did not bode well for the 1961 Grands Prix.

In F1, however, the 1959-60 seasons were triumphant for Cooper. In 1959 Brabham won two Grands Prix, and the Championship, while Moss drove a Walker car to win two Grands Prix and McLaren won his first at Sebring; other Cooper drivers in the Championship top-ten were Trintignant and Gregory. The Constructors' title fell to Cooper.

T51s became a mainstay for independent entrants, especially on the grids in the final season of 2.5-litre GPs (there were nine at Silverstone with Climax, Maserati and Ferrari engines). They were also used in Tasman racing and in the short-lived Intercontinental Formula in 1961.

Drivers (GPs): Lucien Bianchi, Robert Bonomi, Jack Brabham, Chris Bristow, Tony Brooks, Ian Burgess, Giulio Cabianca, Mario Cabral, Chuck Daigh, Colin Davis, Ron Flockhart, Olivier Gendebien, Masten Gregory, Dan Gurney, Bruce Halford, Phil Hill, Pete Lovely, Bruce McLaren, Carlos Menditeguy, Stirling Moss, Gino Munaron, Roy Salvadori, Giorgio Scarlatti, Harry Schell, Henry Taylor, A. Thiele, Maurice Trintignant, Wolfgang von Trips.

Moss in a Walker car leads Brabham in a works car out of the old Gasworks at Monaco. Moss led the race, but retired when a bolt mangled gear teeth, and Brabham went through to score the Cooper team's first Championship victory.

These Coopers lent themselves to conversions and adaptations, exemplified by this Centro-Sud Maserati-engined T51 in the 1960 British GP. Masten Gregory is living up to his reputation as a press-on driver.

T52 Coopers had few reservations about entering Formula Junior as it became an international class, for they could see it would be good for business – they were to sell 17 complete T52s in 1960 and almost as many more as kits to British entrants. Arguably, they went for an over-simplified car, in which Maddocks followed well-known practices, even using some old F2 car components and reverting to a transverse leaf at the rear (where it acted as a top wishbone). Most were fitted with BMC A Series engines, tuned to give around 70bhp and driving through a Citroën gearbox with Cooper/Knight gears;

some cars were to be fitted with DKW engines, one with a Lancia V-4. The MkI FJ car never quite lived up to its early-1960 promise, save that Denny Hulme did well on the Continent and Ken Tyrrell took up the T52 (John Surtees made his four-wheel racing debut with the Tyrrell team, and Henry Taylor won the prestigious Monaco race for Tyrrell).

In its body lines and the rear suspension layout, the T52 looked back a few years. John Surtees (driving here) qualified a T52 for pole in his first car racing appearance, heading Clark in a Team Lotus car.

T53 The 1960 works F1 Cooper-Climax looked a solid purposeful car, lower and sleeker than its predecessor – everybody in the team realized that a considerable advance was called for after Ireland had shown the potential of the Lotus 18 in the Argentine GP (McLaren had won that race in a T51).

The chassis of the 'low-line' still comprised four sturdy main tubes, while coil spring and wishbone suspension was used all round. The FPF delivered 240-250bhp, and drove through a much tougher five-speed gearbox and transaxle designed by Maddocks. Coupled with the reduced frontal area, there was sufficient power for the Cooper to match any other car on fast circuits, where the 1959 cars had been at a disadvantage. A late start meant that the first T53 did not make its debut until May when Brabham drove it to finish second (behind a Lotus) at Silverstone. Then McLaren was second behind Moss in a Walker Lotus at Monaco but after that the T53 came good, and Brabham won five successive Championship races. He was champion, McLaren was runner up. Cooper took the Constructors' title, for the second and last time.

The T53 became the 'customer car' for 1961, with 1.5-litre FPFs the normal power units, although Scuderia Serenissima and Centro-Sud had ineffectual Maserati-powered versions

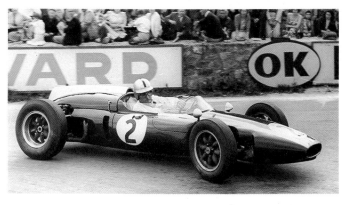

Jack Brabham in the slowest corner at Spa in 1960; he jointly set fastest lap in the Belgian GP with Ferrari driver Phil Hill at 136.01mph, demonstrating that the T53 was an all-round Grand Prix car.

and an Alfa-engined car appeared in South Africa in 1962. Independents scored points here and there, most notably perhaps the strong Yeoman Credit team pair, Salvadori and Surtees, while Brabham ran his own car in non-championship races.

Drivers (GPs): Lorenzo Bandini, Jack Brabham, Ian Burgess, Bernard Collomb, Masten Gregory, Walt Hansgen, M. Harris, Jack Lewis, Tim Mayer, Bruce McLaren, Roger Penske, Roy Salvadori, Hap Sharp, John Surtees.

T55 This was really an interim F1 car, to hold the line with 1.5-litre FPF engines until the new Coventry Climax V-8 was available. It was a lower and slimmer derivative of the T53, with a six-speed version of the 1960 gearbox. The works team picked up a few points with T55s in 1961, before Brabham was committed to the T58 for his final races with Cooper. That year Cooper slumped to fourth in the Constructors' Championship. T55s continued to be used in secondary events, or by the team's number two driver, in 1962, and with 2.5- or 2.7-litre FPFs were run in Tasman races.

Drivers: Jack Brabham, John Love, Tony Maggs, Bruce McLaren.

T56 A great advance on the MkI Junior, the T56 was properly thought through rather than a reach-me-down design. It had a straight-tube chassis, coil spring and wishbone suspension all round and lower lines accentuated by smaller wheels and a less upright position for the driver. The BMC A series engine was still favoured – Coopers had strong BMC associations, with the Mini-Cooper announced in 1961 – although the Ford 105E was an option chosen by several entrants. Driving strength saw Cooper's position maintained, and 22 MkIIs were sold overseas, together with many more which did not carry chassis numbers and were sold in 'complete kit form' in Britain. Tyrrell's team was in the forefront again, with Love and Maggs in 1961. The MkII was used successfully throughout Europe, and in North America.

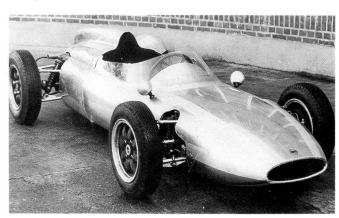

The first T56, looking every inch the part. The bare metal misleads slightly, in that for the first time Cooper used some fibreglass panels in production cars.

T58 This one-off based on the T55 was the prototype car for the Coventry Climax FWMV – Cooper had priority with this new V-8, as reigning champions. The car was first raced in the German GP, but Brabham failed to finish in that race, or in his other two starts in the car.

Driver: Jack Brabham

T59 The 1962 FJ car was outwardly lower and leaner while the most important specification changes were in the revised suspension and the adoption of disc brakes, permitted by the changed regulations. A 1.1-litre version of the BMC A series engine was available (previous Coopers had used 994cc engines, with the 40kg lower weight permitted) but its claimed 98bhp did not come within 10bhp of the rival Ford 105E-based engines. Some 28 cars were exported, with British sales still as un-numbered kits. Ken Tyrrell again ran the leading Cooper team, as pressure from Brabham as well as Lotus increased. His drivers were Maggs, Love and Hulme.

T60 This Grand Prix car was over-shadowed when it first appeared, for its debut came at Zandvoort when the monocoque Lotus 25 and the Porsche flat eight were first raced. It was a workmanlike tubular-framed car designed by Maddocks for the Climax V-8. McLaren drove it to victory in its second GP, at Monaco, and that proved to be Cooper's only Championship race win in the five seasons of the 1.5-litre Formula (he also won at Reims that year, but the race was not a Championship event). Maggs drove the second T60 from mid-season. The team was by no means disgraced, with third place in the Constructors' Championship.

A T60 was used in early-1963 secondary races and both cars were then sold, Bonnier scoring the odd point with Walker's T60. Meanwhile a third car was used for tests by Honda.

Drivers (GPs): Jo Bonnier, Mario Cabral, Tony Maggs, Bruce McLaren, John Rhodes.

The T60 had a slim nose and small front wheels, giving good penetration, and overall was a slim car. Driver is Bruce McLaren, turning away from the harbourside at Monaco on his way to victory in the 1962 GP. Tyre side walls show evidence of contact with kerbs.

T63 This was a prototype for the Mk4 FJ car, using the BMC Hydrolastic suspension in an attempt to build a racing car that would not pitch or dip and would give a consistent handling reponse. It was offered as an option on T65 FJ cars, and one idea was that it would be carried through to an F2 car for 1964. However, tests only showed that it was very difficult to set up for varying circuits and conditions and it was never raced.

T65 There is some confusion about the designation of the fourth-series FJ Coopers, for the type number 67 was also used for the 14 production cars. It had a lighter tubular frame on familiar lines, normal wishbone and coil spring suspension,

and BMC or Ford based engines could be installed (the latter being more successful). Victories for Coopers in that last season of Junior racing were rare.

T66 Another logical progression, for the 1963 Grands Prix. The T66 had modified suspension and marginally slimmer lines, achieved by rearranging the fuel tanks. There were to be mid-season improvements in this aspect.

For much of the year Tyrrell effectively managed the team, as John Cooper recovered from an accident. There were two second placings in Grands Prix, but overall it was another modest year in terms of results. Walker ran a T66 for Bonnier, who scored points with it, and following custom the team cars served into the next season (when Phil Hill drove his first race for the team in a T66 at Aintree).

Drivers (GPs): Edgar Barth, Jo Bonnier, Tony Maggs, Bruce McLaren.

T66 resemblances to T60 are shown in another Monaco shot, of McLaren at Tabac in 1963 on his way to third place. The roll-over bar appears less than adequate.

T69 Apparently the designation for the monocoque F1 project – Maddock's last Cooper design. This comprised a composite sandwiched by aluminium on the outer face and fibreglass on the inner. A hull was completed, but the project was dropped.

T71/T72 Following the design of the T70 Tasman car, a chassis common to the new F2 and F3 was introduced for 1964. The four main side tube arrangement was retained, but with a shaped floor pan in 20swg sheet steel, spot welded to the main frame to give torsional stiffness. In the suspension the front coil spring/shock absorber units were mounted inboard while, again following the Tasman cars, a top radius rod was used at the rear. The BMC Mini Cooper S engine was the basis for the 1-litre F3 unit, rated 88bhp, but as far as F2 was concerned the BMC engine was a flop and the SCA was the obvious choice. The F2 car had extra fuel capacity and was consequently a little corpulent. Production totals were 20 (F3) and 3 (F2).

The suspension looks less than tidy on this T65 – presumably something was gained by the semi-inboard mounting of the front coil spring/ damper units – while the fuselage appears surprisingly broad in this shot of Peter Procter in a Tyrrell car.

The first T72 F3 car. The curious bulge above the engine housed the carburetter. On production cars it was lower and less pronounced.

Ken Tyrrell ran the quasi-works F3 team, and dominated the season in Britain, partly because BMC gave priority to its engines and partly because one of his drivers was Jimmy Stewart's young brother, Jackie. By mid-season he had experienced F2 and his star qualities were such that he was being sought after for F1. The F3 cars did well in European races, but the F2 story was not so happy, with just one win on the very fast Avus circuit. Later an F3 car was modified for F2 with an Alfa Romeo engine in Italy, to no known good end.

T73 The 1964 F1 car was very much along the lines of the contemporary F2/F3 cars, obviously with the Climax V-8 and extra fuel capacity, which was far from adequate (especially for fast circuits where an additional tank was strapped low on the flank). Bruce McLaren was placed second in two Championship races, to provide some comfort in a season that otherwise was largely barren (to the extent that one car did not qualify for the Italian GP). In the first 3-litre season one T73 appeared with a Ferrari sports car V-12, its only GP placing being eleventh in the British race.

Drivers (GPs): Phil Hill, John Love, Bruce McLaren, Jochen Rindt.

T74 This was the one-off forerunner of the 1965 F3 car and was raced in the late summer of 1964. Changes were made largely in suspension geometry.

T75/T76 The 1965 F3 car (T76) and in uprated form the F2 car (T75). Changes were in the suspension, although in their F3 brochures Cooper used the same *Autocar* cutaway drawing to illustrate both the T72 and the T76. The T76 was in fact the last Cooper to sell in double-figure quantities (20), and there were few victories of any consequence. Although Cooper described it as the 'Cooper-BMC', Ford-engined cars were generally placed higher on results lists.

The F2 cars, which should have been prominent, were powered by a BRM four-cylinder engine that was basically one bank of the 1.5-litre V-8, with a quoted power output of 127bhp – hopefully 132bhp later in the year as a response to Cosworth ascendancy. Tyrrell had driving strength, but even that brought nothing better than a second place in just one race. In the three years of the 1-litre F2, Cooper won only one race.

The 1965 cars had radius rods in abundance, by earlier Cooper standards – as well as the pair at the rear, this T75 shows off one running back from the front rocker arm. This is a Tyrrell car being tested by Jacky Ickx, who was to race for Ken in French F2 cars in 1966.

T77 For the final year of the 1.5-litre GP Formula Cooper's car was little changed, a pair designated T77 being run through a lacklustre season which again brought fifth place in the Constructors' Championship. In 1966 an ATS V-8 was independently installed in a T77, and in its one 1966 GP appearance, at Reims, it was 20 seconds off the pole time and was withdrawn.

Drivers: Bruce McLaren, Jochen Rindt.

The additional tank became permanent on the T77, although it still looks an afterthought. This is McLaren in the Belgian GP, where he achieved Cooper's best finish of 1965, third.

T79 This was a one-off built in 1964 for McLaren to use in Tasman races and later acquired by John Love for use in southern Africa. In 1967 he led the South African GP in it, eventually finishing a surprising and brave second.

Driver (GP): John Love.

T80 A period of change following the death of Charles Cooper and Chipstead's acquisition of Cooper seemed to bring the promise of a new dawn – certainly it brought an engine for the 3-litre Formula. To test this Maserati V-12 a T80 was put together using an existing chassis. It was not raced by the works team but was loaned to Walker for a secondary event.

T81 For his first full Cooper design Derrick White produced the marque's first monocoque car, to be run by the team from its new Byfleet HQ and sold to independents. As it comprised two large boxed side members joined by the floor and three bulkheads, the chassis was described as a monocoque for convenience. Each side member housed a 114 litre bag tank (the V-12 was thirsty); the front bulkhead carried the suspension; a bulkhead behind the cockpit provided mountings for the front of the engine and maintained the alignment of those long side members, before they tapered as they extended rearward to a steel ring member which provided attachment points for the suspension. The engine stiffened the rear bay. The suspension followed existing Cooper lines, and in a distinctive feature the front brakes were carried on stub axles slightly inboard of the wheels (an arrangement described as 'inboard-outboard'). The substantial 60-degree V-12, reworked by Alfieri, was rated at 360bhp for 1966.

There were five T81s on several 1966 Grands Prix grids, Rindt showed the car's potential and at the end of the year Surtees drove one to win the Mexican GP – Cooper's first Championship victory since 1962. The last Cooper GP victory came in the first race of 1967, when Pedro Rodriguez won in South Africa.

It was difficult to find a photographic angle to flatter the T81, but this one at least shows a significant occasion, the race in which John Surtees first drove the car at Reims in July 1966. It also shows the 'inboard-outboard' front brakes and cranked lower wishbones. The transverse line across the nose behind the twin badges marks a detachable piece.

The aged V-12 was revised for 1967, when a lighter T81B also appeared. As the main season got under way, however, it was obvious that 3-litre Formula racing was becoming less than favourable to a car/engine combination which had little development potential; after Kyalami, the best results were fourth places. From a challenging third (one point behind Ferrari) in the 1966 Constructors' Championship, Cooper slipped to a distant third (22 points behind Lotus) in 1967. Two T81s and the T81B came out for the first race of 1968, then disappeared.

Drivers (GPs): Chris Amon, Richard Attwood, Jo Bonnier, Vic Elford, Richie Ginther, Jacky Ickx, Guy Ligier, Brian Redman, Alan Rees, Jochen Rindt, Pedro Rodriguez, Jo Siffert, Moises Solana, John Surtees.

T82 A pair of unsuccessful F2 cars was produced for customers in 1966, developed from the 1965 cars. They were outclassed, Gerard's SCA-powered example having a deplorable retirement rate, while despite the efforts of Bonnier and Siffert the BRM-powered example rarely featured in the top ten of a race.

T83 Continuing the line from the T76 this F3 car 'looked right', but was not. The standard power unit was the Ford-Cosworth MAE, as BMC had lost interest in single-seater racing. Seven cars were completed, but there were probably no satisfied customers – a general impression at the time was that while John Cooper was still enthusiasic the new owners were only interested in F1. De Fierlandt won two minor F3 races with a T83 in 1967.

No smiles at an early Goodwood test outing. John Cooper is leaning on a rear wheel. Handling problems led to a front suspension redesign, with outboard coil spring/shock absorber units, but the root of the problem was in aerodynamics, and consequent front-end lift.

T84 The 1967 F2 car turned out to be a one-off, slimmer and with 'inboard-outboard' front brakes, and had the reputation for poor handling that seemed to cling to the last Coopers for secondary formulae. Several drivers raced it, and Rollinson and Gethin got reasonable results.

T85 This was recorded as the 1967 F3 car. Two were apparently built although these do not appear in any racing records.

T86 A more dedicated attempt to produce a 'lightweight' Maserati-powered F1 car, which appeared in mid-1967 and was to have a race record of four retirements, the first from the British GP. It was lighter, lower and less corpulent, and it was also extraordinarily ugly.

Drivers: Jacky Ickx, Jochen Rindt, Ludovico Scarfiotti.

T86B Cooper turned to BRM for an engine to replace the obsolete Italian V-12 in their 1968 F1 car. The BRM V-12 was slimmer than the Italian engine, but this did not mean a return to elegance in the Cooper. Its lines followed the T86, with a full-length monocoque, and Derrick retained the brakes inboard of the suspension uprights at the front. From mid-1968 chassis-mounted aerofoils were fitted.

The BRM V-12 was perhaps the least powerful Grand Prix engine of the year and, that apart, luck did not favour the Cooper team: Scarfiotti was killed in a hill-climb Porsche, and Redman was put out of racing for much of the season when he crashed in the Belgian GP following a suspension failure. Vic Elford and (usually) Lucien Bianchi stood in valiantly. The best results came at Jarama and Monaco, third and fourth in each race. At the end of 1968 Cooper appeared on the Constructors' Championship list for the last time, sixth equal with Honda. The Cooper Grand Prix story did not quite end there, for at Monaco in 1969 Elford drove a privately-owned T86 to seventh place. One T86B was adapted for F5000. An Alfa Romeo-powered T86C was not completed as an F1 car (parts were used in an F5000 car), nor did a similarly-powered T91 take shape.

Drivers (GPs): Lucien Bianchi, Vic Elford, Brian Redman, Ludovico Scarfiotti, Johnny Servoz-Gavin, Robin Widdows.

Cooper-BRM in full flight, driven by Brian Redman towards third place in the 1968 Spanish GP. The unattractive magnesium disc wheels were very light, a sleeker nose was fitted when reasonable temperatures were expected, little nose spoilers were added in the early summer, then larger ones as a high strut-mounted wing was added, roughly above the front mountings of the radius arms.

T90 'A production run of 24 cars has been laid down and it is expected that the Cooper-Chevrolet T90 will be a sure-fire success on both sides of the Atlantic.' The brochure, which also described the car as the Cooper-Vegantune T90, was wildly optimistic and this quite good-looking T86-based F5000/Formula A car was a failure. Two were shown at the 1969 Racing Car Show, and one underwent circuit tests. Both were sold with the rest of the Cooper racing equipment in June 1969 and run among back markers in the British F5000 series, together with two converted F1 Coopers. It was a sad end to an illustrious racing marque's history.

The first T90, unpainted and apparently in John Cooper's parking place. It promised to be a better-looking car than its Formula predecessors, but if it had potential this was never to be exploited.

COSWORTH

This most original and ingenious four wheel drive F1 car was built in 1969 and extensively tested but never raced. Robin Herd based its chassis on a pair of fore-and-aft sponsons between the wheels, with a stressed sheet floor and bulkheads in magnesium, effectively with a double cast bulkhead at the front which formed a box containing the front differential. Each sponson contained three bag tanks. As in other four wheel drive cars of the time, the DFV was installed 'reversed' and coupled to a Cosworth-designed gearbox, which used Hewland parts, behind the cockpit, with a shaft drive to the centre differential on the right. That in turn meant that the driver's seat was slightly offset to the left. For this car a magnesium-block DFV was made, although most of the testing was carried out with an engine from the original 1967 batch of DFVs. There was a very prominent engine oil swirlpot and tank at the rear, and four oil pumps for the transmissions's dry-sump lubrication.

The bodywork was beautifully made by John Thompson, distinctively angular but apparently very effective. Early tests were run with a large 'tea tray' aerofoil, an oil radiator above the rear of the engine, and thin wedges flanking the nose; a small rear wing was later fitted and the nose 'wedges' extended to the full width of the wheels, and in this form the test car survives at the Donington Museum. Its entry for the 1969 British GP was withdrawn, Herd left to become a co-founder of March, and Duckworth abandoned his ideas about redesigning the car.

Trevor Taylor undertook most of the test driving, here at Silverstone, and Mike Costin, Brian Redman and Jackie Stewart also drove the car. The Cosworth had larger wheels than other four wheel drive cars. Like them, it was most effective with most of the drive to the rear wheels.

COWLAN

An acronym of its builders (Coward and Lang) the Cowlan 500cc car first ran in 1947. The basic plot was a Fiat 500 frame and rear-mounted JAP engine (later a Norton) which drove through a BSA gearbox; in other words it was a copy of the Strang. It was sometimes quite quick but never quite achieved results until it passed into the hands of Alf Bottoms who redesigned the rear end and created the prototype JBS.

ML

CREAMER SPECIAL

Sid Creamer was a consistent and successful 500cc special builder and he made a total of five cars, all using space frames. The first was notable for its trailing arm suspension derived from Dick Shattock's Atalanta sports car. Each wheel was suspended by two trailing arms which were sprung by flat laminated springs secured in the centre of the frame. It was not a success due to excessive weight and poor geometry.

Car number two was more conventional with coil spring and double wishbone suspension all round while the third design, of which Creamer made three examples, had a forward seating position, coil spring and double wishbone front suspension, and a de Dion rear end sprung by rubber bands. This design was the best of the bunch and Creamer won half a dozen races.

ML

CRM

G.D. Colquhoun and D.H. Stone built this interesting 500 car in 1951. Its best feature was its lightness, achieved by a space frame and such weight-saving devices as the incorporation of coil springs into the telescopic dampers, although the double wishbone suspension front and rear was supplemented by rubber bands. A BSA engine was mounted at the rear.

ML

CROMARD

Bob Spikins, head of the Laystall Engineering Company, built and raced specials and the Cromard was the apex of his career. It started life with a 1.5-litre Lea-Francis engine in a modified Amilcar chassis fitted with VW suspension but by 1951 it had a new big-tube ladder chassis, VW front suspension, and transverse leaf and swing axle rear suspension located by radius arms. Its engine was an alloy block 1750cc Lea-Francis with four Amal carburettors and this fed about 125bhp through an ENV-Wilson four-speed preselector gearbox.

Although the swing axle rear suspension gave some problems it performed quite well in British races in 1951, but after Spikins was killed in a sports car race in Belgium the Cromard passed to Peter Clarke. It made a single appearance in F2 in 1953.

ML

CROSSLÉ

The Crosslé Car Company, based at Holywood, near Belfast, is the longest-established racing car manufacturer in Ireland by a generous margin. It has seldom built main-line formulae cars as John Crosslé shrewdly looked to markets that were realistic for his company, most frequently in the Ford categories. There were occasional sports-racing cars, Formula Atlantic/B cars, an F5000 venture and some F2 or F3 cars, with more that did not progress beyond the project stage.

Crosslé's first car, a Ford Special, was completed in 1957. The first rear-engined single-seater was the dual-purpose 4F, intended for Formula Junior or 1172cc racing, which was an important category in Ireland. Sports-racing cars helped to establish the name in Europe, while in the late 1960s Formula B successes established it in North America, but real success came with the Formula Ford 16F (more than 40 were sold). It was the first Crosslé designed by Leslie Drysdale, who was to continue with the company as joint designer until he set up the rival Mondiale company in 1983. John Crosslé then took on the design role again, and although production declined in volume he continued building Formula Ford cars through the 1980s. Later in that decade Frank Costin took on a design role.

Formula Junior The 4F was a straightforward rear-engined space frame car introduced in 1961. It had double wishbone front suspension and a swing axle arrangement at the rear, but was notable for its attractive fibreglass bodywork. The second

4F was completed as a Junior, with a Ford 105E engine still at 997cc and not competitive in terms of power output. Crosslé drove it to fourth place in a minor Formula Junior race, then it was converted for 1172cc formula use.

Formula 3 The 1964 6F was important as the first Crosslé to have a fairly normal rear suspension, in the form of a double wishbone layout, and it was offered as an F3 car. The first two, however, were completed for 1172cc racing and the third was delivered as an SCCA Formula C 1.1-litre car. The first F3 Crosslé, therefore, should have been the 17F of 1970 – several drivers (Birrell, Nelson, Watson) were mooted, but the F3 racing plans for this slim space frame car were shelved 'for lack of development time'. Three years later the 26F was to be an F3 derivative of the F2 22F, but again Crosslé and F3 did not come together.

Formula 2 The 1970 18F and 19F were space frame designs for Formula Atlantic/B and F2 respectively, but the differences were slight and with the necessary bag tanks the 18F was run as an F2 car – 18F and 19F made their F2 debuts in the same race, at Mantorp Park in August 1970, when Brian Nelson was eighth in the FVA-engined 18F and Ken Fildes retired the FVA-engined 19F. That year, Nelson started in two more races, the outcomes being an accident and a tenth place; he had two more outings in the car in 1971, but as no development work had been done it was not competitive.

In 1972 the 22F seemed to promise more. It was a compact monocoque car, with a wedge nose and side radiators. Double wishbone front suspension was used, with outboard coil springs/dampers, while at the rear there were lower wishbones, upper transverse link and radius arms, and the rear brakes were inboard. The car was first run with an odd 'midships wing, which had its leading edge ahead of the roll-over bar (an arrangement that was soon discarded). The Hart engine drove through a Hewland FG400. Brian Nelson drove it to win a *formule libre* race at Kirkistown, but it did not appear in mainstream F2. That fate befell a front-radiator 26F shown as an F2 car at the 1973 Racing Car Show.

The 19F before its debut in a libre race at Mondello Park at the end of 1969. It did not appear at an F2 meeting until the Summer of the following year. It was beautifully turned out, but never competitive.

CRS-ALLEGRINI

An Italian F3 one-off which emerged in 1975, built on conventional lines and with a Nova-Toyota engine. It was a narrow-track car, but this seemed to be no advantage on fast circuits or handicap on twisty circuits – it was difficult to judge in a season when a Brabham or a Modus was generally needed to break a succession of March victories. Piercarlo Ghinzani drove the CRS-Allegrini with modest success, scoring two fifths and a sixth in Italian races.

CTA-ARSENAL

This was an outstanding white elephant, stemming from one of those national prestige projects that litter the history of motor racing, and with an injection of Government assistance that led to pressure to race it before it was raceworthy.

It took its name from Le Centre d'Etudes Techniques de l'Automobile et du Cycle (CTA) and the state Arsenal at Chatillon where it was built. Designer Albert Lory had a good reputation, in large part based on his 1926-7 GP Delages. He came up with an apparently sound engine, a two-stage supercharged 90-degree V-8 (60 x 65.5mm, 1482cc) which gave 260bhp in its first tests and was rated at 266bhp when the car reached a grid. It was installed in an archaic chassis of cross-braced box-section side members, and the odd suspension was independent all round, with vertical slide mountings at the wheels, transverse links and torsion bars.

Raymond Sommer drove the first car in practice for the 1947 French GP, when its interesting road-holding habits led to the official announcement that this appearance was a demonstration (far from convincing, as Sommer's best practice lap was nearly half a minute off pole time). At the start of the race the clutch jammed, then freed suddenly, and that broke a half shaft. Two cars were entered for the 1948 French GP, but were withdrawn on the first day of practice as 'unready'. Antonio Lago bought them, but the anticipated input into the GP Talbots never came to pass.

Driver: Raymond Sommer

The CTA-Arsenal was a handsome car, although its proportions seem a little odd – perhaps because the wheels are small compared with its Italian contemporaries. Suspension members are neatly faired, and while the cockpit was commodious the driving position was 'pre-war'. That was probably the least of Sommer's worries as he drove out to practice for the 1947 French GP.

CTG

This was a specialist sub-contracting company, which undertook work for constructors such as Chevron (Roy Baker entered a B48 as a CTG in one 1981 F2 race), Fittipaldi and BRM, and built the F3 Vikings and its own successful Formula Ford 2000 cars from 1977. In 1978 some work was done on a CTG F378 F3 car, but this was never completed.

CUDMORE

An early Australian 500 car, the Cudmore used parts of a Model T chassis for its frame. The front suspension was by parallel links and coil springs while the independent rear was by transverse leaf and lower link. Its most intriguing feature was its engine, a rotary valve two-stroke twin from Japan (presumably liberated after the war) which appeared to be based on a DKW unit. The fact that it had a two-stroke engine tells all about its competition career – no two-stroke ever succeeeded in the 500cc F3. ML

CUTLER

Raymond Cutler's 500 car followed the lines of the first Coopers and was an extremely well turned-out little machine. Where Cutler departed from normal practice was in his insistence on a shaft drive. First he tried feeding the power from its JAP engine through a three-speed Morris gearbox, then through a modified Norton 'box. Trying to achieve shaft-drive with a shaft only a few inches long is an enterprise fraught with problems and Cutler seems to have encountered them all. ML

CYGNUS

This neat ground effects F3 car was designed by Nick Wasyliw and built by him and partner Rob Gustavson late in 1983. It was raced twice by Ian Flux in 1984, who felt that it was a good chassis let down by the only engine available to the little team. It was reworked as the Roni for 1985.

D

DAF

To promote the Variomatic automatic transmission, DAF set up a competitions department, and an F3 programme was initiated in 1965. Initially an Alexis was used for experiments, then a Brabham chassis adapted by The Chequered Flag. For 1967, The Flag (which had built the Gemini FJ cars) built two new cars on Brabham lines but carrying the DAF name. Bold black and white colour schemes accentuated top surfaces that were flatter than Brabhams, but the cars were really distinctive at the rear, where the belt-driven transmissions whirled around. Rob Koch ran the small competitions department, while transmission engineer Win Hendriks adapted the system for a racing car, which primarily meant ensuring that it was matched to high engine revs – Daf looked for top-end power from the Cosworth units rather than flexibility as it was basically running a C.V.T. system, something which has been explored by several F1 teams. There were problems with the transmission, which was affected by climatic conditions, but late in the year team drivers van Lennep and Beckwith each won a race. Then DAF used Tecno chassis for a brief period, before turning away from single-seater racing.

Variomatic racer exposed – without the engine cover that was used in racing. This DAF on test shows the novelties at the rear (those apart, it is very much a mid-1960s F3 car). The rear sub frame appears less substantial than that used by Brabham, while the suspension arrangements had to leave room for the bulky transmission.

DAGRADA

This Milan constructor built a Formula Junior car around the Lancia Appia V-4, which was mounted ahead of the driver with the transmission offset to the right. The ladder-type chassis was conventional, as was the wishbone suspension with coil springs at the front and the transverse leaf spring at the rear. The FJ Dagrada was a stubby car and among its 1959-60 Italian contemporaries only the Faccioli had a shorter wheelbase. Claimed output of the V-4 was 75-80bhp, less than rivals expected from a Fiat 1100, so perhaps Dagrada's apparent success was due to one driver, Giancarlo Baghetti. In 1960 he took on a full British contingent at Albi, was third in his heat and fourth in the final -- a fine achievement as Cooper and Lotus took over the category. Baghetti scored Dagrada's only notable FJ victory, winning a heat and the final of a Juniors-only meeting at Monza in 1960. Before the end of that year, however, Dagrada had given up.

DALBOT

M. Dalbo of Annecy gave his name to his Junior in 1959. It had a rear-mounted Simca engine driving through a Renault Dauphine gearbox, with independent suspension all round. It was not conspicuous on the circuits.

DALLARA

Giampaolo Dallara had a long career as a designer and consultant before his name first appeared on a single-seater, and then it was linked to Wolf on a 1978 F3 car. Before that Dallara, an ex-Maserati, ex-Ferrari engineer, had been largely responsible for early Lamborghini road cars and had achieved his ambition to design racing cars when de Tomaso invited him to undertake F2 and F1 designs.

The 1978 F3 cars, the former Wolf-Dallara cars, served on. Pardini drove one, renamed Emiliani, to win the 1980 Italian Championship. The Dallara F3 cars that came through the second half of the decade were successful in international terms as well as in Italy. Commitment to F3 production, however, meant that Dallara's F3000 car was not a serious contender, and did not seem to have the development potential. Before that could be proved Dallara had moved on to F1, with cars designed by others.

The F1 cars carrying the Bms Dallara label were run by Scuderia Italia and soundly backed by millionaire 'Beppe' Lucchini. A single car was run in 1988, when it was generally rated competent, and in 1989 Dallara was eighth in the Constructors' Championship. That year the administration of the company and the team was split, Vittorio Palazzani becoming overall titular head, while the team was run by Ramazzani and Cantu. Dallara continued in control of technical matters.

381-384 The design which was the basis of a line of F3 cars evolving over four years took shape for 1981, and the 381 was launched into the March-Martini-Ralt dominated Italian series. It was a straightforward monocoque design, with an orthodox suspension layout, and a true picture of its potential did not appear in 1981. In part the Dallara drivers were not among the best, and Dallara was also involved in a Pirelli development programme. Ravaglia, however, was fifth in the Italian F3 Championship.

The first F3 Dallaras had nicely-balanced overall lines and were technically sound, although some suggested that they were imitative. The driver of this blue Trivellato 381 is Roberto Ravaglia.

In the 382 the chassis was strengthened and there were suspension geometry revisions as an effort was made to cure handling shortcomings. There were further modifications, some to the bodywork, during 1982, in a version that became

The blue car (**top**) heading this trio onto the pits straight at Reims in 1966 is a chunky Matra MS5 driven by Beltoise. He was third, in Matra's first finish in a Formula 2 race, and went on to win the F2 race run within the German GP, the only 'non-Brabham' F2 victory in 1966. Attwood follows him here in a Lola T60.

Lotus 69, Tecno and Brabham BT30 – all FVA-powered cars – at London's Crystal Palace in 1970 (**above**). Grand Prix drivers still competed in Formula 2 and the drivers here are the vastly experienced Jochen Rindt in the Team Lotus car and Jackie Stewart in the Coombs Brabham he drove to win this race, sandwiching Regazzoni in the Tecno. Clay was to win the European Championship with the Motul Tecno team

March was prominent in Formula 2 from the beginning of the 1970s to its final races. This 722 (**top**) is heading an Oulton Park pits lane line-up, as Ronnie Peterson waits to lead the field out to the grid for a British championship race in 1972 (he won this race from his team mate Lauda).

Dominant car/driver combination of the 1978 F2 season was the March-BMW 782 and Bruno Giacomelli (**above**), who won eight of the season's twelve championship races. One of his rare failures came in this Donington race, where a Chevron B24 is following his March onto the pits straight.

French cars and drivers were uppermost in Formula 2 in the mid 1970s, notably in 1975 when Jacques Laffite (**top**) overwhelmingly won the European Championship with the Schnitzer-BMW-engined Martin MK 16.

Maurer F2 cars were always very smart, but usually promised more than they delivered. This MM80 (**above**) is in the primitive Thruxton pits during practice for the first race of 1980. Its driver, Markus Höttinger, was to be killed in an accident at the second F2 meeting of the year.

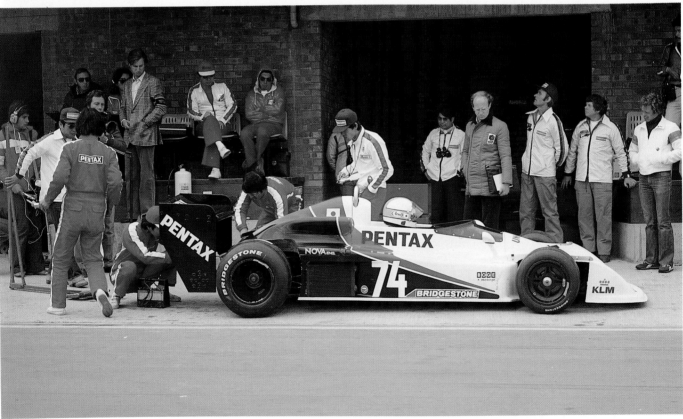

Japanese interest in Formula 2 was strong through its last few years, primarily as engine suppliers. Yamaha's efforts were concentrated on the Japanese series, for example with the engine in this March driven by Geoff Lees in 1985 (**top**). Japanese cars, on the other hand, were rare.

This Nova-BMW 532P was an exception as it fleetingly appeared in Europe in 1978 (**above**), at Donington, where Hoshino drove it to the second retirement of its two-race programme.

known as 382B. Fernando Cazzaniga scored a first victory for the marque at Varano in May. Giannini was fifth in the Italian Championship and Cazzaniga was eighth, while Ravaglia scored odd points for tenth place in the European Championship.

The further revised 383 was a disappointment, although Livio won at Varano in an Alfa-engined car and Forini won a Monza race in a Toyota-engined 383 (the two were second and third in the Italian Championship, but Livio's late-season points were scored in a Ralt). There were no substantial revisions for 1984, when Forini and Barbazza in the works cars were fifth and sixth in the Italian Championship.

385 For the flat-bottom car era that opened in 1985 Dallara introduced the all-new 385, with carbon fibre monocoque and inboard double wishbone pullrod suspension. Outwardly the car was distinguished by shallow side pods with flat undersides and rounded top surfaces which gave an impression of an aerofoil cross section. The 385 was clearly the car to beat in Italy – Forini took the Championship with an Automotor-VW-engined car, while Caffi and Barbazza were second and third in Alfa-engined 385s.

386-9 There was a new monocoque for the 1986 F3 car, a stiffer structure in carbon fibre/kevlar and honeycomb, but outwardly the lines of the fibreglass bodywork were similar (with oil radiator in the left side pod and near-horizontal water radiator in the right pod), as was the double wishbone pullrod suspension. Dallaras had seemed to be at their best on fast circuits, but the 386 soon gained a reputation as an all-round car. In Italy cars with Nova-Alfa engines won 12 of the 15 championship races, and Larini, Apicella and Caffi were 1-2-3 in the Championship. Furthermore Alesi was runner-up in the French series in a car which he ran independently (no mean achievement where local products are so strongly favoured) while Kaufmann and Rosso were second and third in the German Championship in VW-engined 386s.

The 387 in the evolving line confirmed the 1986 ascendancy. The Italian Championship season ended with another Dallara-Alfa 1-2-3 (Bertaggia, Chiesa, Martini), Alesi won the French title in an ORECA 387-Alfa (and that team's 'defection' from the Martini fold summed up the relative qualities of the two F3 cars), and Schneider was German champion with a Spiess-VW-engined car. Suspension changes attuned to tyres would have been needed if more titles were to be taken, for example in the British series, with its different control tyres.

The late-1980s Dallaras were well-proportioned cars, and in aerodynamic respects they were highly efficient. Double rear wings were sometimes used, and the size of the deflectors ahead of the side pods varied. The driver of this Nova-Alfa-engined 388 is Eric Cheli.

The story continued with the 388, which was slightly longer and lighter, with a Dallara gearbox (Hewland internals). Naspetti and Martini topped the Italian points table and eight 388-Alfas were in the top ten. Perhaps more impressively, the top five in France drove Dallaras: Comas and Cheli first and second with Alfa-engined cars and Vidal third with a VW-engined 388. In 1989, however, there was only the Italian title, won by Morbidelli from Reynard driver Tamburini. Morbidelli also won the FIA International Cup in a Forti Corse Alfa-engined 389.

3087 There was nothing unusual about Dallara's entry into F3000, save perhaps that in performance terms it was as great a disappointment as its F3 contemporary was a success. It was built around a carbon fibre monocoque, with double wishbone suspension, pullrod at the front, pushrod at the rear, with inboard coil spring/damper units. Mader-prepared DFV engines were used, with Hewland FT200 gearboxes. The 'works' cars were run by Euroventurini (this combined the resources of Euroracing and Venturini) and Forti Racing also ran one. These cars accounted for 24 race entries in 1987, and that produced one points-scoring finish, a 25 per cent DNQ record and ten finishes.

The Parma constructor was preoccupied with F1 in 1988, but Forti persisted with a car that was theoretically updated (at least it was designated 3087B). Bertaggia started twice in seven attempts, but did finish seventh at Monza, and Croceri failed in four attempts to get one of these inelegant cars to a grid. One was sent to Brazil as Scuderia Italia's Grand Prix entry at the start of the 1988 World Championship season, (the team 'going through the motions' to avoid penalties for missing a race) but it did not qualify – nobody remotely expected it to.

The 3087 was flattered by photography but had none of the good looks that characterized Dallara F3 cars. Marco Apicella gave the car its debut race at Silverstone – seen here – and scored Euroventurini's only F3000 Championship point.

Bms 188 Scuderia Italia Lucchini entered Grand Prix racing with a conventional car, a team whose well-knit approach impressed observers, and, sensibly, a single driver for its 1988 season. Designer Sergio Rinland laid out a long lean car, with conventional monocoque, DFZ engine and double wishbone pullrod suspension. Through the year a variety of front and rear aerofoils was tried. The 188 was first raced in the San Marino GP. Alex Caffi failed to qualify only once and finished in seven GPs with his highest placing seventh in Portugal.

Driver: Alex Caffi.

Dallara made a promising start in F1 with the 188, which was a good-looking car from most angles. Alex Caffi is the driver in this Silverstone practice shot.

Bms 189 To all intents and purposes this was a refined derivative of the 188, although design was credited to Marco Tolentino and Dallara himself. It had a similar composite monocoque and suspension, and Mader DFR engines driving through Dallara/Hewland longitudinal gearboxes. Outwardly the car was fashionably slim. Pirelli tyres were used but proved a mixed blessing. Change during the year was largely in details of aerofoils, bodywork and engine ancillaries.

Dallara was eighth in the 1989 Constructors' Championship, Caffi scoring the team's first point at Monaco. The two drivers failed to get their cars to a grid only three times and were classified 16 times – a 50 per cent finishing record – and de Cesaris was third in Canada.

Drivers: Alex Caffi, Andrea de Cesaris.

The 188 lines were carried over to the handsome 189. Here the driver is de Cesaris, and as he joined the team it almost automatically received Marlboro sponsorship.

DAMW

Deutsches Amt Für Material und Warenprufung was an official East German body which built racing cars until 1956, the best known of which were the EMW sports-racers. The DAMW F2 car of the early 1950s had a dohc version of the BMW 328 engine, a ladder frame chassis with double wishbone and torsion bar front suspension and, at the rear, a de Dion axle sprung by torsion bars and located by an A-frame. Since the same chassis was also used for the EMW sports-racers, it had an offset driving position.

In 1952 the name was changed to EMW and the team was led by Edgar Barth. After the death of Paul Greifzu in 1952, Barth became the leading East German driver. He won the majority of East German races during the next two years and finished fifth in the 1953 Eifelrennen, but in the German GP he was over 1m 40s off the pace, and retired with a blown engine.

DAMW built another F2 car which derived from the Auto Union E Type planned for the 1.5-litre supercharged F1 due to come into force in 1941. Thus it had a rear-mounted unsupercharged V12 engine of 1995cc (62 x 56mm) fitted in a large-tube ladder frame with trailing arm and torsion bar front suspension, a de Dion rear axle sprung by torsion bars and located by lower wishbones and an A-bracket. The engine seems to have suffered from lubrication problems and, before they could be solved, the project was axed. Exactly how much of the car is pure Auto Union and how much was DAMW is still unknown. At least two were made and one is in the Donington Collection.

There were plans to build cars for the 1957-60 F2 but these were squashed and a team of talented ex-BMW and Auto Union engineers were set to work on the Wartburg line.

ML

DANE

Dane Cars of Los Angeles offered two Formula Junior cars, one with a front-mounted BMC engine and BMC gearbox, the other with a rear-mounted Fiat engine and Fiat gearbox. The BMC-engined car had a semi-space frame, wishbone and coil spring front suspension and a live rear axle, while the Fiat-engined car had a ladder chassis with similar front suspension and a de Dion rear end.

DASTLE

Geoffrey Rumble's Dastle company built its first F3 cars in 1972, after specializing in midget cars for short-track racing through the 1960s, with only a tentative venture into the circuit world with a Formula Ford car. There were few F3 Dastles, and they were never front-rank contenders, while some gained odd reputations. One or two had long lives, and an F3 car was still listed by the Send works in 1976.

Mk 9 Geoff Rumble designed his first F3 car around a strong monocoque, with orthodox suspension and a wide track that gave it stability in corners but drag on straights, handicapping the Nova engine on most circuits. An exception was Monaco, where Steve Thompson gave it an apparently encouraging second race. It is best remembered as the car used by the infant Hesketh team, and in particular James Hunt, who drove his last F3 races in one and inadvertently proved the strength of its monocoque in a spectacular Brands Hatch accident (in practice for the same race team mate Horsley crashed the other car).

Mk 10 This 1973 car was on similar lines, with inboard front brakes and a reputation for dubious handling. It was driven by the very experienced Barrie Maskell and development work was put into it, but it was never a serious contender. It eventually reached 'C' form.

The Mk 10 was around for a long time, here being raced more than two years after it was built. Driver Barrie Maskell had a long association with the make.

Mk 12 This came late in 1973, and with a Holbay engine behind him Maskell drove it to a fifth place in an autumn race. It was a derivative of the Mk 10, still with full-width nose and severely angular flanks, and run in 1974 with Nova engines. The Mk 12 was still offered by Dastle in 1976, although the car in which Maskell was sometimes to be found in mid-grid in 1975 had been entered as a Mk 14.

DB

Charles Deutsch and René Bonnet began racing specials in 1939 and had an aerodynamic Citroën special ready to run in the late 1940s. The partners made an immediate impact – Deutsch had imagination and a flair for aerodynamics, Bonnet was pragmatic and could translate ideas into metal. Before long they were established among the best of French special builders, with Panhard-based GT and sports cars.

When F3 became an international category DB was ready with a car which had a box section chassis and a modified Panhard engine and transmission. It had front wheel drive and the engine was forward of the front axle line. Front suspension was by Panhard dual transverse springs and rear suspension was achieved with just a pair of telescopic dampers acting on a solid axle. Compared to, say, a Cooper-Norton, it was overweight, underpowered and ungainly, but for a short while a well-driven example could be quite competitive on the right circuit. By the end of 1952 the handicap of having no more than 36bhp proved too much and the cars faded although the German, Hans Glocker, continued to enjoy some success with one fitted with a BMW flat twin engine. ML

The front of an F3 DB looked a mess, with such oddities as exhausts running forward before turning through 180 degrees, while the rear end was utterly simple. The happy driver of this car is René Bonnet at Rouen in 1952, when his cars still seemed competitive and he chased another driver-constructor, John Cooper, to the chequered flag.

With supercharged 750cc Panhard engines, DB single-seaters appeared in French F2 races, and Johnny Simone actually won some minor events, but against international oppostion the cars were outclassed. DB then built and tested a four wheel drive F2 car with a Panhard engine and gearbox at each end of the car. It ran with a pair of unblown 750cc units but had tests been successful, 850cc engines would have been fitted. Since Bonnet was getting 60bhp from an 850cc engine this would have meant 120bhp in a car weighing less than 450kg, so the theory was not silly. Testing, however, showed up too many practical problems.

DB then used the original single-seater design with an 850cc engine to create the Monomill. These were run in a 'circus' – drivers paid a fee, drew a car, and raced it.

When the 2.5-litre F1 was introduced in 1954 it included a class for 750cc supercharged cars and Deutsch and Bonnet dusted off a couple of their Monomills and fitted them with supercharged 746cc engines. These gave about 85bhp but the car weighed only 350kg compared with weights of over 600kg for most F1 cars.

The F1 DB retained the simple box section chassis with transverse leaf and wishbone ifs and trailing arm and torsion bar irs. It also had magnesium alloy wheels and front disc brakes but since the car was front heavy, it had drum brakes at the rear. This DB is sometimes remembered as being only one of two 750cc supercharged F1 cars to race (the other was a Giaur) but its real distinction is that it was the only post-War front wheel drive F1 car. Two cars were entered for the 1955 Pau GP but they were hopeless. Claude Storez gave up while Paul Armagnac finished eighteen laps in arrears.

After that DB concentrated on the Monomill circus but when Formula Junior became an international category in 1959 the design was dusted off again. It was moderately successful in French FJ races in 1959, when the Italians were absent. In 1960, however, the DBs were hopeless although the French introduced two classes, one for French cars and one for foreign cars. The sight of an eleven-year-old design being lapped by the likes of Lotus and Cooper FJ cars soon lost its novelty value and the DB single seater was finally retired. (See Bonnet).

The F1 DB looked much more substantial, as well as tidier, but the basic make-up was the same. This car is at Pau in April 1955, with Paul Armagnac waiting to practice; he finished the race, thus achieving some sort of distinction.

DEBUIRE

An early French 500 car built by Jean Debuire which used a Zundapp engine and had suspension by torsion bars. ML

DEEP SANDERSON

Westerham Motors of Acton in West London set up a Formula Junior programme in 1959, ostensibly to race-test components to be used on later, and better-known, GT cars. (These lasted through the 1960s, all carrying the marque name Deep Sanderson which derived from the title of a 1920s dance tune 'Deep Henderson' and the name of Westerham's backer.) However, by the end of 1960 an FJ car was being offered for sale, at £1,115.

FJ Deep Sanderson was a dumpy car in its original form, and the nose lines were carried through to the 1961 car, which was lower behind the cockpit, but hardly a match for the Lotus 20 in sleek good looks. The driver of this car is L.J. Fagg, at Goodwood in 1960.

The first two FJ cars had a 'tetrahedron' space frame, which led to the cockpit being narrowest at the point where the human frame is widest, and modified VW suspension. The third car was completed in the summer of 1960 with an orthodox space frame and 'Lawrence Link' trailing links and coil spring/damper suspension designed by Chris Lawrence. This was retained in the fourth car, which became the 1961 model and the first production car. It was lower and slimmer than the first three, and like them had a Lawrencetune-modified Ford 105E engine. Deep Sandersons were raced extensively in 1960-1, but never with any conspicuous success, although Chris Lawrence and Len Bridge were successful at club level. Westerham tended to concentrate on sports/GT cars.

DELANNE

Little is known about this early French 500 car except that it was built by a group of truckies.   ML

DEL CONTESSA

The second Japanese GP, run at Suzuka for Formula Junior cars in May 1964, saw the first race start by a Japanese car conforming to a current formula, anticipating the first F1 Honda by some three months. The Del Contessa was an amateur effort, and looked it – Hino production components featured, including road car suspension and a Contessa engine 'tuned' to give 85bhp at a time when 100bhp was minimal in a Junior. Three came to the grid for that Japanese GP and one finished sixth, well behind the survivors of the European contingent.

DELFIN

A one-off car laid down as a Junior by Jiri Gajdos and built by a group of fellow enthusiasts at the Tatra Koprivnice plant. It was not completed until the last year of the formula and because of its engine probably did not conform with the regulations (but then one wonders how many Eastern bloc cars would have been thrown out by a scrutineer in Western Europe?). It was a square-cut space frame car, with a four-in-line 1100cc engine for which 80bhp was claimed. The interesting aspect was that the power unit was apparently half of a Tatra V-8, but that really made the Delfin a *formule libre* car as the regulations called for an engine from a homologated touring car with, at that time, an annual production run of 1000 units.

DELHAES

Lambert Delhaes was quite successful in 1950/51 in his native Belgium with this 500 car built on Cooper lines and powered by an FN Motocross engine.   ML

DELTA

Maurice Phillippe was in the aviation industry when he became an amateur constructor with a one-off sports car, the MPS, in the mid-1950s, following it with a front-engined Formula Junior car at the end of the decade. This had a Ford

105E engine, multi-tubular frame and independent suspension all round, but like other Juniors inspired by clubmans' cars it was to be overwhelmed in the FJ mainstream.

DEMESSE

A pioneering Belgian 500 car built by Paul Demesse, it used Simca (née Fiat) suspension and its BMW engine was mounted in the front, driving the rear wheels.   ML

DERICHS

In the early 1980s Erwin Derichs was the only German F3 constructor, building just a few cars that were distinctive and uncompetitive. These were laid out around slim honeycomb monocoques, with conventional inboard suspension and Toyota engines. Type numbers from the first in 1982 followed custom, in denoting category and year (for example the 1982 car was D382). They were built to contest the German series, 1982-4, but failed to impress, and since none of their drivers went on to make a name in racing perhaps the shortcomings might not all have been attributable to the machinery.

Derichs built outwardly tidy cars, and this one is flattered by its colour scheme. The roll-over bar seems unusually substantial.

DERRINGTON-FRANCIS

Vic Derrington, a British pioneer in the performance accessories business, and the famous racing mechanic Alf Francis, who had become involved with Colotti the gearbox maker, refettled one of the 1963 ATS F1 cars and used their names on it. Francis built a new space frame with a wheelbase some 15cm shorter than the ATS and clothed it with a smart new body, but the rest was all ATS. Mario Cabral hired it for the 1964 Italian GP and, although he qualified last, he at least made the start which is more than can be said for ten other drivers. Cabral retired with ignition problems and the car never raced again.   ML

DE SANCTIS

Gino De Sanctis and his son Luciano started building racing cars at their Rome Fiat agency in 1958, and continued building for the third-level international formula right through the next decade, albeit rather half-heartedly towards its end as Tecno set a challenging pace in F3. Their Formula Junior cars were modestly successful, and at that time De Sanctis seemed prepared to respond to the pressures of design advances whereas their policy of evolution in Brabham-inspired F3 cars meant that the marque fell behind, and depended too much on the talents of two or three drivers, most notably Jonathan Williams, who gave De Sanctis its best year in 1966. Work started on a monocoque F2 project for him for 1970, but this never appeared, and the perhaps inevitable conjecture about an F1 car at the same time had little substance. The reality that year was a shift into building for minor categories, for the national Formula 850 and for Formula Ford, with just the odd Brabham-like car keeping a presence in F3 as the new decade opened.

Formula Junior Unusually among early Italian Juniors, these cars were rear-engined from the outset. The 1958 prototype had a simple ladder chassis and Fiat mechanical elements, and was raced successfully by Luciano De Sanctis in 1958. It led to the 1959-60 'production' Junior. This retained the ladder frame, with wishbone and coil spring ifs and a swing axle with a transverse leaf spring and radius rods at the rear. The sleek shark-nosed bodywork of the 1958 car gave way to bulky but practical lines.

The car was a winner in 1959, but De Sanctis recognized the trends in 1960 and for 1961 introduced a space-framed Junior with a similar ifs but with a wishbone, inclined coil spring/damper unit and radius rods independent arrangement at the rear. Moreover, Ford 105E engines were used, 'home-tuned' by De Sanctis when most cars were fitted with Cosworth or Holbay units. While most Italian constructors surrendered, De Sanctis cars continued to be competitive, winning just a few Italian races through the rest of the Junior years, with drivers such as Russo ('Geki'), Facetti and Natili. Silvio Moser briefly ran one in F2 in 1964, with a Fiat-based engine.

One of the dumpy first-series production Juniors, with the high tail and curvaceous lines favoured by several Italian constructors. This De Sanctis is driven by Antonio Maglione in 1959.

Formula 3 De Sanctis was a leading contender in Italy in the mid-1960s with F3 cars on Brabham lines, in their space frames and independent suspension layout, which were powered by Ford-based engines. There was little development as such and as time went on this became most noticeable in handling. While the competitive edge was maintained on fast circuits, there was a tendency to rely on the talents of drivers.

In the 1-litre period this tended to be Russo, and more might have been achieved if he had driven regularly for De Sanctis, or if a car had been made available for him for races outside Italy. In 1964 he won five Italian races, including all four ranking events at Monza, but only two of his 1965 F3 wins were scored in a De Sanctis.

In 1966 there was a nominally new car, with a modest development of the existing space frame design, double wishbone suspension all round and a Cosworth MAE driving through a Colotti gearbox. Williams was the lead driver, and he won ten races for De Sanctis that year, securing the Italian F3 Constructors' Championship – a rather hollow title as only Italian makes qualified and national champion Ernesto Brambilla drove a Brabham! There were minor

improvements in the following years, but there were only occasional successes in 1967 and 1968 (when Francisci twice beat the Tecnos) and only one in 1969 when Williams returned to De Sanctis for the Lottery GP; Francisci occasionally appeared with a Nova-engined De Sanctis instead of his Brabham. In the following season ex-F850 driver Marcello Gallo occasionally scored with Francisci's 1969 De Sanctis in Italy (he was third in an Imola race, and sixth in the Italian Championship). After that odd cars helped to fill Italian grids in the first 1.6-litre F3 season.

The 1965 De Sanctis was a competitive F3 car, and looked the part, although there was apparently little concern about the finer points of drag reduction. A leading driver in Italian F3 was 'Geki' (Russo), here at Monza early in 1965.

DESLANDES

One of the first of the French 500 cars, Roger Deslandes' special had a U-shaped sheet metal frame with pannier side tanks, a rear-mounted Triumph Tiger vertical twin, all independent suspension by double wishbones and rubber in torsion and a body similar to a Cooper.   ML

DE TOMASO

Alejandro de Tomaso, an Argentine living in Italy, gave up his racing career in 1959, after he had set up De Tomaso Automobili at Modena and started on a career as a constructor that often seemed to border on dilettante. One of his last races was in the 1959 American GP at Sebring, in an Osca-engined Cooper developed at his new plant, to no good end as he was hopelessly off the pace and lasted only 15 laps. There was a half-hearted attempt to build a pair of Osca-engined F2 cars, very much on Cooper lines, and de Tomaso turned to Cooper copies for Formula Junior, marketing them as Isis.

Assorted single-seaters followed – FJ, F1, F2 and F3 cars, some powered by de Tomaso's own engines, none of them competitive and few developed, until de Tomaso and Frank Williams set up an association in 1969. Williams brought a single-minded sense of purpose to the partnership, and a promising driver, Piers Courage.

Giampaolo Dallara, then known as a Lamborghini road car designer, had been responsible for an F2 de Tomaso in 1969 and undertook an F1 design for 1970. This was a Cosworth kit car and it was beginning to show signs of promise when Courage died in a Zandvoort crash. The team went through the motions for the rest of that season, then de Tomaso turned away from single-seaters.

1.5-litre Formula 2 Late in 1960, as the 1.5-litre F2 was about to expire, a de Tomaso F2 car appeared at the Modena GP, with a Conrero Alfa engine in place of the anticipated Osca engine. Businello crashed it in practice and while it was to reappear as an F1 car in 1961, its F2 career ended before it had started.

1.5-litre Formula 1 De Tomaso got instantly out of his depth with his first venture into F1. Six cars were built, with chassis on scaled-up Isis FJ lines and double wishbone, coil spring and damper independent suspension all round. Four had Osca four-cylinder engines, two had Conrero-developed Alfa Romeo Giulietta engines with special two-plug heads (one of these cars was a rebuild of the 1960 F2 car). Both drove through a de Tomaso five-speed gearbox. Businello recorded the first de Tomaso F1 finish in the oldest car, fifth in the Naples GP.

That was hardly auspicious, but a new F1 de Tomaso appeared in 1962, optimistically entered for the Monaco GP, eventually running in practice for the Italian GP and actually starting a race in the 1963 Rome GP. It was designed by Alberto Massimino with a tubular chassis, the rocker arm inboard front suspension Ing Massimino had designed for Maserati in 1948 and a lower wishbone, upper rocker arms and radius rods rear suspension. Springs were inboard, whereas brakes were outboard. This 801 (the marque's first designation as such) had a new de Tomaso flat eight engine (68 x 51mm, 1488cc) for which 170bhp was claimed. Even if it was obtained, it was not enough by the end of 1962.

The 801 started at Rome, and completed a lap. One of the earlier cars appeared twice with a Ferrari 156 V-6 but Lippi failed to qualify it. A couple of entries with a Holbay Ford wasted time in 1964-5.

Drivers (championship GPs): Roberto Businello, Robert Lippi, Giorgio Scarlatti, Nino Vaccarella.

Formula Junior De Tomaso returned to FJ in 1962, the first of a handful of cars built making an apparently promising debut at Vallelunga late that year. It had a sheet-stiffened tubular chassis (in that year of the Lotus 25 described as 'semi-monocoque'), Massimino's suspension from the 801, Ford-Holbay engine and de Tomaso five-speed gearbox. Bernabei's third place in that Vallelunga race was behind a De Sanctis pair, which serves to put it into perspective, and after that little was achieved.

Formula 3 The 1964 F3 car derived directly from the 1962 Junior, with a Holbay engine that de Tomaso rated at 88bhp. The car showed promise – Mario Casoni actually won a race at Caserta in one, Bernabei gained some good placings and in 1965 one Clay Regazzoni raced one at Monza (to an eighth place).

Formula 2 A one litre F2 car shared the erstwhile FJ chassis layout and was originally promised with a de Tomaso flat four derived from the boxer F1 engine, but appeared with a Ford-based engine. Its appearances were at Rome in 1964 (Bernabei, DNS) and 1965 (Ridolfi, DNQ).

The 1969 de Tomaso was an angular car, with flat sides and a flat top to the nose, where an additional scoop intake was sometimes worn. Jonathan Williams is the driver, in the F2 car's first race, at Monza.

There seemed to be more promise in a car for the 1.6-litre F2. This was designed by Dallara around a box-like hull – basically two cast-magnesium bulkheads joined by fore-and-aft aluminium sheet. It had bottom wishbone, top link, outboard coil spring/damper suspension all round, with radius arms at the rear, a Cosworth FVA and Hewland FT200 gearbox. Jonathan Williams and Jacky Ickx drove it to modest placings in the summer of 1969, then Frank Williams took over and Piers Courage qualified it for the front row of the Rome GP grid, and finished third in one heat. The car was then put away.

The first DFV-powered de Tomaso, looking trim in its race debut in South Africa in 1970.

Formula 1 De Tomaso commissioned Dallara to design an F1 car for 1970. Three 308s, confusingly numbered 505/1,2 and 3 were to be built for the one-driver Williams team. It turned out to be a rather bulky and overweight monocoque car, with double wishbone suspension and outboard coil spring/damper units all round, powered by a DFV which drove through a Hewland DG300. There were minor differences between the three cars, partly in an effort to save weight. The first was written off in a Spanish GP accident, then in the team's noteworthy performance Courage 'finished third in the Silverstone International Trophy. Two retirements followed, and he was running seventh in the Dutch GP when he crashed and died as the car caught fire. The team went through the motions for the rest of the year but to no worthwhile end.

Drivers: Piers Courage, Brian Redman, Tim Schenken.

DHW

D.H. Woods' 1950 front-engined 500cc special was distinguished by being perhaps the longest car built for the formula with, to judge from photographs, a wheelbase as long as a V-16 BRM. Believe it or not, it didn't work.　　ML

DKW SPECIAL

A front-engined, front wheel drive, American Formula Junior car, the DKW Special was built by Erick Sobriety and Jack Sutton around a heavily drilled box channel 'tuning fork' frame, front and rear suspension was independent by transverse leaf springs and lower wishbones, and it was nicely turned out. It was not, however, a success.　　ML

DMRA

The second most interesting thing about D.M.R. Adams' 1948 500 rear-engined F2 special was its suspension – trailing arms and coil springs at the front, wishbones and rubber bands at the rear. It was a nicely built car with a lightweight Dural frame and a rear-mounted JAP engine. The most interesting thing is that after it failed to make any impression in competition, it was sold and its new owner added mudguards and licensed it for road use. ML

DNC

The work of Norman Dewis, this 1951 British 500 car had a rear-mounted Rudge engine driving through a Burman gearbox to a modified G.N. live axle suspended by quarter elliptical springs. That says everything one needs to know about its chances of success. ML

DOLPHIN

This Californian marque flowered briefly during two Formula Junior seasons, with small-production rear-engined cars that promised to be competitive with contemporary European models, especially the 'first-wave' Italian Juniors. Designer John Crosthwaite had worked for Lotus and Cooper, so he perhaps had an idea of what was to come from those contructors.

The first Dolphin followed the original Italian Junior intent, even using a Fiat 1100 engine, locally tuned to give some 75bhp. Second series Mk 1 cars had Super Speed Ford 105E engines, which gave more power to propel lighter cars.

A deep space frame was used, leading to a bulky body with the oddity of an offset cockpit. Double wishbone and coil spring/damper suspension was used all round, and the Dolphin magnesium wheels were a distinctive detail. The Mk1 won first time out, then Dolphin had to weather a succession of transmission failures. Later successes must in part have been due to drivers of the calibre of Ken Miles, for when the Mk2 came the more professional North American drivers were turning to Lotus and it failed to make the impression of the earlier cars.

The Mk 2, which first appeared at a Mexico City race early in 1961, used the same suspension, 105E engine and inverted Fiat gearbox as the Mk 1, but had a new low space frame and a slim body by Dick Troutman.

The Mk 1 Dolphin was an oddly-proportioned car. This Series 2 version was a stand in, run during the second half of 1960

DOMMARTIN

France was relegated to racing's second division in the 1930s and, in an attempt to recapture past glories, a semi-official national racing car project called SEFAC (la Societé d'Etudes et de Fabrication d'Automobiles de Course) was set up and the public was invited to subscribe. Former Salmson designer, Emile Petit, laid down a 2771cc (70 x 90mm) engine with two four-cylinder blocks in parallel and a single supercharger. This produced only 250bhp, when over 400bhp was needed to win. Furthermore the car weighed 910kg so when it appeared at the French GP in 1935 it was thrown out for being overweight. In the next two years it appeared in practice at a couple of events but never started until the 1938 French GP where it blew up after two laps. It ran at Pau the next year but again retired.

Despite this chequered career, in 1948 a company called Dommartin proudly unveiled its Grand Prix contender – it was the SEFAC, rebodied, with the engine bored out to 3619cc. Boldly continuing the radical approach of the line, the Dommartin contrived to be both heavier and less powerful (by 50bhp) than the SEFAC. The money ran out and before it was ready to race the car was abandoned. ML

DRUID

When Royale decided not to go ahead with an F3 car (RP23) designed by Rory Byrne in 1977, the project was taken over by Andreason Racing and Tuning. The detail design was completed by Roger Andreason and Paul Fox and it was offered for sale as the Druid 377. It was a conventional, pretty, design and ease of maintenance was emphasised, but its F3 career was brief and unsuccessful – it did not have the advantage of being run by a top rate team, and it was soon overtaken by ground effect cars. The car achieved respectable results in Formula Atlantic and Formule libre, however, and two further cars were built. ML

The Druid looked sleek, if flattered by this shot of the F3 car without racing numbers or sponsors' decorations. However, the combination of a full-width nose and slender lines between front and rear axle lines was soon to look dated, as ground effects reached F3.

DRW

David Warwick's company produced competition cars in very small numbers from the late 1950s to the early 1970s, usually for minor categories such as Clubman's or Formula Ford. A space frame Clubman's Mk 3 was completed as a Cosworth-engined Formula Junior car in 1961. As a front-engined rear-wheel-drive car it was outmoded by the time it ran, and was converted to Clubman's form.

Jack Murrell, Warwick's partner in DRW, in their company's only FJ car, on test at Brands Hatch.

DS

Sometimes known as the 'Denis', after its creator André Denis, this was a huge front engined French 500 car which would not have looked out of place on an F2 grid. It was based on a Danvignes sports car frame with independent suspension all round by transverse leaf springs. A fan-cooled flat twin Zundapp KS 600 engine, suitably linered down, drove via a Zundapp four-speed box and a long prop shaft to a bevel gear on the back axle which had no differential. With a specification like that, no further comment is needed.   ML

DULON

This constructor built 'production' single-seaters from 1968 until 1977, and there are occasional references to Dulon F3 cars in entry lists. However, no cars left the Didcot plant as F3 cars: odd Formula Atlantic cars may have been converted, but Dulon's own firm proposal to develop an F3 car based on the 1975 Formula Ford 2000 design was abandoned as soon as its entry for a major race was not accepted.

DUQUEINE

Racing car construction was very much a sideline for the Duqueine brothers, whose main business was the manufacture of components for high-tech industries. Their first Duqueine VG (Victor, Gilles) single-seaters were *Formule Renault* cars built at the Villeurbanne plant in 1978. A year later they built a one-off F3 car for Bernard Perroy, and although he was successful with this VG3 a follow-up car did not appear until 1984.

VG4 was laid down for Gilles Duqueine, who had got the driving bug. It was a straightforward car, with carbon fibre monocoque, double wishbone suspension with inboard components, VW engine and Hewland gearbox. It made a good impression in Duqueine's hands and he took three top-six places in early-1985 French races before a road accident put an end to his driving career. Three more VG4s were built for 1986, when Philippe Gache made his name in one, but overall results were not outstanding.

VG5 was announced early in 1987, when four were laid down. The make-up was similar to VG4, with refined lines and Spiess-VW or TOM's Toyota engines in the two works cars, and an Alfa engine in one sold to an independent. These Duqueines made no impression on that year's F3 racing.

VG4 at rest, showing nice nose lines, clean front suspension and a suggestion of asymmetry in the side pods.

DVD

Originally built as a 600cc low-cost racing car in Germany in the late 1940s, D.V. Delfosse's front engined special was converted to run in the 500cc F3 with a Zundapp engine. It had an enveloping body which earned it the nickname 'Flying Saucer'.   ML

DWS

One of the first Australian 500cc cars, Dave Stephenson's special had its single cylinder BSA engine mounted in the front delivering power through the front wheels. The rest of its specification was fairly 'state of the art' with a space frame, coil spring and double wishbone front suspension and swing axles at the rear, also sprung by coil springs.

It was not competitive and later Stephenson built a Cooper copy but spoiled the plot by fitting a Rudge engine.   ML

DYWA

A distinctly sub-standard creation by Dido Monguzzi in 1980, this DFV-powered one-off was laid out to comply with F1 regulations, to be run in the secondary Aurora series races (odd events were held outside Britain, although this was primarily a British championship). The Dywa completed a few slow laps in practice for a race at Monza and then disappeared until it re-emerged as an F3000 car announced for 1985, and appeared once in 1986, as the Monaco.

E

EAGLE

Americans Dan Gurney and Carroll Shelby – the former a prominent Grand Prix driver and both winners of the Le Mans 24-hour Race – launched All-American Racers in 1965, with backing from Goodyear and the primary objective of ending Firestone's reign at Indianapolis. Shelby was soon to break away, and Gurney was anxious to extend his Grand Prix career, as a driver-constructor, so a parallel operation was set up at a base in Rye, Sussex, under the name Anglo-American Racers. The cars to be produced by both AAR outfits were to be Eagles.

The F1 cars were handsome and built to very high standards, with a reputation for good handling, but power units were to prove to be weak points: the Coventry Climax units used at first were stopgaps, while the V-12s purpose-designed for the cars were not over-powerful and were inconsistent. Gurney won a non-Championship F1 race and a Grand Prix in 1967 but in the following year the Anglo-American Racers operation was run down, towards closure.

Through to the mid-1970s Eagles were very successful in USAC racing, with three Indianapolis 500 victories, but in later Indycar years that programme slipped. Meanwhile in the mid-1970s there had been another foray into road racing, in the North American F5000 series when it was jointly sanctioned by the SCCA and USAC, but Eagle failed to break through in this category. Gurney had to turn away from single-seaters altogether in 1986, although he stayed in racing with a Toyota programme, and in 1989 built an Eagle-Toyota GTP car.

Formula 1 The first Eagle was basically laid out by Len Terry to serve for USAC and F1 racing, and in the design he almost inevitably followed the lines of the Lotus 38. The Eagle T1G had a light-alloy monocoque, with wishbone and coil spring/damper suspension. Weslake engines were commissioned, and while this V-12 design by Aubrey Woods was being completed 2.75-litre Coventry Climax FPF engines were used. Gurney scored the first points for his Eagle marque when he finished fifth in the 1966 French GP.

The Gurney-Weslake twin-ohc 60-degree V-12 (72.8 × 60mm, 2997cc) was also built at Rye; the first was completed in the summer of 1966 and raced at Monza a month later. There were teething problems which were never fully overcome, and in respects such as the wide variations in power outputs from engine to engine the team was to be handicapped. The V-12 was not engineered for 'production', or even duplication, and parts were not always interchangeable engine to engine.

Gurney on his way to that famous American victory at Spa in 1967, in one of his handsome blue and white Eagles. This was the fourth car, with titanium and magnesium used in some areas in a necessary and successful effort to reduce weight.

In 1968 Gurney set up his own engine build and maintain facility.

In 1967 Gurney won the Race of Champions and the Belgian Grand Prix. An improved version of the car was developed through the Spring of 1968 while Tony Southgate worked on designs for a lighter and sleeker 1969 car. However, the F1 Eagles ran in only five races in 1968, the effort tailed off, and the second-generation car was never built. The last Eagle seen in a GP was a 1966 FPF-powered car, run independently by Pease in Canada in 1969.

Drivers: Bob Bondurant, Richie Ginther, Dan Gurney, Bruce McLaren, Al Pease, Ludovico Scarfiotti.

Gurney disconsolate in the cockpit after retiring at Monaco in 1968. By then the end was in sight, and there were to be only three more races for Dan and his Grand Prix Eagle.

ECHO

The Echo was built by Mike Siakooles for the brief flowering of the 500cc F3 in California in the late 1950s. It had a neat space frame, modified Fiat front suspension, swing axles suspended by coil springs at the rear and a Norton engine driving through a Burman gearbox. It was one of the prettiest 500 cars ever built but there is no record that it went as well as it looked.   ML

EFAC

A brave French attempt to be different in the formative international year of Formula Junior, 1959. It had a Simca-based engine, which unlike the Renault engines used by other constructors could be at full formula capacity (and in this case was rated at 72bhp), driving through a Fiat gearbox. The ladder-type chassis was staid but the EFAC had independent suspension all round, by wishbones with Neidhart rubber as the springing medium. The car was not successful.

EFFYH

Designed by the Hakonsson brothers and built in Malmo, Sweden between 1948 and 1951, Effyhs won a lot of events in the early days of Scandinavian 500 racing, although much of that took place on ice and loose-surface ovals which were often horse trotting tracks. They were very light cars with space frames, independent front suspension by coil springs and double wishbones, and double wishbone rear suspension having twin transverse quarter elliptical springs mounted on top. Unusually for Europe at the time, Effyhs had roll hoops to protect the driver and, reflecting their short oval origins, side-mounted 'nerf' bars. Ake Johansson won many of the important 1950 Scandinavian road races with an Effyh-JAP,

There is something very 'Cooper' about some aspects of the Effyh, and this example has the short-oval glitter which shows that it was one of a handful exported to the USA in 1951.

often beating visiting British drivers in Coopers.

Around thirty Effyhs were built and they were successful in Scandinavia for some years, particularly on loose surfaces, often fitted with the Swedish SRM engine. Effyh made cars in two specifications, the 'TT' (Tourist Trophy) models being for road circuits, but they made little lasting impact on the international scene.

The Hakonssons also sold complete sets of drawings (for around £3!) and so spawned a large number of clones which went under such names as Bardahl Special, EE Special, Hult, Ivan, JAP, PP and RJ500, and Effyh-inspired cars included Silverbird, Svebe and KG Special.   ML

EHRLICH/EMC

Dr Joseph Ehrlich is forceful, an innovator convinced of the virtues of his innovations, who made his name with his work on motorcycle engines and his EMC motorcycles before turning to cars. A Viennese, he moved to Britain in the late 1930s, and apart from his motorcycle work was a consultant to BMC before he set up his own company in 1958. This undertook work such as machining for other constructors as well as its own research and development. The first F3 car appeared in 1968, and single-seater Ehrlichs or EMCs were built through to the 1980s for Formula Atlantic and Formula Pacific racing as well as F3.

Dr Ehrlich tended to concentrate on engines, and the first chassis were designed and made by Mike Keele. He had built karts, so the first F3 cars showed kart and Brabham influences (EMC manufactured some Brabham components). The first car's space frame was clad in BT21 bodywork, while its engine included EMC, Holbay, Cosworth and other specialists' parts. Roger Keele drove it, and on its occasional race outings it showed promise.

A second car came for 1969, on BT23 lines. Early in the season it showed quite well (fifth in a Monaco heat, eighth in the final), but then EMC disappeared from the circuits for a while. The chassis was dusted down in 1971 – Ehrlich's cars tended to have long lives – when it was designated 606. Jody Scheckter won a Silverstone heat with it, and was fourth in a Mallory Park race before he moved on Merlyn.

The next new car, appearing as an Ehrlich rather than an EMC, was the infamous steel monocoque car, and that was a first. This ES1 was by no means the best car of 1972 as far as handling was concerned, nor did it have the most powerful engines. In 1973 these shortcomings were not overcome, but Derek Lawrence did place fifth and sixth in two British Championship races.

It came out next as an updated car (ES5) with a Vegantune-Ford engine, and Tony Rouff drove it to gain top-six places in 1975. In the Summer of that year there was a distraction as Dr Ehrlich acquired the Lotus 73s that had been in store since their JPS days in 1972, seeing them as a possible basis for his next car. He was always attracted by 'bargains', although in this case Neve raced one only once and they later passed into other hands, again at a bargain price.

Meanwhile, ES5 appeared again in 1976 (when it was sometimes referred to as ES2/5), driven by Mike Tyrrell and then by Richard Hawkins, who won a Mallory Park race in it. As ES6 it was overhauled for the last time, and by then it was venerable.

RP3 in 1977 looked a more complete car – it was perhaps the only Ehrlich with attractive overall lines. Design was by Graham Humphries, and it was built by Sabra Automotive. It was conventional in its suspension and sheet aluminium monocoque, and the Nova-Toyota in the back was carried over from 1976. Pierre Dieudonne drove it, after starting the season with ES6, and found it another difficult car (he was fifth in one British non-Championship race).

RP4 in 1978 was a revision of RP3, and however hard Brett Riley tried he found it uncompetitive. It came out again with a

The long-lasting steel monocoque car in its mid-career form in 1975, driven by Tony Rouff and smoking. The original narrow and shallow nose has given way to this full-width nose.

RP3 was a side-radiator car, with more attractive lines than most Ehrlichs.

full-width nose in 1979, when it was driven by Bryce Wilson, and then a narrow nose from the FA RP5 and side pods were added in 1980. That year Ian Flux was the last Ehrlich F3 driver, rounding off with tenth in the British GP meeting F3 race. RP4 became a Formula Atlantic RP5, and was written off at Brands Hatch. Then Mark Thatcher proved rather destructive of equipment, and Dr Ehrlich turned back to motorcycles and kart engines. He was very successful in both fields in the second half of the 1980s.

RP4 could hardly be described as attractive in its final form. The driver is Ian Flux.

EIFELLAND

This car was entered as an Eifelland Typ 21 for its backer, magnate Gunther Henerici, in the name of his caravan company. In reality it was a March 721 carrying bodywork designed by aerodynamicist Luigi (Lutz) Colani. From the start there seemed to be deficiencies in its aerodynamic qualities – for its first race outing, in South Africa, a standard March nose cone was used and soon a conventional rear wing took the place of the sweeping one-piece curve towards the tail. The singular cockpit surround remained part of the car, although the engine air ducting incorporated in it was ineffectual. Rolf Stommelen tried hard, and to his credit brought it to the finish in six of his eight GP starts in 1972 (best placing tenth). In the summer Henerici sold his caravan interests, and the new owners had no interest in racing; the car was run in Austria by 'Team Stommelen' and was then sold; late in the season it was run in a non-championship race by Hexagon, as a March with a normal 721 body.

Meanwhile, a pair of March 723s with modified noses were run as Eifelland 23s in 1972 F3 races, and in 1974 the F3 Eifelland became the short-lived F3 Rheinland.

Driver: Rolf Stommelen.

One of the odder devices of the 3-litre GP years, the Typ 21 during practice at Brands Hatch. Only the centre part of Colani's original bodywork remains, and that no longer carries the bold acknowledgement to his aerodynamic work that was emblazoned on the car at its launch.

EIGENBAU

The entry lists of most East German F2 races of the late 1940s and early 1950s suggest that by far the most prolific constructor was Eigenbau, in fact in some races every car was an Eigenbau-BMW. Unfortunately 'Eigenbau' is German for 'Special' and in the absence of a contemporary East German motor racing publication East German historians can shed little light on the origins of some of the cars.   ML

ELDEN

This minor marque has experienced varied fortunes since Brian and Peter Hampsheir built the one-off PRH1 sports car in 1961. It became a serious manufacturer in the 1970s – 121 PRH10 Formula Ford cars were built 1972-4 – but then slipped back to the point where it became dormant in 1983, until late in the decade. After being sold and resold, in 1988 it was adopted by Techpro, whose main interests were in mining but who backed Elden to regain its position as a racing car constructor (but not to become a racing team). For the revived company Peter Hampsheir designed F Ford and F Renault cars, but in Elden's background there were also F3 cars, and an abortive F2 project.

PRH9 The prototype F3 car, built in 1972 with a 'skinned frame', wide-based wishbone front suspension, top link, lower wishbone and radius rods at the rear, slim overall lines with unobtrusive radiators alongside the rear of the cockpit, and a Holbay engine. It was extensively tested but raced only twice in 1972, when it was a mid-field runner. For 1973 it was updated with PRH12 bodywork.

PRH9 with its original body, and a more shapely nose than it was to have as PRH12. Mike Catlow is waiting in the cockpit at Snetterton.

PRH12 A definitive F3 car, following PRH9 in layout, but with very different bodywork – full-width nose, higher cockpit sides, engine cover tapering back from the roll-over bar and

Under the skin this was PRH9, and the tail and rear wing treatment was modified after it first appeared at the Racing Car show in London. Driver is again Catlow at Snetterton.

initially exposed pipe runs. Its appearance coincided with a fuel crisis, three were built, and two of them went to the USA. The best F3 placing in 1973 was a third, gained by Andy Sutcliffe at Brands Hatch.

PRH15 A full monocoque F3 car introduced in 1974, with a longer wheelbase and bodywork that gave the impression of a sleek PRH12, with full-width nose, a more pronounced cockpit surround and lower engine cover. Three were completed, one going to the USA.

PRH16 Like PRH9 this was built for Tony Brise to drive, but as in 1972 he took his talents elsewhere. The designer was Andy Smallman, who laid out a monocoque car that gained a reputation for good handling – not in 1974 F2 racing, as was intended, but in F Atlantic where it was driven by Gordon Smiley.

ELF

Formula 2 came to be dubbed 'Formula Elf' in the mid-1970s as under the guidance of François Guitier the French company pursued a sponsorship policy that was both generous and sensible, and in large part was aimed at forwarding a generation of French drivers. Beyond that, its name was applied to an F2 car for the Jabouille/Larrousse Elf-Switzerland team. This 2J was largely designed by Jabouille in 1974, although much was owed to Alpine. It had a 'traditional' space frame, the last in an important formula, narrow track and clean lines, and Alpine components from the pair's recent past were used. (Early in 1975, while the second Elf was completed, the team ran an Alpine as its second car.) The 2J was powered by Schnitzer-BMW engines. Two were built for 1975, when the little team managed by Jean Sage won three races. In 1976 there were three cars, still with the 2J designation but powered by the Renault-Gordini CH1B V-6.

The Elf 2J was a compact well-proportioned car, with a narrow track and short wheelbase. In this 1976 form, with tall airbox above the Renault engine, its lines were even cleaner than in 1975, when the BMW engine air intake arrangement was assymetrical.

Jean-Pierre Jabouille drove them to win three Championship races, and the F2 title, while his team mate Michel Leclere won one race and placed well enough in others to finish fourth in the Championship. Elf's main interest moved on to F1 and these cars were sold to Willi Kauhsen for 1977.

ELFIN (AUS)

The leading Australian constructor of racing and sports-racing cars, Elfin was founded by Cliff and Garrie Cooper. Production exceeded 300 cars in the quarter-century following their first sports-racer in 1958. The use of the family name on their cars was presumably ruled out because of the other Cooper father and son partnership. When local regulations coincided with international formulae, Elfin built cars that conformed, notably for Formula Junior and F5000, while single-seaters were also produced for the Australian National F3 and F2. When FJ was introduced into Australia in 1961 Elfin laid down a car on Lotus 18 lines. Most of the components, such as suspension castings, were made locally, and the Elfin enjoyed a considerable cost advantage over imported British FJ cars. At first it matched them in performance – Matich drove one to win the 1962 Australian FJ Championship – but it lagged in 1963. A multi-purpose design, type 600, came in 1965 and was offered in ANF3 form as well as for other categories.

ELFIN (GB)

The third generation of the Emery family to become involved with racing car construction but Peter, son of Paul, chose not to use the name Emeryson. At the time when the better-known Australian constructor Elfin was becoming established, he laid down his own Formula Junior car and named it Elfin. It appeared late in 1960, and Emery was by no means the first or the last constructor to be misled by the apparent logic of front-wheel drive, as far as circuit cars were concerned. The Elfin was a neat car, with tubular space frame and fibreglass bodywork, and the idea was that BMC or Ford 105E engines could be used. However, the car made no more impact on racing than other front wheel drive machines.

The FJ Elfin had 'traditional' single-seater lines, though some of the drawbacks usually involved (such as excessive frontal area and a long and weighty drive line) were avoided. But it came at a time when the rear-engined layout was demonstrably better.

ELHOO

Finnish 500 cars built by Pentti Loivaranta and Clavi Havana in 1952, the two Elhoos (basically 'LH' after their builders) were

Kieft copies which enjoyed some success in Scandinavian racing, especially in the hands of Loivaranta, who raced his Norton-engined example up to 1960.   ML

ELIOS

The Elios was a home-made Fiat-engined Formula Junior car entered and driven by Mario Pandolfo in the *Coppa Italia* at Vallelunga in 1961. This was nominally an F1 race held to decide the Italian Championship, but since it was hastily arranged the organisers were grateful for any entries. Pandolfo qualified last of ten runners and retired with engine trouble in both heats.   ML

ELPARK

There must have been an air of youthful optimism. and perhaps Wolfsburg influences about this Californian one-off Formula Junior car in 1960. Its designer/builder, one E. Parkinson, chose to mount its Ford 105E engine behind the rear axle line, from whence it drove forward to the gearbox, which in turn had the radiator mounted above it. There seems to be no record of racing achievement, nor of the fright the intrepid driver must have inflicted on himself.

Few Juniors looked more home-built than the Elpark, and few had such an outlandish layout.

ELVA

Frank Nichols' Elva company built sports cars and sports-racing cars for almost five years before its first single-seater came in 1959, for the burgeoning Formula Junior category. The first car was ready for the first FJ race in Britain, at Snetterton in April that year; the Elva was the only car in the FJ class of a *formule libre* event.

It had much in common with the Mk5 sports car, and was front-engined. Keith Marsden was largely responsible for its orthodox design with a tubular frame, wishbone and coil spring/damper ifs, lower arms, trailing radius arms, coil spring/damper rear suspension, and modified BMC gearbox. The engine, set well back in the car, was usually the Rytune BMC A-series unit or a Mitter-prepared DKW engine, which sometimes gave lots of power but was difficult to keep in tune and seldom offered reliability. A linered-down Rootes engine was tried, unsuccessfully, and the car would accept Ford or Goliath engines.

Elva reaped a reward for being first in the British field; sales were good in 1959-60 and the cars were more than a match for early Continental Juniors like the Stanguellini. Some were built to a slightly modified specification by Rytune and marketed as the Scorpion in the USA.

The arrival of rear-engined Juniors meant that Elva had to turn to that configuration, although Charlie Kölb in a front engined Elva-BMC won the 1960 American FJ Championship. The '200' series car was once again straightforward, with a space frame combined with a stressed undertray, wishbones and coil spring/damper ifs, with parallel trailing arms and lower wishbones at the rear. Elva tried to concentrate on Rytune BMC A series engines, but owners tended to turn to Holbay or Cosworth Ford 105Es. This car was first raced late in 1960, but was never more than modestly successful, although 20 were made. The last single-seater Elva – the '300' series – appeared in 1962. Although it was conventional in its layout it was a strong candidate for the lowest production racing car ever made. Unlike Lotus, Elva never ran a serious works team since that would have eaten into profits. The six cars which reached private hands achieved little, except in America where Chuck Dietrich enjoyed some success. After that Elva abandoned single-seaters for the sports car line they knew so well.

Despite the use of a step-down box in the transmission line, the first single-seater Elva (40in overall height) (**above**) was a high car compared with its rear-engined successor (29in) (**below**). In other dimensions the two were closely similar.

EMERYSON

Paul Emery was one of only two men to make cars which complied with each of the first four World Championship formulae, 1950-65. The other was Enzo Ferrari, but Emery not only designed and built his cars himself, he frequently drove them. He could inspire anyone who worked alongside him, and got their hands dirty. Every so often he seemed to be on the brink of becoming an established constructor but one thing he lacked was business sense.

Confusingly, 'Emeryson' was used to name three distinct lines of car: 1930s specials built by Paul's father, George; some 250cc single-seaters made by his son, Peter, who also made the 'Elfin' FJ car; and those made by Paul himself.

Emery's distinctive front wheel drive FJ cars were built in small numbers and there was another break from one-off construction when former Cooper driver Alan Brown sponsored Emeryson Cars Ltd in 1960. This new firm built a range of F1 and FJ cars, with limited success. Hugh Powell, a wealthy American teenager, bought into the company at the end of 1961 and shortly afterwards Brown and the rest of the board resigned. Emery stayed on as designer, but resigned before the end of the 1962 season. His only other connection with F1 was when he prepared a 3-litre version of the Coventry Climax Godiva engine in 1966.

Emeryson Special Mainly the work of Paul, this had a ladder frame, modified Singer coil spring and trailing arm front suspension, an Alta-type independent rear layout with torsion bars, a 1934 dohc Lagonda Rapier engine reduced to 1087cc, an ENV pre-selector gearbox and a two-stage supercharger. Money was short so it was hired to Eric Winterbottom before it had even been bodied and he won a race with it at Gransden Lodge in 1947, and continued to do quite well in minor races.

Paul rebuilt it with a 4.5-litre straight eight Duesenberg engine, tuned to give, he says, nearly 400bhp. A share in the car was sold to Bobby Baird who raced it occasionally but never achieved any success for it had a habit of devouring gearboxes. The Emerys planned an F1 car with an air-cooled flat twelve engine but could not finance it.

500cc Formula 3 Emery designed and built a number of pretty front engined cars which were styled after the Mercedes-Benz W163 and had front wheel drive (ex-BSA three-wheeler) and all-round independent suspension by rubber bands and later by coil springs. They sold in small numbers because buyers could negotiate better starting money with something different and for a time they were competitive. It was typical of Emery that as early as 1950 he had fitted a home-made disc brake to the front of his car, the first disc brake to be used in Europe (the singular is deliberate, it was essentially a transmission brake).

The fwd Emeryson F3 car had well-balanced lines. Drivers had to adopt the crowd-pleasing habit of letting an inside front wheel lift well clear of a track on corners as they battled to stay with rear-engined cars.

Formula 2/Formula 1 When 500cc racing started to become too expensive, Paul built an F2 car in 1953. It had a tubular box frame, coil spring and double wishbone front suspension and a de Dion rear end located by twin trailing arms suspended on coil springs. To keep the drive train as low as possible, a short propshaft led to the gearbox and then a longer shaft went under the backwards-facing differential to a reduction box. It was finished by a pretty body which had the usual Emery hallmark, a small but efficient air intake.

During its life it used, variously, a second hand Aston Martin LB6 engine linered down to 2 litres (unreliable), a second-hand 2-litre Alta engine later enlarged to 2.5 litres and, finally, in 1957, a 2.4-litre Jaguar unit. With an Aston Martin engine Colin Chapman drove his only race in an F1 car, in the 1954 International Trophy where he qualified last and finished 17th and unclassified.

The only major race Emery entered was the 1956 British GP at Silverstone, when he qualified 13 seconds off the pace but quicker than several private Maseratis. His race lasted just four laps before he retired with ignition trouble.

During 1957 Emery developed a Jaguar 2.4-litre engine which he dry-sumped and fitted with his own fuel injection made from a CAV diesel injection pump. In this form it appeared briefly in only one F1 race, at Goodwood, where it retired after four laps. Driven by Roberta (previously Robert) Cowell in hill climbs, however, it was a winner in the Ladies' Class. Emery built a second car for an American customer for use in USAC racing with a fibreglass body and a supercharged 2.5-litre Alta engine.

The erstwhile F2 Emeryson in F1 form in a minor *formule libre* race at Mallory Park in 1956, looking well prepared but distinctly 'bitty'. Driver is Paul Emery, who won the race.

1.5-litre Formula 1/Formula Junior In 1960 former Cooper driver Alan Brown, Dick Clayton and Cecil Libouity backed Emeryson Cars Ltd to build a range of F1 and FJ cars. The result was a single space frame design with front suspension by coil springs and double wishbones while the independent rear was by reverse lower wishbones, coil springs, and twin radius rods. The first car was raced at Brands Hatch in August 1960 in F2 guise. In F1 form, the chassis was modified in detail and Colotti five-speed gearboxes were mated to Climax FPF engines.

In 1961 Ecurie Nationale Belge ran a team of three cars which were fitted with four-cylinder dohc 1484cc (81 x 72mm) 140bhp Maserati 150S engines. Two crashed at Pau and only one World Championship race, Monaco, was entered, but neither car qualified. ENB ordered Lotus 18s but retained the Emerysons, entered them in several races, generally did not turn up, and usually failed to qualify when they did.

Emeryson ran a Mk2 works car for Mike Spence in FJ; Spence won a 100-mile race at Silverstone, the only important race the FJ Emeryson won. Later Spence made his F1 debut in an Emeryson-Climax at Solitude, and ran seventh while holding his car in gear, but soon retired, then finished second in a Brands Hatch race.

Had Emery not had second thoughts about the expense and weight, the Mk3 would have had a fibreglass monocoque but he essayed a more conservative design which was slimmer and lighter than the earlier cars. It did have a semi-monocoque section with pannier fuel tanks contained in a stressed mid-section. In the nose the radiator was almost horizontal and air passed under the car and up through it.

The Mk3 was an improvement on the earlier cars but under-powered. In 1962 Powell ran a two-car F1 team for his guardian, Tony Settember, and John Campbell-Jones. It was too small for Settember and Campbell-Jones proved easily the quicker driver, with a best finish of sixth in the Aintree 200.

The cars appeared in occasional championship races, Campbell-Jones finishing eleventh (and last) at Spa. Settember was eleventh in the British GP, four laps down, and he also managed to qualify (last) at Monza where he retired with a failed head gasket. The car appeared in 1963 under the name 'Scirocco' with a new chassis fitted with V-8 BRM engines.

Drivers (F1): Lucien Bianchi, John Campbell-Jones, Olivier Gendebien, Tony Settember, Mike Spence.

Emery testing his first Junior, which had first run in 1960 as an F2 car. In this form it looks bulky, although the fibreglass bodywork is very smooth.

EMILIANI

This derivative of the 1978 Wolf Dallara was sound enough to win the 1980 Italian F3 championship in the hands of Guido Pardini despite running at various times on Goodyear, M & H or Pirelli rubber. (A test programme carried out by Emiliani, and an early-season win at Vallelunga, led to a wholesale switch to Pirelli by Italian teams). Giampaolo Dallara modified the car, which outwardly had a sleeker body than his original, as well as side pods and skirts for 1979, when Pardini was sixth in the Italian Championship. Toyota engines were used in the Emiliani 380, but Italian enthusiasts were more than happy to proclaim an Italian Championship falling to an Italian team's Italian chassis.

ENB-MASERATI

In 1962, the Ecurie Nationale Belge gathered the useable parts of the Emerysons which it had abused in 1961 and created the ENB-Maserati, comprising Emeryson chassis, a Maserati 150S engine and a new body shell with a twin nostril air intake.

Lucien Bianchi drove the 'new' car in the 1962 Grand Prix de Bruxelles where he qualified nearly half-a-minute off the pace, and retired in the first heat with engine trouble. It then appeared at Pau, where Bianchi crashed, and in the German GP where he qualified it last, nearly two minutes off the pace, and finished last. That was the end of the car's circuit career but it later had some success in hill climbs.   ML

ENSIGN

Morris Nunn entered racing by accident when he bought in a 1.5-litre Cooper-Climax for the family car trading business. That led him to driving, and into F3 in the fierce 1-litre days of the late 1960s, when he did well enough with an ageing Lotus 41 to be offered a Gold Leaf Team Lotus drive. When an F5000 opportunity fell through in 1970 Nunn turned constructor. Backed by Bernard Lewis he set out to build a prototype F3 car virtually single-handed in a lock-up behind his bungalow. That first car proved to be very competitive and others followed, to lead into batch production with the F372.

There was an F2 car for 1972, but that year one of the Team Ensign F3 drivers, Rikki von Opel, asked Nunn to design, build and run an F1 Ensign for him for 1973. The car turned out to be competent, but von Opel's inexperience hardly helped in making it fully raceworthy, and he left for a ride in a developed Brabham in 1974. Nunn kept his team in being, and in 1975 van Lennep scored Ensign's first Constructor's Championship point, although that proved to be a prelude to sponsor problems rather than a period of sustained success. A high point came with tenth place in the 1977 Constructors' Championship. The low points were when a crash in an Ensign ended Clay Regazzoni's racing career in 1980 and when the company almost went under.

In 1981 there were rumours that the team was to be sold but Teddy Yip continued his support and at the end of the year Ensign moved to a new base at Litchfield (hitherto Nunn had stayed near his home town, Walsall). In 1983 the team was amalgamated with Yip's Theodore Racing but that did not bring strength and at the end of the season it faded away. Nunn continued in racing, taking his world-weary look and wide experience to America in a management capacity, and was Emerson Fittipaldi's chief engineer in a triumphant 1989 Indycar programme.

F371/372 In effect these designations applied to the 'pre-production' and 'production' F3 Ensigns, and like later Nunn type numbers also referred to the year. The first car made its debut at the 1971 Racing Car Show, and Bev Bond soon showed that it was a very competitive car. During the year two more were completed (the Ensign premises were hardly suitable for production). The car was built around a square-tube space frame, with stressed alloy side panels, conventional suspension, smooth wedge lines and cleanly ducted side radiators. The 1972 car was closely similar, with a sleek engine cover flowing into a little tail carrying a small rear wing; there was some detail refinement, but development lagged as the F1 Ensign had priority. Dave Baldwin joined Nunn to look after development as customers deserted the marque; he made some progress and Brian Henton helped regain ground by winning with an Ensign. Nunn, however, was about to dispose of his F3 interests. His best year had been 1972, when Mike Walker and Rikki von Opel won in the works cars, and Colin Vandervell also won with an Ensign.

Bev Bond in the original F371 at Brands Hatch in May 1971.

An F2 version was built for John Burton, with wings, larger fuel tankage, bigger brakes and other minor changes. It made no impression at all in F2, never getting beyond practice in 1972 before it was sold.

The F2 version in 1972, with lines that were common to the later F3 cars.

N173-4 The first F1 Ensign, N173 or MN01, was a nicely-made and simple car with striking lines. It comprised an aluminium monocoque, conventional outboard suspension, DFV engine and Hewland FGA400 gearbox. It stood out by virtue of its bodywork, in fibreglass and executed by Specialized Mouldings, from the full-width nose to the rear wing carried on flowing end plates. A dark green and yellow pin stripe finish set it off. Von Opel gave the car its racing debut in the 1973 French GP, and finished 15th; he started in five more GPs that year, then moved on bequeathing the infant F1 enterprise to Nunn, who was to find some 1974 backing from Teddy Yip. A second car was built, with more conventional bodywork. Both cars were used in 1974-5 and N174 (MN02) served on into 1976 (when Amon placed it eighth at Long Beach).

Drivers: Chris Amon, Gijs van Lennep, Rikki von Opel, Brian Redman, Vern Schuppan, Mike Wilds, Roelof Wunderink.

Mo Nunn's first F1 car was nothing if not distinctive, and given adequate resources, and a more experience driver, could have been more than a grid filler in 1973. Here patron von Opel is practising at Monza.

N175/MN04 This Cosworth-Hewland kit car was designed by Dave Baldwin, and financed by the Dutch HB Bewaking company. It was conventional in make-up, with a light-alloy monocoque, rising-rate front suspension and inboard brakes, and in appearance. In the 1975 German GP van Lennep drove it to sixth place, scoring Ensign's first point. A disagreement between Ensign and HB meant that Nunn 'lost' the car and in 1976 it was run by Larry Perkins on a minimal budget, as a Boro.

Drivers: Chris Amon, Gijs van Lennep, Larry Perkins.

Race debut for the N175 was at Paul Ricard in 1975, when it was driven by Gijs van Lennep.

N176/MN05 Baldwin followed MN04 lines in the '05, modifying the suspension and using outboard brakes at the front as Chris Amon did not trust an inboard set up. On circuits it was fast but fragile, Amon crashing twice after component failures and the car was destroyed when Ickx crashed at Watkins Glen. However, it recorded seven finishes, the best being Amon's fifth in Spain.

Drivers: Chris Amon, Hans Binder, Jacky Ickx, Patrick Neve.

MN05 wore three different colour colour schemes – plain red, Citibank's and Tissot's, as here at Monza when it was driven by Ickx.

N177/MN06-08 Ensign weathered the heavy financial problems of 1976 to run a further development version of the second-generation car. In fact, for half of the season there

The N177 was far and away the best of the Ensigns, at least in terms of achievement, and it was a good honest car with no novelties in its make-up. This is Tambay in MN08 in 1977.

were two Ensigns on GP grids, the works car driven by Regazzoni in a happy partnership with Nunn and a Theodore car driven by Tambay. Between them ten points were accrued, giving Ensign its best Championship placing. These cars had to serve through 1978, when the team was run on a minimal budget – again – with a succession of drivers, one of whom, Derek Daly, scored the year's only point. One car ('06) was adapted as a wing car to be used as a spare in 1979.

Drivers: Derek Daly, Harald Ertl, Jacky Ickx, Geoff Lees, Lamberto Leoni, Brett Lunger, Danny Ongais, Nelson Piquet, Clay Regazzoni, Patrick Tambay.

N179/MN11 The one-off 1979 car was Baldwin's last Ensign and was partly funded by Yip. Its monocoque and rocker arm suspension were conventional, but it started its career (at the South African GP meeting, where it did not qualify to start) with radiators built into the scuttle and extending down to the nose. This arrangement was ineffectual (scoops had to be contrived to direct more air over the radiators, and presumably add drag) and the car was rebuilt with conventional radiators in the side pods. It was a wing car, but not a very effective one. As the team struggled, three drivers managed to qualify the car to start in only five races.

Drivers: Derek Daly, Patrick Gaillard, Marc Surer.

In its first form N179 was an outlandish device, but once the radiators were repositioned the existing lines around the front suspension flowed neatly into a conventional nose cone.

N180/MN12, 14 There was adequate sponsorship for 1980, from Unipart, and in the Autumn of 1979 Ralph Bellamy and Nigel Bennett laid out the straightforward N170 – it was designed and the first car built in 68 days. Broadly it followed the then-fashionable Williams FW07. The aluminium monocoque had honeycomb strengthening, rocker arm suspension was used with inboard coil spring/damper units but with outboard brakes all round.

Regazzoni rejoined the team, and while there were problems in the early races the combination was obviously promising. Sadly, however, N180 is remembered as the car in which Regazzoni crashed very heavily when running fourth at Long Beach. The promise faded, in the rest of the year the Ensign entry frequently failed to qualify, there were only two race finishes and no points were scored. One car was modified for 1981, and another built to 'B' specification. Marc Surer drove the latter to score invaluable points for Ensign, notably finishing fourth in the Brazilian GP. After six races, however, his place was taken by Salazar, who brought welcome money to the team. An N180B was overhauled for Guerrero to drive in the opening races of 1982.

Drivers: Patrick Gaillard, Roberto Guerrero, Jan Lammers, Tiff Needell, Clay Regazzoni, Eliseo Salazar, Marc Surer.

N181 Bennett designed the 1982 Ensign along lines which bore an outward resemblance to contemporary Brabhams. For the first time Ensign made extensive use of carbon fibre, with the lower half of the monocoque in aluminium honeycomb and the upper half in Kevlar-reinforced carbon fibre, with carbon fibre side pods. Two were laid down, but only one completed as the little team staggered through another lacklustre season. It turned out to be its last, for Teddy Yip decided to amalgamate it with Shadow, which he had acquired, using the name Theodore. The N181 design was uprated as the Theodore N183 for 1983.

Driver: Roberto Guerrero.

ENVOY

Another of the short-lived racing car names of the early 1960s, when would-be constructors were encouraged by a booming market, only to find that there were hardly enough customers once the majors (Cooper, Lola, Lotus and Elva) had filled their order books. Driver Ian Raby designed the MkI Envoy very much along the lines of 500cc F3 cars of the then-recent past, and with a low selling price in mind. It therefore had a simple ladder-type frame of square tubes, with neat fibreglass bodywork (and a cramped cockpit) and conventional independent suspension all round. The first car had a Barwell-modified BMC A-series engine and Fiat gearbox, a combination hastily replaced with Ford and VW components in the production cars. Nine were built by Sewell and King of Chelmsford in 1960, but only one, sold to an American entrant, achieved worthwhile race finishes. Later in 1960 Raby quit, while Sewell and King set up an association with S.J. Diggory to build and market the FJ Heron. That association was brief and in 1961 a MkII Envoy was developed in a dead end exercise.

N180 was an attractive car, with smooth one-piece bodywork from the nose to the back of the cockpit, and separate glass fibre covers for the broad ground effects side pods.

Designer Ian Raby testing an Envoy, and filling its cockpit – it was laid down as a cheap FJ car, and part of the price was its unsuitability for drivers of average stature. That apart, it was quite pretty.

ERA

ERAs either seem to be part of racing in the 1930s, or to belong to the more recent historic racing scene. However some of those 1930s cars ran in front line races after the War, and one new car was built in the World Championship period – although this was by no means a product of English Racing Automobiles set up by Raymond Mays and Peter Berthon some 20 years earlier.

B-type These cars were built in 1935-6 for *voiturette* racing, four of the thirteen later being uprated, three as C-types (with ifs and other improvements) and one as a D-type. As racing picked up again in 1946 some of the cars were brought out to be raced, notably by Bob Gerard, Mays, Brooke, Hampshire, the Whiteheads, Parnell and others.

Peter Whitehead in his R10B in the 1947 French GP at Lyon, showing off the front axle and the line of the simple main chassis members upswept at the rear – all as redolent of a past age as the paling fence carrying a trackside banner.

E-type This was also a *voiturette,* for the category that gave rise to the classic Alfa Romeo 158. Unhappily this ERA was anything but a classic.

The first was built in 1939 while the construction of the second spanned the war. The engine was a supercharged straight six (63 x 80mm, 1488cc), there was a tubular chassis with torsion bar ifs and de Dion rear suspension with torsion bars and a neat low body. Some development work was done after Johnson took over ERA, but too little, too late. The racing record was largely one of failures to get to grids (including Indianapolis in 1947) or retirements.

The first E-type at Lyon in 1947, when it was owned by Reg Parnell. In this French GP he shared the drive with Wilkinson. In the company of Talbots and Maseratis, it looked quite up-to-the-minute.

G-type ERA was bought by amateur racer Leslie Johnson in 1947 and relocated at Dunstable, where it continues to provide research and development facilities. The company produced this one-off in 1952, with a view to running a full

team in 1953. The chassis was of deep-section and stiff main tubes, coil spring and wishbone ifs and de Dion rear end, and was somewhat under-powered with a dry sump Bristol six-cylinder engine (66 x 96mm, 1971cc). Designer David Hodkin ran the drive shaft to the left of the cockpit. Moss placed it in minor events at Boreham – where he was third, its best placing – Charterhall and Goodwood, but at the end of the season it passed to Bristol, to become the basis of the Type 450 sports-racing car. Two more G-types were planned but not built, and a 2.5-litre project was abandoned after Johnson suffered a heart attack.

The G-type had an unusual but shapely offset single-seater body. It was sometimes run with a four-into-one exhaust, which passed under the rear axle, but here it has stubs and a deflector. Stirling Moss is the driver, in the 1952 British GP at Silverstone (he retired early, as the engine started to fall apart).

ERSKINE STARIDE

Mike Erskine was a small-scale F3 constructor who built cars in the first half of the 1950s, using a space frame, double wishbone front suspension and initially a swing-axle rear set-up, Norton engines and rather ugly bodies. In 1953 Reg Bicknell finished in the top three in three international F3 races, while in 1954 Dennis Taylor achieved similar results with a Staride.

The Staride was not a pretty car, and the driver sat well forward in the chassis. This is the late car with pushrod-operated inboard springs in the rear suspension. The bonnet straps are a nice detail on Anderson's car as it is pushed towards an Aintree grid at the 1955 British GP meeting.

ESO

Eso's main business has always been speedway and moto-cross motorcycles, and remained so when it was absorbed by Jawa. Before that, however, the factory at Divisov in Czechoslovakia built a handful of F3 cars around the Eso 498cc ohv speedway engine that had already been used in odd Czech F3 one-offs. In 1957 when the car appeared Cooper's influence was still overwhelming and the Eso looked like a chunky Cooper. Under the skin it also had a similar tubular chassis and even followed the transverse leaf and wishbone front suspension layout.

ETTORNE

A conventional 1954 British car built by George Henrotte and his father, this was one of the last wholly amateur cars in what had become a professional formula. It still achieved the odd place finish in F3 club events.   ML

EUROBRUN

Swiss slot-machine magnate and sports-car entrant Walter Brun joined forces with Paolo Pavanello in an F1 venture to run for three years from 1988. In that first season Brun found that moving into the big time was far from easy, although Pavanello should have been able to draw on his Euroracing experiences to advise him. Brun looked after the business aspects and aspired to use a German engine and German drivers; Pavanello contributed his base at Senago and design, build and preparation work. In the first season two cars were run, with a best race placing of eleventh to set against 14 failures to qualify. The effort was cut back to a single-car team in 1989, when the high point was one pre-qualification. In both seasons there were implications that the drivers were responsible for mediocrity, but in 1988 the first proposed replacement, Danner, was too tall for the cockpit, while Moreno simply declined the opportunity. In two full seasons, this outfit showed no promise at all and was never a credit to F1 or to its Italo-Swiss founders.

ER188 This bulky car designed by Marco Tolentino and Bruno Zava showed no originality, beyond a certain inelegance. It had double wishbone suspension all round and Mader-prepared Cosworth DFZ engines were used. It was reworked by Zava and George Ryton to serve as an interim car through to the end of the summer of 1989, the principal change being in V-8s, from Cosworth to Judd. Development work in 1988 seemed to be negligible.

Drivers: Gregor Foitek, Oscar Larrauri, Stefano Modena.

ER189 There was a new chassis for the Judd engine, but the car appeared far too late in the year, when it lacked straight-line speed and had handling shortcomings which led to an ER188 rear suspension being reintroduced. The 1989 driver, Foitek, parted company with the team after tests at Monza and for the Italian GP Larrauri returned to Eurobrun to maintain its dismal 1989 record. One car was updated at the beginning of 1989, while the team worked on the Neotech V-12-powered ER190.

Driver: Oscar Larrauri.

EURORACING

When March Engineering withdrew from F3 at the end of 1981, Italian agent Paolo Pavenello, who had run a team with considerable energy and expertise from a Milan base, adapted a pair of 813s for 1982. Under Ing. Marelli these were modified, and renamed Euroracing 101. The chassis, suspension and aerodynamic changes to suit the tyres seemingly failed to overcome the car's tight-corner shortcomings, but made for worthwhile straight-line and fast-bend gains. Alfa Romeo engines were used.

In 1982 team drivers Larrauri and Pirro started in 30 races and won 15, and they dominated the European Championship with nine victories in the 15-race series (Larrauri quite clearly took the title while Pirro was runner up). Euroracing quit F3 on that very high note, to take on the task of running Autodelta's F1 Alfa Romeos.

EVAD

A Formula Junior one-off, adapted by D. Taylor from a Monoposto car. Consequently it was front-engined (a Ford 105E was used), with a tubular chassis, but unlike some other early British Juniors it had all-independent suspension.

Taylor's Evad was a good-looking car, albeit representative of a type soon to be made obsolete. Beyond it on this 1959 Goodwood grid is Fenning's Venom (No 18).

First race for the Eurobrun team was in Brazil in 1988, when both cars were qualified. This shot suggests that cooling arrangements were less than adequate, and shows how low in a chassis a Cosworth DFV sat. Driver is Argentine Oscar Larrauri.

F

FACCIOLI

An early Bologna Junior, with rear-mounted Fiat engine in a tubular chassis and independent suspension all round. It made no impression in its races.

FACETTI

Another of the legion of early Italian Formula Junior constructors, Carlo Facetti achieved some success with his Lancia-engined car. The V-4 was mounted at the rear in a tubular chassis, with coil and wishbone front suspension and a transverse leaf arrangement on the lines Cooper was about to abandon at the rear.

FAIRLEY

When Reg Phillips heard that the 1948 British GP would be supported by a 500 race, he took an Austin Seven chassis and drive train, split the front axle to make independent suspension and stuck a Manx Norton engine forward of the cockpit. With a specification like that it was not quick but at least it finished. Later it was converted into a trials car with a Jowett engine.   ML

FAIRTHORPE

In the 1950s and 1960s, Air Vice Marshal Don 'Pathfinder' Bennett had a knack of discovering niches in the market and attempting to fill them with Fairthorpe cars which, with a little more flair, might have done well. When Formula Junior came along Fairthorpe responded with a front-engined device using many Triumph Herald components (engine, gearbox, front and rear suspension) which had a space frame made of thin tubing and a two-piece aluminium body shaped like a dolphin with a peculiar dorsal fin behind the driver's head. It was completed but apparently never turned a wheel, perhaps because Bennett realised that it was an instant no-hoper. It was dismantled, stored and forgotten until it was rediscovered when the company closed.   ML

FALCON

Japanese efforts in F3 have been spasmodic, at their best in the cars built by constructors like Nova. From its appearance and performance in Iwata's hands at Macau in 1984 this conventional Toyota-engined car was at the other extreme.

FALCONE

This seems an obvious name for an Italian racing car but, at least in the period covered by this book, it has been used only once, for an obscure 500cc F3 car in 1951. This was powered by a Guzzi twin, which was rated at over 45bhp at a time when the favoured Norton engine produced 45bhp at best. It was designed by Giovanni Savonuzzi, who negated any advantage that might have come from more power, more sweetly delivered, by laying it out on 'traditional' front engine/rear drive lines.

FERGUSON

The Harry Ferguson Research company first developed a racing car to demonstrate its four-wheel drive system, and Dunlop Maxaret anti-lock brakes although these were not used in racing. That first car was extensively used for research, enjoyed some competitions success, and led to the P104 Indianapolis car that carried the magic name Novi.

P99 This, the last front-engined Grand Prix car, was designed by Claude Hill and when it appeared in 1961 was first run in Intercontinental guise with a 2.5-litre Coventry Climax FPF; later that year it was run as an F1 car with a 1.5-litre Climax four. These engines were canted to the left in the space frame, to minimize frontal area, and the drive taken via a Ferguson gearbox to a centre differential, thence fore and aft on the left of the car to front and rear differentials. Brakes were inboard.

Project 99 ran into transmission problems in its first race. It was then started in the British GP by Fairman, delayed by an electrical fault and finally was taken over by Moss, only to be disqualified for a push start. Moss then drove it to a convincing victory in the Oulton Park Gold Cup. In 1963 it was driven in Tasman races by Graham Hill and Innes Ireland and then at the behest of Andy Granatelli it was tested at Indianapolis, driven by Jack Fairman.

Drivers (F1): Jack Fairman, Stirling Moss.

Project 99 posed during its August 1963 trials at Indianapolis, Granatelli on the left, Fairman in the offset driving seat.

FERRARI

No name in motor racing has commanded more attention and respect than Ferrari. Through four decades Enzo Ferrari presided over the teams of scarlet cars that carried his name, brought prestige to Italian engineering and a tingle to generations of race enthusiasts. For much of that time he might have exercised control from a distance, at least as far as races were concerned, Fiat might have taken a tighter control of the Ferrari company, there might have been discord among his lieutenants, but throughout this was Enzo Ferrari's team. It is the only team to have contested the World Championship in every season since its inception.

Ferrari cars were often competitive, but sometimes they were outclassed, and it is greatly to Ferrari's credit that he always fielded a team, at worst a single-car team. The team's cars were always more important than its personalities.

Enzo Ferrari raced in the 1920s, and formed Scuderia Ferrari in 1929 to run Alfa Romeos, including the quasi-works team of the 1930s. In 1938 that arrangement fell apart and Ferrari looked to building his own cars. The first ran in the 1940 Mille Miglia. During the Second World War the company specialized in machine tool manufacture, and moved from Modena to Maranello. Immediately after the War Ferrari turned to cars again, to high-performance cars and very soon to Grand Prix cars. The first came in the Autumn of 1948, and from the following year Ferrari became familiar throughout Europe.

The first cars had supercharged V-12 engines, reflecting Ferrari's obsession with that format, but the real challenge came with unsupercharged cars and the Championship fell to Ferrari's four-cylinder cars in 1952-3. The following years were dismal, but the near-collapse of Lancia brought new machinery to Ferrari for 1956 and then in the late 1950s the team ran the last effective front-engined Grand Prix cars.

The old Ferrari belief that engine power was all-important meant that his team almost kept up with the new wave of British constructors with the first-generation rear-engined cars, but lost out badly from the second year of the 1.5-litre Formula as chassis development moved ahead by leaps and bounds. There were distractions, notably the defections by key personnel and, from the mid-1960s, Fiat's interest increased after a Ferrari-Ford liaison plan had been thwarted.

The 3-litre years promised better times, but the second season brought the Cosworth DFV, and a period leading through to the mid-1970s when Ferraris sometimes won races, but not at all regularly. At least that concentrated minds, and wasteful distractions such as sports car racing were set aside.

Ferrari had been slow to accept novelties such as monocoque construction, and was to hesitate before adopting others such as the honeycomb sandwich. In the mid-1970s the classic 312T had put the team back on top, ground effects brought another down-turn, then came turbocharging – a technology Ferrari's people appreciated. The team won championships again, and the Constructors' Championship was the one which Ferrari particularly valued.

Through to the late 1980s the team's fortunes slipped again. There were schisms, particularly as outsiders were brought in by Ferrari and an advanced design centre (GTO Ltd – Guildford Technical Office) was set up a long way from Maranello. As his health started to deteriorate control started to change hands and after his death Fiat instigated a shake-out.

Cesare Fioro was brought in from the all-conquering Lancia rally operation to run the F1 team, and Mansell won the first Grand Prix of the 1989 season, in the radical car designed by John Barnard at GTO on the banks of the River Wey. This car was an effective challenger to McLaren in 1989, and that would have been justification enough for Enzo Ferrari. Before the end of that season Barnard had left, but the fruits of the new technology he had been brought in by Enzo Ferrari to impose on the team were to be picked up by Enrique Scalabroni and Steve Nichols for a very strong pair of drivers.

125 This was the first Grand Prix Ferrari – it should be noted that the first Ferrari to be run in a *grande épreuve* was a stripped sports 166, which Prince Igor Troubetzkoy started in the Monaco GP in May 1948. Gioacchino Colombo designed the 125, which made its race debut in the Italian GP that year. Its heart was an oversquare (55 x 52.5mm, 1496.7cc) 60-degree V-12 with a single-stage Roots-type supercharger. An output of 225bhp was claimed. The tubular chassis was

straightforward, and a double wishbone and transverse leaf spring ifs was used, with a torsion bar sprung swing axle arrangement at the rear.

Lampredi substantially overhauled the design for 1950. With a two-stage supercharger and other improvements engine power went up to 280bhp; a four-speed gearbox in unit with the differential replaced the five-speed gearbox in unit with the clutch; a de Dion arrangement with transverse leaf spring took the place of the swing axle and torsion bars at the rear; wheelbase and track were extended – the original 125 had a reputation for tricky handling.

Sommer placed one of the works trio third in the 125's first race, and late in 1948 Farina scored the first victory for a 125, in the secondary race at Garda. A first *grande épreuve* victory was gained in the 1949 Swiss GP, by Ascari.

In 1949, 125s were sold to independent entrants, most notably to Peter Whitehead, who came close to victory in the French GP and won the Czech GP at the end of the year; he ran an ex-works 1950 car in 1951, continuing in F1 and using it in F2 guise with a 2-litre engine. A short-wheelbase car became the first Thin Wall Special, a 1950 long-wheelbase car with two-stage supercharging was the second Thin Wall. A 2560cc engine was also used in a development programme for the unblown cars.

Drivers (GPs); Alberto Ascari, B. Bira, Felice Bonetto, Giuseppe Farina, Dudley Folland, Raymond Mays, Julio Pola, Ken Richardson, Nando Righetti, Dorino Serafini, Raymond Sommer, Roberto Vallone, Luigi Villoresi, Peter Whitehead.

Whitehead's short-chassis 125 at Zandvoort in 1949 shows off the rather homely lines of the first GP Ferrari.

F2 V-12s The 166 run in stripped form was to all intents and purposes the first F2 Ferrari, and then its V-12 engine was installed in 125 chassis to make a proper F2 car. In supercharged form this model was also to be run in Argentine *formule libre* races. In 1950 a longer and lower F2 car appeared, with mechanical changes similar to those

Raymond Sommer on his way to an easy victory in the 1950 Prix de Berne.

introduced by Lampredi for the F1 machines; many of the shortcomings were overcome and these cars dominated F2, but in 1951 Ferrari was concentrating on new cars and tended to neglect these F2 V-12s, and the works cars were made available to private entrants.

275/340/375 When Aurelio Lampredi took over from Colombo he was a disciple of the unsupercharged (4.5-litre) alternative offered by the F1 regulations, reasoning that it would make for simpler and lighter, less stressed, more reliable and more economical cars. This view was shared by Ferrari, and so a 60-degree sohc V-12 on these lines was laid down for 1950. A full-capacity version was reached in three stages – 72 x 68mm, 3322cc; 80 x 68mm, 4101cc; and 80 x 74.5mm, 4494cc. The maximum power outputs of the progressively numbered 275, 340 and 375 engines were 280bhp, 320bhp and 380bhp. The 275 had an old-style chassis, but for the 340 and 375 a new chassis of rectangular main tubes was designed, with double wishbone and transverse leaf spring front suspension and a de Dion rear suspension with a single transverse leaf spring.

The 275 first appeared in the 1950 Belgian GP, but was seemingly underpowered. The 340 confirmed the unblown policy, and in the Italian GP that year Ascari challenged the all-conquering Alfa 159s with a 375. In 1951 the Ferraris ended the long Alfa reign, the real turning point coming when Gonzalez won the British GP in a Ferrari. A wrong tyre choice at the last GP of the year cost the team's driver the Championship. In 1952 the Grands Prix were run for F2 cars, but the 375s were still run by the works in *formule libre* events, and three cars were sold to independents, while one was progressively modified as the third Thin Wall Special. Ironically, the only successes for those modified for Indianapolis were scored on road circuits.

Drivers (GPs): Alberto Ascari, Froilan Gonzalez, Chico Landi, Dorino Serafini, Piero Taruffi, Luigi Villoresi.

The big unsupercharged Ferraris seemed made for burly drivers – Ascari and Gonzalez were in that mould, and both were very successful with these cars. This is Ascari on his way to victory in the San Remo GP in 1951.

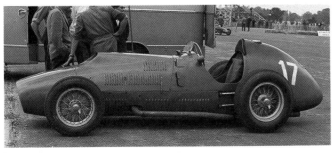

Outwardly the cars changed considerably in their second (*formule libre*) lives –the nose is longer, the intake more pronounced, and a head-rest alters the tail line in this 1952 car.

500 While the V-12 cars were reaching their peak Lampredi was working on a four-cylinder engine, which was authorized and designed very rapidly in 1951 and appeared in 2- and 2.5-litre forms. The larger was actually raced first, run in a car that was a forerunner of the 625 for the 1954 F1 (Taruffi placed it third in its 1951 outing, at Bari). The 500 that was to dominate the two seasons of 2-litre (F2) Championship racing made its race debut at Modena a little later, and in the first European F2 race of 1952, the Syracuse GP, 500s were placed 1-2-3-4, giving a good idea of what was to come.

In 2-litre form the engine, a straightforward dohc unit (90 x 78mm, 1984cc), produced 165bhp in 1952 and up to 180bhp in 1953, although the cars sold to independents had lower rev limits and were reckoned to be distinctly less powerful than the works cars. The engine was set well back in the tubular chassis, making for a well-balanced car, and the suspension followed the 375 pattern.

In World Championship races with the 500 the Ferrari team was beaten only once (at Monza in 1953) and was seldom challenged in secondary races, although independents had a tougher time. The 500 gave Alberto Ascari two Championships, and Mike Hawthorn drove one to his first GP victory, in the dramatic 1953 French race.

Drivers: Alberto Ascari, Bobby Baird, Giuseppe Farina, Rudi Fischer, Mike Hawthorn, Peter Hirt, Roger Laurent, Louis Rosier, Roy Salvadori, P. Scotti, Sergio Sighinalfi, André Simon, Jacques Swaters, Piero Taruffi, Baron de Tornaco, M. de Terra, Luigi Villoresi, Fred Wacker.

The simple, neat and well-balanced Ferrari 500 hardly changed in appearance through two seasons in the front line, although independent cars tended to be run with short noses, and stub exhausts were sometimes used. The 1952 and 1953 seasons belonged to Ascari, here in the 1953 Belgian GP.

625 These cars were rebuilds of the 500s, with a 2498cc (94 x 90mm) version of the four-cylinder engine, rated at 210bhp early in 1954 and 245bhp later that year. The 553 engine was also used in this chassis. Six cars were retained by the works team as a back-up for the 553, but in fact were preferred to it. Others were sold to independents.

A 625 was driven to GP victory in 1954, by Gonzalez at Silverstone. They were competitive in secondary races that year, and served on into 1955, but were placed in the top-six only occasionally, in a season that was bleak for Ferrari, save for Trintignant's lucky win at Monaco.

Drivers: Alberto Ascari, C. Bucci, Giuseppe Farina, Froilan Gonzalez, Mike Hawthorn, Roger Laurent, 'Pierre Levegh', Umberto Maglioli, Robert Manzon, Marquis de Portago, Reg Parnell, Harry Schell, Jacques Swaters, Piero Taruffi, Maurice Trintignant.

Maurice Trintignant in one of the straightforward 625s on the Reims pits straight during practice for the 1954 French GP.

553/555 The first Ferrari with a space frame, and lines that led to it being dubbed 'Squalo' (shark) – rather oddly, as its midriff bulge around the fuel tanks was most unsharklike. It first appeared as an F2 car at the 1953 Italian GP, with a 1997cc four-cylinder engine, and was then brought out in 1954 with a full 2497cc (100 x 79.5mm) version of the power unit for which 240bhp was claimed. Drivers did not like its handling, and changes to the engine position (within restricted limits) did not help. However, a change to coil spring front suspension late in 1954 did make a difference, and Hawthorn drove this revised car to win the Spanish GP.

Squalo and Supersqualo – Gonzalez **(above)** in a 553 in the 1954 French GP and Hawthorn **(below)** in a 555 in the 1955 Dutch GP. Obvious differences are in the nose, lower bonnet line and scuttle.

With a new frame and modified rear suspension, repositioned radiator and lower lines, it became the 555 Supersqualo for 1955. That year many races were cancelled

and the 555s started only 14 times, recording nine finishes with best placings third in Belgium and Italy. The erstwhile Lancia D50s had priority in 1956, although 555s (one with a Lancia V-8) were run in a couple of Argentine races.

Drivers: Eugenio Castellotti, Peter Collins, Giuseppe Farina, Paul Frere, Olivier Gendebien, Froilan Gonzalez, Mike Hawthorn, Umberto Maglioli, Robert Manzon, Harry Schell, Piero Taruffi, Maurice Trintignant.

D50/801 Given cars that were potential world beaters, Ferrari set about transforming them, in part because of his drivers' requirements for the sorts of handling characteristics they were accustomed to. So the Lancia-Ferraris became ever-more D50 derivatives, with original designer (now retained consultant) Jano at odds with Ferrari people such as Bellentani. A 'traditional' tail fuel tank came, the panniers were faired into the body (and ceased to exist as panniers) and the engine no longer had a stressed chassis member role. It was modified by Jano and Bazzi (it became more 'oversquare', at 76 x 68.5mm, 2487cc) to give 265bhp. Contractual problems were avoided, but on-circuit problems were probably invited, as Ferrari ran the cars on Engleberts rather than Pirelli rubber.

In 1956 the team had driving strength in depth, headed by Fangio, who won the World Championship. His GP victories came in Argentina, Britain and Germany, while Collins won in Belgium and France.

More modifications in 1957 included another engine revision (80 x 62mm, 2495cc) to give 275bhp, while suspension revisions included the use of a Supersqualo front set up. All this led to a change of designation, to 801, but not to Championship race victories – in the whole year only three secondary events fell to the Ferrari F1 team.

Drivers: Eugenio Castellotti, Peter Collins, Juan-Manuel Fangio, Olivier Gendebien, Masten Gregory, Mike Hawthorn, Luigi Musso, Cesare Perdisa, Alfonso de Portago, Maurice Trintignant, Wolfgang von Trips.

The process of transforming a Lancia into a Ferrari was well under way in the Spring of 1956, when Fangio drove this D50 with panniers faired into the main body. The circuit is Monaco.

Dino 156 During 1957 much attention focused on this F2 car, named for Enzo Ferrari's son Alfredino, who had been involved with Jano in the design of its V-6 before he died in 1956. The dohc 65-degree engine (70x 64.5mm, 1489cc) initially gave 180bhp, and importantly was to produce 190bhp on the AvGas that became the obligatory F1 fuel in 1958. Its chassis was on 555 lines, with coil spring ifs and 801-type de Dion rear end. It was heavy, but that was offset by the power of the V-6 in its few F2 outings. Late in 1957 it was run with larger engines, finally with 2195cc and 2417cc V-6s, 'field trials' which confirmed that Ferrari was on the right track for the 1958 Grand Prix season.

A 156 designation (156P) was used for an experimental rear-engined car raced once with an F2 engine in 1960.

Ferrari contested only a few F2 races with the Dino 156, usually on fast circuits such Reims (here in 1959, when it was driven by Cliff Allison). The car looks bulky compared with the pursuing Porsche and Cooper.

Dino 246 This neat 'traditional' F1 car emerged in 1958 with the 2147cc (85 x 71mm) V-6 in a tubular chassis derived from the Dino 156 (a purpose-designed chassis lacked ridigity). Ironically, the first Championship race for a Dino 246 ended in the first Championship race victory for a rear-engined 'British kit car'.

Broadly, these Ferraris were successful on fast circuits in 1958, and Hawthorn won the World Championship, albeit with only one Grand Prix victory (in France). The cost was fatal accidents, to Musso and Collins (who had won the British GP). Under Carlo Chiti several changes were made for 1959. Outwardly, lines were sleeker, while disc brakes (essayed in 1958 at Hawthorn's insistence) at last became standard, a 2474cc (86 x 71mm) 290bhp engine, the 256, became available, and at the end of the year a wishbone/coil spring rear suspension was used. The car's advantage on fast circuits was almost whittled away, but Brooks won the GPs at Reims and Avus.

(Above) In its first form the Dino 246 was a solid, chunky car and an attractive representative of a type rapidly becoming outmoded. The upswept exhausts and prominent bonnet-top intake were characteristic of the 1958 car, here driven by Peter Collins at Reims. **(Below)** Ferrari's first rear-engined single-seater in its only F1 appearance. Richie Ginther is the driver in this 1960 Monaco practice shot.

In 1960 independent suspension all round was standard, and the engine was moved back in the chassis and side main tanks adopted in the interests of balance. In the Monaco GP, however, Ferrari ran a rear-engined car.

There was one last victory for the Dino 246 – in the Italian GP – the last for a front-engined car in a *grande épreuve*. The British teams did not contest that race, when the banked track section of the Monza circuit was used to give Ferrari an advantage. The rear-engined 246P had a tubular frame, independent suspension on 1960 Dino 246 lines and the V-6. In its only F1 race Ginther placed it sixth.

Drivers: Cliff Allison, Jean Behra, Tony Brooks, Peter Collins, Olivier Gendebien, Richie Ginther, Froilen Gonzalez, Dan Gurney, Mike Hawthorn, Phil Hill, Willy Mairesse, Luigi Musso, Wolfgang von Trips.

Dino 156 A 156P had been run in 1960, but the familiar Dino 156 was the shark-nose main-line car of 1961, when the power of its V-6 engines more than offset chassis inadequacies. The team dominated the World Championship in the first year of the 1.5 litre Formula. Carlo Chiti was in charge of design for this first regular rear-engined Ferrari. The 65-degree V-6 was developed and a 120-degree dohc V-6 (73 x 58.8mm, 1476cc) introduced. This was lighter, made for a lower centre of gravity and gave 190bhp. Mauro Forghieri, who was to be responsible for most Ferrari racing cars through the next quarter of a century, worked on its development. The rest of the car followed the 246P, with a chassis built up around four large tubes.

The car was a winner from the start, when young Baghetti won the Syracuse GP in a FISA-entered 156, and he sensationally won the French GP in this independent car. That

(Above) The original 156 appeared neither slim nor lightweight – but a typically solid Ferrari. This is Baghetti's FISA car at Reims in 1961, its shark nose battered by stones. The single perspex cover over the intake shows that it has a 65-degree engine; smaller twin covers distinguished cars with the 120-degree V-6. **(Below)** The 'new' 156 in 1963 was more compact and had finer lines. In this shot of Surtees in his first Grand Prix in a Ferrari, at Monaco, the coil spring/damper of the 'British-style' rear suspension is obvious.

apart, the works team was beaten only twice in 1961 – by Moss at his brilliant best. Von Trips won his first GPs (in Holland and Britain) and seemed set for the Drivers' Championship but was killed in an Italian GP accident. The title went to Phil Hill, winner of the Belgian and Italian races. During the off-season several key executives left Ferrari, and the team went into 1962 with the cars revised but still deficient in handling terms and with the V-6 matched by new British V-8s in the power race. That year Ferrari's only F1 victories came in three secondary events.

The 1963 156 was regarded as an interim car, to serve while new engines were completed. Forghieri laid out a lighter space frame, retained the original front suspension but introduced a single top link/lower wishbone/twin radius arm arrangement at the rear. Fuel-injected versions of the V-6 reputedly gave 200bhp. Towards the end of the year this engine was used as a semi-stressed unit in a Forghieri designed semi-monocoque car intended for the V8, dubbed Aero 156, which was used intermittently through 1964.

Drivers: Giancarlo Baghetti, Lorenzo Bandini, Olivier Gendebien, Richie Ginther, Phil Hill, Innes Ireland, Willy Mairesse, Pedro Rodriguez, Ricardo Rodriguez, Ludovico Scarfiotti, John Surtees, Wolfgang von Trips.

158 A V-8 was a rare engine in the Ferrari repertoire, the obvious exception being the Lancia-originated units, and this 1.5-litre unit appeared later than planned, Surtees driving a 158 to a debut win in the 1964 Syracuse GP. The engine was a dohc 90-degree unit (64 x 57.8mm, 1487cc), for which 210bhp was claimed. The chassis had already been used for the Aero 156, and was little modified. Apart from a second placing at Zandvoort, failures in minor components meant that Surtees did not start scoring consistently until the second half of the season, when with victories in Germany and Italy and several second placings he secured the Drivers' Championship. The 158s were also used in early-1965 races.

Drivers: Lorenzo Bandini, Bob Bondurant, John Surtees, Nino Vaccarella.

With the 158 Ferrari achieved simple, smooth body lines to equal the contemporary Lotus and BRM. This is Bandini in the 1964 French GP at Rouen.

1512 With this car Ferrari returned to a 12-cylinder engine, a flat 12 (56 x 50.4mm, 1489cc) rather than a V-12. Its maximum power was 220bhp, but it was temperamental until the closing races of the 1.5-litre formula. It fitted in the 158 chassis, and was first raced towards to the end of 1964. Surtees often preferred to race a 158, and the best GP placing for a 1512 was Bandini's second at Monaco in 1965.

Drivers: Lorenzo Bandini, Pedro Rodriguez, John Surtees.

Through to the summer of 1965 Bandini usually drove the 12-cylinder car, here in the International Trophy at Silverstone. The installation of the flat twelve did not affect the car's lines at all.

246T A one-off intended for Surtees for the early-1966 Tasman series, not used for that as he was recovering from a sports car accident, but a useful second string in the first 3-litre season – Bandini placed it second at Monaco in 1966.

Drivers: Giancarlo Baghetti, Lorenzo Bandini.

Neat marriage of the existing mid-1960s 158 chassis and the 2.4-litre V-6 made for a car that was very competitive in the opening races of the 3-litre Formula. This is Bandini at Monaco.

312 With the 3-litre Formula, pundits proclaimed a return to power, but at first that was not borne out. Ferrari returned to a V-12, then squandered its head start as manager Dragoni was allowed to bluster Surtees out of the team. In any case, approaching economies meant the engine was not drawn from scratch, but derived from a sports car unit – one area of racing in which Ferrari V-12s had really excelled. It was a heavy 60-degree unit (77 x 53.5mm, 2989cc), 360bhp was claimed for it, but 300bhp would have been optimistic for the first race outing. Cylinder head work soon got output to 300bhp, and late in 1966 a three-valve head version was introduced that did deliver power of the order of 360bhp. Chassis design and suspension layout of the 312 was carried over from the late 1.5-litre cars. In a season when much was expected little was achieved. One Championship race was won by Surtees and one by Scarfiotti.

The monocoque was revised for 1967, a little weight was lost and the engine was uprated to give 390bhp. Parkes drove his special 'long-chassis' 312 to win the International Trophy and enjoyed a dead heat with Scarfiotti in the Syracuse race. Bandini died after a ghastly accident at Monaco, Parkes retired from F1 after an accident at Spa, and the season fell apart.

By the time of the Italian GP Forghieri and Rocchi had completed a 48-valve lightweight V-12, good for 390bhp, although not until 1968 did Ferrari's V-12 equal the exemplary DFV. For that year the chassis was updated, and the 312s were competitive.

The Belgian GP saw 312s run with a wing above the engine, mounted to the chassis, and nose trim tabs. In the French GP Ickx became the first driver to win a race in an F1 car equipped with 'wing' aerofoil devices. That was Ferrari's first Grand Prix win for almost two years, and second and third in Britain looked good too, but after that there was just a third and a fourth in Championship races. For once in the forefront in a department other than engines, Ferrari came up with an adjustable aerofoil (automatic or driver-actuated) late in 1968, but the team's advantages were not exploited, in part because of an economy campaign that led to more Fiat support.

In 1969 just one car was run in most races. The 312 chassis was slightly modified, and the engine developed to give 430bhp 'on the bench' but low reliability on tracks. Amon retired five times from seven starts, and quit; Rodriguez took his place, and in the last race for a 312, in his home GP at Mexico City, finished seventh.

Drivers: Andrea de Adamich, Chris Amon, Lorenzo Bandini, Derek Bell, Jacky Ickx, Mike Parkes, Pedro Rodriguez, Ludovico Scarfiotti, John Surtees, Jonathan Williams.

(**Above**) In its first season the 312 appeared a formidable machine, and given competent team management Ferrari could have won the Championship. This is Bandini in the first of the dozen 312s that were to be built, in the French GP. (**Below**) Jacky Ickx during practice for the 1968 French GP, driving 312/0009 equipped with an amidships aerofoil and the longitudinal yellow stripes that marked his personalized Ferraris.

Dino 166 Introduced for F2 in 1967, but raced only once that year, this car comprised a production Dino-based V-6 (initially 86 x 45.8mm, 1596cc then in 1968 79.5 x 53.5mm, 1594cc) in a neat chassis that then conformed to Ferrari's ideas of a monocoque (sheet plus tubes). In 1968 a more serious effort was made with a revised car (primarily, this had a 24-valve engine – 79.5 x 53.5mm, 1594cc). E. Brambilla and Bell, admittedly with some placings in Brabhams, finished third and fourth in the European Championship. In 1969 Bell and Brambilla were fifth and seventh respectively in the Championship, but by then the F2 programme was running down. Meanwhile, Andrea de Adamich had won the Argentine

Temporada between main seasons (although there were some dark suspicions about the size of the engines used by the Ferrari team). In 1968-9 cars with Dino 246 2.4-litre engines were run in the Tasman series for Amon and Bell. Amon won the Championship in 1969.

The pretty little car of 1968 looked a mess in 1969, better when run without the elaborate wing (sometimes with just its supporting structure). This is Tino Brambilla at Thruxton, and he continued with one of the cars as an independent entrant in 1970, with little success.

312B1 This car marked the end of a bleak period. A 1969 agreement with Fiat was to safeguard the future of the Ferrari team, and while its race effort that year might have suffered from the absence of Forghieri he was at least working on a car that was to become a winner, unlikely though that might have seemed as its engine suffered prolonged teething troubles through the summer of 1969. This was a compact flat twelve ('B' in the designation signifying 'boxer', coupled with the then-usual numbers signifying capacity, '3', and the number of cylinders, '12'); the claimed output of this 2991cc (78.5 x 51.5mm) engine in 1970 was 460bhp. It was mounted under a rearward extension of the chassis, which was on familiar sheet alloy and tube lines.

The car was tried with one of the 'old' V-12s, but for 1970 the team was committed to the 312B. It came good in the second half of the season, Ickx winning three Grands Prix and Regazzoni the one that mattered – at Monza.

Drivers: Mario Andretti, Ignazio Giunti, Jacky Ickx, Clay Regazzoni.

The 312B – retrospectively B1 – looked as purposeful as the first 3-litre cars. The low centre of gravity facilitated by the boxer engine is shown in this shot of Ickx in the 1971 Spanish GP.

312B2 An improved car – but not necessarily improved for the better – the B2 had smoother lines, inboard rear suspension and a modified flat twelve (80 x 49.6mm, 2992cc) producing up to 485bhp. Like other teams at the time, Ferrari had handling problems stemming from tyres. Regazzoni gave the B2 a debut victory in the Race of Champions, and Ickx won the Dutch GP with one, but overall the 1971 season was disappointing. Despite constant revisions, to engine and suspension, 1972 was also disappointing with just one GP falling to a B2, driven by Ickx at the Nürburgring. The cars were used early in 1973, until deformable structure regulations made them obsolete.

Drivers: Mario Andretti, Nanni Galli, Jacky Ickx, Arturo Merzario, Clay Regazzoni.

The more penetrating nose of the B2 and the hint of a wedge approach in the overall lines show well in this shot of Merzario in practice for the the 1972 British GP.

312B3 The story of the B3 is a story of transformation. The first car with the designation was an ugly short-wheelbase machine, tested in 1973 and never raced. The second was the first true monocoque Ferrari – a construction that had to be used to meet new regulations. Design was controlled by Sandro Colombo, as Forghieri was suffering one of his periods of banishment from the team. Construction of three chassis was sub-contracted to John Thompson's TC Prototypes company. The car emerged with angular lines, initially smooth, which changed throughout 1973. It was run, for example, with side radiators or nose radiators, but to little good effect until Forghieri was recalled late in the summer.

For 1974 the body lines were less angular, the cockpit was moved forward and the engine was revised to give up to 495bhp. The team was also properly organized (under Montezemelo), with political infighting ruled out, while Lauda and Regazzoni made a good driving pair. Lauda won two Grands Prix, Regga one, and the Ferrari team was solidly back in business.

Drivers: Jacky Ickx, Niki Lauda, Arturo Merzario, Clay Regazzoni.

Jacky Ickx with a pristine 1973 312B3 in nose radiator form.

312T In 1975 the team had a car that gave it a real edge, the 312 Trasversale, taking its 'T' designation from the gearbox installed at a right angle to the fore-and-aft line, and ahead of the rear axle line. This made a responsive car, well suited to Lauda's driving, and Ferrari also had a power advantage over the DFV-powered runners. Lauda won with a 312T in its first race in Europe (the International Trophy), won the third GP in which it was entered (at Monaco) and three more GPs that year, while Regazzoni won two (including the Italian, again). Both Championships fell to the team, for the first time since 1964, the same pair of drivers won the first three GPs of 1976, then the T2 came.

Drivers: Niki Lauda, Giancarlo Martini, Clay Regazzoni.

The 312T was a well-proportioned, handsome car – for once even an air box did not seem an afterthought. This is Clay Regazzoni leaning into the Parabolica on the way to his second Italian GP victory.

312T2 The appearance of cars had to change in 1976 as air boxes were ruled out, and on the 312T this led to neat intakes and trunking alongside the cockpit. In the off season a de Dion rear suspension was tried, but this was not used in racing. The 1976 season saw nuts and bolts aspects overwhelmed by dramatic events on circuits, which was unfortunate for new team manager Audetto. There were disqualifications (and reinstatements) as Lauda and Hunt battled for the drivers' title, there was Lauda's terrible accident at the Nürburgring and his equally dramatic return to racing at Monza. He won three Grands Prix in T2s that year, and while he did not win the Drivers' title these victories helped ensure that Ferrari took the Constructors' Championship.

Ferrari's mid-1970s colour scheme suited the 312Ts well, and in a detail white was used to pick out the cockpit-side trunking on the T2. This is Lauda in 1976.

The T2s served on until the early-1978 races, with slightly more powerful engines and minor revisions, and in 1977 they were very reliable. Lauda won three Championship Grands Prix, and with points piled up with other good placings was World Champion. He quit the team before the last two races. For these Reutemann (who was fourth in the Championship) was joined by Gilles Villeneuve. Ferrari again dominated the Constructors' Championship.

Drivers: Niki Lauda, Clay Regazzoni, Carlos Reutemann, Gilles Villeneuve.

312T3 New less-rounded body lines, a new monocoque and a new front suspension, largely designed to suit the Michelin radial tyres adopted by Ferrari in 1978, distinguished this car. Reutemann won three GPs in T3s, and Villeneuve scored his maiden victory at Montreal, on the circuit later to be named after him. During the off season Ferrari had to experiment with ground effects, running T3s with skirts. Despite shortcomings, these were used in the two opening races of 1979.

Drivers: Carlos Reutemann, Jody Scheckter, Gilles Villeneuve.

This was another good-looking car, which saw Ferrari switch from Goodyears to Michelins and face up to the ground effects era. The colour scheme accentuates the lip along the outside of the side pods, intended to help direct airflow to the rear wing.

312T4-T5 The T4 served for most of the 1979 season – very effectively in that its drivers, Scheckter and Villeneuve, were first and second in the World Championship while the team quite clearly won the Constructors' title. It was a ground effects car, built around a narrow monocoque, but with the handicap of the flat twelve obtruding into an area important in

The bodywork above the actual nose appeared odd on the last 312Ts, although in side elevation the cars looked no more than lower T3s. While the Brabham-Alfas in the background of this shot had V-12s, Ferrari had the problem of achieving reasonable ground effects with a boxer engine. Villeneuve is contemplative in the cockpit, during British GP practice.

ground effects terms. Suspension was tucked out of the under-car airflow, and upper body surfaces were broad and flat. The cars were rebuilt as T5s for 1980, with revised suspension, bodies and aerodynamics, and while it was perhaps not to be expected that the 1978 tally of six Championship victories would be repeated, a wretched failure was a surprise. Ferrari was tenth in the Constructors' Championship, in a sad ending to the 1970-80 story of the illustrious flat twelve 3-litre power unit.

Drivers: Jody Scheckter, Gilles Villeneuve.

126CK The first turbocharged F1 car appeared in the summer of 1980, and was run in practice for that year's Italian GP; its first race start was at Long Beach early in 1981, and it first finished a race at Imola that year. Through the season it underwent a sometimes difficult process of development, as chassis and running gear called for refinement (in mid-1981 Ferrari took on Harvey Postlethwaite to design a new monocoque, to get the team on an equal footing with the British 'kit-car constructors'). Ferrari people, however, had a sure touch with the engine, and the car was powered by a 120-degree V-6 (81 x 48.4mm, 1496cc) which was to serve the team well. It was tested with a Brown-Boveri Comprex supercharger and twin KKK turbochargers.

Ferrari chose to race with the turbo engine, despite its poor throttle response and thirst, and to try to sort out the chassis race by race – in ground effects terms, it was no more than mediocre. Villeneuve was a man to drive over such problems, and he did so to such good effect that in the face of probability he won the Monaco and Spanish GPs. The next best placing for the team was his third, in Canada.

Drivers: Didier Pironi, Gilles Villeneuve.

The 126CK looked cumbersome, and performance generally bore out appearances. This is Villeneuve during practice for his home GP, at Montreal.

126C2 For his first Ferrari chassis Postlethwaite used a honeycomb monocoque, with the rocker arm/inboard coil spring-damper suspension broadly carried over from the 126CK, and the V-6 with turbocharger modifications aimed at further reducing throttle response lag, driving through the transverse gearbox. Through the year the engine was improved and pullrod suspension was introduced, but mechanical developments were overshadowed. Pironi snatched the Imola race from Villeneuve, and at the next GP meeting the Canadian was killed in a practice accident. Tambay took his place and, after Pironi had been seriously injured in a Hockenheim practice accident, he won that German race. Andretti came back to Ferrari for the two late season races. Out of the year's drama and tragedies came success, as Ferrari won the Constructors' Championship.

In a 'B' flat-bottom version the cars served through the first half of 1983, when a revised rear suspension arrangement was introduced. There were two more GP victories (at Imola and Montreal) before the C3 was introduced.

Drivers: Mario Andretti, René Arnoux, Didier Pironi, Patrick Tambay, Gilles Villeneuve.

The C2 was a purposeful car, and successful in a difficult period for the team. As a ground effects car, it did not have to carry the hideously large rear wings used on later turbo cars. This car is driven by Tambay, on his way to victory in the 1982 German GP. Ferraris seemed to wear ever-more decals.

126C3-C4 Although outwardly similar to the C2B, the C3 had Ferrari's first in-house carbon fibre monocoque, which was combined with the earlier car's suspension and of course the turbo V-6, with around 625bhp available. The cars were first raced in the British GP, and Arnoux won the German and Dutch GPs in C3s, to help clinch another Constructors' Championship for Ferrari.

As the C4 the design was developed for 1984, with up to 660bhp on tap, but with two types of engine management systems tried as the 220-litre fuel limit was a worrying new factor. As the year went on it was not the only worry, and although the cars were constantly revised they were only spasmodically competitive. Michele Alboreto – the first Italian driver to race a GP Ferrari since 1975 – won the Belgian GP, but as runners-up in the Constructors' Championship Ferrari did not remotely challenge the dominant McLaren team.

Drivers: Michele Alboreto, René Arnoux, Patrick Tambay.

The 1983-84 flat-bottom Ferraris were not attractive cars, their lines being spoiled by large black rear aerofoils. This C4 is driven by Alboreto.

156/85 There were upheavals on the personality side in 1984. Forghieri was removed from the racing side, this time permanently, and soon took himself off to do what he knew best – design a racing V-12. Ildo Renzetti from Fiat took on engine development, to face the uphill task of attempting to combat the TAG-Porsche power supremacy, in this turning to an alloy-block version of the V-6. Postlethwaite designed a new chassis, and outwardly the car was sleeker. The whole ensemble was subject to revision through the season, when

the engine did not produce enough power and was markedly fragile when attempts to remedy the problem were made by increasing boost. That state of affairs led to a compromise in aerodynamic settings, which were intended to reduce drag but also reduced grip. Alboreto did win two GPs however, in Canada and Germany, and Ferrari was again runner-up to McLaren in the Constructors' Championship.

Drivers: Michele Alboreto, René Arnoux, Stefan Johansson.

The 156/85 was more shapely than its immediate predecessor, especially aft of the cockpit. Driver is René Arnoux, on his way to fourth place in the Brazilian GP, which turned out to be his last race for the team.

F186 In effect this 1986 car was a substantial redesign, and there was a return to iron block engines, which delivered more power, and reliably. Garrett turbos took the place of KKK units during the year. There were handling shortcomings, and traction was poor on some circuits. Fortunes slumped – no GP victories, and a lowly fourth place in the Constructors' Championship.

Drivers: Michele Alboreto, Stefan Johansson.

Johansson – here at Spa – was the most successful Ferrari driver in 1986, persevering through a season that was disappointing for the team.

F187 The year 1987 saw another new start. Gustav Brunner was briefly very prominent in the chassis design team, there was some input into the suspension from John Barnard in distant Shalford and ex-Renault expertise was brought in. A pullrod/double wishbone arrangement was used and there was a new 90-degree V-6 (for which the same internal dimensions were quoted) and 880bhp was claimed for it, driving through a new longitudinal six-speed gearbox. The car looked a winner from the start, but it was not a winner on the circuits until the end of the season, when Berger won the Japanese and Australian GPs. Somewhere in the background was an Indycar project, and perhaps fortunately it remained in the background.

The 1987 design was reworked as the F187/88C for 1988, when there was turmoil in the team as executive and technical personnel went and less frequently came. The car was a little slimmer, the aerofoils were revised, fuel consumption alone meant that in the 150 litres fuel allowance season it did not challenge the McLarens over a race distance (but there was that lucky win at Monza). Some detail refinement work was carried through in the twilight year of turbocharged cars.

Drivers: Michele Alboreto, Gerhard Berger.

An F187 in its slimmed-down 88C form, with bodywork nipped in more sharply behind the engine and a smaller rear wing than the 1987 cars. Gerhard Berger is the driver, in Rio tests.

640 A normally-aspirated development car, the 639, was extensively tested in 1988, but never raced. Later that year this second Barnard design appeared, the 640 (or F189).

Outwardly it was a sharp-nosed car, with a narrow monocoque between bulged flanks housing the radiators for the 65-degree V-12 and bodywork tailing back to a sharply nipped-in rear. Effective aerodynamics were essential as the 600bhp claimed for the V-12 as the season opened was not sufficient for a power battle with Honda-powered McLarens. A double wishbone pushrod suspension system used shock absorbers and torsion bars.

In the face of opposition from lesser men at Fiat, Barnard saw to it that the radical feature of the 640, its electro-hydraulic gearchange, was used through the year. This gearchange had teething problems, miraculously not on one of the cars in the first GP of the year, but its value was to be proved. The driver needed a clutch pedal only at a start. Thereafter two levers ahead of the steering wheel (behind it from the driver's point of view) reacted to touch pressure, the right-hand lever for changes up and the left-hand lever for changes down the seven-speed gearbox. There was no gear linkage in the traditional sense, for operation of clutch and gearbox was by electronically-actuated valves. The 640 was clever and sleek, and also very strong, as Berger's escape from an extremely high-speed accident with only light injuries showed.

Nigel Mansell drove the 640 to a Brazilian GP debut victory, won in Hungary, was twice second and twice third, while Gerhard Berger won in Portugal and was second in two races. Ferrari was third in the Constructors' Championship.

Drivers: Gerhard Berger, Nigel Mansell.

Overall slim and unified lines of the 640 were carried through from nose to tail. There are small bulges to house front suspension members (but one was not needed to accommodate a gear-changing hand), an unobtrusive spine behind the driver's head, and smooth lines flowing into the narrow tail. Mansell is the driver.

FERRY

Pierre Ferry's Paris-based company was early in the Formula Junior field, where it seemed to have a bright future as the category caught on throughout Europe. In the event, its future turned out to be limited in time, and was restricted to local races or the class for French-built cars that more important events sometimes embraced, as an encouragement. The car was rear-engined, but the specification was not advanced, with a ladder-type frame of two large-diameter main tubes and Renault suspension (Dauphine-based at the front, 4CV-based at the rear). The Dauphine engine was used, eventually giving a claimed 75bhp (in international company the Ferry appeared under-powered). It drove through a Pons-Redele Dauphine-based five-speed gearbox. Yves Dassaud was the only driver to make any sort of impression with a Ferry as FJ became really international in 1960, and after that cars faded. Ferry also built the Julien FJ car.

The Ferry Junior had the softer and rounded lines often associated with French single-seaters through to the early 1960s. This car is being driven by Delcarte at Cesenatico in 1959.

FHB

Frank Bacon's pioneer 500cc car of 1946 used a Rudge 'Ulster' engine mounted in the front of an Austin Seven chassis which fed its power through an A7 drive train. The result was a nose-heavy car which was virtually unsteerable and suffered from excess wheelspin. Bacon modified the chassis and put a JAP engine and Burman four-speed gearbox at the rear, which improved the car but still did not make it competitive.

Bacon faded from the scene but bounced back in 1951 with a new special built around a ladder frame, Cooper-style suspension, and some second-hand Cooper body panels. The engine and gearbox came from his second car so he brought together the spirit of the early days of the 500 movement, which he epitomised, and a modern design. ML

FIDGIT

A straightforward pioneering South African 500cc car built by a journalist, P. Harrington-Johnson. A JAP engine was mounted in the back of a home constructed frame and most of the other components came from a Fiat 500. ML

FIRST

Lamberto Leoni's team actually completed an F1 car late in 1988, then did not race it as funds were inadequate and an agreement with March for F3000 apparently precluded an entry into Grands Prix. The conventional Judd-powered 189 was designed by Richard Divila and was tested by Gabriele Tarquini. It was sold to Life Racing Engines to be used as a running test bed for their W-12 engine. The chassis was modified to meet FISA crash test requirements, to be entered in 1990 GPs by Ernesto Vita's Life team.

FITTIPALDI

The first Fittipaldi cars were named for the team's sponsor, Copersucar, on the face of it a Government-approved co-operative of sugar producers. Gradually the Copersucar association was reduced, the name being first hyphenated with Fittipaldi and eventually disappearing. This reflected the changing nature of the team: although some of its major components always had to be imported, the concept and first cars were a genuine effort to make a Brazilian car, but as time went on and the base was moved out of Brazil and then the team was merged with the rump of the Wolf outfit, that dream slipped away. The Fittipaldi team was never significant in GP terms, whether the cars were built in Sao Paulo as Brazilian GP cars or in Reading, an arrangement that made more sense since they were really Cosworth-Hewland kit cars. Wilson Fittipaldi set the team up and was its driver in 1975. Brother Emerson advised from the outset and joined full-time in 1976, to squander his talent, although in 1977-8 and 1980 the team was in the top ten of constructors. In the turbo era Fittipaldi never had adequate financial resources, struggled to survive, and quietly faded away at the end of the 1982 season. Wilson had his collection of cars and Emerson was to reach the top again, as a driver in CART racing late in the decade.

FD01 Richard Divila started design work in October 1973 and a year later the first car was unveiled in Brasilia. It was straightforward mechanically, and in the effort to include a substantial Brazilian content the Embraer aircraft company, which was starting to build an international reputation, was involved as a supplier of specialist components, such as the duralumin parts for the monocoque. Suspension was by double wishbones at the front, parallel lower links, single upper links and radius rods at the rear, with outboard coil spring/damper units. The DFV drove through a Hewland TL200 gearbox. Outwardly the car appeared unusually sleek, from its front wing carried on two forward-reaching prongs to the fully enclosed 'aerodynamic' tail. The water radiator was within that tail, and air was fed to it through NACA ducts and a low-pressure area that was thought to exist under the rear

FD01 in its revised form, with a little snub nose remaining of the original graceful arrangement, tall airbox in place of the low intake outlined by the roll-over bar, and conventional side radiators. The driver is Wilson Fittipaldi.

wing. The first car was crashed at its first race meeting and much of the original shape was discarded, but to little avail. The best Grand Prix placing was tenth and Hoffman used one in the first 1976 race.

Drivers: Wilson Fittipaldi, Ingo Hoffman.

FD04 There was little pretence that this was anything but a Cosworth kit car, apparently workmanlike but hardly competitive. Similar to the first car, save in weight and in some components, the FD04 had nice sharp exterior lines. Two were made in England, the third in Sao Paulo.

Fittipaldi was sixth in three 1976 GPs with this car and did rather better with it in 1977 (fourth in both South American GPs, fifth at Long Beach) before it was superseded.

Drivers: Emerson Fittipaldi, Ingo Hoffman.

The chisel nose, economic body lines, prominent side radiators and well thought out colour scheme characterized FD04. Driver is Emerson Fittipaldi, at Brands Hatch in 1976.

F5 The 'D' disappeared from Fittipaldi designations, as Dave Baldwin designed the car that came in 1977 (it actually made its race debut in the French GP). It followed the lines of Baldwin's Ensign LNF75 and three were built. With them the team mustered one fourth place, in Holland, but the car lacked straight-line speed and had unpredictable handling. Development was hardly feasible as Baldwin left before the car first raced, and Emerson suffered the indignity of not qualifying in Germany and Italy. Caliri's Fly Studio overhauled the design as a wing car for 1978. The suspension was new, with inboard coil spring/damper units, and the Lotus layout with radiators in the side pods was generally followed. Fittipaldi had a mixed season with this F5a, the high point being Emerson's second place in the Brazilian GP. Five other scoring finishes saw the team achieve its highest score, 17 points for seventh place in the Constructors' Championship. Problems with the F6 meant that F5As were used through to the summer of 1979, when the team's only point was scored by

Colin Bennett's heavily revamped Fittipaldi F5A in its 'second life' early in 1980, when it showed promise in Val Musetti's hands.

Emerson in the first race. Meanwhile two of the cars passed to Edwards' Mopar team, primarily for the British national series, where performances were modest in 1979. One of these was substantially reworked by Colin Bennett for 1980, and dubbed 'F5B'.

Driver: Emerson Fittipaldi.

F6 Ralph Bellamy's Fittipaldi design, the F6, looked the part but was a failure. It had a slim monocoque in Embraer honeycomb, with a slender nose and short side pods and the rear end completely enclosed, as an early intention was to run the car without a rear wing. Suspension front and rear was by top rocker arms, lower wishbones and inboard coil spring/damper units. The Cosworth DFV and Hewland FGA400 were naturally used.

The F6 was deficient in ground effects terms, which the F6A that came in mid-summer did not cure. It looked better in the year's last races, but then seemed to lack outright speed.

Driver: Emerson Fittipaldi.

The F6A looked a purposeful car, owing little to earlier Fittipaldis but maintaining the feature of partial fairings for the front suspension upper members. Driver is Emerson Fittipaldi, at Zandvoort in 1979.

F7 Fittipaldi absorbed Wolf before the 1980 season, and that team's WR7 and WR8 appeared in modified form as the interim F7, while a new car was designed by Harvey Postlethwaite. Emerson Fittipaldi and Rosberg finished third in GPs in the first part of 1980, while in his last season as an F1 driver Emerson also scored a fifth and a sixth before the F8 superseded the F7s.

Drivers: Emerson Fittipaldi, Keke Rosberg.

F8 Inevitably, perhaps, this car followed the Wolf pattern in its honeycomb monocoque and suspension (top rocker arms, bottom wishbones, inboard coil springs/dampers all round), and had the same wheelbase and front track dimensions as F7. Outwardly, it had a stubby nose and long side pods filling the space between front and rear wheels. The only points-scoring finish was by Rosberg – fifth in the Italian GP – but the two points earned there were added to the early season scores to place Fittipaldi seventh in the Constructors' Championship.

This pristine F8 had no particularly outstanding qualities or characteristics. In 1980 the last evidence of Copersucar origins had vanished.

One of the three F8s was modified as an F8C for 1981, and two new cars built with the revisions introduced by Gary Thomas. The meagre budget was felt in aspects such as below-par engines and tyres, and no points were scored; 'DNQ' appeared against Rosberg's name five times, and against Serra's nine times.

An F8D was cobbled together for the opening races of 1982, and Serra scored a point with it in the Belgian GP. That was Fittipaldi's last Championship point.

Drivers: Emerson Fittipaldi, Keke Rosberg, Chico Serra.

F9 This car turned out to be a one-off, designed by Richard Divila and Tim Wright, and the Fittipaldi team's swansong – Serra started three races in it, placed seventh in Austria (but lapped twice) and failed to qualify three times. The F9 was another orthodox Cosworth-engined car outclassed in the turbo era, blunt-nosed and deep-bodied, with double wishbone pullrod suspension. As Serra failed to qualify it for the Las Vegas event in 1982 the Fittipaldi team's last race was the Italian GP.

Driver: Chico Serra

In the last two seasons, Fittipaldi cars displayed signs of sponsorship gathered in penny packets, in contrast to the first six years. Serra is driving the F9 in its debut appearance, in practice for the French GP in 1982.

500

This unequivocally named pioneeer Australian 500 car was built by Brian Chatterton and Clem Warburton of Brisbane. It was basically a modified Austin Seven special with a rear-mounted Douglas TT engine and Norton gearbox with the A7 rear axle modified to take chain drive. ML

FLATHER STEEL SPECIAL

Dennis Flather's business was steel and it is therefore curious that this name got through in the days when advertising on cars was banned. Having dabbled with the Marott 500 car, Flather created a Cooper copy chiefly distinguished by the fairings over the front suspension, just like the German Monopoletta. An HRD engine was fitted originally but it was soon apparent that it was short on power and a JAP unit was substituted.

A second Flather was designed in 1954 by Bill Harris (the 'is' of Alexis) and was often driven by him, but without success. ML

Red trio at Silverstone, showing three very different approaches to Formula 1. Ickx leads in a Ferrari 312B2, Peterson is in the very distinctive March 711 and Emerson Fittipaldi follows in a Lotus 72. The Ferrari is red because Ferraris are red, the March red reflects STP and the Lotus red is taken from a cigarette packet colour scheme. Stewart won this 1971 British GP in a blue Tyrrell from Peterson and Fittipaldi.

A year earlier the British GP had been fought out between Rindt and Brabham, in a Lotus 72 and Brabham BT33 respectively, representing very different approaches but on this Brands Hatch occasion giving evenly matched performances. Brabham ran out of fuel when the chequered flag was almost in sight, and coasted past it in second place as Rindt won.

In the 1970s the role of the independent Grand Prix entrant withered, to vanish. As the decade opened the independents were still active – in the 1970 British GP Peterson in Crabbe's Antique Automobiles March 701 narrowly leads Graham Hill in Rob Walker's dark blue Lotus 49C. A McLaren and Amon's works March follow, and the red car at the back of the quintet is John Surtees' TS7, in its debut race.

Elf Team Tyrrell was a meticulous and shrewdly-managed outfit in the early 1970s, and its high standard of car preparation shows in this photograph of Cevert entering the Parabolica at Monza in 002 in the 1971 Italian GP.

Ferrari 312T was another brilliant car of the 1970s, here in its 1975 form and driven by Lauda. That year both championships fell to Ferrari.

McLaren M23 was a sterling design, which like Tyrrell 002 and the Williams FW07 made nonsense of the derogatory implication sometimes built into the use of 'Cosworth kit car'. The low airbox marks this out as an M23 in 1976 form, and so far that matter does James Hunt in the cockpit. Watson follows in a Penske PC4.

In the late 1970s Frank Williams' team became a force in Grand Prix racing with the compact cars in the FW07 series designed by Patrick Head. This is a 1980 FW07B, driven by Alan Jones in the pairing that took both championships. Its skirt is firmly on the Dutch track surface, it was exemplary in ground effects respects and great care was taken to ensure a clean airflow over the upper surfaces.

Wing cars. Others may have dabbled with under-car aerodynamics, but Colin Chapman brought ground effects aerodynamics to racing, where despite skirt bans and flat-bottom regulations this is still a very important aspect of car design. The Lotus 78 (**top**) was the original, though seen here in 1978 rather than 1977. Bristle skirts have given way to rigid skirts, and while this car had looked sleek in 1977 it appeared almost ponderous beside the 79 (**above**) in 1978. The 78 was the car Andretti described as 'Black Beauty'. Drivers are Peterson, in the 78, and Andretti in the 79 he drove to win the World Championship.

There may have been a fair amount of Cooper in the Flather Steel Special, but at least it looked different. Driver is Spike Rhiando, who gave the car its first race at Brands Hatch in April 1951, but is here on one of those scenic British airfield circuits.

FOGLIETTI

This minor Italian constructor introduced a front-engined Formula Junior car in 1958 and continued with it through 1959. It had a tubular chassis and the normal Fiat engine and gearbox, with an offset to allow the drive line to pass to the right of the cockpit. It was a handsome little machine, but like so many of its Italian contemporaries it was out-moded before it turned a wheel.

The F3 Foglietti which appeared in 1964 was a neat rear-engined car, quite conventional in aspects such as its space frame and suspension, and usually with Ford power units (one did run with a DKW engine). It was hardly successful – in the first year of 1-litre F3 odd top-six places fell to Foglietti, but after that the cars were no more than grid fillers.

The F3 Foglietti was a petite, clean-lined car, but that was almost the norm for the mid-1960s. In this photograph the driver is possibly of more interest for he is Antonio Ascari Jr, 'Tonino', son of Alberto, in his only serious season of single-seater racing.

FOOTWORK

The Ohashi Group, an international conglomerate with interests ranging from heavy industry to retailing and hotels, initiated a racing programme with its Footwork Sports Racing Team and became a constructor as Footwork Formula Limited in 1988, discarding the former 'Mooncraft' name for its cars. Owner Watara Ohasi encouraged the team's ambitions with a factory that was appropriate to its target of entering F1 in 1990.

In the event, the Footwork Group acquired a major shareholding in Arrows towards the end of 1989.

The approach was through F3000, with March and Reynard chassis in the Japanese series and occasionally in Europe in 1988; in late-1988 All-Japan F3000 series races Footwork's own MC-031 and MC-040 cars, designed by Takuya Yara, were run and Dave Scott achieved two top-ten placings with the former.

In 1989 a parallel team was set up under John Wickham to contest the European F3000 series. Despite the sensible decision to bring in 'local expertise' there were to be no instant successes – graduation from Japanese racing to European second-level racing was not simple.

MC-041 This was a conventional car, in appearance and make-up, with a carbon fibre monocoque and twin wishbone suspension all round, pushrod at the front and pullrod at the rear. The power of the Mugen engine was almost taken for granted and the car's shortcomings appeared to be in its weight and handling. Ukyo Katayama failed to achieve competitive times and Damon Hill took over the drive in mid-season, at least qualifying the car reasonably well in the rest of the season.

MC-041 looked competent, if a little bulky, but in F3000 in 1989 it was not competitive with Lola and Reynard, or even the solitary March.

FRAZER NASH

Frazer Nash was always prepared to make a single-seater version of its Bristol-engined Le Mans Replica sports car and in 1952 Peter Bell, an entrant who ran his team under the name 'Scuderia Franera', ordered a Mk2 chassis for his driver Ken Wharton. Like the sports car it had a ladder frame, front suspension by transverse leaf and lower wishbones, and a live rear axle suspended by longitudinal torsion bars and located by an 'A' bracket. It was fitted with a tight body with a long air duct and Frazer Nash's usual disc wheels with knock off hub nuts, and looked something like a Cooper-Bristol. However, it was heavier than a Cooper and shared its lack of power, and its road holding was limited by the live rear axle.

The car was raced in the 1952 International Trophy where Wharton finished sixth in his heat and seventh in the final. In the Swiss GP he was way down the grid – 23 seconds off the pace – but he plugged around steadily and, though lapped twice, finished fourth to take the only World Championship points of his career. Wharton was then third in the Eifelrennen, though the major teams were absent, and ninth in his heat of the Monza GP, only to retire in the final when the A bracket broke. At Spa he crashed, then he was back for the Dutch GP two months later, when the back axle broke. The only other appearance was in a minor race at Turnberry when the engine gave up.

A second Frazer Nash single-seater was built for the Scottish amateur Bill Skelly with a different body, while a third car went to the Irish enthusiast, R.E. Odlum. Both confined their racing to club events.   ML

FREIKAISERWAGEN

Not to be confused with the successful pre-War sprint car of the same name, the 1948 500cc car, nicknamed 'Wee Frike', was named after the same men, Joe Fry who drove it and Dick Caesar who designed it. This was one of the original batch of Iotas and, in effect, a prototype for the Iota P1.

At first a Cross rotary-valve motor cycle engine was fitted but it overheated and a JAP engine was substituted. Not far into its career, Fry was killed at the wheel in a sprint event at Blandford. The car passed into the hands of the veteran racer, Jack Moor, who called all his cars 'Wasp' and painted them in yellow and black stripes. Moor fitted a 'double knocker' Norton engine, converted the rear suspension to double wishbones, and this fourth Wasp became quite a successful car.   ML

FREISS

Rhiel Freiss from Alsace made a passing nod to the Franco-German nature of his home region by building the first French 500 car to use a BMW engine. Front engined and very pretty, when the bulk of the driver was removed, it looked like a half-scale model of everyone's idea of a real 1950 racing car but of course it was entirely the wrong way to tackle F3.   ML

FRISCH

A German amateur racer named Frisch called his pioneer 500cc car a 'Cooper', presumably to gain credibility with organizers in the days when German racing was not international, but it was only a Cooper copy.   ML

FRM

Heinz Maltz's Formula Junior Tigerjet seemed to owe something of its inspiration to a cereal packet cut-out racing car, with its 'rocket ship' body – near-oval cross section, small nose intake and a much larger hole at the rear, topped by a large fin. The whole thing was built around a multi-tubular chassis, sat high up on VW-based suspension and was propelled by a Hartmann-tuned DKW engine. This Munich device appears to have no circuit record.

The FJ Tigerjet speaks for itself, as Herr Maltz goes hill climbing. The nose looks as if it might have jet aircraft engine origins.

FRY

A one-off F2 car designed by David Fry and intended for Stuart Lewis-Evans to race in 1959, a plan that was thwarted by his fatal accident. Mike Parkes, who had helped with the design and construction of the car, raced it in British events that year. It was an odd-looking 1.5-litre Climax-engined machine, with a part-monocoque centre section. Lack of success on the circuits spelled the end for the project.

The photograph speaks for the car, which was one of those occasional pieces of racing machinery that really did look different. Parkes is the driver in this Mallory Park shot, sitting much closer to the steering wheel than was fashionable. Most of his upper body projects out of the shallow cockpit, and where did he put his long legs?

G

GARFORD

Gordon Gartside built one of the early British Formula Junior cars, based on a Cooper 500. It had a Ford 105E engine in its tubular chassis clothed in fibreglass bodywork, and independent suspension front and rear.

GAS BARRACUDA

The origins of the name of this obviously American Formula Junior car are lost. It appeared in 1960, with a front-mounted Crosley engine and Fiat gearbox, tubular chassis, wishbone and coil spring front suspension and a live rear axle. That was not a recipe for success. The Crosley was a 750cc engine and the car was entered in one of the additional two power/weight classes which the Americans adopted briefly.

GEMINI

The Chequered Flag team raced an assortment of sports cars for fun in the late 1950s. When Graham Warner decided to take it into single-seater racing he acquired the one-off Moorland Formula Junior car as a basis for a limited-production model and Leslie Redmond came with the project as development engineeer. The name Gemini was chosen simply because it was Warner's birth sign.

Warner was largely responsible for succeeding cars, as The Flag showed signs of becoming a serious constructor, especially as its first mid-engined car was raced successfully by some prominent drivers. That promise was not sustained and in the second half of the 1960s the team reverted to racing other constructors' cars, notably the F3 Brabhams in 1966. There followed a much less happy episode with the quasi-works McLarens. Meanwhile two F3 chassis were built for DAF, to be run with the Dutch company's Variomatic transmission, and campaigned in F3 in 1967. At the end of the decade Warner ran down The Flag's racing commitment, briefly entered the rally world, then gave up competition.

MkII The Moorland design was reworked by Redmond and re-emerged late in 1959 as the Gemini MkII. It was a neatly packaged car with a deep space frame and independent

The nose band picks this out as a works MkII before the Junior Grand Prix at Monaco in 1960. The car looked small and neat among the Italian front-engined contenders although to modern eyes the lower wishbones and fixed-length driveshafts arrangement at the rear looks less than robust.

suspension all round. In common with most of its contemporaries it would accept BMC A series or Ford 105E engines, but a BMC gearbox was standard while like other front-engined cars a transfer box was used to lower the transmission line. It was driven on its debut by Jim Clark in his first single-seater race. The intention was to build six cars but eventually 30 were produced, most of them going to the USA.

MkIII Lotus principles, as demonstrated in the 18, were followed in this car, although outwardly it was admirably sleek where the 18 was bluff. The engine mounting was low, fuel was carried in flank tanks and suspension was a normal wishbones/coil springs/dampers combination with radius arms at the rear. Cosworth's Ford 105E was the usual power unit, driving through a four-speed Renault gearbox in the first car, with a five-speed unit in the definitive cars. These came at the end of 1960 – the prototype had been running since the summer – and were designated MkIIIA, with lighter body and chassis standardized and outwardly a longer nose.

The first MkIII at Brands Hatch in August 1960. The small 13in wheels underlined the visual impression that this was a small car.

MkIV Largely designed by Warner, this appeared almost hesitantly in the spring of 1962, and it did not uphold Gemini's position – FJ's big three in its last two seasons were Lotus, Cooper and Brabham, and the MkIV did not win a major event. It was advanced in specification, with inboard suspension, inboard brakes and a troublesome six-speed gearbox by Jack Knight. Its appearance might have seemed to have owed something to Edwardian wind-cutting ideas, but given a downforce nose instead of a sharp point its side-radiator layout would have been in the forefront a decade later.

A MkIVA came in 1963, the last year of Junior racing, when only Roy Pike posed any sort of a threat in a Gemini, and one appeared in F2 guise in 1964.

The MkIV was distinctly innovative in its lines, which were beautifully smooth. The driver was in a semi-reclining position, and side radiators helped cut the frontal area.

GIAUR

Attilio Giannini was an engine conversion specialist in the 1930s, and after the Second World War he went into partnership with Bernardo Taraschi to build small sports cars carrying the name Giaur (GIAnnini and URania, from Taraschi's earlier cars). A single-seater version was built for the 750cc Italian F3 and when Italy turned to the international half-litre formula in 1951 a variant with a linered-down single-ohc Fiat four-cylinder engine was essayed. The Giaur was beautifully made, but overweight and front-engined, with spiral bevel final drive and rigid rear axle. It was generally no match for machines like Coopers. Taraschi did, however, enjoy moments of glory when he won Italy's first 500cc F3 event at Caracalla, when the category was in an 'exploratory' phase south of the Alps in 1950, and 1951 he led a good-class international field at Genoa, but only briefly and four Cooper exponents finished ahead of him.

A revival in national 750cc racing in 1954 was more attractive than the declining F3, so Giaur turned back to it, while Giannini dallied with a supercharged F1 project which Taraschi drove in the Rome GP. The company then concentrated on its small sports cars and Giannini Automobili reverted to tuning production cars, while Costruzioni Meccaniche Giannini undertook engine conversions and its own power units in the 1960s. The single-seater provided the basis for the Taraschi Junior of 1958.

GILBY

Syd Greene ran a Maserati 250F and sports Maseratis from his Gilby Engineering Company premises in the mid-1950s, and became a minor constructor late in the decade when Len Terry designed the first Gilby, a sports-racing car. For 1961 Terry designed the straightforward space-framed F1 Gilby, which followed conventional lines and had a Coventry Climax FPF engine. The design was modified to accept a BRM V-8 in 1962, initially running with the vertical exhaust stacks that featured on contemporary BRMs. Keith Greene drove it to good placings in secondary events, and was 15th in the 1961 British GP. It was sold to Ian Raby, who raced it in minor events in 1963.

Drivers: Keith Greene, Ian Raby.

The Climax-engined Gilby in the 1961 Brussels GP. The car was wholly conventional, but had distinctive lines around the nose and the cockpit.

GINETTA

The Walklett brothers' company has long been a small-scale sports car specialist, and like others it started on single-seater programmes in the 1960s. The G8 of 1964 was a most original F3 design, in that the chassis comprised a steel perimeter frame with two fibreglass shells bonded together over it (one inner, one outer) to form a strong monocoque. In other respects the G8 was conventional, and outwardly sleek. Three were laid down, and the works car raced by Chris Meek showed promise, before development was halted. At the same time the space frame G9 F2 project was stopped.

A late-1960s return to single-seaters was sensibly cut short when only the G17 and G18 for minor categories had been built, although considerable work was done on the G19 F3 project (based on the Formula Ford G18) and construction of the BRM-powered G20 F1 car was started (both were abandoned).

GLADSTONE

J.P. Gladstone's 500 special had a promising specification for 1949 with its Fiat front suspension and independent rear by rubber in tension, but its builder was short of money and could only fit a very tired JAP engine.   ML

GORDINI

Amédée Gordini made his name in the 1930s with his tuning activities and Simca-Fiat based sports cars, and through to 1951 Gordini remained attached to Simca. The first Simca-Gordini single seater came in 1946, a simple 1100cc car which was light and nimble – virtues that were to apply to most of Gordini's cars. A 1220cc version followed in 1947 and a 1430cc version in 1948, then a 1490cc variant. At that time Simca backed away from Gordini's project for an unsupercharged GP car, so for 1950 he added a supercharger to the four-cylinder engine to transform it into a GP unit.

He also confused his overworked little team by trying to run the same cars in F1 and F2, superchargers being added or taken off as required. He played the same game with a new four-cylinder engine in 1951, when the team achieved nothing and Simca despaired, ending the association.

Gordini seemed to thrive on the financial adversity of the following years, although little development work could be committed to his six-cylinder cars. The first season of F2 World Championship racing in 1952 saw his team score one outstanding victory in a non-title race at Reims and gain some respectable Championship race placings. The six was enlarged for the 2.5-litre Formula, and an eight-cylinder engine introduced, but the tide was flowing strongly against simplistic operations with outmoded cars. The team did not contest a full programme in 1956, and just struggled on into 1957, when an F2 design was not built. That year the team and the marque just faded away, and Amédée Gordini undertook development work for Renault.

Four-cylinder cars The first monoplace Simca-Gordinis were built around Simca 6CV components – four-cylinder pushrod ohv engine (which with only three main bearings was a little fragile), front suspension, rigid rear axle (with torsion bars) and gearbox, with a delicate tubular frame and shapely little body. The first 1100cc engine produced 65bhp, and the 1490cc version was rated at 115bhp in 1948. With a single-stage Wade supercharger the 1.5-litre unit was a Grand Prix engine in 1950, but the GP Simca-Gordini lacked speed as well as stamina. For 1951 there was a new square (78 x 78mm, 1491cc) five-bearing engine.

The original cars did well in *petites cylindrées* races. In F2 there were victories in 1950-1, but the cars were not really strong enough to challenge when main-line Ferraris were around. In 1950 Simca-Gordini drivers gained three World Championship points, but there were none in 1951 when only selected GPs were contested.

Drivers (in GPs): Amédée Gordini, Robert Manzon, André Simon, Maurice Trintignant.

A pretty little blue car – Jean-Pierre Wimille in a Simca-Gordini voiturette at Lausanne in 1948.

Six-cylinder cars For 1952 Gordini designed a straight six (75 x 75mm, 1988cc) on the lines of the previous four, to power F2 cars that in other major respects also followed the last Simca-Gordinis – indeed, the first carried a 1951 body. Such were the constraints on the team that the second car was completed only just in time for the first Championship race. The cars showed well in regional GPs, and there was a great day for the équipe when Behra drove one to beat the otherwise all-conquering Ferrari in a non-Championship race at Reims. In Championship terms Gordini drivers scored 17 points. This was progress but it was also a peak; there were just four points in 1953 as unreliability hit hard.

Drivers: (1952-53 GPs): Jean Behra, B. Bira, Robert Manzon, Robert Mieres, Maurice Trintignant.

The simple lines of the F2 Gordini accurately reflect its make-up, although attractive bodies were contrived on the straight tube chassis. The rigid rear axle was one of the more notorious weak points.

For the 2.5-litre Grands Prix that came in 1954 Gordini enlarged the engine, to 2473cc (80 x 82mm), but economies dictated that with few other minor changes, such as the addition of anti-roll bars, the cars had to serve on. The engine's 220bhp exceeded only a couple of minor British power units and fell well short of German and Italian rivals. As the championship opened, two fifth places fell to Gordinis,

but that level of performance was not matched in 1955, as Gordini worked to complete a new car. In the next year his drivers preferred the old sixes, da Silva Ramos driving one to a last points-scoring finish, at Monaco, while Manzon actually won the secondary Naples race. In 1957 that race saw the last Gordini entry, when a six was run.

Drivers (1954-56 GPs): Elie Bayol, Jean Behra, Robert Manzon, André Pilette, Hernando da Silva Ramos, Harry Schell, André Simon.

The old cars were tidied up a little for 1956, with a revised scuttle line, new screen and cockpit sides. This is Pilette on his way to last place in the French GP.

Eight-cylinder cars A completely new Gordini was a novelty, and the T32 straight eight unveiled at Montlhéry late in the summer of 1955 looked promising. Gordini clung to a ladder-type tubular chassis, but used independent suspension all round and the Messier disc brakes that had been brought in on the late sixes. Its straight eight (75 x 70mm, 2498cc) was the last of the type in a formula car and was initially rated at 250bhp, although that figure was revised down at the end of the year. It had a corpulent body, which was smooth only until the realities of racing called for revision. Only two were built, and they proved large, heavy and uncompetitive. The Gordini eight was last seen at Pau early in 1957.

Drivers: Elie Bayol, André Guelfi, Robert Manzon, André Milhoux, André Pilette, Hernando da Silva Ramos.

Bayol practising at Monaco in 1956. This car has the original full-width nose (a more conventional one was later devised) and the shortest of the three types of exhaust used – the longest extended almost to the rear wheels. The outlet for under-bonnet air (below the mirror) was added in 1956, as was the intake alongside the cockpit for inboard rear brake cooling air.

GOTTENS

The Gottens was a conventional 1951 500 car fitted with a BMW engine but was unusual in that it came from Holland.

ML

GOZZOLI

This car hardly set the 1.6-litre F3 world on fire when it appeared in 1971, or in 1972 when Paulo Minozzi drove a full Italian season in it for Modena Corse – in 13 races, he recorded two finishes, the best a seventh place in a Monza race. It used a Nova-Ford engine, and apparently had no unusual features in its make-up.

GRAC

The Groupe de Recherches Automobiles de Course built cars for *Formule France* at Valence in the second half of the 1960s and entered F3 in 1969 with a car that was so hopeless that both works drivers quit. Patron and designer, Serge Asiomanoff, came back with the promising MT11 in 1970, but Denis Dayan's fatal accident at Rouen spelled the end for this little enterprise. One car was independently adapted for the 1.6-litre F3, with little prospect of success.

MT8 This was a short wheelbase space frame car most notable for its bulky, and by all accounts quite ineffectual, wedge body. Front suspension was by top links, and lower wishbones, with twin radius arms at the rear. The original plan was to use RPM-prepared engines, but GRAC was to turn to Novamotor. The car was raced by Jean Max, for whom tenth place in its debut race at Pau was a high point. He drove a Tecno in 1970.

The parallel M8A had conventional bodywork and was driven by Philippe Vidal, but by mid-season he had gone back to a Tecno.

The MT8 looked quite exceptionally ponderous, and its performance was never exhilarating. Max is driving it towards its best finish, at Pau.

MT11 A plated space frame car, with fibreglass bodywork, as compact as a Tecno and like the Italian car run with its Nova engine exposed. Suspension was similar to the earlier car, and rear brakes were inboard of the wheels, as there was no room within them.

The MT11 was hardly neat, especially with the exposed clutter at the rear, but it promised to be competitive. The backs of the two radiator air outlets are roughly above the sheet strengthening the chassis. The bulge of a side fuel tank can be seen in this Montlhéry shot.

Run as a Veglia-GRAC, the MT11 looked competitive, and Denis Dayan (1969 *Formule France* champion with an MT10) finished fifth between Beuttler and Jarier in the second French F3 race of 1970, but his death after an accident in this car brought the project to an abrupt end.

GRAF

A one-off F3 car devised by driver/entrant Franz Graf in 1966, this was unusual in having a Simca-based engine but was entirely predictable in its modest success rate – one fifth place in a local German event.

GRD

Group Racing Developments came into being under the wing of a Norfolk light engineering company, Griston, in 1971. There was no coincidence in it taking shape as Lotus withdrew from production racing car manufacture, and most of the personnel came from Hethel – Mike Warner, Lotus Racing designer Dave Baldwin, and two leading technicians, Derek Wild and Gordon Huckle (who was credited with the GRD concept). They took a phoenix as the GRD emblem. Jo Marquart, then with Huron, joined them as GRD's designer.

The intention was to move into the market vacated by Lotus Racing, to compete with Brabham – soon to drop customer cars – and March, and the plan seemed to take shape well. GRD merged with DART for 1973, after Denys Dobbie precipitately parted with Rondel (and the Rondel Dart projects) late in 1972, the idea being that DART would run a team closely associated with the works. The arrangement was for five years, but early in 1974 Dobbie pulled out and in November 1974 GRD production abruptly ceased as sales prospects for 1975 were discouraging. Three former employees set up a service operation, then a year later Ralph Firman took this on and the 375 design was adopted as the Van Diemen-GRD F3 car, with new body and other revisions. Effectively GRD soon disappeared.

Through most of GRD's existence a single-seater design served with minor changes for F2 (initially 272), F3 (initially 372) and Formula B/Atlantic; as the design was uprated through succeeding years, the designations followed, hence 275 (F2) and 375 (F3) for 1975. The first car completed, in September 1971 was a 272 for John McConnell, who intended to use it, in F2 form, in Tasman racing and then in Canada as a Formula B car.

Marquart's first GRD design served the company well, and in the early 1970s was outstanding in F3. Robarts' car at Silverstone in 1973 shows the 372/373 characteristics well.

An aluminium bathtub monocoque formed the centre section of the basic design, with tubular sub frames front and rear, conventional suspension and fibreglass bodywork. The lines were distinctive – smooth and wedge-shaped, with prominent side-mounted radiators – but the car did appear large and did exceed formula weights. The biggest change came for 1974, when a front radiator with top exit duct was introduced, allowing for a slimmer body. The nose was slimmer on late cars, and that modification was carried through to the Van Diemen version, together with a larger pylon-mounted rear wing. Updating kits, including new chassis and sub frames, were offered in 1975. The F2 specification included an FG400 gearbox, while the F3 cars had Hewland Mk9 'boxes.

In F2 a works car was run occasionally in 1972, Wisell showing that it could be competitive, and the situation was really no better in 1973 despite the number of teams using GRDs (including DART, Wheatcroft, Team Nippon and Troberg's ambitious Swedish team). But Wheatcroft switched to a March for Williamson in mid season, and GRD did not feature in F2 in 1974.

In F3 the car looked promising from the start, and in 1972 Roger Williamson dominated the season in a Holbay-engined car, while Andy Sutcliffe showed well. In 1973 GRD seemed to rest on its laurels. Alan Jones was consistently successful with a Vegantune-powered 373 and Robarts won some races; other drivers such as Henton turned away from GRD during the season. There seemed to be internal discord at GRD during the year, and then the company began to fade, although a high point was achieved by Zorzi when he won the Monaco F3 race in a Lancia-engined GRD.

The 1974 car followed contemporary fashion, but never fulfilled its promise. For 1975 there was a more shapely nose and a fuller engine cover, as well as a larger rear wing.

GREIFZU

Until his death in a race at Dresden in 1952, Paul Greifzu was a considerable force in post-war German racing with his BMW special, a sleek offset F2 car. Little known outside Germany, he was easily the most successful driver of the immediate post-War period and his performances suggest he might have been of Grand Prix calibre. After his death, his widow entered the car for other drivers in East Germany for a few more years with some success, and today his engine has an honoured place in the Wartburg Museum.   ML

GRENFELL SPECIAL

J. Granville Grenfell built his F3 car in 1951 largely to prove theories. He had raced motorcycles against the likes of Nuvolari in the 1920s when he was a Lancia engineer, and was a little old for active participation in the hurly-burly of half-litre racing (he did test drive his car but Powell-Richards first raced it). In overall terms the car was a rear-engined 500, but at the front it had swing axle suspension with damping by pneumatic struts mounted to the chassis just ahead of the 'instrument panel'. A wide track meant that the front brakes could be mounted inboard of the wire wheels at the front. At the rear Grenfell used a live axle with quarter elliptics. The car, it was reported, worked well, but with a Triumph Twin engine it was never going to be a contender, although it was run until the very end of 500cc F3 racing. It was designated T2, and an assumption is that T1 was Grenfell's first half-litre car, which he built in 1913!

GROSE

Bill Grose's first 500 special was oddly described as looking like a 'mini Mercedes-Benz' – it was actually rear-engined. One of the best-made of the home-constructed cars it was Norton-powered and had all-independent suspension using Standard Eight front units. Grose ran it between 1948 and 1951 without achieving any special success.

Illness kept Bill Grose away from the circuits for nearly two years but he was back in 1953 with a car with a bullet nose and unusual rear suspension; at first glance it appeared to have broad upper wishbones, but these were in fact locating rods for the swing axles, which were sprung by rubber bands. Again, the car reflected credit on its builder but it achieved little in the way of results.   ML

Bill Grose' first F3 car near the end of its career, looking neat and well cared for, but far from handsome with those pressed wheels.

GRS

The designation TC001 was only too appropriate, as this F2 car turned out to be a one-off. It was laid out by one-time ATS and Maurer engineer Günther Richter ('GR') along conventional lines, and built by John Thompson. The power unit was a Mader-BMW, and there were problems with the engine and its installation. The car appeared at only two Championship meetings in 1981 – driver Jochen Dauer had little experience in F2, and started in the GRS once, at Hockenheim where he completed 15 laps. The team had only limited funds and these ran out.

GS

Nicknamed the 'Squanderbug', Gerald Spink's GS1 had a Rudge engine and Norton gearbox mounted in the back of a Dural deep-member chassis with Morgan sliding pillar front suspension and a form of the same system at the rear. It won admiration for its high standard of finish (Spink worked for an aircraft maker) but was too underpowered to be successful.

Spink's second completed 500cc F3 car was designated GS3 and was based on a Fiat Topolino frame, front suspension and steering. The rear set-up was derived from the Monaco, with pivoting suspension arms. Its Norton engine fed power, via chain drive, to both wheels. Like the first GS, it was a well made little car but its roadholding left a lot to be desired.

ML

GVB

A German 500 car constructed like a miniature Grand Prix machine with a front-mounted BMW engine and shaft drive.

ML

GWYNIAD

A pair of Formula Junior cars was built to a design by Les Redmond after the short-lived Heron episode (see also Heron), and followed that car's layout. They were successful in that one actually headed a British FJ race. The cars were also known as the Diggory Gwyniad after Wrexham patron Jim Diggory. If the closely associated Envoy, Heron and Gwyniad ventures could have come together the outcome might have been worthwhile. Diggory ran the Gwyniads for part of the 1961 season, then turned his back on them.

H

HALSON

This was one of the earliest British Formula Junior cars, made by the Halson Trading Company of Newhaven. It followed the front-engined/live rear axle Italian pattern, with a tubular chassis, 'classic' wire wheels, a BMC A series engine and nicely-proportioned overall lines. This was one of the very first British Juniors to compete outside Britain, running at Monaco in 1959.

HAR

Horace Richards was an enthusiast from Smethwick who owned an engineering works which built him an F2 car in 1952. A 2-litre Riley engine was fitted into a ladder frame and suspension was independent all round by unequal length wishbones and torsion bars. An Elektron casting housed the differential and at the front of the casting were two spur gears which allowed the prop shaft to run very low under the driver's seat. Changing them made a total of six final drive ratios available.

It was unusually well made for a one-off, but when it raced, mainly in minor British events, it was invariably on the back row of the grid and generally last to finish. Since it was only ever driven by Richards, there is no way of knowing whether the fault lay with the car or the driver.

When the 2.5-litre F1 came along in 1954, Richards continued to enter his car in non-Championship British F1 events and the odd F2 race until the end of 1955. Richards' usual performance was last on grid and last in the race, often finishing 'not classified'.

A second chassis was built for Bertie Bradnack in 1952, and was apparently to be Bristol-powered. It was entered in a couple of races under the name 'Woden' but did not actually race. Later the chassis was used as the basis of a Jaguar-powered sports car.   ML

HARTMANN

Alfred Hartmann was one of several South German constructors attracted by the paper promise of the DKW three-cylinder two-stroke in the first international season of Formula Junior. By its second season the shortcomings were all too evident, and by its third the engines and the front-engined layout, which Auto Union-DKW apparently encouraged, had largely disappeared. More than most, Hartmann was a DKW man – a member of the works motorcycle team in the 1930s, a rally driver in a DKW after the war, constructor of a DKW-powered sports-racing car in the 1950s, and engine preparation expert. In 1959 he claimed 79bhp from his version of the 980cc engine; that was a little less than some other DKW experts, and like their engines his probably produced the claimed power – for short periods.

All his Juniors, Mk I – Mk III came in 1959, had simple ladder-type chassis, and suspension comprising lower wishbone and transverse spring at the front and transverse leaf spring with rigid axle at the rear. A pair of cars was run in a Hartmann team and a few were sold. The only successes seem to have been in sprints.

HAWKE

David Lazenby, one-time manager of Lotus Components, set up Hawke in 1969 to build cars for minor categories, and that year Tom Walkinshaw won the Scottish Formula Ford championship in one of the DL wedge-shaped space frame cars. This line was followed through in the early 1970s as Hawke moved to Hoddesdon and then on to Ware. In 1974 Mike Keegan, chairman of British Air Ferries, had a controlling interest in the company, and in the next year quite a lot was said about a BAF F1 car that was to be designed by Adrian Reynard and built by Hawke.

The F1 car did not appear but a Reynard-designed F3 car did, and the intention was that once it was proved it would be put into production. It had an aluminium monocoque, with a substantial built-in roll cage, double wishbone front suspension, and despite the full-width nose coil springs/dampers were inboard. At the other end a delta-plan aerofoil was the most obvious feature, as the Nova-Toyota engine was neatly enclosed. Problems with the car were such that Rupert Keegan raced it only once in 1976.

The design was reworked by Pat Symonds, for Jan Lammers to race in the 1977 European F3 series. Outwardly the revised DL18 had a conventional rear wing and a new cockpit surround, which meant that the shapely engine cover had to be discarded. The car was no more successful, Hawke faded, and Lazenby's next racing commitment was to design the Pacer Formula Ford car for 1979.

Hartmann Mk III, with its DKW associations proclaimed by the linked rings badge inside the nose intake, and the standard steel disc wheels.

The Keegan family was never self-effacing and chose to launch DL18 on one of their BAF aircraft on a flight to Le Touquet, where Rupert posed in appropriate company. It was an attractive little car, too . . . .

HAYASHI

While Dome is better known internationally for its endurance cars, its associate company Hayashi had a much longer record in racing. It built single-seaters for a Japanese 500cc category in the 1970s and its first F3 car in 1980, continuing in this category through the first half of the decade, but slipping from the scene in the second half when F3 racing in Japan settled into a Ralt versus Reynard pattern.

The 803 followed March lines closely, with a sheet alloy monocoque, tubular sub frames fore and aft and inboard suspension all round. It was apparently insufficiently rigid, for designer Masao Ono concentrated on this in the 320 of 1981, another Toyota-engined car. It had very prominent side pods on 803 lines, but in the 320 these housed all the radiators and the car had a needle nose in place of the ponderous full-width nose of the 803.

Hayashi 803 marked the Suzuka company's entry into an international single-seater category. Outwardly the treatment was heavy, but under the skin it was seemingly less than robust.

The 1982 321 followed the same neat layout, and one appeared fleetingly in Europe, driven into tenth place in a Silverstone race by Osamu Nakako. It was a ground effects car, and the design was adapted for the flat-bottom regulations that took effect in Japan in 1984, as the 322. This was the last successful Hayashi F3 car.

The following year saw a completely new F3 Hayashi, the 330. Like the Ralt RT30 this was asymmetrical, with a full side pod on the left and a vestigial pod on the right. A sheet alloy tub was used again, with a carbon fibre top. It was not competitive, but was the basis for the 1986 331, which was apparently even less competitive in the Ralt-dominated Japanese series. Nothing had come of Hayashi ambitions to export chassis, for F3 or Formula Atlantic use.

The 321 matched its European contemporaries as a straightforward good-looking car.

HB SPECIAL

Hector Bossaert's front-engined 500 car was one of the first built in Belgium. At first it used a Zundapp engine, then a BMW with which Bossaert achieved the apex of his 500 career with third place in the GP des Frontières meeting at Chimay in 1953.

ML

At least Bossaert's one-off F3 car was different, with its engine ahead of the driver, and a Zundapp unit at that. The designer/constructor is at the wheel, at Brands Hatch in 1952.

HECK-BMW

Ernst Klodwig, an East Berliner, made this mini-Auto Union ('heck' is German for 'rear') in the early 1950s using VW suspension parts, a BMW 328 engine and wheels and, presumably, a VW transmission. One has to say presumably since so little is known about the car, most of its competition history having taken place behind the Iron Curtain. Still, Klodwig not only entered it in the 1952 and 1953 German GPs but drove it to the Nürburgring with all his kit strapped on.

He was obviously long on enthusiasm but on both occasions he qualified at the back of the grid, over two minutes off the pace; although he finished 15th in 1953, he was three laps down. In the East German F2 series, against other BMW specials, Klodwig was on more familiar territory and gave a good account of himself, frequently finishing in the top three.

ML

HERON

This Formula Junior car was the product of a short-lived venture by Sewell and King of Chelmsford and S.J. Diggory Motors of Wrexham. Designed by Les Redmond, it was a

The first Heron, showing the orthodox wishbone and coil spring/damper suspension and relatively generous cockpit. The engine cover 'spine' and white flash is reminiscent of contemporary Coopers.

wholly conventional rear-engined space frame car, using the familiar Ford and VW engine/transmission combination. When it was announced late in 1960 a three car works team was proposed for 1961. Little more was heard of that and the prototype was sold to South Africa for local F1 use, with an Alfa Romeo engine. Sewell and King picked up their Envoy thread, Jim Diggory initiated the Gwyniad FJ car.

The prototype taken to South Africa by Tony Maggs was driven in the 1961 Gold Star series by Ernest Pieterse, who qualified it in mid-field for all four events. His best finish was sixth in the Rand GP. This car re-appeared in the 1964 Rand GP, driven by David Hume, who had problems in the second heat and was not classified.

HESKETH

Lord Alexander Fermor-Hesketh entered racing in 1972, running an F3 team equipped with Dastles – cars which had little to commend them – then moving on to F1 with James Hunt. The team caught popular attention because of its high-life and fun attitude, but the underlying intent was serious. That became apparent in 1973 when Dr Harvey Postlethwaite modified the team's March 731 and Hunt drove it to score 14 World Championship points that year.

It led to Hesketh cars, designed by Postlethwaite and built in the former stables of Hesketh's country home. The cars were quick, although reliability was often questionable. Hesketh was sixth in its first Championship season with its own cars (1974); in 1975 Hunt won the Dutch GP in a Hesketh, and the team was fourth in the Championship.

The apparently carefree approach of the first years had by then given way to a budget-concious approach, and at the end of the year Hesketh was to pull out, after last emotional efforts to find sponsorship had failed – perhaps the team's earlier playboy image had told against it. The then-latest cars were sold to Walter Wolf, but team manager Anthony 'Bubbles' Horsley carried on, running for paying drivers and keeping the name in GP racing. There were more new Heskeths in 1977, but the drivers hardly did justice to them and the team began to run down. It survived into 1978, and the cars lasted longer in British national racing. Hesketh Motors continued to associate the name with motor racing, as an engine rebuild and specialized fabrications company.

308 In this car Postlethwaite extended his 'developed March' theme, laying out a car that was sensible in that there were no design ventures into the unknown. Its monocoque was clothed in flat-topped bodywork that formed a gentle wedge in side elevation, while in plan form the fashionable 'Coke-bottle' lines were followed. Initially nose radiators were used, later they were positioned alongside the DFV. Suspension was orthodox and outboard front and rear, but late in 1974 rubber was first used as the springing medium, at the front.

The car first ran in competition in the Race of Champions, Hunt qualifying for pole but retiring with handling problems. That year he won the International Trophy at Silverstone and in Championship races scored 15 points, with three third places in GPs; Hesketh's sixth place in the Constructors' Championship was a worthy achievement.

In 1975 the car was run in 'B' form, appearing with both rubber cone suspension and normal coil springs. That year Hunt won the Dutch GP, was second in three GPs, and scored 28 of his 33 championship points in 308Bs. Cars were disposed of to independents, who achieved little in 1975, save for Ertl who was twice in the top ten. The 308D was a modest update of the design, which the rump of the team ran alongside 308Bs for paying drivers in 1976.

Drivers: Guy Edwards, Harald Ertl, James Hunt, Alan Jones, Brett Lunger, Torsten Palm, Alex Ribeiro, Rolf Stommelen.

Hunt in the original Hesketh in its patriotic colour scheme, in the 1974 International Trophy, when he scored the first of two victories for the Hesketh team.

Ertl in the British GP two years later, in a 308D entered by Hesketh Racing. Apart from radiators and aerofoils and the lack of a high airbox, the car has not changed greatly in appearance, nor had it in specification.

308C This was a smaller car – reducing frontal area and drag had priority with top designers at the time – with a shallow monocoque which was insufficiently rigid, a neat body with hip radiators, inboard-mounted Aeon rubber units in the

The shallow hull of the 308C can be deduced from the cockpit surround of the first car as Hunt drives it towards it first race finish, at Monza in 1975.

suspension, and of course DFV power. It first appeared in practice for the 1975 German GP, was first raced in the non-Championship Swiss GP, and in two Autumn races Hunt scored points with it. By that time it was being revised and strengthened and the theoretical virtues of narrow track were sacrificed in an effort to improve handling. When Hesketh gave up at the end of 1975 two 308Cs were sold to Walter Wolf re-emerging as Wolf-Williams FWO5s, with further strengthened chassis and suspension (see also Wolf).

Driver: James Hunt.

308E Horsley found the ways and means to carry on through 1977 and into 1978, but at a modest level at a time when modest efforts were not going to win Grands Prix. Frank Dernie designed the 308E on sensibly economic lines, with a conventional specification and outwardly a distinct taper from most angles and a sleek profile in side elevation. Keegan and Ertl achieved Hesketh's best placings in 1977 – seventh and ninth respectively – on the other hand Ashley and Rebaque each managed to qualify only once in six attempts. In 1978 the cars were entered for just seven Championship races, Cheever once getting one to a grid. The company then undertook work for other teams.

Drivers: Ian Ashley, Eddie Cheever, Derek Daly, Harald Ertl, Divina Galica, Rupert Keegan, Hector Rebaque.

The 308E, here in the 1978 colours of the car run briefly for Divina Galica, was attractive but circumstances meant that its potential was never properly exploited, or developed.

HH

Named for its designer, Hermann Holbein, the HH48 was one of the first German post-War F2 cars. Based on BMW 328 mechanicals and looking not unlike a stubby Alfetta, the HH48 and its successor the HH49 had new cylinder heads, a step-down drive train to give a low seating position, and an arrangement whereby the independent rear suspension could be made into a 'live' axle in under ten minutes.

The cars were only moderately successful and that, together with a lack of materials and funds, meant there was no HH50.
ML

HILL

Graham Hill set up his Embassy Racing Team in 1973, initially running a Shadow DN1 and then Lola T370s in 1974. He commissioned a developed version of this car for 1975, when it appeared as the Lola T371 but soon became known as the Hill GH1. Hill drove his last race in one of these cars, at Silverstone. He gave up driving to concentrate on running the team, which shaped up reasonably well in difficult circumstances in 1975, coming eleventh in the Constructors' Championship. It all ended abruptly late that year after tests with a new car at le Castellet. Hill's aircraft crashed in conditions of bad visibility on the approach to Elstree airfield. Graham Hill, designer Andy Smallman and driver Tony Brise were among those killed.

GH1 The car started life as a Lola, and designer Andy Smallman was seconded to the Embassy team by Lola to continue development. Four monocoques were made by TC Prototypes, as Hill's base in an unlovely factory estate west of London was still being set up.

The GH1 was a conventional Cosworth kit car, with double wishbone front suspension, twin lower links, single upper link and radius arms at the rear, and outboard coil spring/damper units all round. The DFV was accompanied by a Hewland FGA400.

The team hardly had time to settle. Hill retired, Stommelen crashed heavily at Barcelona when an experimental carbon-fibre rear wing support failed. Other drivers stood in (Jones most capably) and Hill was fortunate enough to contract Tony Brise. Jones and Brise scored the team's three points.

Drivers: Tony Brise, Graham Hill, Alan Jones, François Migault, Vern Schuppan, Rolf Stommelen.

The Embassy livery complemented the smart lines of GH1. This is Stommelen in the ill-fated GH1/2 in practice for the 1975 Spanish GP.

GH2 Smallman's distinctive little 1976 car was tested late in 1975, and apparently found wanting in several respects. It was of course set aside after Hill's accident, but the single car that was completed survives as a museum exhibit.

Tony Brise driving GH2 in its first check runs at Silverstone. All of Hill's cars looked well in Embassy's white and red colours.

HILL SPECIAL

A lightweight (452lb) 500 car on Kieft lines but with a wider track, this had a multi-tubular frame, double wishbone front suspension and swing axle at the rear, both sprung by rubber bands. A familiar sight at Brands Hatch in the 1950s, it was good enough to win the occasional heat. ML

HONDA

In the 1980s this Japanese company's competitions reputation rested on the solid foundation of its outstanding racing engines. It had earlier ventured into the Grand Prix world as a constructor, with much less assurance and much less success. Honda cars fell a long way short of achieving the dominant position of Honda racing motorcycles, showing a very modest return for a considerable expenditure of effort and ingenuity.

Honda's first move towards F1 came in 1962 when a Cooper chassis was acquired, the intention being to install a V-12 engine. This proved impractical, and work was switched to a complete car project, which took shape as RA271.

RA271 A single car was run in three exploratory GP outings in 1964. It was a space frame design, and interest focussed on its high-revving 60-degree V-12 engine (58.1 × 47mm, 1495cc), and the fact that this was mounted transversely.

Driver: Ronnie Bucknum.

RA272 Outwardly similar to the RA271, this was a more sophisticated monocoque car, with the V-12 carried in a tubular sub frame. In 1965 this engine had a 'safe' upper revs limit of 14,000rpm, and its claimed output of 240bhp at 11,000rpm made it the most powerful engine of the 1.5-litre formula (albeit with limitations such as the narrow effective revs range). A two-car team was run, Ginther taking two sixth places and then at the high altitude of Mexico City winning Honda's first (car) Grand Prix, and the last Grand Prix of the 1.5-litre formula.

Drivers: Ronnie Bucknum, Richie Ginther.

Ginther at Monaco in 1965. The transverse mounting of the V-12 made for a short engine bay and unusual overall proportions.

RA273 This bulky car made its noisy debut towards the end of the first 3-litre season, Ginther running second in the Italian GP before crashing. It had a conventional light alloy monocoque, and conventional suspension, with a 90-degree V-12 (78 × 52.1mm, 2992cc). This had roller bearings throughout, was big, and contributed substantially to the car's dry weight of 740kg (the formula minimum was 500kg in 1966). Its power output approached 400bhp in 1966 and a claimed 412bhp in 1967 was no more than adequate – 1967 was the year the DFV appeared, offering similar power with simplicity and low weight.

As far as Honda was concerned, it was also the year that John Surtees picked up the associations from his motor cycle days, joined the team as driver and technical-cum-general advisor, and was instrumental in setting up a British base. With some minor improvements, the RA273 was run until mid summer, but was discarded as soon as the RA300 was ready. Best placings for the RA273 were a third, in South Africa in 1967, and a fourth-place in each season.

Drivers: Ronnie Bucknum, Richie Ginther, John Surtees.

The RA273 looked a solid lump, and apart from weight there were problems with the engine, the transmission and road holding. This car is driven by John Surtees at Brands Hatch, where he finished second in a Race of Champions heat.

RA300 The 'Hondola', this lighter interim one-off was built by Lola around a monocoque from an Indianapolis car and in Lola's listing designated T130 (unlike the RA273, this monocoque ended at the rear bulkhead and a sub frame supported the engine). Other Lola parts such as suspension units were used as the car was rushed through in the summer of 1967. The engine was rated at 'over 400bhp', probably barely 400bhp, but at least weight was down by more than 100kg with most 'savings' coming in the chassis and fuel system. Surtees drove the RA300 to a surprise victory in its first GP, the Italian, and 1967 was Honda's best season in Constructors' Championship terms, the team being fourth. The RA300 also served at the start of the 1968 season.

Driver: John Surtees.

Surtees in the 'Hondola' that was built at his insistence in 1967. The tubular frame carrying the V-12 shows well, and so do the convoluted exhausts (when the engine was revised for 1968 these emerged low down on the outside).

RA301 The 1968 main-line car followed on from the RA300, with a less tubby monocoque extended to the rear to carry the engine, outboard front suspension, redesigned gearbox and heavily modified engine, outwardly distinguished by its exhausts on the outside and inlet ports in the vee. The output was given as 430bhp, to power a car certainly no lighter than the RA300. Generally a single car was run, but a second which had its rear suspension reworked by Len Terry appeared in the late-season races. In 1968 Honda slipped to sixth in the Constructors' Championship.

Drivers: Jo Bonnier, David Hobbs, John Surtees.

Surtees led at Spa in the RA301, but his best final placing was second in France. By the summer of 1968 the car had a rear wing and prominent nose tabs. This is Surtees in Mexico in 1968, in Honda's last Grand Prix.

RA302 This was an extraordinarily innovative car, with an air-cooled 120-degree V-8 (88 × 61.4mm, 2987cc), modestly rated at 385bhp at 9000rpm when it first appeared, but with development potential. Whether that promise could be found in other parts of the car was open to question. There was a short magnesium-skinned monocoque, with the front suspension mounted to the front bulkhead and the engine suspended from a boom which extended from the rear bulkhead. Little test work was carried out, by Surtees, who was opposed to the entry of the car in the French GP. Its driver, Jo Schlesser, was inexperienced and the exposed engine and its intakes were susceptible to wet conditions; the race started in rain, the V-8 cut out and Schlesser lost control, and died in the fierce fire that followed as the car turned over. A second RA302 was completed, to be driven by Hobbs and Surtees in practice for the Italian GP. It was not raced, and Honda withdrew from the Grands Prix.

Driver: Jo Schlesser.

The RA302 looked compact, but in wheelbase and track dimensions it was only slightly smaller than the Lotus 49, and by the standard set by that car it was an aesthetic mess. Schlesser appears to be fighting it during practice at Rouen.

HOOPER

One of the first Australian 500 cars, this was designed by Jack and William Hooper who were established motor cycle speedway engine tuners. The chassis was a semi-space frame (not properly triangulated) and suspension all round was by double wishbones and lateral quarter elliptical springs. A rear-mounted and highly-tuned pushrod Triumph engine was mated to a Norton gearbox. It was progressively modified and became the 'Norton Special', and later was sold to Austin Tauranac (see Norton Special). ML

HRG

In 1948 Peter Clarke, an HRG enthusiast, commissioned Marcus Chambers to build a single-seater for F2 based on a cut and shut HRG sports car chassis. It had a shortened wheelbase but retained the Vintage-style HRG suspension with solid front and rear axles suspended on quarter elliptical springs. Power came from a modified 1998cc Standard Vanguard engine which gave, at most, 115bhp and which drove through a Standard three-speed gearbox.

It was a case of enthusiasm beating common sense because the car had nothing to commend it except that Cooper Cars made a good job of building the bulbous body. The car ran in a few races in 1949 and was then put to one side. Despite its dismal history it was revived in 1952 and entered for Mike Keen in the International Trophy where Keen, a good driver, failed to qualify. ML

HRUBON

This French F3 car was built for the second season of 1.6-litre F3 racing, 1972, when it failed to make an impact. It was of monocoque construction, with a tubular sub frame for its Nova engine, side radiators and inboard suspension. In overall appearance it was not unlike a contemporary F1 Tyrrell.

HURON

Huron Auto Race Developments was formed at the end of 1970 and did not see out the Summer of 1971. Canadian Jack Smith was the managing director, hence the maple leaf emblem, and his fellow directors were Jo Marquart and Roy Ireland. An ambitious programme which included an F2/F3/Formula Atlantic car, with Formula Ford and sports-racing cars to follow, was announced early in 1971. The first single-seater, completed in the early Spring of 1971, was a monocoque car with semi-stressed engine, nose radiators (with nose-top air exits recalling Marquart's then-recent McLaren past), inboard lower wishbone/top rocker front suspension, and parallel lower links rear suspension with coil springs/dampers outboard but brakes inboard. The programme was hardly under way before it started to fall apart with personnel reshuffles. Expectations that Hawke might take the company over, or acquire its assets as it went into liquidation in the Summer, were not fulfilled. Marquart went off to the infant GRD and the last sign of a Huron was in the layout of an Arian FF car a couple of years later.

HVEZDA

A conventional F3 one-off built by Jirí Bulíček in 1955, with a rear-mounted Jawa ohc engine, ladder frame, transverse leaf front suspension and live rear axle. It was a neat little car and apart from its wire-spoked wheels had the look of a slim-nosed Cooper.

HWM

In retrospect HWM was one of the lesser footnotes to racing history, but in the early 1950s it was very important to British enthusiasts, for the cars were top-ten contenders in Championship races and were driven by some of the outstanding drivers of a new generation.

Hersham and Walton Motors was founded by George Abecassis and John Heath, and its second car was an Alta-powered sports-racer that could be stripped of its simple sports appendages and run in F2 guise. It was raced through 1949 and was the forerunner of the 1950 F2 cars, when a successful team was run. HWM was the first British works team to contest international single-seater events in Europe since 1939.

HWM continued in F2 through its two World Championship years, 1953-4, although there was little development potential in the Alta engine and the cars were increasingly outclassed. A 2.5-litre F1 development was tried in 1954, but this never promised to be competitive; one lingered on into 1955 when single-seaters adapted to take the 3.4-litre Jaguar engine for *formule libre* also appeared. That pointed the way HWM was going – back to sports-car racing. John Heath was killed in a 1956 Mille Miglia accident and HWM racing activities were soon abandoned.

HWM-Alta The first car was a sports car, the second a dual-purpose sports/F2 car, which consequently was over-weight when it was run in formula guise. It had a straightforward tubular chassis, transverse-leaf ifs and a live rear axle with quarter-elliptics. The inclined-ohv Alta four-cylinder engine drove through a preselector gearbox.

1950 F2 Four cars were built as HWMs for F2 racing in 1950, following the general lines of the 1949 car, but with transverse-leaf independent suspension at the rear as well as the front. They were still offset single-seaters, with an eye to mounting sports-car bodies. The Alta engine was rated at 130bhp, which realistically was not enough to allow their drivers to compete with Ferraris and Maseratis, save that there were some performances, notably by young Moss, which showed that paper theories can sometimes be set aside. Claes won at Chimay, Moss was beaten by two Alfa Romeo 158s at Bari and won a heat in the F2 Naples race (where Macklin was second overall), while in the GP de Mons the cars finished 6-7-8-9. The Swiss GP marked the first appearance of HWMs in a grande épreuve, Fisher placing one sixth.

The 'offset single-seater' layout is well shown as Moss rounds the straw bales of the Circuit of the Caracalla Baths in the Prix de Rome, when despite the presence of front-line Ferraris he set the fastest lap (he retired when the car shed a front wheel).

1951 F2 This was a true single seater, with a similar chassis but wishbone and coil spring front suspension on MG TD lines and a Heath rear suspension layout (de Dion axle and quarter elliptics) which proved to be a weak point. Part of the effort to squeeze more power (just a little more power) out of the Alta four took the shape of four Webers. Wilson-type pre-selector gearboxes were still used.

Moss, Macklin, Meyer and Schell all achieved second places in F2 events and Moss won a Castle Combe race. The cars were also run in some F1 races, with occasional reasonable results in secondary events.

Moss again, in the rain at Bremgarten. The car was low and slim, and in dimensions and looks was a match for its Continental counterparts. Stub exhausts were customarily used.

1952-3 F2 There was a new chassis for 1952, approaching a multi-tubular affair, lighter and more rigid, with torsion bars in the de Dion arrangement at the rear, ZF differentials and inboard rear brakes. HWM took over the Alta engine, and new components and improved porting increased power to some 140bhp, or 40bhp less than the contemporary Ferrari four-cylinder engine. Outwardly the tail lines were neater, for while the main fuel tank was at the rear there were two small tanks low on each side, roughly aligned with the front of the cockpit.

The competition was stiffer in F2 and the cars were campaigned hard. There were good placings in secondary events – Frère won the GP des Frontières and Macklin the International Trophy – but in the Grands Prix, Frère's fifth in Belgium was the high point.

The budget did not run to new cars for 1953, but among revisions a change to the de Dion arrangement resulted in a slightly shorter chassis, and the car was also slightly lower, a Jaguar gearbox was adopted and the engine had a new head (180bhp was the quoted power output), so that little save the block remained of the Alta origins. Outwardly, there was a bluff nose, while the exhausts merged into a single pipe. The cars still lacked speed but they were raced a lot, with numerous drivers, through the season. There were, however, only a few top placings, scored in secondary events by Collins, Frère, Giraud-Cabantous and Macklin.

Lots of bumps and bulges, but the 1952 HWM was really a petite car (Frère in the Belgian GP).

A supercharged car was run in New Zealand *formule libre* races in 1954, while there was an F1 effort with a 2.5-litre version of the engine. At first this appeared to be a holding move while the Coventry Climax V-8 was completed, but that unit was not supplied to teams and the HWM GP effort soon petered out.

Drivers (GPs): George Abecassis, Johnny Claes, Peter Collins, Jack Fairman, John Fitch, Paul Frère, Duncan Hamilton, Yves Giraud-Cabantous, Roger Laurent, Lance Macklin, Stirling Moss, Albert Scherrer, Dries van der Lof.

In its seldom-seen 1954 2.5-litre version the car had a more solid look. The flank tank is obvious, the nose lines are from 1953 but the bonnet-top intakes came for 1954. This is Macklin in the French GP.

I

IFA

This Stockholm-built Junior relied on the power of a modified Wartburg engine, which may have made sense to constructor Johansson but does not suggest that it could have been competitive. The rest of the IFA comprised a semi-space frame with wishbone and transverse leaf suspension front and rear.

INTERMECCANICA

This Turin company was set up by Frank Reisner with Canadian capital, initially as a manufacturer of tuning and go-faster components, and it was to develop as a manufacturer of high-performance road cars (Apollo and Italia). Its first complete car was a Formula Junior machine designed by Reisner, with some prompting from Giannini.

It was a rear-engined space frame car, with wishbone and coil spring/damper independent suspension all round, and a Fiat gearbox. Two were built with Peugeot engines linered down to 1092cc to give a claimed 94bhp, with the admission that 85bhp might have been nearer the mark, and one with an 82bhp Fiat 1100. The IM-Fiat was to be offered as the cheap version.

The cars were built for 1961, when new FJ standards were being set, and the only real Intermeccanica success came in Canada, when Jerry Polivka won the national championship in an IM-Peugeot.

The Intermeccanica was by no means a sleek car, and the impression of dumpiness was very strong when it was seen in side elevation. Everything appeared to be very substantial.

IOTA

Iota is the Greek equivalent of the letter 'I' and International Class I is for cars between 350cc and 500cc so it was used both for the title of the 500 Club's magazine and for the cars designed by Dick Caesar, who was one of the main motive forces of the 500 movement. 'Cars' is perhaps too strong a word to describe the first Iotas because in keeping with the original spirit of the movement, which was to encourage the home constructor, the first batch of a dozen Iotas were really only ladder frames and although a rear axle unit was available, as was a structure to take Morgan sliding pillar ifs, suspension was left to the ingenuity of individual makers.

Not only did these machines have no set specification, but builders often gave them individual names such as Stromboli, Milli-Union, Buzzi 2 and Wasp. In 1950 Iota offered a complete car, the P1, which specified Morgan ifs, and a swing axle rear end sprung by rubber bands. By clever design the driver was able to sit further back in the frame than in most rear-engined cars.

By 1950 most of the really serious young drivers in F3 had opted for Coopers and that tipped the scales against the car. In the final of the support race at the British GP Frank Aikens, who had transferred his Triumph engine to the back of his new Iota P1, had a memorable dice with Stirling Moss' Cooper-JAP and was a likely winner, but the JAP engine blew up with the finishing line in sight. That was the apex of achievement for Iota, Aikens and the Triumph engine.   ML

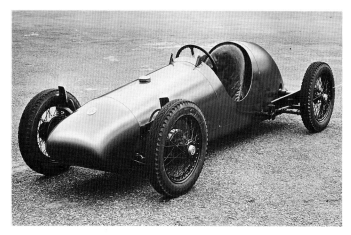

The 'production' Iota, P1.

IOTA-CLARKSON

One of the first batch of Iota frames was bought by Scottish trials driver, Roy Clarkson, who used a JAP engine, Norton gearbox, and sliding pillar suspension all round with transverse leaf springs front and rear. The rear was the unusual end because the hub races were held in guide blocks and took all the cornering and braking forces without assistance from, say, radius rods. A form of de Dion tube, welded to the frame, located the rear sprocket.

Although the rear suspension looked odd in action, the car actually went quite well in sprints. When it passed into other hands it was re-named the Iota-Zephyr.   ML

IRA

In the late 1930s and more recently the initials IRA have had a malevolent connotation but in a more placid period in 1952 they briefly appeared in racing, applied to an F2 car broadly made up of Dubliner Joe Kelly's Alta chassis and a Bristol engine. His rather more ambitious plans for Irish Racing Automobiles did not produce a car.

ISIS

When Alessandro (Alejandro) de Tomaso first attempted to become a constructor he picked on the name Isis for his 1960 copy of a Cooper for Formula Junior. This had a tubular chassis, independent suspension all round, and rear-mounted Fiat 1100 engine. It made no impression on racing.

ISO-MARLBORO

Frank Williams' sponsorship funds ran to new cars in 1973, although that is a little misleading as he still tended to buy used parts. New cars were in any case necessary to replace the Politoys, used early in 1973 in FX3B guise, as deformable structure regulations came into force as the European part of the Championship season opened.

John Clarke designed the Iso-Marlboro IR, a straightforward DFV-powered car, with angular lines in place of the curvaceous FX3's bulges. IR01-4 were built, and three were updated as the first cars with an FW designation for 1975. This update was carried through by Roy Stokoe, as Clarke was long gone (partly because Williams had called in the one-time de Tomaso designer Giampaolo Dallara as a consultant).

The cars were usually grid fillers, and through three seasons several of the drivers who were hopefully entered in them ended up with 'DNS' or 'DNQ' against their names on time sheets. Van Lennep and Ganley each scored a single point in 1973, then in 1974 Merzario was fourth in Italy and sixth in South Africa. In 1975 the cars were entered by Frank Williams Racing Cars or by Williams Ambrozium H7 Racing (the Iso car company's stay in racing was brief, although Marlboro was to have stamina in this respect); the team's only successful outing was in Germany with the FW04 (see also Williams).

Drivers (GPs): Tom Belso, Tony Brise, Nanni Galli, Howden Ganley, Jacky Ickx, Jean-Pierre Jabouille, Jacques Lafitte, Damien Magee, Graham McRae, Arturo Merzario, Henri Pescarolo, Jackie Pretorius, Ian Scheckter, Tim Schenken, Gijs van Lennep, Jo Vonlanthen, Renzo Zorzi.

Iso-Marlboro in its first form, with a nose intake which was to give way to a neat chisel nose in 1974. The messy colour scheme reflected Frank Williams' ability to find at least enough sponsorship to keep his team in being through this period. Driver is Howden Ganley in IR02 in the 1973 Spanish GP.

J

JASON

George Messervey's Triumph-engined 500 special was conventional in most respects; it looked like a Cooper but had Kieft-style suspension (double wishbone front, swing axle rear, sprung by rubber bands) but its rev counter was mounted on the nose in a channel and it had fuel injection, which was novel in F3 in 1956. That bold step forward, however, did not help it rise further than the back of the grid for the one contemporary race in which it seems to have appeared, although it has much more recently featured in historic F3 racing. ML

JAX

This was a BMW-engined F2 car which appeared on the fringe of the 1976 Japanese national scene, driven by German Nico Nicole.

JBS

Early in 1950, the year F3 became an international category, speedway rider Alf Bottoms acquired the Cowlan one-off, primarily for its Norton engine, then set about modifying the car. It became the first JBS, and Bottoms drove it to win at Brands Hatch, Blandford and Reims. For 1951 he introduced a new model, with a properly stressed tubular chassis and tubular wishbone suspension so that any type of power unit could be installed. This JBS was put into production at Feltham, and during 1951 several were raced by prominent drivers, including Aikens, Dryden, Parker and, perhaps above all, Peter Collins early in his career. The JBS became a serious threat to Coopers in F3. However, Bottoms died in a Luxembourg GP accident in May 1951, and although his family continued production into 1952 (when Charles Bottoms grafted a de Dion rear suspension onto one car) the JBS line petered out.

A JBS at Snetterton in 1952, fitted with wire wheels for reasons unknown.

JBW-Maserati

Brian Naylor was a semi-professional driver who made his name in the 1950s by being one of the few British drivers to regularly race in the smaller Continental events. To attract better starting money he ran unusual cars, including his JBW sports cars, which were based on various Lotus models and were built by his chief mechanic Fred Wilkinson. They had Maserati and Ferrari engines.

In 1959 Wilkinson built the JBW F1 car, which followed Cooper lines but had a four-cylinder Maserati 250S engine and a five-speed transaxle. This first JBW had a spasmodic career, plagued by unreliability, mainly in minor races. Its best showing was the 1960 British GP where Naylor qualified 18th from 24 starters and finished twelfth, five laps down.

Another JBW F1 car appeared in 1961 and again it was a Cooper copy, this time with a Maserati 150S engine driving through a five-speed Colotti gearbox. On its debut in the Silver City Trophy at Brands Hatch it was over ten seconds off the pace and retired with overheating. In the Italian GP it ran with a Coventry Climax FPF engine but retired after six laps with a blown engine. It came ninth in the Oulton Park Gold Cup, and finally ran in the Lewis-Evans Trophy at Brands Hatch, where it retired on the first lap. ML

JENNINGS

In the 1950s Bill Jennings was three times South African Champion driving a Riley Special built from the car with which Freddie Dixon had twice won the Tourist Trophy. He followed that with a Porsche-engined single-seater with a space frame and suspension by coil springs and wishbones, rather like the 'Pooper' (Cooper-Porsche) with which fellow-countryman Pete Lovely had so much success in America. Apart from the Gold Star series Jennings entered it in the four 1961 South African *temporada* races and his best result was ninth in the Natal GP. After that neither the car nor the driver appeared again in an international race. ML

JICEY

This ambitious French project was announced in 1948 and was intended to be a production racing car for the gentleman amateur. The concept was a BMW 328 engine, an unspecified gearbox and a welded deep-section chassis made of light alloy. Front suspension was by means of sliding pillars and the independent rear was by double wishbones.

The two Jiceys appeared only occasionally, without distinction, and the marque's only appearance in a major race was the 1950 F2 German Grand Prix where Georges Berger finished ninth, three laps behind Ascari's Ferrari. ML

JLR

Also known as the 'Rowbotham' after its maker, the JLR 500 car looked rather like a Cooper with high ground clearance. Front suspension came from a Fiat 500 and a similar, home-made system was used at the rear. Rowbotham experimented with an engine made from Ariel and JAP parts but normally it ran with a JAP engine, as a make-weight on grids. ML

JOCKO SPECIAL

The possibility that Jocko Maggiacomo's Formula Junior one-off could become the first car of a marque could hardly be entertained, in view of its name, but it was announced early in 1960 as the forerunner of an F1 derivative. Midget and stock car driver Maggiacomo built the car at Poughkeepsie, New York, following the 'Italian school' of 1959 with a front-mounted Fiat engine and Fiat transmission in a space frame and torsion bars of Morris Minor origin in the suspension. This was to be 'stiffened' for the Coventry Climax powered F1 version that never came to pass.

JORDAN SPECIAL

One of the few American 500 cars, this was built by Herb Jordan, an engineer with IBM, and was completed in 1957. It looked like a Cooper and was built around a box channel frame with Fiat Topolino front suspension used at both ends. The car was widely admired for its build quality and for the ingenuity Jordan employed in modifying its AJS engine using Norton and Harley-Davidson components. However, it was no match for imported Cooper-Nortons. ML

JP

In the early 1950s Joseph Potts Ltd of Lanarkshire made a number of 500cc F3 cars along Cooper lines but with coil spring and double wishbone suspension. They were sold mainly in Scotland, the north of England, and in Ireland where they were very successful – indeed, the winners of the 1956 Le Mans race, Ron Flockhart and Ninian Sanderson, both scored many wins in JPs early in their careers, Sanderson being the most consistently successful driver to use one.

From 1953 some JPs were fitted with an unusual de Dion rear axle with parallel double tubes about ten inches apart, joined at each end and by central triangulated tubes. Each de Dion tube was located to the chassis by radius rods hinged on the chassis but welded to each tube, while coil springs were mounted in parallel from the top of the rear of the chassis frame and acted on the lower of the two de Dion tubes. Despite this innovation, or because of it, JP gradually faded away. ML

Overall, the JP was a much neater car than most of its half-litre contemporaries, with better-balanced lines. This one is being driven in typical 500cc elbows-out style by G.A. Brown at Silverstone in 1954.

JR SPECIAL

Jean Terigi's pioneering French 500 car was rear-engined with a Triumph GP engine and a six-speed transmission achieved with twin rear sprockets. Distinguished by an odd tail fin which spoiled otherwise pretty lines, the JR had independent suspension all round by rubber bands. ML

JULIEN

Henri Julien came into racing in 1959, laying out his own Formula Junior car on DB lines, with a simple ladder frame and a Panhard engine, later turning to a BMW engine when the shortcomings of the French power unit were recognized. The front wheel drive car was built by Julien and Pierre Ferry, better known for his rear-engined Junior. M. Julien's FJ efforts, as a driver or as a constructor, were not successful, but he later entered an F3 Matra with great success, and that led to AGS.

K

KAHN

Robert Kahn was a Belgian pioneer of the 500 movement whose first effort was a front-engined car with an FN M86 driving to a live Simca rear axle through a complicated chain system. Later it had a BMW unit and it finished up as a pretty, low car whose performance did not match its good looks.

Kahn then tried making his own V-twin engine but gave it up. His second car, in 1952, was a Cooper copy which achieved little. ML

KAIMANN

This Austrian constructor is known for its Vee and Super Vee cars, and Niki Lauda made his single-seater debut in a Kaimann Vee in 1970. Patron Kurt Bergmann made two ineffectual attempts to take it into F2 in the 1970s. In 1973 Kaimann developed an Opel-based F2 engine that was used in hill climbs in a March 712 chassis, and in 1974 a space frame car was built for Koinigg to race in the European Championship. Koinigg, however, appeared in a Surtees, for the Opel engine came apart at the start of practice when the Kaimann made its only race meeting appearance. In 1976 Bergmann tried again with another space frame, following his Super Vee lines, and a Schnitzer-BMW engine. It was intended for Quester, but again failed to appear on a grid.

KASPAR

Hubert Patthey, a Swiss, was behind the Kaspar 500cc car which had a square tube frame, torsion bar ifs and swing axle rear suspension. It was a pretty car but for reasons which remain obscure, Patthey chose the wheels and tyres with the largest possible diameter and the narrowest possible width – hindsight suggests a different approach might have helped. ML

KAUHSEN

German sports car driver and entrant Willi Kauhsen made expensive, brief and fruitless forays into formula racing in the late 1970s, running former Elf cars under his name in F2 and then building a team of F1 cars.

Kauhsen-Renault The Elf 2J, all-conquering in F2 in 1976, re-appeared in the 1977 entry lists as the Kauhsen-Renault. The more the cars were modified the more their performance deteriorated and lead driver Michel Leclère, fourth in the 1976 F2 championship driving Elf cars, failed to score. Klaus Ludwig left the team in mid-season and, although occasional drivers included such luminaries as Vittorio Brambilla and Alain Prost, the team got nowhere.

WK Undeterred, Kauhsen moved up in 1979, building five F1 cars to a design by Klaus Kapitza (the designation WK referred to Willibald Kauhsen). Outwardly these were competent Cosworth-powered wing cars following Lotus lines, but the aerodynamicists failed to appreciate that the nose of a car lifts under acceleration and dips under braking. Two (004 and 005) were seen at a couple of race meetings, first at the

Spanish GP where Gianfranco Brancatelli was well off the pace in practice and failed to start. After the Belgian GP Kauhsen sensibly gave up, and some of the team's material was sold to Merzario.

F2 Kauhsen at Thruxton early in 1977. Leclère is the driver.

The WK may have followed the Lotus example in layout and intent, but in its lines there was none of the aesthetic appeal that characterized Chapman's cars. Brancatelli is seated well forward in the wheelbase, here doing his best to get the car within striking distance of a qualifying time for the 1979 Spanish GP.

KELLERS

An early Swiss 500 car with a front-mounted Triumph engine driving through car-type transmission. ML

KENT-SMITH

Built by J.B. Kent and G.G. Smith, this British 500 car of the early 1950s had a tubular frame, coil spring and double wishbone front suspension and rubber-sprung swing axles at the back. It was easily distinguished by its pannier fuel tanks strapped to the sides. ML

The Kent-Smith was lower than most of its F3 contemporaries, with the head of its Norton engine projecting above the bodywork and G.G. Smith looking very exposed in a cockpit well forward in the wheelbase.

KG SPECIAL

Two Swedish enthusiasts, K.E. Kronquist and Gred Geitel, built four or five 500 racers in 1948, before Formula 3 as such became an international category. They were 'inspired' by much more successful Effyhs (see Effyh). Even informed Swedish sources can shed little light on their racing career, which was almost exclusively confined to ice and short-oval racing. ML

KIEFT

The first Kieft was built in 1950, and Stirling Moss made the Kieft name on the circuits in the following year as he challenged the dominant Coopers in F3. Kieft moved from Birmingham to a Bridgend industrial estate to start production for 1952. Three years later it was re-established in Wolverhampton, underwent substantial reorganization in 1956 and in 1960 was restructured for the last time under its third owner, at a Birmingham base. 'To win races you must have a Kieft' was the company's slogan, and complete with a JAP engine the 1952 500 was priced at £800. However, although Moss was very fast in a Kieft, some of the customer cars were let down by build quality and by driving techniques that were often coarse by his standards.

Don Parker won the 1952-3 *Autosport* 500cc Championships driving Kiefts and other notable drivers included Ken Wharton and André Loens. In 1953 Bernard Ecclestone acquired a second-hand Kieft. That year the company offered their F3 car in kit form, less engine, for £445. There was the distraction of an abortive F2 project in 1952 and an F1 car was almost completed in 1954. F3 car production continued into that year, although interest had shifted to sports cars.

Cyril Kieft sold his company to Berwyn Baxter at the end of 1954. There was a return to single seaters in 1960, with an FJ car that carried the Kieft name but had none of the old Kieft originality or characteristics.

Formula 3 The first Kiefts appeared in 1950 and had a ladder frame chassis, torsion bar suspension and alloy wheels. They were too heavy to be competitive although they achieved some minor successes in hill climbs when an 1100cc V-twin JAP engine was fitted. The ingenious design of its successor featured a lightweight space frame, front suspension by wishbones and rubber in torsion, swing axles with rubber bands in tension at the rear, and a low cockpit and overall lines. This original design was by Ray Martin, with John A. Cooper and Dean Delamont. There was never a successor as such – Kieft simply followed a policy of evolution, so that by

1954 the cars were lighter, lower and sleeker. It has to be admitted the marque would have faded away in F3 had it not been for the efforts of driver-entrants, especially Don Parker, who meticulously assembled his own cars and used Norton engines prepared by ace tuner Francis Beart. Moss' Martin/Cooper/Delamont car made its debut at Goodwood in May 1951, with a Norton engine, although a JAP unit was specified for 1952 customer cars which were spoiled by being badly made. In 1956 only Don Parker gained top-five placings in Kiefts, with carefully built cars run from his Battersea base, but Parker's cars were so modified they might have been called Parker-Kiefts. In 1957 the name no longer appeared in Cooper-dominated results lists.

Formula 2 One of the original 1950 Kieft chassis was adopted for an F2 project in 1952, beefed up and in effect reversed for the Butterworth flat four engine (with Norton barrels and heads) to be mounted ahead of the driver. Nothing came of this because of insurmountable problems with engine cooling.

Formula 1 This project only fell apart when Coventry Climax took fright at the power outputs claimed for the Mercedes-Benz 2.5-litre GP straight eight and abandoned the FPE V-8. The chassis, designed by Cyril Kieft and Gordon Bedson and completed at Wolverhampton, was a much more substantial tubular affair than the F2 chassis, while the suspension (with conventional springing medium!) derived from Kieft's sports car.

Formula Junior The name Kieft returned to single-seater racing in 1961 under new management, with an FJ car designed by Ron Timmins along conventional rear-engined lines. A Kieft activity through to the early 1960s was modifying Triumph Herald engines, but initial tests in the Junior showed this to be no route to competitive performance and Arden-tuned 105E units were to be used, canted in the chassis. This was a space frame, with wishbone and coil spring/damper suspension. The car showed some early promise, but this was not sustained.

A bare-metal FJ Kieft in early-1961 tests, with the traditional lozenge badge prominent on the driver's helmet but not on the car.

KITCHINER

Tony Kitchiner worked on the Chequered Flag team F2 and F3 cars before setting up on his own to produce F3 cars in West London. The monocoque K2, which made its debut early in 1969 in French F3 races, had an unusually short wheelbase, cantilever-type inboard front suspension, and Broadspeed or Holbay engines. Tested by Cevert, it apparently showed

F3 Kieft lines are well shown in this shot of Don Gray on a wet day at Brands Hatch in 1953 – the stubby nose and tapered tail were constant features, albeit a little sleeker in late cars.

promise, but performances when it was raced by lesser French drivers were not so good, and its best placing was a sixth at Montlhéry. In the summer of 1969 it was converted into a very compact F5000 car, and then at the end of the year it became an F3 car again, in revised form as the K2A. The tubular engine sub frame it had in its F5000 career was retained, while the front suspension was a more conventional double wishbone arrangement, with outboard coil spring/damper units. Two were run in France, without success.

Kitchiner then converted a McLaren M10B into the Kitchmac, before running a McLaren M19 in F5000, and finally turned his back on racing in 1974.

KJ 500

This 1953 500 built by Ken Kitchen and Roy Jones resembled a Ray Martin Kieft (Jones had worked for the company). Details varied from the parent design and the most obvious external difference was the MG wheels with knock-off hub spinners. A four-stud JAP engine drove through a Burman gearbox. The car was used most in hill climbs.   ML

KN

Kenneth Neve was one of the first supporters of the 500 movement and, through the VSCC, was instrumental in making sure there were prestigious meetings in which the first cars could compete, an apparent detail but one of enormous significance in promoting the class. Neve built a rudimentary monocoque from aluminium and ash with Morgan ifs, a GN rear axle sprung by elastic bands and front-mounted Douglas DT engine driving through an Albion gearbox.

The car was not a success, save in the odd straight-line sprint, and a Mk2 version was made with a steel chassis, an Ariel engine and oil-filled dampers at the back, but Neve soon drifted away from 500 events to become more involved in the VSCC.   ML

KOJIMA

In the second half of the 1970s Kojima Engineering of Kyoto seemed poised to become a force in single-seater racing, with F1 cars that were not disgraced in their two races and F2 cars that performed creditably in Japanese racing, by no means a domestic affair as by then the F2 series was contested by leading European drivers and cars.

Matsuhisa Kojima had involved his company in racing through the decade, in national categories and in F2 with March chassis. The F1 cars in 1976-77 were straightforward and competent – lessons had been learned from the Maki fiasco – but despite the proclaimed intentions they were not run outside Japan and that was no basis for a racing programme. The in-house F2 effort carried Kojima through to the end of the decade as a constructor, but led nowhere. In the 1980s the successful Japanese racing products were engines, Honda's in F1 while BMW was displaced by Honda and Yamaha in Japanese F2, although as far as chassis were concerned the last three seasons, 1984-6, were March territory.

KE007 Although designer Masao Ono used Japanese components as far as possible, KE007 was essentially a Cosworth kit car with a Hewland FGA400 gearbox. It had an aluminium monocoque, double wishbone front suspension and parallel lower links, single upper links and twin radius rods at the rear, with coil spring/damper units outboard all round (Kayaba dampers which could be adjusted from the cockpit were used). There was a full-width nose, but radiators were in the flanks. Engine air was ducted along the sides of the very deep cockpit surround. It was raced once, finishing eleventh and last in the 1976 Japanese GP, when qualifying tyres were fitted after a late pit stop and a freak fastest lap was credited to it.

Driver: Masahiro Hasemi.

The all-black KE007 looked particularly sinister in the rain at Fuji in 1976. The cockpit surround was individualistic.

KE008 A pair of F2 cars on March lines, with BMW engines, were raced in 1978, when Kunimitsu Takahasi defeated a top-class field in a championship race at Suzuka.

KE009 A developed version of the KE007 design, tidied up and improved in detail. Two were built and in the 1977 Japanese GP Takahara crashed in the works-entered car while Hoshino finished 11th in 009/2, which was entered by Heros Racing. Nothing came of the suggestion that Kauhsen might enter an 009 in GPs in 1978, so that race marked the end of the short Kojima F1 story (predictably nothing came of rumours of a Honda-engined Kojima for 1978).

Drivers: Kazuyoshi Hoshino, Noritake Takahara.

The Kojima Engineering 009 in the 1977 Japanese GP, looking much neater in conventional respects than KE007. Driver is again Hoshino, who finished the race to give the works team a 100 per cent record.

KE011 Another BMW-engined F2 car on March lines and run in 1979, when it was no match for the Bicester-built March cars that dominated the category (ironically the principal Japanese race, at Suzuka, was won by Hoshino in a Heros Racing March 792, while Pironi lasted only six laps in the sole Kojima).

KURTIS-KRAFT

When America hosted its first World Championship race, at Sebring in 1959, the Indy brigade were fairly contemptuous and reckoned that a well-driven Quarter Mile Midget could put the Europeans in their place (the F1 regulations were then loosely framed so that it was possible to enter one). Rodger Ward, the 1959 Indy winner and one of the greats of the oval tradition, was egged on to enter, and his entry was accepted because it would bring in spectators and would provide a show-down match between F1 and USAC cars. His car was a Kurtis-Kraft Midget with solid axles front and rear suspended by torsion bars, and a 1.7-litre dohc Offenhauser engine with two-speed gear box and two-speed differential. It did have disc brakes, but they were designed to set up the car for sliding on a loose surface and not for road racing.

To test the theory, Ward entered his Midget in a road race meeting at Lime Rock, won a heat and showed up well against Chuck Daigh's Maserati 250F – but then the Maserati was obsolete and Daigh was not an ace. Sebring, with its long straights, was a different matter and Ward's best practice lap was 43.8 seconds off the pace, so it was likely he would finish ten laps down. In the race itself he ran dead last and retired after 20 laps with clutch trouble.   ML

L

LABRANI

Vic Labran's F3 one-off was one of the more competitive 'non-production' cars in British racing in 1951-3, and another one following the Kieft pattern, having a Cooper-style chassis with its driver seated well forward.

LAMBKIN

An improbable name for a racing car, but owed to its Australian constructor Eric Lambkin. His 1959 Junior was conventional in having a front-mounted Fiat 1100 engine in a multi-tubular frame, with unspecified ifs and a live rear axle.

LAMOUREUX

Michel Lamoureux drew on his *Formule Renault* experience when he produced this one-off F3 car for 1983, and it reduced one hardened professional commentator to expletives of disbelief. It was a rather crude device to present at a mid-1980s European F3 Championship meeting, even allowing for the small budget behind it (it was a simple monocoque design). The car appeared at some French meetings, to no worthwhile end.

M. Lamoureux sat well forward in his F3 car, and unfashionably upright. He did crash on occasion, reputedly when his attention strayed, so that very robust roll-over bar was perhaps prudent.

LANCE

This Nova-Ford F3 one-off was run in Germany in 1975. It appeared in a leading position once that year, when it was fourth at Zembach.

LANCIA

Vincenzo Lancia was one of the leading drivers of the formative years of racing but he carefully steered the company he founded away from serious competition. His son, Gianni, was less prudent and took Lancia into top-level sports car racing early in the 1950s, as a prelude to a Grand Prix entry in 1954. The cost was a burden the over-stretched company could not bear, and when it virtually collapsed in 1955 Fiat took over and handed the Grand Prix cars and team material over to Ferrari.

The D50 F1 car was highly original, designer Vittorio Iano departing as far from convention as his Mercedes contemporaries but looking ahead. The 2489cc 90-degree V-8 was a high-revving unit, which initially produced some 260bhp. It was used as a stressed member, with the front suspension and bulkhead bolted to it, and mounted at an angle to give an offset propshaft run for a low cockpit. Outrigged panniers between the wheels carried oil (in the front of the left sponson) and fuel, which improved the airflow. A tail main tank was then the norm, and this of course led to changes in handling as the load was used.

The D50 first appeared at the end of the 1954 season and Ascari took pole for the Spanish GP in its debut. The 1955 race season started well with Ascari winning two secondary Italian races and he was about to take the lead at Monaco when he crashed. His death in a sports car accident a few days later was the catalyst in the Fiat takeover. As Lancia-Ferraris the cars lost their individuality, although they were to win races and give Fangio his fourth World Championship.

Lancia was prominent in GT categories for a while and was to become Fiat's rally arm. As far as single-seaters were concerned, the 1.1-litre V-4 was developed for Formula Junior, but units tuned by specialists such as Dagrada were never really competitive, and in the 1970s Lancia-based F3 engines appeared. Two D50s survive, one at the Biscaretti museum and one in the company's care, as reminders of what might have been.

Drivers: Alberto Ascari, Eugenio Castellotti, Louis Chiron, Luigi Villoresi.

As well as the outrigged panniers of the D50, this shot also shows the tubular wishbones of the front suspension, but not the thin leaf spring. There was a de Dion layout at the back. Although Lancia had used inboard brakes on a sports-racing car, conventional units were fitted to the D50. This car is driven by Castellotti at Monaco in 1955.

LANCIA-MARINO

This obscure special made only one appearance in an F1 race, the 1957 Naples GP. It used Lancia Aurelia components and, driven by Marino Brandoli, qualified 26 seconds off the pace, retiring after nine laps with a burst water hose.   ML

LAWHART

Originally built in 1949 as a sports car, K.G. Hartley's first special was soon converted to run in South African 500cc racing. The basis was a DKW square tube backbone chassis with widened front track (giving a crab effect) and DKW front wheel drive was retained. The engine was a twin cylinder

Lawrence unit which was originally used for pumping out the bilges on Catalina flying boats and this was connected by chain to the DKW transmission.

A second Lawhart, also using a Lawrence engine but this time driving through a Burman gearbox, was a more or less conventional rear-engined car which was influenced by the Ray Martin Kieft. ML

LAYSTALL

UDT-Laystall introduced this car for the last season of 1.5-litre F2 racing in 1960, anticipating that it would be the forerunner of a Grand Prix car. The aim was to emulate Lotus with another 'mini-Vanwall', but the car came at a time when even Ferrari was turning to the rear-engined layout.

A light tubular frame was combined with Cooper front suspension and a wide-wishbone Lotus-like rear suspension. The Coventry Climax FPF was angled at 18 degrees to the right, to cut frontal area slightly, and drove through a five-speed gearbox. Although driver Henry Taylor was no slouch, the car was never competitive and for a full entry into the Grands Prix UDT-Laystall bought rear-engined cars.

The very new Laystall, on slave wheels (BRM pattern Dunlop wheels were specified). The car was not so tightly packaged as the front-engined Lotus 16, nor did it have the elegant lines of the Vanwall.

LDS

L.D. 'Doug' Serrurier, a former South African speedway champion and a leading local driver in the 1950s and 1960s, made 13 LDS specials for his own use and for others, twelve of which were single-seaters eligible both for the South African Gold Star series and the F1 races staged when teams from Europe visited.

Mk1 A copy of a 1957 F1/2 Cooper frame with Serrurier's own modifications, such as front and rear suspension by coil springs and unequal wishbones at a time when Cooper still used transverse leaf springs. Five of these cars were made and they used Porsche, Alfa Romeo and Coventry Climax FPF engines. The most successful was the Alfa-engined car raced by Sam Tingle between 1961 and 1965, who managed to qualify for the 1964 and 1965 South African Grands Prix. The best individual performance, however, was by John Love, who ran one with a Porsche RSK engine and gearbox. In the 1962 Cape GP he qualified quickest of all the locals and only 0.2s behind Tony Maggs in one of the Parnell Coopers.

Mk2 This was based on the 1961 'Low-line' Coopers and, using one fitted with a modified Alfa Romeo Giulietta engine and Hewland five-speed gearbox, Serrurier qualified for both the 1963 and 1964 South African Grands Prix, finishing twelfth in the latter. Four Mk2s were made but the other three were only run in Gold Star series races.

Mk3 A copy of the 'Tasman' Brabham BT11A made for Sam Tingle with the assistance of Brabham as he had just failed to buy the last of the line. It was fitted with a 2.7-litre FPF engine, and Tingle qualified tenth for the 1967 South African GP, ahead of Hill, Siffert and Courage, but failed to finish in the race.

The Mk3 had unmistakeable Brabham lines, and seemingly even more substantial suspension components out in the airflow than the original. The driver is Tingle, in the 1967 South African Grand Prix.

Mk4 Serrurier's own design, although heavily influenced by the Mk3, this car was run with an FPF engine in the 3-litre Gold Star series.

Mk5 The LDS line came to an end in 1965/6 with a pair of cars based on the F2 Brabham BT16. One was fitted with a Ford FJ engine and the other with a 2-litre FPF. ML

LEC

This was one of the more promising independent F1 ventures of the 1970s, brutally cut short. The car was built for David Purley, in the name of the family refrigeration business, whose colours had been carried on other cars he had raced.

The purposeful CRP1 was designed by Mike Pilbeam, and was orthodox in all its main features. The sheet aluminium monocoque was angular, there was double wishbone front suspension, while at the rear parallel lower links, single upper links and radius rods were used, with coil springs/dampers inboard at the front and outboard at the rear. The radiators were alongside the engine, a DFV which drove through a Hewland FGA400 gearbox, and various nose aerofoil configurations were tried.

Lec CRP1 in the Silverstone pits road, Purley in the cockpit, designer Mike Pilbeam on the left, team manager Mike Earle on the right.

Purley gave the car its debut in the Race of Champions in 1977, finishing sixth. He placed it in two Grands Prix, 13th in Belgium (after briefly running second, in freak conditions) and 14th in Sweden. Then he crashed very, very heavily at Silverstone, when the throttle slides jammed open during British GP practice. Purley survived, but quite how is a mystery when the crumpled monocoque in the Donington Museum is examined. Another car was built for him to prove something to himself when his legs had been rebuilt in 1979. After trying it in minor races, he retired, only to be killed when his aerobatic aircraft crashed.

LE GRAND

American cars conforming to the secondary international formulae have been rare since the days of Formula Junior. Four years on, Bruce Eglinton ran a Le Grand Mk 5 in 1967 European F3 races, with some success in minor events. The car followed contemporary Brabham lines, but with some components (such as cast magnesium suspension parts) at a cost level which Brabham would not have contemplated in the BT partnership days, and with the novelty of Airheart brakes.

LENHAM-HURST

The LM1 was a conventional Piper-engined space frame F3 one-off which appeared in the Spring of 1972. Apparently it was an adaptation of the Dave Martin-designed Hamlen Formula Ford car (Hamlen is an anagram of Lenham). Richard Croucher made his F3 race debut in it, in the GP des Frontières at Chimay, but it has no record of race success. Roger Hurst's association with the Lenham Motor Co ended in 1972, and he tended to concentrate on sports-racing cars, still using the marque name Lenham. This was applied to F3 cars with P73 and P87 designations, which were in fact adapted March cars. An F2 project (P81) failed to take shape.

LEPRECHAUN

Designed by Nick Flynn and backed by Redmund Gallagher (managing director of a company which marketed 'Leprechaun' chocolate, not that there was any connection between the two names in the days before sponsorship) this was a 1953 Irish 500cc F3 car. Built with the Kieft in mind, with a space frame, coil springs and double wishbones at the front, swing axles sprung by rubber in tension at the rear, Leprechauns were successful in Ireland but did not repeat that success on rare sorties to Great Britain.   ML

LESTON SPECIAL

Les Leston was one of the slightly larger than life characters in the forefront of 500cc racing in the early 1950s, who turned away from the Cooper which he had raced successfully to his own Leston Special. This was a JBS, substantially rebuilt by Ray Martin, in some respects following Kieft lines. It had a chassis of four main tubes, wishbone front suspension and a swing axle arrangement at the rear.

The Leston started to appear among the top three in major F3 race results in mid-1952 and in the Summer of that year Leston won with it at Orleans and Porrentruy. John Habin also raced it. Leston was successful with his Leston again in 1953, before turning back to the Cooper.

A leading figure in the motor accessory trade was perhaps one of the few driver/entrants who could run his car with whitewall tyres in the 1950s. Otherwise, the Leston Special looks lower and longer than a Cooper as Leston leans to a corner at Oulton Park in 1953.

LEYTON HOUSE

This name was hyphenated to March in 1989 but in the interests of continuity the F1 and F3000 cars for that year are covered in the March entry (in 1990 references to March disappeared).

LIEBL

This Munich-based constructor departed from the normal 1959 Formula Junior pattern, in using a Simca Aronde-based engine and gearbox. In other respects his car conformed, with a ladder chassis, wishbone and coil spring front suspension and live axle with torsion bars at the rear.

LIGIER

Guy Ligier is a well-connected and successful man, an accomplished sportsman who played rugby for France, who drove in a dozen Grands Prix at least well enough to score a World Championship point in 1967, and a powerful businessman in the heavy construction industry. He has friends in high places, including a M. Mitterand who was destined for the highest place in the land and who in times of difficulty was to deploy influence on Ligier's behalf.

Ligier gave up racing after his friend and associate Jo Schlesser was killed in the 1968 French GP, at a time when the first Ligier car was taking shape. All Ligier designations have incorporated 'JS' in honour of Schlesser. The first Ligiers were road-going sports/GT cars, although JS2s were seen in competition. The first out-and-out circuit car was the sports-racing JS3 in 1971 and the JS5 F1 car came in 1976, with the 'right connections' leading to the use of the Matra V-12 rather than the planned Cosworth DFV. That car was competitive and its successor, the JS7, was a Grand Prix winner. The next five Ligier GP victories came with Cosworth engines, then there were two more with Matra-powered JS17s, when the team was Talbot-Ligier for a brief period. A fleeting return to Cosworths in 1983 saw the team slump and no points were scored, a low that was not reached by Ligier again until 1988.

There were distractions like an abortive Indycar project, and the formidable M. Ligier's occasional mercurial decisions were not always an asset to his team. Renault turbo engines did not help much in 1984 but, together with changes in the team, saw Ligier through to respectable Constructors' Championship positions in 1985-6. Rock bottom was reached in 1988 with the hapless JS31. As befits his heavyweight stature, Ligier was back fighting in 1989, with a new base for Ligier F1 at Magny-Cours, a new engineering staff, and new cars to do battle in the blue of France, aiming to improve on the hardly scintillating record of eight Grand Prix victories in twelve seasons. However, the team scored just three Championship points.

JS5 The first F1 Ligier was an impressive machine, designed by a team under former Matra manager Gérard Ducarouge and including Beaujon and Carillo. The Matra engine team had continued development work on the MS73 engine, and in its 1976 form the V-12 was rated at 520bhp. It drove through a Hewland TL200 gearbox. The monocoque was orthodox, as were the twin wishbone/inboard coil spring and damper front suspension, and the rear suspension of upper and lower links, outboard coil spring/damper units and twin radius rods. The bodywork, however, was distinctive. Developed by SERA aerodynamicist Robert Choulet, it was curvaceous, with a concave nose and an enormous airbox which formed a useful billboard for the SEITA tobacco company's emblem. It was worn for only a few races as new regulations which came into force in the spring of 1977 meant that a more modest air intake had to be fitted.

Ligier ran a one-car team in his first GP season, rejecting the F1 experience of Beltoise and Pescarolo in favour of Laffite. Ligier's first race was the Brazilian GP, its first points were scored at Long Beach, and at the end of the first season Ligier had scored 20 to come fifth in the Constructors' Championship.

Driver: Jacques Laffite.

The bulky but smooth JS5 with its first enormous airbox, which housed a reasonably modest intake.

JS7 Broadly, this car followed the JS5, but the different proportions of the MS76 V-12 meant that the weight distribution changed and modifications to the rear suspension and ancillaries were called for. Outwardly the flat sides of the JS5 gave way to rounded flanks, and a finer nose

The JS7 appeared to be another bulky car, but to a degree appearance misled for its wheelbase/track dimensions were similar to other 1979 cars. The nose aerofoil allowed for adjustments that had not been possible with the 1976 arrangement.

mounting a full-width aerofoil was introduced. The engine was troublesome early in the year, then came a first victory in Sweden when Laffite took the lead right at the end of the race. After that performances rather fell away again, with only a second in Holland standing out in the latter half of the season. Ligier slipped to eighth in the Championship.

Uncertainty about sponsorship and Matra's development commitment meant that the team started 1978 with uprated JS7s, primarily with a Hewland FGA in place of the TL 200. Laffite scored with it in two early races.

Driver: Jacques Laffite.

JS9 Modifications to the JS7 led to the JS9, via a 'JS7/9' which showed the directness of the development. During the summer there were further revisions, primarily to the suspension, while in the engine the effective revs range was widened. Laffite's best placings in JS9s were two thirds, and sixth place in the Constructors' Championship was a reasonable outcome at the end of an uncertain year.

Driver: Jacques Laffite.

JS11 The 1979 season opened very positively for Ligier's first two-car team. The JS11 was a Cosworth-powered ground effects car designed by Michel Beaujon and Gérard Ducarouge, with a strong and stiff chassis to withstand the high downloads achieved. Laffite won in Argentina and Brazil, while Depailler took second place in Brazil and won in Spain. Laffite was second in Belgium. A hang gliding accident side-lined Depailler and while his replacement, Jacky Ickx, may have pleased sponsors he was not a front-line driver in F1 terms in 1979. Suspension and aerodynamic revisions in the summer did not improve the cars (Ligier's switch of wind-tunnel contract work to a government establishment in mid-season cannot have helped). Nevertheless, Ligier was third in the Championship.

Drivers: Patrick Depailler, Jacky Ickx, Jacques Laffite.

The strong team before the 1979 season, with the sturdy JS11, autocrat Guy Ligier in its cockpit, and experienced 'joint number one' drivers Depailler and Laffite at his right-hand side. Pronounced upward extensions of the sides ahead of the rear wheels helped the ground effects seal, and enabled the wheel to act as an extractor as it revolved. A dispensation had allowed cigarette sponsorship to continue . . .

JS11/15 The explicit dual designation lasted through 1980, applying to a car built around the 1979 monocoque and front suspension, with revisions at the rear and in the aerodynamics, which were to be further modified through the season. The cars were run in 'fast' and 'slow' configurations, and although the variations in side pods and wings sometimes seemed self-defeating, Ligier's reputation for good handling was generally restored. Pironi and Laffite each won a Grand Prix, and the team achieved its best-ever placing in the Constructors' Championship, second with 66 points. At the end of the year a JS11/15 was used in tests with Michelin tyres.

Drivers: Jacques Laffite, Didier Pironi.

The Gitanes colours were used most effectively on the JS11/15. Pironi is running with a small rear wing at Zandvoort; in common with most 1980 F1 cars a front wing was worn only on slow circuits.

JS17 This was a season of change. The cars were run as Talbot-Ligiers, and while the association with a major company brought with it access to some specialist resources it was a reason for the ageing Matra V-12 to be pressed into service again. In its MS81 form it had no more claimed power than it had been producing three years earlier. Beaujon and Ducarouge – in his last design for the team – came up with a straightforward car, using some carbon fibre in the monocoque and with a large centre fuel cell. Inboard suspension was unremarkable and the team was caught on the hop by 'lowering suspension' systems, but a hydro-pneumatic system on Brabham lines was eventually devised and everything came together in the late summer. Laffite won in Austria, and he won again in Canada, to haul the team to fourth place in the Championship.

The overweight JS17s were slightly revised to serve until the Spring of 1982, but had to be used longer than anticipated as the JS19 fell foul of skirt regulations. The only worthwhile JS17 result that year came when Cheever placed one second at Detroit.

Drivers: Eddie Cheever, Jean-Pierre Jabouille, Jean-Pierre Jarier, Jacques Laffite, Patrick Tambay.

JS17 in January 1981, with allegiances to Talbot and Michelin in its new livery. Drivers are named as Laffite, who had become a permanent feature of the team, and Jabouille, who was to race for Ligier only three times.

JS19 Abruptly the visual continuity of the Ligier line was broken in this Beaujon design – the cockpit was well forward, the engine deck seemed very long, and so did the extension of the bodywork behind the rear wheels. There were very long ground effects side pods and skirts extending to the tail, and

that was not acceptable to the scrutineers at Monaco, where the car made its debut, or in Detroit where Ligier tried again. So the JS19s reappeared at the Dutch GP with the offending parts shortened, and ran in that state for the rest of the year. The monocoque was built up around six sections, with carbon fibre/Kevlar panels. Double wishbone pullrod suspension was used, with inboard coil springs/dampers. The turbo V-6, which was to be by Talbot out of Matra, never did materialize and the cars were underpowered with the V-12. Best placings with this car were two thirds, and Ligier slipped to eighth on the Constructors' points table.

Drivers: Eddie Cheever, Jacques Laffite.

By the end of 1982 the JS19 had lost the smooth unified lines that characterized it when it ran its first tests at Clermont Ferrand five months earlier – in particular the side pods looked an assemblage of odd pieces. Cheever is the driver here, on his way to third place at Las Vegas.

JS21 Matra's inevitable withdrawal meant a return to DFV engines in 1983, and two of the JS19s were in fact converted while the solitary purpose-designed JS21 was completed. Michel Beaujon and Claude Galopin came up with a highly original device, notably in aerodynamic and suspension respects. The car was slim and angular, roughly to a transverse line through the back of its DFV, and from that point a large pod enclosed the radiators and almost embraced the rear wheels. Various single or double rear wings were mounted above this assemblage. Jean-Pierre Labrosse developed a version of the Citroën hydropneumatic suspension for the car, which seemed to work best on slow circuits. The driver pairing did little to arrest Ligier's decline in 1983, when the team failed to score.

Drivers: Raul Boesel, Jean-Pierre Jarier.

The JS21 was at least distinctive, albeit an aesthetic mess and with only a normally-aspirated DFV to cope with lots of drag. Driver is Jarier, at Long Beach, and his car has the Brazilian decals (on the nose and behind the cockpit) which are evidence of the price Boesel paid for his drive.

JS23 At a time when the McLaren MP4 series cars were setting the pace, the JS23 was an also-ran. It had a carbon composite monocoque, orthodox suspension, Michelin tyres and Renault turbo engines. The team had an apparently adequate budget, but the cars were fragile and far from competitive in JS23 or JS23B forms (the latter came in mid-1984, with revised pushrod suspension and bodywork). As number one driver Ligier enrolled Andrea de Cesaris, who scored the team's two points, but often he showed no better than the F1 novice who was his unfortunate team mate.

Drivers: Andrea de Cesaris, François Hesnault.

Red, white and two blues, with neat main bodywork and one of the grotesque rear aerofoils that the power of turbo engines encouraged, the JS23 was a forgettable car.

JS25 In 1985 Ligier regained lost ground, as erstwhile Renault team director and designer Gérard Larrousse and Michel Tétu joined, and Laffite returned. Work on the JS25 was already in hand, so Tétu's immediate role was its development, and disposing of some of the excess weight it carried in a Ligier tradition. The monocoque and front suspension were new, Pirelli tyres were used and during the year the latest EF15 engines were supplied by Renault. Results began to come – Laffite contributed 16 points and de Cesaris three before he was sacked after a spectacular accident (his replacement Streiff scored four).

Drivers: Andrea de Cesaris, Jacques Laffite, Philippe Streiff.

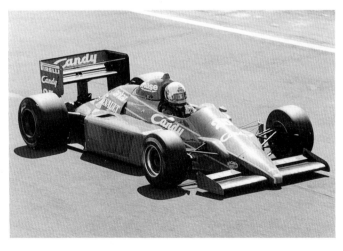

A JS25 in mid-season, with the lighter bodywork, vertical winglets behind the front suspension and cigarette sponsorship deleted from the flanks in deference to television. The hapless de Cesaris is the driver.

JS27 The French Minister of Sport brought influence to bear to enable Ligier to continue using Renault engines in 1986, and caused something of a furore in sporting circles by authorising a grant to the same end. The engines the team got were Mecachrome-prepared, rather than the latest units Renault supplied direct to Lotus. The car was essentially a refined derivative of the JS25 by Michel Tétu, with conventional pushrod suspension (a hydraulic system was tested but not raced) and honeycomb sandwich monocoque

with carbon fibre outer skin. At Detroit a Ligier briefly led a GP again, which was encouraging, but on the other side of the coin Laffite's F1 career ended in a British GP accident. Ligier ended the season fifth in the Constructors' Championship.

Drivers: Philippe Alliott, René Arnoux, Jacques Laffite.

A side elevation shot accentuates the long low appearance of the JS27. Arnoux is the driver, on his way to fourth place in the British GP at Brands Hatch.

JS29 The 1987 F1 Ligier first appeared in 'B' form at the second GP meeting of the year, for Tétu designed the JS29 for the Alfa Romeo 415T light-alloy monobloc turbo engine and early tests showed that this was not all it was cracked up to be. Arnoux said as much in public, which was hardly diplomatic, and that gave Alfa an excuse to cancel the arrangement, for it had been bought by Fiat and Fiat's F1 representative was Ferrari. Tétu rapidly revised the car to take the Megatron (née BMW) turbo engine.

The monocoque was made of aluminium sandwich sheathed in carbon fibre/Kevlar sheet, with the side pods containing the water radiator on the right and oil and turbo coolers on the left. Double wishbone suspension was used, with the front spring/damper units mounted horizontally. Outwardly it was low in its original form, but the Megatron was a taller engine than the Alfa unit, and it was also heavier, so a price was paid in aerodynamics and handling. By mid-season the car had been substantially modified, and ran to the end of the year in JS29C form. In such a confused programme, the team's single point was perhaps an achievement.

Drivers: René Arnoux, Piercarlo Ghinzani.

The luckless Ghinzani practising for the British GP, shortly before he was excluded from the meeting. The car is a JS29C.

JS31 Ligier did not reach bottom in 1987, but for a team that had once ranked among the front runners came close to it in 1988. If Tétu's prime objective was low frontal area, then it was achieved, but beyond that the car could not be made to work. The arrangement of components was odd, with fuel tanks beside the driver's legs, behind his seat and between the Judd engine and the gearbox. The idea was to achieve optimum weight distribution but the plumbing contributed to the old Ligier failing of excess weight. Power steering was an option, intended to ease the task for drivers in the very cramped cockpit, but it was an option soon discarded. A hydraulic suspension proposal went the same way – there were problems enough in the largely unavailing attempts to change the car's handling. Its drivers failed to qualify eight times, and the best Ligier race placing was ninth, twice achieved by Johansson.

Drivers: René Arnoux, Stefan Johansson.

The Loto-Ligier looked smart from some angles, but wholly in the great French tradition of vehicular follies from others. Arnoux is again the driver, in practice at Silverstone.

JS33 By the Spring of 1988 Ligier was looking for a successor to Tétu, and Beaujon started work on a successor to the JS31 in something of a vacuum while a designer was sought. Frank Dernie seemed to be headed towards Magny-Cours but ended up with Lotus in Norfolk and Richard Divila took on the Ligier task. The JS33 was sensibly conventional in the 1989 field of lookalike cars, with Ford DFRs in place of the Judd engines. In the first GP newcomer Olivier Grouillard equalled the team's best placing of 1988, but beyond that there was only a fortunate fifth place for Arnoux in Canada. In B form the JS 33s were brought out again in 1990.

Drivers: René Arnoux, Olivier Grouillard.

After 1988, it was a distinct plus for Ligier to have a car that was entirely conventional. Apart from its blue colour scheme it looked like most others on 1989 grids – not that it always reached the grids. This is Arnoux again, in the Silverstone pits lane.

LINCOLN

An Australian 500 car built by a Mr Douglas who broadly followed Cooper lines but used double wishbones at the rear. Although it seemed to have an edge with its Manx Norton engine, it was let down by poor handling. Mr Douglas had clearly not copied the Cooper closely enough.   ML

LIPPI

The 1958 Italian Formula Junior champion, Roberto Lippi, built his own car during the following year. This did not follow local front-mounted Fiat engine fashion, but used a DKW front-wheel drive three-cylinder engine and transmission set-up at the rear, carried in a ladder-type tubular frame with double wishbone front suspension. Nor did Lippi follow the example of German tuners and bore the engine out to the 1.1-litre limit, claiming 70bhp for it in 980cc form. His independence was poorly rewarded and a Lippi marque did not become established.

LISTER

Brian Lister, usually recalled for his sports-racing cars, built his first single-seater in 1956. Like his sports cars, this F2 car incorporated available components, in this case primarily a Coventry Climax FPE engine and Bristol gearbox. It had a space frame of square-section tubes, with the engine mounted offset and inclined, ahead of the driver. Double wishbone front suspension was used, with a de Dion rear end. The complete car was tiny, and it was a failure.

Lister tried again, with another front-engined F2 car that was completed in the late summer of 1957, and started in an Autumn Goodwood race (when it was not competitive and soon retired). While its make-up was similar the car was not quite so diminutive, and it therefore appeared more convincing. Once again the cockpit was offset and inclined in a space frame, the front suspension coil springs/dampers were inboard and the fuel tanks were alongside the driver's legs. That driver was always to be Archie Scott-Brown, but he was killed in a sports car accident at Spa before the F2 car was raceworthy and the project was abandoned.

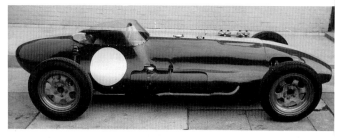

The second F2 Lister, with the carburettors projecting on the left, clean alloy wheels, cockpit set as far back in the relatively long wheelbase as possible, and a fuel tank low down.

LOCKEY

There seems to be no competition history for this British 500cc car of the early 1950s, a neatly finished one-off which reflected credit on its builder. Very much a low-budget effort, it was based on an Austin Seven frame with the Rudge engine in the rear. Remarkably, Tony Lockey was only 15 when he started it and just 17 when it was completed.   ML

LOLA

In 1957 Eric Broadley competed in the British 1172cc 'Ford Ten Special' class with a 'Lola', a car he designed and built himself, and he was sufficiently successful to nurture the dream of becoming a serious driver. The obvious next step was 1100cc sports car racing and again he built his own machine. The Lola-Climax was a superbly made little car, something which was to become a Broadley hallmark, and it was obviously the work of an important new designer. When it appeared in August 1958 Broadley became the first sports car driver to lap Brands Hatch in under a minute. Others soon wanted replicas and Broadley was persuaded to lay down a batch of three cars. Then, during a test session, he invited Peter Ashdown to try his car, realized he was never going to be World Champion and instead signed Ashdown. There followed a dream season in which Lolas won virtually every race they entered and, pound for pound, the Lola Mk1 was probably the best front-engined sports racer ever made.

Other early cars met with less success but a first foray in F1 in 1962 showed that Lola could be competitive at the highest level. The team which ran the first Lola F1 cars seemed to run out of steam before the end of the season and Lola did not become fully involved in F1 again for a quarter of a century. The 1963 Lola Mk6 broke new ground by being the first rear-engined 'big banger' monocoque GT car and among those who were impressed with the concept was Ford. After failing to buy Ferrari, Ford struck a deal whereby Lola became involved in Ford's sports-racing project for a year. The result was the Ford GT40, for which Broadley has rarely received proper credit; less obviously, Lola emerged from the project as a financially stable company.

Over the next few years Lola's cars had mixed fortunes in racing – its small single-seaters were rarely winners but its sports cars and Formula A/5000 cars were often superb. Broadley preferred to stay out of categories where Lola would have had to run a works team, for he claims he is simply no good in that activity and has never regarded himself as a race engineer. Thus Lola only built F1 cars when it was commissioned to do so by another outfit and, for most of its history, the same went for cars for categories such as Indycar racing.

Lola's range changed from year to year as the market changed, but in 1985 Lola made a firm commitment to Indycar and F3000 while being open to joint projects with other teams, which led to supplying cars for both F1 and Group C. In the Indycar field Lola gradually took over March's entire customer car market, largely because it built user-friendly cars which were quick straight out of the box, were made to the required quality, and were backed with excellent service. In F3000 it began on the wrong foot and then recovered and has applied the same formula which won it so many friends in America.

It is unfortunate that the terms of this book exclude most of Lola's best cars. Broadley's company has made an outstanding contribution to motor racing which is not fully reflected by the following entries. Not least among its achievements has been Lola's nurturing of bright young designers and among a very impressive roll call, which began with Tony Southgate in 1960, are John Barnard and Patrick Head whose designs for McLaren and Williams dominated F1 in the 1980s. By the end of 1989 Lola had made a total of 2,245 cars which makes it the most successful production racing car manufacturer ever.   ML

Mk2 Lola's first single-seater was built for Formula Junior and followed the broad layout of the Mk1 sports car with the engine in the front (offset and canted), coil spring and double wishbone front suspension and rear suspension by drive shafts and unequal length trailing wishbones. The specified engine was the Ford 105E which drove through a modified BMC gearbox and drum brakes were inboard at the rear. It was possibly the best front-engined FJ car built, it handled extremely well and rivalled the Lotus 18 for straight-line speed but its engines were never the best (Lotus had an exclusive deal with Cosworth) and the car suffered from frequent engine failures and the complication of its transmission train.

Although 29 were built the Lola Mk2 won only one international race in 1960, but that was a 1-2 at the Nüburgring which tells its own story.

A couple of Mk2s were fitted with Coventry Climax FPF engines and occasionally run as F2 cars in 1960 without any success, but these were private efforts in what had become a professional category so are difficult to assess.

The Mk2 was admirably clean and low of line, but in 1960 the handicap of a front engine mounting was enormous. This Mk2 is at Silverstone.

Mk3 This was a radical rear-engined FJ car with the driver sitting well forward and a central fuel tank. It also had an arrangement whereby the whole of the rear of the car, behind the cockpit, could be removed and replaced in under an hour. Suspension was similar to the Mk2 and the Ford engine drove through a five-speed gearbox which had a Volkswagen casing with internals by Hewland, an arrangement which brought Hewland into the business of making racing car gearboxes and was the first of a long line (and many thousand units) of Hewland 'boxes built inside a VW casing. Innovative it may have been, successful it was not, and not a single win came the way of the eleven which were made. One incident suggests that the car may have been better than the results its drivers achieved might indicate. In a late-season 'second division' F1 race at Brands Hatch, Hugh Dibley qualified in the top half of the field with a Lola Mk3 fitted with a 1,340cc Ford Anglia/ Classic engine which gave away a lot of horses to the Climax FPF engines which powered the rest of the field.

Lola's second-generation Junior, the Mk3, looked the part but was not successful. Its driver was seated in a semi-reclining position, the water radiator was in the nose, oil cooler and carburetter air was taken in through the flanks. This is the prototype, in the little Bromley works early in 1961.

Mk4 Before sponsorship was allowed in Europe some companies by-passed the rules by entering teams under their own name, and among them was the Yeoman Credit finance house. Its racing operation was managed by Reg Parnell (Racing) and for 1962 it commissioned Eric Broadley to design an F1 car for its exclusive use, making it in effect the Lola works team. The Mk4 was a fairly conventional and compact space frame car with suspension front and rear by coil springs, wishbones and radius arms. The first cars had four-cylinder Coventry Climax FPF engines as the team had to

Dawn of the turbo era. Jabouille takes Renault RS01 towards the exit from the Silverstone pits lane during British GP tests in 1977. This was the first public appearance of a turbocharged Grand Prix car, and RS01 was not immediately impressive, while the dull and flat engine note failed to thrill . . .

In the early 1980s Renault's turbo cars had established the marque as a leading GP contender . . . for the first time since 1907. RE30B looked a solid car, yet had elegant lines. Prost drove RE30Bs to two GP victories in 1982 and Arnoux also won two Championship races for Renault.

Under the bodywork of turbo cars the actual engines tended to look small and ancillaries to take up disproportionate space. This is a Renault RE40 (**above**) in 1983, with its carbon fibre composite chassis most obvious around the scuttle and below the fuel cell behind the cockpit. The side pod houses an inclined radiator, KKK turbocharger and waste gate, and (above the 'E') an intercooler.

Before exhaust-driven turbochargers were used in racing, forced induction had meant supercharging. Generally Roots-type superchargers were used but the infamous 1.5-litre BRM had a centrifugal type. Unlike the Renault, the BRM (**left**, in Mk II form) appeared to have an engine compartment full of engine. There were 16 tiny cylinders, 49.53 × 47.8mm compared with 86 × 42.8mm in the Renault V-6. The supercharger was at the front, running at four times engine speed.

Two of the best-known turbo engines were the TAG V-6 (**upper**) and the Honda V-6 (**lower**). The TAG engine was commissioned by McLaren and designed and built by Porsche, whose name appears discreetly ahead of the FISA-badged pop-off valves (on this 1987 engine these restricted turbo boost to four bar). The TAG engine is in a McLaren, the Honda V-6 in a Williams in 1987.

It sometimes seemed that turbo cars were ugly or handsome. **Below left** A Hart-powered Toleman T181C in 1982. **Below right** A BMW-powered Brabham BT56 in 1987.

Ferrari produced a purposeful and attractive second-generation turbo car for 1982 in the 126C2. This car is heading for the Brands Hatch pits exit during GP practice.

wait for its Climax FWMV V8 units. In the early-season minor races of 1962, team leader John Surtees was often the quickest of the four-cylinder brigade and when he got his V8 the combination was one of the quickest three or four in any field.

Surtees showed the potential of car and driver by taking pole in the first World Championship round at Zandvoort, only to crash when a wishbone broke (Surtees thought that the chassis was flexing). He beat Clark, Hill and Brabham in a secondary Mallory Park race. At the Belgian GP, however, when he qualified 11th, one of the car's corners was jacked up and none of the other wheels moved – the frame had flexed to take up the slack. Some extra tubes were hurriedly welded in and Surtees eventually came home fifth.

Surtees and Eric Broadley were to develop a close working relationship, and the car was improved. Surtees' best World Championship placings were second in the British and German GPs but the team's money began to run out and the car slipped down the field. At the end of the season Bowmaker-Yeoman Credit withdrew from racing.

Reg Parnell retained two Lolas for 1963 and entered them alongside the team's Lotus 24 but the cars which had threatened to win in 1962 were now also-rans.

Drivers: Chris Amon, Bob Anderson, Lucien Bianchi, Masten Gregory, Mike Hailwood, Roy Salvadori, John Surtees, Maurice Trintignant.

There was nothing novel in the make-up of the attractive dark green Mk5, but it showed great promise when driven by John Surtees, here in the 1962 German GP.

Mk5 Lola's 1962 FJ car was based on the Mk4 but although it was a great improvement over the Mk3 it was a front-runner rather than a natural winner – Lotus had the best engines and signed the best drivers. Lola did not run an official works team although it had a special relationship with the Midlands Racing Partnership which fielded some good drivers and picked up some wins and a large number of place finishes. After the Lotus works team, the MRP team was probably the best of the rest, both at home and abroad. There was just one victory for a Mk5.

The Mk5A was an update which won eleven national and international races, but to put that into perspective, Lotus won 100½ and Cooper 57½ (they shared a dead heat). One of those races, however, was the Monaco GP support race which

After the Mk3 the 1962 Lola Junior appeared completely orthodox, as indeed it was. This car is driven by Hugh Dibley, at Goodwood.

fell to Richard Attwood in an MRP car (later Attwood became a Monaco specialist) and MRP drivers frequently filled the place positions behind Arundell's works Lotus. Production of Mk5/5As was down to just nine units which compares to the 29 Mk2s and helps to explain why Broadley responded to Ford's approach to become a consultant in the building of the Ford GT40.

Eric Offenstadt converted a Mk5A to run in the new F3 in 1964 and he proved to be easily the most successful driver in French F3 races, winning four and taking many points finishes; he was also the most successful Lola driver in F3 that year.

T53 The first 'post-Ford' car came in 1964, and was the first F3 Lola and the first to use Lola's new type designation. It was the third expression of the Mk5, hence '53', but it was really only a single Mk5A rebuilt for the Midlands Racing Partnership. In a year dominated by the works Coopers run by Ken Tyrrell, Brabham drivers tended to pick up what was left over and the T53 was not a success, one reason being that Lola was preparing to tackle new markets.

T54 Three other Midlands Racing Partnership Mk5A FJ cars were given Cosworth SCA engines and run in F2 in 1964. Attwood won at Vienna as well as taking second places at Pau (splitting the works Lotuses of Clark and Arundell), Albi and the Nürburgring and a third at Aintree just behind Tony Maggs in another T54.

T55 The T54s were updated for F2 in 1964/5, by which time the design was pretty long in the tooth. Most of Lola's effort was going into its T70 Group 7 sports car and its first, and impressive, Indycars. Still, Attwood and Maggs came 1-2 in the Rome GP, Amon won at Solitude and Surtees at Oulton Park and the cars picked up other points finishes, which suggests there was little wrong with handling. But there was the little problem of Clark, who took all of Lotus' five wins, and Rindt leading the Brabham brigade, so three wins with an ageing design was a fair showing. Paul Hawkins also drove a 1500cc Ford-Cosworth powered version in the Mediterranean GP at Pergusa without success. Attwood and Maggs were seventh and tenth in the *Autocar* British Championship, MRP was third in the French Championship.

T60 A conventional but unsuccessful 1965 monocoque car sold mainly for F2. Despite chunky lines it was aerodynamically sound, but most of the best drivers were in Brabhams or Lotuses and among these Brabham, Clark and Rindt dominated the year.

In sleekness of line the T60 almost matched the Lotus 35, but the Ron Harris-Team Lotus cars always seemed to have the best engines, while the apparently bluff Brabhams seemed quicker in a straight line. This MRP T60 is at Vallelunga in 1965.

T61 The 1966 F2 car was an improved T60, made for the Midlands Racing Partnership in 1966. That was the year of the works Brabham-Hondas, and the only two races they did not win were won by Brabham-Cosworths, while the points places were dominated by other Brabhams and the new Matras. The best result for a T61 was David Hobbs' fourth at Barcelona.

T62 The customer 1966 F2/3 model was a conventional monocoque car which made little impact although Surtees ran as high as third with one at Karlskoga before retiring. By this time Lola was having so much success in other fields, notably with USAC cars (Hill won the Indianapolis 500 with a T90) that interest in building cars 'on spec' faded. After the T62, F3 was dropped for some years and F2 designs were undertaken only when conditions were favourable, as in 1967 when BMW commissioned one.

T100 The 1967 F2 car was much improved. Surtees won two races and in one of them, a very wet affair at Mallory Park, he finished 3½ laps ahead of the field. Four were supplied to BMW for use with the 'Apfelbeck' engine. This proved to be extremely troublesome and most of the time Surtees and Hobbs, drivers for the Lola Racing team (a Surtees operation), used Cosworth FVA engines. Still, with the BMW unit, Surtees took second at the Nürburgring in April and Hobbs a third place there in August, which suggests that there was not much wrong with the chassis. This was a normal Lola product, and Lola's 'standard system' suspension components were used front and rear. Using a Cosworth FVA engine Surtees won at Mallory Park and Zandvoort but BMWs works drivers Siffert and Hahne found life very trying without the option of the Ford engine and even when the BMW engine was running properly they could barely run in the top ten. These works cars tended to be referred to as BMWs, and the best placing was Hahne's fourth in the 1967 Eifelrennen. Team Surtees and David Bridges ran T100s in 1968.

T100 obviously followed on from the 1965-66 F2 cars. This is John Surtees in a Lola Racing car, at Crystal Palace.

T102 The developed T100, with a tubular sub frame added to the rear for the simpler BMW engine that superseded the Apfelbeck device. Two were supplied to BMW in 1968 to be run alongside another chassis, from Dornier. The best result from either chassis in F2 was second. Hahne ran one with a 2-litre engine in the very wet and misty 1968 German GP and while he was very slow in practice, he managed to complete the full distance to come tenth of 14 finishers. BMW continued to run T102s into 1969 but Hahne disliked the car, even though he managed a very close second at Hockenheim, and it was soon replaced with a new car designed by Len Terry.

T102 looked a big car by F2 standards and the BMW team drivers were never very happy with its circuit behaviour. Nevertheless, Hahne placed this heavily wing'd example fifth in this Jarama race in 1969.

T130 (Honda RA300) Honda's car for the first year of the 3-litre F1 had a potentially superb V-12 engine (although at first its power and torque bands were decidedly peaky) in a bulky and grossly overweight chassis. John Surtees joined the team in 1967 as the number one driver and to control the preparation and development of the car, which was run from a factory in Slough close to the Lola works.

After struggling with the Honda RA273 for the first half of 1967, Surtees, with the permission of Honda, worked with Eric Broadley to create a new car based on Lola's T90 USAC car monocoque. The tub ended behind the cockpit and the Honda engine was supported on a tubular sub frame, the bodywork was pure Lola and Lola suspension units were used.

T180 (Honda RA301) This was developed from the T130 with input from Surtees, Broadley, Derrick White and Yoshiro Nakamura of Honda. It was supposed to be a lightweight car but Honda's ancillaries meant it was actually heavier than its predecessor. (See Honda.)

T240 This was a conventional 1971 car for the junior formulae. The monocoque design was new, with outboard suspension by double wishbones at the front and lower reversed wishbones at the rear with fixed length drive shafts (the classical Lola solution) and radius rods, and with low-slung angular fuel tanks well back in the wheelbase. Jo Bonnier took one, which was tested by Frank Gardner and Helmut Marko, who raced it once to score one European Championship point; nobody else bought one for F2 or F3 although the cars ran in American Formula B racing. The monocoque was also used for the T330 FA/5000 car of 1972 which the men at Lola regard as the finest single-seater the company has built; at the time it was certainly the most successful and profitable.

T242 A 1972 update of the T240 theoretically available for F2 and F3 but actually only used in Formula B. Lola's small formulae efforts were then concentrated on America until 1976.

T360 This was an F Atlantic car, but one was converted to F2 by the Wella-backed team and entered in British races as a T360B for Ted Wentz. Its deformable structure was made by Gomm and it had a Swindon-BDG engine; it nearly went the distance in the two 1975 Championship F2 races in Britain.

T370 As Graham Hill approached the end of his career as a driver he was unable to command a place with a top team and so created his own with sponsorship from the company marketing Embassy cigarettes. After an indifferent season with a Shadow DN1 in 1973, Hill commissioned Lola to build a new F1 car for 1974.

The T370 was a conventional Cosworth/Hewland British kit car, albeit on the heavy side, which followed the general thinking of Lola's highly successful F5000 car, with front suspension by outboard coil springs and double wishbones

The salient features of the T370 – fine nose, side radiator air exits, large outrigged rear aerofoil and vast air box – all show well in this shot of Graham Hill at Brands Hatch in 1974.

and outboard coil springs at the rear with parallel lower links, single upper links and twin radius arms. The only remarkable thing about the car was its air box which, in profile, presented its sponsor with a huge advertising billboard.

Embassy-Hill began the year with Hill and Guy Edwards as its drivers but neither showed much pace. When Edwards broke his wrist in an accident he was replaced (with relief, perhaps) by Peter Gethin and then Rolf Stommelen; the only points finish all year was Hill's sixth place in Sweden.

Lola T370s were retained for the first three races of 1975, again without success, but then Hill fielded an interim new car originally known as the Lola T371 but then called the GH1. It was the work of former Lola designer, Andy Smallman, and had many Lola design features. (See Hill.)

Drivers: Guy Edwards, Peter Gethin, Graham Hill, Rolf Stommelen.

T450 A conventional 1976 BMW-powered F2 car (three quarter monocoque, tubular sub frame to take the engine, narrow-track outboard suspension and single fuel cell behind the cockpit) which was bought by second division German privateers. The four cars built appeared only spasmodically in a season dominated by Renault-engined cars, they frequently failed to qualify and one tenth place (credited to Roland Binder at the Nürburgring although he was not running at the end) was the best showing all year. One made an abortive appearance with a BDX, Ashley failing to start at Thruxton. Binder entered an uprated car for two 1977 races.

T450 looked attractively slim behind its full-width nose, but five German drivers, a Finn and an Englishman could do nothing with it.

T460 Another F Atlantic car, which sold well for that category and was occasionally competitive in North America. One was tried as an F2 car with a Swindon BDX, without success in its two 1977 appearances.

T470 A 1976 F3 car, similar to the T450. Only one was made, it appeared only occasionally and its best finish was eighth in a race at Thruxton.

T550 A new F2 design for 1977 which apart from its Holbay-Abarth engine had a specification similar to the T450, though 130lb lighter. Only one was built and it did not figure; Roberto Marazzi gave up after just one DNQ.

T570 The 1977 F3 car was broadly based on the T550. It featured the then fashionable front radiator and full-width nose cone and suspension which, in broad terms, harked back to the Mk2. It followed the T470, with the wheelbase slightly increased and the front track slightly narrowed. At the time breaking into F3, especially when the car's fortunes were in the hands of privateers, was an uphill task: the best runners bought proven cars from March, Ralt and Chevron. Mike Blanchet put in a lot of test work, joined in the autumn by Nigel Mansell, who had driven races in a Toyota-powered T570 late in 1977; four were sold but they achieved nothing.

This was another very straightforward car. The works development T570 was sometimes run with a more substantial full-width nose and cockpit surround with the mirrors mounted directly to it. This car is driven by George Aposkitis.

T670 A 1978 F3 car which was a new design but which retained the front radiator and full-width nose cone seen on the development T570 and had a similar paper specification to that car, although front and rear track were narrowed. It might have been competitive in the right hands: as it was its best finish was one fifth place in 1978. Lola's sales director, Mike Blanchet, occasionally drove one fitted with a Chevrolet 'Vega' derived engine in 1979 but that was only because the T770 with which he was due to race in that season did not work with sliding skirts. The lacklustre performance of the car in the hands of a driver capable of winning races points to an engine down on power in a car that was overweight.

A Toyota-engined T670 driven by Slim Borgudd.

T672 An uprated T670, this 1979 F3 car brought the total production for the type up to nine but it had no success whatsoever in F3 and no F Atlantic derivation was made.

T770 This completely new ground effects F3 car was designed by Bob Marston for 1979. It had a narrow chisel nose and front aerofoils and full-length sliding skirts, with a fuselage-type monocoque, side radiators, a tubular sub frame to carry the Chevrolet 'Vega' engine, and inboard suspension front and rear by rocker arms. Compared with the T670 the wheelbase was slightly shortened and front and rear track slightly increased, overall width was slimmer, overall length was slightly shorter and it was 2in higher at 40in.

In testing it was said to be very promising but since the driver was Mike Blanchet, Lola's sales director, he had to keep a brave face while knowing that the car was not competitive. Lola had enormous difficulties with ground effects. In the event Blanchet fell back on the unloved T670 for his spasmodic 1979 season and an ambitious plan for a French outfit to run a full team of T770s came to nothing. One T770, however, was used by Phillipe Alliot who wrote it off early in the season at Donington Park and did not feel inclined to beg for another.

The T770 which Blanchet tested but elected not to use in 1979 was run without skirts (which were then banned) in 1980 as T770/2, and the feeble Vega engine was replaced with a Toyota unit. It showed considerable promise in Blanchet's hands early in the 1980 season, finishing third in its first race and second a week later. Then the private team running the car hit money problems and thereafter its appearances were occasional.

The T770 in its 1979 form, with sliding skirts. This is a test session shot, at Paul Ricard.

T850 This was the 1981 production version of the 1980 Toleman TG280. In a season which saw the arrival of the Ralt-Honda team, Stefan Johansson nonetheless won two races in an 850-Hart and finished fourth in the Championship despite his team being strapped for resources. Properly, these cars were usually known as 'Toleman 850s'. An F Atlantic version, the T860, was also built.

T870 An F3 car completed in the summer of 1983. It was tested but apparently not raced in the formula. It had a similar layout to the T770, with a small nose, side radiators and low engine deck, and a prominent single-pillar rear wing.

THL1 When Carl Haas, Lola's American importer, secured sponsorship for an F1 team, he set up FORCE in a facility close to Heathrow airport. In the absence of a star designer Eric Broadley was engaged as a consultant but the cars were actually drawn by Neil Oatley, Ross Brawn and John Baldwin. Although the Lola connection was tenuous the cars were known as 'Beatrice-Lolas', Beatrice being the sponsor while 'Lola' was included largely because Haas, with Paul Newman, ran the Lola works team in Indycar and was looking to expand his business in the States (see Beatrice).

T950 There was so much doubt and confusion about F3000 in 1985 (the final regulations did not appear until half-way through the first season), that manufacturers adapted existing designs. Lola had only the T900 Indycar chassis on the stocks, but since the T800 had gone well in America much was expected of it. Those who ran the T950 encountered much the same problems as those who bought former F1 cars – in each case the chassis had been designed to take a fuel cell more than double the size required for F3000, with the result that between the cockpit and the engine there was redundant space which did nothing except distribute weight in an unhelpful way. Moreover, aerodynamic requirements of a car running with about 430bhp in F3000 were different from an Indycar with twice that output. The T950 had a honeycomb

monocoque with composite top section, in which the engine acted as a stressed member, and inboard suspension, pushrod at the front, rocker arm at the rear. Seven were ordered but only four were delivered and the best results were a couple of sixth places (scored by Ferté in Mosnier's 'works-status' car with a Nicholson DFV)

By this time Lola had established a complicated system of labelling its types. The '50' of '950' stood for F2/F3000 while the '9' indicated it was the ninth distinct chassis design of a series; had there been an update it would have been the 952 and a further update would have been the 954. Since '00' was the Indycar designation, the 1985 Indycar was the 900.

Mario Hytten's Mader DFV-engined T950 at Silverstone, its lines giving a generous clue to the origins of the design. Like Ferté, Hytten switched to a March during the season.

T86/50 1986 saw Lola introduce a new system of numbering its types, the first figure being the year, the second the category (thus the Indycar design was 86/00). It also started with a clean sheet of paper and produced a bespoke F3000 design, the work of Ralph Bellamy. It looked rather like his March 85B and had similar suspension, pullrod front, rocker arm rear, but the composite carbon fibre/Kevlar monocoque was entirely new and it also benefitted from an intensive wind tunnel programme, the first time that Lola made this claim in its literature. It was designed with the customer in mind, so was notable for its ease of maintenance, but the success of March and Ralt in 1985 gave them a distinct advantage in the market place. Pascal Fabré gave the car a debut win at Silverstone and followed that with a second in the next round, but after that Lola rarely featured in the points.

The engine of the T86/50 was customarily not covered, and that spoiled the sleek good looks of the car. Driver here is Fabré, at Silverstone in a works Mader DFV-engined car.

LC87 Lola returned to F1 in 1987 with a joint project commissioned by Gérard Larrousse acting on behalf of team backer Didier Calmels, hence the designation 'LC' (Larrousse Calmels). Unlike some previous collaborations, Lola committed itself wholeheartedly to this project despite the logistics of building the cars in England and running them from France. Designed by Broadley and Bellamy, the LC87 was a fairly conventional design (carbon composite monocoque, double wishbone and pullrod suspension front and rear, a normally aspirated 3.5-litre Cosworth DFZ engine and a Hewland FGB gearbox), indeed it closely followed the lines of the 87/50 F3000 car. Running a simple car, however, was an ideal way for a new team to ease itself into F1, and the pit lanes regularly saw the unusual sight of Eric Broadley engineering a car.

The team joined the Championship in the second round, at Imola, with a single car for Philippe Alliot. He was to win the normally aspirated category three times in the season as well as picking up three sixth places overall. Most of the work throughout the year was concentrated on shedding weight and steady progress was made all season. Late in the year a second car was run for Yannick Dalmas. Lola finished second to Tyrrell (although a long way behind) in the 'Colin Chapman Cup' which was the Constructors' Championship for the normally aspirated brigade, while in the overall table Lola was ninth.

Drivers: Philippe Alliot, Yannick Dalmas.

In many respects LC87 was closely related to the contemporary Lola F3000 car. The driver here is Alliot, in practice for the British GP.

T87/50 Updated from the 1986 car by Mark Williams, it had the same critical dimensions with a new rear suspension layout using pushrods. The T87/50 made Lola a force to be reckoned with in F3000. It was, by general agreement, the outstanding customer car of the year and was consistent and competitive. Lola won the Japanese F3000 Championship and should have done the same in Europe except that Stefano Modena, running with the vastly experienced Onyx team, was able to make the 'difficult' March 87B work. The Lola worked anywhere, for anyone, and Luis Sala took second place in the Championship, with two of Lola's four wins in the Lola Motorsport car (Trollé and Bailey each won a race). Several T87/50s appeared in 1988, Chiesa winning a point with one.

The French GBDA team enjoyed a close association with the factory with its two-car F3000 team in 1987. Michel Trollé, here at Silverstone, was sixth in the Championship.

LC88 After a promising debut season in F1, Lola allowed itself to be lulled into complacency with the LC88, which was the work of Broadley and Chris Murphy (Bellamy left early in the year). Superficially the car's specification was similar to the 1987 car but with pushrod front suspension. It worked well on

the slower circuits on which the season began, with Alliot usually to be found in mid-grid (once he was as high as twelfth) but the finishing record was poor and the team failed to record a points finish.

Two of the five cars built were modified on a cut and shut basis to run with the Lamborghini V-12 in the first GP of 1989. Designated LC88B, they necessarily had an extended wheelbase, and were overweight. In Brazil the team recorded a DNQ and 12th place.

Drivers: Philippe Alliot, Yannick Dalmas, Pierre-Henri Raphanel, Aguri Suzuki.

T88/50 Lola should have swept the board in the 1988 F3000 Championship but the arrival of Reynard scotched such hopes. The T88/50 was a logical update on the lines laid down in 1986 but featured a new composite monocoque designed by Mark Williams which was much narrower in the areas of the cockpit and the front suspension, and had improved cooling and new pushrod front suspension. On the whole, Lolas went best on the tighter circuits, which suggested that Reynard had found an advantage with its aerodynamic package. Lola took three wins, scored by Grouillard and Foitek, and vied with Reynard to fill the points positions, with second, sixth and seventh on the final table.

Among the numerous Lolas on F3000 grids in 1988 were the three run by the Belgian Sport Auto Racing team, this one driven by reigning French saloon car champion Fabien Giroix, whose single-seater career was to end in a Monza crash.

LC89 Gérard Ducarouge joined Broadley and Murphy on the design team for the LC89, which was a new car built to accommodate the Lamborghini 3512 80 degree V-12 engine and a new Lamborghini transverse gearbox. Both were the work of long-time Ferrari designer Mauro Forghieri. The LC89 appeared in the second race and followed the fashion set by March in 1988 with a very narrow monocoque and long wheelbase, eight inches up on the LC88. Details such as suspension all round by double wishbones and pushrod remained, a set up shared with virtually every car on the GP

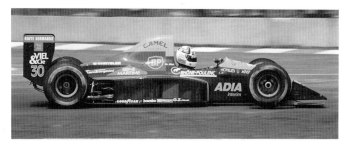

The definitive Lamborghini-engined car had well balanced lines, which related to the preceding F1 car. The driver is Alliot, at Imola.

grids. Alliot gradually worked his way up the grid, race by race, in 1989 while Dalmas in the second car was a regular non-qualifier and was dropped at mid-season.

Much of the season was spent shedding weight and making the engine reliable (a switch to a Bosch management system appeared to help) but only a single points finish was achieved and there were few other times when one of the cars was still around at the finish in any place.

Drivers: Michele Alboreto, Philippe Alliot, Eric Bernard, Yannick Dalmas.

T89/50 Mark Williams' 1989 F3000 car was a subtle update of his 1988 car with particular attention paid to improving driver safety, and with Mugen engines in the DAMS cars, Nicholson or Mader DFVs in other Lolas. It was potentially the best all-round car on the grids but it reached the hands of few drivers who seemed capable of winning. Reynard's aggressive selling techniques had paid off in that it accounted for some 60 per cent of entrants' cars. The French DAMS (Droit Arnoux Motor Sport) team was effectively the Lola works team, and its drivers Erik Comas and Eric Bernard were second and third in the Championship. Comas scored as many points as champion Alesi, but only two outright wins to Alesi's three, and that decided the outcome. It was noticeable that Lolas failed to qualify less often than other cars, which suggests they were better than the number of wins would indicate, a view backed by the fact that Ogawa won the increasingly important Japanese Championship in a Lola.

Once again Lola produced a car that had sleek lines as far back as the cockpit. Behind it the engines, DFV or Mugen, were largely exposed. This DFV-engined T89/50 is driven by Canadian Stéphane Proulx, who was a modest 17th in the Championship.

LOTUS

Colin Chapman's marque was in the forefront of racing for many years, in terms of technical innovation and successes on the circuits, and it also went through periods of failure as well as triumph. After his death in 1982 Team Lotus was kept in racing by his lieutenants, but save for an innovation that in fact had its origins in Chapman's days it tended to have the status of one of several constructors' teams. The 1980s ended with the team at a low ebb – it contested its 400th Grand Prix in 1989, but without adding to the victory score of 79 that had been reached in 1987 – and in some disarray, but that hardly dimmed the brilliance of the past.

Chapman's first single-seater might not have been a Lotus, but a design commissioned by the Clairmonte brothers for F2 in 1952 (it was completed as a sports car). He also worked as a consultant for Vanwall and BRM. The first Lotus single-seaters were never successful in their front-line days, and Chapman had to accept that a rear-engined layout was the right one. Once he did his Lotus cars became pace setters, and until 1971

Lotus was a leading company in the customer car market as well as in its racing teams.

Lotus teams and Lotus private entrants became leading contenders with the 18, and its successors. Innovations included the monocoque principle, introduced with the 25 and to become universal. Chapman was also instrumental in getting Ford backing for the Cosworth DFV engine to power his F1 cars, and in time they were to power every car in F1 except odd Italian machines. He might not have invented 'wings' but he led the way in pushing that branch of automotive aerodynamics forward, almost beyond the point of understanding, as he did with ground effects. From the mid-1960s his ideas were translated into working designs by men like Maurice Phillippe, but he invariably provided the inspiration.

Lotus stopped making customer racing cars in 1971, and from that time the story of Lotus racing cars is the story of Team Lotus. That was usually coupled with a sponsor's name – Gold Leaf Team Lotus in the great days of the 49 (sadly near the end of the great Jim Clark's career). Chapman, perhaps unwittingly, set formula racing on the road to sponsorship that was to become virtually universal. He did not heed the traditionalists when they failed to see that racing was heading towards an expensive new age of high technology. He was not, however, entirely blind to history and by the early 1980s had gathered together a collection of past Lotus models. Among them were many that were outstanding by any racing yardstick: in the world of Grand Prix racing, Lotus won the Constructors' Championship seven times and finished in the top three on the points table 18 times in the years 1960-87.

After Chapman's death his team continued under its manager Peter Warr, who had joined Lotus in 1958 and managed the Grand Prix team in the 1970s before a brief spell with Wolf and Fittipaldi. The long-standing association with Players, which apart from a brief period in the 1970s had run from 1968, finally ended in 1986. In the following year there was the shock of seeing Lotus GP cars in bright yellow Camel colours. Moreover, they brought 'active' suspension into Grand Prix racing, apparently successfully as the 'active' cars won two Grands Prix. But that was to be the last flash of success in the 1980s.

Designer Ducarouge perhaps lost his touch, and things did not go well on the circuits in 1988-90. This led to schisms, and the situation was not improved as drivers and car failed to live up to expectations. The Chapman family, which still controlled the racing team, took action. Team director Peter Warr left and Tony Rudd was seconded from the main Lotus company to become Executive Chairman of Team Lotus International.

12 The first single-seater Lotus as such appeared at the 1956 London Motor Show, but the winter passed before circuit tests were run with a 12. This F2 car seemed as small as a front-engined formula could be. It was built around a lightweight space frame, initially with a double wishbone front suspension and a de Dion arrangement at the rear, soon to be superseded by 'Chapman strut' suspension (a substantial hub casting, long coil spring/shock absorber, radius arm and half shaft). The engine was the Coventry Climax FPF, mounted rigidly and angled down towards the rear to drop the height of the propshaft as it made its way to the Lotus gearbox that was to cause much heartache. The body design emphasised low frontal area and sleekness.

The inauspicious race debut of the 12 came at Goodwood at Easter 1957, Allison retiring as a half shaft failed. A few weeks later Mackay-Fraser recorded the first finish for a single-seater Lotus, second in a short Brands Hatch race.

In 1958 Lotus grew into the Grand Prix world as 12s were run as F1 cars, with 1.96-, 2.0- and 2.2-litre FPFs. Hill made the first race start in an F1 Lotus, in the Silverstone International Trophy, and Allison and Hill started 2.0-litre 12s in that year's Monaco GP, when Allison was sixth (and last). Some 12s served F2 independents into 1959.

Drivers: Cliff Allison, Graham Hill.

The first Grand Prix finish for Team Lotus was recorded by Allison with this car at Monaco in 1958, albeit he was ten laps behind the winner. He gives scale to the whole car.

16 This was a more sophisticated design, outwardly sleeker than the 12 and with a cross-section that appeared nearer to oval than round. The space frame was lightweight to an extent that equated with fragility, suspension followed 12 lines, while in the interests of minimal frontal area the FPF was inclined (at varying degrees) and offset to the centre line so that the transmission ran to the left of the cockpit.

The 16 appeared in F1 and F2 forms, both being raced for the first time at the 1958 French GP meeting, running alongside the 12. Team Lotus' record was far from outstanding: Allison was the fifth F1 finisher in the German GP, but a pit stop had cost almost 20 minutes and overall fifth place had been taken by McLaren in an F2 Cooper, so Hill's fifth in the Italian GP was the best actual F1 result. 1959 was little better, although Ireland was fourth in the Dutch GP and was classified fifth at Sebring. The 16s made few appearances in 1960, several went to Australia, some were cut and shut for various purposes, and in the 1970s some found reliability in historic racing.

Drivers (F1): Cliff Allison, Graham Hill, Innes Ireland, Rodriguez Larreta, Pete Lovely, David Piper, Alan Stacey, Mike Taylor.

Team Lotus 16s at Sebring for the first US GP in 1959. The cast magnesium alloy disc wheels, which combined lightness and strength, were a feature of Lotus racing cars through to the mid-1960s.

18 The first mid-engined Lotus was a chunky car, built around a space frame that was stouter and less complex than the 16's but weighing only a little over 27kg (and fibreglass bodywork added little to that). The suspension used unequal-length

wishbones at the front, with a single lower wishbone and fixed-length driveshaft at the rear, with twin radius rods. On the 'senior' versions Lotus' gearbox was used, for FJ versions VW- or Renault-based 'boxes were specified. This Lotus was built for three classes – F1 and F2, with Climax engines, and Formula Junior where the modified Ford 105E rated at 75bhp in 1960 was the usual power unit. A handful of FJ cars were run with BMC A-series engines and Mitter installed one of his DKW engines in an 18. There were of course other differences, for example in fuel arrangements. In the F1/F2 cars there were many independent variations, for example the Walker cars had revised transmission, in an experiment a Vanwall engine was installed in an 18, and Borgward and Maserati engines were also fitted. There were a lot of these cars around – in 1960 no fewer than 125 FJ 18s were turned out – and there was presumably some 'interchange' between chassis.

Innes Ireland during practice for the 1960 French GP, driving an 18 with a high-speed nose for the very fast Reims circuit and an experimental attempt to feed non-turbulent air to the carburettors.

Stirling Moss during a classic drive in Walker's blue 18 at Monaco in 1961 when he beat the much more powerful Ferraris in the first Championship race of the 1.5-litre Formula.

The FJ version came first, at the 1959 Brands Hatch Boxing Day meeting, and within weeks Ireland led the Argentine GP in an F1 18, before falling away to finish sixth. At Oulton Park at Easter Ireland drove an 18 to score Team Lotus' first F2 victory, and on the Easter Monday won both the F1 and F2 races. Then at Monaco Stirling Moss drove Walker's 18 to score the first GP victory for Lotus. In the Constructors' Championship that year Lotus was runner-up to Cooper. In 1961 Lotus was runner-up to Ferrari, in large part due to Moss' efforts in Walker cars. These were 18s with sleeker bodywork as clashing supplier contracts meant that Lotus could not supply the latest model (the 21) to Walker. Other independent cars were similarly modified, and usually referred to as 18/21 (a Walker 18/21 had a Climax V-8 fitted).

Meanwhile, the 18 had been overwhelmingly successful in FJ racing, and in the last season of the 1.5-litre F2 four races fell to this milestone car.

Drivers (F1 18 and '18/21'): Carlo Abate, Cliff Allison, Gerry Ashmore, Lucien Bianchi, Jo Bonnier, Ian Burgess, John Campbell-Jones, Ron Carter, Jay Chamberlain, Jim Clark, Colin Davis, Graham Eden, Ron Flockhart, Olivier Gendebien, Masten Gregory, Dan Gurney, Bruce Halford, Jim Hall, Carl Hammarlund, Walt Hansgen, Gary Hocking, Innes Ireland, Kurt Kuhnke, Tony Maggs, Willy Mairesse, Ernst Maring, Tony Marsh, Michael May, Stirling Moss, Olle Nygren, Tim Parnell, André Pilette, David Piper, Ernesto Prinroth, Phil Robinson, Lloyd Ruby, Jock Russell, Pete Ryan, Giorgio Scarlatti, Wolfgang Seidel, Gunther Seifert, Tony Shelly, Alan Stacey, Gaetano Starrabba, John Surtees, Henry Taylor, Mike Taylor, Trevor Taylor, Maurice Trintignant, Nino Vaccarella.

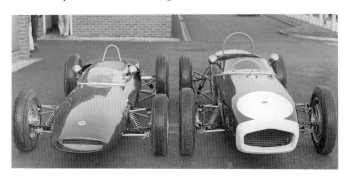

A pairing which makes all the points about reduced frontal area – lowered centre of gravity and sleeker body lines – an 18 Junior (right) and its successor, the 20.

20 An FJ car introduced at the 1961 London Racing Car Show, the 20 was as slippery as the 18 had been square. The driver was seated in a semi-reclining position, a finer nose line was achieved by moving the fuel tank back to behind the driver's seat, smaller front wheels were used, brakes were inboard at the rear (and the 20B had discs in place of drums). Quoted power output of the usual 1098cc Cosworth-Ford 105E was 85bhp. This was another highly successful car, in a very competitive category, and 118 were built.

21 This was an interim car, deriving from the 20 and used to hold the line while Lotus (and other teams) waited for British 1.5-litre F1 V-8s. The familiar FPF was used, driving through a ZF gearbox. It was obviously stronger than the FJ car, and

Clark and Ireland in line ahead in the 1961 French GP, which they finished in third and fourth places. The race was run in extreme heat, so side panels have been removed to aid driver cooling – something that was to be ruled out by Lotus developments in the next year.

other differences included increased fuel tankage, the use of inboard coil spring/shock absorber units at the front and outboard brakes at the rear.

Race debut for the 21 came at Monaco, but the highlight for Team Lotus came at the end of the season when Ireland scored its first Grand Prix victory, at Watkins Glen. He also won two non-Championship races in 21s, yet at the end of the year was dismissed by Chapman. Jim Clark and Trevor Taylor had a rewarding late year expedition to South Africa with 21s, winning four races (several 21s were used by South African independents through the following years). Single cars were briefly used by the Brabham, Filipinetti and Walker teams.

Drivers: C. Barrau, Jack Brabham, Jim Clark, Jim Hall, Innes Ireland, Neville Lederle, Willy Mairesse, Gerhard Mitter, Stirling Moss, H. Muller, E. Pieterse, Jo Siffert, Trevor Taylor.

22 The 1962 FJ car was once again announced at the London Racing Car Show (then a significant pre-season showroom for Lotus Components, responsible for car sales). It was a further refinement, primarily with an inclined engine, almost invariably a MkIV Cosworth-Ford although Mitter again chose DKW power (sic) for his Lotus. As in 1960 (with Clark) and 1961 (with Trevor Taylor) a Team Lotus driver dominated the season – Peter Arundell started in 25 races in 22s, won 18, was placed second in three and retired four times. Niemann ran one in F1 guise, with an enlarged Cosworth engine, in South Africa in 1963-4.

24 Seemingly introduced as an improved 21 space frame car to take either of the new British 1.5-litre V-8s – until in May 1962 it became obvious that for Team Lotus it was a stand-in and that it was actually a customer car. Of the dozen turned out by Lotus, seven eventually had Coventry Climax FWMV V-8s, five had BRM V-8s; Parnell built up additional cars.

The 24 was used by Team Lotus until superseded by 25s. Other leading teams which ran 24s were Walker, UDT-Laystall, Brabham and Bowmaker/Parnell, and 24s appeared on F1 grids through to the end of 1964.

Drivers (F1): Chris Amon, Peter Arundell, Mike Beckwith, Jimmy Blumer, Jo Bonnier, Jack Brabham, John Campbell-Jones, Jim Clark, Bernard Collomb, Paddy Driver, Masten Gregory, Mike Hailwood, Jim Hall, Graham Hill, Phil Hill, Innes Ireland, Tony Maggs, Tim Parnell, Roger Penske, Peter Revson, Hans Schiller, R. Schroeder, Wolfgang Seidel, Gunther Seifert, Hap Sharp, Jo Siffert, Trevor Taylor, Maurice Trintignant, Nino Vaccarella, Heini Walter, Rodger Ward, André Wicky.

A UDT-Laystall BRM-engined 24 at Crystal Palace in 1962, driven by Ireland (who won the race). Apart from its bulkier nose lines, and of course the near-vertical exhaust stacks of that passing BRM fad, it appears almost a 'space frame 25'.

25 This was a most significant car for, avoiding discussion of aircraft and car precedents, with it Chapman introduced monocoque chassis construction to Grand Prix racing. By modern standards it had a simple bathtub structure, with twin side pontoons in light alloy sheet linked by steel bulkheads fore and aft, the instrument panel and the undertray, but it established the principle. It was light, at just under 30kg, yet offered a high degree of stiffness which was to pay dividends in cornering powers as a more supple suspension set-up could be used. It was also a major contribution to safety. Suspension followed the 24 and the Climax FWMV was the normal engine, although some cars were to be re-engined when they were sold out of the works team (for example, Parnell's pair had BRM V-8s, and Hewland gearboxes in place of the ZF originals).

All seven built first served with Team Lotus, and those still on the strength in 1964 were uprated to 25Bs, with smaller wheels and revised suspension. Further detail modifications followed, and in effect Len Terry developed the car as the 33.

A 25 was first raced in the 1962 Dutch GP, and Clark scored the first victory with one in Belgium a month later. The team used 25s through 1964, when a broad yellow stripe was added to the green of the fibreglass bodywork, following the colours used on the Lotus Indianapolis cars in 1963. Independents used them into the second year of the 3-litre formula, with four-cylinder Climax engines or enlarged BRM V-8s.

The Team Lotus 25s won 14 Championship races. In 1963 Clark drove them to win his first World Title, with seven race victories, and that year Lotus won the Constructors' Championship for the first time.

Drivers: Chris Amon, Peter Arundell, Richard Attwood, Giancarlo Baghetti, Bob Bondurant, Jo Bonnier, Jim Clark, Piers Courage, Mike Hailwood, Paul Hawkins, Innes Ireland, Chris Irwin, Tony Maggs, Gerhard Mitter, Pedro Rodriguez, Giacomo Russo, Moises Solana, Mike Spence, Trevor Taylor.

Fine lines characterized the 25, the whole design being beautifully balanced as well as technically innovative. Jim Clark, here at Rouen, enjoyed an outstanding season with the 25 in its first season, 1962.

27 By general consent, FJ had become unrealistically sophisticated and costly by 1962, and for the following season Lotus seemed to hasten the category's demise by introducing a monocoque FJ car. This was actually intended to prove the construction for secondary category customer cars for 1964, when new F2 and F3 regulations were to come into force.

The first monocoque, however, had fibreglass sides which lacked rigidity and it had to be redesigned in alloy. The delay meant that there were few customers, and the quasi-works cars run by Ron Harris' team were not developed and winning until the summer (Arundell won half-a-dozen leading races on the trot, to just beat Hulme to the British Championship).

31 Lotus' first car for the 1-litre F3 was a space frame design deriving from the FJ 22. Only a few were sold in a half-way house season, when many contenders used sleeved-down FJ engines and, as far as Lotus was concerned, 20 or 22 chassis. Only one major FJ race fell to a Lotus (and that was a Janspeed-BMC powered 20/22, driven by Fenning at Silverstone), but then the season was dominated by the combination of J.Y.

Stewart, K. Tyrrell, and Cooper. An 'improved version' was offered for 1965, alongside the more expensive 35. The design was later revived as the Mk51 FF 1600 car.

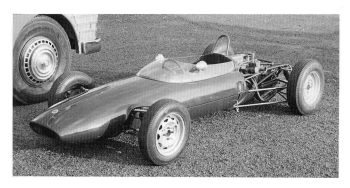

The 31 looked the part, but generally the cars that were raced did not have the best of engines (Cosworth was preoccupied with F2).

32 For the new 1-litre F2, Lotus based a car on the monocoque 27. The tub was in steel, with room for a 41-litre fuel tank in each flank. Suspension was modified, and fully adjustable (that overcame a shortcoming in the 27) and the 115bhp 998cc Cosworth SCA was canted at an angle of 32 degrees, which led to a slightly offset Hewland gearbox/final drive and unequal length driveshafts. Harris ran four cars (of the 12 built) and his drivers won seven races in a season when Brabhams were the cars to beat, Clark taking six and Stewart one. A 32B version with a 2.5-litre Climax engine was built for Tasman racing, and driven by Clark to win five races in early 1965.

Clark trying hard in a 32 in the Oulton Park Gold Cup, when he was beaten by Brabham. The 32 was another neat car, but its monocoque did not give the road-holding/handling advantages theory insisted it should. The oddly angled radius arms show in this shot.

33 In effect this was a development of the 25 – the chassis numbering sequence continued from that model – with the the new wide Dunlops, modified suspension and numerous detail changes. It first appeared in the Spring of 1964, and

The 33 with the BRM V-8 and its low exhausts was perhaps more handsome than the more usual Climax cars. The larger tyres were the main factor in giving an impression that the 33 was much more solid than the 25. This is Hill in Casino Square at Monaco in 1967, during practice for the 33's last race with Team Lotus (he placed this car second in the GP).

from the summer started to take the place of the 25s in the Team Lotus line up. In 1965 it was the mainstay, and continued to be run through the first season of 3-litre Grands Prix, with 2-litre 32-valve Climax V-8s or 2.1-litre BRM V-8s, alongside the 43 with its cumbersome BRM H-16.

Clark and Lotus won the Championship in 1965, with six Championship race victories, but finished well down both points tables in 1966. In the following year Clark won the Tasman Championship with a Climax-engined 33. Once the 49 with the DFV engine arrived in 1967 there was little life in the 33s, even for independents, and the cars disappeared from main-line racing very soon after the last Team Lotus race with them, at Monaco in 1967.

Drivers (GPs): Peter Arundell, Jim Clark, Walt Hansgen, Paul Hawkins, Graham Hill, Pedro Rodriguez, Giacomo Russo, Moises Solana, Mike Spence.

35 F3 was more popular in 1965 but there were few customers for the monocoque 35, which was in a line of evolution from the 27 and 32 and also doubled as an F2 car. Chassis and suspension were standardized, and the 35 would accept a wide range of engines and gearboxes (Cosworth MAE or Holbay engines were the common F3 types, Cosworth SAE or BRM units in F2, with Hewland four-, five- or six- speed 'boxes). In either guise it was a slim car, and looked the part. In 1965 Ron Harris ran cars in both classes; Clark won the British and French F2 Championships for this team, but in F3 the only bright moment came when Revson won at Monaco.

39 An F1 design for the Coventry Climax FWMV flat sixteen, which was never raced as the FWMV proved equal to 1965 challenges – as Clark's achievements with the 33 showed. The chassis of the 39 was adapted for a 2.5-litre Climax FPF (a first Lotus design assignment for Len Terry's successor, Maurice Phillippe). Clark drove the 39 in the 1966 Tasman series, without great success.

41 This F3 car marked a determined fight back into this market in 1966. In it Lotus reverted to a space frame, although the tubes were stiffened with sheet metal diaphragms (foot box, dashboard, rear of cockpit, gearbox area) and undertray. The engine (a Cosworth MAE) was inclined at 30 degrees, and like the gearbox was mounted to contribute to rigidity. The unusually wide track almost drew attention to the slim body – in spite of the tubular structure, the 41 had less frontal area than the 35.

The slippery virtues of the 41 body must in large part have been offset by all those suspension bits and pieces upsetting the airflow.

A quasi-works team was run by Charles Lucas, whose drivers Courage and Pike won half a dozen races, denting Brabham superiority. But above all, this was a customer car; an initial batch of 34 was laid down (price £2475 assembled!) and

final production reached 61. The 41B was an F2 version with an FVA engine, and the number was also applied to the Formula B version in 1967. That year also saw the 41C F3 car with revised suspension, but the sales response was poor as the 41s had gained a reputation for fragility. The '41X' was a one-off derivative with a pronounced wedge body, which Gold Leaf Team Lotus driver John Miles used to score several victories in 1968, when it was modified and became the 55.

Lotus Components ran an F2 41B for Jackie Oliver in 1967. Apart from engine bay modifications, this had wider wheels and tyres. They are reflected on a soaking Mallory Park track on a late spring day in 1967.

43 For an interim 3-litre F1 engine Chapman had to turn to the over-complex and heavy BRM H-16, which was used in a pair of 43s. It was a stressed member, carrying the rear suspension, and it was mounted to a bulkhead behind the cockpit. The short monocoque followed lines laid down in the 38 USAC car. A 43 first appeared in practice for the 1966 Belgian GP, and that car was the only 43 to finish a race, when Jim Clark won the 1966 American GP. A second was completed (a pair started in only one GP, in South Africa in 1967), then the 43s were sold for independent conversions to F5000.

Drivers: Peter Arundell, Jim Clark, Graham Hill.

From most angles the 43 appeared a well proportioned car, in spite of the H-16 lump in the back – engine, transmission and rear suspension exceeded the minimum formula weight! This is the first car, driven by Clark in practice for the Mexican GP.

44 The F2 car for 1966, based on the monocoque of the 35 with the wide suspension of the 41, and with Cosworth engines that were no match for Brabham's Honda units. Three were used by Ron Harris' team, for which Clark and Arundell were in distant third and tenth places on the Championship table; the third car was driven by several drivers.

48 A new car for the new 1.6-litre F2, although it was first used in the Australian GP. It had a full monocoque, with a tubular sub frame for the Cosworth FVA engine. In 1967 Clark won three races, against another Brabham tide, but his team mate Graham Hill could do no better than two second places.

The cars were brought out again in 1968, and because there were no F1 cars available at the time of the presentation one of the 48s was the single-seater featured at the announcement of Gold Leaf Team Lotus. Clark, sadly, was driving a GLTL 48 when he was killed in a high-speed crash at Hockenheim.

A sight that shocked the motor sport Establishment one day early in 1968 – a road racing car painted in a sponsor's colours, to be entered in races carrying a sponsor's name. The sailor's head just had to go, but nothing could be done about the overall scheme. From a low angle this freshly repainted 48 looks particularly sleek.

49 This was a landmark car. After the uncertain first year of 3-litre Grand Prix racing it set a true standard. It was laid out for the even more astonishing Cosworth-Ford DFV engine – Colin Chapman was instrumental in bringing together Keith Duckworth and Ford's Harley Copp and Walter Hayes, and they committed Ford to back the design and development of the DFV. It was to be exclusive to Lotus for the 1967 season, and the 49 was designed to complement it.

It was a straightforward car, with timeless lines in its first form. The cross-section of its monocoque was determined by the cross-section of the 90-degree V-8 (85.7 x 64.8mm, 2993cc), and this was bolted to the bulkhead behind the cockpit and served a load-bearing role. The rear suspension sub frame was bolted to the block and cylinder heads, with braking loads fed forward into the monocoque through twin radius arms. A dozen 49s carried chassis numbers, although three were rebuilds and one was an exhibition car and never raced. A 2.5-litre Cosworth DFW-engined version (49T) was run in Tasman races. The 49B of 1968 had a longer wheelbase, modifications in areas such as the rear sub frame, wider wheels and a semi-wedge body. Strutted 'wings' were carried from the French GP of that year, until both GLTL 49s crashed heavily as a result of rear aerofoil failures on the bumpy Barcelona circuit in 1969, when such devices were precipitately banned.

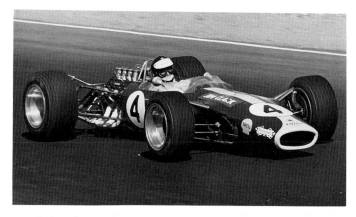

Jim Clark on his way to his 25th World Championship race victory at Kyalami, as 1968 opened. This was also the last race for an F1 car in the old Team Lotus colours. The car is 49/R4, new but virtually to original specification, although in details – such as the front suspension – had been uprated and ZF components in the transmission were soon to give way to Hewland gearboxes. In a detail showing on the nose of R4 Shell has taken the place of Lotus' traditional supplier, Esso. This car was sold to Rob Walker and destroyed in a garage fire.

The 49 was driven by champions – Jimmy Clark won his 25th and last Grand Prix victory in one, Emerson Fittipaldi drove his first F1 race for Lotus in one and Graham Hill won his second World Championship with 49s. It was in the front line for four years, at the centre of the great wings controversy, central to the introduction of sponsorship to Grand Prix racing, driven to a debut race victory by Clark in Holland in 1967 and the last of its twelve Championship race victories was scored by Rindt at Monaco in 1970. A 49 was the last private owner car to win a Grand Prix, when Jo Siffert won in Rob Walker's 49/7 at Brands Hatch in 1968. The Lotus 49 was one of the great Grand Prix cars.

Drivers: Mario Andretti, Richard Attwood, Giancarlo Baghetti, Jo Bonnier, Bill Brack, Dave Charlton, Jim Clark, Emerson Fittipaldi, Wilson Fittipaldi, Graham Hill, Pete Lovely, Jackie Oliver, Jochen Rindt, Jo Siffert, Moises Solana, Tony Trimmer, Eppie Weitzes.

Two 49Bs in the 1968 Mexican GP, Graham Hill in the GLTL 49/R6 and Jo Siffert in Walker's 49/R7. Hill's car has a driver-adjustable rear aerofoil, which could be feathered for minimum drag on straights. Walker's blue car has normal wings. Hill won this race.

55 The '41X' F3 car, revised and run as a GLTL entry in 1968.

56B The spare 56 from the 1968 USAC programme had a Pratt & Whitney gas turbine equivalent to a 3-litre piston engine installed in 1970, and it was raced in some F1 events in 1971. It was a four-wheel drive car, which suffered a variety of niggling setbacks, as well as throttle lag. Its first race was the Race of Champions, and in the Silverstone International Trophy, on a more suitable circuit, it showed promise. Its best GP result was eighth in Italy, driven by Fittipaldi and run in black and gold colours, and its active career ended when Fittipaldi finished second in a non-Championship race at Hockenheim.

Drivers: Emerson Fittipaldi, Dave Walker, Reine Wisell.

In common with other four wheel drive cars, the 56B had identical front and rear wheels. It also had Lotus' wedge lines, a forward driving position (imposed by the length of the power unit), much larger ducts for brake cooling air than the track cars and aerofoils not used on the 56 two years earlier. Driver is Australian Dave Walker, during Silverstone tests.

57 An F2 car with de Dion suspension that was tested in 1968 but never raced.

58 The 57 revised for further tests, with a Cosworth DFW engine and ZF gearbox. If tests had shown worthwhile advantages the project might have been pursued for F1, as it was it never raced.

59/59B This design for F2 (59B) and F3 marked a Lotus effort to rebuild fortunes in the secondary categories. Dave Baldwin designed a fairly complex square tube space frame, but in the main the cars were orthodox. The body was not admired, and apparently was not very efficient in aerodynamic respects, but handling qualities were first class.

Roy Winkelman Racing was the principal F2 team, works-blessed but without the status Ron Harris teams had in the past. Rindt and Hill were its 'name' drivers, and the Austrian dominated in the 1969 F2 season.

There was a GLTL F3 team (drivers Pike and Nunn), while works help got 59s into the hands of other good drivers – Kottulinsky and Ikuzawa won with 59s, as did Emerson Fittipaldi – but in overall terms the season belonged to Tecno.

The 59 was an uncharacteristically bluff car, but it handled well and put the power on the road efficiently – what more could an F3 driver ask for at the end of the 1960s? Better aerodynamic penetration, perhaps, and that came in the 59B with a more shapely nose on 69 lines.

63 In laying out the complex 63, Lotus at least had experience of four wheel drive with the 56, and Phillippe followed that precedent in some respects. The car, of course, had much in common with the contemporary 64 Indianapolis car. The DFV was 'reversed' in the chassis, with the clutch behind the driver's seat and the gearbox on the left, drive being taken fore and aft to ZF final drives. In components such as the fabricated suspension it was a substantial car by Lotus standards.

Regular 1969 team drivers Hill and Rindt did not like the 63, although ironically when Rindt was persuaded to race it, in the Gold Cup, he achieved its best result (second). John Miles drove it most, making five starts, and in nine races 63s recorded seven retirements.

Drivers: Mario Andretti, Jo Bonnier, John Miles, Jochen Rindt.

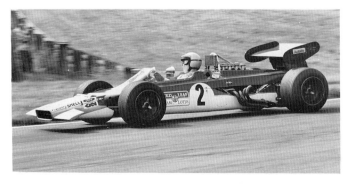

The odd overall appearance of the 63 does not call for comment, save that it was sleeker than other four wheel drive F1 cars. The bodywork shows the upper line of the open bathtub monocoque. Rindt is the driver, at Oulton Park.

69 This number was used for single seaters built for four categories, F2, F3, Formula B/Atlantic and Formula Ford. Although there were close outward similarities, the specifications were not similar – the F3 car inherited the 59 square tube frame, while because of new bag tank regulations the F2 car had a monocoque centre section with tubular frames front and rear (59 to 69 'conversion' was possible). Various Ford-based engines were seen in the F3 cars during the final 1-litre F3 season (1970), while under the 1.6-litre regulations the very successful GLTL cars used Ford-based Novamotor units. In F2 Cosworth FVAs were used.

The 69 became popular in F3, and in 1971 Dave Walker was clearly the top driver – from 32 starts the single-car GLTL team scored 25 victories. That team did not contest F2 races, and in 1970 Rindt formed his own team with Bernie Ecclestone – in effect out of the Winkleman team – and he won four of the ten races he started. In the final year of 1.6-litre F2 racing, Emerson Fittipaldi won three European Trophy races in a Team Bardahl 69. With the 70, an unsuccessful Formula A/5000 car, these were the last Lotus production racing cars, and Lotus Racing Limited, which took the place of Lotus Components for 1971, ceased operations after a very brief life.

The naked engine bay spoils the lines of this acrobatic F3 69, driven by Dave Walker at Cadwell Park in 1971.

The 69 in F2 form, at the 1971 Racing Car Show. From this angle the slightly more rounded flanks distinguished it from the space frame car.

72 This successor to the 49 was also destined to serve longer than envisaged in the Grand Prix front line, although Chapman in no way saw this as a short-term car. He sought advantages over other teams using DFV engines and the concept for Phillippe to turn into metal and fibreglass was radical – a refined wedge with radiators amidships and ultra low to enhance aerodynamic efficiency, with torsion bar rising rate suspension, and inboard brakes. Suspension loads were light and the tyres were well away from brake heat, so soft tyres could be used with grip advantages (problems did arise when Lotus switched from Firestone to Goodyear, and tyres that were not designed with the 72 in mind had to be used).

The suspension was to be modified very early in the 72's career, when it looked as if the stunning car that had been unveiled might not be what it promised. Later the hull had to be reclad to meet changing regulations, various 'wings' were used and from mid-1971 assorted airboxes were fitted. The first changes led to 72B, more early suspension refinements to 72C, the 72D had twin radius rods at the rear and subsequent modifications before the 72E in 1975 and then 72F which was longer and had coil spring rear suspension with 'helper' coil springs at the front.

The first 72, on the day it was first shown to the Press, at Hethel early in 1970. NACA ducts took in cooling air for the disc brakes, 'chimneys' above them expelled that air and extractors were placed on them in pits after fast running to maintain a flow of air.

72/7 driven by Fittipaldi at Monza in 1973. The radiator pods have been integrated into the deformable structure and a very large wing extends well behind the rear wheels.

From 1972 the cars were run as John Player Specials, in black and gold livery. The 72 was first raced in Spain in 1970, and by the early summer was fully raceworthy – Rindt won the Dutch, French, British and German GPs in succession. Then in practice at Monza he was fatally injured in an accident that started when the right front brakeshaft failed. By finishing first and third in 72s in the US Grand Prix, Fittipaldi and Wisell ensured that Rindt's tally of points was not equalled and he thus became the sport's first posthumous champion.

The following year was largely barren, but in 1972 both Championships fell to the team (Fittipaldi taking the Drivers' title) and Lotus won the Constructors' title with the 72s in 1973. Peterson won three Championship races in 72s in 1974, but the car was slipping out of the front rank. There was little hope of victories in 1975, when the team concentrated on Peterson with the second car run for several drivers. The black 72s were last raced at Watkins Glen at the end of 1975, when Peterson placed one fifth. Nominally, nine of these handsome machines were built – there were rebuilds to the extent that new numbers would have been justified – and in six years the 72s added 20 Grand Prix victories to the Lotus tally. As early as 1970 a 72 had been sold, to Rob Walker for Graham Hill to

drive, Dave Charlton ran one of the 1970 cars from 1972 (in the colours of another cigarette company!) and two more went to South Africa. Odd 72s lingered on in minor British events in the late 1970s.

Drivers (GPS): Dave Charlton, Jim Crawford, Paddy Driver, Emerson Fittipaldi, Brian Henton, Graham Hill, Jacky Ickx, Eddie Keijan, John Miles, Ronnie Peterson, Jochen Rindt, Ian Scheckter, Tim Schenken, Tony Trimmer, Jack Tunmer, Dave Walker, John Watson, Reine Wisell.

73 This was an F3 car which according to the publicists was to complement the 72, a pair being run in JPTL black and gold colours. It had a monocoque centre section, with sub frames mounting the front suspension and the Nova engine/transmission/rear suspension, side-mounted radiators and inboard brakes. It may have been advanced, but it was altogether too complicated for F3 and that led to lack of progress as the 1972 season wore on. One of the original pair was then used for Novamotor F2 engine tests and a 73B was developed late in 1972, but set aside as Lotus and the sponsors turned away from F3. In 1975 Dr Ehrlich acquired the 73s, running one late that year as an Ehrlich-Lotus.

The sleekness of the 72 did not transfer to its little brother. Tony Trimmer – here at Mallory Park in the 73's first race – stepped back to F3 for what proved a frustrating season, with his best result a second place at Monaco.

74 The Texaco Star F2 cars, designed by Ralph Bellamy and using some features from the 72 – torsion bar suspension, inboard front brakes and hip radiators (water on the right, oil on the left). Lotus' 907 light-alloy engine was developed by Novamotor for this car, to give a claimed 275bhp. Team manager Jim Endruweit had the driving services of Emerson Fittipaldi and Ronnie Peterson. On paper it was a winning combination but on the circuits a flop.

Although a CART Lotus was to be built in the mid-1980s it was never raced, so the 74 was the last Lotus single-seater to be raced by a works team in a category outside F1.

A good-looking car, although a predominantly white Lotus seemed odd in 1973. That year saw Fittipaldi score Lotus' 50th Grand Prix victory, but no such fortune attended his efforts in the 74.

76 Team and sponsor desperately wanted this to be known as the John Player Special, and the idea was an updated and lighter 72. Torsion bar suspension was retained, so were inboard brakes, and there was a novel electronic clutch (once the car started from rest, this could be operated with a gear-lever button). It was, however, raced with a normal clutch and drivers preferred 72s. In mid-summer 1974 the 72 back end was grafted onto a 76 tub, and soon both 76s had 72 backs to make curious hybrids which were raced in late events.

Drivers: Jacky Ickx, Ronnie Peterson, Tim Schenken.

A 76 on stage at its flamboyant launch. In racing, a normal rear wing took the place of the biplane arrangement, and the radiators were to be moved forward to just behind the front wheels in an effort to improve weight distribution.

77 The 'John Player Special MkII' was a experimental car, eventually the product of the labours by several designers – Geoff ·Aldridge (monocoque) and Martin Ogilvie (suspension), with some input by Len Terry (suspension) and then Tony Southgate. Dubbed the 'adjustacar' it allowed for variations in track and wheelbase (facilitated as the brake callipers doubled as suspension pick-up points), while weight distribution could be changed. A driver-adjustable rear anti-roll bar came in mid season and then skirts, to partly control under-car airflow. In all this the slim monocoque, DFV and Hewland gearbox were almost overlooked.

Early in the year Peterson despaired and left, but Andretti committed himself to Lotus and through the year Nilsson gained in stature with the team. The performance of the 77 steadily improved, and at the end of the year Andretti drove one to victory in the Japanese GP.

Drivers: Mario Andretti, Bob Evans, Gunnar Nilsson, Ronnie Peterson.

78 A most significant Grand Prix car, the JPS MkIII established ground effects as a far-reaching development and put Team Lotus back in the forefront. But for some trivial reasons it would have been back on top. Once again Chapman laid down the principles, Bellamy, Ogilvie, aerodynamicist Peter Wright and others translated them into the car. It had a slim sandwich monocoque with wide side pods containing radiators, a fuel tank each, and the 'inverted wing section', with a skirt at the outer bottom edges extending down to the track to seal in the airflow (the skirt was a row of bristles on the first car, but rigid skirts soon came). The front track was wide, with suspension members interfering with the air flow to the side pods as little as possible. Andretti won four Grands Prix in 1977, Nilsson one. No drivers won as many as Andretti, no team won as many as Lotus, but both Championships eluded the team.

In 1978 Andretti and Peterson each won a GP before the 79 superseded the 78, but there was a sad footnote to the 78's career. Ronnie Peterson had to go to the start of the 1979 Italian GP in one, as his 79 had been damaged in the warm-up session, and he was fatally injured in a start-line accident. Independent Hector Rebaque ran a 78 into 1979, and in that year the first 78 appeared in the minor British F1 series.

Drivers: Mario Andretti, Gunnar Nilsson, Ronnie Peterson, Hector Rebaque.

In 1978 the 78 was rated a handsome car, but in that respect it was to be overshadowed by its successor. This is the 78/2 early in 1978, when rigid skirts were well established. The nose radiator is the oil cooler – air passed through the water radiators at the sides was exhausted through the pod tops (roughly alongside the mirrors). Driver is Peterson, on his way to victory in South Africa.

79 More than a refined 78, this was in many eyes the most elegant car of the 3-litre formula. It was an exemplary ground effects car, and it was a Championship car. Its side pods were wholeheartedly devoted to ground effects – there was a radiator in each (water on the right, oil on the left), but there were no fuel tanks in them as a single cell between cockpit and engine sufficed and the rear suspension was kept out of the airflow. In most other areas development was simple and although a Lotus gearbox built by Getrag and incorporating a freewheel was essayed, Lotus reverted to a Hewland FG400 for the main season. The 79 was the car of the year, and it was reliable. Andretti won six GPs in 1978, one of them in a 78; Peterson won two (one in a 78) and was second four times.

The front of the 77 looked a mess in the first half of the 1976 season, and certainly the inboard front brakes and suspension mounted to the callipers seemed to be at aerodynamic odds with the slender monocoque. Terry introduced outboard brakes (with Ralt production suspension uprights) which cleaned things up a little. Andretti, who made positive contributions to the car's development progress, sits patiently in the cockpit in this early-season shot.

Andretti was World Champion by a wide margin, and Lotus was clear winner of the Constructors' title.

In 1979 the 80 proved troublesome, and for most of the season Team Lotus had to rely on its 79s. Although prospects did not look bad as the season opened it soon became obvious that the pace-setting car of 1978 had been matched very quickly. There were points-scoring finishes, but no victories

Drivers: Mario Andretti, Jean-Pierre Jarier, Ronnie Peterson, Hector Rebaque, Carlos Reutemann.

JPS MkIV was an elegant car from almost any angle, and in 1978 it was almost unchallenged on the circuits. This is Andretti in 79/4 at Monza.

80 An attempt to extend ground effects parameters, with side pods (and skirts) curving to continue inside the rear wheels. It even had skirts under the nose, but they were soon worn away and were replaced by a conventional nose with aerofoil winglets. The main skirts did not move up and down in their slides predictably, and if one jammed the ground effects seal could be broken, which could make life difficult for a driver. Andretti did place an 80 third in the 1979 Spanish GP, but this unhappy model was raced only three times.

Drivers: Mario Andretti, Carlos Reutemann.

When the 80 was announced it did not have conventional aerofoils, but these were soon added. Sometimes there was an additional tier between the tops of the fins at the back, which presumably was felt to contribute unwanted drag at the fast Silverstone circuit where this test shot was taken. With new sponsors, Team Lotus cars (79s as well as 80s) were run in green colours in 1979.

81 A conservative approach made sense in 1980, and the 81 was a 'careful blend of the 79 and lessons learned from the 80' – according to the Press announcement. It was built around a basic sheet aluminium structure that derived from the 80, and a mid-season replacement monocoque led to the 81B designation. Elio de Angelis scored a second and a third early in the season, and there were a few other mildly encouraging performances (former team test driver Mansell was given a first GP drive in the first 81B in Austria and showed well

despite considerable problems). The 81 continued in use into 1981; de Angelis scored with 81s three times before the 87 came and Mansell's first scoring finish came with one in Belgium.

Drivers: Mario Andretti, Elio de Angelis, Nigel Mansell.

Another change of colours, to the flashy blue, red and silver of David Thieme's Essex petroleum company. The 81 tended to be raced without nose fins, which made it look even more stubby. This car is posed at Team Lotus HQ – is that really Andretti under the helmet?

86 An experimental dual-chassis car using an 81 monocoque. Completed in the Autumn of 1980 it was used for tests but never raced.

87 This actually appeared after the 88, and took the team place intended for that car in 1981. It was conventional, using 88 running gear – 88 to 87 (and vice versa) conversions were made in mid-season. A moulded carbon-composite monocoque was used. Some weight was saved in the second half of the season, and the 87B led directly to the 91.

Drivers in 87s scored 13 points in Lotus' 1981 total of 22, which as the team was in turmoil for much of the year was not at all bad. By the early summer of that year the Team Lotus cars were black and gold again. The two 87Bs were used in the opening GP of 1982.

Drivers: Elio de Angelis, Nigel Mansell.

Traditional Team Lotus pose with a new car – drivers Mansell and de Angelis flank Colin Chapman. The 87 still shows some allegiance to Essex (where the radiator air was exhausted through the sides) but in the main this is another JPS.

88 This was the controversial 'dual-chassis' concept presented as a raceworthy car, entered for races, and rejected by officialdom. It had a main chassis comprising bodywork, carrying side pods and radiators, and aerofoils; within it there was the monocoque, engine and transmission, and suspension. The first chassis was carried on coil spring/damper units attached to the suspension uprights. The idea was to achieve generous ground effects downforce, without the undue stress and strain drivers were having to bear with rock-hard ground effects suspension.

Protests forced it out of racing and it was modified as the 88B, which although acceptable to the RAC at the 1981 British GP meeting was not acceptable to anybody else in authority. Piles of paper marked its passing.

The nearest the 88 came to racing was in practice sessions, for the last time at Silverstone in 88B form.

91 In many ways this might have been designated '87C', the prime objective being a stronger, and above all lighter, derivative of the 87. Lotus still used DFVs, so could not afford excess weight, and a very strong and rigid tub was achieved with a carbon fibre/Kevlar Nomex sandwich, weighing only just over 18kg. Suspension was very stiff, aerodynamic qualities good. Three wheelbase variations were built into the design, as was a controversial detail shared with other teams using DFVs – water-cooled brakes, which seemed to some to be an unnecessary weight.

With this car Lotus went some way towards recovering competitiveness, most notably when Elio de Angelis won the Austrian Grand Prix.

Drivers: Elio de Angelis, Nigel Mansell.

Colin Chapman with the first 91 outside Ketteringham Hall. This was to be his last Grand Prix Lotus, but at least he was to see it win a Grand Prix.

92 A pair of 91s converted to comply with flat-bottom regulations for the opening races of the season, very much as stand-ins while the 93T was prepared. One was used in active suspension trials.

Drivers: Elio de Angelis, Nigel Mansell.

93T Lotus' first turbo car was powered by the Renault EF4B V-6, but as the team was pulled together under Peter Warr construction was sluggish, with only one car being available for the first Championship races. That was not the bad news it might have been, for the 93T was a cumbersome uncompetitive device, and as soon as Gérard Ducarouge joined as designer in the early summer of 1983 work started on a new car.

Drivers: Elio de Angelis, Nigel Mansell.

The 93T looked a bulky car, and it proved ineffectual. The relationship with Pirelli was short-lived.

94T Ducarouge worked quickly, using the tub of the 91 as a basis for the 94T, and the first was ready for the British GP. It looked neater, was lighter, had a weight distribution which complemented its Pirelli rubber (coincidentally the tyre company reverted to stiffer tyres), was never a winner, but started Team Lotus back on the road towards winning. In his first race in a 94T, at Silverstone, Mansell finished fourth, and at Brands Hatch at the end of the European season he was third in the GP d'Europe.

Drivers: Elio de Angelis, Nigel Mansell.

Mansell poses with a 94T during a break in tests at Donington. The car's lines compare favourably with the 93T, and it is obviously equipped for refuelling pit stops.

95T Once again Team Lotus had a car that was instantly competitive, for although at the end of 1984 the best results were three third places, component failures or driver error had probably cost victories. However, third place in the Constructors' Championship was Lotus' best since 1978.

The 95T was the first all-new Lotus since the dual-chassis episode, but nevertheless appeared in a line of evolution. The return to Goodyears was important. This time team manager Peter Warr and designer Gérard Ducarouge pose with the new car.

There was nothing revolutionary about the 95T, which was built around a carbon-composite monocoque with pullrod suspension, but it restored Lotus' old reputation for good handling. It was also more than a match for the works Renaults, and this was one factor that led to Lotus being favoured with better engines in 1985.

Drivers: Elio de Angelis, Nigel Mansell.

97T This car was a derivative, with aerodynamic refinements and Renault EF15 engines for races, delivering more power at some cost in reliability. There was strength in the driver pair too – de Angelis finished 11 times in 1985, every time in a scoring position and with a victory at Imola, while Ayrton Senna finished nine times, winning in Portugal and Belgium. Lotus was again third in the Constructors' Championship.

Drivers: Elio de Angelis, Ayrton Senna.

Senna on his way to a maiden GP victory in Portugal in 1985. Aerodynamic novelties are the vertical deflectors in the front suspension, intended to reduce turbulence, and the small 'winglets' at the rear of the side pods.

98T Although this car appeared to be a straight successor to the 97T, Ducarouge departed from previous practice in using a one-piece moulded carbon-composite chassis. While the front suspension was carried over from 1985 there was a new set-up at the rear, used for most of the year's races, and an hydraulic adjustable ride height system was used in conjunction with this. Renault made works-prepared EF15B engines available – other teams using the V-6 were supplied by the Mecachrome preparation company – and the higher-revving pneumatic valve operation type was sometimes used.

As was becoming customary, four cars were built. Lotus was actually in contention for the Championships for much of the year, eventually taking third place again on the Constructors' points table. Attention tended to focus on Ayrton Senna, who scored points ten times and won two Grands Prix; team mate Johnny Dumfries occupied the number two seat.

Drivers: Johnny Dumfries, Ayrton Senna.

Last of the black and gold cars. Dumfries in full flight in 98T. The vertical 'winglets' are not fitted at the front, although they continued in erratic use through 1986.

99T The outward change was the adoption of yellow and blue Camel colours – that apart, the family resemblance was strong. Under the skin, however, there was a Honda 80-degree V-6 and many more ancillaries than with the Renault engine; there was also a Lotus six-speed gearbox, and active suspension. Although the car was tested with a revised 'normal' suspension arrangement, Senna was insistent on the active system, and he was a power in the team. Thus the 99T became the first F1 car to race with active suspension, in the Brazilian GP, and the first to win with it (at Monaco). Shortcomings in aerodynamics led to a substantial summer redesign, primarily to clean the airflow to the various rear wings used, while there was also criticism of the chassis.

This time six cars were built, three for R & D use in Britain and Japan. Lotus was third in the Constructors' Championship and Senna third in the Drivers' Championship, having scored in 11 races and again having won two Grands Prix.

Drivers: Satoru Nakajima, Ayrton Senna.

The same Ketteringham Hall door is in the background, but much else has changed. Senna is firmly in the driving seat of the first 99T. Nakajima, who was suspected of coming as part of the Honda package but who scored well in the Championship, sits beside the cockpit. A very large front wing is fitted. Overall, a high gloss finish accentuates the car's sleek lines.

100T Lotus slipped badly in 1988. The car looked right, with the needle-nosed lines adopted by most designers as a regulation requiring drivers' feet to be behind the centre line of the front wheels came into force, and it had an apparently competent 'passive' suspension system, as well as the advantage of Honda power. Fiddling with aerodynamics, track, wheelbase and so on brought little improvement in fortunes – best placings were thirds, scored by Piquet in the first races of the season (at Rio and Imola) and in the final race at Adelaide. He was sixth in the Championship, and while Lotus slipped only one place on the Constructors' points table, the team's score was little more than a tenth of McLaren's.

Drivers: Satoru Nakajima, Nelson Piquet.

A 100T pulling a lot of wing at Rio, and in lots of detail looking much less tidy than the 1987 car. The driver is Nelson Piquet.

101 Technical direction was taken over by Frank Dernie, whose recent reputation was as an aerodynamicist – he perhaps tended to be more concerned with that aspect than with, say, suspension. That comprised double wishbones, pullrod at the front, pushrod at the rear, with the front springs in blisters low on the sides of the hull and those at the rear fitted in neatly ahead of the Lotus longitudinal six-speed gearbox. The car was slim at the nose, widening at the cockpit to lines which followed through along the fuel cell and engine areas. For a normally-aspirated engine, Lotus looked to the Judd CV 90-degree V-8 and there was some fuss early in the year about exclusive Tickford developments including a five-valve head, which did appear briefly and soon disappeared. By the end of the year one of the cars was being tested with a Lamborghini V-12 in preparation for the 1990 102.

This car was an improvement on Ducarouge's last Lotus, but some of its promise was illusory and some was dissipated – the number one driver seemed demotivated for part of the season. At the Belgian GP meeting neither car qualified, and that was a low point first in Lotus Grand Prix racing history. Piquet salvaged something with two fourth placings and two other points-scoring finishes, while in his last race for the team Nakajima achieved his best result, fourth in Adelaide.

Drivers: Satoru Nakajima, Nelson Piquet.

The needle nose of the 101 seems overwhelmed by a large front wing in early tests at Snetterton. Cockpit sides and engine cover are deep, flanks are tidy, rear suspension is out of the airstream as far as possible. Driver is Nelson Piquet.

LOVA

One of the rare Dutch attempts to build a racing car, this Junior of 1963 was laid out around a rear-mounted DKW engine, which by that time was *passé* in all save its Wartburg form in East European cars. It was another of those cars for which there is no record of racing achievement.

LOWENO

André Loens was a well-known F3 campaigner with, amongst others, a Kieft in the mid-1950s. In 1956 he came up with his own Loweno Special, a low, blunt-nosed rear-engined car of no great distinction. Loens did, however, achieve some success with it in the dwindling number of Continental 500cc races in 1957.

LTE

The LTE-Brillant was a German 500 of the early 1950s, designed and built by Ferdi Lehder following his first 500, the Juwel. It had lower wishbone/top link suspension, a tubular chassis and rather flattened yet corpulent lines that reflected

the need to house a BMW boxer engine. The bodywork might have been attractive without its many little scoops and louvres. Lehder also raced it, enjoying some success in German national races in 1950, but not enough for the production programme that was talked about to come to pass.

LUCANGELI

Sergio Lucangeli of Ancona entered Formula Junior with a Fiat-engined car in 1959, but unlike most of his compatriots he mounted the engine at the rear (it drove through the inevitable Fiat gearbox). The car had a multi-tubular chassis, with independent suspension all round.

LYNCAR

Martin Slater was a one-time racing driver who had the ability to build a Formula Junior car for his own use and later undertook design work with Lola, March and Brabham. In 1971 his first Lyncar, 001 for Formula Atlantic, appeared; that was followed by four more Formula Atlantic cars and the DFV-powered 004 hill-climb car. One of the Formula Atlantic cars, 005, was used by Nicholson McLaren Engines expert John Nicholson to win the 1973 Championship, and that led to a commission to build an F1 car.

This emerged as Lyncar 006 in 1973, and was a sensibly straightforward car. Its aluminium monocoque was fabricated by Maurice Gomm, the F Atlantic suspension was followed and outboard brakes were used. There was a full-width nose and one of the more shapely engine air boxes of the period.

Nicholson contested a limited programme, finishing in the two British non-Championship races in 1974 but failing to qualify for the British GP. In the same races in 1975 he actually finished in only one, the International Trophy, but was classified 17th in the GP. He had always said that his F1 racing was an experiment; presumably he discovered something, because he moved to power boat racing, while continuing to build F1 engines for McLaren.

The Lyncar was run in modified form by Emilio de Villota in some British national series races in 1976-7, when he won a Mallory Park race before moving on to a McLaren M23 as he pursued his own learning curve.

Driver (GPs): John Nicholson.

As a simple and sensible machine for a modest team, Lyncar 006 was well suited to the Aurora series, here in 1977 with new nose and a low-line engine cover. Driver is Spanish bank manager Emilio de Villota.

LYNX (AUS)

Ron Tauranac laid down the car that was to become the first Lynx before he moved to Britain to join Jack Brabham, and six were completed in 1960, but most not in the F3 form Tauranac had envisaged. The design was substantially modified as the basis for the MkII Junior in 1961. Double wishbone suspension replaced the original transverse leaf arrangement at the back, and nose radiators and plumbing were installed for the engines which replaced the original motorcycle units. The Lynx MkIII was also a Junior, introduced in 1963, with a new space frame clothed in sleek bodywork. Eight were built before Lynx stopped making cars.

LYNX (GB)

Godfrey Hall's one-off F3 car was developed from his Monoposto category Ralt-based car of 1983, with somewhat earlier suspension components and a Toyota engine. This GH2 was run as a Class B car, that is at least a year old at the start of the season – which its component parts were even if the whole was new to F3. In that sub-division of the British series Hall scored points in six races.

M

MAC

A 500cc car which appeared in 1948, John Gibbs' MAC had a rear-mounted JAP engine, an Albion gearbox, a Fiat 500 frame and a rear axle from a Raleigh three wheeler. ML

MACKAY

Built by W.T. Mackay, between 1947 and 1949, this nicely-made little '500' was clearly influenced by the Cooper and used Fiat 500 front suspension at both ends. A modified Triumph twin engine and standard Triumph gearbox were used, and the whole thing was assembled for £150. Although it was not always successful it was often cited as an example of how a special builder could make a low-cost 500 car to professional standards. ML

MACKSON

This 1952 F3 car had then-familiar components, but striking looks. It had a tubular chassis, a twin-ohc Norton engine, wishbone ifs and swing axle rear on Kieft lines. Its lines, however, were advanced, for it was lower and sleeker than its F3 contemporaries. The name was owed to its Guildford constructors, McGee and Bedson (Gordon Bedson, the designer). Three were built, but none of the drivers who raced a Mackson – they included Burgess and Wharton – was successful with it.

This was a better-balanced and more unified design than many half-litre cars.

MACO

Ernst Maring built attractive-looking F3 cars in very small numbers through the second half of the 1970s, never quite breaking through to real success, and also produced an F2 car, very hesitantly. He was an F3 and F2 driver, and a Super Vee constructor, and all that was in the background of his first F3 cars. These were usually run in the German series, where Maco enjoyed the support of top sponsors through the middle years of the decade, and were seen as far afield as Monaco. Maring adopted a conventional model designation system, combining category and year – 374 for the 1974 F3 car.

Formula 3 These cars were conventional in make up, usually attractive in appearance; outwardly the first cars had resemblances to GRDs, but soon a distinctive bodywork line was developed for the side-radiator cars. An early 374 was run with a Nova Ford twin-cam engine, but save for occasional use of a BMW engine, Nova-Toyota power units became the norm.

The most successful 374 driver was Maring himself, for he took second place in races at the Nürburgring, Ulm and, three times, at Hockenheim. Giorgio Francia also drove a Maco in 1974, with some success.

A tidied-up car came for 1976, when the opposition was stiffer and in races of any stature that year just two second places fell to 376 drivers, Kern and Maring, both at the 'ring, while there were a few other top-six placings and Leppke was tenth at Monaco. Cosmetic work led to the 376B in 1977, when BMW engines were also seen in Maco chassis; Niggermeier and Korten managed top placings in German Championship events, the latter scoring a second and a third. There was even less success in 1978, and Maring flew the flag for the last time with the 379 in 1979, when he was fourth in the German Championship (ironically, this was won by his former driver, Korten, with a March).

'Second-series' Maco F3 cars had odd proportions in profile, whereas most of Maring's cars were attractive. This car is being driven by Peter Wisskirchen.

A later car that is more representative of Maco's economical and attractive lines (the characteristic radiator intake was carried over for several seasons). This virgin-white car is being driven by Korten in 1977.

Formula 2 Maco entered F2 in 1978, with the 278. This turned out to be a very limited exercise with a derivative of the F3 car powered by a BMW M12. It was entered for the three German F2 races for Korten, who failed to qualify it for the two Hockenheim races and finished a distant 15th in the Nürburgring event.

MAGNUM

Successful attempts to break into the tantalizing F3 car market in the 1980s could be counted on the fingers of a rude gesture. Magnum nearly made it, but race wins came only in secondary series and there were none in the British championship, where success was essential if the F3 Magnums were to be widely accepted. The first cars, the 813 F3 prototype and 81A Formula Atlantic derivative, were built by Automotive Designs Ltd at Northampton, then from 1982 John Robinson's Magnum Racing Cars continued in the Ralt-dominated world of F3, handicapped in racing and development aspects by a lack of resources. Reality perhaps suggested that a category where there was more room to manoeuvre in terms of unit costings might have been more appropriate for the painstaking approach adopted at the Corby factory (the 863 F3 car was to be laid out with possible F3000 use in mind). In 1986 Magnum Race Engines developed a VW-based F3 engine for 1987.

813 This design started life as a Theodore F1 project by Len Bailey and was picked up by Automotive Designs in the summer of 1980 and revised for F3. The prototype was completed for tests in the autumn of that year. The car had a narrow monocoque with a single fuel cell behind the cockpit and wide side pods incorporating radiators and giving clear ground effects airflow to clean rear exits. To this end coil spring/damper units were inboard, and those at the rear were mounted above the gearbox. A Toyota engine was used. The car seemed to perform well in tests and survived an early-1981 crash but made no impression in racing in 1981.

A narrow nose, deep cockpit surround and generous side pods were characteristic of the first F3 Magnum.

823 This was Robinson's development of the original design and was sometimes raced in 1982, driven by David Leslie, but gave its constructor little encouragement to continue along the same lines.

833 A new design by Robinson, which looked much neater and started its first race from pole position (oddly the 833 usually went much better at Silverstone than other circuits). The car had a honeycomb monocoque and a one-piece undertray as the search for better under-car aerodynamics continued; in the suspension the existing lines were followed, and it used a Quaife differential, which was unique in F3. On the British F3 points table at the end of 1983 this was the best non-Ralt, for Leslie had scored with it in eleven races (there were only two other non-Ralt scores).

843 In 1984 a Magnum won an F3 race, but a victory by Bo Martinsson at a circuit like Anderstorp was not news to set the F3 world alight. The car was an improved version of the 833, but tidier and, as ever with the Robinsons, beautifully made. It was only run in the Spring races in Britain, when Cor Euser often qualified it well but scored only a single point.

853 Magnum started the flat-bottom era with a new design, again with a honeycomb chassis and with the rocking lever suspension arrangement at the rear used for the last time. Pushrod suspension was fitted. Four cars were laid down, one of each of the first pair with a Toyota engine, the other with a VW unit (a third tubular sub frame for Alfa engines was available). The combination of a pair of inexperienced Finnish drivers and Magnums did not work, and once again it was left to Euser to show the Magnum potential, right at the end of the year when he took pole at Zandvoort and finished fourth in the race.

Robinson's Magnums had rounded lines, yet never appeared sleek. In 853 suspension members at the rear emerge through curving panels. The driver is Cor Euser.

863 This was another derivative car, although the honeycomb monocoque was new, notably in its cast aluminium bulkheads, and there was pushrod suspension at the rear as well as the front. An F3000 variant was envisaged. On the circuits in 1986 the 863 showed promise in tests that was not reflected in races, in part because drivers lacked experience.

An 863 showing its very clean lines in the Silverstone pits lane late in 1986, but showing virtually no signs of sponsorship. The driver is Californian Fulton Haight.

873/883 A development of the 863 came for 1987, although it was not seen in races. At the front a less rounded nose was fitted, while at the rear use of a Staffs Silent Gears 'box made for narrower and lower bodywork and meant that the coil springs/dampers were mounted alongside the gearbox. Magnum's one uncompetitive race appearance in 1988 signalled the end of the line.

MAKI

This Japanese entry into F1 was unveiled to the wide Grand Prix world in 1974 at a rather odd function in a London hotel, and the first car appeared in public in practice at Brands Hatch. It was claimed to be the forerunner of an advanced automotive engineering programme that was to include a 3-litre F1 engine, but most of that programme failed to materialize. Unconvincing 'Cosworth kit cars' did materialize, designed by Kenji Mimura, who was also team manager, with some input by Masao Ono, who was to be responsible for the Kojima. Although they were entered more frequently the cars showed up for only eight race meetings, and when the Maki entry for the 1976 Japanese GP did not reach the grid the racing enterprise folded.

F-101 At a glance this seemed a competent Cosworth-powered car, but closer inspection in pits lanes led to misgivings about the strength of its construction. It had outboard suspension on orthodox lines and rather bulky bodywork. It was a true kit car in that most components were bought in – Hewland FGA400 gearbox, Lucas fuel injection and ignition, Koni dampers, Lockheed brakes, and so on. Howden Ganley failed to qualify it for the British and German GPs – its only two appearances – and at the Nürburgring it crashed very heavily after suspension failure. The team was back with a revised and sleeker car in 1975, when Hiroshi Fuchida and Tony Trimmer failed to get it to the start of a Championship race (twice each). Trimmer eventually made Maki's only race start, in the Swiss GP at Dijon, finishing 13th and last.

Driver: Tony Trimmer

First appearance for the Maki in its patriotic colours was in practice at Brands Hatch in 1974, when Howden Ganley failed to qualify to start in the British GP.

F-102A This was an angular car, with a slim and deep monocoque and slender radiator pods alongside the DFV engine giving it unusual lines. It was patently not raceworthy when Trimmer attempted to qualify it for the 1976 Japanese GP, and it ran for only eight timed laps.

MANX SPECIAL

Jack Walkem's 500cc special was one of the top cars in Australia in the mid-1950s. As its name suggests, it had a Manx Norton engine while front suspension followed Cooper lines (transverse leaf and lower wishbones) and the swing axle and rubber band rear suspension was inspired by Kieft. ML

MARCH

During 1968-9, two innovations occupied the minds of many people in motor racing: the ready availability of the best engine in the world, the Cosworth DFV, and the FIA's decision to allow American-style sponsorship. This meant that anyone could enter F1 provided he had a designer and a sponsor, and one of the first people to recognise this was Max Mosley, a barrister who exchanged his wig and gown for overalls and helmet at weekends to race in F2. He not only understood the equation but was a friend of Robin Herd who was then being touted as potentially the best racing car designer of all. Max went to work on the problem, realizing that he was never going to be World Champion but that he could put together a World Championship package, provided he could get the support of Robin Herd.

Alan Rees, a very good driver who had not quite made it to F1, had just hung up his helmet and turned to team management. Together with Graham Coaker, he had looked over available production racing cars and decided there was room for another outfit in the market. Alan was a close friend of Robin Herd and before long, Robin had Alan speaking in one ear, Max in the other, and virtually every other team, except Ferrari, made him an offer because he was the star designer of the future.

Typically, Robin stuck with his friends, and he was able to bring together the Mosley proposal and the Rees idea. A company was formed to enter F1 and make production cars in order to give it financial stability. The parties concerned seemed to bring together the elements necessary for success: Herd on design; Mosley to look after commercial affairs; Rees, the one distinguished racer among them, would run the racing side; and Coaker, an engineer and an amateur F3 driver, would supervise production. The four friends each put up £2,500 as initial capital and decided to call the company 'March', an acronym of their names.

Although the company was under-financed, Max Mosley sold the idea so well that suppliers extended credit, customers put down deposits and a sponsor was found to support the works teams. A fairly rudimentary F3 car appeared late in 1969 and showed some promise, and this formed the basis of the first customer cars which were made for F2, F3, Formula Atlantic and Formula Ford 1600. Meanwhile Robin also designed an F1 car and, once that was out of the way, a Can-Am car.

March also supplied F1 cars to Team Tyrrell, which was led by reigning World Champion Jackie Stewart, to Andy Granatelli who was Mario Andretti's entrant and to some privateers. Although the F1 cars showed initial promise there was little development potential in them, and while March finished third in the Constructors' Championship, with up to seven cars entered in races plus some of the best drivers around, it should really have won it.

The basic problem was that too much was done in too short a time, with the result that while all the cars could run at the front, not one had the necessary extra edge. As a result March was never able to attract the extra sponsorship which would have given it financial stability and it was soon apparent that the production car side was underwriting the F1 effort. Production interests versus F1 became a theme running through the company's history and led to Graham Coaker leaving after twelve months and Alan Rees a year later.

At the end of its first year, March made a profit of only £3,000 and still owed an enormous sum to its suppliers, so was virtually bankrupt. A constant juggling of cash became another theme in the March story, which explains some of the odd deals made and why, apart from occasional flashes of promise, it never achieved much in F1 although its customer cars were often superb.

At the end of 1977 the production versus F1 conflict was resolved when Max Mosley tired of running a team on a shoestring and left. For a while March prospered as a production-car only company until it was hit by the recession of 1980. At the beginning of 1981 it was bankrupt in all but name but was saved by a decision to enter the American Indycar market. Over the next few years it became extremely successful in America and made a lot of money, so much so that the decision could be taken to diversify into consultancy and to work towards the day when it could leave the volatile production racing car market and concentrate on servicing industry and major manufacturers who wished to go racing.

March re-entered F1 at the beginning of 1987 and shortly afterwards was launched as a Public Limited Company, but within a year or so it was facing bankruptcy again, partly due to some poor management decisions and partly due to complacency which meant it had not maintained its competitive edge in the market, a problem compounded by a reputation for poor quality. In order to improve this it bought Ralt Cars at the end of 1988 but shortly afterwards had to disclose a massive loss to its shareholders. By that time many of the senior managers had been replaced and the embryo consultancy business had been closed down.

In order to get out of trouble March stopped making production cars except for Ralts and the 'Wildcats' (modified 1985 F3000 cars with Buick engines) which were used in the American Racing Series, and entered agreements with Alfa Romeo and Porsche to build Indycars for them. Early in 1989 its F1 and F3000 operations were sold to Leyton House, its Japanese F1 sponsor, which also bought the March name in F1 and F3000 until 1999. It was separated from March Group PLC, although the personnel remained unchanged and indeed Ian Phillips, the team manager, became Managing Director while Adrian Newey, the concept designer and Tim Holloway, the mechanical designer, became directors. The emphasis shifted to the use of Leyton House rather than March, the 1990 F1 cars being named Leyton House.

By the end of 1989 Robin Herd, the last surviving co-founder, had severed day to day links with the company, although he remained the largest shareholder. March Group PLC began to diversify as a financial management company although it renewed its contracts to service Porsche and Alfa Romeo in Indycar racing and was actively seeking a partner for Group C. Thus the most successful production car manufacturer over a twenty year period became a service company for selected manufacturers and, for the first time in its history, was able to build up to a quality and not down to a price.   ML

The first two numbers in each March type are the year, while the third denotes the category – thus the 693 is the 1969 F3 car.

693 March's first car had a simple square-tube space frame, and used Lotus and Brabham components. Ronnie Peterson brought it home third in a top class F3 field on its debut at

The first March, the simple and bluff 693, which at least served to suggest to the racing world that March was seriously in business. Driver is James Hunt.

Cadwell Park in late September. It was raced by the works in only two more events: Peterson crashed at Monthléry and substitute driver, James Hunt, had a lacklustre outing at Brands Hatch.

701 March's first F1 car was designed to be reliable rather than innovative although assistant designer Peter Wright attempted to get some extra downforce by shaping the small side fuel tanks like the sidepod profiles of a ground effects car (later, at Lotus, Wright designed the first ground effects car). For the rest it was a conventional DFV-powered machine with a bath tub aluminium monocoque with cast magnesium bulkheads and outboard suspension by coil springs and wishbones. It was a good enough car to take the first two places on the grid, with equal times, on its début in South Africa and to win three of its first four races. However, two wins were by default and only one, the Spanish GP won by Stewart, was in a World Championship event.

The 701 flattered to deceive, for there was no development in it and it was soon outclassed by the Lotus 72 and the Ferrari T312. Even some of the world's best drivers could not make it into a natural winner – by the end of the year Tyrrell had built his own car and Granatelli had converted the tub of his 701 into a flower box. Most new teams would envy March's third place in the Constructors' Championship, but in order to get the project off the ground Max Mosley had so hyped the company that most people regarded it as a poor showing.

Drivers: Ray Allen, Chris Amon, Mario Andretti, Derek Bell, Mike Beuttler, John Cannon, François Cevert, Hubert Hahne, Jean-Pierre Jarier, John Love, Jean Max, François Mazet, Ronnie Peterson, Johnny Servoz-Gavin, Jo Siffert, Jackie Stewart, Tony Trimmer.

The 701 was obviously from the same stable as 693, short and stubby. Its DFV was conspicuously naked and one eye-catching feature was the inverted aerofoil section fuel tank on each side. This 701 is being driven in a demonstration by Jo Siffert.

702 March's first F2 car was based on the 693 but it was disappointing through most of 1970, in particular the 'multi-purpose' space frame design used stronger tubes for F2, and it was a heavy car. FVA engines were usual. A season's development and new, lighter, chassis frames made it competitive by the end of the year but its only win came in the non-Championship German F2 GP when, both driving 'heavy' 702s, Xavier Perrot led home Hannelore Werner. This remains the best result ever achieved by a woman in an F2 race.

703 Most of the comments on the 702 apply to the F3 version, regarded as heavy, and not too effective in the matter of putting power on the road. It scored only occasional place finishes, mainly in the hands of Dave Morgan, but considerable progress was made throughout the year.

711 One of the most distinctive F1 cars of the 1970s, the 711 had a body designed by Frank Costin, who had pioneered serious aerodynamics on single-seaters with Vanwall in the mid-1950s. Underneath the startling body it was basically a refined Lotus 72, but then the chassis was designed by Geoff Ferris who had assisted on the Lotus. Like the 72, it was designed with inboard front brakes but a breakage in the model's first race saw a rapid change to outboard brakes. Front suspension was by double wishbones, with inboard coil springs/dampers, while at the rear lower wishbones and upper trailing arms were used with outboard coil springs/dampers.

After the star driver line-up of the previous year March had to tighten its belt so ran the young Ronnie Peterson as number one, with the Spanish amateur Alex Soler-Roig buying the second seat until he gave up in disgust. These cars both used the Cosworth DFV engine but a deal was struck with Autodelta to use a version of the Alfa Romeo T33/3 sports car engine for two of Alfa's protégés, who tended to alternate in the car.

For once Frank Costin goofed on his calculations, and parts of the body he designed had to be discarded because it led to over-heating. When Peterson received one of the latest-spec DFVs, however, he proved both himself and the car, and although he did not win a race he finished runner-up to Stewart in the Drivers' Championship and was largely responsible for March tying with Ferrari for third spot in the Constructors' Championship.

Drivers: Andrea de Adamich, Ray Allen, Skip Barber, Derek Bell, Mike Beuttler, John Cannon, 'Nanni' Galli, Jean-Pierre Jarier, Niki Lauda, John Love, Jean Max, François Mazet, Xavier Perrot, Henri Pescarolo, Ronnie Peterson, Allan Rollinson, Jo Siffert, Alex Soler-Roig.

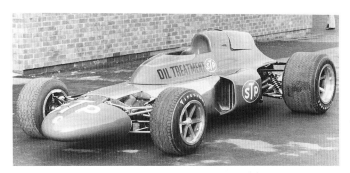

An incomplete 711 rolled out for publicity shots (**above**) shows how sleek it was before wings and mirrors were added. This car has an Alfa Romeo badge on the nose, in a position where it would be obliterated by the aerofoil mounting. The nose wing (**below**) meant that this was another March with a distinctive feature. Driver of this car running without engine cover or radiator fairings is Peterson, at Zandvoort.

712 This 1971 monocoque chassis with semi-stressed engine supported on a tubular sub-frame laid down a design which remained in production for some years with relatively minor modifications. The overall layout derived from the 693 with suspension similar to the 701, the radiator was front-mounted and the engine (usually a Cosworth FVA) was a semi-stressed member. It was the class of the field, winning ten races (five of them non-Championship) and gave Ronnie Peterson six wins and the F2 title, while other March drivers to win F2 races

were Mike Beuttler, Carlos Pace, Dieter Quester and Henri Pescarolo. Quester's victory was scored with a BMW engine.

This was a sleek car, despite the appearance of 'clutter' in this shot. Driver is Peterson, early in the 1971 season, before inboard rear brakes were used on his car. Very little of the tread of the right rear tyre is actually a contact patch with the road.

713 A choice of space frame or monocoque chassis was offered for the 1971 F3 car. The 713S had a round tube space frame and a body similar to the 712. For some reason – perhaps lower costs – most went to Germany. The 713M was a monocoque car, similar in its make up to 712 although detail differences were considerable. Roger Williamson drove one to win one British F3 Championship and was runner-up to Dave Walker's works Lotus in the other. It gained a reputation for being easy to run and to drive, but no other front runner used one for the whole season. The 713M was adopted as the base design for all March F3 cars until 1978.

Without aerofoils, the 713 looked much cleaner than its F2 counterpart. The driver is Lauda, at Hockenheim.

721 March began the 1972 season with a detailed up-date of the 711 and even used the same body for the first race. Soon the Costin 'Spitfire' front wing gave way to a chisel nose (on all but the car the German Eifelland caravan company ran). The 721 was primarily designed for customers, although only Eifelland and Frank Williams were tempted, but it was used by the works until the 721X was ready.

The 721X was to have been the technical breakthrough which would catapult March to the forefront of constructors. The 721X used a 721 monocoque but the rear springs were mounted high and operated through cranks and levers. The main driving force of the concept was to create a low polar moment of inertia by distributing the weight nearer to the centre of the car by using an Alfa Romeo-style gearbox (Alfa gears in a March casing) which was in front of the rear axle line. There was nothing wrong with the theory – Porsche and Alfa Romeo had both used the layout – but March was using customer Goodyear tyres and they were designed to work with a conventional layout.

Since the most important parameter of racing car design is to keep the tyres happy, the 721X was an unmitigated disaster, for the front tyres were so overloaded that in a bend the car would first produce enormous understeer and then, eventually, enormous oversteer. It was not helped by the Alfa Romeo transmission, which was fairly primitive, but even using other makers' gears did not improve matters. When it became clear that the great technical breakthrough was a miasma, March turned to the 721G.

When Mike Beuttler's backers ordered a new car March offered the 721G on a sale or return basis. Its designation 'G' stood for the Guiness Book of Records for it was created in just nine days. Earlier in the season John Cannon had ordered a modified F2 car to run in F5000 and it had been quick enough to take pole on its début. The 721G followed this line of thinking in that to a beefed-up F2 monocoque were added F1 specification suspension and brakes, and of course a DFV engine. It was immediately apparent that it was a vast improvement over March's other two 1972 F1 cars and from then until the end of 1977 all March F1 cars would be modified versions of its F2 design. Incidentally, March must be the only manufacturer ever to build three distinctly different F1 models and a total of eleven cars in one season.

Had March begun the year with the 721G it might have been developed into a winner but as it was its best finish was third (German GP, Peterson). The constant chopping and changing undermined the confidence of both the works drivers, who left at the end of the season.

Drivers: Skip Barber, Mike Beuttler, Luiz Bueno, Jean-Pierre Jarier, Niki Lauda, François Migault, Carlos Pace, Henri Pescarolo, Ronnie Peterson, Rolf Stommelen, John Watson.

721X hardly looked convincing, and it was a failure. Herd, Peterson and Mosley pose with the first car. Salient visible features are the full-width nose, elaborate and strong roll-over cage, exposed engine and high rear suspension members.

721G was a sensible and expedient mid-season development, looking what it was – a DFV powered F2 car.

722 Broadly this car was the same as the 712 but had new bodywork with a chisel nose and side radiators. In the rear suspension, parallel lower arms replaced the former lower wishbone. March lost its way with this one, which did not have the subtle harmony of the 712, and it took only one Championship win (driven by Peterson) although Niki Lauda won the minor four-race British F2 Championship. In the following year the 722 was competitive in F Atlantic.

The 722 seemed to be a competent successor to 712, but tht promise was not fulfilled in racing. Body lines look aerodynamcially effective, suspension is markedly outboard.

723 As with the 722, March took a backwards step with this car, and on the circuits it was not helped by the antics of the outfit to whom the works team was entrusted. All the top British drivers who bought one quickly switched to Ensign and GRD. The F Atlantic version was very successful in Britain and America and dominated both series.

731 Strictly speaking, there was never a 731 outside the paperwork because all the cars which bore the designation were 721Gs with the radiators moved from the sides to the front of the cars, narrow track suspension, a longer wheelbase and add-on deformable side structures to comply with new regulations. March began the year with hardly any money so ran only a single car, for Jean-Pierre Jarier, until he started to do so well in F2 that it was obviously a mistake to divert his attention with outings in a low-budget F1 car. Mike Beuttler continued to drive his private car, one ex-works car was sold to Lord Hesketh for James Hunt to drive, and the others were offered for hire. Roger Williamson was one who drove a 'rental' car, David Purley was another, and it was David who tried to save Roger's life when he crashed during the Dutch GP after a front tyre failed.

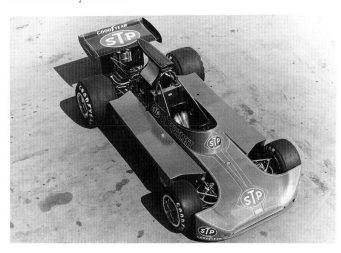

The close relationship between the 731 and 721G is not immediately obvious, but economy had dictated that these cars were simply updated 721Gs.

James Hunt proved he was a star in the making and although he only ran in six races he ended the year with a superb second place behind Peterson's Lotus in the soaking wet United States GP. (The Hesketh car was developed by former March designer, Dr Harvey Postlethwaite). Hunt showed there was nothing much wrong with the March concept, so while the company was ready to withdraw from F1 to concentrate on its production cars, the thought that a win in a World Championship had been less than a second away persuaded March to stay and fight.

Drivers: Mike Beuttler, James Hunt, Jean-Pierre Jarier, Henri Pescarolo, David Purley, Roger Williamson, Reine Wisell.

732 A development of the 1971 (not 1972) car, with a front radiator set in a full-width nose. This step backwards came as a result of James Hunt being loaned a 712 late in the 1972 season – his performance in it highlighted the problems of the 'improved' car. March was aided by an exclusive deal, for one year, to use BMW engines, and Jean-Pierre Jarier was almost unbeatable in F2, taking seven of March's eleven Championship wins, the others falling to Williamson, Vittorio Brambilla (twice) and Jacques Coloun. Through the year several independents turned to March, for the well-developed car was superior in braking, cornering and acceleration, although any straight line advantage may have been marginal. The works March team continued to use BMW engines until the end of European F2 in 1984, Herd's relationship with BMW often over-ruling his head when superior engines such as Renault and Honda units were offered.

Any description of the full-width nosed 732 is secondary to the obvious exuberance of Jarier in full flight.

733 Although drivers defected from March in 1972, in 1973 they dumped their GRDs and Ensigns in mid-season and came back to the 733. This was a short and narrow car, with excellent aerodynamic qualities; 15 major race wins were scored with Holbay engines, six with Nova engines. 733 drivers won all three British Championships (Tony Brise won

The car to beat in F3 in 1973. The louvred engine cover was standard, but 733s were also run with engines open to the elements.

two and Ian Taylor the third) plus the Italian and Swedish series which went to Carlo Giorgio and Conny Andersson respectively. The Atlantic derivative was a successful customer car in the category.

741 March followed the established practice of adapting an F2 car for F1, and in essence it remained a 1971 design. The radiators were positioned at the sides again and the wheelbase and front and rear tracks were both extended but there was nothing to excite the technically-minded. That said, the 741 was a competent DFV-powered car which while not a winner was capable of being a consistent points-finisher. March was short of money as usual, and as a result was not able to guarantee its preferred driver, Howden Ganley, a secure position alongside Hans Stuck. Ganley left when he had a firm offer from Maki, and was replaced by Vittorio Brambilla.

Stuck looked like a star in the making until he tangled with Hunt at Monaco and although he was physically unscathed after a nasty shunt he was never the same driver again. Although the car had potential about the only thing which can be said about March's 1974 season was that the final result was Brambilla 3, Stuck 2 – the number of tubs each destroyed. However, they did score enough points to place March ninth in the Constructors' Championship.

Drivers: Vittorio Brambilla, Howden Ganley, James Hunt, Hans-Joachim Stuck, Noritaka Takahara, Mike Wilds, Reine Wisell.

742 Customer cars were up-dates of 1973 models but the works cars had F1 style nose cones, side radiators, revised suspension geometry and F1 style brakes. These modifications made them superior to customer cars and this caused a great deal of resentment among buyers, so much so that the Bob Harper team quickly switched to Chevrons. Works drivers Patrick Depailler (four outright wins, one maximum points score) and Hans Stuck (three wins) finished 1-2 in the European F2 Championship. In a season in which March failed to win only one European Championship race, other wins fell to Peterson and Lafitte and 742s also dominated the European Hill Climb Championship.

Dominant drivers of the 1974 F2 Championship were Depailler (Elf March) and Stuck (Jagermeister March), here side by side at the start of a Hockenheim race.

743 The dominant F3 car of 1973. Works driver Brian Henton won 17 British F3 races and both Championships with a Holbay-engined car, Giorgio Francia won most German races in a Nova-Toyota-engined 743 (but Binder and Andersson had odd wins in a similar car), Colombo won in Italy and Tom Pryce won the Monaco race in a Holbay-engined 743. Keegan was still winning with a 743 in 1977.

751 Based on a new wider, lower, and stiffer monocoque with built-in deformable structures, but still made to the broad principles of the 1971 F2 car, the 751 had a longer wheelbase and narrower track than the 741 and was the only single-seater

March made in 1975 which worked properly (mainly due to the Vee lay-out of the Cosworth DFV which made for a very stiff installation). The team began the season with Brambilla but he was soon joined by Lella Lombardi who, by coming sixth in the shortened Spanish GP, scored half a point. She is still the only woman to have scored in the World Championship.

Brambilla put in a number of fine drives, showing particular finesse in the wet. He put a works March on pole in Sweden (a March first in a World Championship event but achieved by Robin Herd waving the pit board in front of the timing beam at the right moment). Brambilla led the Swedish race until his brakes faded (March could not afford F1-spec brakes), drove superbly in a downpour at Silverstone and emerged an easy winner in Austria. The Austrian race was another very wet affair and was stopped early so only half points were awarded but that was still the first World Championship win by a works March. Brambilla raised his arms in the air as he took the flag, braked and promptly crashed.

The works cars were joined by March 751 run by Penske Racing for Mark Donohue, but that was all too brief an arrangement for after only two races Donohue suffered a fatal accident at the Osterreichring. Penske's own PC3 which appeared late in the season was based on the 751, with some of the parts being interchangeable. Hans Stuck also raced a 751 after he was able to buy the team's test car which, in typical March fashion, generated short-term cash but blunted its long-term competitiveness.

Drivers: Vittorio Brambilla, Mark Donohue, Lella Lombardi, Hans Stuck.

The 751 had to be a workmanlike and economical car – that suited March resources at the time.

752 This lower F2 car had a wider and stiffer monocoque with built-in deformable structures. A last-minute change of rear tyre size by Goodyear upset calculations, which were already awry since the works tested with the much lighter Ford engine on the grounds that it was cheaper to run. A 741-style nose

A pristine 752 in the very smart livery used by the Project 3 team on the car driven by Peterson at Thruxton in 1975.

cone and side radiators were retained but the body from the nose cone to the front of the cockpit was much smoother. Although the 752-BMW won five Championship races (Leclère won two, others went to Flammini, Tambay and Brambilla) the Championship went to Laffite's Martini-BMW. Leclère and Flammini, however, also won non-Championship races and Noritake Takahara took the Japanese F2 Championship so 1975 was only a relatively poor year for March.

753 This retained the 1971 narrow tub and narrow track, a full-width nose but side radiators. Bodywork was smooth and while any of the year's F3 engines could be installed Nova-Toyota units were favoured. Works drivers Gunnar Nilsson and Alex-Dias Ribeiro came 1-2 in the British Championship and Brancatelli, Andersson, Deutsch and Mantova won in Europe. There was, however, a cloud on the horizon – the first Ralt RT1s began to appear and proved a thorn in March's side.

The 753 was sleeker than its F3 predecessor, but still a solid-looking car. This is Conny Andersson's car.

761 The most successful of the March F2-based DFV-powered cars, the 761 had a stiffer monocoque than the 751 on which it was based, an even longer wheelbase and wider track. Suspension was still outboard all round, and the team used different nose cones depending on the nature of the circuit, flank radiators were retained, neatly faired, and air boxes ranged from tall and narrow to later regulation low intakes. Two teams were run, and after the first race of the season back door wheeling and dealing saw Peterson replace Lombardi. Once he had a properly made car, Peterson became a front runner and often led races until let down by mechanical problems (brakes were an Achilles' heel) but he did manage a memorable win at Monza in the Italian GP, the only full-length World Championship race won by a works March. As Peterson showed his class and revived his career Brambilla tended to

Among March F1 cars the 761 was a rare success, especially in Peterson's hands.

try too hard (he had three big crashes during the German GP weekend) but he showed he had lost none of his touch with a wonderful drive in the last race of the year, the extremely wet Japanese GP. For all that it was a good year, March was only seventh in the Constructors' Championship. There was no joy for the independents who ran these cars in 1977.

Drivers: Vittorio Brambilla, Michael Bleekemolen, Bernard de Dryver, Boy Hayje, Brian Henton, Mikki Kozarowitsky, Brett Lunger, Arturo Merzario, Patrick Neve, Ronnie Peterson, Hans Stuck, Andy Sutcliffe.

761B A slightly modified 761 with a shorter wheelbase, the 761B formed the basis of March's 1977 effort but suffered like all Marches that year in that none of them could make effective use of Goodyear's new tyres. Inexperienced drivers Ian Scheckter and Alex-Dias Ribeiro were run (the former was the most successful March driver ever, with six South African Championships to his credit). Robin Herd made F2 his top priority, so that March could keep works BMW engines. Mosley grew tired of the unequal struggle when running the F1 team and left March to work full-time for FOCA. There were no Constructors' Championship points for March in 1977, despite as many as seven 761 and 761B being entered for one race (the British GP).

Drivers: Brian Henton, Arturo Merzario, Alex-Dias Ribeiro, Ian Scheckter, Hans Stuck.

This shot of a 761B shows the large flank radiators of the 761/761B, and also the first signs of Frank Williams' Saudia sponsorship, for it is the car Neve drove for Williams in 1977.

762 This was an uprated 752 with slightly changed rear suspension (a lower wishbone replaced the former parallel arms), fractionally longer track and narrower wheelbase. Although the 762 won five races, three were taken by Stuck who was a graded driver drafted in on behalf of BMW to uphold honour, so they did not carry points for the Championship. Flammini scored two wins which did carry points but the Championship was dominated by Renault-

engined cars. March could have used this unit (its V-6 configuration made for a much stiffer installation which was its major advantage) but it was rejected because of loyalty to BMW. As with the 752, odd independent cars were tried with Lancia engines, but the points-scoring alteration to the BMW M12 was the Hart 420R. Noritake Takahara (762-BMW) again won the Japanese F2 Championship – virtually every car in the series was a March.

763 A lightly revised 753 with 762-style rear suspension. In a works car Bruno Giacomelli won the lesser of the two British F3 Championships and might have taken the BP series but was punted off in the last round by Rupert Keegan. However Bruno did win at Monaco. Conny Andersson just 'lost' the European title, and other notable winners with 763s included Brancatelli and Ghinzani. All used Nova-Toyota engines, but interestingly a Unipart-backed team ran 763s with Holbay-Triumph engines. The Formula Atlantic variant dominated both North American series with both going to Gilles Villeneuve.

A neat 763 posed in the Silverstone pits lane before the start of the 1976 season.

771 Intended as March's main weapon for 1977, the 771 had an entirely different monocoque to the production cars, with a front radiator, and was lighter, with the weight being distributed more to the middle, in the manner of ground effects F1 cars. In the event it proved to be no advance and only one was raced. Ian Scheckter finished in it only once, tenth in the Dutch GP, and retired three times.

Driver: Ian Scheckter.

2-4-0 March's six-wheeled car was primarily intended to attract sponsorship, so when it was first shown to the Press it was little more than a full-sized model. The idea had enormous potential since it had less drag and better traction and braking than any other F1 car, and it could have been a wonderful ground effects car since it could have accommodated huge under-car venturi. Unfortunately, after the special gear casing had been drawn it looked very

Economical lines typified the mid-1970s March cars for secondary categories. This Hart-engined 762 was driven to fourth place in the 1976 Thruxton F2 race by Eddie Cheever.

Robin Herd showing off his six-wheeled car at its Press launch (the author is leaning on a Bicester wall and seemingly ignoring him).

expensive, so some of the ribs were erased; when the car ran, the forces generated by its close-coupled four wheel drive twisted the casing and caused havoc in the transmission.

There never was a single six-wheeler but the transmission was bolted onto several 761s. A car was loaned to Roy Lane who won hill climbs with it, provided it rained – in the dry the higher cornering forces caused it to be unreliable. Oddly enough, although the six-wheeler never raced it was March's most profitable car as it was in great demand for exhibitions and Scalextric paid royalties on models.

772 This further update of the 1975 model was no opposition to the Renault-engined cars in F2 racing in 1977 when Martini set the pace. Some March teams were in disarray and some drivers in F2 and F3 switched to other marques. The 772P F2 car (P for 'prototype') run by the works was built around the narrow (pre-1975) F Atlantic tub under pressure from BMW, who threatened to withdraw works engines if results were not forthcoming. Had Bruno Giacomelli had one from the start of the season he probably would have taken the title, and graded driver Jochen Mass also won two races with the 772P. The last round of the Championship was won by Giacomelli with the prototype 782, which was a derivative of the 772P.

772P-BMW at Thruxton in 1977, driven by Alex Ribeiro, who had occasional F2 drives that year, one in a Hart-engined 772P.

773 This was a further up-date of the 1975 F3 car, still with narrow tub, which seemed suited to all types of circuit. Stephen South won one of the two British F3 Championships with a 763-Toyota and Piercarlo Ghinzani took the European title. Brett Riley was the only other driver to win major F3 races with a 773.

The 773 had a March outline that was soon to be discarded. This is South's Team BP car.

781 Basically this was a lightly revised 771 which was used with limited success in the British (Aurora) F1 Championship. One of the two cars had limited fuel capacity as the races were only 100 miles long, and plans to run the second car in some World Championship events came to nothing.

782 This car had a new slim monocoque with the driver moved forward in the wheelbase and a nose radiator. It derived from the car with which Giacomelli won the last round of the 1977 series. With the withdrawal of Renault at the end of 1977, March scooped the market – deservedly as the 782 was one of the best March F2 cars. The works cars ran half-length sliding skirts during the latter part of the season but these were more cosmetic than anything. Giacomelli won eight races and the title in a works car, aided by Herd who no longer had the stress of running an F1 team, while Marc Surer was Championship runner up, with no victories but a string of scoring finishes in a BMW Junior team car. Fifteen of the 21 drivers who scored points did so with 782s. Ribeiro in a Hart-powered car also won a race, at the Nürburgring, while Brian Henton, operating on a shoestring with a 782-Hart, revived his career with some stirring drives.

783 A light up-date of previous models served for this F3 car, which had a more angular tub as the company had bought some new metal folding equipment. Few were made, no outstanding driver had a whole season in one, although Mansell and Warwick drove 783s for part of the year and Teo Fabi won three European Championship races. March still held on to its pre-eminence in American Atlantic racing, but its days of dominance were numbered.

792 March's first true ground effects car with full-length sliding skirts, new narrow tub with honeycomb inserts and engine as a stressed member with steel sideframes. The inboard front suspension was by lower wishbones and top rocker arms, rear suspension was by lower wishbones, top and bottom links, single radius arms and inboard springs. Wheelbase and track dimensions were similar to the earlier F1 cars and the radiator was mounted in a slim nose cone with side wings. There were endless problems as the works and customers came to grips with ground effects, which more than quadrupled the spring rates required to make the system work. In the early part of the season there were many chassis and body breakages due to the extra stresses being generated, and the 792 could be beaten by a well-sorted 782. Still, progress was made and 792 drivers won six races (a 782 won one) and works driver Marc Surer took the F2 Championship by a whisker after the brakes on Henton's Ralt failed on the penultimate lap while he was leading the final round. Most 792s had BMW engines, but once again there were a few with Hart power units.

This was not a pretty car, but it was an effective racing machine. The 'square' nose is obvious in this shot – in profile it was a fine wedge – and other features are the inboard suspension, low build and clean lines. The driver is European champion Marc Surer.

79C This was a ground effects F3 car based on the 792 and built as a prototype. It was tested by Chico Serra but as the customer 793s were winning most races, and sliding skirts were permitted only for 1979, it was not raced.

793 Broadly similar to the 1978 F3 car, with front radiators and full-width nosecones, the March 793 had sliding skirts but was not a serious 'ground effects' design since little work was done on the venturi and its outboard suspension was not ideal. It completely dominated British F3 racing but against negligible opposition – top runners Serra, Thackwell, de Cesaris, Johansson and Acheson all drove 793s in 1979.

A relatively slim hull and broad side pods are obvious elements of a ground effects car, but the full-width nose and outboard suspension seemed to be contradictions. However, in British F3 the 793 was supreme in 1979.

802 This F2 car had the same monocoque and layout as the 792 but with chisel nose, front aerofoils, side radiators, and venturi sidepods though without sliding skirts. It was another superb customer car, one of the best March ever made, but in the Championship it was beaten by the well-funded Toleman-Hart team. March still took three victories and Teo Fabi was third in the Championship behind the Tolemans of Henton and Warwick.

A works BMW-powered 802 in the Silverstone pits lane during pre-season tests.

803 This car had a front-mounted radiator in a short chisel nose with side wings, improved venturi side pods and rocker arm front suspension with inboard springs. The 803 began the season with outboard rear suspension but a rocker arm rear

system was adopted at mid-season which went some way to answering customer complaints. Many drivers preferred the 793, however, and six of the nine March victories in the British series were won in 793s. March was in a shaky financial position and could not afford to produce aerodynamic packages for both Britain and Europe because it had begun to suffer the effects of the general economic recession, and the 803 did not work well on British control tyres. However, Michele Alboreto won the European Championship (where tyres were 'free') in a Pavanello Euroracing developed Alfa-engined 803.

The major success for the 803 was achieved by Euroracing with their Alfa-engined cars. This one is driven by Alboreto.

811 Although called a 'March' this F1 car was made for March Grand Prix, a joint venture between John Macdonald's RAM Racing and Robin Herd which had no connection with March Engineering of Bicester. To circumvent the usual problems of design and development, it was decided to copy the Williams FW07 RAM had been running and the cars were built by March Engines at Cowley, a special projects outfit owned by Herd.

The cars were straightforward Coswoth DFV/Hewland FGA machines, but made on the cheap, and when the first one proved heavy, because March did not use the exotic materials which Williams employed, it was lightened by using thinner gauge sheeting. The result was that the tubs flexed, the cars proved virtually undriveable, and very soon Macdonald and Herd had fallen out. Gordon Coppuck took his place as Chief Engineer for a limited spell and then handed over to Adrian Reynard. Between them they managed to make the car into a reasonable proposition which Derek Daly typically qualified around row ten of a grid. Eliseo Salazar had left in disgust, taking his sponsorship to Ensign. Ironically the March 81C, which founded the company's fortunes in Indycar racing, was based on the 811, but that was built by March Engineering, with input from George Bignotti. Daly failed to qualify for the first six races, then finished four times in eight attempts with his best finish seventh in the British GP.

Drivers: Derek Daly, Eliseo Salazar.

An 811 in its early form, before Adrian Reynard introduced a short-chassis version and initiated a weight-cutting programme. Driver is Derek Daly.

812 A new monocoque and body marked out the 1981 F2 car but the rocker arm suspension was similar to the 802. It was another good customer car but this time was beaten by the works Ralt-Hondas which had superior power and, perhaps, a tyre advantage. Still, three European victories fell to March drivers – Thierry Boutsen was Championship runner-up – and Satoru Nakajima won the Japanese series in a 812-Honda.

The 812 had clean lines and BMW engines – BMW Motorsport or Mader units in the works cars, while some independents used Heidegger BMW engines. Tyres were more crucial. This car carries a Pirelli decal, and Corrado Fabi was one driver who stuck with the Italian rubber, but Boutsen did better with Bridgestones.

813 Broadly similar to 812, the 1981 F3 car had smaller critical dimensions and front-mounted radiator in a similar bluff nose cone. Mauro Baldi won the European Championship with an

813-Alfa Romeo but March could not afford to build a version to work on British control rubber (the only March drivers in the top ten of the British Championship were fourth and ninth). At the end of the season March stopped making F3 cars in order to concentrate on F2, Indycar and sports cars, which made more money. In 1982 Euroracing 101s, actually modified 813s, dominated the European F3 Championship.

821 This F1 car retained the March name although the team had become entirely separate and Herd had nothing to do with it. Adrian Reynard, now the Chief Engineer, was able to shed weight and bring the car, still basically inspired by the Williams FW07, to the level it should have been at the start of 1981, but everybody else had made further advances. Macdonald landed a major sponsor in Rothmans but when the cars did not produce immediate results Rothmans threatened to withdraw. One of the problems lay with the Pirelli tyres, and in desperation Macdonald switched to Avons, but then Avon withdrew from racing. While the team was able to buy all the stock there could be no improvement, while Pirelli made enormous strides.

Rothmans withdrew its sponsorship when both cars failed to qualify at Monaco so a planned development programme had to be axed. The team limped to the end of the year and although a new 1983 car was called a RAM-March it existed only on paper. Onyx Race Engineering entered a car for Villotta in five races, and he failed to qualify five times.

Drivers: Raul Boesel, Rupert Keegan, Jochen Mass.

The 821 was well sponsored, looked purposeful, and was another failure. This car is driven by Raul Boesel in Brazil in 1982.

822 An update of the 812 but with a slightly narrower tub, improved aerodynamics, and new rear suspension geometry, this turned out to be one of the very best March F2 cars. Works drivers Corrado Fabi (five wins) and Johnny Cecotto (three wins) came 1-2 in the European F2 Championship despite a massive effort by Honda who backed both Ralt and Spirit. Satoru Nakajima won the Japanese Championship in an 822-Honda.

Last of the March F3 cars, the 813. Driver is 1981 European Champion Mauro Baldi, in an Alfa-engined car.

This was another pace-setting March-BMW, running on Michelin tyres. Driver is Johnny Cecotto.

832 For F2 in 1983, March had a new monocoque and aerodynamic package – the monocoque was necessary to meet survival cell regulations – but generally Bellamy followed the 822 concept. It worked very well in the early part of the season, giving Beppe Gabbiani four wins from five starts in a car run by Onyx Race Engineering, which had taken on the 'works' F2 team. There was a fundamental weakness in the tub and later on the cars became very difficult to drive as the tubs grew tired. The works responded with add-on stiffeners, including a carbon fibre top section, but had the tubs been replaced the title might not have gone to Jonathan Palmer's Ralt-Honda. The Onyx 832s were third, fifth and seventh in the Championship, with independents also scoring. Geoff Lees won the Japanese Championship in an 832-Honda which, with the engine's V-6 configuration, had an inherently stiffer installation.

Christian Danner in one of the 'official' 832s. Engines were supplied by BMW Motorsport, tyres by Michelin, and initially the car was particularly effective on fast circuits. Then it slipped off the pace, and there were component failures to compound problems.

842 A new honeycomb monocoque designed by Ralph Bellamy was introduced, with composite top section and honeycomb and machined aluminium bulkheads, for the 1984 F2 car, which also had a flat bottom to comply with new regulations, BMW engine tilted at four degrees to the horizontal driving through a Hewland FT200 and a new pullrod front suspension. Although many at March thought this was the best F2 car the company made, it seems that the suspension was insufficiently rigid, and the Onyx-run works team made the wrong choice of tyre supplier. March took only one race win in the final European Championship season, to bring the March total of European F2 Championship victories to 77. Satoru Nakajima took his third Japanese F2 title with an 842-Honda, Johansson was second in a similar car, and the next four places were taken by BMW-powered 842s.

The 842 was a svelte little car, with the monocoque forming much of the 'bodywork'. This is an early-season test shot.

85B March's first F3000 car, designed by Ralph Bellamy, was an 842 with a two-inch longer monocoque. It was the best customer car available in F3000 because its weight

distribution was right. In its make-up the aluminium honeycomb/carbon fibre monoque followed the 842 precisely, and the DFV engine fitted it neatly. Front suspension was a double wishbone pushrod layout while at the rear there was a lower wishbone and top rocker arm arrangement. Christian Danner won the inaugural F3000 Championship with three race wins with a privately entered 85B, Emanuele Pirro won twice and Ivan Capelli also took a victory. By the end of the season March dominated F3000 both in terms of numbers on the grids and finishers in the points, the 85Bs winning seven of the twelve races.

This F3000 car derived from the last 'European' F2 March, distinguished by its engine, slab sides and larger rear wing. This car is driven by Emanuele Pirro, who was third in the first F3000 Championship.

85J This F2 car was virtually the same as the 842, and was built for the Japanese Championship. Once again, this was won by Satoru Nakajima with Honda power.

Another 842 derivative, and very closely related, was the 85J for the Japanese F2 series that was totally dominated by March in its final seasons.

86B Designed by Andy Brown, this car had the same mechanicals and tub as the 85B but was changed in detail to fit a complete revision of aerodynamics, notably re-profiled side pods moved eight inches forward and a high engine cover. Ivan Capelli won the F3000 Championship with an 86B run on a very tight budget, and his two wins were backed by two by Pirro and a single victory for Philippe Alliot. March, riding high on its 1985 season, captured most orders and the best teams and drivers.

The DFV-powered 86B was aerodynamically cleaner than the 85B, especially at the back where a preoccupation was the airflow to the rear wing. The driver is Pirro again, at Silverstone.

Juniors (**top**). The red cars are Ron Harris' pair of Lola Mk 5s in the Crystal Palace paddock in 1962. The cars are neat and slim machines, as is the Lotus behind the Minor, but the real interest must be in the setting: this was an important secondary meeting and there are works cars around, but there is not a single transporter in sight, let alone a mobile home, there are no barriers to keep the small boy away from the Lotus and no sponsors' messages to be seen. That could even be a traditional British summer event warm beer tent in the distance . . .

A typical F3 grid towards the end of the 1960s (**above**), with a good crowd enjoying June sunshine at the minor Mallory Park circuit. The cars on the front row of the grid are a Lotus 59 (Roy Pike), a Chevron B9 (Barrie Maskell) and a Brabham BT28 (Tim Schenken). There are two more 59s on the second row (Ikuzawa and Nunn) and a green Tecno in the middle of row 3.

Tom Pryce's March 743 (**top**) glittering in the Monaco sun in 1974. He stepped down from F1 to dominate this prestigious race with the essentially simple Holbay-engined March.

Through the 1980s Formula 3 was largely the province of two British constructors, one French and one Italian. The British pair are represented in this 1987 Silverstone grid shot (**above**), with Thomas Danielsson nearest the camera in a Reynard 873 and Damon Hill on the outside in a Ralt RT31.

There seemed to be a consensus among designers in the late 1970s, too, shown in a 1978 Ralt (**upper**) and a 1981 Martini (**lower**). Tauranac's basic RT1 design was by then four years old, but much refined and still very much a winning car. The origins of the Martini MK34 also dated back four years but during that time Martini had not put in enough development work to keep the marque right in the forefront. Both cars were driven by men on their way to Formula 1, Nelson Piquet in the Ralt and Emanuele Pirro in the Martini.

Formula 3000 cigarette packets. The Onyx 87B (**top**) is a DFV-engined car driven by Stefano Modena in 1987. The Eddie Jordan Racing Reynard 89Ds (**above**) are Mugen-engined cars, driven by Jean Alesi and Martin Donnelly in 1989.

86J A further update of the 842 for the Japanese F2 Championship, which was won yet again by Nakajima in a Honda-powered car. He won only one race in the eight-race series, but scored well in every one, whereas Championship runner-up Kazuyoshi Hoshino won three in an 86J but retired twice. Nine of the first ten in the All-Japan Championship drove 86Js; Thackwell was fourth in an 85J. Hoshino drove a March to win the last-ever F2 race.

87P After ten years out of F1, March returned in 1987 with a one-car team which was set up as a separate company within the March group, March Racing. The decision to enter F1 was made late in 1986 so the new season started before the 871 was ready but, in order to qualify for possible FOCA membership, March had to appear at the first race. Thus the 87P (an 87B F3000 car with 871 body and suspension) appeared in practice for the Brazilian GP. Because it had limited fuel tanks, being an F3000 chassis, there was no hope of it completing the race. It qualified to run, all the team's engines were wrecked during practice, and it did not start.

871 March Racing's real 1987 F1 car was designed by Gordon Coppuck, who borrowed heavily from Andy Brown's F3000 car while both were being drawn. It was a fairly conventional design with a carbon fibre monocoque, pullrod suspension front and rear, and Cosworth DFZ engine. Not too much was expected from it since the season was to be a learning year for all concerned. Ivan Capelli, who brought sponsorship from Leyton House, the leisure division of a huge Japanese company, was given the seat and he surprised everyone by coming sixth in only his fourth race, at Monaco.

By mid-season Capelli was a frequent front-runner in the 'atmo' class which he won in Austria and Portugal. Had the team had better service from its engine builder it is likely that Capelli could have finished higher than fourth in the Jim Clark Trophy (for drivers with normally aspirated engines). So acute was the problem with engine supply that on occasion Capelli was forced to use a 3.3-litre Cosworth DFL sports-car engine. The single point scored meant that March was equal eleventh in the Constructors' Championship.

Driver: Ivan Capelli.

The blue 871 performed creditably in 1987. Generally it was run in this form, without an engine cover although an airbox was tried.

87B The 1987 F3000 car had a monocoque designed by Andy Brown with composite top section. Mechanically it was similar to the 842-86B series, and DFV engines were again used, with March gearboxes that had Hewland internals. It had the reputation of being tricky to set up and not as easy to drive as its rivals from Lola and Ralt. Stefano Modena won the F3000 Championship – he was an outstanding driver, who was run by the very experienced works-associated Onyx team. However, there was general dissatisfaction with this car, which marked the beginning of March's decline in the category.

The 87B was compact and seemingly workmanlike, but fine tuning to race competitiveness was difficult. This ORECA team car is driven by Yannick Dalmas, who was fifth in the 1987 F3000 Championship.

881 Adrian Newey, who was March Racing's first choice as designer, was unable to join the team before the middle of 1987 due to commitments in CART (with the Lola works team) but when he was free he set to work on a design which won the ultimate accolade in racing – it was widely copied the following year. The main advance was in aerodynamics, and the 881 was a very slender car with a longer wheelbase than most, and narrower front and rear tracks. For 1988, March switched from Cosworth to Judd engines.

The 881 was too rigid to perform well on the slower circuits early in the season and was plagued by transmission problems due to a faulty batch of crown wheels and pinions. Further, the Judd V-8 suffered loss of power during the course of a race but the cause was soon identified and rectified. On faster circuits the 881 came into its own and Gugelmin and Capelli were often the fastest non-turbo qualifiers. In very wet conditions, Gugelmin came home fourth in the British GP. Mauricio Gugelmin was brought in alongside Capelli, for new rules stipulated that each team should run two cars (that was March Racing's plan in any case).

Two more highlights of the season came in Portugal where Capelli qualified third and came home second, splitting the McLarens of Prost and Senna, and in Japan where Capelli actually overtook Prost to lead. True it was for only 400 yards but it was the first time a non-turbo car had led a GP since 1984. March was sixth in the Constructors' Championship, only a point behind Lotus and Arrows.

Drivers: Ivan Capelli, Mauricio Gugelmin.

The highly successful 881, showing its trend-setting slim lines and clean front suspension. Driver is Ivan Capelli.

88B Described as a new car, this was actually an updated 87B at a time when a new design was desperately needed, due to the form shown by Lola and the arrival on the scene of Reynard, which swept F3000 at its first attempt. The 88B was a very difficult car in every way and virtually wiped March out of F3000 in Europe and Japan where even Leyton House, its F1 sponsor, switched chassis after only one race. Extensive work, mainly by Gordon Coppuck, made it reasonably competitive by mid-season and Pierluigi Martini won at Enna and took some good points finishes, but by then the damage to March's reputation had been done.

Martini in a First Racing 88B, the only team to win with an F3000 March in 1988, total defeat being staved off by Martini's inspired driving, back-up development by March and field work by team engineer Richard Divila.

CG891 Newey's 1989 car was a development of the thinking behind the 881 but was entirely new and even slimmer behind the driver (March Racing commissioned a narrow-angle engine from Judd for its exclusive use). The initials 'CG' were added to the type number in memory of Cesare Gariboldi, Capelli's mentor, who had played an important part in setting up the team and who died in a road accident at the end of 1988. The March Group PLC financial crisis of late 1988 meant that the CG891 arrived late (it raced for the first time at Monaco) and the team never caught up.

In the event, the CG891 proved disappointing. Others who copied the 881 made greater advances and some mistakes were made in the area of suspension geometry. Gugelmin had finished third in the first race of the season in an 881 but apart from the odd flash of promise in qualifying (Capelli was fourth on the grid in Mexico) the CG891 was rarely competitive except on very fast circuits (Capelli held second place at Paul Ricard) and all too often the cars retired, for a variety of reasons. March slumped to twelfth in the Constructors' Championship as, technically, the name disappeared from F1 again.

Drivers: Ivan Capelli, Mauricio Gugelmin.

The last Grand Prix March was a disappointment and visually there was little to mark it out from a gaggle of similar cars.

89B This entirely new F3000 designed by Ralph Bellamy had an all-composite monocoque (the first customer car in March's history to be so made), pullrod suspension front and

rear and Judd engines. It was a big improvement on the 88B but when it was not quick straight from the box most of its few European customers switched makes. Fabrizio Giovanardi won at Vallelunga and celebrated by switching to a Reynard and sliding down the grid. For most of the season only a single works-run March appeared in European F3000, a championship the marque had won for its first four years, as attention was concentrated on Japanese races, where the 89B backed by Leyton House was reasonably competitive. This group bought the F3000 project in May, 1989, when it became a separate company, Leyton Engineering, under the managing directorship of Mike Smith, who had been the F3000 Project Manager at March Engineering.

MAROTT

Dennis Flather's long-serving Marott 500 car was a Marwyn which began with a water-cooled two cylinder Scott engine (MARwyn-scOTT). It went through many changes, including a number of engines, and Flather managed to make a dreadful base machine into something approaching a competent, but not competitive, car.   ML

MARSHALL

An early Australian 500 car built by J. Marshall, this was a conventional device built around a simple ladder frame and originally fitted with a Triumph engine, later replaced by a JAP unit. Road-holding was not of a high order.   ML

MARTIN

A pair of Martin Specials appeared in British F3 races in the Spring of 1953, when Dennis Taylor drove one to a debut victory at Castle Combe, and the cars then featured amongst the leaders here and there for the rest of the season. Ray Martin built his cars in small numbers, on Kieft lines and with the swing-axle rear suspension that enjoyed a brief vogue (he had been partly responsible for successful early Kiefts). Norton engines were generally used. Charles Headland, a Cooper driver in 1952 and Kieft driver in 1953, ran one of these cars quite successfully as a Martin-Headland in 1954, winning a major Silverstone race.

MARTINI

Tico Martini is a naturalized Frenchman, born of Italian parents, who built his first competitions car in Jersey in 1962. This was a kart-like hill climb machine with a 650cc Triumph motorcycle engine. A year later he was looking after the technical side of the Knight brothers' Winfield Racing Drivers' School at Magny Cours, and he took his next steps towards becoming a racing car constructor in a garage at the track. Since then Martini cars have carried an MW or MK (Martini-Winfield or Martini-Knight) designation, although the proper factory that was later set up was a short distance away.

The first Martini F3 car was built for the school team, and from 1969 Martini achieved both sales and successes in the class. Interest tended to fluctuate with French self-interest, as *Formule France* and *Formule Renault* sometimes demanded priority. In the mid-1970s F3 was important again in France, and Hugues de Chaunac (at the time a director of Automobiles Martini) ran the works-associated ORECA team which at the end of the decade was supreme – the combination of the MK27 and Alain Prost was almost unbeatable, and Renault tended to refer to the successful Renault-engined Martinis as 'Renaults'!

A venture into F1 in 1978 was a disaster, following very rewarding F2 seasons 1975-7. Martini is fourth in an overall table of victories in the most recent years of F2 racing, 1967-84, although a return to the class in 1983 was not an outstanding success and Martini decided against entering F3000, the 'successor' to F2.

In the 1980s Martini fortunes in F3 varied. As the decade opened a lack of development seemed to be a handicap, but the marque bounced back, especially in France and the prestigious Monaco race. Later in the decade, however, Martini's first carbon fibre car was a lemon, and despite the long association ORECA turned to Dallara for F3 in 1987 (and in 1989 took the French title for the sixth time in successive years), while in 1990 de Chaunac moved to AGS. Through those closing years of the 1980s Martini won only occasional F3 races and lagged behind the other members of the quartet that had dominated F3, but in the perspective of recent history, Martini's status was assured.

MW1 This was a one-off space frame car which had much in common with the first batch of *Formule France* cars built in 1968. It was generally regarded as Brabham-inspired, and with a Lucas-Cosworth engine had performance equivalent to a BT21B. Appropriately, its race debut came at Magny-Cours, on May 1 1968; Etienne Vigoreux (a Winfield school 'graduate') led the first heat at that meeting and was placed sixth on aggregate after suspension problems.

MW3 In effect this was a purpose-developed F3 car, again with space frame but on a shorter wheelbase. It was not seen often in 1969, when it was driven by Lafitte, but it was raced more extensively in 1970, with a Novamotor engine and usually driven by Mieusset.

MW4 This came in a line of gentle evolution, and was the last step towards Martini's really serious entry into F3. The space frame and Nova engine were retained. Its race debut was at Pau, and initially it was driven by Salomon, then Laffite scored Martini's first top-three placing with it, at Magny-Cours.

MW5 This 1970 car is generally considered to mark Martini's arrival as a force in F3. In specification it did not represent a great advance, but it gained a reputation for good handling and the Nova engine used was the equal of any save the works development units. With it the little side tanks that came to be regarded as a Martini characteristic were introduced. Salomon showed its potential with good results early in the season, then in September Jaussaud scored Martini's first important race victory, with an MW5 at Nogaro. After the season James Hunt put in some test work with an MW5.

MW7 With this 1971 car Martini's presence in F3 started to become numerically significant, as production just reached double figures. It followed the tried and tested lines – space frame, double wishbone outboard suspension and Nova engine, with low flat-topped bodywork. Its drivers usually had to give best to their Alpine compatriots, but Migault won with an MW7 while Dolhem, Coulon and others were well placed in Martinis.

Among the features of early Martinis were low overall lines and little bulges housing the fuel tanks low down alongside the cockpits. This MW7 is running without aerofoils at Pau in 1971. The driver is Jose Dolhem.

MK9 The space frame was retained in the 1972 F3 car, while Holbay engines came to be preferred to the less sophisticated Nova units. The biggest change, however, was in the adoption of a full-width nose and engine cover as attention was paid to airflow efficiency. In French racing the Alpines again had the edge, but towards the end of the year Coulon won in a Martini at Magny-Cours and Montlhéry.

MK12 Physically the changes in the 1973 F3 car were not great, but the combination of Jacques Laffite and Martini came good and took the French Championship from Alpine. The rather heavy space frame was retained, the bodywork was a little smoother (but engines covers tended to be left off) and Holbay engines were generally used, although odd independent cars ran with Vegantune units. Apart from his Championship, Laffite won the F3 race that is somehow the most important in prestige terms, the Grand Prix Monaco F3. Then, almost abruptly, the French turned away from F3 at the end of the season, preferring Super Renault where the Martini line was continued.

MK16 Tico Martini's first F2 car came in 1975. It was quite straightforward, with an open bathtub aluminium monocoque, orthodox double wishbone suspension, a fairly bulky body with front-mounted radiator and full-width nose, and Schnitzer-BMW engine. There was little need for change through the season, beyond some suspension modifications. Jacques Laffite drove the MK16 to win six of the races in the Championship series and take the title with 60 points – the runner-up scored 36. The single-car team was run by de Chaunac, and adequately sponsored.

In 1976 the MK16 was modified to take the Renault-Gordini CH1B V-6, and used in early-season races while a second MK19 was completed. Arnoux placed it second in the opening F2 race of the year.

The first F2 Martini was a solid-looking car, sound rather than sensational, well prepared and highly successful.

MK19 The definitive 1976 F2 car was powered by the Renault V-6, and although this was heavier than the BMW engines the complete car was lighter than the MK16. It followed that car closely, save in the rear suspension, as the V-6 was wider. The 90-degree 24-valve unit produced just over 300bhp in 1976, and drove through a six-speed gearbox. Team drivers Arnoux (three race victories) and Tambay (one victory) were second and third in the European F2 championship. In 1977 three French drivers entered MK19s with BMW engines, in nine attempts achieving three finishes.

The first MK19 looking very smooth. Outward changes were to be in details, for example in the nose, in the engine cover and in the redistribution of decals.

MK21 Through 1976 there were rumours of a French return to F3, and of a monocoque Martini for the category. A Martini did appear in 1977, but rarely as there were no F3 races in France. There was the Monaco race, however, and that fell to Pironi in the Martini. It was the conventional MK21, with a Novamotor Toyota engine, and the same car was raced in 1978. Very similar 21Bs appeared that year, Toyota-powered save for a works car run with a Gordini-developed Renault 20TS engine. This was driven by Alain Prost and hardly set new standards, although in the Autumn he won the Jarama round of the European F3 Championship. Odd 21Bs appeared in 1979, but generally were not competitive.

The 21B was a run-of-the-mill F3 car of the late 1970s.

MK22 For the last season of Martini's first venture into F2, and the last of an Elf-backed F2 campaign, a mildly revised version of the MK19 was produced. This Mk22 was reputedly a more nervous car, but Arnoux won three races and the European title with it, while Pironi won once and was third on the points

table. Confusingly, Giancarlo Martini also ran a Martini MK22 in 1977, but achieved little with it; Naddeo entered it in five 1978 races, and achieved nothing beyond five DNQs.

The brand new MK22 at Magny-Cours, showing off the still-bulky but sleek bodywork. Yellow was the principal colour, with blue cockpit surround and engine cover. Lined up behind the car are Pironi, Tico Martini, Hugues de Chaunac and Arnoux.

MK23 This car marked a move into F1 that almost brought Martini down. It followed the F2 line of development, and indeed there were similarities. There was a monocoque hull, front suspension by lower wishbones and upper rocking arms (and for the first time on a Martini, coil springs/dampers were inboard) and rear suspension by parallel links and radius rods. A Cosworth DFV drove through a Hewland FGA400 gearbox. Something more than a simple Cosworth kit car was called for in the ground effects era, and the Martini was never in with a chance. It was entered for eight races, and Arnoux got it past the flag three times (with its best placings ninth in Belgium and Austria). Sponsorship was inadequate and the little team did not qualify for FOCA benefits. Before the end of the 1978 season it was pulled out, and Martini set about rebuilding the business.

Martini's unhappy F1 car, travelling at speed past the Paul Ricard pits exit road. Its slender nose and side radiators are obvious, but there are no skirts and this is the 1978 French GP. Arnoux at least placed it in this race, 14th.

MK27 This was a car to restore morale and fortunes. A well-sponsored but remarkably economical one-car, one-driver team was run in the European F3 Championship. Frequently there was no spare, so Prost's approach had to be near-faultless. He won 7 of the 11 Championship races he started (as well as the Monaco event) and took the title with 67 points. The runner-up scored 28. The abundant supply of Renault engines, the band of experienced technicians, the biggest budget and the best driver were all deployed to good effect.

The MK27 was down to the minimum weight limit, with a simple hull and tubular engine bay. The engine in the works car was the Renault unit, lighter than the Nova-Toyota engines to be found in the backs of independent MK27s (and the odd 21/27).

A side shot gives the impression of mass concentrated towards the rear. The side plates suggest that the pods were larger than they actually were. In view of Renault publicity assertions that the title-winning car was a Renault, the company name has little space on Prost's car.

MK31 Although Ferté drove an uprated MK27 (sometimes referred to as a 27/31) in 1980, most of the Martinis in F3 that year were Toyota-engined MK31s, and very effective they were. The MK31 was a mildly developed version of MK27. Boutsen seemed to be running away with the European Championship until his team was caught out by tyre developments. Nevertheless, places from second to sixth went to Martini drivers in 1980.

The MK31 was closely related to MK27, but in 1980 was more effective with Toyota engines. Mauro Baldi, here on his cooling-down lap after a convincing victory at Monaco, scored three European Championship race victories and was equal third in the points table. Success came after he turned away from the Dudot-developed Renault engine.

MK34 In chassis terms, this was another development, and many pundits reckoned a development too many when a new car was called for. Novamotor Alfa Romeo engines were the fashionable, and successful, power units and used by seven of the eight MK34 drivers who scored in the European Championship (where Alain Ferté, Alliot and Streiff finished second, third and fourth behind March driver Baldi).

Two MK34s at Monaco – a slow sinuous circuit where these cars were competitive in 1981. Drivers are Alliot and Ferté, who went on to win the race.

MK37 This was a new F3 design, built around an aluminium monocoque which was claimed to be more rigid and was certainly slimmer, in the interests of ground effects. Front suspension was by top rockers and lower wishbones with parallel links at the rear; front coil springs/dampers were inboard while at the rear they were mounted above the gearbox. Alfa engines were generally used. Save for Ferté's repeat win at Monaco, and another at twisting Magny-Cours, the 1982 season was disappointing as the MK37 had handling problems as well as straight-line speed shortcomings.

MK37 looks clean if substantial, but it turned out to be disappointing for the team and works drivers Ferté (driving this car) and Alliot. Work to make the bodywork sleeker brought little reward and it was never competitive in terms of straight line speed.

MK39 There was little improvement in 1983, when Martini representation in the European series was very thin. MK39 was an evolutionary car, with detail modifications, for

MK37-MK39 looked more substantial that their predecessors but were effective only on circuits like Monaco. This is Michel Ferté in the Principality in 1983.

example in the suspension, and Alfa engines were normal. ORECA MK39 driver Michel Ferté received Michelin's favours, which saw him win the Monaco race and narrowly beat Ralt driver Hesnault in the French series.

MK42 Slightly out of sequence, but logically here as it carries the Martini F3 story through to the end of the ground effects era, the MK42 came for 1984 as the last development of the family, and again it was Nova-Alfa-powered. MK42s were prominent in the French series (accounting for the top five places at the end of the season), but in international racing Martini owed everything to the skill and occasional good luck of Ivan Capelli. He won four European Championship races, and the title, and he won at Monaco. Tarres used some MK42 elements in a hybrid run in one 1984 F2 race.

The clean lines of the ground effects F3 Martinis show well in this Monaco pits shot. Bernard Santal crashed out of the race on the first lap, and scored once in the European series before turning to a Ralt and doing rather better.

001 Martini returned to F2 for its last two seasons, with Mader-BMW-engined cars which followed the general lines of their March contemporaries but were not particularly effective on the circuits – on the one hand more power was needed to combat Honda, on the other hand more sophisticated cars were needed to combat the Ralts powered by Honda. Michel Ferté started in three 1983 races and Theys in one. Alliot was the only driver to contest a full season, finishing in four races (of twelve) with two fifth places.

001 showed some promise, bearing out the appearance of a competent car. Vertical stripes on the flanks are a substitute for a cigarette brand name on this car driven by Michel Ferté.

002 Improvements, mainly in aerodynamic aspects, paid off in 1984, when the Martini F2 car was the best of the BMW-powered runners, although Michel Ferté's third place in the Championship was remote from the Ralt-Honda drivers who headed it (his score included two second places and three places). His ORECA team mate Theys was eleventh on the table, and brother Alain had one outing, for a fifth place.

Aerodynamic improvements on 002 show in little tabs and fins at the rear, the engine cover and end plates to the wings. Driver is again Michel Ferté.

MK45 Martini regained its leading position in European F3 in 1985 with this 'flat-bottom' car, a petite machine with orthodox mechanical elements. ORECA's two drivers, Raphanel and Dalmas, headed the French Championship table, while Weidler won the German title. In the more competitive Italian series, Larini made his name with a Coloni MK45, but his team mate Caffi turned away from the Martini he drove early in the season. Dalmas won the Monaco race.

MK45 was a more attractive car than its immediate predecessors, with side pods reminiscent of the MK27s. The driver is Denis Morin, a hard-trying mid-field runner in the French series.

MK49 The main-line F3 Martini for 1986 was little changed in chassis respects as an all-new design was being developed, but the ORECA MK49s had VW engines (other teams stayed with Alfa engines). Dalmas was French champion, and by the grace of Michelin gained Martini's eighth consecutive Monaco victory. His team mate Trollé was third in the French series, but the only other middling achievement was Rensing's sixth place with an MK49 in the German Championship. Desperation led to an MK49 chassis being fitted with MK52 suspension in 1987 – a hybrid which failed to produce results.

MK52 This had Martini's first carbon composite chassis, and it was a failure despite a long gestation period. The sleek car had new pushrod suspension and generally looked the part. The best placings for an MK52 were two fourths achieved by Rensing with a VW-engined car in the German series.

MK55 The 1988 F3 Martini was another car that had attractive characteristics, but failed. Lionel Robert won a single French race with a VW-engined car, while Frank Biela won two in Germany; Robert also looked like being the leading Martini driver in 1989, but in the late Summer he switched from his MK55 to a Dallara. Just before that he put contemporary performances in perspective by taking pole for a Montlhéry race in his Class B MK55, leading for several laps and finishing second.

MK58 This 1989 car did nothing to restore Martini fortunes, for at the end of the season there were fifth and tenth places for VW-engined cars in the French series, and an eighth in the German series, to show for another redesign.

MARWYN

In late 1947 Marwyn became the first outfit to offer 500cc cars for sale (£445, complete) and said it was laying down a batch of thirty cars. Cooper beat it to actual delivery and total Marwyn production did not exceed single figures. The prototype had a ladder frame with an MG beam front axle suspended on semi-elliptic springs, while the rear-mounted Triumph engine delivered its power to a live axle suspended on quarter elliptics. Production models had independent suspension all round but enjoyed no success largely due to the bold innovation of using a floppy chassis and having ridiculously high ground clearance.

In 1949 Marwyn produced a new model with a longer and stiffer chassis, Standard Eight ifs, improved rear axle location, smaller wheels and much lower ground clearance, while by then the Speedway JAP engine had become standard. Gray of Emsworth, who later built the Vanwall bodies, clothed it with a neat shell but it was too late to regain the initiative and few were made.   ML

A stubby little early Marwyn hill-climbing, and with that card front number presumably not attaining startling speed. In this view it was a well-balanced car, its lines complemented by its wire wheels, but it had ridiculously high ground clearance.

MASERATI

The Maseratis that played a prominent role as racing was re-established after the Second World War were four-cylinder cars that had been laid down in 1939 for *vettureta* racing, and this line was followed through after the War, under the control of the Orsi family. They retained the Maserati name (even the trident of Bologna badge). The new company that three of the Maserati brothers set up became Osca (see also Osca). In 1948 a substantially revised four-cylinder Maserati appeared, and became a mainstay of independent teams in the early 1.5-litre Grand Prix years.

Maseratis slowly became less significant until 1954, when the outstanding 250F was introduced. This ran until 1958 with works status, by which time Maserati's own GP effort had been undermined by the follies of sports car racing and problems in the Orsi empire. A 250F derivative carrying the name Tec-Mec was completed, and Maserati engines were used in the Cooper GP cars in the second half of the 1960s, but for more than a quarter of a century Maseratis have been road cars.

4CL The first of the four-cylinder line, schemed by Ernesto Maserati in 1939 on very straightforward lines – channel-section main chassis members, wishbone and torsion bar front suspension and dohc engine (78 x 78mm, 1490cc). The 4CLT cars built just after the war had a tubular chassis. In the immediate post-war races Maserati did not run a team and the principal Maseratis were campaigned by Scuderia Milano, which numbered Nuvolari and Sommer among its drivers.

In May 1946 Tazio Nuvolari leads Milano team mate Sommer over the cobbles and tram tracks of the Prado circuit in the first heat of the Marseilles GP – Nuvolari's first race since 1939. Their 4CLs are nicely-balanced cars, redolent of late-1930s practices.

4CLT In the Orsi era the design was reworked by Alberto Massimino, who used the 4CLT chassis with revised suspension and a twin-supercharged engine, for which 260bhp was claimed. With a lower body, this 'San Remo' Maserati – so named for its first race appearance in the 1948 San Remo GP – looked substantially different.

In 1948 the principal Maserati team was Scuderia Ambrosiana, whose leading drivers were Ascari and Villoresi (once relieved by Nuvolari), while Bira and Parnell were other prominent users. In 1949 Squadra Achille Varzi ran cars for Fangio and Campos, Platé 4CLT/48s for Bira and de Graffenried, and Milano a car for Farina. A slightly modified version designated 4CLT/50 followed, but in 1950 the works Alfa team was back in business and only Ferrari mounted an effective challenge. There were still four-cylinder Maseratis around in abundance, but in 1950-1 their GP role was in filling grids, although they were still useful machines in secondary races.

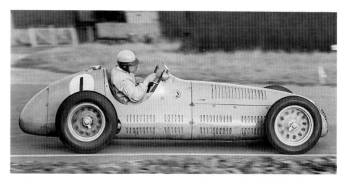

Parnell in an Ambrosiana 4CLT/48 at Goodwood.

The Ruggeri brothers commissioned Mario Speluzzi to modify the 4CLT design for their Scuderia Milano; these cars were known as Maserati-Milano, and soon just as Milano (see also Milano). Two of the Maserati brothers essayed a 4CLT/48 update as an Osca (see also Osca), with little success. Another revision was undertaken by Swiss entrant Enrico Platé for the first F2 championship season. The engine capacity was increased to 1995cc (unsupercharged) and the chassis revised. The Maserati-Platé was a stand-in for 1952, and none of the three converted were successful. De Graffenried finished third in two minor French races, while in the handful of Grands Prix the team contested the best placing was his sixth in the Swiss GP, lapped four times.

Drivers (Championship GPs): 'B. Bira', Felice Bonetto, Louis Chiron, Gianfranco Comotti, Froilan Gonzalez, Emmanuel de Graffenried, David Hampshire, David Murray, Reg Parnell, Enrico Platé, Franco Rol, Harry Schell.

Schell in one of the shortened Maserati-Platé F2 adaptations in the 1952 French GP at Rouen.

A6GCM/A6SSG For 1952 Orsi authorized a new F2 car, before it was known that this would be the world championship category, and Massimino took the A6GCS sports car as a basis. The chassis and rear suspension followed the 4CLT/48, there was a wishbone and coil spring front suspension, while the engine was a straight six (75 x 75mm, 1988cc).

A works team was run spasmodically in 1952, as early outings showed that development was needed. By the Italian GP progress had been made, as Gonzalez was able to challenge the dominant Ferraris.

For 1953 the car was modified, as the A6SSG, with 1997cc engines rated at 190bhp. Fangio and Gonzalez mounted a serious challenge to Ferrari, Fangio eventually defeating the 'other Italian team' in a dramatic Italian GP. Meanwhile, independent entrants also enjoyed some success with these cars.

In 1953 Maserati matched Ferrari on fast circuits such as Reims, Spa and Monza. This is Gonzalez, characteristically crouched in the cockpit in the French GP.

Drivers: Gino Bianco, 'B. Bira', Felice Bonetto, Heitel Cantoni, Johnny Claes, Juan-Manuel Fangio, Jan Flinterman, Oscar Galvez, Emilio Giletti, Froilan Gonzalez, Emmanuel de Graffenried, Chico Landi, Hermann Lang, Sergio Mantovani, Onofré Marimon, Luigi Musso, Nello Pagani, Franco Rol.

250F The specification of this car promised no more than a competent successor to the 2-litre cars of 1952-3. But it was to become the one outstanding Grand Prix Maserati, serving four seasons in the front line and on intermittently through another three, thus covering the span of the 2.5-litre formula. In the hand of top-flight drivers it could challenge the more advanced cars run by much more generously-funded teams. It had considerable development potential, and especially in its later forms was a most handsome car.

Colombo, who had undertaken development of the 2-litre cars, contributed to the design, with Bellentani and Alfieri. The definitive 250F – some A6GCMs were 'converted' with 250F engines as stand-in cars – emerged with a stiff multi-tubular chassis (not a space frame as such), wishbone and coil spring front suspension and a de Dion arrangement at the rear in place of the traditionally weak Maserati rigid axle, and a straight six (84 x 75mm, 1497cc) which gave 240bhp in 1954 and 270bhp in 1957.

Throughout the car's 'production' life – 29 were built – there were numerous changes and variants, quite apart from uprating, including lightweight cars, short-wheelbase 'Piccolo' cars, V-12-engined cars and the Tec-Mec. Along the way the standard bodies became slimmer, a streamlined car was tried in 1955, offset cockpits were introduced. Among independent cars, the 250Fs run by Moss and the Owen Organization had notable modifications, both having disc brakes and Moss' being tried with fuel injection. A works V-12 car also appeared in the 1957 Race of Two Worlds at Monza with a 3.5-litre engine, and the 4.2-litre Maserati Eldorado Special run in that event in 1958 used some 250F components.

Fangio on his way to victory in the 1954 Belgian Grand Prix in one of the original 250Fs. It seems to have as many louvres as the 4CLT/48.

Almost every driver of the 1950s seems to have raced a 250F and the car was a mainstay of independent teams and entrants. A 250F won the first race in which it was run, driven by Fangio in Argentina in 1954, and the great man won his fifth world title when he drove 250Fs in 1957. More than 40 races fell to 250Fs, including eight Championship events (in modern terms that might not sound impressive, but in 1954-7 there were only 28 such races). A 250F ran in the first race of the 2.5-litre formula, and in the last. It was also successful in southern hemisphere *formule libre* racing.

As far as a works team was concerned, the Maserati racing department closed at the end of 1957, but work was still undertaken for private owners and two Piccolo 250Fs were completed, one to be driven by Fangio in his last Grand Prix.

Drivers (F1): Chris Amon, Alberto Ascari, Jean Behra, Carel Godin de Beaufort, 'B. Bira', Jo Bonnier, Jack Brabham, Keith Campbell, Ettore Chimeri, Louis Chiron, Johnny Claes, Peter Collins, Antonio Creus, Colin Davis, Bob Drake, Jack Fairman, Juan-Manuel Fangio, Maria Theresa de Filippis, John Fitch, Bob Gerard, Gerino Gerini, Francesco Godia-Sales, Froilan Gonzalez, Horace Gould, Emmanuel de Graffenried, Masten Gregory, Pablo Gulle, Bruce Halford, Mike Hawthorn, Hans Herrman, Ken Kavanagh, Jean Lucas, Lance Macklin, Umberto Maglioli, Sergio Mantovani, Onofré Marimon, Luigi Musso, Cesare Perdisa, Luigi Piotti, Louis Rosier, Jim Russel, Roy Salvadori, Giorgio Scarlatti, Harry Schell, Carroll Shelby, André Simon, Bob Stilwell, Piero Taruffi, André Testut, Alessandro de Tomaso, Luigi Villoresi, Ottorino Volonterio, Peter Walker, Ken Wharton.

Fangio in his last race, driving one of Buell's Piccolo cars at Reims. It looks smaller, smoother and neater than any preceding 250Fs, which indeed it was.

Apart from its strange nose this Piccolo car is unmistakably a 250F. It had started life as 2504 in 1954, was revised in this form by the El Salvador team to run alongside the two 'genuine' Piccolo cars, and is here being driven by Jensen in New Zealand in 1959. It was later remodified to appear as a normal 250F.

MATHE

Otto Mathe of Innsbruck, one of few Austrian constructors, essayed a Formula Junior car following the 'South German school' in 1959. It had a ladder frame, rear-mounted DKW engine driving through a Porsche gearbox, torsion bar front suspension and a wishbone and transverse leaf arrangement at the rear.

MATRA

Matra – Mécanique-Aviation-Traction – came into existence in 1942, out of the CAPRA aviation industry sub-contraction company that had been founded by Michel Chassagny. After the war it moved into the missile field, then its interests spread through other high-tech activities and almost by accident into sports cars. Chassagny had an interest in his friend René Bonnet's company, and as it was about to collapse in 1964 Matra took it over and by continuing production of the Bonnet Djet as the Matra Djet entered the motor industry.

Jean-Luc Lagardère ran this Matra Sports subsidiary and set up a modest competitions department, under Claude le Guezec, to contest rallies and pick up the single-seater thread from Bonnet's Formula Junior cars. In the Spring of 1965 a pair of F3 cars was built, in time for the Monaco Junior GP. Matra wanted success, and French instincts were subordinated to that end, in that the Renault-based engines used in FJ and F2 Bonnets, and indeed in the first Alpine F3 cars, were not used. The first *monoplace* Matra had Ford-based Cosworth power units.

Jean-Pierre Beltoise's victory in the all-important Reims F3 race on July 4, 1965 ensured that the Matra Sports programme would continue. As far as single-seaters were concerned, it ran until 1972, and relatively few cars were built, but they played a key role in the restoration of French racing fortunes.

An alliance with Ken Tyrrell (and Jackie Stewart) was also critical. In effect, Tyrrell took Matra into F2 in 1966 and into F1 in 1968, although that was the year that Matra entered the Grand Prix arena 'in its own right', with backing from Elf and other suppliers, and from the French Government to the tune of six million francs, which in theory was a loan (and perhaps eight times Tyrrell's budget for his first F1 season).

Matra campaigned cars powered by an in-house V-12, while Tyrrell ran DFV-powered Matras very successfully (Matra never did win a GP with its own V-12 cars while Tyrrell won nine). Then Matra became closely associated with Simca, and that meant that Matras with engines so closely linked to Ford were no longer acceptable for Simca had been swallowed up by Chrysler, and a change in the regulations applying to fuel tanks conveniently ruled out the existing cars after 1969. Tyrrell went his way and Matra persevered in F1 until the end of 1972, but the team's main successes came in sports car racing.

The V-12 was brought out for Grand Prix use again in 1977, when it at last powered a GP-winning car – a Ligier. Two more GPs fell to Ligier-Matras in 1981, but in 1982 the V-12 was clearly outclassed. Matra did not return to single-seater racing and in modern motoring the name is more clearly identified with projects such as the MPV that became the Renault Espace, but the blue cars produced by Matra Sports ('SA Engins Matra' from 1969) had done much to revive French motor racing fortunes and the general French interest in racing in the late 1960s.

MS1 In most respects this was an extremely conventional F3 car, a forerunner which the Matra engineers used to feel their way quickly into the category. To that end its suspension followed 'British' lines, and the track and wheelbase dimensions were the mean of the F3 cars shown at the London Racing Car Show early in 1965. The Cosworth engine drove through a Hewland gearbox.

There was one great departure, in the monocoque. The side pontoons were built to such a high standard that bag fuel tanks were not needed and each could therefore be braced by lateral bulkheads, which made for great stiffness. Aerospace workmanship saw to it that they did not leak, and slightly later cars on these lines were to serve through three seasons without fuel tank leaks.

MS5 This was the definitive F3 car, which made its race debut at Monaco in 1965. Five were built that year, others followed and some remained in use until 1969, when they were ruled out. Beltoise and Jaussaud secured the 1965 French championship for Matra, but the cars did not become commonplace. In 1966 there were nine wins in major F3 races, above all Beltoise' at Monaco, but none outside France, which in Matra eyes had absolute priority. In 1967 Matra dominated the Argentine F3 Temporada, Beltoise winning four races, while in Europe Pescarolo won at Monaco and Jabouille at Reims. The powerful works team was withdrawn at the end of the 1967 season. Hitherto only a very few MS5s had been run by independents: Fenning had won at Reims in 1966 in a Tyrrell car while Ecurie Crio ran MS5s in 1967. That year's works cars were sold to French entrants for 1968, when they made little impact. Meanwhile, at a BP dinner after the 1965 Trophées de France F2 series, Lagardère agreed to lend Tyrrell a car for tests with a BRM F2 engine, and that led to a two-car F2 team for 1966 – Matra International.

MS5 was a solid, chunky car. Appropriately, in view of the chauvinistic overtones, Beltoise' car in the 1966 European F3 race at Brands Hatch late in 1966 has 'France' plastered on its nose.

MS6 The F2 Matras raced in 1966 were usually entered, and generally known, as MS5s – modification was simple, as even the engine capacity for F2 and F3 was the same – but authoritative French sources designate the F2 cars MS6. The rigid chassis was well-sorted and there was a lot of talent in the works and the Tyrrell and Coombs teams that ran the cars. Most started the year with BRM engines but most switched to Cosworth engines. The problem was Brabham, running Honda engines and unbeatable until the last F2 race of the year. However, to make up the numbers for the German GP an F2 category was included and the first three of its four finishers were Beltoise, Hahne and Schlesser, all Matra-mounted.

Sole victory in Matra's first year in F2 fell to Jean-Pierre Beltoise with this Cosworth-powered car at the Nürburgring.

MS7 The first Matra theme was carried through to this car, the last the company built for a secondary category. Effective riveting still distinguished the four-bulkhead monocoque; the side members carried 120 litres of fuel for the 1.6-litre engines of the new F2 (the FVA was favoured, driving through a Hewland gearbox). Few changes were made through to the end of the MS7's active life – the air scoop that had been so prominent ahead of the cockpit surround was dropped, and for a while the cars were loaded with high aerofoils. Jacky Ickx won the European title with Tyrrell cars in 1967, Beltoise won it with works cars in 1968, Servoz-Gavin with Matra International cars in 1969.

A Matra Sports MS7 with a full complement of well-braced aerofoils, driven by Beltoise in 1969. Appendages such as exhausts, wider wheels and beefier suspension make it look more substantial than its predecessors. For hot-weather races a larger nose intake was substituted. The inboard front/outboard rear suspension arrangement shows clearly in this shot.

MS9 This was a test bed, but it was raced once. It comprised a modified MS7 chassis and sports-racing car suspension components, and was originally intended for development work with Matra's V-12 (which had been announced early in 1967). Ken Tyrrell, however, arranged to marry Matra chassis and his DFV engines, so MS9 was modified for a DFV, which served its stressed member role despite the retention of a light sub frame linking monocoque and rear suspension. Stewart qualified it for the front row of the 1968 South African GP grid, and it ran well in the race before the engine failed (at least that spared the team the problem of a refuelling stop).

Driver: Jackie Stewart.

MS10 This was built expressly for Tyrrell, Stewart and the DFV, and this combination means that Matra is a successful marque in Grand Prix history. Designer Bernard Boyer followed established Matra practices in the monocoque, retaining the frame linking monocoque and rear suspension,

MS10/02 looking remarkably naked as Stewart drives towards Matra's first GP victory, on a rain-soaked Zandvoort track in June 1968. Some of the early excess weight had been 'lost' in this car. The deep channel offset from the centre of the Dunlop rain tyres is obvious. The nose carries small trim tabs, and three GPs later – when Stewart again won on a wet circuit – the car was raced with a modest rear aerofoil.

and using the side pontoons as compartmentalized fuel tanks (with a 190-litre capacity). The suspension followed proven lines, with broad-based front wishbones at the front, top links, lower wishbones and twin radius arms at the rear, and the inboard front/outboard rear spring/damper arrangements. After the car's first outings the sports-car-derived components were hastily replaced. Transmission was through Hewland DG300 or FG400 gearboxes.

The race debut came in the Race of Champions at Brands Hatch, and Beltoise drove the car in its first GP, in Spain. The MS10's third GP, in Holland, saw Stewart score Matra's first World Championship victory. The Scot was to win two more GPs with MS10s in 1968 (the German and US races) and the South African GP in 1969 before the car was superseded. Only two MS10s were built, so the return on investment was high.

Drivers: Jean-Pierre Beltoise, 'Johnny' Servoz-Gavin, Jackie Stewart.

MS11 The all-French 'Matra-Matra' had a V-12 designed by a team headed by Georges Martin. It was a 60-degree unit (79.7 x 50mm) initially rated at 390bhp – disappointingly less than the simpler Cosworth V-8. Installed in a car it looked most untidy beside a DFV. Its six exhaust pipes gave forth abundant noise – questionably music or an appalling shriek – and it overheated, seriously. As it was not designed to perform a stressed role, box-section members were run back from the rear of the monocoque to support it, thus adding to the weight of the car, which was to increase again later in 1968 when larger fuel tanks were added. Otherwise, the MS11 followed the same general lines as the MS10.

Its racing debut came at Monaco in 1968 and the high point when Beltoise finished second in Germany. Beyond that an MS11 was used for tests with an hydraulic four wheel drive system and later with a new V-12 for the 1970 season (Matra's representation in GPs was left to Tyrrell in 1969).

Drivers: Jean-Pierre Beltoise, Henri Pescarolo.

Beltoise inadvertently shows off the untidy rear end of the MS11 at Zandvoort in 1968.

MS80 The most successful F1 Matra served for less than a full season, and only two were built in a deliberate economy programme. The MS80 gained the Constructors' Championship for Matra International (Tyrrell), or for Matra-Ford or for France depending on the point of view of the reporter, while Stewart won five Championship GPs and the drivers' title. His wins came in the Spanish, Dutch, French, British and Italian races.

Boyer followed the rigid structural lines of earlier Matras, but outwardly the extended flanks gave 'Coke bottle' lines (tanks in these brought fuel capacity up to 210 litres, centred around the cg, as the subsidiary tank behind the driver in the MS10 had not been a satisfactory arrangement). Suspension was outboard all round, and geometry was revised to suit

smaller (13in) wheels and new generation Dunlops. Rear brakes, however, were inboard. The car ran with a 'biplane' aerofoil arrangement before such extravagances were banned, was aesthetically most attractive with an engine cover merging into a low rear aerofoil and was cleverly run in the Italian GP in 'low-drag' form with no aerofoils.

At the end of the season the cars were retired; Matra lost its way; Tyrrell had seen the way to go.

Drivers: Jean-Pierre Beltoise, Jackie Stewart.

MS80 in its most attractive form, with the aerodynamic fences on its nose that were a characteristic and the wider rear wheels that came in mid-season. This is Stewart driving in the '69 German GP.

MS84 Matra built a one-off four wheel drive car, partly at the behest of Matra International, and it was at least more successful than the others essayed in 1969. It had a space frame, with the DFV and gearbox in effect turned through 180 degrees, and a Ferguson four wheel drive system (the project engineer was Derek Gardner). Torque split was variable, initially 25:75 front:rear, but by the end of the season MS84 was being run as a rear wheel drive car. There was a substantial weight penalty (595kg compared with the 535kg of an MS80) as well as extra complication. Servoz-Gavin drove the MS84 to sixth place in the Canadian GP, to score a point in his first outing in the car.

Drivers: Jean-Pierre Beltoise, 'Johnny' Servoz-Gavin.

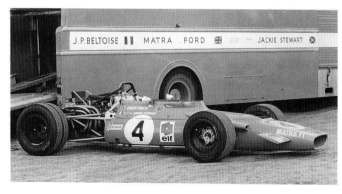

Outwardly, MS84 resembled other Matra-Fords, but from this angle the exhausts arrangement shows that it was radically different. Although the car is on wet tyres in this photograph, the opportunity to prove the superiority of four wheel drive on a wet circuit did not come. While other Matras have been preserved, this one-off was broken up.

MS120 The Matra works team was on its own in 1970, in large part because of a commercial liaison with Simca – unlike Ford, the Chrysler company was prepared to market Matra's road-going sports car – and also because of factors such as Lagardère's pride. Much was to be made of the 'all-French' nature of the new car, which overlooked contributions by Hewland, Lucas, Goodyear and others.

Georges Martin reworked the V-12, stiffening the crankcase so that it could act as a stressed member and revising the cylinder heads. Power output more or less kept pace with the DFV, while consumption was at least better than the old V-12 and reliability was good, perhaps reflecting sports car successes.

Boyer's new car was angular, naturally had bag tanks, and as a consequence was less stiff than its predecessors. The sloping flat surfaces contributed some downforce, while a wide-chord aerofoil normally sat above the rear axle line (it was sometimes left off). Suspension was similar to the MS80.

Beltoise placed an MS120 in the points five times in 1970, his best finishes being third in Belgium and Italy, while Pescarolo was third at Monaco. Matra was sixth in the Constructors' Championship, and that turned out to be the zenith for the Velizy team.

However, there was confidence in the MS120B, based on Amon's victory in a non-Championship Argentine race, with one of the original MS120s. The 1971 car had a stiffer monocoque, less angular lines and a full-width nose. Amon scored points in three races, with a third placing (in Spain) once again the best showing. Beltoise failed to score at all.

Two of the MS120Bs were rebuilt as MS120Cs for the one-driver team in 1972. The lines were rounder, there were detail improvements, and a little more horespower was found. Yet Amon sometimes preferred the surviving MS120B until the one and only MS120D was ready in mid-season. It was a little lighter, with smoother lines. First time out in it he led the French GP, before a pit stop with a puncture cost him the lead. He stormed back to finish third, again the best placing of Matra's F1 season. It was also its last. Matra found success and publicity in sports car racing, and years later the V-12 did power Grand Prix-winning Ligiers. MS120D was apparently modified for tests with a development V-12 in 1974, but nothing came of this. The Matra *monoplace* line ended in 1972.

Drivers: Chris Amon, Jean-Pierre Beltoise, Henri Pescarolo.

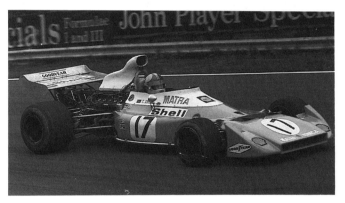

Last of the line, the Matra MS120D in 1972.

MAURER

Businessman Willy Maurer came in to F2 as a constructor in 1979, with a low-key effort to test the water. A sound team in 1980 ran into an accident streak, but with a cohesive programme in 1981 Maurer became a front-running team. For that year Gustav Brunner designed the best-engineered and best-looking car of the season and the team gave up its own engine preparation and turned to proven Mader power units. The manufacturing base had already been moved to the one-time Chevron factory at Bolton, where it was run by Paul Owens (another ex-Chevron man, Dave Wilson, had played an important role in pulling the team together in 1980).

In 1981 Maurer led F2 races, and won at Vallelunga, but there was a season-long controversy about the car's adjustable

skirts. The MM82s won, too, in spite of more skirt problems and some lack of harmony in the team – the patron tended to be autocratic. Moreover, a problem seemed to be that the wins were unexpected and Maurer did not have the strength of character within the team to build upon them. Maurer slipped in 1983, and then the team did not come out at all in 1984, as Herr Maurer became disillusioned – his drivers, he reckoned, had not adhered to their letters of contract or acknowledged their spirit. The F1 programme he apparently wanted badly never came to pass, although work on a Brunner-designed DFV-powered car was initiated late in 1981. Thus the black-liveried Mampe cars that had briefly promised so much disappeared from the European circuits.

MM1 Conventional construction, but with unusually wide track, and distinctive looks characterized this car which failed to make any impression at all in the 1979 F2 Championship. The driver, Armin Hahne, was inexperienced, while the team was plunged into an environment where March, Chevron and Ralt had lots of know-how. The closure of Chevron was a stroke of luck for this German would-be constructor.

Compact MM1 stood out in the 1979 F2 crowd, from its needle nose to individual rear wing treatment. Driver is Hahne.

MM80 Brunner looked first and foremost to a stiffer monocoque for this car, under 1979 bodywork, until a sleeker body with a conventional nose aerofoil and single-pillar rear wing came in the Spring. The wide track was also retained initially, until its shortcomings on fast circuits were recognized. The team's BMW M12 engines were prepared in-house, under Franz Pucher.

Howden Ganley was briefly a consultant, before the ex-Chevron people were taken on. There were trivial mechanical failures that could be attributed to a team's bedding-in period, and there were more serious setbacks, when Markus Hottinger was killed in a Hockenheim accident and number one driver Eje Elgh broke an arm in a test accident (in the F2 Tiga). Replacement driver (for two events) Gaillard came close to victory at Pau and Gabbiani came close at Enna but both retired late in those races. However the Italian became

The MM80 looked more purposeful than the first Maurer, had less colour to relieve the black by which the cars became known. Beppe Gabbiani is the driver.

the first driver to score a Championship point in a Maurer, at Enna. Henzler was also drafted into the team, to be placed eighth at Mugello. The first race victory for a Maurer was scored by Tony Martin in a Mazda-engined MM80 in a South African Formula Atlantic race early in 1981.

MM81 Outwardly this was a compact and slim car. It had a honeycomb monocoque and titanium was used extensively where less exotic metals served on other cars. Rivals reckoned they were run with sliding skirts, but formal protests only produced the findings that nothing in the design actually led to rules being broken. There were still handling problems, leading to a redesign of the side pods in mid season.

The team cars were well prepared and with the switch to Mader engines they were competitive. Guerrero won the Championship race at Thruxton and Elgh won at Vallelunga, but the pair were only seventh and third respectively in the Championship.

The MM81 was an effective racing package, which did not quite live up to expectations. Roberto Guerrero scored the marque's first F2 Championship race victory in the Spring 1981 event at Thruxton.

MM82 This car maintained Maurer's reputation for high-quality engineering and aesthetics, but in the eyes of many it was flawed by another ground effects controversy. Some carbon fibre was used with honeycomb in this monocoque, track was narrower front and rear, suspension geometry was revised to suit Michelins, spring/damper units were inboard and there was a new gearbox. There was also an ingenious dual-spring arrangement to keep the skirts in contact with the track surface whenever the car was moving (but they could be locked 'up' by a driver). It was apparently not illegal but 'not in the spirit', and some felt it generated too much downforce for the power of F2 engines. In that department Maurer surprised rivals – and caused some dissent in Maurer ranks –by using some short-stroke (and reputedly short-life) Heidegger BMW engines in the car driven by Germany's *comingman* Stefan Bellof.

The MM82 was another clean-lined car, with no afterthoughts or extemporized bulges breaking its lines and even the normally untidy Maurer exhaust arrangements packed away. This car is driven by 'occasional' driver Alain Ferté.

He won the first two races of the 1982 season (his own first two F2 races) but finished only fourth in the Championship, one place and seven points ahead of team mate Gabbiani. In a complicated arrangement a third team car was run from Germany for Peter Schindler, who turned out not to be a *comingman*. There were some customer cars around which were not fitted with the trick skirt arrangements, and Jelinski scored in a Schafer Racing Maurer.

MM83 The lines were similar and the design by Paul Brown was close to MM82 but with a carbon fibre monocoque and pullrod rising rate suspension. There were no squabbles about skirts, as FISA had settled that issue. The team started the year with Heidegger engines, reverting to Mader units in the summer. (Maurer claimed poor performance, Heidegger claimed poor payment record and enforced repossession.) The team was separated from the factory and run from Germany, to little good end. Before the end of the season Paul Owens gave up his two-car, then one-car effort. Bellof did take the flag at Pau, only to be disqualified as the car was underweight, and he was ninth in the Championship. Joint tenth on the final points table was Acheson, who drove an Owens-run car until the summer. The only other driver to score was Alain Ferté, and he left in the summer after a legal run-in with Maurer.

Last of a line of pretty little cars, although unreliability and disagreements with organizers and suppliers meant that the talents of Stefan Bellof (driving here) were poorly rewarded.

MBM

Peter Monteverdi was a sports car driver who built his first special in 1951 and later in the decade initiated the Bamosa (Bale-Monteverdi-Sauter) single-seater project. Sauter went

The MBM Junior had a deep body, substantial front suspension members and wheels from the same Porsche source and prominent coil spring/damper units at the rear. The finicky DKW two-stroke was the normal power unit, hence the car's best performances were in hill climbs rather than longer events on circuits.

on his own way, to build a Formula Junior car, while Monteverdi picked up his design as a Junior, working with DKW tuner Mantzel, hence MBM (Monteverdi-Bale-Mantzel). Their rear-engined FJ MBM used Porsche front suspension and other components, had independent rear suspension, and was normally powered by 1-litre/85bhp or 1.1-litre/95bhp DKW-based two-strokes, although a Ford alternative was to be listed. The car was built in small numbers through to 1962, and a few were sold to the USA as 'Machans'.

The multi-tubular chassis was the basis for an F1 car, which had a flat four Porsche engine and wide-base wishbone front suspension. It appeared in 1961, when Monteverdi completed two racing laps in the non-Championship Solitude GP, then crashed heavily at Hockenheim. The remains of this car are buried under the concrete floor of Monteverdi's museum but a sister car which was never raced is exhibited there.

In the mid-1960s Monteverdi turned to the more familiar road-going GT cars that bear his name. In 1990 he returned to Formula 1 when he took over Onyx, the team being renamed Monteverdi-Onyx.

MBMG

In 1952, H.H.G. Monk unveiled his F3 challenger, which was the nearest that a British 500 constructor came to the Italian approach. It was a largish, front engined, rear drive, car based on a P type MG with the engine reduced to 496cc by using a short throw crank, which had four Amal carburetters and four exhaust pipes and drove through a Norton gearbox. It did not take F3 by storm but was an interesting, if spasmodic, addition to grids for some years.   ML

McCANDLESS

Rex McCandless was an innovator, best known for his racing Norton designs (notably the 'Featherbed'), who should also be recalled for his work on four-wheel drive and four-wheel steering, and his use of engines as stressed members, all back in the 1950s. In the middle of that decade he built a pair of F3 cars, far removed from the Cooper pattern. These McCandless Specials had front-mounted Norton engines (usually part exposed, sometimes cowled) and the features they were built to demonstrate: four-wheel drive and transmission braking. The driver sat low alongside the backbone of the frame.

In 1954-5 the cars were normally raced by McCandless and Laurie McGladery, sometimes by technician Freddie Smith. They ventured out of Ireland only rarely, but in the then-flourishing local racing scene, at circuits such as Kirkistown, they were competitive in F3 and FL events. Then in 1956 McCandless turned to a sports car, which was a short-lived project, although one survives in the Belfast Transport Museum.

McGUIRE

Australian driver Brian McGuire ran the Williams FW04 in British national races in 1976, and updated it for 1977 as the McGuire BM1. It was entered for only one GP, the British, when McGuire was hopelessly off the pace in practice and failed to qualify. He set his GP aspirations aside, returned to the British series, and was killed in a practice crash in the BM1 at Brands Hatch later in 1977.

McLAREN

Bruce McLaren was a successful Grand Prix driver with the Cooper team, setting up Bruce McLaren Motor Racing in 1963 to run a team of Coopers in the Tasman series, then moving towards becoming a constructor with the Zerex Special sports-racing car. The first McLaren as such, the M1A sports-racing car, appeared in 1964 and was adopted as a production car by Trojan. The M1B came in 1965 and a the end of that season Bruce McLaren broke with Cooper, to take his embryo company into the single-seater field.

The M2A single-seater test car had been built in 1965 and the first McLaren single-seater to race, the M2B, was completed late that year, for the 1966 F1 season. It was not successful, largely because of the engines used. The BRM-powered cars that followed showed promise, then came Robin Herd's last McLaren design, the Cosworth-powered M7. Bruce drove an M7A to join the select band of driver-constructors who have won in one of their own cars, in Belgium in 1968. With these handsome orange cars, McLaren was established as a front-running team in the Grands Prix as well as in sports-car racing.

Bruce McLaren's death while he was testing a sports-racing car at Goodwood in 1970 was an enormous blow to the sport in general. His wife and his associates kept the company and its racing teams in the forefront through to the second half of the 1970s.

The sports-racing car team was to be discontinued at the end of 1972, but in top-flight single-seater racing the first half of the 1970s was a golden period for McLaren. The M16 started on an enormously successful run in US track racing, and in 1973 the M23, a Grand Prix classic, came from the same design approach. This was to bring the Constructors' Championship to McLaren for the first time, in 1974, and Emerson Fittipaldi and James Hunt were to win World Championships with it. The M23 was also the first McLaren to wear the red and white Marlboro colours, which were still carried by McLaren F1 cars in the 1990s in one of the longest of all sponsorship associations.

Fortunes declined later in the 1970s, especially in the opening seasons of the ground effects era. The company was to all intents and purposes taken over by Ron Dennis' Project Four team in 1980 – a merger was proclaimed, but at best it was a shotgun marriage, with a Philip Morris finger on the trigger. It was reformed as McLaren International, but the initial arrangement whereby Bruce McLaren's one-time partner and a major shareholder in Team McLaren, Teddy Mayer, continued as joint managing director lasted for no more than the agreed two years. Under Dennis, the company became Marlboro-McLaren and then Honda-Marlboro-McLaren, while car designations were to change to reflect the incorporation of Project Four.

John Barnard became technical director and his innovative MP4s were to gain an outstanding record. But that had to be set against the new standards set by Ron Dennis. He correctly saw how F1 would evolve in the 1980s, and set out to keep McLaren in the forefront. The first McLaren base had been a glorified hut at Feltham, and a move to nearby Colnbrook came in 1965; McLaren International's first base was at Woking, immaculately clean but in adapted buildings which became cramped, so in 1988 a short move was made to a new and most impressive purpose-built factory. There the research and development activities Dennis regarded as essential could really be deployed, and departments from engineering to marketing could operate efficiently (and efficiency might be one Dennis watchword).

Success was imperative, and in that light the bold move in commissioning a turbocharged engine from Porsche and obtaining financial backing for it from Techniques d'Avant Garde (TAG) seems less than breath-taking. It succeeded, as did the partnership with Honda that came for 1988. The whole enterprise was effective beyond outside expectation.

M2 The first McLaren single-seater, M2A, was built as a Firestone test vehicle designed by Robin Herd and built around a Mallite composite material monocoque (Mallite was a sandwich, of aluminium/wood/aluminium) with inboard suspension. Its engine was a 4.5-litre Traco-Oldsmobile V-8. Apart from its value to the tyre company it was used to prove the monocoque construction and systems.

M2B was an F1 car, with the light, strong and rigid Mallite monocoque and orthodox suspension, with coil springs/ dampers inboard at the front. For a power unit McLaren looked to the Ford twin-ohc Indianapolis V-8 which was tried in two 3-litre forms and eventually used as a 95.66 × 52.07mm (2995cc) unit. It was big and heavy, and gave some 300bhp with a narrow effective revs band. McLaren turned to a Serenissima V-8 – the Italian company had F1 ambitions, and in 1969 there were to be rumours of a Serenissima F1 car. This engine was less powerful but more compact, and Bruce McLaren scored a point with it in an M2B in the British GP. Late in the year he reverted to the Ford V-8 and with it placed an M2B fifth in the US GP. Two cars of a projected trio were completed but a second team entry, for Amon, never appeared in a race.

Driver: Bruce McLaren.

The size of the Ford engine in M2B is only too obvious in this shot of McLaren at Monaco in 1966. The car looked much neater with the Serenissima unit, apart from its exhausts twisting between suspension members (the Ford exhausts were in the vee).

M4 The M4A was a simple design by Herd, which came first for F2 in 1967, to be followed by the F3 version intended for production by Trojan for Formula B as well as F3.

It had a constant diameter bathtub aluminium monocoque with fuel tanks in the sides plus a seat tank and conventional suspension (wishbones located by long radius arms front and rear, with outboard springs) using some parts such as uprights from sports-racing McLarens. The F2 power unit was the Cosworth FVA, driving through a Hewland FT200 gearbox.

In F2 it was not outstanding, Bruce McLaren racing one eight times in 1967 (best placing second at Rouen) while Courage drove the quasi-works Coombs car (best placing second at Zandvoort). In 1968 the Chequered Flag team ran the cars, and once again a second place (by Widdows at Pau) was the high point, before the team faded. The Flag also ran the 'official' F3 team in 1968, but this car was disappointing, winning just one important race (Mike Walker at Oulton Park).

Meanwhile the M4B had been contrived as a one-off F1 stand-in for 1967. This was a conversion of an M4A, powered by a BRM 2.1-litre V-12, with additional fuel tanks prominent

on each flank. McLaren drove it in five races, to a best finish at Monaco where he was fourth. It was damaged when he crashed in the Dutch GP, and was later destroyed.

Driver (M4B): Bruce McLaren.

An M4A of The Chequered Flag team in 1968, looking every inch a typical F3 car of the period. However, the design had already served as the basis of a Grand Prix car.

The M4B which showed so well at Monaco in 1967. It has bulged sides and a bunch of exhausts emerging low at the rear, otherwise it looks the same neat little car. For this event it also had the short 'Monaco nose'.

M5A Another F1 one-off, but purpose-built for a BRM V-12 in full 3-litre capacity. The chassis followed M4 lines but the main fuel tanks were within the side pontoons so there were no extemporary bulges (additional fuel was carried above and below the driver's legs and the extensions from the monocoque that supported the V-12). Suspension followed existing lines. This car was competitive – McLaren challenged for the lead in the Canadian and Italian GPs with it in 1967, but it was placed in the points only once, when Hulme was fifth in the 1968 South African GP. After that it was sold to Jo Bonnier who raced it late in 1968, and was sixth in the Italian GP.

Drivers: Jo Bonnier, Denny Hulme, Bruce McLaren.

Bonnier in M5A during practice at Monaco in 1968, followed by McLaren in an M7A.

M7A-D This was the first noteworthy single-seater McLaren, basically laid out by Robin Herd with the design completed by McLaren and Herd's successor-to-be Gordon Coppuck. An open-topped (bathtub) monocoque of riveted and bonded aluminium was used, with suspension comprising lower wishbones and top links at the front and double wishbones with radius arms at the rear (coil springs/dampers outboard all round), and DFV engine with Hewland DG300 gearbox. It was a winner first time out, in the two British non-Championship races in the Spring of 1968, and then at Spa Bruce McLaren won the Belgian GP in one of his orange cars. Late that year Hulme won in Italy and Canada. The cars were modified in detail, for example with two types of little 'external' fuel tanks and of course with 'wings', initially odd little things mounted above the DFV and braced to the roll bar. They served on through 1969, with a second the best placing in a GP, and appeared in 1970. In 1968 McLaren was second in the Constructors' Championship, but in 1969 and 1970 was fourth. One M7A was converted for F5000 after that year.

One came out as 'M7B' in 1969, with broad sponsons containing fuel tanks faired into the body. Initially it was used by the works team, then entered by Colin Crabbe for Elford until written off in a German GP accident.

M7C was another one-off, which was built around the full monocoque hull of the M10 F5000 car, with M7A suspension. It was Bruce McLaren's usual race car in 1969 (he scored a second and two thirds with it), then it was sold to Team Surtees and later passed to Ecurie Bonnier. In 1970 an M7D appeared and was around for half a season, although it ran in only one GP. It was a new car, with an Alfa Romeo V-8, used by de Adamich until an Alfa-engined M14 was ready.

Drivers: Andrea de Adamich, Jo Bonnier, Vic Elford, Peter Gethin, Dan Gurney, Denny Hulme, Bruce McLaren, Basil van Rooyen, John Surtees, Reine Wisell.

Like so many cars of the period, M7s looked incomplete without engine covers – otherwise M7A was an attractive car. This is Bruce McLaren, on his way to a debut victory, in the 1968 Race of Champions.

Hulme on his way to a victory, in Canada late in the same year. His car has the extra fuel tank alongside the cockpit (not outrigged as it had been earlier) and a small wing.

M7C probably rated a new designation, but was numbered in the M7 sequence. This is Bruce McLaren, testing it with a full set of aerofoils at Silverstone.

M9A A four-wheel drive car, designed by Jo Marquart and, in common with other 1969 cars, built before it was realized that 4-wd was not the way forward in F1. The DFV was 'reversed' in the monocoque chassis and the McLaren-devised transmission followed Ferguson lines. Equal-size small wheels were used front and rear. It started in only one race, falling out of the British GP with rear suspension failure.

Driver: Derek Bell

Derek Bell waiting in the cockpit of M9A in the Silverstone pits lane during practice for the 1969 British Grand Prix. A feature of the car was the broad aerofoils at the rear.

M14A/D Essentially this was a derivative of the M7C, with modifications to the monocoque to improve fuel tankage, suspension and in other details. It was a moderately successful car in 1970 (when McLaren tied with Brabham for fourth place in the Constructors' Championship) and was used on into 1971; the first of these seasons was particularly difficult, for Bruce McLaren was killed and Hulme was handicapped while his hands, burned in an Indianapolis accident, healed.

M14D picked up the Alfa Romeo engine theme, one car being completed early in the summer of 1970; its best placing was eighth in the Italian GP (when Galli failed to qualify the M7D, otherwise there would have been two Alfa-engined cars on a GP grid at Monza).

Drivers: Andrea de Adamich, Peter Gethin, Dan Gurney, Denny Hulme, Bruce McLaren.

Obviously a derivative of the M7s, M14A was another no-nonsense McLaren.

M19A/C This was a new design, by Ralph Bellamy as Coppuck was committed to the Indianapolis cars (and Marquart left to join Huron). It had an aluminium monocoque with fibreglass bodywork, and novelty was concentrated in the suspension, which was a problem area. Rising-rate suspension was devised, with inboard coil springs/dampers, and it seems that this was not compatible with the car's aerodynamics, or changes in tyres. Outwardly the M19A had pronounced 'coke-bottle' lines – it was low, with sides swelling out below the cockpit surround – with neat aerofoils and later an airbox which sat oddly above an otherwise exposed DFV. The best race result in 1971 was Donohue's third in the Canadian GP, in his first race with the car Penske had acquired as he looked to Formula 1.

M19As were run early in 1972 with conventional rear suspension. That year the M19C, a slightly refined version, appeared and was to be used into 1973, until it was ruled out by deformable structure regulations. In 1972 the traditional McLaren orange gave way to Yardley colours. The year started well, as Hulme was second in the opening race in Argentina and then won the South African GP in an M19A; later there was a second and third in Austria. McLaren was third in the 1973 Championship.

Drivers: Mark Donohue, Peter Gethin, David Hobbs, Denny Hulme, Jackie Oliver, Brian Redman, Peter Revson, Jody Scheckter.

M19A in 1972, outwardly with revised aerofoils and airbox, and of course Yardley livery. This is Hulme, on his way to victory in the South African GP.

M21 This F2 car designed by Bellamy turned out to be a one-off, as production plans were shelved. It was a monocoque car, with lower wishbones in the suspension at both ends, with a single top link and (rearward) radius rod at the front, transverse link and twin radius rods at the rear. The Broadspeed BDA was one power unit, but it came to be known as a Cosworth BDA-engined car. The Impact quasi-works team ran Jody Scheckter in the M21, through a difficult season, as despite the early efforts by Hulme and Gethin it was never fully sorted out. Scheckter won one race with it, at Crystal Palace.

M21 looked a neat, small car, with a low monocoque and large cockpit surround. In this Brands Hatch shot it appears dwarfed by its rear aerofoil, but the camera distorts.

M23 This was one of the outstanding Grand Prix cars of the 1970s. It was Coppuck's first full F1 design, with lines deriving from his very successful M16 Indianapolis cars and some elements, notably the suspension, carried over from the final M19C layout. It had a narrow monocoque conforming to the deformable structure requirements and the integral side pods which housed radiators also contributed to safety in this respect, as well as lateral stiffness. The DFV drove through a Hewland FG400. The M23 was functional, well-mannered as far as the drivers were concerned, with no problem areas when it came to setting it up for circuits or conditions. It was to serve for more than four seasons, and win 16 Championship races.

The debut race for the M23 was in South Africa, where Hulme started from pole and finished fifth.

The M23/8 driven by Hunt in the controversial 1976 British GP is little changed, save in aspects like the engine cover and air intakes, for high air boxes had been ruled out that year.

In 1973 the 'Yardley Macs' won three GPs (Hulme winning in Sweden, Revson in Britain and Canada); Marlboro colours came in the following year and have been carried by McLaren GP cars ever since (in 1974 a single Yardley-backed car was run in parallel with the works cars for Hailwood). Hulme won in Argentina in 1974, at the start of his last single-seater season, while Emerson Fittipaldi won three GPs and the Drivers' Championship, and he was runner-up in 1975 with two GP victories. In the extraordinary 1976 season, Hunt drove M23s to narrowly take the title from Lauda, with GP victories in Spain, France, Germany, Holland, Canada and the USA. In the seasons when the team ran M23s, 1973-7, McLaren was third, first, third, second and third in the Constructors' Championship (some of the 1973 and 1977 points were scored by M19Cs and M26s). The cars served on in second-level racing.

Drivers: Dave Charlton, Emerson Fittipaldi, Bruno Giacomelli, Mike Hailwood, David Hobbs, Denny Hulme, James Hunt, Jacky Ickx, Brett Lunger, Nelson Piquet, Peter Revson, Jody Scheckter, Gilles Villeneuve, Emilio de Villota.

M26 This Coppuck design was the replacement for the ageing M23s, following the proven lines of that car but lower and lighter, 'cleaner through the air', with honeycomb monocoque construction and M23 suspension. The first was completed in the summer of 1976 but it did not supplant the M23 until the 1977 season was well under way. During that long gestation period, the radiator positioning problems posed by the low monocoque were solved by moving the oil radiator to the nose. It was another forgiving car, but it had a relatively short competitive life as Lotus introduced ground effects and made it obsolescent. James Hunt won three 1977 GPs with M26s (at Silverstone, Watkins Glen and Fuji). In 1978 the team's best placing with an M26 was Hunt's third in the French GP, and McLaren slipped from third in the 1977 Championship to eighth in 1978.

Drivers: Bruno Giacomelli, James Hunt, Brett Lunger, Jochen Mass, Patrick Tambay.

There was little frontal area gain with the M26, although it looked less bulky than M23. Usually M26s were seen in familiar red and white colours, but this one (M26/6) was run by the BS Fabrications team for Brett Lunger in L & M livery in 1978.

M28 This ground effects car followed the Lotus example, and was deliberately as large as the regulations permitted, in a search for maximum under-car airflow. To the same end its suspension was inboard all round. A honeycomb monocoque formed the basis, with very broad side pods which contained radiators and a fuel cell (there was a third cell behind the cockpit). The M28 was insufficiently rigid, lived up to its bulky appearance with a low top speed, and gained a reputation for poor grip. The design was revised here and there, and the cars

rebuilt, but the real solution was a successor (this was ready by mid-1979). Best placing was Watson's fourth at Monaco, with a car designated M28C.

Drivers: Patrick Tambay, John Watson.

The colour scheme on the cockpit surround tends to disguise the fact that M28 had very large side pods and the radiator air top exit below the mirror.

M29 This replacement for M28 came commendably quickly once shortcomings in M28 were accepted. It had a sheet metal monocoque in place of the honeycomb construction, a single central fuel cell, shorter wheelbase and narrower track, and later in the year revised suspension, under-car aerodynamics and outboard rear brakes. Once again the best placing in 1979 was fourth, scored by Watson at Silverstone in the M29's debut race.

The car was revised for 1980, as the M29C, with the late-1979 alterations and some loss of weight. Development continued up to the point when M30 came in mid season. In 1979 Watson was fourth with M29s at Long Beach and Montreal. Two of the cars were used early in 1981.

Drivers: Andrea de Cesaris, Alain Prost, Patrick Tambay, John Watson.

M29 was a more compact car than M28, again with its cockpit well forward in the wheelbase. The driver is John Watson, testing at Silverstone.

M30 This was the last of Gordon Coppuck's designs for McLaren, and indeed the last of the old company's cars. Compared with the M29 it was stiffer, with brakes outboard all round, and had improved aerodynamics. It turned out to be a one-off, and a short-lived one-off at that – it was first raced in the 1980 Dutch GP and destroyed in a practice accident at Watkins Glen late that year, after starting in just three races.

Prost seems dwarfed in the M30 cockpit during tests at Brands Hatch.

MP4/1-1C The new designation denoted Marlboro-Project Four, and that indicated the origins of the design in the backer and Ron Dennis' team before it was merged with McLaren – in the background some design work had been done by John Barnard before McLaren International came into being. Outwardly this car was as sleek as its immediate Colnbrook predecessors had been bulky. Carbon fibre was used extensively for major components such as the slim monocoque (this 'space-age' material had previously been used in racing cars for incidental parts, and McLaren turned to Hercules Incorporated of Salt Lake City to make the monocoque sections). Carbon fibre is costly, but in this employment it made for a light and very rigid monocoque, which also had outstanding impact-resistant qualities.

The rest of the car was relatively conventional. From its introduction early in 1981 Cosworth DFV engines were used, while the Dennis-initiated TAG-financed Porsche turbo engine was developed for it. A first victory for the MP series was scored by John Watson in the 1981 British GP, the next did not come until 1982 when Lauda won at Long Beach. That was in a 'B' car, which was revised in detail in a search for better aerodynamics and, with Michelin, for better grip (MP4s were also run with narrower rear tyres than the turbo cars, which gave a tiny drag gain). The MP4/1C was a 'flat-bottom' car, powered by DFV or DFY engines, which served in 1983 until McLaren's turbo car appeared. McLaren fortunes certainly looked up under the new regime: the team was sixth in the 1981 Constructors' Championship, a close second to Ferrari in 1982.

Drivers: Andrea de Cesaris, Niki Lauda, John Watson.

MP4 set the tone for all Barnard McLarens with its beautifully sleek lines. The car made its public debut in practice for the 1981 US Grand Prix (West) at Long Beach, driven by John Watson.

MP4/1D-1E An adapted 'Cosworth' MP4 was used as a development vehicle (D) for the TAG turbocharged engine, running tests for the first time at Silverstone in July 1983. MP4/1E was the first race car with this engine, completed very quickly for Lauda to use in the Dutch GP. It was an adaptation of the existing design, pending a true second-generation Barnard F1 McLaren design, but it did not appear so, for the V-6 and its ancillaries (primarily turbochargers and

MP4/1E looked bulkier than the Cosworth-engined cars, but was still a very sleek machine. The driver is Lauda, in the car's debut race at Zandvoort.

intercoolers) seemed made for the chassis. The engine was an 80 degree V-6 (82 × 47.3mm, 1499cc) with two KKK turbochargers producing some 750bhp in race trim. The turbo cars made seven starts in late-1983 races, and in that bedding-in phase for the chassis/engine partnership recorded no finishes.

Drivers: Niki Lauda, John Watson.

MP4/2 In its A, B and C forms the MP4/2 saw McLaren through three seasons, to two Constructors' Championships and three Drivers' Championships. Although this was a new design, in some respects it was a redesign, for example in the monocoque and allowing for a shorter engine and a larger (220 litre) fuel tank. Broad side pods were retained, with turbochargers further forward, and they curved in at the rear to completely enclose engine and gearbox with careful regard to aerodynamics. The 1984 car suspension had lower wishbones with top rocker arms and of course inboard coil springs/dampers; revisions were to bring a pushrod system front and rear in 1985.

There were 16 Championship races in 1984, and McLaren won twelve (Prost won seven, Lauda five); in 1985 Prost won five GPs, but Lauda won only at Zandvoort.

There were more changes in the 'C', for example in subtle aerodynamic refinement as the fuel allowance was cut to 195 litres and in the rear suspension. But there were fuel consumption problems, and McLaren's season was just a little less than brilliant. Prost won four GPs (and the drivers' title), but his new team mate Rosberg did not score a single win.

Drivers: Niki Lauda, Alain Prost, Keke Rosberg.

From some angles, MP4/2 looked a big car, but this shot of Prost in 1984 shows that the monocoque was narrow. The airflow to those gaping intakes was presumably clean through the front suspension. The diffuser panel that was an important aerodynamic element can just be made out on either side of the gearbox. The 'winglets' at the rear were banned at the end of 1984.

MP4/3 There was a new car for 1987, the last McLaren with the TAG engine. It was designed by Steve Nichols, albeit following proven lines laid down by Barnard (who left to set up Ferrari's GTO). Suspension and transmission were carried over, but there was a new body that certainly appeared more slippery, in a break with McLaren practice there were side outlets for radiator air, and there were new aerofoils. Porsche put some development work into the engine but the V-6 was virtually at the end of its F1 life and on top of that a spasm of unreliability set in. During the season one chassis was to be devoted to test vehicle use for a Honda engine. Prost won three GPs in 1987, and although McLaren was runner up in the Constructors' Championship it was a long way behind Williams on the points table.

Drivers: Stefan Johansson, Alain Prost.

In profile MP4/3 was a very attractive car. The black bars on the engine cover of Prost's car in practice for the British GP are a device adopted when TV and other regulations barred cigarette advertising.

MP4/4 This was a totally new car, with design controlled by Technical Director Gordon Murray and directly handled by Project Leader Steve Nichols. The major change was the switch to a Honda engine, the turbocharged RA168-E, which had been redesigned for just one season's racing, primarily so that it sat lower in a chassis. There were no departures in the chassis, the shorter 150-litre fuel cell compensating in length for the regulation that foot pedals had to be behind the centre line of the front wheels in 1988 cars. Unequal-length wishbone suspension was used, pullrod at the front, pushrod at the rear, with the shock absorbers vertical inside the slender nose bodywork. A new six-speed McLaren gearbox was introduced. The team had the immensely strong driver pairing of Prost and Senna, who accounted for 15 of the season's 16 Grands Prix. McLaren won the Constructors' Championship with 199 points. The next six teams on the final table scored 192 points between them. Meanwhile, from the summer, MP4/4 chassis had been used for tests with Honda's 3.5-litre V-10 for 1989.

Drivers: Alain Prost, Ayrton Senna.

Unlike its turbo predecessors, MP4/4 was not an elegant car, but it was mightily effective. This is Senna on home ground, in the 1988 Brazilian Grand Prix.

MP4/5 Design and development of a normally-aspirated car ran in parallel with the MP4/4, with the design group headed by Neil Oatley. The monocoque was new, there was double wishbone suspension (pullrod at the front, pushrod at the rear), and the Honda RA109-E 72-degree V-10 (92 × 52.5mm, 3490cc) was credited with a power output not far short of 700bhp, driving through a McLaren six-speed longitudinal gearbox (a transverse 'box came in mid season).

The McLaren team had problems in 1989, when mechanical difficulties tended to be overshadowed by personal clashes between the two drivers. Nevertheless, at the end of the season Prost and Senna were first and second in the Drivers' Championship, with ten GP victories between them, while McLaren conclusively won the Constructors' Championship again.

Drivers: Alain Prost, Ayrton Senna.

Outward characteristics of MP4/5 were a low and fine nose, the relatively open cockpit usually favoured by McLaren, high engine cover and short side pods swept down to the rear. The driver is Senna again.

McNAMARA

This short-lived constructor is best recalled for its Formula Vee cars and its outstandingly ugly USAC cars. They won odd minor events and an SAE award for race car engineering, perhaps because a German-built Indianapolis car was such a great rarity. Between these extremes Francis McNamara, an expatriate American, built some modestly successful F3 cars at his plant at Lenggries in Southern Germany.

The McNamara MkIII, which appeared in 1969, was designed by Austrian Jo Karasek. It had a space frame and suspension on Brabham lines (some Brabham components were used on the first cars). That year Austrians Helmut Marko and Werner Reidl gained odd top-six places in major F3 events. The IIIB with modified suspension came in 1970, and found favour with another Austrian, one Niki Lauda. One-time Lotus F1 driver Peter Arundell briefly ran the works F3 team. The 1971 version of the Indianapolis car brought problems with STP, the customer, and McNamara also had personal problems, which centred around the sudden death of his wife, his subsequent disappearance, and the active interest of Interpol. There were no more McNamara racing cars.

The MkIII F3 car was the only McNamara to have attractive lines, and then only in side elevation, where there was a hint of the 'wedge' theme then popular.

MELKUS

Heinz Melkus of Dresden continued to be described as a driving instructor through to the early 1960s when he was already established as the leading racing car constructor in East Germany and was respected throughout the Eastern bloc. His ingenuity was ill-served by the need to use components originating in Eastern Europe and this meant that his Formula Junior and F3 cars could never really be competitive in Western races, although they were bravely run in West Germany. Once racing in the East was directed away from the international formulae, Melkus' cars similarly faded.

Formula Junior Melkus built his first Junior in 1959 using AWE-Wartburg components, four-speed gearbox, brakes, steering and so on, and of course the three-cylinder engine. (This was actually the original A-U engine, which had a slightly longer stroke than the DKW derivative used by Melkus' West German contemporaries). He chose to keep it in its 980cc form, claiming an output of 68bhp in 1960. The engine was slightly offset behind the cockpit in a tubular frame. Front suspension was a double wishbone arrangement, with a de Dion rear axle.

A handful of these Juniors was built, setting a standard and example for other East European constructors. On home ground they were successful, and Willy Lehmann scored a rare victory for an East German car at Hockenheim in 1960. Later Juniors appeared slim and rakish, for Melkus had turned to a horizontal engine installation to achieve a low overall height. By the end of the Junior period Melkus looked to power outputs of 85-90bhp. Small-scale production continued, and it appears that some cars went to the Soviet Union. Late cars were converted for F3 use in the mid-1960s.

The early Junior Melkus was a dumpy car, with bodywork partly enclosing suspension components front and rear.

In the late Juniors the suspension members still looked very substantial, but the overall appearance of solidity had gone, the engine was on its side under smooth tapered rear bodywork and coil springs were out in the airflow.

F3 Essentially, Melkus had to use the same equipment in his F3 cars, and as in the West these were straight conversions from FJ cars in 1964. After that there was little development, while cars continued to be built in small numbers and sold in the Eastern bloc. There were closed East European F3 Championships, but in open international competition little was achieved; when drivers were brave, or occasionally lucky, a Melkus scraped into the top six of a 'second division' central European race (indeed, Melkus himself was second in a predominantly Brabham and Lotus field at Aspern in 1965). Work on the cars was concentrated on improved aerodynamic efficiency, with slippery bodies, inboard suspension and carefully ducted radiator outlets (used air being carried right through to the tail in two side tunnels), for despite painstaking work on the single-carburetter version of the Wartburg engine no more than 85bhp was claimed in 1965. Generally the outclassed engines meant that these cars could not be competitive, and when the 1.6-litre F3 was introduced in 1971 East European motor sport authorities were no longer interested in external competition.

The 1967 Melkus was a good-looking car by any F3 standard, and at that time was the most effective single-seater in East European racing.

MERCEDES-BENZ

This great German company signalled its intention to return to the Grand Prix arena by running a trio of 1939 cars in two Argentine *formule libre* races in 1951 (none too successfully), and then entering sports car racing very successfully with the 300SL in 1952. The Grand Prix comeback in 1954 was dramatic in an 'anniversary year' – Mercedes had re-entered GP racing in 1914 and 1934 – with a team that mixed the old and the new. Its manager was almost a throwback; its car was startling, and accepted without question by contemporary pundits (although with hindsight it can be seen to have been a dead end); and its number one driver was to bring success to the venture, for Juan Manual Fangio scored 41 World Championship points driving Mercedes in 1954 while his team mates amassed 20 between them.

The W196 bristled with novelty, so far as F1 was concerned. It had a tubular space frame, independent suspension front and rear, the latter by low-pivot swing axles, inboard brakes, and a straight eight with direct fuel injection and desmodromic (positively operated) valve gear which was laid over at 37 degrees to the horizontal to reduce frontal area. Initially the cars were run with full-width bodywork, but shortcomings meant that normal open-wheel bodies were hastily made and used on all save the fastest circuits where the *stromlinienwagen* were still used. A short wheelbase version was built in 1955, necessarily with outboard front brakes.

The engine was initially rated at 257bhp, then up to 290bhp in its second racing season, and save for a Gordini unit was the last straight eight to be seen in main-line single-seater racing.

The W196s were run in twelve World Championship races in 1954-5, winning nine before Mercedes withdrew from racing. Although expenditure was miniscule by today's standards, compared with their Italian rivals in the mid-1950s Mercedes threw money and resources into the programme, and fortunately for the reputation of the 'Silver Arrows' they threw some of it in the direction of the greatest drivers of the period, Fangio in 1954-5 and Moss in 1955.

Drivers: Juan-Manuel Fangio, Hans Herrmann, Karl Kling, Hermann Lang, Stirling Moss, André Simon, Piero Taruffi.

The first race for the W196 was the 1954 French GP at Reims, won by Fangio in one of the streamlined cars.

Stirling Moss in a conventional open-wheel W196 on his way to victory in the 1955 British GP at Aintree, where he headed a team 1-2-3-4. In this form the car appeared purposeful although far from handsome.

MERLYN

Colchester Racing Developments' first Merlyns were Formula Junior cars, and as far as single-seaters were concerned this largely remained the upper level of aspirations. There were some F3 and F2 cars, but it was most successful in Formula Ford in terms of race successes and production numbers. Like so many companies in motor sport the team had its origins in enthusiasm, and the first one-off came before the formation of Merlyn by John Barrington Lewis and Richard Neale at a modest base in a village near Colchester.

Some of the early Merlyns had unusual features, but soon the company followed the path of convention. The F2 effort was spasmodic, and F3 tended to be neglected at times, which was unfortunate as it meant that some promising cars were side-lined instead of being developed. By the mid-1970s Merlyn was building for only the Ford categories, and before the end of the decade that effort had ceased.

Mk1 This was a conventional one-off Formula Junior car designed by Selwyn Hayward and built in 1960. It had a multi-tubular frame, front-mounted Ford 105E engine, double wishbone front suspension, with lower wishbones at the rear and the prominent coil spring/damper units that featured on several of its contemporaries. It came to be regarded as a development car but apparently was never raced.

Mk2 The production version of Merlyn's first Junior, although 'production' seems a grand term to apply to the quartet that was built in 1961-2. Two stayed in England, two went to America, but they were of course out-moded on both sides of the Atlantic by 1962.

Mk3 Inevitably Merlyn turned to the rear-engined layout with the Mk3. A slim knife-edged nose made this a distinctive car (there was a radiator air intake under the nose). Disc brakes were fitted all round, inboard at the rear, Hewland gearboxes were used and 105E engines were normal. The car was good, but not outstanding; it was first raced at the end of 1961, and 16 were built.

Overall the Mk3 Merlyn was a sleek car and the lines were well balanced. The driver of this works car is Ian Raby.

Mk5 This was an attempt to improve on the Mk3 in 1963, with a similar simple space frame, a little narrower in the body and wider in the track. Initially the front coil spring/damper units were inboard, mounted horizontally and rod-operated, but Merlyn could not make this arrangement work and reverted to an outboard layout. At times the Mk5 seemed competitive, but Formula Junior passed without a major race falling to Merlyn.

Mk7 A dual-category car for the 1-litre F2 and F3 that came in 1964, with appropriate engines (Cosworth SCA and Holbay respectively), wider wheels on the F2 car and so on. Common to both was a space frame with sheet stiffening around the cockpit, conventional wishbones and coil springs suspension, inboard at the front, and clean body lines. In F3 Chris Irwin showed that the car had real potential by running with the class pace-setters at times, while towards the end of 1964 when Irwin was taking top-three places in F3 David Hobbs began to show well in F2. However, there were no prominent race wins.

Mk7 in Cosworth-engined F2 guise, looking very Lotus-like around the nose. David Hobbs is the driver, at Brands Hatch in 1964.

Mk9 A derivative of the Mk7 in 1965, for F2 and F3, and as the Mk9A for F3 in 1966. Changes were in details, for example in dropping the sheet stiffening around the cockpit, while the Mk9A had outboard front suspension. The F2 effort seemed half-hearted and Irwin did not score in 1965 (nor did Hobbs in his one 1966 F2 start in a Mk9). In F3 Fenning's good performances included a win at Monthléry in 1965, when Irwin was second in the Monaco race; in 1966 there were just odd sixth places in secondary F3 races.

Mk10 In effect the two 1966 Mk9As were prototypes of the Mk10. A dozen of these were to be built in 1967, and their sales appeal depended on low price rather than on advances in specification, for this was little different to the Mk9A. Drivers like Dave Walker began to get results – in 1967 he headed a Merlyn 1-2-3-4 at Opatija, which sounds remarkable until the quality of the opposition is taken into account! There were fourths and fifths in other races, and Tony Lanfranchi started his association with Merlyn (third at Pergusa). Independents used the cars in 1968.

The Mk10 proved quite a good buy, as well as an economic one, for independents. It was a very straightforward car, with suspension outboard all round.

Mk12 An FVA-powered F2 car built for the 1968 season, and in layout a derivative of the Mk10, with Hewland FT200 gearboxes. A quasi-works pair was run by Bob Gerard, and during the season no fewer than nine drivers occupied their cockpits (the best placings were Hart's seventh at Jarama and Rollinson's eighth at Vallelunga). The cars came out again as Mk12As in 1969. Chris Williams was fatally injured in a test accident in one, and while the other was further revised in detail it was raced only occasionally. Bag tank requirements ruled out further developments, although Mk15 was a Formula B variant.

Mk14 A one-off F3 development car, entrusted to Lanfranchi to race in 1968, which led to the Mk14A production version late in the same year. It was very much in the Merlyn line of

Mk14A was a workmanlike car, but few were seen. Lanfranchi is the driver, at Brands Hatch.

development, this time stemming from the Mk12. Lanfranchi occasionally finished well placed, once second, but this car never quite matched up to expectations.

Mk 21 Merlyn returned to F3 with a new car in 1971, setting aside the abortive Mk18. The Mk21 was a space frame car, with conventional double wishbone suspension and inboard rear brakes, prominent bulges on the flanks housing the tanks and a nose on Brabham lines. Holbay engines were used. The Mk21 seemed set to revive Merlyn F3 fortunes, in large part because of forceful driving by Scheckter, who won races at Oulton Park, Mallory Park and Thruxton.

There was nothing particularly distinguished about the Mk21, save some drives by the then up-and-coming Jody Scheckter (here at Outlton Park).

Mk22 The Mk21 revised in detail, and in its bodywork. It was not developed, or even raced consistently through the 1972-73 seasons, when Hakan Dalqvist had occasional good races in it.

Mk27 Although this car was announced for 1975 there was to be no F3 revival for Merlyn.

MERZARIO

Arturo Merzario drove for leading Grand Prix teams and for grid-filling Grand Prix teams, though he was more successful in sports-racing cars, and after his active front-line career was over he turned out in odd F3 races. His last F1 efforts were in his own cars, under-financed and uncompetitive devices, and he persevered as a constructor in F2 into the 1980s. One can only wonder at his unwavering optimisim ....

A1 Piola's drawings, handed to the Press at Monza in 1977, suggested a sleek car. In the metal in 1978 Merzario F1 A1/01 turned out to be cumbersome, and that impression was

A1 was a side radiator car, with intakes for the inclined water radiators just behind the front wheels and flank oil radiators alongside the DFV. The engine air intakes are reminiscent of the Ferraris Merzario once drove.

reinforced by the man's slight stature. A fair amount of his March 751 found its way into this DFV-Hewland kit car. There was a double wishbone front suspension, with upper and lower links and twin radius rods at the rear, and outboard coil spring/damper units all round, and it had the shortest wheelbase of any of the 1978 F1 cars. A second A1 was built with revised front suspension.

In 1978 Merzario qualified eight times in 16 attempts, but failed to finish a single race. The second car was mildly uprated for the first four races of 1979, when Merzario kept up the 1978 average, with two DNQ and two DNF.

Driver: Arturo Merzario.

A2 This was a first attempt to build a wing car, and the design (attributed to Merzario and Simon Hadfield) was constrained by the need for simplicity and low cost. The monocoque was apparently too fat for the ground effects airflow to work properly, but in respects such as its inboard suspension and the use of honeycomb materials it was up to date. However, it was far from competitive: Merzario failed to qualify it twice, Brancatelli failed once.

Driver: Arturo Merzario.

Merzario's 1979 F1 cars looked as lithe as his 1978 car had appeared dumpy, but the main dimensions were similar.

A4 By the middle of the 1979 season Merzario had abandoned construction of a second A2 and turned to A4, which was based on the abortive Kauhsen and had the benefit of attention from designer Giampaolo Dallara. In that it had a slender monocoque with its fuel cell behind the cockpit its side pods were adequate for the 'under wings'. Quite why absorbing the effects of one failed team was expected to restore the fortunes of another is not clear. The last seven GPs of 1979 saw an unbroken run of DNQs . . . .

M1 Merzario blew a little smoke screen around his move 'down' to F2 in 1980 with the contention that his new car was designed to take a DFV engine in place of a BMW when the time was right. The M1 followed A4's ground effects layout but in departments such as its inboard rocker arm suspension was patently ineffectual. Merzario entered himself in nine races, started in three and placed ninth at Thruxton; Dacco and Necchi racked up eight retirements and two finishes. M1 ran only in F2 form.

There were echoes of Merzario's F1 cars in his M1, in the lines of the nose and other parts as well as in a dismal performance record.

M2 A derivative for 1981, which Merzario drove occasionally (reputedly to maintain a presence as a start-money special) while Marco Brand drove it twice. The team's number one cars were March 812s.

M28 Merzario ran March 822s in 1982, modifying them to no good end through the season, then for 1983 he introduced the M28. Designed by Ernesto Degan, this had a honeycomb monocoque, with carbon fibre elements, pullrod suspension and Mader BMW engines. It showed signs of structural inadequacies and was unreliable. Two drivers quit the team in mid season. Degan sorted out details and Dallest later placed an M28 seventh at Misano (although that was also last, he had run in the leading six) and was twice eighth, so there might have been potential in the car. That year an Alfa-engined Merzario 283 flitted across the local F3 scene, driven by Roberto Campominosi.

M84 As the final F2 season opened Merzario presented another new car. Well, Degan claimed it was an all new design although the specification was similar to the M28's. Stefano Livio started an M28 from the back of six grids (he was regarded as a brave man), and among his three finishes was tenth at Silverstone. Other drivers made three starts in M84s so that Merzario's team had a better than 50 per cent overall finishing record in his last season as a constructor. His M84s were seen for the last time in the summer.

The last Merzario was not an elegant car, and appearances also did it justice in that it was not small and nimble. This car is running early tests.

MEUB

A Frankfurt-built Formula Junior car of 1959, rear-engined, with a ladder frame, wishbone and transverse leaf front suspension and a torsion bar sprung rigid axle at the rear. Main components followed German convention of the early Junior period, with engine and transmission coming from DKW. This car recorded only one worthwhile result, when Philippe Meub placed it third in a poorly-supported race at La Châtre in 1960.

MEZZOLITRE

A fairly large but very pretty front-engined front-wheel drive 1951 500cc car with rubber suspension, the Mezzolitre was designed by Gordon Bashford, Chief Engineer of Rover, for two of his colleagues who actually built them. BSA engines, developed in cooperation with the works, were used and although not winners, the cars did not disgrace themselves. One, successively modified, graced the British scene for a number of years. ML

MH

A conventional 500cc car which appeared in Germany in 1952. At least three were made but they achieved little. **ML**

MILANO

When the organisers of the 1949 Italian Grand Prix offered a bonus to any entrant of two cars to a new design, the Ruggeri brothers, who ran Scuderia Milano, modified two Maserati 4CLT/48s and entered them under the name Milano. They shortened the wheelbase, changed the bodywork, enlarged the brakes and had Mario Speluzzi, who specialised in marine engines, tweak the supercharging to tease 30bhp more than standard: this was enough to qualify for the bounty.

Giuseppe Farina and Piero Taruffi drove the cars in the race, when only the works Ferraris in the thin field were quicker. Farina gave up after 18 laps because he was unable to match the Ferraris, but Taruffi came home third.

The Ruggeri brothers designed a new chassis to take their Speluzzi engines in 1950. These were tubular ladder frames with double wishbone and torsion bar front suspension, but they were less certain about the rear so one car had a de Dion axle with a transverse leaf spring, while the other had twin trailing links and transverse leaf irs. It was never raced under the Milano banner.

The new cars took a long time to complete and, in the interim, Felice Bonetto drove one of the original Maserati-Milanos in the 1950 Swiss and French Grands Prix, to fifth and retirement respectively.

The first Milano appeared in the non-Championship Grand Prix des Nations at Geneva, driven by Gianfranco Comotti, but it dropped out after eight laps while Bonetto, in a 1949 car, finished eighth.

At the Freiburg hill climb pre-War Auto Union driver Paul Pietsch set FTD in a 1949 car, which made the Ruggeri brothers think that there was nothing wrong with their cars. They were misled – for in the Pescara GP, Bonetto, in the de Dion Milano, was timed at only 152mph on the long straight, more than 30mph slower than Fangio's Alfa Romeo.

A single Milano turned up for the 1950 Italian GP, for Comotti, and for this race Speluzzi came up with a twin-plug cylinder head which gave a claimed 320bhp. Its performance did not back the claim and it retired after 16 laps. A couple of cars were entered in the Barcelona GP for local drivers and one finished tenth. The previously unraced second chassis formed the basis of the 1955 Arzani-Volpini F1 car. **ML**

Drivers: Felice Bonetto, Gianfranco Comotti, Guiseppe Farina, Francesco Godia-Sales, José Jover, Paul Pietsch, Piero Taruffi.

MILLI-UNION

G.H. Millington's Milli-Union was an early Iota fitted with Morgan ifs and a pushrod Norton engine. Little was achieved with it. **ML**

MINARDI

Giancarlo Minardi took the major step from entrant of an independent March F2 team to constructor in the same category in 1980, and another when he moved into F1 in 1985. Through the decade the little team persevered, and was

respected for that as actual race successes were rare – just one win in an F2 Championship event.

Minardi's base is at Faenza, where Signor Minardi has a truck dealership. The first cars were designed by one-time Ferrari men Caliri and Marmiroli at their Fly studio in Bologna, where the first F2 car was completed in February 1980. Successive F2 cars sometimes showed flashes of real promise, but as a constructor Minardi had a tough apprenticeship. His F1 plans were laid in good time for the team to move up as F2 wound down, although Caliri's first F1 Minardi was laid down as a dual-purpose car, with F3000 also in mind. The team then went through another tough apprenticeship, running a single car in 1985.

From 1986 two cars were run, but Minardi's first 60 Grands Prix produced just one Championship point, in 1988. Hence the joy when the team scored three points in the 1989 British GP. Minardi's first decade was sustained more by enthusiasm than rewards.

GM75 The first Minardi followed standard ground effects lines – March 792 lines to a degree – with a fairly narrow monocoque and full-length side pods. The body was attractive, the engineering beneath it provoked some unkind comments. Osella-BMW engines were proposed, but Mader-BMW units were used. There were development problems, not eased as Pirelli changed tyre specifications.   Once the season settled regular driver Angel Guerra did a competent job, finishing nine times in eleven European F2 Championship starts, and scoring in five. Gabbiani drove occasionally but less happily. Dacco used a GM75 to qualify for the last rows of grids in 1981 and did a little better with it in the following two seasons, when it was run as an M275.

GM75 was a shapely car, with a neat colour scheme lost under all the decals. This is Argentine driver Guerra at Silverstone in 1980.

Minardi FLY281 In most respects a derivative of the first Minardi, this was a more refined car, slimmer and with better downforce characteristics. It was laid down to accept Mader-BMW or Ferrari engines, but development with the Italian V-6 was sluggish. (Guerra returned, after an F1 accident, to give a Minardi-Ferrari its first race late in the summer and the car came out once in 1982 as well.)

FLY 281 was not an outstanding car, but Michele Alboreto drove it forcefully, winning on his home circuit, Misano.

Eventually the cars and the tyres worked well, and might have worked better in 1981 if Minardi resources had stretched to a proper test and development programme. As it was, Alboreto took pole in Pau and then scored Minardi's first victory, at Misano. It was also Minardi's only F2 victory.

With revised bodies the cars were run as 281Bs in 1982, when the anticipated successor with a carbon fibre monocoque did not materialize, in part because of the confused ground effects situation. Nannini scored eight Championship points, for tenth place on the overall table. The 281B was used by the team four times in 1983, as it struggled to make the 283 raceworthy.

283 F1 was very much in mind when this car was laid out, with an engine bay that would have accepted a DFV in place of a Mader-BMW. The monocoque was a mix of honeycomb and carbon fibre (used in the side panel skins), and this time Caliri used pullrod suspension all round. In racing the season looked better – Nannini was seventh in the Championship and Martini tenth.

For the last F2 season the design was updated but, perhaps in part because the summer of 1984 saw the first F1 Minardi unveiled, the team's racing fortunes slipped. Nannini was again tenth in the Championship.

The 283 was another good-looking car with the cockpit well forward in a long wheelbase. Nannini was a spirited driver (here at Thruxton).

M85 The first F1 Minardi was completed in July 1984, but was not raced until the following year. Caliri had moved in-house to design the F1 cars and look after their development so the external lines and much of the make-up of the 283 were carried over. There were differences, such as pullrod front/pushrod rear suspension. It was laid out with several possible engines in mind, initially the Alfa V-8, until Alfa Romeo disposed of Chiti, who then set up Motori Moderni. Minardi's partner, Gianpiero Mancini, had an interest in Motori Moderni and the MM V-6 turbo was selected. It was designed and built very quickly, but for the first two races the M85 was propelled by Cosworth.

Caliri followed his F2 pattern faithfully in the M85, although the F1 car looked bulkier. Driver is Martini, at Silverstone.

The car was overweight, had a tendency to understeer, was sadly underpowered with the MM V-6 and was driven by Pierluigi Martini who was out of his depth in F1. He finished three times, his best placing being eighth (and last) in Austria.

The design was modified as the M185B for 1986, when it was still a heavy car but had improved handling characteristics. Two were built, a 1985 car serving as the spare for the two drivers. Each failed to qualify once and an M85B was classified just once, when Nannini was 14th in Mexico.

Drivers: Andrea de Cesaris, Pierluigi Martini, Alessandro Nannini.

M3085 Basically, this F3000 car was an adaptation of the 283 in its 1984 form, with a Nicholson DFV engine. It appeared at two 1986 Championship meetings, when it was sadly off the pace and was not qualified to start in either race.

M86 A single new car was run from the summer of 1986, and eventually four appeared, to serve the team through 1987. In design terms it was a straight derivative, lighter with a carbon fibre monocoque and with sleeker lines but still powered by Chiti's V-6 and still using Minardi's own gearbox. De Cesaris and Nannini both raced the 1986 car, the former placing it eighth in Mexico. Nannini was eleventh in two 1987 races, when the team recorded just four finishes, one achieved by the team's 'paying driver'.

Drivers: Adrian Campos, Andrea de Cesaris, Alessandro Nannini.

Minardi's original basic colour scheme was seen for the last time in 1987, on a visibly lower car. Driver is second-string Spaniard Adrian Campos.

M188 This was Caliri's last design for Minardi, changed regulations meaning that little was carried over save the rear end (suspension and gearbox). The carbon fibre monocoque allowed for a fuel tank which extended forward on both sides of the cockpit, which in turn meant that the engine could be mounted well forward. In an odd front suspension, horizontal top-mounted dampers were inter-linked. This was not successful, nor was Caliri's own revision. He left and Aldo Costa took over the design role. He soon came up with a more satisfactory conventional front suspension. The team became

M188 had a short wheelbase and more balanced lines, with lower rear bodywork as a DFZ took the place of the bulky MM V-6. Driver is Perez Sala, in Brazil in 1988.

a Cosworth DFZ customer, to advantage (Minardis were placed 13 times in 1988). Campos was shown the door after five races, Martini came back wiser and more experienced and scored a point, in Detroit.

In B form the cars were used in the early 1989 races, showing more speed and usually qualifying well. Minardi was nominated as Subaru's official team, and in the background was a Subaru flat twelve, designed by Chiti and produced by Motori Moderni. It was tested in an M188, but never raced.

Drivers: Adrian Campos, Pierluigi Martini, Luis Perez Sala.

M189 This car did not make its race debut until the fourth GP of 1989, and from the eighth GP it was the first Minardi to make an impact in F1. Designer Aldo Costa and aerodynamicist Nigel Couperthwaite laid out a car that was orthodox by 1989 standards, using the updated B188 suspension, Cosworth DFR engines as Chiti's confection faded, and Pirelli tyres which gave advantages in some conditions. Outwardly it was another slender-nosed car, with longer side pods than the B188.

There were new-car teething problems, but the second half of the season witnessed the transformation of Minardi from a no-hoper team to a good little 'un as from the British GP (fifth and sixth) its drivers started scoring points. Moreover, Martini often qualified an M189 in exhalted company, briefly led a GP, and scored well enough to lift Minardi to equal tenth in the Constructors' Championship.

Drivers: Paolo Barilla, Pierluigi Martini, Luis Sala.

Somebody deserves credit for harmonizing a potentially messy collection of colours and sponsors' decals (yellow nose and engine cover, white and black bands, black end plates on the aerofoils). This is Martini in the M189/3.

MINOS

This was an F2 one-off which Australian Bobby Muir based on his 1975 Birrana Formula Atlantic car, using a BDX engine. He qualified it for its F2 debut at Thruxton in 1976, but made no impression in the race. He was then so far off the pace in the Minos during practice at Pau that he put it aside and persuaded his backers (Bob and Marj Brown) to invest in a Chevron B35.

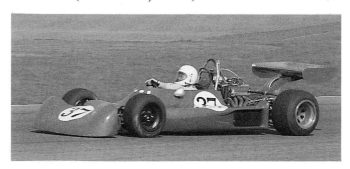

In its one Thruxton race the Minos in no way belied its unpretentious origins, and in 1976 rather more was called for to compete with Elf, Martini, March, Chevron et al.

MIRAGE

This Mirage was a single-seater originating in Italy, which made three ineffectual appearances at F2 championship meetings in 1979-80. It was a conventional BMW-engined car which Sergio Mignotti qualified to start at Mugello in 1979, only to retire in the race; he twice failed to make the grid at Vallelunga with his Mirage.

MITTER

Gerhard Mitter was a one-time racing motor cyclist, a racing driver, a DKW agent and tuning specialist and a designer, who briefly turned constructor in the early Formula Junior years. He campaigned his prototype car in 1959, with some success in hill climbs.

The car naturally had strong DKW associations, first and foremost with the three-cylinder engine enlarged to 1097cc and driving through the front wheels (this was claimed to be the first front-wheel drive Junior). A space frame carried the DKW-based suspension, lower wishbones and top transverse leaf spring at the front and a dead axle with transverse leaf spring and single radius rod at the rear. The Deek four-speed gearbox was used.

For 1960 Mitter built a small batch of improved cars, with the engine rated at 85bhp, a similar space frame and mechanical specification, and fibreglass bodies with no claim to elegance. These cars were not notably successful, and Mitter concentrated on engine preparation (he supplied DKW engines to Elva for FJ cars) and for his own racing used his DKW engines in Lotus chassis, before he began to concentrate on sports cars. Mitter was also the second 'M' in the original MBM outfit.

The first Mitter was a spindly device, with wheelbase and track dimensions so close to the other German and Italian front-engined Juniors in 1959 that there seemed to be a consensus. Mitter is driving the car at Innsbruck.

The 'production model' in 1960, still a front wheel drive car, with Elva cast wheels and one of the least attractive noses in racing. Mitter is again the driver, in a hill climb.

MODUS

Modus Cars was set up in 1973 as a division of Teddy Savory's group of companies at Watton in Norfolk, at a time when his building, construction, farming and other activities seemed to be prospering. Savory was an enthusiast, who had raced saloons and turned to entering drivers in F3. In 1973 Jo Marquart joined Modus from GRD and Modus moved towards becoming a constructor. Tony Brise was another factor (he came close to winning the Formula Atlantic championship with the Modus team in 1973) and so was Jorg Obermoser. He had an association with GRD in 1972, whereby he was to take Marquart-designed F3 and sports cars in component form and complete them in Germany, to market as ToJ. After Marquart moved to Modus, Obermoser commissioned cars from the new company.

The first Modus single-seater, an F3 car, was announced early in 1974. Cars for F5000, Formula Atlantic, Super Vee and Super Renault, and sports-racing cars, were to follow, and so with a little more trouble was an F2 car. By the end of 1974 there was even talk of F1, but late in 1976 it all ended abruptly. The group had not been prospering and the racing division was closed in November. The manufacturing rights passed to Andreason early in 1976. Nothing came of that, but Modus had made a mark on racing in the 1970s.

M1 The first Modus was a conventional front-radiator design, introduced to serve for Super Vee (M2) and F Atlantic (M3) as well as F3, while, in time, a Super Renault version was to come. It was built around a straightforward monocoque and was to be developed through three seasons, mainly in its suspension. There were double wishbones at the front, and initially at the rear, where twin parallel lower links were substituted for 1976. In 1975 a narrower track had been introduced. Ford twin-cam engines, prepared by Neil Brown, Holbay, Nova and others were favoured at first, but increasingly Nova-Toyota units were used, while in Germany BMW units were installed.

Perhaps the outstanding result of 1974 was not a win but Tony Brise's second place at Monaco – a very worthwhile achievement for an infant company. But Arnott did put an M1 on pole for its debut race at Oulton Park, while Danny Sullivan scored Modus' first win, and his first F3 win, at Thruxton. The peak year in F3 was 1975 when the works cars were driven by Eddie Cheever (he won the fifth and sixth F3 races he started, and that was good for Modus' reputation too) and Sullivan also won races. Kottulinsky won in Germany with a Schnitzer-BMW-engined M1 and Nordstrom with a Nova-Toyota Modus. Only two of the major F3 races in 1976 fell to M1s (Riley's winning M1 at Silverstone had a Neil Brown Triumph engine).

Marquart's Modus cars had individualistic lines, with short full-width nose, angular flanks and often bulbous engine covers, which did not always envelop the roll-over bar as on this 1975 team car. The colour scheme was primarily orange. This is Danny Sullivan at Thruxton.

M7 Modus' F2 ambitions were set aside until sponsorship justified building cars, and that came with Ian Grob in 1976. The M7 was most closely related to that year's Atlantic car, and did not resemble earlier Modus cars – it had a small nose carrying a full-width aerofoil, radiators in large side pods and prominent cockpit surround. Hart 420R engines were used, while a BMW unit could have been installed. This car was troublesome. Grob was entered for eleven races, failed to qualify for six, and his highest placing was fifth at the Nürburgring. Sullivan failed to qualify at Mugello. These dozen outings made up the M7's career.

MOLTENI

An early French Formula Junior car, built in 1959 and naturally rear-engined as it used a Renault Dauphine engine (at 996cc, which made the claim of 70bhp perhaps optimistic) driving through a Renault four-speed 'box. It had a tubular chassis and double wishbone suspension front and rear. There seems to be no record of success in racing.

MONACO (GB)

Built for George Hartwell by the Monaco Motor and Engineering Company of Watford the most distinctive thing about this early 500cc car was its five foot wheelbase (roughly 150cm). Front suspension was Fiat 500 with coil springs at the rear and the sohc Norton engine was mounted at the back on the offside of the chassis. The drive went forwards to a countershaft and then back via chains and sockets to both rear wheels, there being no axle as such. Eventually it received a pretty body and while it was never competitive on courses which had corners, it was rapid in a straight line and did well in speed trials.   ML

MONACO (I)

Among the entries for the mid-1986 F3000 Championship race at Imola was the Monaco 001, or Monte Carlo 001, entered by Ecurie Monaco. This turned out to be the Dywa from 1980, with a Mader DFV engine installed in its little-altered chassis. It would have been surprising if Fulvio Ballabio had managed to qualify this hack machine at Imola, and true to its showing at Monza in 1980 it failed to make the race. Seemingly, it was renamed in a ploy to attract sponsorship from the Principality.

MONNIER

Maurice Monnier, a Belgian, built this wire-wheeled single-seater based on BMW 328 components in the late 1940s and he drove it in a handful of minor F2 races each year, except 1951, until 1953. Unfortunately his usual result was 'did not finish' or 'running but not classified'

By 1953 Monnier was clearly losing interest and others drove the car; M. Noreille came fifth in a minor race at Monthléry in May 1953 and Georges Mulnard drove it in the 1953 Grand Prix des Frontiéres at Chimay where it failed to complete a lap. It was sold Pierre Bastien who entered it in the 1954 Chimay race but was over a minute off the pace and retired around half distance with a broken oil pipe.   ML

MONO JK

Julius Kubinsky (JK) was a special builder based in Brno who produced sports-racing cars in the 1950s and, intriguingly, a single-seater one-off that complied with F1, although it never appeared in an F1 race. It seems that it ran somewhere, as it was timed at a speed of more than 140mph (so it would hardly have been competitive if it had run in F1 company). Like other Czech would-be constructors, Kubinsky had to use production components, in this case with Porsche-type ifs and a Roots-supercharged version of the Lancia V-4, with a 1498cc capacity. Kubinsky later built a 500cc F3 car.

MONOPOL/ MONOPOLETTA

Helmut Polensky built one of the first post-war German F2 cars, the Monopol. This was based on BMW 328 mechanicals in Polensky's own chassis with torsion bar suspension, but it was unusual in that it was rear-engined, transmission being by a VW gearbox. It was fairly successful in German races at a time when Germany was exluded from international competition.

When the 500cc F3 became international, Polensky built a car for the formula, the Monopoletta. Its suspension followed Cooper lines but was hidden, front and rear, behind fairings, the driver sat further forward, the body panels were designed to stress the tubular chassis, and the 'knock off' wire wheels had lightweight alloy rims. The Monopoletta first came to prominence when a BMW-powered example driven by Walter Schlüter won an important national race at the Nürburgring in 1950, beating a couple of locally-owned Cooper JAPs. However, when the cars came up against good British opposition they were outclassed. Polensky later drove for the Porsche works team.   ML

The Monopoletta was a compact and well-balanced package, which promised well. These two cars on a Nürburgring grid in 1950 show the distinctive suspension fairings. Drivers are Walter Polensky in No 2 and Walter Schlüter in No 4.

MOORLAND

One of the first British Formula Junior cars, laid down by Len Terry before he started on his own Terrier Junior. It was seen through to completion by Les Redmond, but only as a one-off because financial backing was withdrawn. An orthodox front-engined car, it raced in the early summer of 1959; then following tests by Graham Warner at Brands Hatch in the July was 'adopted' by The Chequered Flag team. The design was refined by Redmond and put into production as the Gemini MkII.

MORE COLLEGE

A one-off Japanese F3 car, with an up-to-date specification and Toyota engine. It was run in the 1986 All-Japan series, apparently without showing any signs of becoming remotely competitive.

MORETTI *see* BRANCA

MORONI

Another of the first-generation Italian Formula Junior lookalikes, with a front-mounted Fiat 1100 engine and Fiat gearbox, but unlike most of its contemporaries with independent suspension all round.

MOTUL

In 1972 Rondel Racing – Ron Dennis and Neil Trundle – ran a team of Brabham BT38s in F2 but the season did not go too well. Reutemann had an early accident and throughout it seemed that the principals did not have an easy relationship with Brabham. So a car to be named for the team's main sponsor, Motul, was laid down for 1973, and first ran in the Autumn of 1972.

Designed by Ray Jessop, the M1 was essentially straightforward, but not so simply developed to raceworthiness. In part this might have been due to Rondel preoccupation with sponsorship problems, which meant that the six-car effort originally planned had to be scaled down. In part it was due to engine problems – BDAs, BDGs or FVDs were seen in the backs of the M1s at various times (the FVD, an Alan Smith version of the sports car FVC, turned out not to be homologated), but most races were won by the new BMW engine which was exclusive to March.

The team's graded drivers, Pescarolo and Schenken, each won a race, and two of the drivers who were eligible for European Championship points, Wollek and Pryce in a Titan-backed M1, both finished a race in second place behind a graded driver and thus scored maximum points. Wollek was sixth in the Championship, Pryce eleventh and Jaussaud 17th. The Motuls were not raced in F2 in 1974, most being sold to the USA for Formula B use.

The F2 Motul appeared as a no-nonsense racing machine, slab-sided and bluff-nosed, changing in detail such as the addition of little tabs to direct airflow at the radiator air exits and with stalk-mounted mirrors in place of cockpit-surround mirrors.

MRD

Motor Racing Developments' first car appeared unobtrusively at a Goodwood meeting in August 1961, entered and driven by Tasmanian Gavin Youl. He drew attention to the car by placing it second in the Formula Junior race. It had been built in a shed at Esher and was a sensible and workmanlike car, outwardly with no eye-catching characteristics at a time when new FJ cars were commonplace. The space frame, coil spring and wishbone suspension and Holbay-Ford engine were not remarkable. However, this was the first Brabham, designed by Ron Tauranac, and a one-off as Jack was still a Cooper driver and building FJ cars for sale was a major Cooper concern. At the end of that season Brabham left Cooper, and by then the vulgar connotations of MRD in France had been explained, so the successors to the prototype – for that, in essence, was what the MRD was – were Brabhams.

The MRD in the Goodwood paddock. It lacked the professional finish of contemporary Lotus and Cooper FJ cars, although it was slimmer than most. The Australian flag below the roll bar was appropriate to Brabham, Tauranac and Youl.

MRE

This short-lived marque, which disappeared as it was taken over to become Tiga in 1975, is chiefly recalled for its production Formula Ford cars in the early 1970s. Its 1973 F3 venture hardly took off; the Max Boxtrom-designed space frame car, a simple adaptation of the F Ford model, appeared competent but was not competitive, apparently let down by its engines in the final season of 1.6-litre F3 racing, and not developed.

The straightforward F3 MRE, apparently posed in a public park before it was taken to its first race meeting. Circuit performances in the hands of Barrie Maskell and Mike Tyrrell were disappointing.

MUSTANG

A one-off Formula Junior car built in Brno in 1962 by Vladimir Valenta. It was a space-framed car with low lines in common with others powered by the Wartburg engine and double wishbone suspension all round. There seems to be no record of racing success.

N

NARDI

Enrico Nardi's name lives on through a range of accessories, especially steering wheels, but he also enjoyed a long career as a special builder and helped to build the Auto Avio 815s (the first cars built by Enzo Ferrari after he severed his links with Alfa Romeo). Some of his post-war sports cars had limited production runs and he also built single-seaters for the national 750 formula (a 500cc F3 version with Gilera engine was announced in 1951). In 1952 a Nardi F2 car was built, and in 1952-3 it could have run in World Championship events. It used a Lancia Aurelia engine and gearbox/final drive unit (although Gianni Lancia was reported to be 'interested' he apparently refrained from other comment, let alone involvement). The 1991cc V-6 (72 × 81.5mm) initially gave a hopeless 110bhp, and the 140bhp ultimately claimed for it was still inadequate by at least 40bhp, especially as the complete car weighed in at a hefty 670kg/1475lb.

Unusually for an Italian racing car of the period the engine was mounted at the rear and it had an odd triangulated tubular frame, with massive main tubes. Aurelia front suspension was used, with a wishbone and transverse leaf arrangement at the rear; the rear drum brakes were inboard, while the front brake drums were on the outside of the centre-lock wheels. Nardi and Valenzano tested the car when it was completed in September 1952 and accepted that it would not be competitive. The Nardi joined the ranks of unraced might-have-beens.

NARVAL

Bernard Lagier introduced this F3 car on Brabham BT35 lines early in 1972, built around a space frame but with less rounded bodywork than its inspiration (Lagier had been a Brabham driver, and MRD's agent). The car appeared in two versions, one with a full-width nose and Nova engine, the other intended as a school car with a BMW 2002 engine and other variations such as Dunlop 'long-life' tyres.

In F3 racing the odds against a newcomer in the early 1970s were as great as they were in the 1980s, and the planned two-car team never really took off. Christian Ethuin, however, showed well in the solitary works Narval JC3, with a third place at Chimay in 1972.

The 'school' version of the Narval, which had a more attractive nose than its racing counterpart. Chassis and suspension were identical, but the BMW engine meant exhausts on the right, whereas in the Nova-engined car they were on the left.

NEMO

Designer Max Boxstrom envisaged a multi-role car, for F2, F3 and Formula B, when he laid out the Nemo, but only two F3 cars were built, by the Race Cars International team in 1970. The basis was a light-alloy monocoque, with a sub frame carrying the engine and conventional suspension. The prototype was first raced in July 1970 and appeared spasmodically through to the end of that season, showing some promise but suffering teething troubles – the RCI driver preferred to race the team's other cars. At the end of the year the project was put up for sale by Brendan McInerney, and the design, cars and spares were acquired for a song by Tony Kitchiner (who never did build a K4 around the Nemo).

The Nemo stood out among its contemporaries, largely because its monocoque was slim and deep. An intention was that repairs should be as simple as with a space frame car as this was a period of transition in the 'customer-car' categories, and that was one reason for the external plumbing. The substantial sub frame mounting of the engine can be seen.

NERI

One of the few middle-period Italian Formula Junior cars, and another that failed to impress. It had a rear-mounted Fiat engine in a tubular chassis, wishbone and top link suspension front and rear, and the suggestion that a Colotti-Dauphine gearbox could be an alternative to the normal Fiat 'box.

NETUAR

The Netuar was an F1 Cooper copy, made by Rauten Hartmann ('Netuar' is Rauten backwards) and fitted with a Peugeot engine. Hartmann drove it in the Rand GP in 1961-4 and achieved a remarkable record of consistency. In 1961 he qualified last, and retired, in 1962 he failed to qualify but the following year he bounced back with last on the grid and last classified finisher. He seemed to lose his way in 1964 when he set only second slowest qualifying time, but went some way to redressing the matter by being last classified finisher in the first heat and retiring in the second.　　ML

NIKE

Ken Nicholls had, and has, a reputation as a space frame specialist, but in the 1970s his North Devon company built single-seater Nikes. Most were for lesser categories (Formula Ford or Clubmans cars) but there were two pairs of F3 cars.

Although these seem to have been used for other purposes (one of each was sold for hill climbs) they were F3 cars and are included here. Joint designers were Mark Erwood and Ken Nicholls. The Mk6B was based on the F Ford Mk6 in 1971 and was a straightforward space frame car with a Holbay engine driving through a Hewland 'box. Later it turned up as a Monoposto championship car, before being excluded from that category. The Mk11 was a monocoque car, with a tubular engine bay and, like the Mk6B, orthodox double wishbone suspension.

NORTH STAR

This rather dumpy tubular-framed British Formula Junior car appeared in 1963, when the only route to success in this category was with a proprietary chassis from one of the majors.

NORTON DOMINATOR SPECIAL

Les Penna built this Australian 500 special which appeared in 1955, seven years after Norton's first Dominator motor cycle. The engine choice is evident but a less obvious feature of this very pretty car, which had coil spring suspension and alloy wheels, was the fact that the ladder frame was built around Ford Model T side rails.

NORTON SPECIAL

A pioneering Australian 500 car built by Bill Hooper in 1948, before a proper 500cc class existed, the Norton Special was bought by Austin Tauranac in 1953 and was modified by him in conjunction with his brother Ron. When it became, in effect, an early Ralt it featured a new space frame and all independent suspension by upper wishbones and lower transverse leaf springs, the reverse of conventional practice.   ML

NOTA

Nota Engineering was a Sydney company, formed by Guy Buckingham, which built sports cars and single-seaters in small numbers from the late 1950s through to the 1970s, and continued with one-off sports cars into the 1980s. Its first F Junior car was an adapted front-engined clubman's car, but this was followed in 1962 by a notably low space-frame car on

Nota's rear-engined single-seater in F Junior guise in 1962, driven by David Hill.

Lotus 20/22 lines, using a Ford 105E-based engine. Its layout was followed through in ANF3 and F Ford cars, but by the end of the 1960s Nota was concentrating on production of its rear-engined sports car (eventually more than 100 of these Mini Cooper-powered cars were built).

NOVA (I)

Another of the short-lived Formula Junior cars of the early Italian primitive period, using Fiat components (1100 engine and gearbox) in a ladder-type chassis with the engine ahead of the cockpit, wishbone and coil spring front suspension and a live rear axle. There is no record of achievement, or of the car's fate.

NOVA (J)

Shinsuke Yamanashi formed Nova Engineering in 1973, with driver Hiroshi Kazato and designer Kikuo Kaira, at a base set up at Fuji. The first car was for F2, then the premier category in Japan, but it was not completed until 1974. F2 cars that became familiar to European competitors in Japan followed, and one was run in Europe. An F3 effort was short-lived, and that car was driven in Britain by Satoru Nakajima, who was destined to be Japanese F2 Champion five times, including a hat trick run in 1984-6. Those were March years in Japanese F2, with the competition being between tyre companies or between engine suppliers, or maybe between local drivers and Europeans. The 'local' engines had not been available to Nova in the 1970s. In the 1980s Nova Engineering ran other constructors' cars in F2 and F3000.

Formula 2 Kazato was the moving force behind the first F2 Nova, drawing on his experience of racing in Europe, but the project was set back by his death. The 02 was eventually completed, only to be virtually destroyed in a 1974 Suzuka accident before its first race, and although it was rebuilt to be raced in 1975 this was largely as a lead-in to the 512.

The 512 had vague wedge lines, and looked ponderous. However, it was effective, especially in the hands of Kazuyoshi Hoshino.

On the other hand 532P did not appear out of place among European cars. The driver is Hoshino again.

Supreme exploitation of a loophole in the regulations, the Brabham BT46B 'fan car' (**top and above**). Designers Murray and North managed to create a ground effects car in spite of the Alfa flat-12 engine (its cylinder heads occupied much of the region needed for venturi tunnels). Skirts sealed the car to the track, and under-car air was drawn up through a radiator mounted atop the engine by the large fan at the rear, where the air was exhausted. There were splendid arguments about the primary use of the air, moveable aerodynamic devices, and so on. The car was never declared illegal, but after it had raced once (and won) it was very effectively barred. It made one more appearance after its Swedish GP victory in 1978, at a Donington Park demonstration where these photographs were taken.

Seat fitting is part of a new driver/new car routine. The departure from normal at the March Bicester plant early in 1975 was Lella Lombardi in the cockpit (**right**). Her race performances were generally unimpressive, although she scored half a point in the shortened Spanish GP – an achievement still not equalled by another woman. The team soon welcomed her replacement, but her abrupt dismissal was perhaps less than fair, as March historian Mike Lawrence points out, for a faulty bulkhead endowed her 751 with quirky cornering habits.

Peterson sitting in a bathtub. The shallow monocoque was favoured by Gardner in his Tyrrells and shows well in this P34 (**above**) without its deep cockpit surround. So does the forward roll-over bar ahead of the steering wheel, and those four little front wheels. Aluminium, and aluminium honeycomb, was used in most monocoques through to the 1980s, and Head's Williams were among the last F1 cars to feature it. Work of the highest quality is obvious in this FW08C in 1983 (**above right**). Laffite is in the cockpit, a Brabham BT52 is being pushed past, an Alfa Romeo 183T gently smokes behind it. Carbon fibre moulded monocoques were introduced in Barnard's MP4/1 McLarens in 1981. This is the very slender monocoque of a 1987 MP4/3 (**right**). Without bodywork the cockpit looks very open.

Regazzoni with Ferrari's chief engineer Mauro Forghieri at Monza in 1976. The neat engine air intakes and ducting alongside the cockpit were a feature of the well-balanced 312T2, and another was the smooth low engine deck (made possible by the flat-12) which contributed to a clean airflow to the rear wing.

The slogan 'watching in the comfort of your own . . .' hardly applies, but drivers no longer look to the man with the clip board – they can keep in touch with rivals' practice times through a small screen. Berger is doing that in a Ferrari F1/87. A small upright was once a feature of a low sprint car's nose, to ensure that a timing beam was broken, but nowadays one or two aerials sprout from GP cars, usually one for driver communication and perhaps one for engine and systems telemetry.

March returned to Grand Prix racing in 1987, with the straightforward 871 (**top**), the talented Ivan Capelli, and adequate backing from the Leyton House group, which was to take over completely two years later. The car's colours might not have been to everybody's taste, and a car with an exposed DFZ brought a homely touch to Formula 1. But at the end of the year there was a Championship point to show for effort.

After a season out of racing, Brabham (**above**) returned in 1989, which turned out to be a year fraught with off-track problems for the team. But its BT58s looked as smart as any Brabhams in the 1980s, and in racing were by no means unsuccessful.

This turned out to be quite conventional, with an aluminium monocoque, double wishbone front suspension, and top links, parallel lower links and radius arms at the rear, and outboard coil springs/dampers. A BMW engine drove through a Hewland FG400. Together with the F2 Kojima, the 512 was a match for most locally-owned European cars in JAF racing. Takahara used the second 512 to win the 1976 Japanese Drivers' Championship, and in 1977 the title was won by Hoshino, who drove a Heros Racing 512B. (Lotus F1 driver of the future, Nakajima, was third, racing a Nova in his first F2 season.)

That year the 522 had made little impression, unlike the 1978 532P. This had a similar specification and Matsuura BMW engines were used. The 532P lived up to the 512 record in Japanese racing, and Hoshino started in two 1978 European Championship races in a Heros 532P, retiring at Rouen and Donington. Then Heros, Hoshino, Nakajima and seemingly everybody else involved in racing at this level in Japan turned to March.

Formula 3 Nova's F3 effort is recalled for Nakajima's brief European foray with an adapted FH1300 car in 1978 and especially for a destructive start accident at the British GP meeting. This 513 was a conventional car, with a Toyota engine in its F3 guise.

Satoru Nakajima during his short European campaign with the unobtrusive little Nova 513.

O

OBM

A sports BMW 328 converted into an offset single-seater F2 car by Oscar Moore in 1948. He raced it with some success in secondary Continental events, notably placing it third in the 2-litre class of the 1949 GP des Frontières and fifth in the 1950 Luxembourg GP.

OCELOT

Ocelot Engineering of Washington DC responded to the first flush of enthusiasm for Formula Junior with a car that outwardly followed 1958-9 convention, in that it had a front-mounted engine in a tubular frame. However, the engine was a linered Peugeot 203 unit and it drove through a Chevrolet four-speed gearbox, while the torsion bar front suspension derived from a Morris Minor and there was a wishbone and Watts linkage arrangement at the rear. Perhaps it is not surprising that there is no record of Ocelot racing success.

ONYX

Mike Earle entered racing in the mid-1960s and soon became a highly respected team manager, running the F5000 Church Farm team, the Pygmée F2 team for a year, David Purley's Lec ventures and some lesser teams before he set up Onyx Race Engineering in 1979. With this he maintained his standing, most notably running the March F2 and F3000 factory teams through five successful seasons from 1983. In 1987 his F1 plans began to take shape, and in 1988 Paul Shakespeare backed this project, then early in 1989 Van Rossem's Moneytron financial company acquired the major shareholding and the team became Moneytron Onyx.

As its first F1 season got under way (hesitantly) Onyx moved from its long-established base at Littlehampton to more spacious premises at Fontwell. Relations between Moneytron boss J.P. Van Rossem and the Onyx partners Mike Earle and Joe Chamberlain quickly became strained and Earle and Chamberlain left the company in December 1989. Within weeks, Van Rossem pulled out, after the arrangement he felt he had with Porsche fell through, but the team was bought by the Swiss, Peter Monteverdi, once a constructor as MBM.

While it followed 1989 F1 lines, ORE-1 had a deeper nose and neatly-sculpted flanks. The colour scheme was predominantly blue, with a broad pink-edged white lateral stripe and a sign of Earle's continuing Marlboro association. The driver is Gachot, at Monaco.

ORE-1 Onyx designer Alan Jenkins had a background with Project 4/McLaren and Penske, and his first design for the new marque was a clean, conventional, late-1980s car. A carbon fibre and aluminium honeycomb monocoque was used, with pushrod inboard suspension all round. Cosworth DFR engines prepared by Brian Hart drove through Onyx/Xtrac six-speed transverse gearboxes. The season was not easy for teams with 'customer' eight-cylinder engines, and the car was not quickly sorted out. But once it was raceworthy, Johansson and/or Gachot started to pre-qualify fairly regularly, and once over that hurdle to qualify for grids. Johansson scored the team's first points when he finished fifth in the 1989 French GP, and he was third in the Portugese GP. Gachot apparently criticized the team and sponsor too loudly, and was replaced. Necessarily, the cars had to be used again early in 1990.

Drivers: Bertrand Gachot, Stefan Johansson, J.J. Lehto.

ORCA

Le Mans-based ORCA announced its conventional Toyota-engined F3 B301 for 1979, when nothing came of the enterprise.

OSCA

Three of the surviving Maserati brothers, Ernesto, Ettore and Bindo, sold the original Maserati company in 1937 but were retained on a ten-year service contract. When that expired in 1947, they set up as independent constructors again at San Lazzaro di Savena on the outskirts of Bologna. Officine Specializate Costruzioni Automobili Fratelli Maserati was known as OSCA Maserati, and soon as Osca. It specialized in small sports cars, but also produced a few single-seaters. These were generally ineffectual, although Colin Davis did drive an Osca when he won the Italian Formula Junior Championship in 1960. Two years later the brothers, then advanced in years, sold out to MV.

4.5-litre Osca's shaky entry into the single-seater business was with an engine initially intended to uprate the supercharged 1.5-litre Maserati 4CLT/48, which was no longer competitive. 'Uprating' was largely confined to offering an unsupercharged V-12 (78 x 78mm, 4472cc) which owed a lot to an abortive Gordini project. (Gordini had an option to use the engine for his own cars.) In 1951 it was rated at 300bhp,

Bira pushing the Osca-engined Maserati hard at Goodwood in 1951. Outwardly, the Osca nose considerably changed the Maserati lines.

but the only taker for a 4CLT conversion was Bira, who won a short Goodwood race with a car best described as a 'Maserati-Osca'. A new 4.5-litre Osca was completed later in 1951 with a more up to date chassis/suspension specification. It appeared in the Italian GP, when Franco Rol's best lap in it was some 14 seconds slower than Farina's fastest race lap. Later it was converted into a sports car.

Drivers: B. Bira, Franco Rol.

2-litre Adapted sports Oscas were run in F2 in the early 1950s, and when this became the Championship category in 1952 it offered the brothers a real chance to get back into the big time. They came up with a workmanlike car with an oversquare straight six (76 x 73mm, 1987cc) for which an output of more than 150bhp was claimed. The car was wholly orthodox, with double wishbone/coil spring front suspension and a de Dion rear end, at first with inboard rear brakes.

One was run by Elie Bayol in 1952, and he was joined by Louis Chiron in 1953. Both put in respectable performances, but both were handicapped as independents and the cars were no match for the dominant Ferraris. Bayol did win two secondary French races in 1953.

Veteran Louis Chiron in the 1953 French Grand Prix.

1.5-litre In 1957 the brothers slowly developed another F2 car, which in most respects was an adaptation of their sports-racers but had a four-cylinder engine (78 x 75mm, 1490cc) boasting desmodromic valve gear. Alessandro de Tomaso bought the car, which never started in a race, but when he built some F1 cars in 1961 the Osca engine was one of two specified power units.

An Osca Junior with a Scuderia Serenissima badge, at Monaco in 1960. The offset of the cockpit is obvious, the lines are clean, there are even little bonnet straps. The 1960 Monaco FJ race was totally dominated by rear-engined cars.

Formula Junior
The last single-seater Osca was also the most successful, in that Colin Davis used one ('in tandem' with a Taraschi) to win the Italian Championship in 1960 and several were sold in Italy and the USA. It was a handsome little car in a totally 'traditional' fashion – ladder frame, ifs and live rear axle, with front-mounted Fiat engine, transmission offset to the left, cockpit offset to the right – but by 1960 that line of development was at a dead end.

OSCAR

Oscar was a minor Japanese constructor in the 1980s, moving to the fringes of success with the conventional Toyota-engined SK86F F3 car in 1986, when Hideo Fukuyama won an All-Japan Championship race at Tsukuba.

OSELLA

Enzo Osella, a one-time sports car driver, became directly involved with the Abarth sports-racing car effort in the late 1960s, running the Abarth-Osella team (effectively the Abarth works team) from 1969. As Abarth was absorbed by Fiat, Osella continued with the sports-racers under his own name, but even in Italy these had a limited future and he looked to single-seaters to maintain his racing car operation at Volpiano near Turin.

The 2-litre F2 was an obvious category to move into: it was close to Osella's experience in aspects such as car performance, and some of the changes, such as a switch to BMW engines, could be carried through in parallel with the development of the last sports-racers. The first F2 FA appeared late in 1974, and looked promising. Francia did score 16 points in the 1975 European F2 championship, when the FA2/75 was fast but fragile, but Migault was the only driver to score in an Osella in 1976, and then only a single point. The team came close to disintegration, and was to stay away for two seasons. The hoped-for sales of the F2 car had not materialized, and an F3 FA was a sideline. An Osella team returned to the F2 Championship in 1979, when Eddie Cheever won three races – Osella's only single-seater race victories.

By that time Osella was heading towards F1, entering a single car in 1980. Although its equipment was not the best it stayed in the Grands Prix through the decade, scoring just seven Constructors' Championship points in 130 races. Why persist? There cannot have been commercial justification, but to Osella's credit that was not the be-all; there was satisfaction and pride in just being there.

Late in 1989 the team was under-pinned as its principal sponsor from that season, Fondmetal, acquired a majority shareholding.

FA2/75-76 The FA2 designation was applied to all the F2 cars, the first appearing in the final race of 1974, when Merzario drove it at Vallelunga. It was a conventional and economical monocoque design by Osella and Tomaini, with suspension on contemporary March lines. At first it had smooth but rather bulbous bodywork, especially around the engine bay, and a March-like full-width nose. The cockpit surround and engine cover were more slender in 1976, with a needle nose and full-width wing. BMW works engines were used in 1975-6, and some Schnitzer BMW engines in 1976.

While 1975 had seen progress with two cars, four works cars were run in the opening 1976 races, an 'Italian pair' and cars for Hans Binder and François Migault. That year there were balance and handling problems from the start, there were too many DNQs and by the early summer the outfit was falling apart. In June there was just one works car around, for Migault, and he was gone by the autumn when Merzario was back again. One Charly Kiser made the odd ineffectual appearance in an FA2/76.

FA2/75, when the F2 Osella showed promise, although the lines of the car were not distinguished. The driver is Giorgio Francia.

FA2/76 marked Osella's low point in F2, although this version of the car looked neat and suited to its purpose. François Migault is the driver.

FA2/79 A lay off was only sensible, then late in 1978 FA2/79 started tests. Basically this was the old design reworked as a wing car by Giorgio Stirano. It was lighter and sleeker, had Osella's effective short-stroke BMW engine, and Pirelli radials. As the season went on a new and stiffer monocoque was introduced, as was inboard front suspension, and more weight was shed. This was the successful F2 Osella – Cheever's win in the first race of the 1979 Championship season was the first for an Italian car in F2 since the Tecno's days and as well as that Silverstone victory he won at Pau and Zandvoort.

FA2/79, the Osella that won, although Cheever looks less than confident in this pre-1979 season publicity shot. From this point of view the most notable change during the season came as the front suspension coil spring/damper units were moved inboard.

FA1A Launched at the end of 1979, this first F1 Osella was a wing car designed by technical director Stirano, with the FA1 designation that was to be carried by F1 cars through the 1980s. Its monocoque took the form of a tubular frame with stressed aluminium skins, suspension was by upper arms, lower wishbones and inboard coil spring/damper units, and a DFV engine drove through a Hewland FGB gearbox. The car looked bulky, and it was overweight by some 45kg. Cheever recorded four DNQs and seven retirements (in eleven GPS) before FA1B was introduced.

Driver: Eddie Cheever.

Eddie Cheever and Enzo Osella with the first FA1A. It was sometimes run without nose aerofoils, and with an oil cooler under the rear wing.

FA1B Giorgio Valentini and Osella laid out this car, which first appeared in the 1980 Italian GP, when Cheever was twelfth to record the team's only finish in its first GP season. It was lighter than the first car, with a monocoque of conventional construction, stiffened with carbon fibre and slimmer to allow for more generous side pods (and a claimed five per cent increase in downforce). The suspension was revised and the DFV/FGB combination retained.

Three more were built for 1981, when Osella started the season with a rent-a-drive pair and then called on the experienced Jarier in order to get some results on the board. He obliged with three good finishes to set against one retirement before the FA1C became available. Overall results were desperately unimpressive: 17 DNQs, 5 retirements, 4 finishes. On top of that there were sponsorship problems.

Drivers: Giorgio Francia, Beppe Gabbiani, Piercarlo Ghinzani, Miguel-Angel Guerra, Jean-Pierre Jarier.

The FA1B looked even bulkier than its predecessor. This pre-season group with the first car is made up of Gabbiani and Guerra, and the designer and patron.

FA1C Following precedent, a new car was introduced for the Italian GP and it was used through most of the following season. Giorgio Valentini designed it around an aluminium sheet/honeycomb monocoque, with the suspension layout of the earlier cars but a very short (104in/264cm) wheelbase.

Osella scored points in 1982, but Jarier's fourth place at Imola was next to last as only 5 of the 14 starters were running at the end of that San Marino GP. Then his team mate, F1 novice Riccardo Paletti, died in a Canadian GP start accident and for the rest of the year a single car was run, Jarier finishing only once more.

Drivers: Jean-Pierre Jarier, Riccardo Paletti.

FA1C looked broad around the cockpit for a wing car. It seemed well suited to a street circuit at Long Beach, where Jarier (driving here) qualified tenth, but then he failed to qualify at Monaco.

FA1D An uprated FA1C introduced in the summer of 1982 was referred to as FA1D, and was further modified by Peirotta for the first races under flat bottom regulations until FA1E was built. This was the last DFV-powered Osella, and one was converted to become the first Alfa-powered FA1E.

Drivers: Corrado Fabi, Piercarlo Ghinzani.

FA1E The converted FA1D with the Alfa Romeo 1260 V-12 was first raced at Imola in 1983, and it was soon followed by the FA1Es. Designed by Tony Southgate, these had tubs built by Auto Racing Technology, slender sheet-aluminium jobs with carbon tops. Double wishbone pushrod front suspension was used, with a top rocker arm and lower wishbone arrangement at the rear and inboard coil spring/damper units all round. The Alfa engine drove through an Alfa gearbox. It was all to little avail – the Alfa-engined cars finished three times (from 19 entries) in 1983 and one appeared, ineffectually, at Imola in 1984.

Drivers: Corrado Fabi, Jo Gartner, Piercarlo Ghinzani.

The first Alfa-engined Osella. The definitive FA1E had a more slender nose and the upper front suspension members were not shrouded, while there were twin air intakes on the engine deck. The rear-mounted radiator pods were retained. The driver in this shot is Ghinzani.

FA1F The association with Alfa Romeo continued in 1984, and to help Osella into the turbo era an Alfa 183T was made available and modified as the first FA1F for the opening races of the year. However, the team gave the first event a miss and the car was destroyed at Kyalami in practice for the second.

The design of Osella's own FA1F was simply credited to 'Osella'. The car had double wishbone suspension all round, pullrod at the front, pushrod at the rear, with a conventional monocoque chassis and the Alfa turbo engine and gearbox combination. Outwardly it was another short-nosed car, with radiator pods running from the line of the back of the cockpit with very prominent top air outlets.

Its debut came at the Belgian GP meeting, and two were available from the early summer. Both drivers qualified regularly and each scored a fifth place (Ghinzani at Dallas, Gartner at Monza) to give Osella its best Championship season – tenth on the 1984 Constructors' table. An FA1F was brought out again for the single-car team early in 1985, and as the second car for the two-car team in 1986, Ghinzani and Berg each finishing one race in it.

Drivers: Allen Berg, Jo Gartner, Piercarlo Ghinzani.

There was little distinctive about the mid-1980s Osellas, save that the FA1Fs finished races in points-scoring positions. This is Gartner in a brand-new car at Brands Hatch in 1984.

FA1G This was a derivative, lighter, with a smaller carbon fibre monocoque, pushrod suspension all round, cleaner Kevlar bodywork and the 1985 Alfa turbo engine driving through a Hewland-based Osella-developed five-speed gearbox. It was generally a back-of-the-grid car. Ghinzani returned for seven races, then Rothengatter took his place and managed the best Osella finish of the season – seventh out of eight classified cars in the Australian GP. The FA1G was used by three drivers in 1986, Ghinzani finishing just one race in it, and was used five times in 1987.

Drivers: Allen Berg, Alex Caffi, Christian Danner, Franco Forini, Piercarlo Ghinzani, Huub Rothengatter, Gabriele Tarquini.

The lines of the FA1G show largely evolutionary changes, with the side pods back to full length and smoother bodywork behind the cockpit. This is Ghinzani warming up at Silverstone in 1985.

FA1H First seen incomplete at the 1986 San Marino GP; complete for the Belgian GP but not raceworthy; raced in the French GP and crashed in the British GP and not seen again, although design work was in large part carried over to the 'I'. It had improved bodywork, revised pushrod front/pullrod rear suspension, the Alfa turbo rather than the anticipated Motori Moderni engine, and a Hewland DGB gearbox. In its two race practice outings it showed no sign of being competitive.

Driver: Piercarlo Ghinzani.

FA1I In most respects this was the H revived and also attributed to Petrotta, with revised suspension and aerodynamics, Alfa engine and Hewland gearbox. Through the 1987 season minor modifications were made to suspension and aerodynamics, while towards the end of the year small changes were tried with a view to 1988. Caffi managed one finish from twelve starts in this car. In 1988 it came out once, when Larini failed to qualify it.

Driver: Alex Caffi.

The number of small sponsors underlines Osella's habitual shoestring operation, as Larini attempts to qualify FA1I in Brazil in 1988.

FA1-M89 There was sponsorship for Osella to run two cars again in 1989, the unrewarding seasons with Alfa engines were history and Antonio Tomaini designed a car that in appearance and specification made up lost ground. FA1-M89 had a fashionably slim carbon fibre monocoque, with pullrod double wishbone suspension front and rear, Mader-prepared Ford DFR engine and longitudinal Hewland DGB400 gearbox.

Unlike its predecessors, this car promised well, and Larini did run as high as third with an Osella in one race. But he was classified a finisher only once (at Imola) and seven times failed to pre-qualify; Ghinzani contributed 13 failures to that dismal score, and his race achievements in his last season amounted to three retirements. Osella had little to celebrate at the end of a decade.

Drivers: Piercarlo Ghinzani, Nicola Larini.

FA1-M89 had a slender nose, short side pods and a high engine cover. The driver is the talented Larini, at Silverstone.

P

PALLISER

This south-west London based constructor had a brief existence, with its first production car appearing in 1968 and the little plant closing early in 1972. Its cars carried a WD plus category designation – W being designer Len Wimhurst and D being patron Hugh Dibley (an airline pilot and sports car racer). A Formula Atlantic car (which never did appear in the alternative F2 form suggested) was followed by successful Formula Ford models before the Palliser F3 car made its debut at Silverstone in April 1970.

This WDF3 was a neat and conventional space frame car, and as was common practice among small-scale constructors at the time the space frame was contracted out, to Arch Motors. A Broadspeed engine was used for the first race, but Manctilow and Ehrlich prepared engines were later used in WDF3/1. Roger Keele was the regular driver and his best finish was fourth in an Oulton Park race.

A second WDF3 was run in 1971, both cars initially with BRM engines. A few top-six places fell to the Palliser drivers (Lawrence and Lamplough) despite handling and engine shortcomings. In 1972 Damien Magee showed the potential of the car, racing WDF3/2 with minor modifications and a Novamotor engine and taking early-season second places at Brands Hatch and Oulton Park. But with Palliser Racing Design no longer in business the car rapidly became obsolescent. The Palliser name fleetingly re-appeared in the mid-1970s, and Len Wimhurst designed the LRL376 F3 car for 1976, but nothing came of this.

WDF3 was a clean-lined car, with a broader cross-section at the cockpit than most of its contemporaries. This is the first car, at Brands Hatch in the summer of 1971.

PARKER SPECIAL

Don Parker won more British 500cc races than anyone else – he was a good driver and a very small man whose cars could be made smaller and lighter than most. His Parker Special was built for him by Charlie Smith, the designer of the CFS, and followed Cooper lines, although it had wire wheels and was much lighter than production Coopers. Some idea of the advantage his all-up power/weight ratio gave him can be gauged by the fact that at the 1949 Brighton Speed Trials with a JAP engine in his car he was 2.47 seconds quicker than a Cooper-Norton with an engine tuned by Francis Beart.

In 1952-5 Parker drove a works Kieft, but this more properly might be considered a Parker Special as Don lightened and assembled a kit of parts with the assistance of Ray Martin, the original designer, because Kiefts were notoriously badly made.   ML

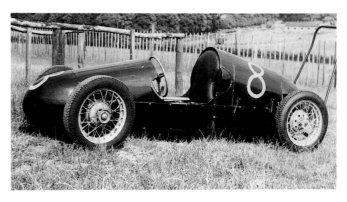

The Parker Special had more solid looks than most 500cc one-offs, and in 1951 (when it was photographed at Brands Hatch) its wire wheels did not look out of place.

PARNELL

Reg Parnell (Racing) commissioned an F1 car design on Lotus 25 lines from Les Redmond in 1963 but the team acquired three of the Team Lotus 25s in 1964 and dropped the project (components already prepared were used in a sports-racing car).

In 1967 a Lotus 33 modified by Tim Parnell was run as a Parnell in three F2 races. It had an FVA engine and Hewland HD5 gearbox. Mike Spence got it through to the end of one race, finishing ninth at Silverstone.

PARNELLI

Velco Miletich and former leading USAC driver Rufus Parnelli Jones set up Vel's Parnelli Jones Racing with Firestone backing in 1969, initially to contest USAC events, then Formula A (F5000) before moving on to F1 in 1974. For this programme VPJ contracted several prominent Team Lotus personnel, including designer Maurice Phillippe. He laid out a car on Lotus 72 lines, with an overall wedge shape, hip radiators, torsion bar suspension, inboard brakes front and rear and the familiar Cosworth/Hewland engine/transmission combination.

Designated VPJ4 – the first three cars were for USAC racing – this attractive car made its debut in the 1974 Canadian GP, when Andretti placed it seventh. After this encouraging start

This shot of Andretti during practice for the 1974 United States GP shows off the 'Lotus 72' lines of the VPJ4, with the nicely-angled hip radiators an improvement on that source of inspiration.

Firestone's withdrawal at the end of the year was a major setback. Jones lost interest in F1, leaving Miletich, and, increasingly, Andretti to carry the team. In 1975 Andretti started in twelve championship races, led the Spanish GP before retiring, and finished fourth in Sweden.

Little development work was undertaken through the season, but towards the end of the year the design was revised with coil springs and outboard brakes. Further refinement, with sleeker bodywork above and alongside the engine, led to the re-designation VPJ4B for 1976. After just two races the Vel's Parnelli Jones team was wound up.

The broad flat upper surface of the wedge nose, ducting for the outboard front brakes and sleeker lines towards the rear of the 'B' are features in this 1976 Kyalami pits shot.

PARSENN

Designed by Keith Steadman for Jeremy Fry (brother of Joe) in 1949, the Parsenn was the lightest 500 of its day. Its space frame was made up of narrow steel tubing which ended behind the cockpit, and a separate sub frame took the engine and gearbox. Suspension was independent all round by rubber, bushes in torsion at the front, while the swing axle rear was by rubber rings in compression. Looking like a miniature Auto Union, this JAP-engined car spent most of its life on the hills and in sprints, where it was often a class winner, and it went pretty well in its odd circuit races as well.

ML

PEARCE

London motor trader and accessory dealer John Pearce devised a Ferrari-engined Cooper special in 1966 and ran it in two GPs. Chris Lawrence placed it eleventh and last in the British race and retired in Germany. Pearce was then encouraged to undertake a new car for 1967. Three were built,

appearing as unprepossessing space frame cars; one was intended for the Ferrari V-12, while two were built for the light-alloy Martin V-8. This engine had been race-tested in an F2 Lotus, and early in 1967 was run in the first Pearce chassis, which was to be damaged in a Brands Hatch test accident. The three Pearce cars were entered for the Silverstone International Trophy, but were destroyed in a fire at the circuit two days before practice.

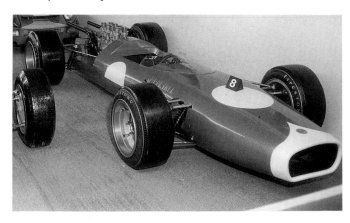

The first Pearce was exhibited at the 1967 Racing Car Show, with a Martin V-8 installed but apparently incomplete as the cigar fuselage seemingly has no provision for a roll-over bar to be fitted, and it was perhaps expedient to fit similar-sized wheels all round.

PETTY

Created by Norton tuning specialist Ray Petty, this handsome 500 car first appeared at the 1955 Boxing Day Brands Hatch meeting in the hands of A.V. Cowley. It was a slim, neat, space frame car notable for its suspension – inboard coil springs and rocker arms at the front and a de Dion rear axle sprung by a transverse leaf spring.

Early in 1956 it was beginning to show some promise when its driver was involved in a controversial driving incident which resulted in a life ban from motor racing. Later it performed creditably in the hands of an inexperienced driver but was never able to show its true potential. ML

PILBEAM

Mike Pilbeam's first racing car was built for the 1172 clubman's category in 1959 and he designed several 1172 cars before moving on to work for constructors such as BRM and Lotus. He set up Pilbeam Racing Designs in 1975, to design and build competition cars. Some, such as the F1 Lec and the Wheatcrofts, appeared with the commissioning team's badges, some appeared as Pilbeams. All too often these seemed to be under-financed. While it followed that they may not have been adequately developed, the implication of a lack of continuity misleads to a degree, for Pilbeam had a continuing work load, ranging from hill climb and sports car designs to detail work for front-line constructors.

However, within the formulae covered by this book Pilbeam cars did appear spasmodically. The first was actually an F2 car, MP42, in 1979; that was disappointing, and short-lived, and the F3 cars of the early 1980s promised more, but they failed to establish Pilbeam as a formula racing marque.

Formula 2 A single ground effects MP42 was run by Mike Earle's Onyx team at the start of the 1979 F2 season. It followed orthodox lines, with a shallow bathtub hull, front radiators and fuel tank between cockpit and Hart engine, inboard front suspension but outboard components at the rear, and side pods that looked the part but were changed after the first race appearance. There were new car problems, as the MP42 was hardly tested before the season, and its European F2 Championship career ended after the fourth race of the year; Neve finished one race in it (15th at Hockenheim) and retired three times.

Formula 3 The first car for this category, MP44, was completed late in 1979, using the monocoque of the MP42. It ran with skirts, driven in a few British Championship races by John Bright (the Toyota engine and gearbox from his March were used). During the off-season it was modified and ran tests in narrow-track, full-width nose form. The MP45 came later in 1980, amounting to a reworked MP44. It was not raced regularly, and the backing for badly-needed development was just not available. That could be reported of MP51, which was run in late-1981 races, was distinguished by its pylon-mounted front wing, and proved over-weight and seldom competitive. It was modified for 1982, outwardly with a conventional front wing, with a Judd-developed Brabham-VW engine; further revisions in the summer of that year failed to enhance its potential.

MP44 running tests. The angular side pods look temporary, and were to be superseded by lower pods with a less pronounced wedge line.

MP51 in its 1982 form, at Oulton Park

PLW

An Italian Formula Junior car on Stanguellini lines, with a front-mounted Fiat 1100 engine and Fiat gearbox, a semi-space frame tubular chassis, ifs by wishbones and coil spring/damper units and a live rear axle with transverse leaf spring. This car from Vigerano made no impact on the crowded look-a-like scene in 1959.

POGGI

This was yet another racing car from Modena, and yet another Italian Junior that was destined to have a short life. A front-engined car, it was designed by Eugenio Poggi, with some input by Massimino (who had left Stanguellini at the beginning of 1959 as the first Poggi was about to take shape). The initials PM appeared intertwined on the nose of the car, and it was sometimes known as the PM-Poggi. Contemporaries also referred to it as a Tec-Mec.

The car had a tubular frame, unequal-length wishbone ifs and a live rear axle with the unusual feature of cantilever quarter-elliptical springs. The rest was conventional, with Fiat 1100 engine and Fiat gearbox. The first car appeared in the Spring of 1959, the last of a handful built came out a year later.

Borrani knock-on wire wheels seem very appropriate to this handsome little car, anachronistic though it was in 1960 when this photograph, of one of the Ecurie Vienne cars, was taken.

POLITOYS

This was the first Williams, the FX3 appearing here as it was entered for its two 1972 races as a Politoys. It was a straightforward DFV-powered car, with a monocoque on 'Coke-bottle' lines and conventional suspension. It was designed by Len Bailey for 1971, but Williams' then-customary shortage of funds meant that it was not completed until 1972, when it was to be raced alongside the team's March cars. While it was still a Politoys the design was worked over by Ron Tauranac. It finally appeared for the British GP, when Pescarolo grappled with handling problems before crashing (something apparently broke, but as the Frenchman seemed crash-happy that year dark thoughts were inevitable!). FX3

The dark blue Politoys was not a distinguished car, in appearance or performance. Nevertheless, Chris Amon is obviously pushing it hard at Brands Hatch in the 1972 John Player Challenge Trophy race.

reappeared at the end of the season, when Amon retired it from a non-Championship race.

This car, and a new one, came out again in 1973 as an Iso-Marlboro (see also Iso-Marlboro); that year an FX3B also appeared.

Drivers (GP): Nanni Galli, Howden Ganley, Henri Pescarolo, Jackie Pretorius.

PORSCHE

Porsche's racing reputation has been built on years of sports and sports-racing successes and on the F1 engine, commissioned by TAG and discreetly labelled 'Made by Porsche', that powered McLarens to 26 race victories in the mid-1980s. The company's own ventures into the principal single-seater categories have been less successful. In the background, the first Auto Unions of the 1930s were Porsche designs and carried the design studio number 22, while the advanced Cisitalia GP project of the late 1940s was *Typ 360*.

In the 1950s 'central-seat' RSKs appeared in F2, and there were several independent efforts with adapted sports cars or using Porsche components. Outstanding among these was Jean Behra's conversion of an RSK, carried out for him in Modena in 1959. He was never able to race it because of conflicting contracts before he died at the wheel of a 'proper' RSK but other drivers achieved good results with it. Porsche engines were used in cars such as Pete Lovely's 'Pooper', which was very competitive in US racing. Otto Mathé's open-wheeler was successful in ice races and an independent Indianapolis creation used one 901 flat six ahead of its driver and another 901 engine behind him, but that was not remotely competitive. The factory had entered F2 in 1957 with 550As, and the full-width sports bodies were actually an advantage on fast circuits.

In main-line terms, Porsche entered open-wheel F2 cars successfully in the late 1950s, entered F1 less successfully in the early 1960s, and in the 1980s succumbed to the lure of Indycar racing.

718/2 and 787 The first single-seater built as such was little more than an open-wheel RSK (or 718), with the air-cooled flat four (85 x 66mm, 1498cc). Five more, slightly modified, were built for 1960, when a works team was run and a car made available to the prominent independent entrant Rob Walker. Largely thanks to Stirling Moss, Porsche won the F2 championship that year, and the German GP, run for F2 cars only on the rarely-used Nürburgring *Sudschleife*, fell to Bonnier in a Porsche.

These cars were, of course, Grand Prix cars as the 1.5-litre regulations came in 1961, and were used through that season, alongside the closely-similar 787 derivative which was hardly an improvement and was set aside. In 1962 the 718/2s were sold to independents, notably Dutch driver Carel Godin de Beaufort, who scored Championship points but died at the wheel of his 718 in a 1964 German GP accident.

Best placings were Gurney's runner-up finishes in the 1961 French, Italian and American GPs, and Porsche ended the year third in the Constructors' Championship.

A 1962 development 787 with an engine reworked by Michael May was not followed through.

Drivers (F1 events): Edgar Barth, Jo Bonnier, Carel Godin de Beaufort, Dan Gurney, Ludwig Heimrath, Hans Herrmann, Ben Pon, Heinz Schiller, Wolfgang Seidel, Nino Vaccarella, Heini Walter.

804 If Porsche was to stay in GP racing, a car designed for the job was obviously needed. The *Typ 904* was a space frame car, low and sleek compared with its predecessors, with suspension front and rear by twin wishbones and longitudinal torsion bars. Porsche was not then ready to abandon air cooling, so the 1492cc (66 × 54.5mm) *Typ 753* flat eight engine designed by Honich and Mezger was surmounted by a familiar plastic fan. These cars actually had disc brakes – despite its reputation for innovation, Porsche was the last firm to use drum brakes in F1.

The team seldom challenged the dominant British teams in 1962, but Dan Gurney did win the French GP. He was lucky, as cars ahead of him dropped out. At the end of the year Ferry Porsche decided that F1 was too costly and that success could be found more easily and less expensively in sports car fields where the competition was not so intense.

Driver: Jo Bonnier, Dan Gurney.

Lanky Dan Gurney protruding out of the otherwise low and sleek 804, in the 1962 German GP.

PRA

Although no competition history is known for this 1953 British 500 car designed by C. Preston, it was interesting in that it was built along the lines of a pre-War Mercedes-Benz. It had a tubular frame in the front of which was mounted an sohc Norton engine which, uniquely for a British 500, drove to the rear wheels via a shaft. Like the Mercedes W163, front suspension was by coil springs and wishbones, a de Dion rear axle was used and, like its inspiration, it had wire wheels. The car still exists.   ML

The car's homely appearance is well shown in this shot of Dan Gurney driving 718/2-03 out of the Watkins Glen pits road for the 1961 US Grand Prix, when he was to finish second.

PROJECT FOUR

This was Ron Dennis' Marlboro-backed F2 team in the late 1970s and 1980, when it was to be run down in favour of an F1 programme for which a design was commissioned. This was conceived around a carbon fibre monocoque by John Barnard, and this novel tub was to be made by an American specialist. Before design work was finished Project Four merged with McLaren.

PROMOT

An F3 one-off built towards the end of the period when Eastern bloc motor sport authorities admitted this formula. A Wartburg-engined car, it was raced in 1970 by Kris Frank.

PROTOS

This highly original F2 design was commissioned for the Ron Harris team, in part at the instigation of driver/engineer Brian Hart, who had been impressed by Frank Costin's aerodynamic work. In the Protos, Costin followed his penchant for timber construction, using a bonded plywood monocoque, with metal bulkheads and a tubular sub frame to carry the FVA engine, while wooden ribs on the flanks contained the fuel tanks and supported the outer skin. The lines were very slippery, and aerodynamic refinement was carried through to front suspension members and the distinctive cockpit screen. Suspension comprised lower wishbones, raked fabricated upper arms and inboard coil springs/dampers at the front, while at the rear there were conventional lower wishbones with parallel upper transverse rods and radius arms. The car was overweight and the ground clearance was too high, but in its only season, 1967, it was competitive on fast circuits (its best placing was a second at Hockenheim). In a major accident, it proved admirably crash-resistant.

One of the three Protos built survives as a museum exhibit, another privately. Its distinctive and sleek lines show well from this angle, as does the 'screen which was part-way to a bubble cockpit cover.

PSW

P. Scorch built this odd-looking German 500cc car, which resembled nothing so much as a 1920s GN although it did have all-independent suspension by transverse leaf springs. A reversed water-cooled DKW two-stroke engine was mounted at the back and drove through a normal front wheel drive unit.

PUMA

Alan McKechnie's team undertook construction of an ingenious F3 car designed by Tony Hilder around a full monocoque chassis in Mallite (the light alloy/balsa wood sandwich used by Herd in McLaren's 1966 F1 car) with torsion bar suspension, which was to be at the root of some acrimony in the team. Although construction started in 1969 it did not appear on the circuits until 1971, showing some promise in Bob Evans' hands before a test accident apparently put an end to it (Evans was put out of racing only briefly).

However, the car, or maybe another car – that depends on how many new blades are joined to new handles before you have a new shovel – was built up with a BDA engine and a spare tub for the Rothmans 50,000 formule libre event at Brands Hatch in 1972. Best regarded as a Formula Atlantic car and sometimes given the designation HM23, it failed to come to the grid. It next appeared as the 377 F3 car for Nigel Mansell to drive his first races in that category in 1977. Team manager John Thornburn had faith in Mansell, but one suspects very little in a car that was admitted to be a lash up with revised suspension (Lola uprights, Chevron wishbones at the front and March at the rear), a March nose, a GP Metalcraft rear wing and borrowed engines. It was quick through corners, slow on straights and retired from its two races.

The Puma in its original form, Bob Evans driving in 1971.

PYGMÉE

The first Pygmée was an F3 car built by Marius Dal Bo for his son Patrick to race in 1965. Successive one-off F3 cars followed from the base at Dal Bo's Annecy heating equipment plant in 1966-7, when they were regarded as brave but under-resourced efforts, and attempts were made to get Formule France production established. In F3 the Pygmées were taken more seriously in 1968 – late that year Patrick Dal Bo scored Pygmée's first significant F3 victory, in a Montlhéry end-of-season race against strong Tecno/Matra/Brabham opposition (he had won a minor race in 1966).

The monocoque of the 1968 F3 car was carried over as the basis of an entry into F2 in 1969. An F3 programme was continued erratically through 1969-70, while priority was given to F2 and continuing efforts to market Formule France cars. The F2 programme got off to a disastrous start, and the attempt to run a four-car team in 1970 spread resources too thin, with predictable results; 1971 seemed more promising, as did 1972 when the BE Racing Team (Banting, Earle) undertook to run three strong drivers. BERT ran out of finance in mid-season, and Pygmée faded away at the end of the 1973 season. Through five muddled F2 seasons Pygmée drivers had scored just nine European Championship points.

ML

There seems to have been little or no cohesion in the early F3 programme, rather MDB one-offs with distinct 'bitza' qualities, with Brabham-type space frames or in 1967 a monocoque noted for its flexibility. Holbay engines tended to be used. The name started to appear among the top six on results sheets soon after the first car was built. Notably Dal Bo was second to Bondurant at Monza and fifth at Monthléry in the Autumn. He scored a first victory in 1966 at Opatija in Yugoslavia, (although beating opposition no more serious than a trio of East German Wartburg-powered cars), and then was second at the Sachsenring (more meritoriously Jean Sage was third in a Monthléry race). South African Trevor Blokdyk reinforced the driving side in 1967, so the Dal Bos must have been disappointed that the best result was his second at Jyllandsring, although Patrick did score in the top six as the equipe moved towards professionalism.

MDB10 One of the 1968 Pygmée F3 cars was a straight derivative of the *Formule France*/F3 space frame designs of previous years, moving further away from the Brabham inspiration. Double wishbone front suspension was retained, with top link, lower wishbone and radius arms at the rear, and outboard coil spring/damper units all round. Although Holbay engines were still used (with Hewland gearboxes), Dal Bo started his own engine development programme. Of the works pair, Offenstadt tended to drive the space frame car, and odd examples appeared in the hands of independents.

MDB11 The second 1968 F3 car was also a derivative, having a simple but more rigid aluminium bathtub monocoque and tubular engine bay, with similar suspension and engine/transmission arrangements to the space frame car. Like that machine, it suggested that Pygmée was making progress, particularly in handling. As the season wore on it became increasingly competitive, Patrick Dal Bo ventured as far afield as Zandvoort (for a fourth place) and finally won the Coupe de Salon at Monthléry.

MDB12 This car marked the 1969 move into F2. It was based on the monocoque F3 car, with similar suspension and theoretically good penetration with its low drooping nose line (the radiator was mounted on the rear axle line). FVA engines were used. Dal Bo scored a single European Championship point at Pergusa, but nothing was achieved beyond that. There were problems with handling and team morale (Offenstadt quit in mid season).

The brand-new MDB12, appearing sleek and with items such as the rear view mirrors and exhausts yet to be fitted (from this angle the latter would have hidden the oil catch tank). The team tended to run it without an engine cover.

MDB14 The 1969-70 F3 car, neglected while F2 took priority and probably not helped by the Pygmée-developed engines used when it occasionally appeared. The only top-six finish in F3 in those years was Dal Bo's sixth at La Chatre in 1969.

MDB15 Backing from Elf meant that Pygmée could run a proper works team in 1970, but the curious choice was to run four cars and Pygmée was not up to keeping that number in the field (so 'did not arrive' frequently appeared against Pygmée drivers' names in race bulletins). This car had a full monocoque, with tubular engine bay, double wishbone suspension all round with inboard coil spring/damper units at the front, longer wheelbase, sidepods with top exits, full sets of wings and sometimes Matra-like nose strakes. At the beginning of the year Pygmée FVAs were used, but Cosworth FVAs were soon substituted. Beltoise led one race, and Jabouille scored European Championship points, two of them by coincidence at Pergusa. The appalling overall record was three finishes to set against 31 failures to qualify or retirements, in addition to no-shows. In the following year Mieusset and Roussin successfully campaigned MDB15s in hill climbs.

MDB16 This first appeared as a chisel-nosed car with the cockpit surround rising above wide flat-topped fairings enshrouding the side radiators. Cooling arrangements were ineffectual, apparently for aerodynamic reasons, so after the opening F2 races of 1971 it was rebuilt with nose radiators. Dal Bo reverted to a bathtub monocoque, with front and rear sub frames, and to outboard coil spring/damper units in the otherwise similar front suspension. Two cars were run, but graded driver Beltoise did not appear at all the F2 races. There were signs of reliability, but there were no top-six finishes.

The revised MDB16 was a chunky car. The original bodywork followed the rising line of the cockpit surround, ending above the top rocker arm mount housing.

Dal Bo shows off the finer nose lines of MDB17 as he brakes for the Thruxton chicane in the team's only good 1972 race, its last good race.

MDB17 For Pygmée 1972 was the half year of BERT, when the team was to be run from an English base. The car was a sleeker development of the front-radiator MDB16. The intention was to use the Aubrey Woods-developed Amon BDA, but that was lacking in almost every respect so Pygmée developed 1.8- and 1.9-litre BDAs for the car. Pace led races, but the team's only finish was at Thruxton, when Dal Bo was fourth overall (second non-graded driver). Schafer attempted to run one of these cars in 1973.

MDB18 This was a simple update of the MDB17, and a two-car team was proposed for 1973. This hardly came to pass as Patrick Dal Bo gave up, which must have undermined the whole project, and Migault started in only a few races. The passing of Pygmée was hardly noticed.

Q

QUASAR

This minor Italian constructor built a handful of cars for 1.6-litre F3, on wholly conventional lines and with Novamotor Ford engines. The first appeared in the summer of 1971, when one of those pseudonymous drivers 'Gero' placed it fifth in two races. Two teams ran Quasars in 1972, when 'Gero' and Marazzi each had a best showing of a seventh place, but in the summer both drivers turned to Brabhams.

QUODRA

Don Philp had raced an F2 Cooper-Climax with some success in South Africa, where he was highly rated as a driver, but his Quodra was less successful. It was based on the 1960 works Cooper 'Lowline' with a space frame built by Philp (his old Cooper was cannibalised to provide parts). It ran in three of the four 1961 'temporada' races and on each occasion qualified in mid-field but failed to be classified as a finisher.

ML

R

RAF

This Italian Formula Junior car of 1961 used Lancia main components (Appia engine, for which 80bhp was claimed, and Aurelia gearbox). The engine was mounted behind the cockpit in a tubular frame, with double wishbone front suspension and lower wishbones, top links and radius arms at the rear, with torsion bar springs. Such a specification was an adventurous departure from the Italian main stream, but there seem to have been no rewards in racing success.

RAINERI

One of the 1958 crop of Italian Formula Junior cars conforming to the local pattern, with tubular chassis, Fiat independent suspension all round, Fiat 1100 engine and four-speed gearbox. The only novel offering was the option of a Goliath engine, but there is no record that this was ever taken up. Luigi Nobile had a little success with the front-engined car. By 1960 Luigi Raineri had turned to a rear-engined layout, using a Lancia engine in a space frame car but achieving no worthwhile results with it.

RAK

The enthusiastic Polish quartet behind Rak, Brun, Jankowski, Kulczynski and Przybysz, moved on from sports-racing cars to their first single-seater in 1961. This was a slender rear-engined Formula Junior car, with a tubular chassis and double wishbone suspension all round, and apparently a Triumph-based engine. It was run in local events through to 1963.

The Junior led to a more serious venture, into F3, and a small number of Rak single-seaters was built with official blessing. These were space frame cars, with double wishbone front suspension and lower wishbones with top link and radius arms at the rear. Alternative engines suggested were Ford or Wartburg based, while before he had a serious accident in 1966 Jankowski managed a couple of top-six placings in East German F3 races with a Skoda-powered Rak. After that the Rak line faded away, before the East European organizers gave up F3.

The Wartburg-engined Rak appeared low and lean even among its mid-1960s East European contemporaries, and this car at a Krakow meeting seems to be fitted with a silencer.

RALT

Ron Tauranac was attracted to motor racing in 1946, built his first competition car with his brother for his own use in local Australian events, and built another for his brother. Their initials, Ron coupled with Austin Lewis and Tauranac, gave the world Ralt. The first Ralts were not far removed from early Coopers in spirit or layout – simple tubular-framed rear-engined cars, powered by pushrod Norton engines that were progressively modified until little of the original remained. In parallel the cars were developed, and Jack Brabham gave a hand with machining while Ron Tauranac undertook some fettling work on Jack's Coopers. The two were rivals in early-1950s hill climbs but were to become firm associates.

Tauranac built more one-off Ralts in his spare time, and the fourth eventually became the basis of a production batch of Vincent-powered sprint cars. By the time they were laid down for 1959, Tauranac was ready to accept Brabham's invitiation to set up a partnership in England. The production batch was sold 'part-made' (Ron's term) to become Lynx rather than Ralt.

In England Tauranac started the Motor Racing Developments company with Brabham, as an engine preparation business. The first MRD Formula Junior car was built in 1961, and it became the first Brabham. Tauranac designed and built a string of successful Brabhams through to Jack's retirement and later took over the company before selling to Bernie Ecclestone. He designed a couple of Trojans, worked with Williams, and briefly retired.

In 1974 he re-established Ralt in a modest plant at Woking. In 1975 the first RT1 was completed. Ten were built that year; nine years later the 500th Ralt was delivered. Ralts were enormously successful in categories such as Atlantic and Super Vee, as well as in F3 and F2, where Tauranac found himself working with Honda again for the first time since the all-conquering F2 Brabham-Hondas of 1966. Although he had seen Ralt essentially as a commercial enterprise producing customer cars, he was running a works team again.

In 1988 he sold out again, to March, and this time carried on as a consultant. The Ralt design and engineering base was moved to the March Engineering Colnbrook plant in 1989. Ralt became responsible for cars for the junior formulae, leaving March to concentrate on categories such as F3000.

Through the Tauranac days the man was reflected in his Ralts, which were always down to earth and essentially practical. If a simple and low-cost component would do a job, then it was to be preferred to a complex high-cost item – a straightforward approach which is not always followed in major teams. Similarly, the base design served for the range of customer cars and, save when a change in regulations (for example requiring 'flat-bottom' cars) intervened, a design was allowed to evolve rather than made obsolescent by successors season by season.

RT1 The first 'new-generation' Ralts were F3 cars, but among the ten completed in the first year were three in Formula Atlantic form and three for F2. The basic specification was common, with an aluminium alloy monocoque, sub frame behind the cockpit, bolt-on deformable structures when these were called for, and tanks in the side sponsons varying according to purpose (on the right only in the F3 car, on both sides in F2 cars). Double wishbone suspension was used at the front, single top link with lower wishbones and twin radius arms at the rear. Outwardly a bluff full-width nose characterized the car (the Tauranac philosophy being that a hole of that size had to be punched through the air anyway), and while rear wings were usually carried on end plates some F3 cars were to have central pillar mountings.

There were other detail variations, for example with a narrower track being introduced on F3 cars for 1976, while F2 engines called for modifications usually affecting the wheelbase (BMW, Ferrari, Hart and Swindon engines were used). Through the production life of the RT1, which ran to four years and some 150 cars, there were numerous detail revisions, but the major components and hence spares were carried over from year to year.

In racing the RT1 was most familiar in F3, with Nova-Toyota engines. A first major victory was scored by Larry Perkins at Monza in June 1975; for the next two years RT1s were more common on the Continent, but in 1978 they were dominant in the British Championship. In F2, 1977 was the best season for RT1s, with Cheever and Hoffman second and seventh in BMW-engined cars in the European Championship.

Slab-sided RT1/2 driven by Larry Perkins in a Thruxton F3 race in 1975.

Three years on, Ingo Hoffman in an RT1 in F2 guise, with wider wheels helping to give the car a much more susbstantial appearance.

RT2 The 1979 F2 car was the first departure from the 1975 concept, and was an exception in the Ralt story as it was a short-life car produced exclusively for the Toleman team – Rory Byrne played a role in the build phase and after a disappointing start introduced modifications which made the car a winner (and led to the Toleman TG280 in 1980). It was a sleek ground effects car, with inboard front suspension,

RT2 in the black livery adopted part-way through the car's only season. This car had the Byrne side pods and a modified rear wing, while a spring-loaded skirt is very obvious. Rad Dougall is the driver, at Donington.

outboard rear suspension, side radiators and a central fuel tank between the cockpit and the Hart 420R engine. Byrne shaved weight, introduced new side pods and made many detail changes. Brian Henton was Championship runner-up, with two outright race wins (and another disallowed), while his team mate Rad Dougall had a Ralt for only half the season.

RT3 This car also came for the 1979 season, but its F3 career went on and on and more than 150 were sold. It was the car to beat in 1980, became almost universal in the British series and was a winner in other championships. Among drivers who won titles with it was Ayrton Senna da Silva, who was British F3 champion in 1983 – the year Pierluigi Martini won the European championship with an RT3-Alfa. Like some other Tauranac cars, however, it took a while for it to catch on, or be developed into a winner.

The RT3 was a very stiff ground effects car, with an aluminium monocoque (honeycomb bulkheads), inboard suspension all round, a central fuel tank and Hewland Mk 9 gearbox. Variations came first and foremost in engines – Toyotas then the lighter VW or Alfa units – and in modifications by teams as they sought the slightest advantage.

Ralt introduced modifications as production went on, an addition to the designation giving the year (eg RT3/81, RT3/82). A notable change was the adoption of pushrod front suspension for 1984, while FT200 gearboxes were more widely used. That year also saw the last European F3 Championship, which had comprised 130 races, 1975-84. Ralt RT1s and RT3s won 50 of them, more than any other marque.

Although the RT30 was introduced for the new 'flat-bottom' era that came in 1985, RT3s were still raced, modified by independents. A few top-six placings fell to these cars, but they were soon outclassed.

A pair of immaculate David Price Racing RT3s in 1982, with the finer noses devised by that team and nose aerofoils designed to give a cleaner airflow to the all-important side pods. These cars had John Judd VW engines, then rated at 160bhp.

RT4 An F Atlantic car but run in F2 in 1981-2 by Ray Mallock, with a BDX or Hart engine. He finished three times in five F2 starts.

RH6 The changed letter in the designation indicated the Ralt-Honda alliance for F2, and '6' was to be retained for five seasons, when three new model numbers might have been justified. The project stemmed from an approach by Honda at the beginning of 1980, the car making a less than auspicious debut in mid season. By the end of 1980 it was competitive.

Inevitably, in view of the time span, it followed RT2 lines, with a light-alloy monocoque. The engine was used as a stressed member and a Hewland FT200 was fitted. Front suspension was by top rocker arm and bottom wishbone, with inboard dampers, while top and bottom wishbones were used at the rear. For 1981 there were refinements in areas such as aerodynamics, while an enforced change from Goodyear to Pirelli had to be accepted. Setting a pattern that ran through to 1983, the RH6 was distinctly overweight.

Honda had to modify the iron-block V-6 (90 x 50.3mm, 1996cc) so that it did not interfere with the ground effects venturi. It was initially rated at 300bhp at 10,500rpm, but for 1981 330bhp at 12,000rpm was claimed, albeit with a narrow effective revs range.

In 1980 Nigel Mansell opened the Ralt-Honda scoring with a fifth place at Zandvoort, and Geoff Lees led the last race of the year. He continued with the team in 1981, and the combination came good halfway through the season – Lees won three races and was champion, while team mate Mike Thackwell won once before the setback of a severe accident.

RH6/82 was half-jokingly designated RH6H by Tauranac, as it had a honeycomb monocoque (one of the first outside F1). Its cockpit was further forward and the suspension was substantially modified, especially at the back where the track was wider and an inboard arrangement used. Bridgestone tyres were to prove a dubious asset.

In 1982 Honda had undermined the partnership by linking up with a rival team, Ralts suffered accidents early and late in the year, and all the momentum of the previous year was lost. Acheson and Palmer were sixth and ninth in the Championship. That was to be put right in the next two seasons.

RH6/83 had a slightly revised monocoque, wide front track with pullrod suspension, Michelin tyres and around 340bhp to propel Palmer and Thackwell. They were convincingly first and second in the Championship, with seven race wins (from twelve) between them.

Early RH6, in a primarily green colour scheme, driven by Mansell.

Late RH6 – a very different car, under the skin as well as in its clean lines. The blue-and-white RH6/84 dominated the last F2 season. New Zealander Mike Thackwell is the driver.

RH6/84 was further refined, revised in ground effects respects to maintain downforce under new 4cm clearance regulations (which in this case meant a wooden – rubbing – underside) and with aerodynamic appendages developed in a wind tunnel – a first in the Ralt story. The car was at last close to the 515kg mimimum weight limit, and while the V-6 was only a little more powerful it had a much wider usable power band. The team cleaned up in the last European F2 Championship season, Thackwell winning seven races and the title while his team mate Roberto Moreno was runner-up with two wins. Meanwhile, Team Ikuzawa ran an RH6/84 with some success in the Japanese F2 series, the car looking most unfamiliar as a black and gold John Player Special.

RB20 Ralt naturally entered F3000 as the category replaced F2 in 1985, and had a prototype car running during the preceding Autumn. The honeycomb chassis of the F2 car was used, together with the front suspension, while at the rear the pullrod operated coil spring/damper units were mounted horizontally on the Hewland gearbox. Judd-prepared DFV engines were used in the team cars. The 'B' designation was for Bridgestone, tyre suppliers and sponsors.

These were interim cars – the chassis was in its third season – but Mike Thackwell won four races in the twelve-race series and John Nielsen won one; the pair were second and fourth on the end-of-season points table.

RB20 was obviously a Ralt, although the red and white colours were new to the team. This car is driven by Mike Thackwell, exiting the Thruxton chicane during practice for the second race of the new formula.

RT30 With this successor to the RT3 an F3 type numbering system intended to run through to RT39 was introduced. The 'flat-bottom' regulations meant that a new design was called for, and this car was laid down with production very much in mind – Ralt had 60 orders before it was first shown early in 1985.

It followed Ralt practice in having an aluminium monocoque, with no 'exotic' composite materials (although the dash bulkhead was in honeycomb). A tubular sub frame mounted the engine, usually a VW-based unit, although odd Alfa-powered cars appeared on the Continent and TOM's Toyota began to make an impression (Morimoto won the 1986 Japanese F3 championship with a Ralt-Toyota). Pullrod suspension was used all round, with the damper at the rear atop the Hewland Mk 9 in 1985 but conventionally alongside it in the RT30/86.

The car was strikingly asymmetric. Tauranac reasoned that one radiator called for one side pod. So there it was on the left, with the required 'lateral protection panel' projecting on the right. Overall, the aerodynamics of this arrangement were proved in wind-tunnel tests.

The RT30 was the dominant F3 car of 1985-6. The important British title fell to Gugelmin in 1985, and while this went to a Reynard driver in 1986, 22 Ralt drivers scored points in that year, but only six Reynard drivers.

The immediately noticeable novelty of the RT30 was the absence of a side pod on the right, where a slim protection panel met the regulation requirements. Driver is Mauricio Gugelmin, in 1985.

RT20 Tauranac went back to a 'traditional' sheet aluminium monocoque, with very adequate stiffening bulkheads and honeycomb sections around the cockpit and fuel cell, in the 1986 F3000 car. The suspension was refined, pushrod at the front, with the coil spring/damper units mounted horizontally above the driver's legs and the 1985 pullrod arrangement at the rear.

The works RT20s were powered by Honda V-8s – a John Judd/Neil Walter design – which were reckoned to be closely similar to the DFV in bhp terms at the regulation 9000rpm maximum, but lighter. Drive was through a Hewland FT200, which also showed a useful weight saving over the FGB used in 1985, so the car was actually under the weight limit and ballast could be used to advantage. Only one race fell to a works car, scored by Mike Thackwell.

Independent teams did better with DFV-powered RT20s, notably the Pavesi team which used Mader-prepared engines. Martini and Sala both won twice, Luis Sala winning the first Birmingham Superprix in monsoon conditions. This team sometimes used its RT20s in 1987, and for the second-string drivers in 1988.

Independent RT20 – the Bromley Motorsport Judd DFV-powered car, driven by Roberto Moreno in practice at Birmingham in 1986.

RT21 Once again F3000 Ralt works cars had Honda engines – actually Judd – while the customer cars had Cosworths. The aluminium monocoque incorporated honeycomb panels between the bulkheads for rigidity, while composite materials were used in selected areas towards the same end. In the double wishbone pushrod front suspension the spring/damper units were mounted above the footbox; the pullrod layout was retained at the rear.

The works drivers often set the pace in racing, but in end-of-season points terms Moreno and Gugelmin were third and fourth, with one race win apiece.

DFV-engined RT21 on the grid at Silverstone. Pier Luigi Martini is the driver, before the only race in which the Pavesi team scored points with its 1987 Ralts.

RT31 This F3 car had features in common with the RT21, for example in the honeycomb panels on the inside of the monocoque and the spring/damper units above the driver's legs (in this case they were angled backwards). Overall the bodywork was slimmer and smoother than the RT30.

Alfa Romeo, Nissan, Toyota or VW engines could be installed. Gary Brabham modified his RT31 so that its Spiess-VW engine sat lower in the chassis (he also adopted a Staff Silent Gears 'box, in place of the usual Hewland five- or six-speed Mk 9).

In the British Championship honours were shared fairly evenly between Reynard and Ralt, but this Ralt was not outstandingly successful in other national championships. In 1989 a Brabham Racing RT31 was used for tests with the the first Mazda F3 engine.

Damon Hill and Martin Donnelly pose in the Silverstone pits lane with a TOM's Toyota-powered RT31. Its non-radiator side is again prominent.

RT22 The final season for Ralt in F3000 was very disappointing. The new car had Tauranac's first all carbon fibre monocoque and the tried suspension. Works cars had John Judd 'Honda' V-8s, while customer cars were still Cosworth-powered. Pre-season tests seemed promising, but putting the power of either engine on the road seemed to pose insuperable problems. Hence there were frequent driver changes and very few points-scoring finishes.

GEM Cosworth-powered RT22 in the 1988 International Trophy. With the engine cover in place this was an attractive car, but looks were not reflected in performance. Driver in this shot is Andy Wallace, in the last of his four drives in an RT22 before he switched to another car.

RT32 To a degree Ralt followed Gary Brabham's 1987 experiments, and the 1988 F3 car had engine mountings 30mm lower (for all four power units that might be used, the engine companies collaborating in this) and Hewland contributed a gearbox with a cast magnesium casing. The monocoque comprised an aluminium honeycomb lower section bonded and riveted to a carbon fibre composite top – more expensive, but with increased torsional rigidity and better driver protection. Pushrod suspension was used all round. In part because the Spiess VW engines needed two water radiators the RT32 appeared conventional, with twin side pods.

In racing, the Ralts again shared the honour with Reynards in the British Championship; at the top of the table Lehto (who had rather special Toyota engines) ended the season ahead of Gary Brabham (who had rather special Spiess units). Elsewhere only the Swedish championship fell to Ralt.

Gary Brabham running without an engine cover, at Brands Hatch – with it in place, the car looked much sleeker (and the sponsors got better exposure). There are vertical 'deflectors' at both ends of the short side pod.

RT33 This was a cleaner 1989 derivative of the RT32, with most attention paid to aerodynamics, especially in 'unseen' areas such as the tail and in the reprofiled side pods. One of the West Surrey Racing team cars was the first to run in England with a Mugen F3 engine, in a season when as much interest focussed on power plants as on chassis. It was also a year when Ralt regained its old ascendancy in the British F3

Championship, with McNish, David Brabham and Higgins taking the top three places with RT33s, with Mugen, VW and Mugen engines respectively. The 1989 Japanese F3 series was dominated by Mugen-powered Ralts. RT33s uprated by leading teams such as Bowman Racing proved competitive with RT34s in 1990.

RT33 was a clean-lined car, and a very effective piece of racing machinery. This car is driven by David Brabham.

RAM (GB)

John Macdonald and Mick Ralph were business partners in the early 1970s. Macdonald was manager of a group of London garages and a racing driver, in saloons and in F3 with a March, a Brabham BT38 and, in 1973, a rebuilt GRD. This was run by Ralph Macdonald Racing, the forerunner of RAM Racing, which entered F5000 in 1975, running Alan Jones in a March. That was an exemplary tight operation and its success led RAM into the Grand Prix world with a pair of Brabham BT44s, and failure. RAM returned to the Aurora British national series in 1976, then planned a move back to F1 with a March 781. That venture failed, and RAM went back to the British national series, this time running Williams FW07s, which were used in another return to F1 in 1980.

In the following year RAM brought the name March back to the Grands Prix – the only direct involvement was through Robin Herd's March engines company, not with March Engineering – and once again life was not easy as the team failed to qualify for race after race. Eventually Adrian Reynard transformed the March into a car in which a driver could at least qualify to join a GP grid. For 1983 the team built its own cars, retaining the March name for the F1 status this carried. The 1984 car was a RAM in name as well as in fact, but it brought no real change in fortunes, nor did its successor in 1985. Sponsors withdrew, potential new backers were not impressed by tests at Rio early in 1986, and the team collapsed – at a late-1985 creditors' meeting debts of more than £1m were admitted. Macdonald stayed with the sport, as a manager in minor categories, with a passing FISA management role in the World Sports-Prototype Series for 1989.

01 Known as RAM-March 01, or March-RAM 01, this was a very straightforward Cosworth DFV-powered car designed by Dave Kelly. Three were built, and several drivers struggled to qualify them. Salazar succeeded in the first GP of 1983, and finished too (15th); Acheson succeeded at the last GP, and finished (12th). Schlesser and Jacques Villeneuve failed in their two attempts. The first car was adapted to take a Hart engine for the beginning of the 1984 season, when Palmer drove it.

Drivers: Kenny Acheson, Jonathan Palmer, Eliseo Salazar.

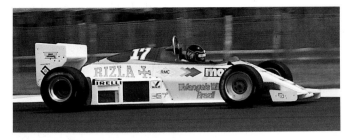

01 had convincing lines, but convincing performances were rare. This is Acheson, trying to qualify for the British GP.

02 The March name was discarded in 1984, when RAM turned to the Hart 415T for the essential turbo engine and Kelly designed another outwardly neat car for it. This was quite conventional, around a carbon-composite monocoque and with prominent side pods, but it lacked both downforce and high speed, which did not leave much to admire except the excellent preparation. A thorough test programme might have led to improvements, but RAM just did not have the resources. Matters did improve, in that the team recorded only four DNQs, but no points were scored in nine finishes.

Drivers: Philippe Alliot, Jonathan Palmer, Mike Thackwell.

At first sight this was another attractive car, but at times it was almost cumbersome. Driver is Jonathan Palmer, at Brands Hatch in his first full F1 season.

03 RAM started 1985 with a bigger budget, and in Gustav Brunner had a designer with a growing reputation. His 03 had slim lines, the monocoque also serving as bodywork, it was low and light, had pullrod suspension and had the latest Hart 740bhp engines to propel it. His staff included designer-to-be Sergio Rinland, but still the results did not come. Alliott managed only one finish in the year, and the team suffered an enormous setback when Winkelhock was killed in a sports car race after he had twice finished GPs in a RAM. Towards the end of the season the principal sponsor, Skoal Bandit, pulled out and RAM missed the last two races. An 03 was tested in a new colour scheme early in 1986 but the hoped-for Australian sponsorship deal was not finalized and so RAM slipped out of GP racing, while the very smart F3000 derivative of 03 with shorter monocoque and side pods and DFV engine appeared only spasmodically.

Drivers: Kenny Acheson, Philippe Alliot, Manfred Winkelhock.

End of the road – Alliot in the 1985 GP d'Europe, RAM's last F1 race, with the Brunner-designed 03 that turned out to be such a disappointment.

RAM (I)

Rome American Engineering essayed a Junior in that first flush of Italian enthusiasm for Lurani's formula, with a 1959 car on the Stanguellini pattern – front-mounted Fiat 1100 engine in a tubular chassis, all-round independent suspension with Fiat production origins and a Fiat gearbox. There was a slight deviation in the use of fibreglass bodywork. As its racing history is not recorded it was presumably unremarkable.

RAY

Bert Ray launched a successful line of Formula Ford cars from his South London plant in 1973 and two years later introduced an F3 car for the driver who put Ray on the map, Stephen South. Variously designated BR3 and 375, it was a monocoque car with a rear frame for the Novamotor engine, side radiators and double wishbone suspension with outboard coil spring/damper units. Its deep cockpit surround and wide-nose aerofoil mounted clear of the bodywork made it distinctive (its appearance was not improved when a large nose cone was fitted).

The 1975 racing season started well, as in the early events South placed the Ray third (at Aintree), fifth and sixth. But then the Ray slipped down qualifying and race orders. South drove a March in 1976, and, although an F376 was announced for that season, F3 turned out to be a one-off experience for Ray.

Bert Ray's F3 car was petite, but there seem to be drag-inducing elements in the airflow. The driver is South, at Thruxton.

RAYBERG

The first phase of Formula Junior encouraged many one-offs such as this car built by Aberg in 1960, and like most it was destined for club-level use. Like the Venom, also built by Aberg, the Rayberg used Cooper 500 components and had a Downton-tuned BMC engine.

RBS

An abortive F2 venture by René Berté in 1957 – he apparently got his special to Reims for the major summer meeting, but failed to get it to the start.

REALPHA

The Realpha was a slim Alfa Romeo-engined Cooper copy built in Rhodesia by Ray Reed and driven by him in the 1964 Rand GP where it was off the pace and failed to finish. Then it was entered in the 1965 South African GP three weeks later under the name 'RE' (Ray's Engineering) but failed to appear. Reed died soon afterwards in an air crash.   ML

REBAQUE

Hector Rebaque was a Mexican entrant/driver, who started in 41 Grands Prix in 1977-81. In the first two of those seasons he drove a Lotus 78 and a Lotus 79. He continued with the Ian Dawson run Lotus pair into 1979, becoming disillusioned as there was no development input and the spares position was uncertain. He commissioned the Rebaque HR100, which followed Lotus 79 lines in its monocoque and other respects, and contemporary Williams in side pods and suspension. Design work was under the control of Geoff Ferris at Penske's Poole base, where the HR100 was built (to a typically high standard). It was entered for three late-1979 Grands Prix and started only once, in Canada. Then it was set aside, as there were tyre-supply and race-entry problems, and Rebaque drove the second works Brabham in 1980-1.

Driver: Hector Rebaque.

REEVES RUDGE

An early Australian 500, built by Norman Rook but taken over by A.F. Reeves, it had a tubular frame with transverse leaf and lower wishbone front suspension, and swing axles suspended by another transverse leaf spring at the rear. Its chances were not enhanced by fitting a Rudge engine.   ML

RENAULT

Renault brought the turbocharger into road racing, and that mixed blessing apart, Renault Sport was a major force in the Grand Prix world through one of its crucial periods. The Régie never reaped full benefits from its pioneering or its vast investment, for championships never fell to the team or its drivers. However, the programme was successful in many ways, and then in the second half of the 1980s Renault turned to an approach that was sensible for a major manufacturer, becoming a supplier of a major component, its engine, to smaller and more efficient outfits.

Renault's F1 programme effectively had its origins in the Alpine-Renault sports-racing cars which were run from 1972. These were powered by the Renault-Gordini CH1 V-6, also used in F2 by Elf and Martini. A turbocharged version of this engine, the CHS, came in 1975 and was used in the single-seater A500 *Laboratoire*, built by Alpine in 1976 as a lead-in to an F1 car announced at the end of 1976. The RS01 was built at the Renault-Gordini Viry-Châtillon plant, as Alpine's activities had been wound down, and it made a less-than-momentous race debut at Silverstone in 1977.

That was, however, a development season, as to a large degree was 1978. That year there were race finishes, the first Renault Grand Prix victory since 1906 came in the French GP in 1979, and the distinctive yellow and black cars were Championship contenders in the following seasons. Somehow the final breakthrough never came. In some

respects the team was caught out by other advances, schisms took their toll and the leading driver was made a scapegoat in 1983 (Prost moved on to win a record number of Grands Prix). In 1984 most of the executives who were racing men left and a 'non-believer' was appointed Renault Sport Director.

The announcement of the team's withdrawal came in the summer of 1985, although engine development continued and the turbo unit was supplied to Lotus, Ligier and Tyrrell. Lotus was favoured with advanced versions, and won five Grands Prix with the V-6. Renault abandoned that F1 activity at the end of 1986, but picked it up again in 1989 when normally-aspirated RS01 V-10 engines were supplied to the Williams team, which won two Grands Prix with them in that first season.

The RS (Renault Sport) designation gave way to RE (Renault Elf) in 1980, as a gesture to a major sponsor. The turbo Renaults won 15 Grands Prix, from 123 races contested, but the team was never better than runner-up in the Constructors' Championship, in 1983.

RS01 In all save its engine this was a conventional car, designed by André de Cortanze around an aluminium monocoque and with attractive moulded bodywork. Suspension was orthodox, with double wishbones at the front, parallel lower links, single upper links and radius rods at the rear; coil spring damper units were inboard at the front, outboard at the rear. The EF1 engine (86 x 42.8mm, 1492cc) was developed by Bernard Dudot – the one executive who was to be a member of the team throughout its life – from the Castaing-designed sports-car CH V-6. In its initial form, the EF1 had a single Garrett turbo and was rated at 500bhp at 11,000rpm, and there were formidable over-heating and throttle lag problems to be overcome.

Its race debut came in the 1977 British GP, when it retired (it failed to finish a race that year). In 1978 development continued and only once were there problems in qualifying (in Canada, where it had failed to get onto the grid in 1977) and it finished five times (once not classified) from 14 starts. Jabouille scored Renault's first points with a fourth place in the US Grand Prix. In 1979 he was joined by Arnoux, and RS01s were used until the RS10 was ready.

Drivers: René Arnoux, Jean-Pierre Jabouille.

RS01/2 in its 1978 form. Earlier RS01s had been run with different aerofoils and nose intakes, with varied engine covers, with conventional mirrors on the cockpit surround, no bodywork around the radiators, and so on. Jabouille is the driver in this French GP shot.

RS10 Michel Tétu, previously with Ligier, was responsible for Renault's first ground effects car, longer than its predecessors with a slender monocoque typical of the wing car, and with more elegant lines ending in a large rear aerofoil. Twin KKK turbochargers were used, giving improved throttle response as well as some 520bhp to pull the big wings, and there were other detail improvements. Reliability was still elusive.

Nevertheless, a two-car team was run with some confidence, and the big breakthrough came when Jabouille won the French GP at Dijon in RS11 and Arnoux was third in RS12. Four cars were built (RS10-12 and 14).

Drivers: René Arnoux, Jean-Pierre Jabouille.

RE20 The 1980 cars were derivatives, refined in aerodynamic areas and engine ancillaries, while through the year other modifications were introduced, with much attention being paid to brakes. The team won three GPs, in Brazil, South Africa and Austria, but there were too many failures, a particular weak point being valve springs. RE20-25 were used.

The design was modified for 1981, as the RE20B. This was an interim car, on a longer wheelbase, for the first season of racing without sliding-skirt ground effects. In that the Renault team was caught out as suspension-lowering devices appeared, and the RE20B was outclassed.

Drivers: René Arnoux, Jean-Pierre Jabouille, Alain Prost.

The first 'RE' cars were distinctly longer and sleeker. Minor body variations were to appear during 1980. This was Jabouille's last full season, for after a crash in Canada he re-appeared only briefly in F1.

RE30 This was a new design – lighter, shorter, generally more compact and simpler in constructional respects – with Renault's Type 30 gearbox (using Hewland internals) and the engine still modestly rated at 540bhp. With RE30-35 the team was very competitive, winning three GPs (France, Holland and Italy), although it was still dogged by failures, with a retirement rate of more than 50 per cent.

The 'B' versions of the RE30 run in 1982 were lighter to the extent of being under the mimimum weight, and at least in the early-season races were equipped to carry water ballast. The Renault chassis was becoming outmoded, and once again the cars were unreliable (this time the fuel system was often a cause of retirements). There was a retirement rate approaching 60 per cent to set against four GP victories in the 1982 South African, Brazilian, French and Italian races.

Prost made his mark with the team and in points terms was the first Renault driver to finish the season within striking distance of the drivers' title, seven points behind the 1981 champion. The RE30's lines were much sharper.

Three were modified as 'flat-bottom' RE30Cs for the opening race of 1983, and one was also used in the second event before the 'full set' of RE40s was available. The V-6 gave up to 650bhp.

Drivers: René Arnoux, Eddie Cheever, Alain Prost.

The finer nose and lower engine deck of the RE30s are shown off in this shot of an RE30B.

RE40 This flat-bottom car was the first Renault-Elf to use a carbon fibre chassis, built by the Hurel-Dubois aerospace company. Tétu adopted pullrod suspension, aerodynamics were improved and there was an exhaust system which in conjunction with a wide 'underwing' was reckoned by some to promote ground effects (protests were dismissed – 'designed to direct high-temperature gasses away from the rear tyres' proclaimed Renault). Prost won four Grands Prix in 1983 (the French, Belgian, British and Austrian races), seemed set to win the Championship, was let down too often by the cars (turbo overheating being a culprit this time, despite water injection cooling), was made the scapegoat for failure and quit.

Drivers: Eddie Cheever, Alain Prost.

RE40 was a handsome car. The non-spill filler for the pit-stop races of the period is just behind the cockpit.

RE50 For 1984 an alloy-block version of the engine, with Garrett AiResearch turbochargers, gave 750bhp, but in that first year of fuel consumption restrictions (220 litres for a race) there were problems in that area. The new chassis had to be rethought in mid season, in particular as the front suspension pick-up points were suspect. Warwick came close to winning races, but the finishing record was as poor as ever

(12 finishes in 31 starts) and Renault slumped to fifth in the Constructors' Championship.

Drivers: Patrick Tambay, Derek Warwick.

The actual hull/engine/gearbox package of the RE50 was compact and the pullrod front suspension was clean, but the side pods and wings made for a substantial frontal area. This car is driven by Warwick.

RE60 The end of the line came in 1985 with a car designed by Tétu but built after he had left (together with another key member of the team, Gérard Larrousse). It was a little more compact, but overweight – that shortcoming was to be corrected during the year in the RE60B. The fifth RE60 was converted to that specification, and although it was supposedly a low-budget season, two new cars were built. Dudot improved the EF4 to give 760bhp while the new EF15 (80.1 x 49.4mm, 1494cc) was rated at 810bhp, or up to 1000bhp with qualifying boost. Lotus, however, made better use of Renault turbos in 1985, when the Renault team was seventh in the Constructors' Championship table. During the summer, the Régie announced that the team was to be wound up, and eight years of endeavour came to a subdued end in Australia.

Drivers: François Hesnault, Patrick Tambay, Derek Warwick.

One of the last Grand Prix Renaults, in one of the last (moderately) successful races – Patrick Tambay in RE60/4 on his way to third place in the 1985 Portugese GP. The team livery was still predominantly yellow and black, with bold white flanks and red racing numbers, but the scheme was less unified than it had been in earlier seasons.

RENNMAX

A name with a Germanic ring was chosen by Bob Britton when he built his first racing car in Sydney in 1961. He followed the dominant British school in that car and in his production models built between 1961 and 1978. As far as the international formulae are concerned, these included a handful of cars for Formula Junior, which had been introduced into Australia in 1961. The FJ car was a space frame design on Lotus 22 lines. Britton then turned to Formula Vee, Formula Ford and sports-racing cars, and built occasional ANF2 cars.

REVIS

In 1951 Reg Bicknell built himself a car on Cooper lines but with double wishbone suspension sprung by Metalastic bushes. The Revis was soon found to be overweight so Bicknell built a new, shorter frame which put the driver further forward, and at the same time changed the rear suspension to swing axles. In 1952 Bicknell and the Revis were one of the most successful combinations in British 500 racing and although he dallied, successfully, with a Staride in 1953 he returned to the Revis and continued winning. He had a very good 1954 season when the car sported a full-width nose but then he became side-tracked with a Borgward-powered sports racer which was not a success. Bicknell was a Lotus works driver for sports cars in 1956 and then he faded from the scene. ML

Bicknell with his Revis in its second form, at Snetterton in 1952.

REYNARD

Adrian Reynard has applied an outstanding talent to racing cars since the mid-1970s, not perhaps as a driver but certainly as a designer, a consultant and a constructor, yet not to the point of excluding other activities such as recreational flying.

His approach to the sport was as an aspiring driver in 1972, and he built his first car in 1973, setting up as a constructor with Bill Stone, late of March (years later, in 1982, Stone was the engineer trying to make something of March F1 cars for the hapless RAM team). Reynard Racing Cars' 1974 output was one car, in 1984 it was 151 and set to rise rapidly. By that time Rick Gorne was a co-director and former Chevron/Maurer engineer Paul Owens was production and technical manager. The company had a modern factory at Bicester, with its associate Sabre Automotive fabrications company (and incidentally, as well as the more usual dealer network, Reynard Racing Cars Inc was established in Boston, Mass.).

Reynard cars were immensely successful in Formula Ford and Formula Ford 2000, and that set the scene for the first F3 car, which was completed in February 1985. In the second half of the 1980s Reynard cars more than maintained the success record, while it grew in business terms. The first F3000 Reynard came in 1988, and won first time out, and at the end of 1989 there was an F1 car, albeit a test vehicle, which was the 1056th Reynard chassis. Meanwhile the company had built all the cars for a booming third-level class (where they carried another company's name), had been commissioned to build a batch of 40 cars for a Mexican F3 series in 1990, and in 1989 was the largest racing car constructor in the world.

If there were shortcomings, they were to be found in the realization that Reynards were usually more expensive than equivalents from other constructors (although the 1989 F3000 car was cheaper than the March) and were perhaps less user-friendly – if a team deviated from the optimum laid down at Bicester, then the competitive edge could be lost and prove very difficult to retrieve. But the standard products were winners, mopping up championships from Formula Ford to F3000, to an extent that more widely lauded constructors and designers could not aspire to match.

853 Concept work leading to the first F3 Reynard started in the summer of 1983 and design work in 1984, leading to the completion of the first car early in 1985. It was laid down with a view to production in quantity and it had the first unitary carbon fibre/composite monocoque laid out with that in mind. The monocoque shell weighed just over 18kg/40lb, before bulkheads, mounting plates and roll-over hoop were bonded in. There was an aluminium floor panel and a controversial nose box. Inboard pushrod suspension was used all round (designed to shear away from pick-up points on impact, to minimize hull damage). The 853 was designed to take a range of engines.

If 1985 was a season of coming to terms with F3 it was successful enough. The relatively minor Swedish Championship was the only one to fall to a Reynard-equipped team, but there were race wins in most European series and Reynard driver Wallace was runner-up in the important British Championship.

Most cars had VW-based engines, but in an effort that turned out to be a footnote, albeit an interesting one, Saab engines were run in some series, and at least the engine supplier saw Thomas Danielsson win the Swedish series.

The 853 had attractive lines, and in this case a successful overall colour scheme. However, the Nicholson McLaren Engines 16-valve Saab units were not successful. The 'clean' appearance of the right side is due to the enclosure of the restrictor, as air was fed to it via a plenum chamber throught the side pod.

863 This car looked similar to the 853, but there were changes to the monocoque and suspension, while the aerodynamics were refined. VW-based engines were used in 863s run in the British series (Andy Wallace won the title) and this time in the 863 which Schonstrom drove to take the Swedish Championship. Wallace also won the important Macau race.

The sharper nose and larger front wing were two 'identification points' on the 863. At the end of the British Championship season Wallace is waiting as a Silverstone grid forms up.

873 The basic design was carried over to the 1987 F3 car, which had narrower track and longer wheelbase and improved aerodynamic qualities in part resulting from a narrower engine bay (achieved with a multi-purpose modular gearbox and oil tank casing which carried the rear suspension links and anti-roll bar). Thirty 873s were ordered before the car was first shown (at the Essen Show) and increased production was possible in Reynard's larger factory premises.

In 1987 a Reynard R & D team was run with 873s powered by Nova-Alfa Romeo engines (Philippe Favre's car was in Racing for Geneva colours). Johnny Herbert clearly won the British Championship, while Dave Coyne had the highest score in the EFDA Euroseries, both with VW-based engines, and Ross Cheever won the Japanese series with a Toda-Toyota-powered car.

A pair of 873s, driven by Herbert (2) and McCarthy (1). The sleeker engine cover shows well from this angle.

883 Numerically Reynard was strongly represented in F3 in 1988, with a car that had a new tub. Pre-season test accidents seemed to point to structural weaknesses in this area, but the furore passed. By mid-season the only Reynard-equipped team challenging for British Championship honours, Pacific Racing, was running a development car and one significant improvement was to contrive a lower engine position for the

TOM's Toyota power unit. The third element in the combination that brought a third successive title to Reynard was the driving skill of Jyrki Jarvilehto (sensibly called J.J. Lehto for an international audience). Meanwhile Winkelhock and Rensing were first and third in the German Championship in Spiess-VW-powered 883s.

There were subtle changes in the lines of Reynard's F3 car for 1988, although the brash, bright Camel colours tended to distract. This is Favre, at the start of a season with Alfa-powered cars that was none too fruitful.

88D Reynard's first F3000 car was an immediate winner: four leading teams chose it before the start of the 1988 season, and an 88D won the first race of that year's Championship. Roberto Moreno went on to win the title with a Bromley Motorsport 88D, while Donnelly was third in a Q8 Team Ford car. The 88D was based on the F3 car, with design work under Malcolm Oastler and Adrian Reynard. It had a one-piece carbon fibre/ kevlar/aluminium honeycomb composite monocoque, double wishbone suspension with pushrod inboard coil spring/damper units, a Cosworth DFV engine and Hewland FGB transaxle. It looked the part, and did the job.

88D had solid and purposeful lines, although these were not enhanced by the colour scheme of the Q8 Team Ford examples.

89D The 1989 F3000 car had a new monocoque, similar suspension but slightly longer wheelbase, revised nose and outwardly sleeker side pods, and a high engine cover with air ducted to the intakes of Mugen, Judd or Cosworth engines.

Obvious changes from the 88D are the side pods, engine cover and rear aerofoil. This is J.J. Lehto in a Pacific Racing car, a combination which did not have a happy first year in F3000.

The Mugen engine gave no great advantage, but its introduction by Eddie Jordan Racing, the team which ran Alesi and Donnelly, was felt to be a major factor in the steep increase in the costs of F3000 racing. Late in the year one car was adapted for tests with a Mugen F1 engine, and the basic monocoque was also used for the 903 F3 car. In racing the leading 89Ds in the European Championship were first (Alesi, with Mugen engines), third (Apicella, with Judd engines) and sixth (Chiesa, with Cosworth engines).

893 The make-up of the 1989 F3 car was similar to its predecessor, with more aerodynamic improvement, but there was as much significance in other aspects. It was for example the vehicle that ushered in the Paul Stewart Racing team, which brought big names, big money and a new standard of professionalism to F3, and was one of the teams that introduced the Mugen (Honda MF-204) engine to European F3.

In terms of championship successes, the 893 had a better record outside Britain: Gounon was French champion with an Alfa-engined 893, Nilsson was Swedish champion with a VW-engined 893, Tamburini (Alfa) was runner-up in Italy and Frentzen (VW) runner-up in Germany. The best overall Lucas Championship position was Rydell's fourth with a Spiess-VW powered car.

This shot shows off the lines of the 893, but in 1989 the personalities of this team were felt to be more important – Paul Stewart and father Jackie are standing behind the cockpit.

RG SPECIAL

Roger Gerbout's special started life in 1949 with a Lombard engine and was an occasional, unsuccessful, entrant in minor F2 races. Fitted with a BMW unit it appeared in the 1954 *Grand Prix des Frontières,* where it qualified last by a big margin and retired early in the race. ML

RHEINLAND

A short-lived German F3 car which was seen in national races in 1974, this was the F3 Eifelland renamed. Modest results were achieved by Harald Ertl.

RIAL

Gunther Schmid of ATS fame, or notoriety, returned to the F1 world in 1988 with a car named for his brand of wheels, and the comeback was with a strong paper asset in the form of a car designed by Gustav Brunner – another link with the ATS past. Brunner, however, was soon to move on again. A tight one-car team was run in 1988, and as the driver was Andrea de Cesaris there was a fair amount of accident damage to be repaired as well as the odd good result. Two cars were run in 1989, with no more return in terms of points, and with some aggravation in the team (and driver changes). One of the blue cars qualified for a grid only once in every seven attempts and Schmid withdrew the team at the end of the season.

ARC1 This was dubbed 'the blue Ferrari', and forward of its engine it did indeed resemble the Ferrari F1/87 that Brunner had been involved with. He insisted, however, that the two designs had nothing in common, in particular pointing to the fact that the Rial was roomier. The make-up of ARC1 was largely conventional, although in the double wishbone/pullrod suspension the dampers were mounted longitudinally. Cosworth DFV engines were used. At the first outing the fuel capacity was inadequate, this apparently reflecting Brunner's obsession with keeping weight to the formula minimum, and maybe even an expectation that the car would not go for a full race distance. De Cesaris ran as high as sixth in that debut race in Brazil and through the season he usually qualified without problems. He finished in four GPs and scored points with his fourth place in the USA.

Driver: Andrea de Cesaris.

First time out for Rial, in Brazil. The compact blue car is running without an engine cover, with small fuel tankage and 'illegal' oil cooler, both rectified before the second race of the season.

ARC2 This was an updated version of Brunner's design by Bell, Fober and Goodrich, with a strengthened monocoque, cleaner aerodynamics, a nicely curved sweeping engine cover and side pods that were to be altered during the season. The team's fortunes did not change and only Danner's fourth place in the American Grand Prix broke a dismal run of failures.

Drivers: Christian Danner, Gregor Foitek, Pierre-Henri Raphanel, Volker Weidler.

The 1989 Rial was the sleekest car of the year. Whatever its significance in German, a schoolboy English rendering of the name on the outer endplate of the front wing seemed only too appropriate: Mr Junko.

RICHTER

This was also known as the GRS TC001, as it was laid out for one-time ATS and Maurer technician Günther Richter ('GR') and the designation turned out to be only too appropriate as it was a one-off. It was entirely conventional, and built by John Thompson. The power unit was a Mader-BMW, and its cooling arrangements were a major problem. The car was entered for five F2 championship races in 1981 and appeared three times, driven by Jochen Dauer. He had little F2 experience and it started once, at Hockenheim, where it completed 15 laps. The team had limited funds, and these ran out. Richter joined Zakspeed.

RISPAL

This early French Formula Junior car was built by a Renault distributor in Bordeaux, and it naturally incorporated many Renault components, which at that time meant a Dauphine engine and transmission, already conveniently arranged for a rear-engined car. The Rispal had a tubular frame, ifs by wishbones and coil spring/damper units, and swing-axle rear suspension.

RONDEL

Rondel Racing was a prominent F2 team, run by Ron Dennis and Neil Trundle in the first half of the 1970s. It commissioned the design and construction of cars that eventually appeared with other names, notably the F2 Motul (see Motul) and an F1 car by Ray Jessop which was taken over and renamed the Token RJ02 by two other Rondel directors when it was almost complete in 1974. At that time the Rondel outfit ran into financial doldrums. History repeated itself in 1980, as Project Four – also run by Dennis – initiated an F1 programme around a John Barnard-designed car, which was to have a carbon fibre monocoque chassis. Project Four, or P4, was to become part of the McLaren designation.

RONI

Rob Gustavson and Nick Wasyliw substantially revised their Cygnus F3 one-off as the Roni T85 (ROby + NIck) for 1985, primarily with completely revised suspension to meet the flat-bottom regulations. Another mediocre engine was used, but as this was made available free of charge it was appreciated. Ian Flux raced it twice and it was tested through the Autumn,

The maroon Roni, here at Snetterton during tests, had attractive lines and was yet another promising car which was never developed to its potential.

when Dave Scott confirmed Flux's evaluation of the chassis and despite that poor engine both drivers set times that were almost competitive. The little team lacked the resources to develop the car and in 1987 it was sold to Sweden, where it was used for promotional purposes.

ROUGIER

Looking like a scaled-down version of the Grand Prix Osca, this pioneer French 500cc car of 1950 used Simca (née Fiat) parts and was huge, about the size of an F2 car. It was soon apparent this was not the way to go.   ML

ROVER

In 1948 three Rover development engineers, Peter Wilks, George Mackay and Spencer King, built an F2 car from Rover components, and while it was a hobby for them, the company gave it some support. The engine was a 1996cc (63.5 x 105mm) version of the 2.1-litre straight six unit which powered the new Rover 75 and had overhead pushrod inlet valves and side exhaust valves. It was installed in a box-section chassis using production Rover ifs (coil springs and wishbones) and a de Dion rear axle suspended on quarter elliptic springs.

The car gave the three friends some amusement in minor British races until 1951, when it was sold to Gerry Dunham, who re-christened it 'DHS' (Dunham and Haines Special, after his motor business). Dunham ran it in minor F2 races – it was never going to win but he drove it well and often qualified and finished ahead of more recent cars. In 1954 it appeared in two F1 races and in one, admittedly only a five-lapper at Goodwood, Dunham brought it home fourth. Later it was handed over to Frank Lockhart, who had been a salesman at Dunham and Haines, and driver and car have been a feature of Historic racing for years.   ML

ROWE

An interesting concept from Australia, this front engined Douglas-powered car was designed by Keith Rowe to run in 500cc F3 and serve as a two-seater roadster, just like some Italian Formula 750 cars and East European F3 cars. The chassis began life under a Fiat, and other bits came from other cars.   ML

ROYALE

The origins of Royale were in the car trade, and in the enthusiasm that led Bob King to Coventry Climax engine tuning and then to an engine company, Racing Preparations, while he also found a personal outlet in racing. The business was centred on Climax engines and naturally declined in the second half of the 1960s, so Racing Preparations turned to cars. The first Royale Formula Ford RP1 was completed in 1968 (RP being retained for designations, while 'Royale' derived from the Park Royal district of London where the factory was situated as well as being a pun on the founder's name).

By 1971, when the first F3 car was completed, the company had become the second-largest racing car manufacturer in Britain and had moved to Huntingdon (where the largest, Lola, was based). In less happy circumstances it was to move again, to Little Staughton in 1974.

Bob King retired for health reasons two years later, and the company continued under Alan Cornock, who had been with it since the Racing Preparations days. It survived a very difficult period by concentrating on cars for the lesser categories, Ford, Ford 2000, Super Vee and then just the Ford categories, and successful designs by Rory Byrne saw it through to the end of the decade. Production dropped dramatically in the early 1980s and Royale went into liquidation in 1984. Cornock later revived it, to build small sports-racing cars.

RP8 This was announced in 1970 as a Formula Atlantic/B/3 car, but only two were built and neither ran in F3 form.

RP11 When the prototype RP11 F3 car appeared late in 1971 there were no long-term plans for it. However, in Tom Pryce's hands it was immediately competitive, and when he drove it to a clear victory in the first round of the 1972 British championship the company's F3 expectations were aroused.

It was a monocoque car, with outboard suspension, hip radiators and a Vegantune engine. That specification was carried over to the RP11A production version, outwardly distinguished by its engine cover with a pronounced fin. A dozen were built in 1972. Royale was not geared up to run a works car in this category, Pryce moved on very successfully to Formula Atlantic with the RP12 and none of the customers – drivers included Ashley, Bond and Sutcliffe – could match his pace in an RP11A.

The first F3 Royale was a pretty little car, and driven by Tom Pryce it was also pretty sensational, most notably in this first race at Brands Hatch.

RP15 This was a one-off F2 conversion of an F Atlantic RP12 for Manfred Schurti in 1973, with a similar make up to RP11. Its BDA let it down at its only race appearance, at Nivelles.

RP20 Announced late in 1973, this was to be the definitive follow-up to RP15 and for F3 or F Atlantic use (different tubular engine sub frames to bolt to the back of the monocoque were to make it truly interchangeable). An RP20 was raced only once, in F Atlantic form.

RP23 An F3 design by Rory Byrne, which was sold when work had started, to become the Druid (see Druid).

RRA

Geoff Richardson contrived three specials carrying the initials RRA (Richardson Racing Automobiles) and raced them in British second- and third-level events through more than a dozen seasons, until trends began to swing too harshly against amateurs enjoying themselves in racing above club level.

The first car started life as Maclure's 'IFS Riley Special' in the 1930s. Owned by Richardson from 1948, it went through a series of new handles and new blades, so that its origins were lost – a new chassis, a new central-seat body, new suspension, an ERA engine in place of the Riley unit and finally an Alta engine.

It was followed in 1957 by an RRA built up around a 1955-6 Aston Martin Tasman chassis with a Jaguar 2.4-litre engine, which Richardson ran in the International Trophy but soon abandoned (its new owner 'converted' it into a 'new' DB3S sports car). The third RRA was a Cooper T43 with a Connaught engine, run in secondary F1 races in 1960 and two Inter-Continental races in 1961, when it was far from competitive.

Geoff Richardson in his first RRA in its monoposto form.

RSM

An obscure US Formula Junior one-off built in 1960, with its DKW engine and transmission behind the cockpit in a chassis of square tubes. The torsion bar front suspension had Wolfsburg origins and there was a wishbone and transverse leaf spring set-up at the rear.

RUDGE SPECIAL

An early Australian 500 car, built by Ted Huggins. He used a lightened BSA frame, front suspension and front wheel drive from the same source and a front-mounted Rudge engine. Rear suspension was by quarter elliptical springs and radius arms. It took nearly three years to complete but so far as race results were concerned, Huggins need not have bothered.

ML

S

SAAB

Formula Junior tempted Saab to essay a pair of front wheel drive single-seaters in 1960, using the company's 96 saloon fwd engine/transmission components and suspension (which most unusually for a racing car of that period meant a beam rear axle), in a simple stressed-skin sheet metal and glass fibre chassis/body. In appropriate blue and yellow colours they were driven in Scandinavian races, by Erik Carlsson among others.

The Saab Junior had simple lines, and a reputation for good straight-line speed coupled with tricky handling. Whatever it might have proved as a test vehicle, it was not a competitive racing car. Saab's chief engineer, Rolf Mellde, appears less than happy during tests – with the engine ahead of the driven wheels, and something of the order of 70 per cent of the all-up weight over those wheels, it had a reputation for understeer to the point of extravagance.

SACHA-GORDINE

Sacha Gordine, a French film producer who had driven in rallies, announced an ambitious programme to put France back on the racing map in 1952. This involved the simultaneous development of 1.5-, 2-, 2.5-, 3- and 4.5-litre V-8 engines, some of which were to be supercharged, and cars for F1, F2 and Le Mans. In order not to be confused with Gordini, who might have worked miracles had Gordine given him a fraction of what he was prepared to spend, Gordine put a hyphen in his name. Gordine's cars were built regardless of cost and for the 1953 World Championship he proposed that no fewer than five would be prepared.

His designer, M. Vigna, specified torsion bar and trailing link front suspension and a rear-engined layout but more conservatively chose a ladder chassis and de Dion rear axle sprung on torsion bars located by twin trailing arms. Magnesium was used extensively.

In F2 form the 'over-square' dohc V-8 engine was fed by four twin-choke carburetters and was claimed to give 191bhp at 8,000rpm which, if true, would have made it the most powerful car in the World Championship. A five-speed gearbox was unusual at the time. The 17in wire wheels stood well proud of the bonnet line for this was the lowest single-seater of its time, and with twin nostril air intakes feeding two small radiators it was years ahead of its time in style.

With two of the five cars nearly complete, Gordine unveiled the project early in 1953 and filed an entry for the Pau GP in April with a sports car predicted for Le Mans. Then he realised he was frittering away all his money, and as suddenly as it had begun the project was closed down. ML

SADLER

A front engined Formula Junior car built at St Catherine's, Ontario in 1959 – a Canadian single-seater is a rarity. It had a simple multi-tubular chassis with a BMC A Series engine mounted at an angle to the fore-and-aft line, so that the transmission passed alongside the driver. There was a live rear axle, but the coil spring/damper units of the suspension were neatly tucked in the bodywork of the high Elva-like tail.

SAFIR

The first Safir was the Token RJ02 (see also Token), acquired by John Thorpe and renamed for his engineering company. It was run in two British F1 races in 1975, finishing last in both.

The major part of Safir's modest budget that year was dedicated to a one-off F3 car designed by Ray Jessop. The RJ03 was a competent car, very much on Ralt lines with a full-width nose, flat-sided hull and orthodox wide-track suspension. Economy meant that Holbay-Ford Pinto and then Holbay-Ford twin-cam engines were used. Belgian Patrick Neve was the ideal driver for the little team – quick and sensible. The only win came in a secondary event, but Neve was second in the Monaco and British GP meeting F3 races.

A slightly revised RJ03 was run in 1976 with a Nova-Toyota engine and in the second half of the season Tiff Needell gained some top-six placings with it. Ray Jessop died early in the year and the development potential in the car was not exploited.

The essentially straightforward Safir F3 car in 1975.

SANA

Gordon Fowell designed a low Formula Atlantic car that was built as a one-off by John Thompson and made a good impression in its first race, a Spring 1976 event when it was driven by Cyd Williams. As a result of that showing, an F3 version was put in hand for Terry Perkins for the Monaco GP meeting F3 race that year. He qualified it for the last row of the grid for a heat, but its apparently malevolent handling in the race caused him to give up. Maybe the designer's notion that his suspension was correct for all conditions so that provision for adjustment of roll bars was not necessary contributed to the problem. The car had a monocoque chassis, full-width nose, wedge lines to its bodywork and a Brown-Ford engine. That was not the most potent unit around in 1976, but no matter as far as the Sana was concerned, for it was not a lasting feature of the F3 scene.

SAUTER

This Swiss Formula Junior car was built by one of the trio responsible for the MBM (see also MBM), which it closely resembled in appearance and specification. It had a multi-tubular chassis clothed in fibreglass bodywork, Porsche-derived independent front and rear suspension and gearbox, and a Mantzel DKW engine.

Save in details this could be an MBM. It is the one-off Sauter, driven by Heini Walter at Cesenatico in 1960.

SAXON

A one-off Formula Junior car built by C. S. MacArthur when serving with the British Forces in Germany in 1959 and raced there and in England. It had a rear-mounted BMC A Series engine, rated at a modest 68bhp, in a tubular semi-space frame chassis with wishbone and coil spring ifs and swinging axle, coil springs and radius arms rear suspension. A second Saxon, which came in 1960, was a modified 500cc Mackson fitted with a DKW engine.

SCAMPOLO

Scampolo competition cars appeared in West and East Germany in the 1950s and 1960s, and the progenitor of the DDR Scampolo, Willy Lehmann, was also involved with other marques.

Walter Arnold and Walter Komossa built DKW-powered sports-racing cars at Recklinghausen in the early 1950s, and soon built a 500cc F3 car. This looked ungainly and was unusual in its use of a water-cooled two-stroke DKW engine,

Scampolo at Luxembourg-Findel in 1952, when the GP de Luxembourg was the most important race on the international F3 calendar. Komossa looks very cheerful, although here as elsewhere his BMW-engined car was outclassed.

which drove through an adapted DKW front-wheel drive system. Constructors were repeatedly to discover the shortcomings of the DKW engine on into the Formula Junior years; when Arnold and Komossa did so, they revised the car to use a BMW flat twin driving through a VW transmission, were reported to have tried a Norton engine, and soon renamed the car 'Condor' (confusingly as there was another F3 Condor in Germany). Scampolo and/or Condor do not feature on the results sheets of races where there was a serious entry.

In the other Germany that then pursued its own very separate existence, Willy Lehmann of Bittefeld used the Scampolo name for a Formula Junior car. It was rear-engined, with a multi-tubular chassis and de Dion rear suspension. In common with other East German constructors, Lehmann suffered under the handicap of having to use local components (primarily a Wartburg engine). Lehmann next appeared with SEG in the 1-litre F3 years (see SEG).

The redoubtable Willy Lehmann giving an FJ Scampolo-Wartburg some welly in a South German race in 1960. The car is obviously immaculate, and although it appears large its lines are clean.

SCARAB

Lance Reventlow had some success as a sports driver, and brought together a group of talented people in his Scarab programme, initially to build a very small number of sports-racing cars, which proved to be very competitive in the USA. An ambitious F1 car was laid down for 1959, on front engined lines with a Troutman and Barnes space frame and all-independent suspension. Prolonged development time spent on the in-house engine (a twin ohc four-cylinder unit with desmodromic valve gear and fuel injection) delayed the car's appearance until 1960, and it was obsolete by the time it reached the circuits. Daigh qualified one to start just once in

Lance Reventlow in one of his handsome blue and white Scarabs during practice for the 1960 US GP.

the early summer GPs in Europe, so that part of the programme was sensibly abandoned; later one was placed tenth in the US GP. One of the two cars then completed was modified for the short-lived Intercontinental Formula in 1961, but was no more successful in that guise. A third car was made up from parts. The last single-seater Scarab from Reventlow Automobiles Incorporated was a rear engined car for Formula 366; it had a stock-block 5-litre Chevrolet V-8, but as the category (which was superseded by F5000) also allowed for 3-litre racing engines it could have doubled as a GP car if the project had been pursued.

In the early 1980s the name Scarab was used for unrelated Formula Vee cars built in Britain.

Drivers: Chuck Daigh, Lance Reventlow.

SCORPION

The name adopted by Rytune for 'export' versions of the front-engined Elva Formula Junior car, normally DKW-engined and with a closely-similar chassis and running gear specification. The body was of fibreglass and did not follow precisely the same lines as the Elva equivalent. This was effectively the North American version and provided a means of keeping the cash flowing after Frank Nichols' original agent was convicted of financial irregularities.

A photograph giving the lie to recollections that the front-engined Stanguellini was bulkier than its 1959-60 Elva counterpart. On this occasion the Italian car was the winner, and the race carried a most illustrious title – Vanderbilt Cup Race – run moreover at the Roosevelt Raceway. The white Scorpion was driven by Pedro Rodriguez.

SCOTT

Driver Richard Scott took an ambitious step when he commissioned Patrick Head to design a car for the 1973 F2 season, with the brief that it was to be uncomplicated and simple to run as the little team had a very tight budget. Grand Prix Metalcraft made the aluminium monocoque, conventional suspension was used, there was a full-width

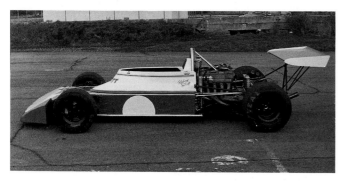

The simplicity of the one-off Scott is obvious in this shot of the new car.

nose with air ducted to twin radiators, and the BDA engine drove through a Hewland FT200. Between those components was the only unusual feature of the car (new to F2), a spacer which extended the wheelbase by some 12cm and in effect pushed the cockpit further forward in it.

Scott's enterprise was poorly rewarded. Five races absorbed the budget, and the only good showing in a 1973 race was at the Nürburgring, when Scott worked the car up through the field to seventh place. Later the design was used as the basis for the successful Delta F2000 car.

SEG

Willy Lehmann (see also Scampolo), best known as a prominent driver in East European Formula Junior and F3 racing through the 1960s, was behind this Wartburg-engined F3 car in the mid-1960s. It was a well-built space frame car, low and with clean lines as obvious efforts were made to compensate for the power (sic) of its engine, but Lehmann's only top-six finishes with it in major races were at the Sachsenring, where he was fourth in mediocre company in 1965 and 1966.

Beside some of its East European contemporaries, the double wishbone and other suspension members of the SEG-Wartburg appeared almost spindly. The body lines were beautifully smooth.

SELEX

This Barcelona constructor built its first F3 car in 1969 and its last in 1983, as the Avidesa. However, throughout the 1970s Miguel Molons' company was mainly concerned with SEAT Formula 1430 and 1.8-litre *Formula Nacional* cars, and by the second half of the 1980s its only interest in competition motoring was in specialist shock absorbers.

The 1978-9 ST8 was a neat and tidy car, unlike some of the Selex F1430 machines of the mid-1970s. The driver is Marcos Molons, son of the patron.

The F3 ST2 was a short-wheelbase space frame car with wide-based wishbone suspension and a Novamotor engine, in concept and make-up not unlike the F3 Tecno. It was first raced in 1970, by Salvator Canellas, in international events but without success.

The growth of national racing was strong in 1971-2 and F3 was set aside. Late in the decade a monocoque that had been designed for a *Formula Nacional* car was used as the basis for the F3 ST8. This had a conventional front radiator, outboard suspension layout and Nova-Toyota engine. It lacked the stimulus which a national F3 Championship might have brought, and in Spanish terms tended to be headed by Spanish drivers in March or Ralt cars when it appeared at odd European Championship races. However, a developed version did lead to the Avidesa, which showed enough promise to confirm the capability of Selex but was the last F3 car to be built in Barcelona.

SENIOR

Yet another one-off that flitted across the British Formula Junior scene in its formative period, and given a rather juvenile name by its Scottish originators, the Bertram brothers. There is no record of achievement.

SERVAL

A rear-engined French special following typical 500cc lines but fitted with an HRD twin. It appeared in the Grand Prix de Cinquantenaire at Roubaix in 1950. Driven by M. Foury, it retired early.   ML

SHADOW

Don Nichols formed Advanced Vehicle Systems in 1968 and its first vehicle to be seen on circuits was the extraordinary sports-racing car driven by Jackie Oliver in 1970 CanAm races. Two years later an AVS base was set up in England, to build and race UOP Shadows in F1 as well as CanAm, the latter soon to be dropped. The UOP title tended to be dropped too, although Universal Oil Products stayed with the team until 1975, and the cars apparently ran on its lead-free fuel.

After the first car, Shadows promised to become leading contenders, but Nichols suffered heavy blows – Peter Revson's fatal crash during tests at Kyalami and the bizarre death of Tom Pryce in a race on the same circuit, the loss of sponsors and the struggle to maintain a GP team on minimal funds, and the defection of the team's executives.

Only one Championship race fell to Shadow, and after Alan Jones' victory in the 1977 Austrian GP the team increasingly battled to survive. Surrender came early in the summer of 1980. Teddy Yip acquired the shareholding of Shadow Cars, adopting the last design for his own Theodore team.

DN1 Designer Tony Southgate followed fashionable 'Coke bottle' lines in his first Shadow, which had a fine slim nose, hip radiators and outboard suspension. It was also his first DFV-engined car, and his failure to make sufficient allowance for the excessive vibrations of the V-8, allied to the fact that the tub was not stiff enough, led to problems through much of the season. However, Follmer's car held together through Shadow's first GP, in South Africa, where he scored a point. For the rest of that first season fortunes were mixed – cars were written off but at its end Shadow was eighth in the Constructors' Championship. The DN1s were used in the early-1974 races.

While the team cars were black, another DN1 was run in the largely white colours of Graham Hill's infant Embassy-sponsored team.

Drivers: George Follmer, Graham Hill, Jean-Pierre Jarier, Jackie Oliver, Brian Redman.

The first Shadows stood out in the black of the team's principal sponsor. In details such as the nose, the car was modified through 1973, and a more compact engine airbox was adopted. This is Oliver in DN1/4, at Silverstone.

DN3 In effect Southgate modified the first design, with longer wheelbase, wider track, stiffer tub and improved aerodynamics. There was a setback when Revson crashed during tests, after a promising first outing in a non-Championship race. Oliver had taken on full-time management work with Shadow so Jarier became the team's constant driver through the year, with Redman, briefly Roos, and then the immensely talented Tom Pryce in the second car. One car was mildly uprated as a DN3B, using some DN5 parts, for the two South American races that opened the 1975 season. Meanwhile, eighth place in the 1974 Constructors' Championship suggested that little progress had been made.

Drivers: Jean-Pierre Jarier, Tom Pryce, Brian Redman, Peter Revson, Bertil Roos.

DN3 looked long and lean, but that angular airbox did little to improve its appearance. Everybody seems very relaxed as Tom Pryce prepares to go out onto the track during Italian GP practice in 1974.

DN5 A further development of the design, improved in detail and showing a promise that was never quite fulfilled. Tom Pryce scored Shadow's first F1 victory in the Race of Champions at Brands Hatch, Jarier took pole in Argentina and Brazil, Pryce and Jarier both led the British GP (and both crashed), and the Welshman started scoring consistently in the late summer, to haul Shadow into sixth place on the Constructors' table – the team's best ever.

The DN7 was short-lived, so in 'B' form the cars had to serve on through 1976, Pryce again scoring well early in the year, and into 1977. DN6 was an F5000 derivative of DN5, with many F1 car parts and Chevrolet, later Dodge, engines.

Drivers: Jean-Pierre Jarier, Tom Pryce, Renzo Zorzi.

The DN5 served into a third season, still in black livery despite changes of sponsorship. This is newcomer Zorzi with a car in DN5B form in Argentina in 1977.

DN7 This turned out to be a one-off, with a short life, although when it made its race debut in the 1975 Austrian GP Nichols must have felt that it promised a new beginning. A new chassis was built for the Matra V-12, then rated at some 500bhp compared with the DFV's 470bhp, albeit at some cost in fuel consumption. In its fast-circuit appearances, at the Osterreichring and Monza, when the DN7 was driven by Jarier, this 'extra' power was not translated into an all-out speed advantage. Nobody really knew if that would have come once the chassis/engine combination had bedded in, for French politics were brought into play and the Matra engines were supplied exclusively to Ligier in 1976.

Driver: Jean-Pierre Jarier.

Jarier in DN7 in the 1975 Italian GP.

DN8 Southgate laid down the DN8 for 1976, but shortage of funds meant that the first was not raced until the summer and the second was not completed until the beginning of the next season. By then Southgate was long gone, to Lotus, although the design Dave Wass took over bore his mark, following the lines of his earlier Shadows, with a shallow monocoque. Southgate was to return to the team to develop the car in 1977, then leave again as one of the group which set up Arrows. After Pryce's death Alan Jones joined the team, and in Austria he drove a slightly modified DN8 to score Shadow's only GP victory. Further good placings saw the team seventh on the 1977 Constructors Championship table.

Drivers: Jean-Pierre Jarier, Alan Jones, Arturo Merzario, Jackie Oliver, Riccardo Patrese, Tom Pryce, Clay Regazzoni, Renzo Zorzi.

The DN8 when new, driven in mid-1976 tests by Tom Pryce. Very large radiators, mounted fore-and-aft alongside the engine, took the place of the stepped side pod arrangement in the 1977 revised car, when the engine deck was lowered, larger front wings with prominent end plates were run and there was another attempt to contrive skirts, which were little more convincing than this first effort.

DN9 The Shadow team struggled on after the defection of most of its key staff, and its first ground effects car came for the Spring races. This DN9 was designed by Southgate, whose work was picked up by John Baldwin, and outwardly was a more angular car. Its specification was absolutely straightforward, the team focussing its attention on survival. Stuck and Regazzoni each scored a fifth and team survival was achieved honourably. One of the five DN9s was run by the Interscope team, but Ongais failed to qualify it.

The cars were modified to 'B' specification by Richard Owen and John Gentry for 1979, when principal changes were to the suspension and in attempts to generate more downforce with new side pods. It was another downbeat season, saved at the last race when de Angelis scored Shadow's only points of the year.

Drivers: Elio de Angelis, Jan Lammers, Clay Regazzoni, Hans Stuck.

DN9B with the sponsor's rather lurid colour scheme, driven by Lammers in the 1979 Dutch GP.

DN11 Yet again a Shadow was a joint design, as one designer, Gentry, left and Owen and Vic Morris carried on. Front suspension was new, rear suspension was carried over from a mid-1979 redesign for the DN9B, radiators were in the side pods and there was a needle nose quite unlike the previous Southgate noses. There was however little money and so drivers who could bring sponsors to the team were sought. Kennedy brought some, but hopes that Italians would bring more came to nothing, so at the last minute Johansson was enrolled, then replaced by Lees. He was the only driver to qualify a DN11 for a grid.

Driver: Geoff Lees.

DN12 This short wheelbase car designed by Morris and Chuck Graemiger was a forlorn hope. It appeared at the 1980 Belgian GP, and a second car was ready for the Spanish GP. The entrant was still Shadow Cars, but the owner was Teddy Yip and by the Spanish GP the entrant was Theodore Shadow. He decided not to contest a full season when neither driver qualified at Paul Ricard, although a DN12 was to start a race in 1981 as a Theodore.

Drivers: David Kennedy, Geoff Lees.

Benetton (**top**) became Ford's favoured team in the second half of the 1980s, running cars in a very distinctive colour scheme. This is Pirro in a 189.

Williams' 1989 alliance with Renault would have seemed improbable earlier in the 1980s, but was successful in its first season with the French V-10 engine in the FW12C. Later in 1989 the FW13 (**above**) was introduced (photographed when Patrese was driving it in initial tests).

With less immediate success a Forghieri-designed Lamborghini V-12 was introduced in the Lola LC89 (**left**).

A Ferrari 640 (**left**) shows the slender monocoque that became universal at the end of the 1980s, in this car coupled with curvaceous side pods which had deep radiator intakes well forward in the wheelbase and were cut in as far as possible at the rear – in aerodynamic respects this was rated highly efficient. The driver is Mansell.

In a comparison, the late turbo Ferrari driven by Johansson (**below left**) has a wider monocoque – although the cockpit fits the driver just as tightly – very large intakes at the front of each side pod and more aerodynamic clutter at the rear.

Lotus had bright new colours in 1987, Honda engines, and active suspension on the 99T (**right**). That novelty lasted through the season and Senna (driving here) won races with it. Other teams ran development cars in tests with active, or reactive, suspension systems but the Lotus lead was not immediately followed in racing, or used by Lotus in the next season.

The Tyrrell Racing Organization has sometimes fallen on hard times, running unsponsored cars. In the first part of the 1989 season its DFR-powered 018s (**right**) were run in a pleasing royal blue, then sponsorship came, with the prospect of a more secure existence in the 1990s. The driver in this shot is Jonathan Palmer.

Alain Prost and Marlboro McLaren made the outstanding partnership of
the 1980s, and it ended with the decade. Here he is alone on the streets
of Phoenix in a 1989 MP4/5.

SHANNON

This one-off created by Aiden Jones and Paul Emery in 1966 was one of racing's oddities. It appeared once as an F1 car, and it was still popping up as an F3 car in some races as the decade ended. A monocoque car, it looked inadequate for its first use – and it was not strong – but with the passage of time came to appear rather bulky. In its 1966 form it was powered by one of the Coventry Climax FPE V-8s, which had originally been intended for the 2.5-litre Formula a dozen years earlier but were never used in racing, and which had been acquired by Emery. He enlarged them and modified them to run on pump fuel, with Tecalamit fuel injection (apparently 312bhp was achieved on test). Trevor Taylor retired the Shannon on the first lap of the 1966 British GP. As an F3 car it became known as the Mk1, latterly powered by an EMC engine and driven by Australian John Wilson through to 1969.

Driver: (F1): Trevor Taylor.

A rare sighting of the Coventry Climax FPE as adapted by Paul Emery, in the back of the 1966 Shannon.

SIGMA

Completed early in 1969, this product of a research and study group was intended to demonstrate racing car passive safety, for example incorporating a driver 'survival cell', multi-layer Pirelli fuel tanks outside the main structure, a comprehensive fire extinguisher system, wide sponsons protruding outside the wheels to prevent interlocking, and rear bodywork to safeguard against wheels throwing up track debris or water at following drivers. It was built around contemporary Ferrari F1 components, but the bodywork meant that it was not eligible to race (the formula requirement was that no bodywork should protrude beyond the inner faces of the wheels) and it was in any case substantially overweight at 590kg when the F1 minimum was 520kg.

The Sigma had sleek lines – as they were the work of its constructor, Pininfarina, that was only to be expected – but with the oddity of a wing mounted almost centrally and to the bodywork (which suggested a failure to appreciate the forces generated by such aerofoils).

SILVERBIRD

An Effyh clone (see Effyh) powered by a BSA engine and built by Robert Nelleman, a Dane, in 1949. A second car had a JAP engine and was largely used for short-oval racing. ML

SIMCA-SURVA

Henri Otterbein, a Frenchman, originally made his front engined 500 special as a supercharged car using a Simca (née Fiat) as the basis. It was converted to match F3 regulations and although it was never remotely likely to be successful, Otterbein raced it for many years, even making the occasional trip abroad. ML

SIMON MG

This contender in early American Formula Junior races began life as one of the Roger Barlow Simca Specials which dominated their class in SCCA racing for some years. One was taken over by Harvey Simon and given an MG engine, and when FJ arrived Simon stripped off the road equipment and ran it in the unique American 1300cc class. Apparently its road-holding and traction were outstanding but its bulk and weight lost time on the straights. ML

SIRMAC

Before Bernard Boyer became known as an F1 engineer he devised one of the few French Formula Junior cars, his Sirmac proving competitive with early-1960s Cooper and Lotus cars, let alone German and Italian cars. It was straightforward in make-up, with a tubular chassis and a Renault Dauphine engine bored out to 66mm to give a capacity of 1094cc. The cockpit was well back in the wheelbase, and this contributed to the Sirmac's reputation for good handling to partly offset the engine's relative lack of power, at least on sinuous circuits and the hill climbs where Boyer enjoyed some success.

Posed outside the entrance to Montlhéry, the Sirmac shows attractive lines – the bodywork was by a Paris coachbuilder – and its original cast light alloy wheels.

SKODA

This Czech company has built up a worthy international reputation in rallies, with dependable and sometimes surprisingly quick class winners, but its racing has largely been in national sports car events or East European single-seater categories.

In 1960 the Skoda Junior Venezuela appeared, as an independent venture by S. Vivaldi and S. Severini, with a rear-mounted 1098cc 440-derived engine, rated at a modest 78bhp. As the name implies, it was raced in Venezuela, by Stefano Soriani.

In 1965 the company took a serious look at the then-new 1-litre F3, turning out a batch of ten space frame cars with 1000MB-based engines. These developed some 75bhp at 7500rpm, at a time when Cosworth was setting the F3 pace with units that could be relied on to give 100bhp. That order of output was claimed for the Skoda engine later in the decade, when a works team was run in East European events. One car appeared in a 1969 Austrian race as a back marker. Skoda's wider international aspirations had quickly been abandoned and soon Formula Skoda was devised, to keep the name alive in local circuit racing.

The F3 Skoda had clean lines and minimal suspension interference with the airflow to help compensate for its engine's lack of competitive power. However, some of the suspension members appear none too substantial on this show car. The wheels look like Cooper reach-me-downs.

SMITH

Ken Smith built his F3 one-off in 1948 on unashamedly Cooper lines, and he raced it for fun in the face of unreliability. It was a dumpy little device with a blunt nose and unattractive disc wheels. His second car, which won an award for the most successful home constructor in 1951, was built round a specially-commissioned Buckler space frame, and it was successful for three seasons – in 1953 he still had a car capable of beating 'constructor-built' cars in the hands of people like Bueb, Russell and Lewis-Evans (he did just that in a Silverstone 100-mile race). The third Smith was built for him by Creamer in 1954, following Cooper lines.

Wire wheels and a steering wheel that appears strangely large are details that set Smith's third 500 apart from the Cooper-dominated grids of 1954. Cyril Posthumus commented on this photograph "trying to look and go like Don Parker's Parker".

SMITH

Gerald G. Smith built and raced a Kent-Smith 500cc F3 car then turned his hand to F2 in 1957. His front-engined car was later sold to Jack Perkins and he produced another for 1958. This also used a front-mounted Climax engine and made a few race appearances, driven in 1958 by Alan Stacey and once in 1959 by Ashdown. In 1960 Smith modified an FJ Lola as Lola-Smith, but this was apparently not a success for it faded away.

SMS

Jeff Sparrowe's 1948 500 car had a rear-mounted Rudge engine in an Austin Seven chassis with split axle (A7) ifs. Needless to say, it did not change the face of motor racing. A later SMS was actually a modified Marwyn.   ML

SPARTON

This small-scale manufacturer of cars for minor single-seater categories was set up by Norman Pierce and Paul Jackson in 1977 and ventured into F3 in 1983-4, with the SE420, when Sparton was based at Lingfield in Surrey. The SE420 followed the lines of the Formula Ford 2000 model and therefore was hardly sophisticated in F3 company, yet it maintained Sparton's reputation for well-engineered cars. The SE420 was first raced with a VW-based engine by Jeff Ward in the summer of 1983. He did not score in the Marlboro championship and late in the year Paul Jackson took it over for three races, when it showed promise. After tests Ayrton Senna (da Silva, as he then was) was reported to speak well of it. A second car was built with revised bodywork for 1984, to be run for Jackson by Valour Racing. He scored two top-ten places with it – the highest being eighth at Zolder – but in mid-season turned to a Valour Ralt. A Sparton appeared among the 1985 Marlboro series Class B entries, but with it the name faded from F3.

The neat, economical lines of the first F3 Sparton, with the broad side pods of the ground effects era, which then had one more full season to run. Perhaps a constructor new to the category should have bided his time.

SPIDER

This inappropriately named single-seater was a Holbay-powered F3 one-off by Borje Bjorkquist on Brabham lines. It appeared at some Scandinavian meetings in 1965.

SPIRIT

Spirit Racing was formed in 1981 by John Wickham and ex-McLaren, ex-March designer Gordon Coppuck, with backing from Honda and Bridgestone. Their 201 was almost immediately competitive in F2 in 1982 and they moved on to F1 in 1983 – a significant move as it brought the Japanese car company back into Grand Prix racing. The potential of the turbo engine was demonstrated in the second half of the season, whereupon Honda abandoned Spirit for Williams in 1984, but at least helped Spirit in a switch to Hart engines.

Beyond that, the little equipe was under-financed and struggled to survive into 1985, when it gave up. A nucleus undertook car restoration and then Spirit returned, as Spirit Motorsport, to run an F3000 team.

201 This neat F2 car was conventional in its aluminium honeycomb monocoque and suspension, tailor-made for the Honda V-6. There were teething problems, usually with minor components, but Thierry Boutsen won three races and was third in the Championship; Stefan Johansson was quick but retired too often. A major headache was that Bridgestone supplied dry crossply tyres and wet radials and it took over an hour to change the car. In the final round at Enna, Boutsen had a chance of the title but the organisers delayed the start to ensure a wet/dry race, so helping an Italian, Corrado Fabi.

For 1983 two cars were converted to take BMW F2 engines by the Emco-backed team. Jo Gartner won at Pau in a Spirit-BMW and was sixth in the Championship.

Boutsen testing a 201 at Silverstone early in 1982. A much larger front aerofoil was used when the car was raced, to cure excess understeer.

The 201C in the Silverstone pits lane during tests, showing off its hybrid make-up – virtually the F2 car back to the cockpit, then a mobile test rig behind it. Although 30kg lighter than the first F2 conversion, this car was substantially overweight.

A more significant conversion saw 201/B71 run as an F1 development car late in 1982, and 201/4 appear at the 1983 Race of Champions with a Honda RA163-E turbocharged V-6, beefed-up transmission and an extraordinary amount of ancillaries which with the addition of short and wide side pods and large triple aerofoils made the car look unusually ponderous behind the cockpit. A lighter car, designated 201C, was built for the team's GP debut at Silverstone. However, problems meant that the first car was raced there, and in three other GPs, while Johansson started the 201C twice. He finished three times, his best placing being seventh at Zandvoort.

Driver: Stefan Johansson.

101 Built in the late summer of 1983, but not run in any of the late-season races, this was the only purpose-designed F1 Spirit. In October 1983 Honda withdrew support and engines, so the design was reworked for the Hart 415T turbo engine (which could not be used as a stressed member). A shortage of Hart engines meant that it was also run with a Cosworth DFV. This was one of the smallest and most compact cars in F1, lighter than the 201s, while the angled radiators and intercoolers were much less prominent than on the Honda-engined cars.

The little team was dogged by a lack of funds. Emerson Fittipaldi tested the first 101, but a deal with the Brazilian could not be financed and less-than-competent Fulvio Ballabio financed a test programme. Baldi started 101s in seven races (best placing eighth), Rothengatter in seven (best placing eighth); each driver failed to qualify once.

Two cars were revised to D specification for 1985, with changes to radiators and suspension, and Mauro Baldi started in three races before the team ceased operation.

Drivers: Mauro Baldi, Huub Rothengatter.

101 in its 1984 Hart-engined form, albeit with a Honda 'acknowledgement' ahead of the angled radiators. The more prominent sponsorship emblems did not mean long-term support. Driven by Mauro Baldi, this car is perhaps dragging too much rear wing for its Hart engine.

SPRINT AUTO

A one-off Italian Formula Junior car, front-engined with a tubular chassis, wishbone and transverse leaf suspension at both ends, the almost inevitable Fiat 1100 engine and 600 gearbox, and no known racing record.

SPROG

A pioneering Australian 500 car, Bob Burnett-Read's Sprog D Type ('D' for the pre-war Auto Union D-wagen) had a channel section and tube frame, Fiat 500 front suspension, swing axles and transverse leaf rear suspension, and a rear mounted BSA twin-cylinder engine.   ML

STANGUELLINI

Vittorio Stanguellini followed a well-marked Italian path when he started tuning saloons at his Fiat agency in Modena in 1935, and then built his first Stanguellini sports cars around Fiat components in 1946. By the beginning of the 1950s his small capacity sports cars were enjoying considerable success in Italian races, though little further afield, as when Stanguellini ventured to Le Mans. An offset single-seater open-wheel 1.5-litre car derived from this series and was tested by Ascari in 1949, then raced by Sighinolfi in secondary events such as the Circuit of Garda in 1950. Stanguellini also built record cars.

His National 750 design dating from 1955 was an ideal basis for a Formula Junior car as that formula was launched in Italy in 1958 – Stanguellini was the first constructor to build a batch of cars for sale, after a prototype had been demonstrated by Fangio at Modena in November 1957. By the end of 1959 more than a hundred had been sold, and it was the dominant car in that first international season, Michael May driving one to win the International Junior Championship while among *comingmen* who raced Stanguellini were von Trips and Bandini.

Formula Junior The first FJ Stanguellini were front-engined cars, largely built around Fiat components. A simple tubular chassis was used, with some body panels contributing to ridigity, and the cockpit was offset to the left with the prop shaft alongside the driver (but these were still very high cars). The early cars had a coil-sprung live rear axle, an independent set-up (with inboard rear brakes) coming in 1960.

By that time the new wave of British cars had taken over FJ, and the front-engined layout was obsolete. Stanguellini attempted to regain lost ground with the rear-engined Delfino Junior, a striking 'nostril-nosed' space frame car with the coil springs/dampers of the front suspension best described as partially inboard, and inboard rear discs. The engine, inclined to the left at 45 degrees, was the Fiat 1100/103, rated at a modest 90bhp at 7500rpm for that 1961 use.

The only really successful Stanguellini was the first FJ car. It was a traditional Italian racing car down to its wire wheels, well made and attractive in a style that was rapidly passing when this car ran at Monaco in 1959.

Formula 3 The Delfino turned out to be a one-off, but in 1963 Stanguellini looked to the forthcoming F3, and was apparently ready for it with a low, clean-lined car. This had inboard front suspension (but the rear brakes were outboard) and once again the Fiat 1100-based engine was used, as a 65 x 75mm unit giving 85bhp. It was not competitive and, apart from its appearance in the back of an adapted Cooper, nothing was seen of the F2 version.

Stanguellini stuck with the Fiat engine in square form (68 x 68mm) in his last single-seater, in 1966. The engine was rated at 105bhp at 9000rpm, but that figure might be regarded with a suspicion of Italian optimism. It was inclined in the space frame chassis at 30 degrees. With the aerodynamic lines looking 'right' (bodywork was by Gran Sport in Modena) prospects for this dual-category F2/F3 car must have seemed good, but the reality was disappointment and Stanguellini abandoned the world of competition motoring.

STANLEY-BRM

The original BRM endeavour lasted for 24 years, but as the holding company, Rubery Owen, withdrew support late in 1974 BRM was put into liquidation. Louis Stanley saw this as an opportunity to clear the decks, unhappily clearing them of some of the remaining worthwhile personnel as he launched Stanley-BRM. This proved that resounding press statements do not produce effective racing cars – the P207 which was the only new car to emerge was an abysmal failure (see BRM).

STARKE

A 1964 home-built F2 car, with a tubular chassis, DKW engine and VW transmission. It all sounds remarkably similar to German Formula Junior essays of five years earlier, and true to the record of those cars Karl Starke only ran his F2 machine in local events.

STEBRO

Stebro was a Canadian outfit which made conventional Formula Junior cars (space frame, coil spring and double wishbone front suspension, lower wishbone, transverse link and twin radius arms at the rear) and while these were not distinguished two entrants managed to get them accepted for the 1963 US GP. Only one turned up, fitted with a 1500cc version of the Ford 105E engine which gave around 110bhp. Peter Broeker qualified it last, 15 seconds off the pace, but by keeping going was seventh at the end, tantalisingly close to a World Championship point despite the fact he was a mighty 22 laps in arrears.

In 1964 Broeker drove a Stebro in a couple of European F2 races but was embarrassingly slow.   ML

STELLA III

An obsure Russian 500 car of 1951. All that is known is that it had a rear-mounted ZIS 342 engine.   ML

STONE

A shoestring early British 500 car which proved that a Rudge engine in the back of a cut and shut Morris 15cwt van chassis was not a trendsetting specification.   ML

STRANG

Colin Strang, a New Zealander domiciled in England, was the first really successful builder of a 500cc racing car. In the early days of the category he was the star who beat everyone, even the Coopers, but while John and Charles Cooper got their car into production, the Strang remained a one-off.

Basically, Strang took a Fiat 500 chassis and put a Vincent-HRD motor cycle engine and gearbox behind the driver. Beyond that simple statement there was a wealth of subtle thinking. The frame was lightened and stiffened – in the face of then-current lore which said that an ultra-lightweight car would never hold the road properly – and the steering was improved. He retained the original Fiat quarter elliptical rear springs and created his own solid rear axle, which he located properly, and he obtained more power from his engine than even the Vincent works had done.

Strang won the first 500cc competition at Prescott in May 1946 and twelve months later had won all seven events which he had entered. This remarkable start could not continue indefinitely and although he updated his car, and was still a leading contender in 1949, others overtook him. He eventually sold the car, had a race in a Kieft and disappeared from the scene.   ML

STROMBOLI

Adrian Butler and Bruce Mardon completed the first of the original batch of Iotas with this name. It had modified Morgan ifs and rear swing axles which were sprung by a transverse leaf spring. A Douglas flat twin was mounted at the rear, but this type of engine was notoriously difficult to tune properly and was one reason why Stromboli was never successful.   ML

STRUŽKA

This 1951 Czech 500cc car was also run with cycle wings and sidelights, and in that guise it appeared a wondrous throwback to the sporty cyclecars of the early 1920s. The engine was mounted in a drilled sub-frame ahead of the front wheels, which were driven via chains, and as that engine was a single-cylinder Jawa ohc unit it had to be housed under a hump on the nose, which was accentuated as the rest of the car was very low. Transverse leaf front suspension was used, with a simple axle at the rear. In 1952 Stružka converted it into a sports car, with a 600cc Aero Minor engine.

SUPERNOVA

This short-lived Sussex-based constructor built one of the better looking Super Vee cars in 1975 and followed it with the one-off SF3 F3 car in 1976, when it showed well at the beginning of the season as Cuicci placed it third in an Oulton Park race. It was a slender car with a front radiator (and nose reminiscent of Trojans), outboard suspension all round, and a Brown Ford twin-cam engine.

SURTEES

John Surtees became a constructor by accident. He was acting as Len Terry's agent in the Leda F5000 project and when the shortcomings in the prototype Leda became obvious he took

it over. To honour Surtees' commitment it was redesigned and became the TS5, and fortunately the workshop facilities to build it existed; within a year the base was to be relocated at Edenbridge in Kent, where all subsequent Surtees cars were built. The earlier numbers, prefixed JS rather than TS, referred to motorcycle projects, JS4 for example being a special frame for a Ducati engine.

When the TS5 came in 1969 the Surtees Racing Organization comprised Team Surtees and TS Research and Development Ltd, which was the engineering and construction side. The TS7 F1 car came in 1970, and that year John Surtees scored his first World Championship points in his own car. He was soon to give up race driving to concentrate on running the businesses as well as the cars in the field. His own assessment is that Team Surtees did F5000 and F2 very well but never succeeded properly in F1. A tyre company withdrawal left it exposed, sponsors let it down, and too often it was a shoestring operation, at a time when F1 was becoming sophisticated and very costly.

John Surtees' health was poor in the Autumn of 1978, he was disillusioned and had been at odds with some of his FOCA colleagues. As a result he rationally decided to abandon F1, and although he had thoughts about continuing as a constructor in other categories he also closed down the whole motor racing operation.

F5000 cars were fundamental to the first half of Team Surtees' history, which could appear fragmented if they were ignored (as they are elsewhere in this book when incidental to the mainstream line of a constructor such as Lotus).

TS5 This F5000/Formula A car stemmed from the Leda, and was intended first and foremost as an independents' car, although a works team was run as part of the development programme. It had a full monocoque chassis, conventional suspension and followed the contemporary pattern with its 5-litre Chevrolet V-8, driving through a Hewland gearbox. Engines were BRM-Surtees or Traco prepared. Prominent TS5 drivers included David Hobbs, Andrea de Adamich and Trevor Taylor, who was runner-up in the 1969 Guards F5000 Championship.

A modified car was run in 1970 and used to prove some parts intended for the TS7 F1 car, but the TS7A found no customers in Britain. Several accidents led to the works team being withdrawn before the end of the season. The planned TS6 successor never came to pass.

The TS5 looked balanced and a solid car, and build quality was high. The original Surtees colour scheme, red with a broad white arrowhead pattern, suited it well. This is Hobbs at Mondello Park in July 1969, on his way to a first race victory for Team Surtees.

TS7 The first F1 Surtees was completed in time to run trials at Goodwood before the 1970 British GP. John Surtees laid down the lines of the car, and detail draughting work was by Peter Connew and Shahab Ahmed. It followed the TS5 in broad respects, although outwardly it was not similar, being small, with a distinctively slab-sided tub and delta nose aerofoil. Suspension was orthodox, inboard at the front, while a DFV engine and Hewland DG300 gearbox were used. A second, slightly different and lighter, TS7 was ready by the late summer of 1970. Surtees ran as high as seventh in the car's debut race at Brands Hatch and was fifth in the Canadian GP; between those races he won the Oulton Park Gold Cup. That was to be one of two races he won in his own GP cars, for he repeated the victory with a TS9 in 1971.

Drivers: Derek Bell, John Surtees.

The purposeful TS7 stood out, with drooping nose (the radiator was angled at 30 degrees to the horizontal), angular flanks and relative shallowness around the cockpit. This is John Surtees in TS7/001 in the car's GP debut race at Brands Hatch.

TS8 This was another straightforward F5000 car, generally more successful than the TS5 in one of the better years of racing in this category. Mike Hailwood drove the works car to a win straight out of the box and ended the season as runner-up in the Rothmans Championship. The planned Formula A team fell through, so McKechnie took over the TS8 built for it, and Alan Rollinson drove this car to two victories. The cars reappeared in 1972, when Steve Thompson won a race in one (this car lingered on in British F5000 through the next season).

TS9 As it first appeared, this was obviously a derivative of the TS7, longer in the wheelbase and wider in the track, lower and with a changed nose line. It ran in this form from its debut at Kyalami until the end of the season when the side-mounted radiators first tried in the late summer were standardized.

Further modifications led to the TS9B in 1972, when the team cars were sometimes competitive, but were also too many failures for trivial reasons.

Hailwood in particular drove TS9s hard, finishing fourth in the 1971 Italian GP but only 0.14sec behind the winner in that classic blanket finish, and taking second in the same race in 1972.

Drivers: Andrea de Adamich, Mike Hailwood, James Hunt, John Love, Carlos Pace, Tim Schenken, Rolf Stommelen, John Surtees.

The TS9s carried full sponsorship colours in 1971. In this car spectators could see more of the driver than his helmet (John Surtees is the driver, in his last full season and on his way to his best GP placing of the year, fifth at Zandvoort).

TS9B looked a very different car, with full-width nose 'pierced' to allow a free flow of air to the side radiators. Hesketh hired one for James Hunt to make his F1 debut in the 1973 Race of Champions.

TS10 This car marked Surtees' very successful move into F2. It had the familiar lines, with a flat-sided monocoque and radiators in a full-width nose, and the engine was a semi-stressed member (with a tubular sub frame that tended to flex, leading to early problems). The works cars used Hart-developed BDA engines, which gave something away in capacity terms (at 1850cc) but in terms of power lost out only at the top end, and they were very reliable.

Hailwood was the lead driver for the works team run by Pete Briggs, and he convincingly won the 1972 European title; during the year Pace took Surtees' place as the second driver. Two cars sold to independents did not feature in results tables.

The 'arrow' motif was revived on the TS10s, this one just wheeled out at Edenbridge and yet to have appendages such as rear-view mirrors attached.

TS11 The singleton 1972 F5000 car was based on the TS9, with Smith-Chevrolet power. It was run very successfully by Epstein's Speed International team, in that Gijs van Lennep drove it to win the European Championship, with only two race victories (out of 14 races) but consistent points-scoring performances. It served on for half a season with Epstein's 1973 team.

Meanwhile, after a modified works TS8 had been wrecked in a Teretoga accident during a 1972 Tasman race a replacement was contrived with a TS11 monocoque and TS8-style nose radiators, for Hailwood to complete the series (he was second in the Championship).

TS14 In hindsight this car was crucial in the Team Surtees story, for it marked the start of its decline. It was ready too far in advance, designed and built to conform with deformable structure regulations that were then relaxed, leaving Surtees with an overweight car. In part, too, a Firestone change of policy told against the TS14 – it was very quick in its first tests, but devoured front tyres, and in an unhappy coincidence Firestone ran down their development programme as withdrawal was anticipated. There were also destructive accidents, to set against best GP placings of a third and a fourth (both achieved by Pace).

A sandwich construction monocoque was used in the TS14, the combination of a full-width nose and side radiators was repeated, and this time suspension was outboard all round. In the TS14A used by the team in 1973 (five were built) some weight was shed, and through the year there were detail modifications.

The type was first raced at Monza in 1972, when Surtees drove it in his last Grand Prix and failed to finish. He was to continue test driving almost to the end of his days as a constructor.

Drivers: Mike Hailwood, Jochen Mass, Carlos Pace, John Surtees.

Not the tidiest Surtees, and although its drivers had confidence in it, not the most successful. Carlos Pace (above) was the team's most successful driver in 1973.

TS15 1973 was the year BMW arrived in F2 with an exclusive deal with March, and although he had good Hart engines Surtees had to settle for second place in the Championship with the consolation of running the best 'non-BMW' team. Mass drove hard, won two races, was second in the Championship; Derek Bell drove TS15s occasionally and was eighth on the points table.

A version was then built to take the 3.4-litre Cosworth-developed Ford GA V-6, for the revised F5000. This was encouraged by Ford's executives but, in that period of shilly-shally Ford sports policies, minds were changed, and this TS17 never appeared in a race.

TS15 was compact and competent, but never powered by engines that would have enabled its drivers to compete on level terms with the dominant March-BMWs of 1973.

TS16 This followed the TS14 pattern, and through two seasons the principal changes were to be in radiator positions. Aerodynamically, it was a good straight-line car, although Surtees did not have the best of DFVs to fully exploit this, and it

was another overweight car. All of the contracted sponsorship monies for 1974 failed to materialize, and in 1974 the team was reduced to running a single car (1974 had ended disastrously, too, when Helmut Koinigg was killed in a practice crash, driving TS16/03 at Watkins Glen).

Pace placed a TS16 in the points once in 1974, then left the team in mid-season; in 1975 John Watson finished well in three non-Championship F1 races but failed to score in the Championship.

Drivers: Derek Bell, Jose Dolhem, Jean-Pierre Jabouille, Leo Kinnunen, Helmut Koinigg, Jochen Mass, Carlos Pace, Dieter Quester, John Watson.

Obsolescent F1 cars had a useful possible second life in the British F5000 series in the second half of the 1970s – this is TS16/04 being driven by Divina Galica for the Shellsport-Whiting team in 1976. It is largely in its 1975 GP form, and one of the radiators, angled only slightly to the fore-and-aft line, is just visible.

TS19 As the Pilbeam design for the F1 TS18 never took shape, the next Surtees was the TS19, which made its debut in the 1976 South African GP. Design was credited to John Surtees and Ken Sears, and the car promised well. It had a distinctive shape – a broad flat nose and pyramid-section through the main hull, with a tight cockpit surround above it – had outboard suspension all round and the usual DFV/Hewland DG400 combination in the back.

Surtees was back on the Constructors' Championship points table in 1976, Alan Jones scoring the team's seven points, while Brett Lunger showed well in the second car of the works team. The TS19 was brought out again in 1977, when the driving strength was less strong. Brambilla was the constant, and there was a string of second drivers. Nevertheless, six points were accrued. Single entries were made with TS19s in the opening races of 1978.

Drivers: Hans Binder, Vittorio Brambilla, Alan Jones, Brett Lunger, Larry Perkins, Henri Pescarolo, Vern Schuppan, Noritake Takahara.

Alan Jones' determination exploited the sound little TS19 in 1976. In detail the car showed some outward variations through the year, for example being seen with a slit intake across almost the full width of the nose.

TS20 This was a refined car on similar lines to the TS19, seemingly with potential. It was, however, a conventional car when ground effects was really taking hold and it was not ready for the early races. There were also tyre problems, as in 1978 Goodyear adopted a two-tier policy and Team Surtees was not among the favoured. Furthermore, John Surtees was not fully fit, drivers Brambilla and Keegan were both injured during the year, and while Arnoux came in and demonstrated that better results could have been achieved with the car he probably had an eye on a Renault seat (Arnoux visited Surtees in hospital and offered to drive for him). Everything seemed to conspire against Surtees in 1978, and later that year he decided to give up.

Before that a TS21 had been put in hand, and a model tested in a wind tunnel. The car was never completed, but its ground effects elements were married to a TS20 (TS20B, or TS20+) and at the end of the 1979 season Gordon Smiley put in some times in British national series races that hinted at what might have been. In 1980 this car was destroyed when Ray Mallock crashed at Thruxton.

Drivers (GPs): René Arnoux, Vittorio Brambilla, Rupert Keegan.

John Surtees at a sponsor's presentation of his last GP car, the attractive TS20. Surtees' full-width nose had at last been abandoned, and in 'pre-ground-effects' terms the car gives every appearance of aerodynamic efficiency.

The only ground effects Surtees and the last Surtees was this adaptation of a TS20, with its front suspension members tucked away out of the airflow to the side pods, which contained 'normal' radiators replacing the longitudinal rads on the original. In this shot the TS20+ is being driven by Ray Mallock in the Oulton Park Gold Cup.

SVA

One of the most obscure of all F1 cars, the SVA had a supercharged 1100cc Fiat engine and was entered in the 1950 San Remo GP by Ecurie Espadon. Swiss privateer Rudolf Fischer was allowed to start from the back of the grid without managing to set a practice time, but retired on the first lap with a broken oil pipe. ML

SVEBE

The first Svebe, with a DKW 800cc engine and front wheel drive, was built by Sven Andersson and Bengt Peterson in Sweden in 1947. When the 500 movement began to take root the following year a 500cc JAP engine was substituted and the cars were quite successful in sprints and hill climbs. Then followed a hard look at the Effyh 500 car, and the next Svebes were lightened clones which were quite successful until, after making about seven examples, the two friends recognized that Coopers were both faster and cheaper to run. In the early 1960s Andersson built a few F3 Brabham copies for Bengt Peterson's son, Ronnie. ML

SVEZDA

The Svezda Salut was a compact 1952 Russian 500 car which looked not unlike a Cooper. Press releases from the USSR suggested that it was a serious F3 car, and photographs showed one receiving the chequered flag at the end of a 'race'. The 1950s were peppered with rumours of Russian racing cars, which included the Kharkov 'F1 project', and the propaganda was reinforced by sports commissars visiting Western circuits and muttering about serious Soviet intentions. It was all propaganda, however, and magazines which published photographs of the race-winning Svezda suggested, perhaps correctly, that it was a staged picture. Photographs of the 350cc Svezda record car (looking like a model of John Cobb's Railton Special) were also released but nobody took them seriously. ML

SWALLOW

Swallow Racing came into being to run a Pilbeam in Formula Ford 2000 in 1981 and progressed to F3 with a Reynard in 1985. That year Dave Rendall started design work on the team's own car, which emerged early in 1987 as the Swallow 387. It was built around a composite chassis, with pullrod suspension all round and initially a Judd VW engine mounted at an angle of 14 degrees, driving through a Staffs Silent Gears 'box.

Several drivers tested the 387, and save for minor traction shortcomings the results were encouraging, although seemingly undermined by a lack of continuity and the fact that the team ran Reynard 873s in parallel. Donnelly and Schonstrom scored in those in the British Championship, while Tim Davies failed to score in the Swallow.

SWICA

Pierre Rechsteiner, Formula Ford driver in the late 1970s, one-time on-circuit service engineer for Mader, who runs a car preparation company and teams for minor categories from a base near Lausanne, explored the business of being a constructor with an F3 car in 1985. It was a conventional Spiess-VW-engined machine, its monocoque having an aluminium sheet lower section bonded to a carbon fibre upper section, and it appeared bulkier than its French and British contemporaries. Rechsteiner Racing concentrated on the French F3 series, without great success, and in 1988 reverted to running other constructors' cars, in Formula Ford, French F3 and historic series, while Rechsteiner looked to the possibility of building more F3 cars in the 1990s.

T

TALBOT

For a quarter of a century spanning the Second World War the French presence in top-line single-seater racing was largely maintained by Italian-born constructors – Ettore Bugatti and Amédée Gordini, and between them chronologically there was Antonio Lago. Tony Lago is forever associated with those big blue cars that seemed so very 'French' in the first World Championship seasons (they seemed big, but in dimensions such as wheelbase they were smaller than late-1980s F1 cars, although substantially heavier).

In the background was the Sunbeam-Talbot-Darracq combine, which collapsed in the mid-1930s. Lago took on the French factory, and in 1936 the sports cars that were the basis of the post-war Talbot GP cars were introduced. Stripped sports cars were run in late-1930s GPs. The sports and racing cars that came after the Second World War were often referred to as Lago-Talbots.

A pre-war Talbot single-seater was naturally used in the recovery period and its layout was picked up in the T26C. This was never competitive with Italian front-line cars in terms of power, outright speed and acceleration, but it was economical and reliable, and drivers picked up placings in early Championship races, and wins in secondary events into the 1950s. Lago apparently had thoughts about a supercharged F1 car, but in its last decade the Talbot company turned its attention (and limited budget) towards sports cars.

In 1959 the company passed to Simca, and thus in time the marque name passed on to Peugeot, and was used for road cars built at Chrysler's former European plant. In 1980 the group announced plans to enter F1 in the following year, using the marque name Talbot. BMW motor sport supremo Jochen Neerspach joined Talbot to set up a competitions department, and the plan was to take over a BMW turbo engine project that seemed to be languishing and commission a chassis from a specialist constructor. That fell through abruptly as BMW announced their Brabham liaison four months later, but the name Talbot did feature on GP entry lists again in 1981-2, when Ligier ran Matra-engined cars as Talbot-Ligiers. These echoed tradition in being big and heavy cars.

Monoplace Built in 1939 around sports car components, this one-off was raced after the war alongside slightly earlier offset single-seaters. Common to all, and to succeeding cars, was a box-section chassis, ifs and rigid rear axle, and a straight six driving through a Wilson pre-selector gearbox. Louis Chiron drove the Monoplace to win the 1947 French GP and placed it second at Monaco in 1948, the first year of F1 as such.

Louis Chiron on his way to victory in the 1947 GP de l'ACF at Lyon (it has to be remarked that Alfa did not contest the race). The Talbot was run by Paul Vallée's Ecurie France.

T26C It is perhaps over-statment to credit Lago and Carlo Marchetti with the design of this car, for it seemed to evolve out of the Monoplace and post-war sports cars. 14 were to be built. The chassis and suspension remained unchanged, the 4485cc (93 x 110mm) pushrod ohv straight six was rated at 240bhp in 1948, and from the Wilson pre-selector gearbox the transmission was offset to run to the right of the driver. In 1950 a bonnet-side air intake distinguished the cars with reworked engines, which gave 280bhp but were less reliable. At the same time a little of the excess weight was trimmed.

The Type 26C made its race debut at Monaco in 1948, and in the following year two major GPs fell to Talbots, Louis Rosier winning the Belgian race (that was reputedly a factor in Ferrari's switch to unsupercharged engines) and Louis Chiron winning the GP de France at Reims (not, incidentally, the French GP as such – that was a sports car race in 1949). Thereafter top five placings were the best that Talbot entrants could look for (Rosier taking two third places in 1950 Championship races and a fourth in 1951), while odd secondary races fell to the cars. In 1952-53 Whiteford won the Australian GP in a T26C.

Drivers (Championship GPs): Eugène Chaboud, Louis Chiron, Yves Ciraud-Cabantous, Johnny Claes, Gianfranco Comotti, Philippe Etancelin, Giuseppe Farina, George Grignard, Duncan Hamilton, 'Pierre Levegh', Henri Louveau, G. Mairesse, Eugène Martin, André Pilette, Charles Pozzi, Georges Raph, Louis Rosier, Raymond Sommer, J. Swaters.

The great Raymond Sommer at Bremgarten in 1949, the Swiss cobbles seeming most appropriate to the classic 'Vintage' lines of the Lago-Talbot.

TARASCHI

Bernardo Taraschi was involved with small sports cars, the Giaur and the Urania, before building Formula Junior cars under his own name for a brief period and then reverting to that Italian performance car staple business of tuning Fiats. The Taraschi Junior was introduced in 1958 with the customary Fiat 1100cc engine mounted ahead of the driver in a ladder-type chassis. Wishbones and coil springs front suspension was used but at the rear there was a de Dion type axle – unique in an Italian Junior. The bodywork was smooth but bulky, with the cockpit offset to the left, clear of the transmission line. Zannini won FJ races for Taraschi in 1958, and Taraschi scored one of his marque's last victories at Caserta in 1960. The 1959 season, however, was the most successful, when Colin Davis saw off the best of the Continental front-engined runners in several Italian and French races. A Taraschi was one of the first Juniors to appear in the USA. Like most 'traditional' Italian front-engined constructors, Taraschi was overwhelmed by the new wave of British cars from 1960.

Borrani wheels, louvred flanks and nice nose and tail lines mark the Taraschi out as an Italian racing car of the old school. Signor Fiordelesi had modified nose and tail of this one against Cesenatico scenery in 1959.

TARK

It seems a little unreal that the few constructors which have produced more than a thousand single-seater racing cars include among their number one based in Tallinn (hence the alternative name used for some of the cars, Estonia). Tallinna Autode Remondi Katsetehas had its origins in a group of enthusiasts and the spindly F3 car, Estonia 1, they built in 1958. Production started in 1960, with an order from the Soviet Central Auto Club (they did things differently East of the old Iron Curtain!) and TARK was established in the following year.

Most of its cars were built for local classes, run to regulations framed around local components such as Lada, Wartburg or Moskvich engines, although occasionally the Central Club would make a bulk purchase of Western tyres, or an item such as a Colotti or Hewland gearbox would become available. Generally, 'exotic' materials did not come into use until the 1980s, and the monocoque did not feature in the TARK repertoire until the second half of the decade.

Among the cars for Formula Vostock and other local categories were some built to the main-line formulae, although these were not seen outside Eastern Europe. Essentially TARK and its first designer, Ants Seiler, had to look abroad for inspiration. The first F3 cars owed something to the Czech Eso while Melkus was a source of inspiration and of two-stroke tuning know-how in the later 1960s, before Western practices were followed.

In 1989 the first moves towards genuine international exposure were announced by Novotec in Germany, although when a car first appeared at Hockenheim its engine blew up. This exploration of F3 with the Tark-Moskvich served to show that it was sadly under-powered, but races with a Spiess-VW engine suggested there was little wrong with the Eufra-built chassis. After the announcement of a two-year programme to develop an F1 car Novotec remained silent on that subject.

Formula 3 The Mk1 Estonia was a one-off 500cc F3 car in 1959. This came to be regarded as a prototype – Mk 2 was a development car and Mk3 the definitive production version. All had tubular frames, with a single-cylinder Serpukhov 36bhp motorcycle engine behind the cockpit and a four-speed gearbox. The 32 production cars, which set TARK up as a constructor, were delivered in 1960-1, when as an international formula 500cc racing was extinct.

TARK picked up the F3 thread again in 1964 with a conversion of the Mk9 Formula Junior car using a 1-litre Wartburg engine, for which the Junior output of up to 85bhp was claimed. It was installed horizontally, making for very low overall lines. A 1.6-litre Moskvich-engined Mk16 appeared for 1971 F3, but that effort was deflected to the local 1.3-litre F3, in line with bloc policy of not contesting in fields where national products could be shown up.

There was another return in 1989, with a car that looked up to the minute in many respects – slim hull (the chassis was made in West Germany by Eufra, which had an autoclave), side pods to conform with international safety requirements and house radiators, inboard suspension and so on. In the second race in the 1989 German Championship, Argentine driver Victor Rosso placed a Spiess-VW engined TARK second, between two Reynards, showing promise not repeated in that season.

Late-1960s TARK F3 machines were slim-bodied cars with a wide track.

Perhaps the F3 car seen in Germany in 1989 and at the 1990 London Racing Car show was a pioneer? It was a smart grey machine with a rather spindly red hammer and sickle ahead of the cockpit, the slightly enigmatic slogan 'Racing Cooperation East West' on its flanks and Moskvich on the engine cover. It was actually assembled at Paderborn by Novotec.

Formula Junior The Mk5 laid down by Roman Bertelov followed 'semi space frame' lines and proved to be a one-off. Its rear-mounted Wartburg engine produced some 65bhp, which meant that it was competitive only in Eastern bloc terms, with cars such as Melkus-Wartburgs.

Bertelov's successor, Kalle Keel, designed the more sophisticated Mk9 to follow it in 1963. It was slimmer and lower, with a space frame, double wishbone suspension with inboard coil spring/damper units and an 80-85bhp version of the Wartburg engine. It was the basis of the short-lived 1-litre F3 car.

TATRA

This very old company is best known for the large rear-engined saloons that in Western countries might have been categorized in the gentleman's express class, and followed in a line of evolution, rather than development, from the mid-1930s. Its single-seaters of the early 1950s naturally conformed to this layout, and while they were really no more than *formule libre* specials they were another interesting strand. Since the T607 single-seaters were around when the 2.5-litre Grand Prix formula was announced they could just conceivably be regarded as eligible to run under its regulations, although before it came into force they had been retired to the Tatra museum, and in no way were they Grand Prix cars.

The T607 was built around a full space frame – that was to become common in front-line racing some time later – with a double wishbone front suspension and a swing axle at the rear and torsion bar springing. The pushrod ohv V-8 from the 603 saloon was apparently used in three capacities – 2490cc, 2545cc and 2472cc – but obviously was not generously powerful in any of these forms. The cars were run in a few local races, and were used to break modest national records.

The T607 was a surprisingly small car, narrow-tracked and with narrow wheels, but with overall lines that would not have looked out of place on a grid in the late 1950s. The pleated seat back and large steering wheel are straight out of a late-1940s Italian specification.

TCA

The initials stood for Trips-Colotti-Automobili, or for those north of the Alps for Trips-Colotti-Auto Union, and the 1960 Formula Junior car had a formidable pedigree. Leading F1 driver Wolfgang von Trips was the patron, Valerio Colotti was the designer, Fantuzzi built the bodies and Tec Mec the production cars (the prototype was built by von Trips' mechanic, Neri). The weak link was perhaps the three-cylinder DKW two-stroke regarded as the standard power unit.

The car was a rear-engined space-framed job, with suspension front and rear by lower wishbone and upper transverse spring, and while outwardly it appeared large it was well proportioned. The DKW engine and gearbox internals were specified (in the latter case Colotti allowed for DKW, Fiat or VW casings). Like other DKW-engined Juniors, the TCA was fast but lacked stamina.

Stausberg hill-climbing in a TCA in 1960. This was an activity better suited to the DKW two-stroke than circuit racing, for the engines quickly lost tune and a particular weakness was over-heating in the middle cylinder.

TECHNIC

This one-off F3 car was built in 1977 by CTG on the lines of the previous year's Viking. It appeared in practice for just one race, but never came to a grid.

TEC-MEC

This F1 enterprise was ill-timed, in that it took shape slowly as a front-engined design at the time when the rear-engined layout had been proved. It began and ended as a one-off derived from the Maserati 250F, designer Valerio Colotti setting up Studio Tecnica Meccanica when the Maserati team was closed down and obtaining some backing to continue his line of development for the 250F. Colotti then moved on as the first car, designated Tec-Mec 415 by the syndicate that took it over, reached completion.

The car had a tubular space frame, ifs by wishbones and coil springs, irs by wishbones and transverse leaf spring, disc brakes and front-mounted 250F engine. Testing was sluggish, but eventually the American among the backers got the car to Florida for the 1959 United States GP. It was off the pace in practice and lasted seven laps in the race. This was its only race, save for historic events after it had been brought to England by Tom Wheatcroft. Tec-Mec also made up a *formule libre* cut and shut job on a 250F.

When Colotti sold the studio in 1959 Automobili Tec Mec essayed a Formula Junior car. This was rear-engined (almost inevitably in Italy in the early Junior years the power unit was basically Fiat) and had independent suspension all round. It made no more impression than the F1 car.

Driver: Fritz d'Orey.

TECNO

Luciano and Gianfranco Pederzani formed their Tecnokart company in Bologna in 1962 as an offshoot of a hydraulic pump manufacturer. Around a decade later it was running a

Grand Prix team but rapidly approaching racing extinction. The Tecnokart Kaimano 100/200 and Piuma karts won many national, European and world championships through the 1960s. In mid-decade Tecno had launched a delightful little F4 car, the K250, with a 250cc engine (usually a Ducati), and that had led to a generally similar car for the Italian Formula 850. In 1966 the first F3 Tecno appeared, on similar kart-inspired lines.

The F3 car was third first time out, at Mugello, and in 1967 a European Championship race fell to a Tecno team car. In the next two years they took the Championship. Several national championships also fell to Tecno drivers – the Italian, of course, the French and the Swedish. As the 1970s opened Tecno had a foothold in F2 – Cevert had scored the marque's first F2 win at Reims in 1969, and Regazzoni won the Championship in 1970.

These were tough chunky little cars, controllable and 'chuckable' in the manner of karts, and with character well matched to some of the men who drove them. They evolved from the 1967 F3/1968 F2 designs, and tended to be designated by year of manufacture. Occasionally a novelty was introduced, for example the full-width F2 nose in 1970, and sometimes something went wrong – notoriously the flimsy wheels of 1970. Generally Tecno seemed set on a fair course into the 1970s, despite the retirement of older brother Luciano in 1969, but in 1972 the expected Tecno F2 team did not appear, while Tecno cars had almost disappeared from F3 as the 1.6-litre regulations came in 1971. Tecno had gone into F1, and that effort demanded all of its resources, which were never abundant. It proved to be a fatal move. The sponsor was among the most understanding in the sport, the drivers and the team manager were good, but the machinery through 1972 and 1973 was appalling.

Formula 3 Broadly the first F3 Tecno in 1966 was a scaled-up K250, Cosworth-engined with unashamedly outboard suspension, a forward driving position in the short wheelbase giving it a dumpy appearance. It enabled the brothers to find their feet in F3 and come up with a more practical car for 1967. This was naturally a space frame car, still on a short wheelbase and with unchanged suspension (double wishbones and coil spring/damper ifs at the front and rear, with long radius arms at the back). It was efficient in aerodynamic respects, for it could match any other car on straights. as well as in corners. Development occupied the works pair for most of the year, and as it ended Clay Regazzoni scored Tecno's first international win, in Spain.

Success came with a rush. In 1968 Tecno sold a lot of cars, and introduced their own version of the Cosworth MAE, claiming up to 125bhp. Racing Team Holland ran Tecno-DAFs for Beckwith and Van Lennep. Works drivers Regazzoni and Bernabei won with the 'normal' cars, and so did Cevert, Peterson, Jaussaud, Wisell and Mohr, between them piling up 32 victories in the year's 65 major F3 international races.

The 1969 story was similar – only detail changes to the car and a great run of success, none greater than Ronnie Peterson's in a Novamotor-engined Tecno. He won 14 races, including the all-important Monaco F3 event despite the fact that, belying appearances, the car was not at its best on a tight street circuit. Picchi won the Italian Championship, clinching the title in the final race of the season. Jaussaud did most of the winning for Tecno in 1970, a season when few top drivers appeared in the cars, winning seven events. In 1971 there were just a couple of victories.

Formula 2 Tecno moved into F2 with space frame short-wheelbase cars closely related to the F3 machines, initially with Cosworth engines but soon with Tecno's own versions of basic Ford units. The layout served through to 1971, with only detail changes.

In 1968 two Tecno teams ran in some European Championship races and showed the cars' potential. Regazzoni was entered for eleven races and scored 13 points with his best placing a third at Crystal Palace. He was involved in heavy accidents, as was team mate Jaussaud. The 1969 emphasis was on a works team and Cevert scored Tecno's first F2 win at Reims.

A more substantially modified car came in mid-1970. It retained the basic tubular chassis with minor changes to the suspension but the body was wider and flatter, behind a big full-width nose cone which ducted radiator air to each side. There was some surprise when Regazzoni won the Championship, one of his race victories coming in a 68 and three in the 'new' 70. Cevert also scored well, with one win. There was little change for 1971, when Tecno's BDA was powerful but unreliable. That flaw dogged most aspects of the team's season as the F1 programme loomed. Cevert was successful only in the first part of the season when he won two Championship races and one non-title event.

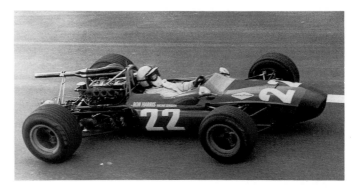

From some angles the early F2 Tecno appeared to consist of engine, wheels and suspension, with a small nacelle for the driver. This shot of a Ron Harris car, driven by Pedro Rodriguez, shows how close it was to the F3 car, the obvious differences being behind the cockpit.

Aesthetically the F3 Tecno had nothing to commend it, save fitness for purpose. This is Jean-Pierre Jaussaud in a Tecno 69 at Montlhéry.

The late cars looked more substantial, but in fact were very similar in make-up. This is Cevert in 1971.

Formula 1 Luciano Pederzani committed Tecno to move into the very different environment of F1 in 1971 and decided against a proprietary engine. Italian constructors have long had an ability to run up an engine very quickly although many have not actually been very good. Tecno was no exception and its first flat twelve (80.98 x 48.46mm, 2005cc) was on the test bench in the late summer of 1971, with 460bhp at 11,000rpm and safe to 13,500rpm claimed. The chassis comprised a space frame with sheet steel welded to the bottom and sides, and outrigged frames to carry the fuel tanks. The engine/Hewland DG400 was a stressed unit. Front suspension was a double wishbone arrangement with outboard and near upright coil springs/dampers, while at the back were lower wishbones, upper links, similar coil springs/dampers and radius arms.

The first car was not ready for late-1971 races, as had been hoped, but the delay enabled Tecno and Martini to get together. Then it was realized that the car exceeded maximum width dimensions, so it had to be rebuilt, with rounded flanks. The delayed race debut came in the Belgian GP, and a hard year brought no reward beyond third place in a minor race at Vallelunga. Ron Tauranac reworked the rear suspension, but further changes were called for.

Alan McCall designed a new monocoque chassis for 1973, while driver Chris Amon persuaded the sponsor to invite Gordon Fowell to design an alternative, via Goral ('a consortium of independent designers'). The McCall car, PA123-006, which had similar suspension to the 1972 PA123s, first raced in the Belgian GP, when Amon became the only driver to score a Championship point in a Tecno. It was raced to three more retirements, while the Goral E731 proved hopeless. Amon quit, Tecno gave up and before the end of the 1973 season Martini sponsorship went to Brabham.

Drivers: Chris Amon, Derek Bell, Nanni Galli.

The original PA123, bulky and over-size. The full-width nose contained a large radiator, as the flat twelve had a tendency to overheat; the two small slots are for brake cooling air.

The angular McCall car, driven by Amon in Belgium in 1973.

TELNA

André Halnet, a Belgian, based his front-engined 500 car on the Kahn MkI which had been built by Robert Kahn. It was front-engined with front wheel drive, sliding pillar ifs and independent rear suspension by transverse leaf and lower wishbones. Unlike the Khan, however, it was built high and horrid and from a distance could have been mistaken for a 1920s cyclecar. At first a Saroléa engine was fitted but this was soon replaced by a JAP unit. Either way it did not matter a great deal for the Telna was never a competitive car, though it did have a long competition life. On at least one occasion it was entered under the name ECI 3, which was clearly a ruse designed to confuse historians.   ML

TERRIER

Len Terry, best known as a journeyman F1, Indianapolis and F5000 car designer, built his first Terriers for Clubman's racing, and Brian Hart drove a Mk2 to a string of victories in 1958. While Terry was designing Gilby sports-racing and F1 cars he also ran the company building Mk2s. The basic design was easily adapted for the Mk4 Formula Junior car, which was intended to be an 'economy' car (hence the use of components such as an Austin A35 gearbox). It was a semi-space frame car, with independent suspension all round (twin wishbones at the front, lower wishbones, deep hub carrier and prominent coil spring/damper units at the rear). A twin downdraught Webers conversion of the Ford 105E engine was used. By the time it was introduced in 1960, economy was no more a way to racing success in Formula Junior than a front-engined layout.

The Terrier Junior was an exemplary front-engined car, but in 1960 nothing could overcome the handicap of a man in the cockpit between engine and driven wheels. The driver in this Terrier is Brian Hart, at Snetterton in the early summer of 1960.

THEODORE

Macau-based entrepreneur Theodore 'Teddy' Yip was active in Far East racing before he sponsored Brian Redman in F5000 in 1974. He was then involved with several drivers before he backed the second Ensign in 1977, when it was driven by Patrick Tambay. That led him into F1, and in 1978 he ran his own car from the one-time Ralt plant. It was a failure, and so were the Wolf cars he ran later that year.

While he still held interests in both Ensign and Shadow, he turned back to the British Aurora series, where Divina Galica drove one of his Wolf cars to become the first woman to win a race in an F1 car. Yip then took over Shadow as a basis for a new Theodore Grand Prix team, the DN12 being redesignated TR2 for early 1981 outings. For that year's championship races the TY01 was laid down, but little was achieved with it, and nothing with TY02 in 1982. Theodore Racing and Ensign were amalgamated for 1983 and ran an uprated version of the previous year's Ensigns as Theodores with an Ensign designation. With no prospect of developing a turbo car for 1984, Yip and Mo Nunn turned to CART racing.

TR1 This very unremarkable Cosworth kit car was designed by Ron Tauranac, and apart from its bluff lines it was wholly conventional. Two were built, and entered for five Championship races, but never qualified. However, Rosberg not only started in the Silverstone International Trophy, he won it – a result that owed everything to his skill in torrential rain.

TR1/1 in the old Ralt shops, not quite complete in that the bodywork normally extended above the radiators. TR1/2 had a revised nose, with a larger intake.

TY01 A ground effects car designed by Tony Southgate, this was competent rather than distinguished, and run-of-the-mill. Yet TY01 was usually a qualifier, and Tambay drove one (of the three built) to score the first of the two Championship points that were to accrue to Theodore. It started life with a pylon-mounted front wing but during 1981 gained a normal nose aerofoil. TY01s were used into 1982.

Drivers: Patrick Tambay, Marc Surer, Derek Daly.

TY01 in its early form, running on Avon tyres. And if old tyres marking a corner seem out of place in the 1980s, this car was photographed during a demonstration event at Dubai.

TY02
Another Southgate design, and a pair were built around aluminium-honeycomb monocoques and on straightforward ground effects lines. At best they were back-of-the-grid qualifiers (and all too often they did not qualify); driver changes through the year did not help, but just one finish (and that a 14th place) in the 1982 season was hardly encouraging.

Drivers: Tommy Byrne, Derek Daly, Jan Lammers, Geoff Lees.

The broad side pods of a ground effects car are very obvious in this shot of Byrne during practice at Hockenheim in TY02/1. He failed to qualify in his first outing in the car.

N183 This was a revised version of Nigel Bennett's Ensign N181 design, the single car completed (as an Ensign) in 1982 being uprated and joined by two more. The principal improvement was the introduction of carbon fibre reinforcement around the cockpit. Between them, paying drivers Cecotto and Guerrero failed to qualify only five times, and the ex-motor cyclist scored Theodore's second and last point, at Long Beach.

Drivers: Johnny Cecotto, Roberto Guerrero, Brian Henton.

Brian Henton had a one-off drive in an N183 at Brands Hatch, placing it fourth in the 1983 Race of Champions, while regular team driver Guerrero was seventh and last.

THIN WALL SPECIAL

The Thin Wall Specials, forerunners of the Vanwalls, were Ferraris modified to varying extents by Vandervell's racing team, more significant for what they represented than for what they were in the metal. Through them there was a growth in professionalism that was necessary as Britain played a larger role in racing.

The first two were Tipo 125 supercharged V-12 cars, a single-stage 1949 version (actually bought for BRM) and a 1950 two-stage supercharged car on loan. Neither met Vandervell's exacting requirements. The second was rebuilt as a

4.5-litre unsupercharged car, and then came a long-wheelbase car which was to be extensively modified, in the engine, transmission and running gear, and was also fitted with disc brakes. Through it the team learned a lot about the business of car development and racing, while they worked towards the first Vanwall.

By the time this Thin Wall was raced, F1 was no longer the World Championship category, but in short British F1 and *formule libre* races it was happily pitted against the V-16 BRM and assorted lesser cars. In the hands of Collins, Farina, Gonzalez, Hawthorn and Taruffi it provided great entertainment. Not that entertainment in these little events was uppermost in G.A. Vandervell's mind.

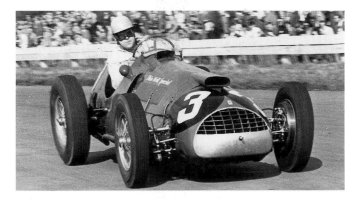

Third Thin Wall, driven by Parnell at Goodwood in 1951.

Fourth and last Thin Wall, driven by Collins at Silverstone in 1952. The blatant commercial words reflect that Vandervell was powerful enough to have his way in the presentation of his cars, prompting a comparison with the put-down of Jack Brabham when he attempted to run a Cooper as a 'Redex Special' a few years later.

THUNDER

This LM39 was a locally-built BMW-engined F2 car which did not remotely challenge the March domination of top-line Japanese racing in 1979.

TIGA

Howden Ganley and Tim Schenken, New Zealand and Australian one-time F1 drivers, took over MRE and its Formula Ford production in 1975, and produced their first Tiga in 1976. With designer Martin Read they concentrated on Formula Ford (both 1600 and 2000) and small sports cars, allowing the distraction of an F1 project in 1978. This came close to realization – major components such as chassis and suspension were gathered together but never actually assembled. That year Schenken launched Team Tiga, to run F3

drivers, initially in March and Ralt chassis. (Eventually Schenken was to strike off on his own in team management, before moving on to motor sports organization in the second half of the 1980s.)

The team led to the F381, an F3 car designed by Ganley and Colin Smith. This was a conventional car, but only a one-off. As it was run occasionally alongside Schenken's Ralts it was never fully developed. Weaver drove the F381, and scored points in one British Championship round in 1981.

Meanwhile the Tiga F280 F2 car had shown some promise, until driver Hans-Georg Bürger was fatally injured in a warm-up accident at Zandvoort in 1980. It was a quite straightforward BMW-powered ground effects car with a light alloy monocoque, quite deliberately laid out as a scaled-down F1 car and therefore not intended for possible production in quantity. It was completed slowly, the finance it was hoped would come with Eje Elgh did not (nor did Elgh). After Bürger's death the fate of the design was to be used as the basis for a CanAm Tiga.

In the early 1980s Tiga built a range of cars for the lesser single-seater categories, in round terms up to the level of Formula Atlantic including the FA82 Australian Championship car, before concentrating on sports cars.

The F280 was a ground effects car built to high standards, which showed some promise in early tests. Bürger started it in five F2 races in 1980, when his best placing was eighth.

TIGER CUB

In 1948 South African enthusiasts, Orlando Fregona and Don Hall, took a Fiat 500 chassis, lightened it, put a Triumph Tiger 100 engine and gearbox in the back, added twin master brake cylinders (probably the first 500cc car to have them) and clothed it in a fairly rudimentary body. The result was 'Tiger Cub' and with Fregona at the wheel it was the most successful 500 car in South Africa until Cooper MkVs began to appear in the summer of 1951/2.   ML

TIGER-KITTEN

One of the first 500cc specials, Clive Lones' Tiger-Kitten used an Austin Seven frame and suspension, Morris 8 hydraulic brakes and a front-mounted JAP engine. At first it was underpowered and overweight, and the cockpit was offset, but Lones soon narrowed and lightened his car, threw away the Austin front axle and substituted Morgan sliding pillar ifs, and obtained a 'five stud' JAP engine. Thanks partly to Lones' ability behind the wheel (he had been competing since the 1920s) this pretty and well-made little car was a leading contender in the early years of the 500 movement and, on occasion, won events.

Later Lones entered a second Tiger Kitten but this was in fact the prototype Iota P1 given a new name. After that Lones bought a Cooper and plugged on to complete nearly thirty years in motor sport.   ML

TIGER SPECIAL

Australian E. Millier basically cut and shut the chassis of a 1930 Morris Minor, complete with semi-elliptical springing front and rear, and put a Triumph Tiger twin at the back to make a 500cc car, but it did not win races. ML

TITAN

As the 1967 season wound down Charles Lucas Engineering introduced the Titan Mk3, which was greeted as a most promising newcomer to F3. To a degree that promise was fulfilled in 1968, only for the company to change its policy and offer its car construction business for sale in order to concentrate on engine development.

Lucas had run the 1966 Lotus works F3 team, and continued with one 41 (driven by Lucas) in 1967 alongside Stiller's Brabhams. Thus there was a background of experience behind the Mk3 (Mk1 was a sports-racer, Mk2 an F2 project). It was a conventional space frame design by Roy Thomas, naturally with Lucas' own version of the Cosworth MAE engine.

A works pair was run in 1968 for 'Luke' and Roy Pike, who was responsible for development and also came good in racing, winning in France, Belgium and Eire as well as England. Leo Kinnunen enjoyed some success in Scandinavia in 1968 and 1969, but other independents seemed to find the Mk3 a tricky car.

The Mk3A that came late in 1968 had revised suspension and space frame stiffened with sheet metal panels. It turned out to be a one-off and was sold to Ben Moore, who then proceeded to run Charles Lucas in it in 1969. He scored one brilliant win at Silverstone but through much of the season was handicapped by increasingly uncompetitive tyres.

The Mk3 Titan was a clean competent car in the late-1960s F3 pattern. The short-lived marque's most successful driver was American Roy Pike, here at Brands Hatch in 1968.

TMS

The unpretentious TMS 833, run in the 1983 Swedish F3 Championship by Mats Carlsson, was a home-built one-off, with Toyota engine and Hewland gearbox. Carlsson was runner-up in the Championship, among a gaggle of Ralt RT3 drivers.

ToJ

Jorg Obermoser was a prominent German supplier of electrical industrial equipment as the 1970s opened, an enthusiast with some saloon racing experience who saw an opportunity to become a constructor in 1972. That year he undertook to distribute GRD racing cars in Germany and adjacent countries, but then as designer Jo Marquart moved to Modus so Obermoser transferred his affiliation.

The first ToJ was a GRD 2-litre sports-racing car design (ToJ SC02) and a 1974 Modus project was ToJ SC03 for the same category, with bodywork designed by Achim Storz in an arrangement that was to come to apply to single-seaters. That year Obermoser also handled F3 sales. ToJ continued in parallel with Modus, and for a while after the collapse of that company. Although the 1977 F2 effort was paltry, Peter Scharmann won the German F3 championship with a ToJ. By then Obermoser had despaired of becoming established as a constructor.

Formula 3 At the start of the 1975 season the Modus-type cars run in Germany tended to be regarded as Modus/ToJ, correctly as apart from bodywork they were Modus M1s (and M1s were also run in Germany). As the year wore on they were increasingly referred to as ToJ. The 1976 car was no match for the dominant March/Ralt/Chevron trio, nor even for Maco in most German races, but towards the end of the year Keke Rosberg began to get results with F301.

The F302 in 1978 followed the existing chassis and running gear lines, with bodywork that in plan tapered from the back of the cockpit forward to a narrow nose that was distinctly unfashionable. Austrian Peter Scharmann ran a car in the gold Warsteiner colours that had been associated with ToJ since its inception, and used BMW and Toyota engines through a year when good placings saw him win the German championship.

Last of the ToJ line, the F302 driven by Scharmann. Its body lines were neat, and suspension components were unashamedly hung out in the breeze. It worked well, and in the right hands might have achieved much.

Formula 2 The 1976 ToJ F2 car preceded its Modus equivalent, with a chassis on similar lines and the narrow-track approach. Outwardly, however, ToJ followed its own path, with a not very handsome body, small nose carrying a full-width wing and a cockpit that gave the impression of wrapping round the driver. Heidegger BMW engines were used. Handling was a problem, improved after a spring change of tyres but never good despite later suspension modifications, stronger bulkheads to beef up the monocoque and loss of weight. Saloon car ace Hans Heyer scored a European Championship point in a ToJ at Hockenheim, in his first-ever single-seater race, but had only one more outing. Rosberg worked hard and scored a fourth and two fifths from eight races with F201s (his was usually the only car run). In the last race of the season, and the last for a works ToJ, Obermoser just failed to qualify one of his cars. Odd ToJ F2 cars appeared, occasionally and quite ineffectually, in 1977 and 1978.

F201 was not a handsome car, and results were to reflect its looks.

TOJEIRO

Examples of the Britannia Formula Junior car designed by John Tojeiro carried his name, as he had an interest in this minor and short-lived constructor. If his intention was to prolong its existence, however, he failed, for the car was not competitive under either name.

TOKEN

The Token was a short-lived Cosworth kit car, which made little impact in 1974 and faded away as the Safir in 1975. Had the economic times been more propitious it might have been significant – it was conceived as Ron Dennis' first F1 car, for the Rondel team in which he was a partner with Neil Trundle, and less than ten years later Dennis was to make a great impact on F1.

The Token RJ02 reflected designer Ray Jessop in being an honest and workmanlike design. It had a slim monocoque, conventional suspension, DFV power and a Hewland FGA400 gearbox, with attractive overall lines. The name Token was derived from Tony Vlassopoulo and Ken Grob, who took it over when Rondel retreated from F1.

Tom Pryce bringing the neat little Token into the narrow Silverstone pits lane during its very brief practice for its first race start – he completed only three laps in practice and 15 in the race before gear linkage failure led to retirement from the International Trophy.

The car showed promise in its debut race, but started in only three GPs in 1974, when Ian Ashley finished in the German and Austrian races, 14th and 13th respectively. RJ02 reappeared as the Safir in the two British non-Championship races in 1975, when Trimmer placed it 12th in the Race of Champions and 14th in the International Trophy.

Driver: Ian Ashley.

TOLEMAN

Toleman Group people were involved in British racing through most of the 1970s, with Ford Escorts and devices with DFV F1 engines that masqueraded as a Capri or a VW. The group moved on to a Formula Ford 2000 team that cleaned up in 1977, and then entered F2, backing a March for Rad Dougall in 1978. That year ex-Royale designer Rory Byrne joined and was to design Tolemans, and Benettons when the team was taken over. Meanwhile, Toleman ran quasi-works Ralts in 1979, drivers Henton and Dougall finishing the season second and fifth respectively in the F2 championship.

This provided a springboard for 1980, when Toleman became a constructor and the Byrne-designed cars dominated the season. Through it, Toleman worked towards an entry into F1 which came in 1981, when the combination of a new car with a new power unit, in a new environment, was a 'character-building' challenge. By the mid-1980s Toleman cars were serious contenders, although somewhat unreliable, but tyre problems early in 1985 were solved only by buying the Spirit's team's contract. That year the cars ran in Benetton colours, and for 1986 the whole enterprise was taken over by the Italian company, the team continuing with Byrne-designed cars named Benettons.

TG280 The first Toleman was a neat, clean-lined car which dominated the 1980 F2 Championship. Designed by Byrne and team engineer John Gentry, it had an aluminium alloy monocoque and conventional suspension, the novelties being the Hart engine and Pirelli tyres. These made significant contributions to Toleman's success, for the engines were very reliable and the tyres were much better than the Goodyears most F2 teams used. A 'B' version with revised front suspension came during the season. Henton and Warwick were a clear first and second in the Championship.

BS Fabrications built the first batch of chassis in 1980, while customer cars for 1981 were built by Lola as Toleman T850s, with a quasi-works team being run by Docking-Spitzley, for whom Johansson won races.

Attractive livery complemented the clean lines of the F2 car, photographed as Stephen South drove it during its first tests, at Goodwood. South split with the team in acrimonious circumstances.

TG81 Toleman's first F1 car was far from handsome and in 1981 there was little to show for boldness: Brian Hart was commissioned to produce the 415T engine (the first British turbocharged F1 engine which ran tests in an adapted F2 Toleman late in 1980) and Pirelli tyres were used. The monocoque was still in aluminium, with rocker arm suspension. Henton and Warwick failed to qualify until late in the season and then only managed one race apiece. An uprated TG181 was used in 1982, until the TG183 was ready. That year drivers with TG181Cs failed to qualify ten times, Warwick making the grid for all but two races.

Drivers: Teo Fabi, Brian Henton, Derek Warwick.

The ungainly T181s waiting to practice, at the 'minor teams' end of the Silverstone pits in 1981.

TG183 This had the look of an F1 car of the 1980s when it ran its first tests in August 1982, and it also showed Toleman's technical progress, with a much stiffer carbon fibre composite chassis, the Hart 415T used as a semi-stressed member, pullrod suspension and better aerodynamics. The first car was used twice in 1982.

Derek Warwick testing the first TG183 at Silverstone in 1982 (**above**) and in a TG183B in the 1983 European Grand Prix at Brands Hatch (**below**), the first race when both Toleman drivers finished in the points.

The TG183B, on the other hand, was not a pretty car, with a very large nose aerofoil incorporating radiators (the underside also generated some ground effect) and a double rear aerofoil that looked cumbersome (but worked) and improved turbo intercoolers. In 1983 a Toleman driver failed to qualify only once, and the team ended the 1983 season with ten Championship points. The TG183Bs were used in early-1984 races.

Drivers: Derek Warwick, Teo Fabi, Bruno Giacomelli, Ayrton Senna, Johnny Cecotto.

TG184 In most respects this car followed convention, although the distinctive double rear wing was retained. Essentially, the TG183 monocoque was used, with pullrod front suspension and pushrods at the rear, radiators were in the side pods (water and oil on the right, turbo intercooler on the left), while revised aerodynamics gave additional downforce. Senna came close to winning at Monaco, and was well placed in Tolemans at Brands Hatch and Estoril; Cecotto crashed heavily at Brands Hatch, ending his GP career.

Drivers: Ayrton Senna, Johnny Cecotto, Stefan Johansson, Pierluigi Martini.

The first TG184. The colour scheme was to change, but Toleman's mid-season switch to Goodyear tyres seemed more significant in performance terms, and was to have later repercussions.

TG185 Described as a refined TG184, this last Toleman had a new monocoque (the first produced in-house), sleeker aerodynamics treatment with a fully enclosed engine, a three-tier rear wing, and a Toleman-developed five-speed gearbox. Tyre supply problems meant that the team missed the first three races, then ran a single car until the summer, dogged by unreliability.

Drivers: Teo Fabi, Piercarlo Ghinzani.

TG185 as it was announced, on anonymous tyres (which were unsuitable for racing) and barren of sponsorship – the tiny 'Virgin' on the nose acknowledged the use of the West London canal-side premises where it was launched on a snowy day early in 1985. Later it was painted in Benetton colours, presaging the team's future.

TREVELLICK

R.J. Trevellick's 1951 500 special was fairly conventional, with a chassis similar to an Iota, Standard 8 front suspension, BSA rear suspension, and, at first, a Douglas engine. It stayed on the scene for some years, was gradually modified, and two other cars appeared. The three sometimes appeared under the grand name of Trevellick Racing Cars. ML

TRIMAX

Alvin 'Spike' Rhiando was a larger than life Canadian who tried his hand at virtually every type of low-cost motor sport, including midget cars and speedway riding. He became one of the best-known of the early 500 racers, especially after he won the support race for the 1948 British GP in a Cooper-JAP. During 1949 he evolved the Trimax, so-named because it was designed to take three sizes of engine, 500cc, 750cc and 1,100cc.

It had a bath tub monocoque chassis made from Dural sheeting with bag tanks contained in the side members, uncannily like the Lotus 25, and suspension followed Porsche lines with trailing arms at the front and swing axles at the rear, but sprung by adjustable 'Metalastik' bonded rubber units. The steering system reflected the days of the cyclecar with chains and cables moving a central pivot from whence came dual track rods, and while its hydraulic front brakes were conventional enough, at the rear a single (drum) brake operated on the transmission.

It was quite a large car, distinguished by pretty cast alloy wheels, but was too heavy to be truly competitive. Rhiando drifted out of racing. ML

TROJAN

In the early 1970s, Trojan built the McLaren M8E and M8FP 'customer' cars at Croydon, and looked to building runs of the M21 F2 car or a variant of the M19 F1 car for F5000/Formula A. In the event the McLaren association ended, and Trojan went ahead with their own cars for a very brief period, even venturing into F1, at the most modest level. The T101 and T102 were F5000 cars.

T103 Much of Ron Tauranac's design work for the T102 was economically applied to this limited-budget F1 car, which was entered for just eight of the 1974 championship Grands Prix – even the two British non-Championship F1 races were ignored, unusually for a British-based minor team at that time.

Unlike distant forebears that carried the name Trojan, there was nothing unconventional about the T103, which even looked dully sensible. It was photographed on the equally dull Nivelles-Baulers circuit, where Schenken placed it tenth in the 1974 Belgian GP.

It used the monocoque of the T102 and was powered by a Cosworth DFV, which drove through a Hewland gearbox. The T103 started in six GPs, finishing 14th in its debut in Spain, twice finishing tenth and retiring three times. As the budget ran out the programme was closed down after the 1974 Italian GP.

Driver: Tim Schenken.

TUI

Alan McCall is another name on the roll call of constructors who did not get the right breaks. The New Zealander was a McLaren mechanic when he completed his first Tui F3 car early in 1970; seven years later he turned away from a North American Formula Atlantic programme with the ageing design. Along the way he had designed the only F1 Tecno to score a point, run Hexagon's F1 Brabham, and had associations with other teams.

The first car followed McLaren lines, and indeed in areas such as its suspension McLaren components were used. It had an aluminium monocoque with the engine (initially a second-hand Broadspeed unit) serving as a stressed member. A racing programme got under way slowly, with driver Bert Hawthorne, bringing half a season of teething problems and accidents but no success, before that F3 ran its term.

In 1972 McCall achieved an ambition by getting into F2 with the car slightly modified from its 1971 Formula B (that is, Atlantic) form with a longer wheelbase, revised suspension and Hart BDA engine. Early in the year it was entered as the Leda-Tui AM29; when a new car was built it was run as the Tui BH2. The little team was rocked in the Spring when Hawthorne was killed in an accident at Hockenheim. Dave Morgan and John Watson drove the second car in some European championship events, the high points being when Morgan put the Tui on pole for a heat at Albi and when Watson finished fifth at Rouen. McCall then became preoccupied with Tecno, and the Tui next turned up in North America, updated again for Formula Atlantic.

Alan McCall's Tui in F2 form in 1972.

TURNER

John Webb (not of Brands Hatch) commissioned special builder Jack Turner, who had converted his MG K3 Magnette into a single-seater, to build an F2 car for the 1953 season. Like Turner's sports specials it had a lozenge-shaped ladder frame and transverse leaf springing, and was fitted with an aluminium block 1750cc Lea-Francis engine enlarged to 1960cc with a twin-plug aluminium head by Turner. It also had SU fuel injection adapted from the SU aircraft system and supervised by the works. In this form it gave a claimed 145bhp at 6500rpm and drove via an Armstrong-Siddeley preselector gearbox to an EMV differential mounted on the chassis.

Webb drove it in some minor British F2 events in 1953 where it was always at the back of the field. The following year he tried a 2.5-litre Alta engine but the story was the same and its best performance was in the 1954 International Trophy when Jack Fairman drove it and came 13th from 15 finishers in the Final. At least on that occasion it finished, most of its races ended in retirement.

Turner also built a water-cooled dohc 500cc engine which was fitted into a Kieft F3 car but proved disappointing since it gave only about 36bhp.   ML

TYRRELL

Ken Tyrrell is an enthusiast and a fighter, and as far as his Grand Prix team and its survival are concerned the two have gone hand in hand. Too often the team has been grievously under-financed, particularly in the 1980s, when it was also on the receiving end of some questionable rough justice. In many seasons its equipment has not been of the best, and at one point it almost seemed that stagnation had set in – though that impression was misleading. Through the decade this was one of the more friendly teams, perhaps because commercialism was not its only motivation.

Tyrrell turned his back on driving – he had been good but not outstanding in the 500cc F3 days – to build up a sound reputation as an entrant/team manager in the 1960s, running Formula Junior, F3 and F2 Coopers and then F2 Matras for drivers of the calibre of John Surtees, Jacky Ickx and above all Jackie Stewart. He was ambitious to take the Tyrrell Racing Organization into F1, and the opportunity came with the Cosworth DFV engine – ordered in 1968, before Tyrrell had a car for it, or the finance. The car came in the form of a Matra, and the chassis cost him nothing.

Stewart drove Tyrrell's blue Matras to nine Grand Prix victories in 1968-9, but the French constructor was not prepared to build a new car to be powered by Ford-labelled engines in 1970, and nor was Tyrrell prepared to abandon the proven engine and the relationship with the Ford company. He turned to March 701s, but these were never more than stand-ins and late in the Summer of 1970 Tyrrell 001 appeared.

The 001 was the first of a line, the early chassis being individually numbered, type numbers coming almost incidentally with 006 in 1973 and then more deliberately with 007. These early cars were designed for Elf-Team Tyrrell by Derek Gardner, who stayed with the team to see his six-wheeled racing car theories put into practice, succeed to a degree and then become a dead end. Maurice Phillippe took his place and remained with Tyrrell through a long period that saw more disappointments than triumphs. One of the low points came in 1984, when the team's Championship race placings were retrospectively disallowed as an alleged illegal additive was found in the water injection system of one of its cars.

Throughout Tyrrell persevered, sometimes with front-line drivers, sometimes with understanding, adequate, sponsors, but often struggling. In 1988 Tyrrell became the elder statesman among constructors as Ferrari died, and in that year changes came. Harvey Postlethwaite joined as chief designer, and Phillippe and his designer colleague Brian Lisles soon left.

Then came the transformation of the Ockham base that had been temporary since Jackie Stewart was the number one driver. By 1989 the premises were appropriate headquarters for a modern F1 constructor; there was a new management

structure, with Ken Tyrrell becoming chairman, his son Bob managing director, Postlethwaite engineering director and aerodynamicist Jean-Claude Migeot in charge of research and development. Former Ferrari chief mechanic Joan Villadelprat soon joined as team manager. Early in 1990 came news of an association with McLaren, in a marketing department linked with TAG/McLaren Marketing Services. On the face of it, Tyrrell therefore entered the 1990s as strongly placed as at any time since the first half of the 1970s, and in a vastly changed world, too.

001 The first Tyrrell was designed in great secrecy, Gardner working at his home (where a mock-up was built in his garage). In some general respects he followed the lines of the Matra MS80, and 001 had a similar 'coke bottle' planform, while another distinctive feature was the broad-nose aerofoil above the radiator intake. Construction was conventional, around an alloy monocoque, with double wishbone front suspension, and single top links, twin lower links and radius arms at the rear. The car was first run in the Oulton Park Gold Cup, then in three late-season Grands Prix, where it showed potential but failed to finish a race.

Driver: Jackie Stewart.

The 001 prepared for its debut. The general lines show well, as do the broad-based lower wishbones of the front suspension, the 'spine' which deflected air from the radiator around the cockpit and the bulge for the gear-changing hand on the right of the surround.

002-004 These cars were in effect refined versions of 001, longer (002 was built for Cevert, taller than Stewart) and with numerous detail improvements. Black engine airboxes were used from the 1971 Dutch GP onwards, and full-width noses in racing from the French GP, while components such as double-disc brakes appeared and novelties such as a rear wing incorporating radiators were tried. The first Grand Prix victory for a Tyrrell fell to Stewart, driving 003 in Spain; he also won the Championship races in Monaco, France, Britain, Germany and Canada to clearly take the drivers' title, while Cevert won the US GP in 002. Tyrrell won the Constructors' Championship, scoring more than twice as many points as the runner up.

These cars came out again in 1972, when Stewart brought his tally of Championship race victories with 003 to eight, as he won the Argentine and French GPs. 004 was built as a spare, and raced three times by the team before it was sold to South Africa.

Drivers: François Cevert, Patrick Depailler, Eddie Keizan, Jackie Stewart.

Jackie Stewart in 003 during tests at Silverstone. The car has the full-width nose and the first effective engine airbox seen in racing.

005-006 These much more angular cars, shorter and lower, came in mid-1972. In detail they retained nose water radiators but had oil radiators alongside the rear of the cockpit, clean lines around the engine bay, large airboxes by 1973 and, save for a brief period, brakes were outboard all round, as was the suspension. Two duplicates of 006 were built for 1973, when the team won in South Africa, Belgium, Monaco, Holland and

The pristine 005 – the lines of this chunky little car were distinctive and cockpit surround strakes were to feature on later Tyrrells. Airbox contours flow into the rear wing; mirrors have yet to be fitted to this new car.

Jackie Stewart at Monza in 1973 in 006/2, with high airbox and more prominent inboard front brake cooling vents than 005.

Germany, but was second in the Championship. Cevert crashed fatally in 006/3 at Watkins Glen at the end of the season, Stewart retired, and Tyrrell had to rebuild his team around two new drivers, using these cars for the opening races of 1974.

Drivers: Chris Amon, François Cevert, Patrick Depailler, Jody Scheckter, Jackie Stewart.

007 Although three 006 cars had been built, 007 was the first number intended to cover the cars of a batch – four were laid down and raced from the start of the 1974 European season. That year they had torsion bar suspension and inboard front brakes, replaced in 1975 with coil spring/shock absorber suspension and outboard brakes. In 1975 two more 007s were built, to serve into 1976. Two were entered independently in GPs when sold out of Tyrrell service. Scheckter won three GPs in 007s, in Sweden and Britain in 1974 and in South Africa in 1975, but in Constructors' Championship terms the team slipped, to third in 1974 and fifth in 1975.

Drivers: Patrick Depailler, K. Hoshino, Jean-Pierre Jabouille, Alessandro Pesenti-Rossi, Jody Scheckter.

Ken Tyrrell with the first 007, obviously longer and sleeker than its predecessors.

P34 This car was the sensation of 1976, probably earning a worthwile return for its sponsors through photographic exposure before it ever raced. From the cockpit back it was conventional, but behind its broad nose Gardner used four small wheels, to improve penetration and, through increased tyre contact, to improve cornering and braking. Suspension was by double wishbones and coil springs/dampers. Scheckter and Depailler placed P34s first and second in the Swedish GP, and through the rest of the year the cars were placed second in six races. Development lagged in 1977, especially with the small tyres, while the cars (in new sponsorship colours) grew bulkier and heavier, in part as the front track was increased in efforts to get the little tyres to 'work'. This was the first season when a Tyrrell car failed to win a race.

Drivers: Patrick Depailler, Ronnie Peterson, Jody Scheckter.

The first P34 posed in the Silverstone pits lane – Tyrrell looks pleased, Derek Gardner is quizzical, Patrick Depailler obviously thinks he should get on with the job. Windows were to be inserted in the cockpit surround below the mirrors, so that drivers could watch the behaviour of those little wheels, and the flat surface between the wheels was raised along its outer edge, to the height of the front tyres.

008 Phillippe's first design for Tyrrell, compact but quite conventional and never a real championship contender. It had a shallow monocoque, double wishbone front suspension with inboard springs/dampers, and upper and lower links, radius rods and outboard springs at the rear. Depailler did drive 008/3 to his first GP victory, at Monaco, but overall this was the year that ground effects arrived and this Tyrrell was outmoded. Five cars were built, and a succession of scoring finishes earned Tyrrell a respectable fourth place in the Constructors' Championship – the team was not to equal that in the next ten seasons.

Drivers: Patrick Depailler, Didier Pironi.

The shallow monocoque and deep cockpit surround and engine cover show in this shot of a well-balanced 008. It also shows signs that Tyrrell still had adequate sponsorship in 1978.

009 Introduced for 1979, this was a ground effects design following Lotus 79 lines, with rocker-arm front suspension and double wishbone rear suspension. It seemed competitive as the year opened but after that never looked a winner. The four third placings gained were just about what it merited, and other points-scoring finishes saw Tyrrell fifth in the Constructors' Championship again.

Drivers: Derek Daly, Jean-Pierre Jarier, Geoff Lees, Didier Pironi.

010 Another clone, this time inspired by the Williams FW07. It appeared as well built as all Tyrrells, but uncharacteristically was involved in two heavy accidents attributed to structural failures. The 010 had to serve on into 1981 for resources were very limited as the team battled to survive. One of the bright spots was that Tyrrell brought Alboreto into his driver line up, and that immediately underlined the need for a better car. In

1980-1 Tyrrell was sixth and eighth in the Constructors' Championship, all but two of the 1981 points scored with 010s.

Drivers: Michele Alboreto, Eddie Cheever, Derek Daly, Jean-Pierre Jarier, Ricardo Zunino.

Broad side pods mark 009 out as a ground effects car. These proclaimed the name Tyrrell until sponsorship came from Candy, from the sixth GP of the year.

010 was a handsome car, but the results achieved with it were barely respectable as it carried Tyrrell into his second decade as a constructor.

011 The '1981 Tyrrell' did not appear until halfway through that season. It was a stiffer car, complying with driver safety cell regulations due to come into force in 1982, and its efficacy in that respect was proved very early in a test accident. It had narrower track, pullrod suspension and fixed skirts. An 011 was placed in the points just once in 1981. The car was substantially modified for 1982, when Alboreto scored in the last seven races, and won the final GP, at Las Vegas. The 011 was further modified, to 'flat-bottom' form, for 1983; that year a Tyrrell was the last DFV-powered car to win a Grand Prix, when Alboreto won at Detroit (actually with a DFY).

Drivers: Michele Alboreto, Slim Borgudd, Eddie Cheever, Brian Henton, Danny Sullivan.

The 011 started life as a white car, with evidence of some secondary sponsorship; in 1982, when Alboreto drove this car to win at Las Vegas, 011s were predominantly black. Throughout they appeared very solid.

012 Shorter, slimmer, with a carbon fibre aluminium honeycomb monocoque and still relying on non-turbo Cosworth power, 012 appeared for the last four races of 1983 and ran through 1984, a year of strife as Tyrrell had to forfeit points scored (notably from a fine second at Detroit) after a 'hydrocarbon content' was found in an engine's water injection system. These cars were powered by the Cosworth DFY, and for a time were the only normally-aspirated entries in GPs (hence Tyrrell's reluctance to agree to a reduced fuel capacity limit, which perhaps cost him the support of the turbo teams in his battle with FISA). They continued in 1985, until 015 was ready, and two were used in the first season of F3000.

Drivers: Michele Alboreto, Stefan Bellof, Martin Brundle, Stefan Johansson, Danny Sullivan.

Without turbo power, Tyrrell could not afford the drag of large aerofoils, but that extraordinary rear wing on the inelegant 012 was soon discarded.

014 Tyrrell arranged to use Renault turbo engines in 1985, albeit not as a favoured customer for the latest units (those went to Lotus) and supplied through Mecachrome. In most respects, 014 followed established Tyrrell lines in chassis and running gear, with wider track and longer wheelbase. The first 014s were raced from mid-season, and on into 1986 when the team had a major sponsor again (Data General). At least Tyrrell returned to the top ten in the Championship, ninth in 1985 when Bellof scored all the points in Cosworth-engined cars.

Drivers: Stefan Bellof, Martin Brundle, Ivan Capelli, Stefan Johansson, Philippe Streiff.

014 looked a solid car, but a workmanlike appearance was not enough – no points were scored with it in 1985 and only two in 1986, before it was superseded.

015 This can be seen as an uprated 014, with pushrod suspension all round, rear brakes moved outboard, softer body lines with the Renault engine completely enclosed and radiator air exhausted through the tops of the side pods. It was run in Data General colours, with some success – Tyrrell was seventh in the 1986 Constructors' Championship table, Brundle's fourth in Australia being the best race placing.

Drivers: Martin Brundle, Philippe Streiff.

As Data Team Tyrrell, the team regained respectability with the predominantly white 015.

016 Tyrrell turned away from turbocharged engines with obvious relief, to contest the non-turbo division with DG016, designed by Brian Lisles and Maurice Phillippe and powered by Cosworth's DFZ V-8. Construction was conventional, and while the cars looked bulky they were reliable and effective, the team clearly winning the Colin Chapman Cup (for entrants), Jonathan Palmer equally clearly taking the Jim Clark Cup (for drivers), while Tyrrell was sixth equal in the overall Constructors' Championship.

Drivers: Jonathan Palmer, Philippe Streiff.

Streiff appears dwarfed in the cockpit of the first DG016.

017 The 1987 season had been one of encouraging recovery for Tyrrell, but it was followed by a slump with 017. This appeared less convincing despite its sleeker lines, which did not in fact give aerodynamic advantages, and it seemed not to benefit from clever detail work (including lowering the engine). Palmer did score points, but his team mate often failed to qualify, so although the team retained its top-ten place in the Constructors' Championship it was beating only the rag, tag and bobtail on the Grands Prix grids. From the Summer Postlethwaite was at work on a successor, but until that was ready three 017s were prepared for the early 1989 races. The principal modification in '017B' was the introduction of a Tyrrell-designed six-speed gearbox mounted longitudinally (this was being developed for 018). The only race for these cars was the Brazilian GP, when Palmer placed one seventh.

Drivers: Michele Alboreto, Julian Bailey, Jonathan Palmer.

Palmer testing an 017 at Silverstone early in 1988.

018 The Tyrrell Racing Organization's team was fifth on the 1989 Constructors' Championship table, the highest place since 1979, yet the outcome of the season was perhaps a disappointment. Harvey Postlethwaite laid out a state of the art car, with the slimmest nose among grids of cars noted for that characteristic, on an in-house carbon-composite monocoque, with a Cosworth DFR engine and the Tyrrell-developed gearbox. A front suspension novelty accounted for the fine lines of the nose – it was a double-wishbone layout but there was only a single damper, just ahead of the instrument panel and operated by a transverse rocker and pushrods. There was a more normal double wishbone pushrod arrangement at the rear. In 1990 Pirelli tyres were to be used. The team was not generously financed in 1989, indeed to all outward appearances hardly financed at all until mid-season, when sponsors were proclaimed and Camel yellow was spliced to Tyrrell blue. A driver change after six races turned out not to be a great set-back, for new boy Jean Alesi finished fourth in his first GP (in France), after running as high as second. The best final placing of the year was achieved by Alboreto, third in Mexico, and in 1990 the team had its best result for years when in the first race Alesi led to half distance and finished second, the other car being placed sixth.

Drivers: Michele Alboreto, Jean Alesi, Satoru Nakajima, Jonathan Palmer.

A new look for Tyrrell. The dark triangle just ahead of the mirrors was the cover for the single Koni shock absorber. Engine air intake was within the loop of the roll-over bar. This first car was first seen in all-over royal blue colours; by the summer of 1989 the engine cover was yellow; in 1990 the cars came out for the first races in white and royal blue.

U

UNDERWOOD

In the early days of the 500 movement, A.A.D. Underwood took a Fiat 500 frame, used Fiat front suspension for the independent rear and then rather spoiled a promising idea by using a water-cooled two-cylinder Scott engine.　　ML

URD

These initials are remembered for a minor German constructor's sports-racing cars, but a URD 376 powered by a Nova-Toyota engine also flitted across the German F3 scene in 1976. Its driver, Werner Fischer, did not feature in the top ten of a major F3 race.

U2

Arthur Mallock's cars are usually associated with club racing categories and with very clever chassis engineering within constricting regulations, and since Mk1 in 1958 U2s have always been front-engined cars. In the 1960s and 1970s a few were built for international formulae, where the rear-engined layout was de rigeur and their appearance was distinctive. John Harwood drove a front-engined U2 to win a Formula Junior race in Germany in 1960, and later there were occasional finishes in F3 and even F2. In 1978 a Formula Atlantic version of the Mk20 was essayed, but by that time the Mallock family was concentrating on clubman's cars, as it did through the 1980s, when consultancy work also became an important activity for the little Northamptonshire company.

Mk2 This was the first production U2, and two cars were completed in FJ form. A ladder-type chassis was used, with Ford swing axle front suspension and a BMC rigid rear axle with quarter-elliptic springs. John Harwood won a secondary Nürburgring FJ race in a U2 late in 1960.

Arthur Mallock in his first FJ U2 in 1960. Its bluff lines contrast with the sleekness of later front-engined U2s.

Mk3 Primarily a sports car, the Mk3 also appeared in 1-litre F3 guise in 1964. This was the first U2 to have coil spring rear suspension. The F3 theme was not pursued at the time.

Mk6 In this 1966-8 car wishbone front suspension was adopted and while it was primarily a clubman's sports-racing car it also appeared as a road car (6R) and in F2 races in 1967 with a twin-cam engine. In this form Arthur Mallock raced it in British events and at nearby Continental circuits. His best placing was ninth at Mallory Park in 1967 and at Crystal Palace that year there was a second U2 in the F2 field, driven (to retirement) by one Max Mosley.

Mk11B Another spin-off from the clubman's programme, and another F3 one-off (although it was hoped it might lead to a team for 1972). Ray Mallock raced this car in 1971, when his best placing was sixth in good company in a Castle Combe race. This car was later fitted with an FVA for *libre* use.

Mk12 The first U2 with a de Dion rear suspension layout. Ray Mallock placed it fourth in a Silverstone F3 race and qualified it well elsewhere, but development for this cut-throat category lagged and the team's F3 engines were never of the best. Although there were to be cars such as the Mk13 F2 essay and the Formula Atlantic Mk 20B, this 1972 car ended the Mallocks' ventures into the main-line formulae.

V

VAN DIEMEN

Ralph Firman took over the 375 after GRD closed down, introducing it as the first F3 Van Diemen in 1976. As the VG376 it had new bodywork with more effective aerodynamics but it was nevertheless an ageing design. Jac Nelleman was the only driver to score top-ten placings with a 376 in 1976, and then turned to a Modus, while an odd Van Diemen-GRD lingered on in Scandinavian racing in 1977. Firman concentrated on cars for lesser single-seater categories, a known market for Van Diemen and one where the company thrived.

VAN HOOL

Marcel van Hool, a Belgian truck and coach operator, made two attempts to enter F2 with cars carrying his name. Both cars were built in Spain, both owing something to March, but neither was successful. The first was reported to be complete in the summer of 1974 but never appeared on an F2 grid. Nor did the 1976 car, which had torsion bar front suspension and a BMW engine, although de Dryver attempted to qualify it for that season's opening race, at Hockenheim. (His other F2 appearances that year were with the team's back-up March 752, which suggests something.)

VANWALL

Guy Anthony Vandervell was a hard-nosed industrialist who supported the early BRM endeavours but could not long suffer committee-minded bureaucracy or an element of gentlemanly amateurism, so he set out to build up his own team to beat the Italians – that was the target he felt mattered in the 1950s.

His first F1 car had been a Ferrari, named Thin Wall Special after his company's shell bearings and purchased to give the BRM team some experience in actually running a car. Other Ferraris followed (see also Thin Wall), and were raced by the Vanwall team while its own 2-litre F2 project got under way. That car was completed only as 2.5-litre F1 came in, so it was raced with 2-litre, 2.3-litre and then 2.5-litre versions of the four-cylinder engine that had been largely designed by Norton engineer Leo Kusmicki.

For the following year four cars were built with chassis and rear suspension designed by Colin Chapman, and the tall sleek bodies by Frank Costin that were so distinctive in a stolid green. These were also the basis of the 1957-8 cars, which won nine Championship races and the first Constructors' Cup in 1958. Tony Vandervell's prime racing ambition was fulfilled, and as ill-health took a toll his Vanwall team was run down to a part-time basis, fading away on a low note in 1961. Vanwalls did not carry type or mark numbers, chassis numbers tended to be repeated and each year's output tended to be used as parts bins for the following season's cars.

1954-5 The first Vanwall as such, run as the Vanwall Special, had a chassis on Ferrari lines built by Cooper, and in its first 2-litre form was distinguished by an ugly surface radiator. It was used through most of 1954 and written off in a Spanish GP practice accident. Four more cars were built on closely similar lines for 1955, and at the end of that season were broken up. Harry Schell drove one to score Vanwall's first race victory, in a heat of the Crystal Palace International Trophy in July 1955.

Drivers: Alan Brown, Peter Collins, Mike Hawthorn, Harry Schell, Desmond Titterington, Ken Wharton.

The first Vanwall, driven by Peter Collins during practice for the 1954 British GP. At that stage it had a 2.3-litre engine and the surface radiator on top of the nose was shrouded.

The 1955 cars – this is Wharton at Monza – had conventional nose radiators, and for this high-speed circuit the front suspension is partly faired.

1956-58 The Chapman/Costin cars, the first four being built using some parts from the 1955 VW1-4. Moss drove one to Vanwall's first significant victory, in the 1956 International Trophy, while Schell battled with the leaders in the French GP. The standard of workmanship was high, but the cars were too often let down by niggling faults.

These cars were in part carried over to 1957, when coil spring rear suspension was introduced and additional cars completed as the team reached its full strength, in its drivers as well as materials. One car was tried with a streamlined body, and another had a lightweight chassis. In the British GP Moss took over the unwell Tony Brooks' VW4 to score an historic victory.

The abiding Vanwall shape, shown off by Moss in the 1958 British GP. The height of the car is accentuated by its high cockpit surround, and the air intake arrangements, from the slim nose to the NACA flush ducts, never called for extemporary revision.

Five cars were improved in detail for 1958, but little effort was made to save weight despite the loss of power as methanol fuel gave way to Avgas (down from a maximum of 285bhp in 1957 to just under 260bhp in 1958). It was a season of triumph as Vanwalls dominated the GPs but one which ended in tragedy as Stuart Lewis-Evans was fatally injured in an accident in the Moroccan GP. Tony Vandervell formally announced the end of the full team.

Drivers: Tony Brooks, Stirling Moss, Froilan Gonzalez, Mike Hawthorn, Stuart Lewis-Evans, Roy Salvadori, Harry Schell, Piero Taruffi, Maurice Trintignant.

1959-60 One car was rebuilt in a more compact and lighter form and driven by Brooks in the 1959 British GP and secondary British events in 1960. It was also used to prove an independent rear suspension designed by Colotti. Together with a gearbox behind the final drive, this was used on VW11, the 'lowline' car that was the last Vanwall to start in a Grand Prix, the 1960 French race. This was also its only race.

Driver: Tony Brooks.

The 'lowline' Vanwall at Reims in 1960. Brooks qualified it 14th on the 20-car grid but retired after three pit stops in the Grand Prix.

1961 Vanwall experimented with a Vanwall-engined Lotus 18 in 1960, then came up with a rear-engined car (VW14) with a 2.6-litre engine for the abortive Intercontinental Formula in the following year. It placed fifth in its only race, the International Trophy.

VENOM (GB)

An F3 Cooper converted into a Formula Junior car by E.E. Fenning, with a BMC A series engine. It served for the first season of Junior racing in Britain.

The Cooper 500 origins of Fenning's Venom were obvious as seen here in No. 18.

VENOM (USA)

One of the small crop of American Formula cars built to take advantage of the local modification to the regulations which admitted engines under 1 litre (and up to 1.3 litres) with appropriate weight adjustments, and thus made the 750cc ohc Crosley unit eligible. In the Venom this engine was mounted ahead of the cockpit and drove through a Crosley three-speed gearbox. A live rear axle completed a specification which promised little and delivered little in circuit terms.

VERITAS

In 1948 former BMW engineers Ernst Loof and Lorenz Dietrich built a number of sports cars using the BMW 328 engine in a tubular chassis based on the design which won the 1940 Gran Premio de Brescia, sometimes called the '1940 Mille Miglia'. These were highly successful in Germany, in both sports car events and F2 races. Despite a ban on their export some were dismantled and exported as 'spares' to appear in France under other names. Loof developed the BMW engine and then designed his own unit, which was built by Heinkel. This followed the broad lines of the 328 engine but was cast in alloy and had 'square' dimensions of 75 x 75mm which gave it a capacity of 1988cc. In competition trim, with three Solex carburettors and running on methanol, it gave a useful 140bhp.

This was fitted into a single-seater which had a ladder chassis and independent suspension all round by double wishbones and longitudinal torsion bars. Some BMW components were used but Loof designed his own five-speed gearbox.

Germany was banned from international competition until 1950, but Veritas was quite successful at home, and as a competent production car it helped bring on a number of leading German drivers. It seems that Veritas became too ambitious for its slight resources (it also made a 750cc sports car using Panhard parts) and it folded in 1950. Dietrich left but Loof revived it in a small workshop at the Nürburgring. Later that same year he unveiled a single-seater, with an all-enveloping body and de Dion rear axle, which became known as the Veritas-Meteor to distinguish it from the RS open-wheeler. The apex of Veritas achievement came when Paul Pietsch won the 1951 Eifelrennen in a Meteor.

By the time F2 was elevated to Championship status, however, the drive had gone out of the marque and it was struggling. International events rarely saw a Veritas though the Belgian amateur, Arthur Legat, entered his home GP in 1952 (he was extremely slow). Five cars started the German GP but only one finished, Fritz Reiss in seventh and two laps down. Legat entered his car in the Belgian GP in 1953 but was again very slow and retired after one lap. Six cars started the German GP and three finished, in ninth, twelfth and sixteenth places.

During 1953 Loof realised that he could not keep pace with new developments so he closed his works and returned to BMW. Sadly, he died of a brain tumour three years later.

VIKING

This ambitious F3 effort was nominally Swedish, through its co-designer and team promoter Tore Helle, Rotel sponsors and drivers. However, Len Terry had a hand in the design and the first cars were largely built by CTG Racing Developments, for the 1976 season.

The TH1A was a sophisticated car by F3 standards, with a sheet aluminium monocoque, conventional suspension and the almost universal Nova-Toyota engines. Outwardly a low nose line contrasted oddly with an engine cover that swept sharply down from the top of the roll-over bar and then the rear wing was carried on swept-back end plate supports. Three were built for the team, and there was optimistic talk of a Swedish factory being established to undertake production. By mid-1976 Helle had run into financial problems and disbanded the team; Conny Ljungfeldt arranged finance on a hand-to-mouth basis for the surviving team car that he continued to run, while the design rights reverted to Terry and CTG sought backing to run a one- or two-car team.

Originally a trio of talented drivers had been brought together, but Eje Elgh quit after accidents in the prototype car, and Borgudd soon followed. Ljungfeldt was the only successful Viking driver (pun not intended), winning the 1976 Swedish championship and a heat at Monaco. One car re-emerged, fleetingly, in 1977 as a Technic.

Basically the Viking was a low and flat car, but with an extraordinary hump over the engine and a nose that just seemed to be a muddle (that wing is independent of the outrigged fairings intended to direct airflow around the front wheels). Driver is Ljungfeldt.

VISION

Domination of a British clubman's racing category in the mid-1980s led Paul Gibson to initiate a Vision F3 project late in 1986, although the VT388TA did not appear until 1988. Designed by Dave Amey, it turned out to be an over-sophisticated car for F3 production (F3000 use was in mind), built around a carbon-fibre/honeycomb chassis with pushrod suspension all round and a TOM's Toyota engine. It was developed through the summer of 1988 and revisions

The F3 Vision on test at Silverstone.

incorporated by the end of the year were expected to lead to the definitive VF388/9 for a two-car team in 1989. In fact a single VF389 did not get beyond the test stage, and late in 1989 the whole ambitious F3 project, which had over-extended Vision and made no impression on the circuits, was sold off to sprint exponent Rodney Eyles.

VM

A Tatra-based F1 car created by Viglielmo Matozza who filed an entry for the 1954 Grand Prix des Frontières. Matozza had put in some 'all-nighters' to complete the car and fell asleep after he arrived at Chimay; by the time he awoke it was too late to practice. It was not entered in any other F1 race.   ML

VOLPINI

This Italian constructor is usually recalled for its Formula Junior cars, but earlier in the 1950s Volpini appeared in F3. Italy never really took to half-litre racing, and in the overall scene that was unfortunate – real international competition for the British cars would have been a valuable stimulant and if there was one possible threat that would get a reaction from the British 500 Establishment it was that somebody would come up with properly-developed MV- or Gilera-engined cars. The Volpini cars run in 1953 had Gilera engines, and were run with some success, in France as well as Italy. Seemingly the development effort was not there.

Volpini was then a secondary name in the first Italian F Junior seasons. The car was front-engined, invariably with a Fiat 1100 unit, had a simple ladder frame chassis, unequal-length wishbone and coil spring/damper front suspension and a live rear axle. The transmission was dropped, but the driver still perched high in the car.

The Volpini Junior was priced to compete with Stanguellini in the market that was familiar ground to a Milan-based constructor, but offered little competition in terms of race performances.

As it lacked even the modestly advanced feature of an offset cockpit, the Volpini looked dated among the front-engined Juniors at Monaco in 1959. It was also seen with a larger oval nose intake.

VOTORINI

Built by Californian Bob Allinger, the Votorini started life as a cycle-winged sports car, but when Formula Junior came along he removed the wings, lights and spare wheel and joined the fray. The car had a simple frame, a front-mounted Fiat 1100 engine, and coil spring front and solid rear suspension. Needless to say it did not take the formula by storm.   ML

VSM

Victor van den Brempt was a Belgian pioneer of the 500 movement and his first car, the 'Dofin', was actually a two seater which appeared occasionally in 500cc races. This used a modified Fiat frame and engine driving through a DKW front wheel drive transmission. His second car, the VSM of 1950, also combined a Fiat engine and DKW transmission, but on this occasion they were installed in a purpose-built ladder frame and DKW suspension was employed. Like the 'Dofin' this was a two-seater and van den Brempt had plans to enter long distance sports car events, but he seems to have confined himself to odd F3 races where, not surprisingly, the car proved to be too heavy for the job.   ML

VW

Built by Arthur Rosenhammer, who later drove for the EMW sports car team, and looking something like a miniature Auto Union, this car began life with a 750cc BMW engine and was thought to be perhaps the fastest unblown 750cc car of its time. It was easily adapted to 500cc racing. To a light tubular frame, Rosenhammer added Volkswagen front suspension while the rear-mounted BMW engine was mated to a VW gearbox, final drive and rear suspension and a Beetle also supplied the wheels and brakes. Touted at the time as the German Car Most Likely to Succeed (it didn't) at least one other was built, for Hans Luck, and that had a markedly different body.   ML

W

WACO

A conventional British 500 car built by Jeremy Webster and raced by him in 1951. At the end of that year he was called up for National Service so he slotted in a Harley Davison engine and converted it for road use. ML

WAGNER

Fritz Wagner, who had been involved with German sports-car projects, devised an F3000 car for 1987. In a tradition of chauvinism that has sometimes made life difficult for German constructors, he chose to use a German engine, a BMW straight six. The only advantage it could have offered was a slim engine bay. The Wagner car was reported to have run on test, but it never appeared at a race meeting.

WAINER

This minor Milanese constructor had more stamina than many of its contemporaries spawned by Formula Junior, although patron Gianfranco Mantovani did not seem anxious for Wainer to become a large-scale outfit, and at times concentrated on running Corrado Manfredini. The cars were sometimes known as Wainer-Mantovani, and some carried a turtle emblem in honour of Nuvolari.

Wainer built one of the first Juniors in 1958 – a rear-engined car, very much on British F3 lines. There was a chassis of two main tubes, with secondary tubular members, Fiat-derived wishbone and transverse leaf suspension and an 1100 engine and transmission. Standard parts were used as far as possible, to keep the price down, and the Wainer substantially undercut early Stanguellini in this respect. Manfredini enjoyed some success in minor FJ races in 1958-9. Wainer proved more flexible than other Italian FJ builders, and for the last two seasons of the formula offered an up-to-the-minute Ford-powered space frame car. It was seldom seen outside Italy, but performed reasonably well there – in 1963 Colin Davis came out of semi-retirement to place one second in the important Lottery GP at Monza, Ernesto Brambilla scored another good second and there were other top three placings.

The first Wainer was a stubby little car, with a home-built look about it. Its race debut was on ice, at Cortina d'Ampezzo, when Manfredini won.

The 1962 Junior, with a nostril nose that was presumably inspired by the 1961 World Championship Ferrari. Driver is Corrado Manfredini.

The Wainer 893 was an unprepossessing slab-sided car, with the very shallow side pod that was a fashionable way to meet a safety regulation.

The design carried Wainer through into the F3 era that opened in 1964, when two second placings (one by E. Brambilla) were a modest record. In 1965 Giacomo Russo scored a rare race victory for Wainer, at Vallelunga, while Manfredini came back into the frame, runner-up in a Monza race. He scored top-six placings in 1966, when the effort was running out of steam, and production ended. However, that was not the end of Wainer in F3 as odd cars appeared in the 1980s, some still as Wainer-Mantovani, for example a 1985 honeycomb monocoque car which posed problems as Marino Mantovani struggled to make it competitive (he failed). At the end of the decade there was a more determined effort with the one-off 893 driven by Franco Forini; this failed to make any impression in the Italian Championship, and the Swiss driver's season cannot have been improved as the team was accused of fuel irregularities.

WALKER-CLIMAX

In 1959 Rob Walker, the most successful of all post-War private entrants, ran F1 and F2 Coopers for Stirling Moss and Maurice Trintignant. They rewarded him by winning regularly, but the Coopers left much to be desired and Alf Francis, Walker's chief mechanic, and ex-Maserati designer Valerio Colotti, designed a replacement. The result looked like a Cooper but it had a proper space frame, all independent suspension by coil springs and double wishbones and Borrani wire wheels. The Coventry Climax 2.5-litre FPF engine sat vertically, making for a high engine cover, and the bulbous pannier fuel tanks were held in place by rubber bands. As with the Walker Coopers, a five-speed Colotti gearbox was used.

Work on the car was slow, partly because the Lotus 18 made it virtually redundant before it was completed. When it was tested in 1961 the 1.5-litre F1 was operating and the Walker was too bulky and heavy to be competitive. The original car therefore did not race, although it still exists, and a second, lighter, car was not completed because Moss was happy with the Lotus. ML

WALKER SPECIAL

A pretty 500 car made by H.W. Walker in 1953, the Walker Special was easily distinguished by its high engine cover. It had a multi-tubular frame, Cooper-style front suspension and swing axles at the rear suspended by rubber in tension. It was a commendable effort, although never a winner. ML

WALTON

One of the most successful of early Australian 500 cars, and a race winner, Bruce Walton's JAP-powered special had Cooper-style suspension and a lightweight chassis, the lower part being box section with triangulated tubes above. ML

WEHRLIN

R.W. Wehrlin was a pioneer of the 500 movement in Switzerland. The car he built in 1948 had a front-mounted JAP engine in a Fiat 500 chassis and was completed by a neat body on the lines of the Grand Prix Alta. ML

WENZ

A rare instance of an American 500 car, this was built by Californian Bob Wenz who was inspired by reading of the Strang Special. His car followed similar lines and was built on a Fiat chassis but it might have been more successful had he not used an Ariel 'Red Hunter' engine, which was never seriously considered in the UK. ML

WGM SPECIAL

An interesting Australian 500 car from 1955, this was the work of Morrie Wheeler and Jack Gow who were both designers with the Commonwealth Aircraft Corporation. It featured a Y-shaped chassis, a front-mounted Matchless engine driving through the front wheels, and rubber suspension. It was also the first car in Australia (including imports) which had disc brakes, and these were designed and built by Wheeler and Gow. Despite this promising paper specification its ground clearance was too high and it was horrid to the eye. ML

WHARTON

The popular all-rounder, Ken Wharton, had in his stable an MG J4-engined sprint car based on an Austin Seven with split axle ifs and a skimpy body. On odd occasions he fitted a highly tuned BSA vertical twin engine which, when it ran on song, made the Wharton one of the quickest of the early 500cc cars. The engine never ran on song for more than a few minutes at a time and the experiment was abandoned. ML

WHEATCROFT

Tom Wheatcroft has usually been single-minded in his enterprises, so his vacillating policy with the single-seaters that bore his name was surprising. Whatever he may have said at introductions or at times of decision, he probably did not become a constructor with the conviction he applied to

rebuilding the Donington Park circuit. His museum-associated workshops provided the plant to build cars, and his first thoughts were for an F1 car for his protégé Roger Williamson. Later, towards the end of 1974, he commissioned Mike Pilbeam to design a car for Formula Atlantic. He did not look to F2, yet that was where the car raced. Wheatcroft lost interest in running cars after a while, but the name of his minor marque lived on in South African Formula Atlantic and through John Bright's efforts in F3.

R18 This petite car appeared in the Spring of 1975, its characteristics being a full-width nose, slim hull defining the body lines back to hip radiators, and double wishbone suspension with inboard coil spring/damper units at the front. A single fuel tank behind the cockpit helped maintain the slender appearance. The car was also light. It made its debut as intended, in Formula Atlantic form in Richard Morgan's hands, then it was badly damaged in a test accident (when Henton was driving). Morgan did win Atlantic races in the replacement car, but meanwhile Wheatcroft had decided to run an F2 version.

This first raced at Silverstone in August 1975, when Henton finished third. The F2 R18 had the obligatory deformable structure, neatly achieved with additions to the lower sides of the hull, increased fuel capacity and a Hart-BDA engine driving through a Hewland FT200 gearbox. After its F2 race, this car went to South Africa for Formula Atlantic.

The Formula Atlantic car Morgan had driven re-appeared in F3 form in 1977, modified in Wheatcroft's workshop by John Bright and fitted with a Nova-Toyota engine. That year Bright scored in the British Championship only once, but he did win a non-title race – at Donington Park. He used the car again in early-1978 races.

The F3 R18 looking very smart but lamentably barren of sponsorship for Bright's shoestring operation.

The compact but not notably sleek Wheatcroft-Abarth at Thruxton in 1976, when the engine made splendid noises but let down the car and driver Brian Henton. The basic colour was dark green with orange relief along the cockpit sides.

P26 This was another small car, again with a full-width nose, with the flanks neatly flared to the hip radiators, a large rear wing and prominent air box above the engine. This was an Abarth straight six (86 × 57mm), which had been designed by Iacoponi of Ferrari to become the Fiat-Abarth 260. Fiat set it aside and Holbay took on its development. In practice for its first race in P26 at Thruxton in 1976, it ran its bearings, and never came to a grid in a Wheatcroft. The P26 started in two 1977 F2 races with a Hart engine, and retired in both.

WHITE-LLOYD

Anthony White began his 500 with a Lloyd backbone chassis (Lloyd was a short-lived maker from Grimsby which made small-engined road cars) and to that he added 'parallelogram' ifs and swing axle irs, both sprung by transverse leaf springs, and a rear-mounted JAP engine. It appeared in 1948, and was nicely made, but the backbone chassis meant that the driver sat high, which did nothing for the centre of gravity, and the car was not successful. ML

WILLIAMS

Frank Williams is a perfectionist and a realist, and he soon recognized that he was by no means outstanding among the lower echelons of racing drivers in the mid-1960s, so he became an entrant, running an F2 Brabham BT23C for Piers Courage and then an ex-works F1 Brabham BT26. The equipe worked well, and Courage placed the immaculate Brabham second in two Championship Grands Prix in 1969.

That was a step towards Williams' fulfilment of an ambition to run a full Grand Prix team, and in 1970 he fielded the works de Tomaso. But that was a sombre year – Courage died in a Dutch GP accident – and in 1971 Williams reverted to the role of customer car entrant, with a March.

His own Politoys (see Politoys) came in 1972, and was followed by the Iso-Marlboros. These were later redesignated Williams FW01-03, and in 1975 kept the company of the first 'new' Williams, FW04. The team was run on the tightest of budgets, and the opportunities offered by joining forces with Walter Wolf for 1976 were welcome (the erstwhile Hesketh 308Cs were run as FW05s), although the marriage soon palled.

In 1977 Williams ran a March again, and although the season was barren in terms of race achievements he formed the association with Saudi Arabian businessmen who were to provide financial security for five years and allow the team to lay down the first F1 cars designed by Patrick Head.

The FW06 was promising and the FW07 was outstanding. The team's first GP victory was scored by Regazzoni at Silverstone in 1979 and in 1980-1 Williams won the Constructors' Championship. A period of relative disappointment followed, and ironically the TAG company that Williams had brought into racing backed a Porsche turbo engine for McLaren. Rather than become a second customer for the German engines, Williams chose to develop a relationship with Honda, and in time that was to be very rewarding, bringing the 1986-7 Championships to Williams-Honda.

The team operated from a sophisticated base at Didcot, and had the strength in depth to ride the terrible blow of Frank Williams' crippling road accident in 1986. In 1989 a conference centre was added to the Didcot facilities.

Honda moved its association to McLaren, and Williams suffered a lean year in 1988, with the FW12 powered by normally-aspirated Judd engines in that final turbo season. Frank Williams developed an alliance with his one-time arch-opponent Renault for 1989, and that proved fruitful surprisingly quickly, with Williams-Renault victories coming in the first half of the season and in the final race of the year. That fittingly rounded off a decade when Frank Williams' team had generally been in the forefront, after a first decade that had been largely concerned with a struggle to survive.

FW01-03 The erstwhile Iso-Marlboro IR cars, redesignated after Iso abruptly stopped paying in the Spring of 1974 and uprated for use by the team in 1975, when the regular drivers were Merzario and Laffite with eight stand-ins. The team was run on a budget that would have been inadequate for a single top-line F3 season less than a decade later – Williams even bought scrubbed tyres from other teams. Late in 1977 FW03 reappeared as the Apollon-Williams, entered for the Italian GP for Loris Kessel, who did not remotely approach qualifying times before crashing.

FW03 in its final Williams form, in this shot most notably with a full-width nose and a sleeker airbox, in common with FW04. Driver is François Migault, failing to qualify for the French GP grid, in part another victim of the unreliability that resulted from the team's hand-to-mouth existence.

FW04 A one-off development of the existing FW cars by Ray Stokoe, whose main contribution was a lighter slimmer and more angular monocoque. Just once, in the 1975 German GP, other teams suffered problems and Laffite drove FW04 through to a timely second place. It was acquired by Brian McGuire, who attempted to uprate it for GPs as a McGuire in 1977, and died in it in a Brands Hatch accident.

Drivers: Jacques Laffite, Arturo Merzario, Renzo Zorzi.

FW05 This designation was applied to the Hesketh 308Cs when they were taken over by the Wolf team (see Wolf).

FW06 During 1977 Patrick Head designed the first Williams to make a real impact on racing – the neat, straightforward and light FW06. It had a conventional monocoque and suspension, and almost inevitably the DFV engine. Three were built and driven by Alan Jones through 1978, and the cars served on until the FW07 was ready in the Spring of 1979. By that time the FW06 was outclassed by ground effects cars, but Jones had scored points (notably another second for the team, in the US GP); his driving coupled with the car to serve notice that the revived and well-backed Williams team was to be taken seriously. The cars were sold on, and had useful second lives in the British national series.

Drivers (GPs): Alan Jones, Clay Regazzoni.

The arrow lines of the FW06 show well in this launch photograph. The nose houses the oil cooler (the water radiators were in the flanks) and the wide-chord front wing which was to give way to a narrower 'foil with more prominent end plates. The basic white and green colour scheme was constant, but there were changes of lettering (notably in the presentation of 'Saudia') and another sponsor's decal was to take the place of the Williams badge on the nose.

FW07 Williams' – and Head's – first ground effects car was exemplary, and to a greater extent than the FW06 it marked the team's transition from a 'British kit car' builder to a fully-fledged constructor with the resources to dedicate time and effort to research and test programmes.

The FW07 had an aluminium honeycomb monocoque and conventional suspension (upper rocking arm/lower wishbone/inboard coil spring-damper) which was necessarily very stiff so as to remain consistent with the very heavy downloads. The side pods were broad, yet the overall lines were elegant. A large radiator was positioned at the front of each, oil on the left, water on the right. The cars were brought out as the 1979 European season opened – a litte late as there were minor failures and incidents which meant that despite obvious speed the results did not come until high summer. Before that this had been the first Williams car to lead races, then Regazzoni won the British GP at Silverstone and in the second half of the year Jones won the German, Austrian, Dutch and Canadian GPs. The team was runner-up in the Constructors' Championship.

RAM acquired three FW07s to race in 1980, although they seldom reached the grids. Keegan achieved a top-ten placing, de Villota achieved very little, Lees and Cogan failed to qualify in their attempts. But during the winter off-season, Alan Jones did win the non-Championship Australian GP in a works car.

The Constructors' title fell to Williams by a wide margin in 1980, when his drivers Jones and Reutemann were first and third respectively in the Drivers' Championship (between them they won the GPs of Argentina, Monaco, France, Britain, Canada and the US GP East). The car used was modified as the FW07B, with a stiffer monocoque and extended under-car aerodynamics; in this form it suffered 'porpoising', but shorter 'underwings' made it sanitary.

Reutemann drove an FW07B to win the 1981 South African GP, before the FW07C complying with the skirts ban appeared. In its first form Jones and Reutemann drove FW07Cs to win the Long Beach and Brazil GPs, then the team

was caught up in the scramble to follow the Brabham example and develop a suspension-lowering system to circumvent the ban. In aerodynamic respects the cars were not quite right again until the summer. Reutemann won the team's fourth GP of the year in Belgium, where his own incredible run of 15 scoring finishes in consecutive GPs ended, and the next victory did not come until the last race of the year, at Las Vegas (also Jones' last race for Williams). For the second time Williams Grand Prix Engineering was champion constructor. The FW07Cs were run in the first three GPs of 1982, when Reutemann and Rosberg each finished second in a race. The Argentine abruptly retired, and Andretti stood in for one race with Williams.

Drivers (GPs): Mario Andretti, Emilio de Villota, Alan Jones, Carlos Reutemann, Keke Rosberg.

The economy of line that became a Head and Williams hallmark was shown to advantage in the FW07C, here in its definitive form. Driver is Carlos Reutemann, on his way to his last GP victory, in Belgium in 1981.

FW08 Once again Williams waited for the European season before introducing a new car, the short-wheelbase, short-chassis FW08. In most respects it followed FW07, but apart from being more compact it was stiffer and eventually had better aerodynamic qualities. It was at least down to the minimum weight and carried the water 'ballast' that enjoyed a brief and dubious vogue.

Keke Rosberg was the principal driver in 1982, consistently successful so that although he won only one GP (the Swiss race, at Dijon in France) he won the Championship, although Williams slipped to fourth on the constructors' table.

FW08 had been designed with a six-wheel configuration as a possible development, and FW08/01 was converted to run an evaluation programme in the Autumn of 1982. As well as the drag and tyre contact patch advantages from using four small wheels at the rear, increased downforce resulted from the larger underwings possible. But for 1983 six-wheeled cars were barred from F1.

The six-wheeler during October 1982 tests. It used an FW08 hull, which was shorter with this possible application in mind. The camera does not distort the length of car behind the cockpit, and the front wheels were larger (15in) than the rear four (13in).

For that year an FW08 was converted to comply with the 'flat-bottom' regulations and FW08Cs were built. Outwardly this car looked markedly different, with very short pods containing radiators alongside the engine. The latter was the DFV, near the end of its illustrious career and outclassed in power terms. The only GP to fall to the team was the Monaco race, won by Rosberg. Otherwise Keke and Laffite scored enough points to retain fourth place for Williams on the Constructors' table.

Drivers: Derek Daly, Jacques Laffite, Jonathan Palmer, Keke Rosberg.

The FW08, here in its 'C' form at Spa in 1983, was a neat and nimble car. Its 'mini-pods' compare with those on its ground effects predecessors. Intake scoops were sometimes seen on the engine cover.

FW09 Williams' first turbo car was ready for tests early in the Autumn of 1983 and ran in a 'race test' in the South African GP that wound up the championship year (Rosberg drove it to an encouraging fifth place). The power unit was the Honda RA163-E 80-degree V-6 with IHI turbochargers, which was undoubtedly powerful but had 'on-off' power curves. Head still used an aluminium honeycomb monocoque which was not stiff enough, and introduced a new pullrod rear suspension. This was superseded in the FW09B that came in mid-1984, and also had Williams' own six-speed gearbox.

From late 1983 the team was based in its new Didcot factory. In racing the 1984 season was not rewarding, in part as the team had to learn to use the new power unit. Understeer was a persistent problem. Rosberg won one GP, at Dallas, but Williams was only sixth in the Constructors' Championship.

Drivers: Jacques Laffite, Keke Rosberg.

FW09 in its first form, during 1983 tests. The whole car appeared more solid than the FW08, and less attractive. Long side pods were used again.

FW10 Head finally turned to a carbon composite monocoque for the 1985 car, and the nine chassis were all made in-house, for the Williams factory included an autoclave. Pushrod suspension, naturally with inboard spring-damper units, was used at the front while at the rear top rockers operated the inboard spring-damper units until mid season, when pullrod rear suspension was introduced on the 'FW10B'. The gearbox was revised and usually carbon brakes were used.

The cars did not seem wholly competitive early in 1985, but Rosberg won in Detroit and the team came on very strongly late in the year, when Mansell won the European and South African GPs while Rosberg won the Australian GP. The team was equal third in the Constructors' Championship.

Drivers: Nigel Mansell, Keke Rosberg.

After the FW09, the lines of FW cars appeared smooth again. These were Williams' first cars since the March 761 of 1976 which did not carry signs of Saudia support.

FW11 In a year, 1986, when Frank Williams was largely absent following his road accident his team pulled together strongly and dominated the Constructors' Championship. The FW11 evolved from the FW10, was even more neatly packaged, albeit slightly longer and wider in the wheelbase dimensions, and had 'F' Honda engines that were adequately powerful even in race-boost trim (this was the year of the 195-litre fuel allowance per race). Most problems resulted from minor failures but it was not until the Austrian GP that both cars failed to finish a race.

Nelson Piquet won in Brazil, Germany, Hungary and Italy, Nigel Mansell won in Belgium, Canada, France, Britain and Portugal and in championship terms lost out spectacularly as a rear tyre exploded at Adelaide.

For 1987 the design was improved in details such as cooling arrangements, and seven of the new monocoques built were for the FW11B, while the revised Honda V-6 was more powerful and more fuel-efficient. The new factor was the hydraulic computer-controlled active (or 're-active' in

Mansell and Piquet at the Paul Ricard circuit in 1987, when they came first and second in the French GP. The FW11B was an immensely effective racing machine, and good-looking in spite of the plethora of sponsorship decals.

response to Lotus bleats) suspension system, which was intended to give a constant ride height through a race and was extensively tested before it was raced, at Monza, where Piquet used it on his race-winning FW11B. By that time it was known that Honda had decided to break the contract with Williams prematurely, despite the success of the partnership. In 1987 Williams was again the Champion constructor, Piquet was World Champion (with wins in Germany, Hungary and Italy) while Mansell was runner up, with victories at Imola, Paul Ricard, Silverstone, the Osterreichring, Jerez and Mexico City.

Drivers: Nigel Mansell, Riccardo Patrese, Nelson Piquet.

FW12 The team was perhaps misled by the performance of the 'reactive' suspension in 1987, and for the next season, when perforce a normally-aspirated engine had to be used, concentrated on saving weight. The engine was the Judd CV8 3.5 litre V-8, driving through the Williams transverse gearbox (which incorporated Hewland gears). From the first race meeting the electronic controls of the gas/hydraulic suspension behaved unpredictably, and half the season passed before the instant decision was taken at the British GP to convert to conventional suspension overnight. It worked, in that Mansell was second at Silverstone. There were no victories for Williams that year – seventh in the Championship was another trough – but it transpired that 1988 had been a holding season.

Drivers: Nigel Mansell, Riccardo Patrese.

Mansell testing an FW12 with 're-active' suspension at Silverstone.

FW12C Williams Grand Prix Engineering and Renault signed an agreement covering collaboration and the supply of engines for three years. Williams once again had an exclusive, and it was soon shown competitive, engine; Renault had the front-line team that was vital if the programme was to go ahead.

The RS1 67-degree V-10 had run on a dynamometer in January 1988 and in the Autumn it was circuit tested in a FW12. The FW12 was modified, for example with a wheelbase extended by some 15cm to take the French V-10, and a new designation might have been expected. But Head's FW13 was programmed to come later in the 1989 season.

The FW12C looked low and sleek compared with its predecessors and this gave the impression that the wheelbase was considerably longer than FW12. Unusually for a Williams, radiator air exhausted through the flanks. Boutsen is the driver in this Italian GP shot.

Meanwhile the FW12C was just competitive, Patrese finishing second in three consecutive GPs, while Thierry Boutsen scored his maiden GP victory in Canada. However, through the summer it was being run to the limit of its potential, and because of 'new car' problems with its successor one was used as late as the Spanish GP, when Patrese placed it fifth.

Drivers: Thierry Boutsen, Riccardo Patrese.

FW13 Although purpose-designed for the Renault engine, this was an evolutionary car. Its chassis was slimmer than the FW12's and intended for a season's use, and there was a new front suspension, but the rear suspension of the FW12C was used for the first races.

The settling-in period was not too happy as there were handling problems and both cars were put out of their debut race (in Portugal) with clogged radiators. Nevertheless, the FW13s were second and third in their third race (in Japan) and Boutsen won in Australia; with the FW12C and FW13 Williams finished second in the 1989 Constructors' Championship. The cars appeared in B form in 1990, with modified bodywork and aerodynamic appendages.

Drivers: Thierry Boutsen, Riccardo Patrese.

Patrese driving the first FW13 in its initial tests, in mid-September 1989.

WILLYS-GAVEA

When this Brazilian project was announced early in 1966, it was proclaimed that the simple chassis and running gear could be developed for F1, as well as the intended F2 and F3 uses. The tubular frame and double-wishbone suspension, however, were constructed with rudimentary circuits uppermost in the designer's brief and so the device could hardly have been expected to progress beyond local use, and it didn't.

WISHART

This South African 500cc car of the early 1950s had a BSA engine in a chassis derived from Cooper and JBS. The work of A.G. Wishart of Durban, it was one of the most beautifully made amateur 500s to appear anywhere.   ML

WOJCIEHOWSKI

Records of this 1959 Polish Formula Junior venture are scanty, beyond the basic facts that it had a rear-mounted Wartburg engine in a tubular chassis.

WOLF

Austrian-born Canadian Walter Wolf came into Grand Prix racing when he backed the struggling Williams team from late in 1975. He acquired the equipment of the dissolved Hesketh team for use in 1976, when the cars carried Williams designations and were sometimes referred to as 'Wolf-Williams'. Wolf took over 60 per cent of the Williams company, and within a year Frank Williams was in an impossible position and quit to regain his cherished independence.

For 1977 Wolf set up a powerful team, with Harvey Postlethwaite to design a new car, Peter Warr persuaded to leave Lotus to manage affairs, and just one driver – Scheckter – who won three Grands Prix. That was the only good season, however, for Wolf had no immediate response to ground effects. The F1 team failed to score in 1979 and during the following winter it was merged with Fittipaldi as Walter Wolf turned his back on racing. There was also a Wolf-backed F3 effort, with Dallara cars having a WD designation, and sponsorship in Japanese F2 racing as well as European F3 in 1980.

FW05 Two of the three cars had been completed as Hesketh 308Cs, and modifications for 1976 only meant that they were heavier and not competitive. Five drivers achieved ten finishes, eight retirements and, woundingly, five DNQs.

Drivers: Warwick Brown, Jacky Ickx, Michel Leclère, Arturo Merzario.

An erstwhile Hesketh in Wolf's black and gold colours, driven by Ickx at Brands Hatch, when his failure to qualify the car for the British GP led to his dismissal from the team.

WR1-4 This was a distinctive and workmanlike design by Postlethwaite, with a 'wedge' theme to its outward lines in plan as well as in profile, and mechanically a conventional Cosworth DFV/Hewland FGA400 package. Jody Scheckter drove WR1/1 to a debut victory in Argentina, and used the same car to win in Monaco and Canada. Beyond that he scored two second places and four thirds in a remarkable display of mechanical and team reliability. The cars served on for the first races of 1978, when they were outmoded. However, Rahal was given a run in one at the end of the year, while Teddy Yip entered Rosberg in one of the two Theodore cars in mid-summer races, to no good end. WR4 was run by Theodore during the first half of the 1980 British national F1 series, unremarkably save that Desiré Wilson won the Easter race at Brands Hatch in it, the first race to be won by a woman driver in an F1 car.

Drivers: Bobby Rahal, Keke Rosberg, Jody Scheckter.

WR1/1, with Wolf's Canadian allegiance prominently displayed. The car appears solid and purposeful, and a unified design – there were to be no 'tacked-on' afterthoughts in 1977.

WR5-6 The opening race of 1978 showed that there was no development life in the first Wolf design. Postlethwaite quickly designed a ground effects car, and WR5 was equally rapidly built. It was an ugly device, in large part because of the oil cooler mounted ahead of the cockpit. Its circuit habits were tricky, so WR6 was completed with wider track (two cars carried this number, as the first WR6 was written off in a warm-up accident at Monza). Scheckter was second in the German and Canadian GPs, the team's best results of the year. In mid-1979 Kennedy drove WR6/2 in British national races and he too found that its ground effects were not consistently effective.

Driver: Jody Scheckter.

A WR6 was run in a few late-1979 sideshow races in the British national F1 series, retaining its basically black livery. Here Kennedy ponders in the Brands Hatch pits lane during practice for his first race in it (he finished third).

WR7-9 These three cars were at least better-looking machines, although much less effective – the team's record in 1979 comprised twelve retirements (and one failure to qualify) to set against two finishes. There were persistent aerodynamic balance and suspension problems, and the cars were not competitive in straight-line speed terms.

Postlethwaite introduced his folded honeycomb aluminium monocoque construction with this design, which in aspects such as suspension was conventional. It was, of course, DFV powered. Its debut in Argentina was accompanied by a furore as clutch-driven impeller blades were used to draw air through the oil cooler, and that was ruled out as a 'moveable aerodynamic device'.

That apart, the last Wolf was in the news only when Hunt gave up in mid season; like James, his successor Rosberg was classified only once in his 'half' of the year. Through that period team morale was in sharp decline, as a disappointing end was in sight. WR8-9 became the first two Fittipaldi F7s.

Drivers: James Hunt, Keke Rosberg.

WR7 in pristine condition, and suggesting promise that was never delivered.

Wolf-Dallara Giampaolo Dallara had a considerable reputation to apply to the design of the F3 WD1 (or WR) which, like some of his later cars, did not quite live up to the billing. Three were built, two for Walter Wolf Racing and one for an Italian independent. WD1 was a neat little car, but its monocoque proved too lightly built and its tendency to flex led to rebuilds in a more rigid form. Suspension was conventional, Nova-Toyota engines were used, and drive was through Hewland FT200 'boxes. Results were not outstanding, although Bobby Rahal enhanced his reputation with the car, notably in practice at Monaco and at the Nürburgring. As Wolf-Dallara the cars served only through 1978, although one was to re-emerge as the Emiliani.

Competent once initial shortcomings were 'redesigned out', but not outstanding, the WD1 wore Walter Wolf's familiar black colours. This one is driven by Rahal at Monaco in 1978.

Y

YEOVIL

This American Formula Junior car was of no merit in terms of racing achievement, but of interest for its unusual combination of major components – a Hansa-Goliath engine fitted with twin Holley carbs (80bhp was claimed) and driving through a VW gearbox. Beyond that, the engine was behind the cockpit in a semi-space frame with wishbone and transverse leaf spring front suspension and a swinging arm arrangement at the rear.

YIMKIN

The little Yimkin Engineering company formed by Don Sim and Mike Handley, with the unlikely-sounding address of Cadogan Lane, London SW1, specialized in BMC engine tuning and in clubman's sports cars. The idea of an 'economy' Formula Junior car was attractive in view of the club-level FJ category that was being propounded in 1960. That idea never took off, but two FJ versions of the Yimkin sports car were sold. The FJ car had a front-mounted engine (BMC or Ford) in a tubular chassis, with ifs and live rear axle, and glass-fibre bodywork. Yimkin ceased operations at the end of 1960 and Sim later made the Diva GT car.

Z

ZAKSPEED

Erich Zakowski's team built up a solid reputation in saloon car racing in the late 1960s, adopting the name Zakspeed in 1970. It became more and more closely involved with Ford, and developed cars such as the Group 5 Escort and turbo Capris before undertaking Ford's hapless Group C car in 1982-4. By 1983 Zakowski was looking towards F1, and the compact Zakspeed Formula Racing division was set up. Its turbocharged four-cylinder F1 engine (90.4 x 58.25mm, 1495cc) ran for the first time in September 1984 and the 841 car was announced late that month.

Despite considerable experience with turbo engines, Zak's commitment to an in-house engine was bold, and it was poorly rewarded in the four seasons in which it was raced. The power output of the early units may have been the claimed 700bhp, and in 1986 800-1100bhp (race or practice tune) may well have been achieved, but in competitive terms output was never quite sufficient. The cars looked neat but were not very effective despite the best efforts of some drivers, and through those turbo seasons a Zakspeed finished in the points only once.

For 1989 Zakspeed was again innovative – in its use of a Yamaha engine – but it also had inexperienced drivers, and the combination of new machinery and new drivers meant that it featured most regularly on the list of entries that failed to progress beyond the pre-qualifying stage. At the end of the year it was withdrawn, to devote a season to saloon racing and development of the Yamaha engine.

841 Although it was announced in September 1984 this first F1 Zakspeed was not raced until the following year, and then only in the European races on the Championship calendar. It was a state of the art design by Paul Brown (ex-Chevron, March and Maurer) around a carbon fibre/Kevlar monocoque, with double-wishbone front suspension and pullrod rear suspension. The race debut was in the Portugese GP and the only finish in nine GPs entered came at Monaco, where Palmer was eleventh.

Drivers: Christian Danner, Jonathan Palmer.

Dr Palmer poses with the team's two 841s, both in the red and white livery of the sponsoring cigarette company. He was the only driver for most of the season, but after he was injured in a sports car Danner took his place.

861 The design was refined for the team's second season, in particular weight was shed, aerodynamics improved and a new engine management system introduced. In detail during the season carbon fibre brakes were introduced, there were

new fuel injection arrangements, Garrett turbochargers were used in place of KKK units, and detail aerodynamic work was carried out. Performances did not improve proportionately, in part because resources were stretched when a second car was run through most of the season. Thirty entries reaped a return of ten finishes, Palmer's eighth at Detroit being the best. The cars were also used early in 1987.

Drivers: Jonathan Palmer, Huub Rothengatter.

861/1 on the inside and 861/2 on the outside during practice at Monaco in 1986. Respective drivers were Rothengatter, who failed to qualify, and Palmer who was twelfth in the race. 861/1 had 'winglets' at the rear of the side pods, 861/2 vertical deflectors.

871 Attributed to the 'Zakspeed Design Group', this was a further development of the existing design, although continuity paid few dividends. Frontal area was reduced, aerodynamics were improved (although perhaps only on paper) there was revised wishbone/pullrod suspension that was to be further revised as 1987 went on, and there was a new gearbox. The first car was ready for the second GP of the year, when Brundle drove it to score Zakspeed's first Championship points. Thereafter development lagged, and although some wind tunnel work was done adequate downforce proved elusive.

Drivers: Martin Brundle, Christian Danner.

871/3 during practice for the British GP when Brundle qualified it 17th. He usually managed a top-20 place on a grid, which reflected credit on him rather than the car, for he was classified in only four races; team mate Danner finished six times.

881 In its last year with its own turbo engine Zakspeed's fortunes slipped further – the turbos were supposed to hold a residual advantage over 'atmo' engines, but the 2.5-bar boost pressure regulations seemed to reduce the power of the

Zakspeed engine to par with the best normally-aspirated units, and it was unreliable. The 1987 chassis was uprated and the bodywork refined, but the cars were never competitive. Team leader Ghinzani was classified three times (best placing 14th), Schneider once (12th); as much to the point, respective DNQ annotations were eighth and tenth.

Drivers: Piercarlo Ghinzani, Bernd Schneider.

Once again a Zakspeed 'looked right', but the 881 was not. This is Schneider attempting to qualify 881/1 for the British GP – he did not get it to the grid.

891 This car marked a new beginning for Zakspeed. It was designed under the direction of Gustav Brunner by Nino Frisson, who had joined from Ferrari in mid-1988. Outwardly it seemed small and less neat than its predecessors, carried the same West colour scheme, and pullrod suspension was used again. But the engine was the 40-valve Yamaha OX88 V-8, and it drove through Zakspeed's new transverse gearbox. That amount of novelty called for experienced development drivers, and neither Schneider nor Suzuki was experienced. With almost inevitable regularity the Zakspeeds failed to get past the pre-qualifying hurdle, although Schneider did get one onto the grids for the last two races of 1989.

Driver: Bernd Schneider.

A side elevation shot that compares with the 881 (above), showing the 'humped-back' lines of the 891. Driver is Bernd Schneider.

ZIG

Luxembourg has not contributed many racing cars, but in 1951 came the Zig 500cc F3 car which was a Cooper copy with a BMW engine. Several were made but they achieved little.

ML

ZIMMERMAN

Willi Zimmermann parted company with his German contemporaries who used DKW engines in Formula Junior cars as his Cooper-inspired one-off was rear-engined. His Herbster-built car also had a space frame rather than a simpler ladder-type chassis. Independent suspension was by transverse leaf spring and lower wishbone, front and rear. A Goliath-Hansa flat four was used in 1959, then replaced by a DKW engine in a slightly modified car for 1960.

Zimmermann, here in its 1960 form with proprietary road wheels, was a solid-looking car. The telescopic dampers with no associated coil springs appear odd, but were not unusual among the South German constructors of the time.

THE FORMULAE

Through most of the period covered by this book there have been three principal single-seater international racing categories, the term formula being used as it became universally accepted after the Second World War. In the 1950s and from the mid 1960s to the mid 1980s these were Formula 3, Formula 2 and Formula 1, in a neat ascending order from a 'finishing school' class to the Grand Prix formula.

However, Formula 2 was allowed to lapse in 1954, as the then-new Formula 1 was apparently successful enough to make it superfluous. That turned out to be a false conclusion and F2 was 're-introduced' in 1957. It lapsed again in 1961, when a 1.5-litre capacity limit was in force for Formula 1. Formula Junior, which had International status since 1959, was then the only category enjoying that status below Formula 1, for a brief period effectively serving as F2 and F3. Those categories were revived in 1964. In 1985 Formula 2 was discontinued in favour of Formula 3000, although it was continued for two years in Japan. In 1952-53 the World Championship Grand Prix were run to Formula 2 regulations, for there were too few teams prepared to compete with Formula 1 cars.

Regulations were once fairly loose, now they are precise, rigid and rigidly applied. Loopholes have been few and far between, and when one has been found FISA or 'interested parties' have moved swiftly, usually to close it – not always successfully, as in the 'lowering suspension' episode which extended the life of ground effects in Formula 1.

FORMULA 1

When racing picked up after the Second World War grids were made up of late-1930s cars, and *formule libre* rules were applied so that the organizers of events could at least get fields together. By 1947, however, there was sufficient confidence for the Formula A that had been framed for 1941 to be promulgated as Formula 1. Save for the 1952-53 seasons, Formula 1 has been the Grand Prix formula since then (that original Formula 1 remained in force until the end of 1953, albeit in a secondary role). Like all successful sets of regulations, it was framed around engine capacities and this policy has generally been followed through four decades of World Championship racing, although as the sport has become less simplistic the number of subsidiary rules has multiplied, and when things have got a little foolish, for example in the turbocharged engine era, attempts to curb performance have depended on other restrictions.

Grand Prix does not quite equate with World Championship historically, for in 1950-60 the Indianapolis 500 was a Championship event, although it was not run to F1 regulations – engines apart, the small matter of race distance was overlooked in one of those spasmodic attempts to establish Grand Prix racing in the USA. Ironically, these came closest to success when they were not marketing inspired, back in the Edwardian period . . . .

These, then, are the basic regulations that have governed Grand Prix racing since 1947:

1947-53 Maximum engine capacity 1.5 litres (supercharged engines) or 4.5 litres (normally aspirated engines). No weight, dimensional or fuel restrictions, but for World Championship races (from 1950) a minimum distance of 300km (186 miles) or duration of three hours was imposed.

1954-60 Maximum engine capacity 750cc (supercharged engines) or 2.5 litres (normally aspirated engines).

Minimum WC race distance 500km (310.7 miles) or three hours; in 1958 a minimum distance of 300km/186 miles and a maximum distance of 500km/310.7 miles and a minimum race duration of two hours was substituted. 'Commercial' fuel, defined as 100-130 octane Avgas, mandatory from 1958.

1961-65 Minimum engine capacity 1.3 litres, maximum capacity 1.5 litres, both normally aspirated (supercharged engines not permitted). 'Commercial' fuel with a maximum octane rating of 100 stipulated. Minimum weight 450kg/992lb, including oil and water. Aircraft-type fuel tanks, self-starter and separate emergency braking required.

1966-85 Maximum engine capacity 1.5 litres (supercharged or turbocharged engines) or 3 litres (normally aspirated engines). Initial minimum weight 500kg/1102lb. WC race distance to be between 300km/186 miles and 400km/248.5 miles.

During the life of this formula many changes were introduced, principally:

1969 On-board fire extinguishers required, roll-over bar requirements defined. During the season the dimensions and positions of aerofoils ('wings') were severely restricted following failures, and movable aerodynamic devices were banned.

1970 Minimum weight 530kg/1102lb. Bag fuel tanks stipulated, which meant that monocoque construction became necessary.

1972 Minimum weight 550kg/1212lb. Engines with more than 12 cylinders barred. Maximum car width 130cm/51.18in.

1973 Minimum weight 575kg/1268lb, maximum fuel tank capacity 250 litres/55 Imp. gallons. Deformable structure fuel tank protection required, and dry-break fuel line couplings. Race distance 200 miles/321.8km or two hours, whichever was the shorter.

1974 Rear aerofoil overhang limited to 1m/39in behind centre line of rear wheels.

1976 Further restriction on overhang of aerofoils (80cm/30in at rear, 120cm/45in at front). Other dimensions stipulated: max. height above lowest sprung part 85cm/33.5in (this had effect of reducing airbox height), max. overall car width 215cm/84.7in, max. tyre width 21in (c. 53cm), max. rear wheel rim diameter 13in (c. 33cm). Forward roll-over bar mandatory.

1977 Maximum overall height 95cm/37in above the ground. Race distance 250km/155 miles – 322km/200 miles, or minimum two hours.

1978 Single 250-litre fuel cell stipulated.

1979 Maximum overall car length 5m/198in.

1981 Minimum weight 585kg/1290lb. Sliding skirts banned and 6cm/2.36in ground clearance required.

1982 Survival cell cockpit stipulated, including 30cm/11.8in pedal box.

1983 Minimum weight 540kg/1190lb. Flat bottom required, to ensure ground clearance and put an end to suspension lowering devices. Aerofoil sizes further restricted (for example, rear wing width 100cm/39in). Four-wheel cars stipulated, thus ruling out six-wheelers, and four-wheel drive banned.

1984 Fuel cell capacity restricted to 220 litres/ 48.4 Imp. gal, and refuelling during a race banned. Race distance 300km/186 miles – 320km/199 miles, or two hours.

1985 Ancillary aerofoils ('winglets') at rear banned. Crash-tested nose box required.

1986 Turbocharged engines only, with maximum capacity of 1.5 litres. Fuel cell capacity 195 litres/48.4 Imp. gal.

1987 Maximum engine capacity 1.5 litres (turbocharged) or 3.5 litres (normally aspirated), respective minimum car weights 540kg/1190lb and 500kg/1102lb. Turbo engine boost restricted to 4 bar in 1987, 2.5 bar in 1988 (4 and 2.5 times ambient barometric pressure, enforced by use of FISA 'pop-off' valves). Turbo car fuel capacity 150 litres/33 Imp. gal. in 1988. Multi-stage or liquid-cooled turbochargers banned.

1988 Requirement that drivers' feet should be behind front axle line introduced. No fuel restriction for cars with normally-aspirated engines.

1989 Normally aspirated engines with a maximum capacity of 3.5 litres only (turbocharged engines banned). Race distance 305km/199 miles or two hours, whichever was the shorter.

INTERCONTINENTAL FORMULA

This was a misguided attempt by the British Establishment to extend the life of the 2.5 litre Formula 1 in a reaction against the 1.5-litre Formula 1 in 1961. It admitted cars with unsupercharged engines of 2-3 litres, and did not last into a second season.

FORMULA 2

A secondary category was almost as old as racing, 'light car' classes being firmly established in the city-to-city races early in the Century. More specifically, the 1930s Formula B approach was picked up in a new Formula 2 in 1948, and this almost suddenly became the World Championship category in 1952-53, as race organizers realized that it would not be possible to assemble fields of competitive Formula 1 cars. To all intents and purposes Formula Junior took the place of Formula 2 in 1961-64, when the 1957-60 F2 regulations in effect became Formula 1. As the second-level formula, F2 gave way to F3000 in Europe in 1985, but continued as the principal racing class in Japan until the end of 1986.

Australia had its own Formula 2, ('ANF2' is the convenient initials reference used in this book) from 1964; maximum capacities were 1.1 litres (1964-65), 1.5 litres (also 1964, when it was not ANF2, 1966-68), 1.6 litres (from 1969); throughout there were other limitations, for example requiring engines based on touring car units from 1978. Formula B (USA), Formula Atlantic and Formula Pacific were closely related – chassis served for all of them, and F Atlantic cars were sometimes converted to run in F2 (an expedient that might have been economical but did not make for competitive cars). Generally, 1.6-litre production-based engines were stipulated for these categories, although for a while a Formula Atlantic series built around Mazda engines was run in South Africa. The regulations for the South American Formula 2 in the 1980s bore little relationship to the mainstream international Formula 2.

Another 'economical' 1.6 litre category, Formula Mondial, was contrived along the same lines as these classes in 1984.

The basic Formula 2 regulations were:

1948 Maximum engine capacity 500cc (supercharged) or 2 litres (normally aspirated).

1954 Formula 2 lapsed.

1957 Maximum engine capacity 1.5 litres (normally aspirated).

1961 Formula 2 lapsed.

1964 Maximum engine capacity 1 litre (normally aspirated).

1967 Maximum engine capacity 1.6 litres (normally aspirated).

1972 Maximum engine capacity 2 litres (normally aspirated); production-based engines stipulated.

1976 Maximum engine capacity 2 litres (normally aspirated); specialist racing engines admitted.

1984 European Formula 2 discontinued at the end of the season.

1986 Japanese Formula 2 discontinued at the end of the season.

FORMULA 3000

This second-level class was introduced in Europe in 1985, when it took the place of Formula 2 and marked the end of the European Formula 3 Championship. Normally aspirated engines with a capacity of up to 3 litres (and no more than 12 cylinders) were admitted, and engine speed was restricted to 9000rpm by an electronic limiter approved by FISA and common to all cars. Cars were to have flat bottoms, a maximum width of 200cm/78.7in and a minimum weight of 540kg/1190lb. Maximum wheel diameter was laid down (13in, with the wheel and tyre combination not the exceed 24.5in) and each car was limited to ten tyres for official practice in the first season, twelve in 1986; the choice of tyres was free in 1985, but in 1986 control tyres (Avons) were stipulated. The maximum race distance for a European Championship even was 210km/130 miles, including the formation lap.

FORMULA JUNIOR

Formula Junior, based on a national 750 class, was introduced in Italy, the most important Europan country (in motor racing terms) where the 500cc Formula 3 had never caught on. Giovanni Lurani saw it as an ab initio category for Italian drivers, but that idea was swept away as it became an International category in 1959, and then during the period of the 1.5-litre Formula 1 it effectively took the places of F2 and F3. Briefly, it was the most genuinely international of all formulae, but the overwhelming success of sophisticated British cars soon had a constricting effect.

Formula Junior admitted cars with engines of 1000cc or 1100cc, according to the weight of the car, 360kg/793lb or 400kg/882lb respectively. Engine and gearbox had to derive from a homologated touring car, and the braking system had to be the same as that on the car for which the engine was built. North American and Australian regulations differed in admitting engines up to 1.5 litres and ohc units, because there were few locally-built power units conforming to FIA requirements.

FORMULA 3

The first Formula 3 had its origins in the British 500cc movement, which saw its first official race in 1947. It was adopted as the third-level international racing category in 1950, and that first F3 ran on until 1960, with 500cc events still being organized when it had been superseded by F Junior. A 1-litre Formula was introduced in 1964 and ran until 1970. In 1971 the maximum engine capacity was 1.6 litres, but power output was restricted by a limit on engine air supply. The capacity limit was raised to 2 litres in 1974, when engines were still to be based on production units. The most significant subsidiary regulation came in 1985, when 'flat-bottom' cars were stipulated.

Australian National F3 differed considerably, primarily in engine regulations, for example in allowing only sohc 1.3-litre engines through its final years (ANF3 was phased out at the end of 1977).

FORMULA 5000

Formula 5000, Formula A in the USA, is another major category mentioned in this book. It was a 'big-engine' single-seater category built around 5-litre mass-production engines, which almost invariably meant American V-8s. In other respects – chassis, suspension, brakes, aerofoils and so on – it reflected contemporary F1 practices, and after a few promising seasons from its introduction in 1969 it became a very expensive category, with restricted international appeal. In the USA, Formula A gave way to a curious CanAm category, single-seaters with full-width bodywork, while in Britain a series for near-obsolescent F1 cars and F2 cars took its place.

THE CONSTRUCTORS' CHAMPIONSHIP

Introduced in 1958, this was always a manufacturers' rather than teams' championship, for even in the days when independent teams were prominent in Grand Prix racing any points they scored were credited to the marque. It complements the drivers' championship, with a similar points scoring system.

The first five cars scored 8, 6, 4, 3 and 2 points in the first two seasons, then a point was awarded for sixth place and in 1962 a win scored nine points. However, only the highest-placed car of a marque scored in the first 20 seasons; since 1979 all the points scored by the first six have counted. Beyond that, only the best results from specified numbers of Grand Prix have counted, 6 from 11 in the first year, then 5 or 6 from 8-10 until 1966, then the season was split so that specified numbers of races in each half of the season counted. Since 1981 the best 11 results have scored. Half points have occasionally been awarded for shortened races. Points scored in the first half of a season have had real value in recent years, for example qualifying a constructor for admission to a travel expenses pool, or avoiding race pre-qualifying and giving automatic admission to race practice (the letters 'DNPQ' having an awful finality as they mean that a driver from the 'poor end' of a pits lane is denied the opportunity to even attempt to set a grid time).

In this list engine manufacturers are not hyphenated to cars – reference to the A-Z entries gives this information – and only scoring points totals are given:

1958 Vanwall, 48; Ferrari, 40; Cooper, 31; BRM, 18; Maserati, 9; Lotus, 6.

1959 Cooper, 40; Ferrari, 32; BRM, 18; Lotus, 5.

1960 Cooper, 48; Lotus, 34; Ferrari, 26; BRM, 8.

1961 Ferrari, 40; Lotus, 32; Porsche, 22; Cooper, 14; BRM, 7.

1962 BRM, 42; Lotus, 36; Cooper, 29; Lola, 19; Ferrari and Porsche, 18; Brabham, 6.

1963 Lotus, 54; BRM, 36; Brabham, 28; Ferrari, 26; Cooper, 25; BRP, 6; Porsche, 5.

1964 Ferrari, 45; BRM, 42; Lotus, 37; Brabham, 33, Cooper, 16; BRP, 5.

1965 Lotus, 54; BRM, 45; Brabham, 27; Ferrari, 26; Cooper, 14; Honda 11.

1966 Brabham, 42; Ferrari, 31; Cooper, 30; BRM, 22; Lotus, 18; Eagle, 4; Honda and McLaren, 3.

1967 Brabham, 63; Lotus, 50; Cooper, 28; Ferrari and Honda, 20; BRM, 17; Eagle, 13; McLaren, 3.

1968 Lotus, 62; McLaren 51; Matra, 45; Ferrari, 32; BRM, 28; Cooper and Honda, 14; Brabham, 10.

1969 Matra, 66; Brabham, 51; Lotus, 47; McLaren, 40; Ferrari and BRM, 7.

1970 Lotus, 59; Ferrari, 55; March, 48; Brabham and McLaren, 35; BRM and Matra, 23; Surtees, 3.

1971 Tyrrell, 73; BRM, 36; March, 34; Ferrari, 33; Lotus, 21; McLaren, 10; Matra, 9; Surtees, 8; Brabham, 5.

1972 Lotus, 61; Tyrrell, 51; McLaren, 47; Ferrari, 33; Surtees, 18; March, 15; BRM, 14; Matra, 12; Brabham, 7.

1972 Lotus, 61; Tyrrell, 51; McLaren, 47; Ferrari, 33; Surtees, 18; March, 15; BRM, 14; Matra, 12; Brabham, 7.

1973 Lotus, 92; Tyrrell, 82; McLaren, 58; Brabham, 22; March, 14; Ferrari and BRM, 12; Shadow, 9; Surtees, 7; Iso (Williams), 2; Tecno, 1.

1974 McLaren, 73; Ferrari, 65; Tyrrell, 52; Lotus, 42; Brabham, 35; Hesketh, 15; BRM, 10; Shadow, 7; March, 6; Iso (Williams), 4; Surtees, 3; Lola, 1.

1975 Ferrari, 72½; Brabham, 54; McLaren, 53; Hesketh, 33; Tyrrell, 25; Shadow, 9½; Lotus, 9; March, 6½; Williams, 6; Parnelli, 5; Lola, 3; Penske, 2; Ensign, 1.

1976 Ferrari, 83; McLaren, 74; Tyrrell, 71; Lotus, 29; Penske and Ligier, 20; March, 19; Shadow, 10; Brabham, 9; Surtees, 7; Fittipaldi, 3; Ensign, 2; Parnelli, 1.

1977 Ferrari, 95; Lotus, 62; McLaren, 60; Wolf, 55; Brabham and Tyrrell, 27; Shadow, 23; Ligier, 18; Fittipaldi, 11; Ensign, 10; Surtees, 6; ATS (Penske), 1.

1978 Lotus, 86; Ferrari, 58; Brabham, 53; Tyrrell, 38; Wolf, 24; Ligier, 19; Fittipaldi, 17; McLaren, 15; Williams and Arrows, 11; Shadow, 6; Renault, 3; Surtees and Ensign, 1

1979 Ferrari, 113; Williams, 75; Ligier, 61; Lotus, 39; Tyrrell, 28; Renault, 26; McLaren, 15; Brabham, 7; Arrows, 5; Shadow, 3; ATS, 2; Fittipaldi, 1.

1980 Williams, 120; Ligier, 66; Brabham, 55; Renault, 38; Lotus, 14; Tyrrell, 12; Arrows, Fittipaldi and McLaren, 11; Ferrari, 8; Alfa Romeo, 4.

1981 Williams, 95; Brabham, 61; Renault, 54; Ligier, 44; McLaren, 28; Lotus, 22; Alfa Romeo, Arrows and Tyrrell, 10; Ensign, 5; Theodore and ATS, 1.

1982 Ferrari, 74; McLaren, 69; Renault, 62; Williams, 58; Brabham, 41; Lotus, 30; Tyrrell, 25; Ligier, 20; Alfa Romeo, 7; Arrows, 5; ATS, 4; Osella, 3; Fittipaldi, 1.

1983 Ferrari, 89; Renault, 79; Brabham, 72; Williams, 38; McLaren, 34; Alfa Romeo, 18; Lotus, 13; Tyrrell, 12; Toleman, 10; Arrows, 4; Theodore. 1.

1984 McLaren, 143½; Ferrari, 57½, Lotus, 47; Brabham, 38; Renault, 34; Williams, 25½; Toleman, 16; Alfa Romeo, 11; Arrows, 6; Ligier, 3; Osella, 2; ATS, 1. Tyrrell scored 13 points, which were disallowed by FISA.

1985 McLaren, 90; Ferrari, 82; Williams and Lotus, 71; Brabham, 26; Ligier, 23; Renault, 16; Arrows, 14; Tyrrell, 7.

1986 Williams, 141; McLaren, 96; Lotus, 58; Ferrari, 37; Ligier, 29; Benetton, 19; Tyrrell, 11; Lola, 6; Brabham, 2; Arrows, 1.

1987 Williams, 137; McLaren, 76; Lotus, 64; Ferrari, 53; Benetton, 28; Arrows and Tyrrell, 11; Brabham, 10; Lola, 3; Zakspeed, 2; AGS, Ligier and March, 1.

1988 McLaren, 199; Ferrari, 65; Benetton, 39; Arrows and Lotus, 23; March, 22; Williams, 20; Tyrrell, 5; Rial, 3; Minardi, 1.

1989 McLaren, 141; Williams, 77; Ferrari, 59; Benetton, 39; Tyrrell, 16; Lotus, 15; Arrows, 13; Dallara and Brabham, 8; Minardi and Onyx, 6; March, 4; Ligier and Rial, 3; AGS and Lola, 1.

INDEX